LAW, RECORDS AND INFORMATION MANAGEMENT

The Court Cases

LAW, RECORDS AND INFORMATION MANAGEMENT

The Court Cases

Donald S. Skupsky, JD, CRM

John C. Montaña, JD

Information Requirements Clearinghouse

Denver, Colorado

"This publication is designed to provide accurate and authoritative information in regard to the subject matter covered. It is sold with the understanding that the publisher and author are not engaged in rendering legal, accounting or other professional services. If legal advice or other expert assistance is required, the services of a competent professional person should be sought." Excerpt from the Declaration of Principles jointly adopted by a Committee of the American Bar Association and a Committee of Publishers and Associations.

Information Requirements Clearinghouse
5600 South Quebec Street, Suite 250C
Englewood, Colorado 80111
(303) 721-7500

Printed in the United States of America
98 97 96 95 94   5 4 3 2 1

Library of Congress Catalog Card Number: 94-77173

ISBN 0-929316-32-0

Table of Contents

Preface

Organizations create and maintain records to:

- Organize and retrieve relevant information to support and facilitate operations and activities;

- Comply with legal requirements imposed by statutes and regulations; and

- Provide support for organization actions and avoid adverse consequences during litigation, government investigation and audit.

In this third situation — litigation, government investigation and audit — the sufficiency or legality of an organization's records and information management program may be challenged. Attempts to admit records into evidence may be contested by the other party. The absence of records may raise questions of improper destruction.

Judges have examined a variety of records and information management practices in court cases. Their decisions and commentary articulate a series of principles that apply to the overall design, implementation and management of a records and information management program. Adherence to these principles enables records to pass judicial scrutiny. Failure could result in sanctions, fines, penalties and other adverse consequences.

Although no single case definitively provides the formula to produce legally-sufficient records, the judicial statements, taken together, identify acceptable and unacceptable practices. This book provides both the actual language used by the courts and detailed analysis of how to incorporate the conclusions in a records and information management program.

This book does not examine nor analyze specific statutory and regulatory recordkeeping requirements imposed by state and federal government agencies.[1] Nor does it deal with unique litigation issues such as discovery strategies, attorney-client privilege, and standards of review, although, some of these issues were raised in cases selected for inclusion.

This book provides the detail and depth of analysis needed by lawyers, plus significant excerpts from relevant cases to reduce additional research and facilitate independent analysis. Records and information managers will also find it to be a valuable reference when designing and implementing record and information management systems, providing insight into the legal thought process and addressing issues with legal counsel.

Readers will begin with varying backgrounds and understanding of legal issues. We deliberately provided basic background information on the business records exception to the hearsay rule, as well as statutory and judicial definitions of "business", "business record", and other basic terms. Lawyers not involved in litigation and non-lawyers will find this material both useful and necessary in understanding judicial treatment of records management issues. Legal principles and conclusions found later in the book depend on a consistent and uniform understanding of the basic issues.

Some basic legal principles may be contrary to commonly-held perceptions. For example, readers unfamiliar with the process of introducing business records into evidence may even be surprised

---

1   *See Legal Requirements for Business Records, Information Requirements Clearinghouse*, updated annually, for federal and state statutory and regulatory recordkeeping requirements.

to discover that not all records kept by their organization will be admissible as business records. Yet, knowing what judges expect from record and information management systems is critical to designing systems that can withstand legal challenge.

All cases referred to in the body of the book have been edited and reproduced in Appendix C. References in the footnotes preceded by an "*" do not appear in the appendix.

We wish to thank Katherine Gerland and Paul E. Tenorio, student law clerks, for assisting in the research and editing for this book and Dan Campbell, Nora F. Goodman, George S. Kondos, Whitney S. Minkler, Carter Simpson, David O. Stephens, and Benjamin Wright for reviewing this book and providing extremely valuable insight. Finally, we wish to thank Toni P. Mote, Administrative Associate, for painstakingly typing and editing the text of this book, including the detailed appendices.

Introduction

What is a Records and Information Management Program?

Traditionally, people, capital and property represented the vital resources of an organization. Without them, some believe that organizations could not retain their competitive advantage.

Today, information increasingly is being viewed as another vital resource, without which an organization cannot function effectively. Employees need complete, accurate and timely information to do their jobs. When employees leave, organizations retains their expertise in the form of information that they leave behind.

Records preserve and perpetuate information. An effective records and information management program ensures that records will be created, maintained and disposed of in a timely, efficient and cost-effective manner. Additionally, the program preserves information required by the organization for legal or operational purposes for the requisite period.

Even efficient organizations accumulate paper in file cabinets, records storage areas, and valuable office space causing staff to waste time finding important information. Organizations also waste valuable office space and incur significant costs to maintain valueless information.

Many records retention and microfilm programs have been developed with the specific intent of either eliminating paper records or reducing the amount of storage space required. The elimination of valueless information within a records retention program improves the organization's ability to handle the valuable information. By getting rid of the junk, filing errors are reduced and valuable information can be retrieved faster. A well managed records retention and microfilming program lowers costs and increases efficiency.

Records need to be accessible and convenient for some period after they are created. Eventually, they begin to lose their value. At some time in the future, records may not be needed for any legal, user or other reason. A records retention program provides a "back door" for records by eliminating the accumulation of valueless records.

Unfortunately, the cost-savings offered by a records retention program or even by records management may not motivate top management to act. Some managers may feel that the records problem will "go away by itself" or that they cannot justify even modest expenditures for such a "minor problem."

The compelling legal reasons for developing an effective records retention program may get their attention. A properly designed and implemented records retention program ensures compliance with relevant laws and protects an organization during litigation, government investigation or audit.

Traditionally, attorneys have advised clients to "keep everything forever in case they were sued." Unfortunately, some organizations experienced litigation during which certain records, that could have been destroyed in the regular course of business, proved detrimental to their case. The problems of long-term retention—coupled with the huge costs of long-term storage—have changed attitudes. More attorneys and records managers now follow the emerging philosophy: throw away records as soon as possible.

A properly designed records retention program correctly determines how long to keep records for legal purposes and ensures that users have them to do their jobs. The program also ensures that records will be destroyed when they are no longer needed. Records that are needed for legal, user or other legitimate reasons will continue to exist; otherwise, they will be destroyed.

The entire records and information management program may be subject to judicial scrutiny. Before records can be introduced into evidence, the attorney must establish a foundation by showing that the process or system the organization used did produce accurate records. When a duty to preserve records exists, the records retention program ensures that individuals affected receive prompt notice to preserve relevant records. When the duty to preserve records ends and other legal, user or historical retention periods terminate, the records retention program ensures that valueless records will legally be destroyed. Finally, an effective records and information management program enables the organization to quickly and completely identify relevant information for litigation or to confirm that no relevant information exists. Through systematic, documented procedures, training and audit, the records and information management program provides the controls and confirmation of accuracy necessary to meet the legal duties imposed by the courts.

The records and information management program is the combination of people, equipment, processes and procedures to manage the records and information in an organization. The program could include the following components:

- *Record series* — standard identification and numbering system for records.

- *Records retention* — establishment of periods and procedures for destruction of records and ensuring legal compliance and acceptance of the procedures.

- *Forms management* — design and coordination of new forms created in the organization.

- *Active records management* — design and implementation of standard, space-efficient filing systems and file tracking systems within the organization.

• *Inactive records management* — establishment of procedures and facilities for storage of records while inactive.

• *Data and Information Management* — establishment of database management systems, networks, electronic mail, electronic data interchange and other electronic information systems.

• *Image management* — reproduction of original paper records using microfilm or electronic imaging systems to produce a duplicate of records and facilitate retrieval of information.

• *Vital records and disaster recovery* — establishment of programs to ensure that records and information necessary for the continued operation of the organization will be available in case of disaster such as explosion, fire, hurricane, flood, etc.

Benefits of a Records and Information Management Program

Why should an organization develop a records and information management program?

The benefits of a good records and information management program include:

• Improved capability to find the right information

• Improved capability to find information quickly

• Fewer misfiles or lost records

• Improved compliance with legal requirements

• Reduced costs

Some of these key benefits result when paper records are eliminated. The use of sophisticated electronic information management systems, reproduction of paper records onto microfilm or electronic imaging systems, and destruction of paper records under a records retention program all provide significant benefits.

Cost Savings

Accumulating records in inactive filing areas, working areas, closets, basements, and off-site storage areas costs money, reduces efficiency and strains limited staff resources. A recent study by the Texas State Government estimated that it costs $1,206.20 per year to maintain a single five-drawer file cabinet in office space.[1]

The cost to maintain hundreds or thousands of file cabinets in a large organization is substantial. When the information is needed to conduct business or comply with the law, the expense may be justified. But when organizations store valueless records that are no longer needed for any operational or legal purpose, the expense is unnecessary and wasteful. A records retention program could save an organization money in several ways.

- *Space Savings.* Records occupy space in valuable and expensive offices. Even when records are transferred to remote records centers, an organization pays either to manage the storage space or to lease space and services from another.

  Office space used to store valueless records is not available for offices, conference rooms, and other types of productive work areas. Staff may even be cramped into inefficient space. Expansion may be precluded. The resulting loss of productivity could be significant. By eliminating valueless records, the space can be reallocated to accommodate future records or for other productive purposes.

- *Staff Savings.* Managing valueless records wastes staff time. By destroying valueless records, staff becomes available for other, more productive tasks, such as better managing valuable records. The savings in staff time is particularly important for those organizations that allocate only a marginal staff for records management.

- *Equipment Savings.* After destroying valueless records, existing equipment can be used again to store future records. An appro-

---

[1] Eugenia K. Brumm, Ph.D., "A Cost/Benefit Analysis of the Records Management Program of the State of Texas", *Records Management Quarterly*, Vol. 27, No. 2, p.30 (April 1993).

priate records retention program will ensure that old, valueless
records are removed from the storage equipment and destroyed
as new, valuable ones are created or received. New equipment is
only needed to replace worn or outmoded equipment or if the
volume of new records exceeds the destruction of old ones.

Improved Access to Valuable Information

A records retention program also improves the access to valuable information. When valueless records are regularly destroyed,
current information can be located and retrieved much faster. Staff
can be assigned to manage and control the important records,
instead of "managing" valueless records.

Record users will appreciate the retention program. They can
save time and effort locating and reviewing current records, rather
than wasting time handling valueless ones. Decisions also will be
based on current, rather than outdated, information.

Consistency of Records Destruction

A records retention program establishes the timetable and the
procedures for destroying records. Records will be destroyed at the
designated time. The program ensures that an organization will
not destroy records prematurely. Staff will destroy records systematically according to organization policy, reducing the risk of inconsistent, reckless or personally-motivated destruction of records.

Legal Compliance

A good records retention program also ensures compliance with
the multitude of laws affecting records. The federal government
alone has issued over ten thousand laws affecting records. The fifty
states and territories plus some foreign countries have issued laws
for records. Organizations must comply with those laws that affect
them based on the jurisdictions in which they do business, location
of offices and staff, types of products manufactured or sold, impact
of business on the environment and many other factors subject to

regulation. Given the large number of records-related laws, how can an organization comply with all the laws affecting its records?

Knowledge of the relevant laws and legal responsibilities is the first step. Implementing the legal conclusion in a records and information management program is the next. An effective records retention program, for example, requires adequate legal research to determine which records must be kept and for how long. Only then can an organization be confident that records are being retained according to law and being destroyed appropriately.

Legal research to determine recordkeeping requirements can be difficult and time-consuming. Manual and automated legal research tools can facilitate the process. However, recordkeeping provisions often contain inconsistent language and may appear in untitled paragraphs following many pages of prose. Additionally, many state regulations are not available in law libraries or even through automated legal research systems.

While adequate legal research facilitates compliance with laws affecting records, it may still be impossible to ensure full compliance due to the difficulty of this type of research. The methodology followed for both legal research and records retention must then provide additional safeguards to protect an organization from omissions and errors in research and legal analysis.

Protection During Litigation, Government Investigation or Audit

An effective records and information management program also protects the organization during litigation, government investigation or audit. The program ensures that designated records exist and that other records do not exist. It also ensures that records will be maintained whenever a legal duty exists to maintain those records, even if the retention program would have otherwise allowed destruction.

Legal counsel and comptrollers often have difficulty locating records in defense of the organization's position. Unfortunately, staff does not know where the records are, how they are organized, or whether they have been destroyed. Searching for the information takes time and money.

A well-managed records and information program helps to identify records needed to support a claim as well as those requested by an adversary. The program significantly reduces the time and cost of locating information and helps identify information relevant to the case.

The protection afforded by an effective records retention program not only reduces the cost of litigation, government investigation or audit, but may have a major impact on the outcome. When necessary records exist and can be found, an organization can defend its claims. When necessary records no longer exist for unexplained reasons or can no longer be found, an organization can lose rights, incur significant fines and penalties, or suffer adverse consequences or sanctions during litigation.

Records and Information Management Costs in Litigation

While a records and information management program will provide better access to valuable information, improve efficiency and reduce costs, it will also facilitate the litigation process. Many efficiencies appropriate to litigation management are equally appropriate to business needs. Therefore, procedures designed to improve response to litigation needs are likely to improve the overall business efficiency of the records management program. Similarly, increased efficiency in the overall records management program is likely to yield similar results when demands are made during litigation. Meeting the demands of litigation can and should be an integral part of the overall records management program.

While this book addresses the legal issues affecting records and information, the costs of producing large quantities of documents for commercial litigation cannot be ignored. The efficiency offered by today's modern records and information management systems help reduce these costs while facilitating compliance with court orders.

Hundreds of thousands or millions of documents may be produced under court order during years of protracted litigation. In *Hense v. G. D. Searle & Co.*,[2] the parties produced over 750,000 documents related to the products liability issues. Litigation lasted six years before being dismissed prior to trial. The plaintiff's pretrial expenditures alone were over $250,000.

Document production may entail costs other than direct legal expenses. In *Transamerica Computer Co. v. International Business Machines Corp.*,[3] the court ordered IBM to identify and copy over 17 million pages of documents in a three-month period. Since many of the documents were protected by either the attorney-client privilege or the attorneys' work product doctrine, each page had to be carefully screened prior to release. The company hired outside attorneys and clerical help to conduct the multiple-level review process for each document.

Documents came from 30 IBM branch offices, one district office, five regional headquarters, one plant, corporate headquarters, data processing group headquarters, data processing division headquarters, systems development division headquarters, and world trade headquarters. Each document underwent the following steps:

- A trained analyst reviewed each page to determine if it was potentially privileged.

- The analyst removed potentially privileged documents from the original file folder and placed them in green folders, on end within the original folder.

- A clerk then removed the green folder from the box of documents, and made certain that the green folder identified the box number, a folder name, and other information, from the original folder.

- A more experienced lawyer then reviewed the green folders to verify whether the documents were privileged or partially privi-

---

2 *Hense v. G. D. Searle & Co.*, 452 N.W.2d 440 (Iowa 1990).
3 **Transamerica Computer Co. v. International Business Machines Corp.*, 573 F.2d 646 (9th Cir. 1978).

leged. Any non-privileged material was placed back into the file for production to the other party.

- Partially privileged material was then placed in blue folders with instructions for masking privileged material prior to copying. Fully privileged material was logged on forms pursuant to the court's order.

- An experienced attorney reviewed the documents selected for production one last time.

- Non-privileged and partially privileged, but masked, documents were copied.

Of the 17 million pages, some 491,000 were withheld as privileged. In spite of these arduous procedures, approximately 5,800 pages of privileged documents may still have been inadvertently provided to the other party. Miraculously, IBM met the three-month deadline imposed by the court for completing this task.

The high cost of this Herculean effort remains unreported. The production costs constituted only a portion of the total litigation costs.

These costs are not limited to parties to the litigation. In an antitrust suit filed by the United States against the three major television networks,[4] the defendants subpoenaed documents from five non-party motion picture studios. The studios incurred costs of over $2 million to hire more than 93 extra workers to identify and produce some 600,000 documents. The studios moved to recover these costs in 1980, but waited for repayment until 1986 when the court finally awarded reimbursement for some, but not all, of the $2 million expended.

There are other, less obvious, costs associated with such production. Employee efficiency drops as more and more employee time is expended on the document production process, rather than on normal business activities. Efficiency of the business as a whole

---

4   *See *United States v. Columbia Broadcasting System, Inc.*, 103 F.R.D. 365 (C.D.Ca. 1984).

suffers as records needed for normal business purposes are removed from files and assembled for production. If, as is frequently the case, the production process extends over a period of months or years, planning and decision-making may be hampered, and morale may suffer.

These costs cannot be entirely avoided. Faced with a court order to produce records, an individual or business has little choice but to comply, or face the very real possibility of sanctions, including dismissal or default judgment. Further, even when one party is spared the cost of producing documents to other party, it still must bear the cost of searching its own records to identify information to support its own contentions in the matter.

Even if the cost of document production for litigation cannot be avoided, it can be minimized if:

- Current staff can perform document production without compromising regular duties.

- Current staff can quickly and efficiently find the documents.

When the organization quickly meets its discovery obligations, it reduces the time, effort and cost expended on the pretrial stages of litigation. Thus, one goal of the records management program should be the quick and cost-effective resolution of document production demands associated with litigation, without the need for additional staff.

Part I. The Attributes of Business Records

Chapter 1. Business Records

Organizations and individuals create records such as wills, deeds, ledgers, invoices, memoranda, letters, and computer records. Some of these records are used to conduct daily business activities, establish legal rights and duties or serve as valuable references. These records may become the subject of litigation or may be used to support claims of the parties in litigation.

1.1. Records Defined

No single definition for "records" applies to all organizations. Rules of evidence provide definitions of records that may be admitted into evidence, laws provide definitions for government records, national associations provide definitions for purposes of standardizing industry definitions and individual organizations provide definitions for their own internal operational use.

The Uniform Rules of Evidence do not use the term "records," preferring instead to use the more traditional legal verbiage "writings and recordings:"

> (1) *Writings and recordings*. "Writings" and "recordings" consist of letters, words, sounds, or numbers, or their equivalent, set down by handwriting, typewriting, printing, photostating, photographing, magnetic impulse, mechanical or electronic recording, or other form of data compilation.

(2) Photographs. "Photographs" include still photographs, X-ray films, video tapes, and motion pictures.

(3) Original. An "original" of a writing or recording is the writing or recording itself or any counterpart intended to have the same effect by a person executing or issuing it. An "original" of a photograph includes the negative or any print therefrom. If data are stored in a computer or similar device, any printout or other output readable by sight, shown to reflect the data accurately, is an "original."

(4) Duplicate. A "duplicate" is a counterpart produced by the same impression as the original, or from the same matrix, or by means of photography, including enlargements and miniatures, or by mechanical or electronic rerecording, or by chemical reproduction, or by other equivalent techniques which accurately reproduces the original.[5]

The status given a particular record by a court is critical to its admissibility at trial. A record of an organization may meet any of the definitions stated above and still not be admissible in evidence. Only a record that qualifies as a "business record" is generally viewed by the courts as presumptively trustworthy in determining its admissibility into evidence to prove the truth of its contents.

The Federal Records Act defines federal government records as follows:

[A]ll books, papers, maps, photographs, machine readable [i.e., electronic] materials, or other documentary materials, regardless of physical form or characteristics, made or received by an agency of the United States Government under Federal law or in connection with the transaction or public business and preserved or appropriate for preservation by that agency . . . as evidence of the organization, functions, policies, decisions, procedures, operations, or other activities of the Government or because of the informational value of data in them. . . .[6]

---

5   Fed.R.Evid. 1001.
6   44 U.S.C. 3301.

Record can also be defined by practical definitions developed by the records and information management industry. ARMA International, Inc.[7] defines records as follows:

> Recorded information, regardless of medium or characteristics.[8]

The Association for Information and Image Management (AIIM) defines records as follows:

> Information preserved by any technique in any medium, now known, or later developed, that can be recognized by ordinary human sensory capabilities either directly or with the aid of technology.[9]

An organization will regularly create or receive materials that conform to one or more of the definitions for records but do not necessarily constitute the final, official information or position of the organization. While the definitions of records address the processes by which records can be created, organizations often establish their internal policies and procedures based on the intent of the creator or the reliance placed on the records by the organization. The records management terms "official records", "unofficial records" and "non-record material" provide some additional perspectives on the reasons for different treatment of records versus other, similar material.

1.1.1. Official Records

An "official record" reflects the final, official recorded position of an organization related to the specific content of the record. ARMA, International defines an official record as:

> A record which is legally recognized as establishing some fact.[10]

---

7 Also known as the Association of Records Managers and Administrators, Inc.
8 *Glossary of Records Management Terms*, ARMA International (1989).
9 *Performance Guideline for the Legal Acceptance of Records Produced by Information Technology Systems*, Part II, ANSI/AIIM TR31, 1993.
10 *Glossary of Records Management Terms*

Official records reflect the intent of an organization both to commit to a position and to record that position. These records reflect the information and position that the organization believes is true and complete, will rely upon to conduct its affairs and hopes others will also rely upon.

These will be the records an organization will likely attempt to introduce into evidence as "business records" under the rules of evidence.[11] Official records consequently must be subject to rigorous procedures for creation, modification and destruction under a records management and a records retention program.

1.1.2. Unofficial Records

Official records can be distinguished from drafts, work-in-progress, handwritten notes, copies of documents, word processing electronic records used to create official signed documents, unsigned letters and other material that is either in a preliminary state of development or has not yet been authorized or approved by an appropriate person. These "unofficial records" do not yet reflect the official position of the organization and remain subject to change before completion.

In *S. C. Johnson & Son, Inc. v. Louisville & Nashville Railroad Co.,*[12] plaintiff destroyed handwritten notes regarding the condition of products damaged in shipment after converting the information to a typed memorandum documenting his findings. An employee testified that the notes were destroyed because they were illegible to others and that all the necessary information had been included in the memorandum.

The court rejected the defendant's claim that relevant information contained in the notes could help determine whether the findings in the memorandum were accurate, and accepted the records destruction. Even though the notes were not destroyed

---

11   *See Business Records Defined*, below.
12   *S. C. Johnson & Son, Inc. v. Louisville & Nashville Railroad Co.*, 695 F.2d 253 (7th.Cir. 1982).

under any company policy, the court found no reason to believe that the plaintiff destroyed the notes in bad faith. Although the court did not distinguish between official and unofficial records, the court did conclude that the important information from the hand-written notes had been transferred to the final memorandum.[13]

Unofficial records should be covered by some procedure indicating that unofficial records may be destroyed when superseded, when the information has been transcribed to another record or when no longer useful. In no event should unofficial records be kept longer than the official versions. Unofficial records may generally be modified and destroyed at any time without the need for the formal procedures otherwise required in a records management or records retention program, until they become official records of an organization or unless they become subject to a duty to preserve.[14] They might also be admissible when introduced into evidence by a party opponent to litigation.[15]

1.1.3. Non-Record Material

"Non-record material" consists of library material, printed publications, commercially-available computer software, blank forms and other materials that do not reflect the recorded position of the organization.

ARMA International defines non-record material as:

> . . . records not usually included within the scope of official records, e.g., administrative record, convenience file, day file, reference material, publications, etc.[16]

---

13 *See also Shinrone, Inc. v. Tasco, Inc.*, 283 N.W.2d 280 (Iowa 1979) (destruction of veterinarian's handwritten log was not grounds for a best evidence objection where the log was transcribed by a typist and verified prior to destruction, and the transcription was entered into evidence.

14 *See* Chapter 6 for details related to the duty to preserve relevant records while litigation is pending, imminent or foreseeable.

15 *See* Chapter 3 for admitting records that are an admission by a party opponent.

16 *Glossary of Records Management Terms*, ARMA International (1988).

The Federal Records Act also specifies certain non-record material that is excluded from its definition of records:

> . . . Library and museum material made or acquired and preserved solely for reference or exhibition purposes, extra copies of documents preserved only for convenience of reference, and stocks of publications and of processed documents are not included.[17]

Since non-records are not records they will not be subject to the same scrutiny as official or even unofficial records. Non-record material may be created, modified and destroyed without the formal procedures otherwise required for a records management or records retention program. Typically, organizations permit non-record material to be destroyed without the need for a records retention schedule.

1.2. Business Defined

The first step in defining a business record is to define "business." Several statutory definitions are widely used, and all define business very broadly.

> The term "business" shall include every kind of business, profession, occupation, calling or operation of institutions, whether carried on for profit or not.[18]

> "Business" includes every kind of private business, profession, occupation, calling or operation of private institutions, whether carried on for profit or not.[19]

The Federal Rules of Evidence, and the related Uniform Rules of Evidence, define business in a similarly broad fashion.

---

17   44 U.S.C. 3301.
18   The *Uniform Business Records as Evidence Act*, adopted in Arizona, California, Connecticut, Idaho, Minnesota, Missouri, New Jersey, New York, North Dakota, Ohio, Pennsylvania, Rhode Island, South Carolina, Tennessee, Vermont and Washington.
19   The *Uniform Preservation of Private Business Records Act*, adopted in Colorado, Georgia, Illinois, Maryland, New Hampshire, Oklahoma, and Texas.

The term "business" . . . includes business, institution, association, profession, occupation and calling of every kind, whether or not conducted for profit. [20]

At least 35 states and one territory have adopted the *Uniform Rules of Evidence*, containing wording identical or substantially identical to Fed.R.Evid. 803[21].

The term "business" in all these definitions clearly includes government, non-profit organizations, charitable and religious organizations and most other organizations or professions.

The business records exception to the hearsay rule,[22] refers to "records of regularly conducted activity." It is the regularity of the activity and the need to keep accurate records for the purposes of the activity that define a business for the purposes of the business records exception to the hearsay rule. Judicial decisions reflect this emphasis on the regularity of the activity, rather than its commercial or business nature, as the key to whether it produces business records. As a result, courts have accepted a wide variety of activities as businesses in the business records context.

Regularly conducted activities, such as the state forensics laboratories,[23] coroners offices, hospitals, police departments, and attorneys,[24] are businesses within the meaning of the business records exception. The term business has even been extended to illegal activities such as loansharking operations.[25]

---

20 Fed.R.Evid. 803(6).
21 Alaska, Arizona, Arkansas, Colorado, Delaware, Florida, Hawaii, Idaho, Iowa, Kentucky, Louisiana, Maine, Michigan, Minnesota, Mississippi, Montana, Nebraska, Nevada, New Jersey, New Mexico, North Carolina, North Dakota, Ohio, Oklahoma, Oregon, Puerto Rico, Rhode Island, South Dakota, Tennessee, Texas, Utah, Vermont, Washington, West Virginia, Wisconsin and Wyoming
22 Fed.R.Evid. 803(6).
23 *United States v. Farmer*, 820 F.Supp. 259 (W.D.Va. 1993).
24 See generally, Monarch Federal Savings and Loan Assn. v. Genser, 383 A.2d 475 (N.J.Supr. 1977).
25 See *People v. Kennedy*, 503 N.E.2d 501, 505 (1986), wherein the court, although concluding that an inadequate foundation had been laid for the admission of a loan shark's records into evidence, nonetheless concluded that a loansharking operation was a business within the meaning of the business records exception, noting: "[The] principles of efficient accounting apply just as readily to an illicit enterprise as they do to a licit business" (quoting *United States v. Baxter*, 492 F.2d 150, 164, *cert. denied* 416 U.S. 940, 94 S.Ct. 1946, 40 L.Ed. 292).

1.3. Business Records Defined

A showing that the creator or custodian of a record is a business does not, in and of itself, confer upon that record status as a business record for the purposes of litigation.

A distinction must first be drawn between the everyday usage of the term "business records" and the definition of that term as used in judicial proceedings. In common usage, all types of records produced on paper, microfilm, computer, optical disk or other media will likely to be viewed as business records. This common view is inadequate, however, if these records will be used in litigation.

An organization whose records contain favorable information will likely seek to have them admitted as business records. In order to do so, however, these records must meet the judicial interpretation of the definition of business records. The records must meet specified criteria for creation and maintenance in order for the court to be satisfied that they are sufficiently trustworthy to be received into evidence.

In contrast, records created or adopted by the opposing party that contain unfavorable information or information favorable to the other party, need not meet these criteria in order to be admissible into evidence.[26] The mere fact that the organization created records which contain information unfavorable to its own position is an indicator of reliability sufficient to justify their admission.

Thus, if an organization maintains documents which do not meet the judicial requirements for trustworthiness and the documents subsequently become relevant in a lawsuit, the organization may find itself in the position of being unable to admit those documents favorable to its case, while its opponent is able to bring into evidence equivalent documents, perhaps from the same files, which are unfavorable to the organization's position. When developing and implementing a records management program, attention must be given to the distinction between records, documents,

---

26   Fed.R.Evid. 801(d)(2).

and other everyday data compilations, and the statutory definition of business records. As used in this volume, business records will refer to those records that meet the statutory definition for business records as construed by the courts. When such terms as "records," "documents," or "data" are used, they will refer to records in the everyday sense, which may or may not meet the statutory definition for business records.

1.4. Court Cases Defining Business Records

Business records are hearsay.[27] "Hearsay" is normally inadmissible in evidence, but records which meet the definition of business records are admissible notwithstanding that they are hearsay. The business records exception to the hearsay rule sets forth the definition for a business record which serves as the starting point for any judicial inquiry into the status of an information compilation as a business record:

> *Records of regularly conducted activity.* A memorandum, report, record, or data compilation, in any form, of acts, events, conditions, opinions, or diagnoses, made at or near the time by, or from information transmitted by, a person with knowledge, if kept in the course of a regularly conducted business activity, and if it was the regular practice of that business activity to make the memorandum, report, record, or data compilation, all as shown by the testimony of the custodian or other qualified witness, unless the source of information or the method or circumstances of preparation indicate lack of trustworthiness.[28]

Thus, from a judicial standpoint, a record or data compilation must have four qualities in order to qualify as a business record —

- It must be made at or near the time of the event that it records;

- It must be made by or from information transmitted by a person with knowledge of the event;

---

27 *See* Chapter 3 generally for a discussion of the business records exception to the hearsay rule.
28 Fed.R.Evid. 803(6).

- It must be made in the course of a regularly conducted business activity; and

- It must have been the regular practice of that business activity to make a document or data compilation.

The presence of these factors is deemed to be indicative of the reliability of the records.

> [Business] records must be kept pursuant to some routine *procedure* designed to assure their accuracy, . . . they must be created for *motives* that would tend to assure accuracy . . . and they must not themselves be mere accumulations of hearsay or uninformed opinion.[29]

> A business record is recognized as an exception to the hearsay rule because it is made in the regular course of business and therefore possesses certain "hallmarks of authenticity."[30]

> The basic theory [of the Uniform Business Records As Evidence Act] is that records which are properly shown to have been kept as required normally possess a circumstantial probability of trustworthiness, and therefore ought to be received in evidence unless the trial court, after examining them and hearing the manner of their preparation explained, entertains serious doubt as to whether they are dependable or worthy of confidence.[31]

Courts consider business records to include data compilations, electronic records and even some unusual forms of records. Any recorded information which meets the criteria for admissibility may be viewed by a court as a business record.

In *Rice v. United States,*[32] a baggage strap tag and claim check, recovered from a stolen suitcase, were held to be business records where testimony demonstrated that they were prepared by a bus company employee in the regular course of business and pursuant

---

29 *United States v. Fendley*, 522 F.2d 181, 184 (5th Cir. 1975) (quoting *United States v. Miller*, 500, F.2d 751, 754 (5th Cir. 1974)).

30 *United States v. Farmer*, 820 F.Supp. 259, 264 (W.D.Va. 1993).

31 *Monarch Federal Savings and Loans Assn. v. Genser*, 383 A.2d 475, 480 (N.J.Super. 1977) (quoting *Mahoney v. Minsky*, 188 A.2d 166, 218 (1963)).

32 *Rice v. United States*, 411 F.2d 485 (1969).

to established procedures. In *Hill v. Joseph T. Ryerson & Son* [33] the court concluded that a number painted on a piece of pipe by a warehouse employee was admissible as a business record of the employer, even though the pipe had subsequently passed into the hands of a purchaser. The court emphasized that regularity and trustworthiness, rather than the method of storage or retention by the maker is the key to the admissibility of business records. [34]

Armstrong v. Executive Office of the President, [35] strongly suggests that, in the absence of a rational policy classifying them otherwise, E-mail messages are records subject to normal retention procedures. The court rejected the assertion that an E-mail communication could be defined as a non-record merely by a conclusory statement that such was the case. The court also concluded that, in the absence of a policy excluding them from status as records, E-mail messages would be treated as records by the court. *Armstrong* is not directly applicable to business records, because it was decided in the context of the *Federal Records Act,* [36] which is applicable only to records of federal agencies. The court's conclusions are nonetheless applicable to business records by analogy. Electronically generated or transmitted information of any kind has at least the potential to be a business record. Thus, a records management program must include electronically created data compilations such as E-mail.

Another important aspect of *Armstrong* was the court's distinction between electronic records format and paper printouts of the same record. The court concluded that the paper record did not contain some information contained in the electronic record, such as date and time of delivery, and list of recipients. In the court's view, retention of a paper printout did not satisfy a requirement that a complete copy of the original record be kept.

Hill, Rice, and *Armstrong* have broad implications for the records management program. Information not normally perceived of as business records may have the status of business

---

[33] *Hill v. Joseph T. Ryerson & Son, Inc.,* 268 S.E.2d 296 (W.Va. 1980).
[34] *Id.* at 310.
[35] *Armstrong v. Executive Office of the President,* 1 F.3d 127 (D.C.C. 1993).
[36] 41 U.S.C. 2101 *et. seq.*

records, whether or not so intended by their creator or custodian. In such a case, a duty to preserve them may arise.

Records may also be needed as business records for admission in subsequent litigation. If tags, labels, or other forms are discarded, or computer disks erased after litigation, on a theory that they are no longer needed, sanctions may ensue in subsequent, similar litigation for failing to preserve these records.

Similarly, an organization may encounter a surprise in subsequent litigation unless computer data are viewed as potential business records and adequately provided for in the records retention program. Electronic mail may contain informal language, terse comments and incomplete information. When entered into evidence by a sophisticated opponent, the information can prove quite damaging.

The records management program can provide significant guidance for the treatment of business records versus non-business records. Word processing files, electronic mail, voice mail, databases and other data compilations often will be used to create business records and simply to transact business. By themselves, they may constitute non-records —tools or development materials — rather than the business records themselves.

1.5. The Status of Non-Business Records

Some records do not meet the judicial criteria for business records. These records may still be valuable for the effective operation of the organization and may be subject to a legal duty to preserve. The duty to preserve records and data is not dependent upon their status as business records, but is instead dependent upon the informational content of the document or data compilation in question.

The records management program must address non-business records in the same fashion that it deals with its business records. Their retention and destruction must be governed by business and legal requirements reflected in the records retention policy.

1.6. Records Management System Design Considerations

The records management program controls the creation of business records and should establish appropriate procedures to ensure that records qualify as business records for purposes of admissibility into evidence.

This does not mean that records that do not qualify as business records will necessarily be inadmissible at trial. Other hearsay exceptions cover a variety of records.

But favorable records created by an organization that do not qualify as business records may not qualify for admission into evidence under any other exception. A records management program that places an emphasis on procedural requirements for business records can therefore help the organization in litigation without benefiting the opposing party.

A poor records management program can significantly disadvantage a party in litigation. Opponents who find favorable records within the opponent's files will probably be able to admit them whether or not they qualify as business records. Thus, the opposing party need not be concerned with whether they are business records when it seeks to admit them at trial.

The records management program must address two evidence issues. First, many records which appear to be routine business records may not meet the statutory definition of business records for the purpose of admission at trial. Second, many types of information that do not appear to be business records may meet the judicial criteria, and thus be admissible as business records.

When examining a record or data compilation to determine whether it qualifies for status as a business record in connection with litigation, attention must be given to the following factors:

- Was it made at or near the time of the event or condition that it records, or from information transmitted by a person with knowledge of that event or condition?

- Was the entity that created the document or data compilation a business?

- Was it the regular practice of that business to make the document or data compilation?

- Do the circumstances of preparation indicate trustworthiness, as, for example, by relying on the record for the conduct of the day-to-day business activities?

- Can each of the above be demonstrated by a custodian or other qualified person?

If each of the above can be answered in the affirmative, then the document or data compilation in question probably qualifies as a business record for the purposes of litigation.

The records management program should be designed and conducted in a manner that facilitates easy and persuasive demonstration of compliance with the above factors.

- The program should include written procedures that document the circumstance related to records creation and maintenance.

- The program should document the types of records maintained by the organization.

- The system should periodically be audited to confirm the accuracy of the procedures.

- The records manager, custodian or other witness ultimately used at trial should be familiar with the records management program and procedures, and be able to clearly testify regarding the creation, maintenance and disposition of records.

The inability to prove or explain the process or system used to produce records could result in the exclusion of evidence necessary to support claims in litigation.

Chapter 2. Form of Records

The law does not generally require that business records be created or stored on a particular medium.[37] Rather, as stated by the court in *United States v. De Georgia*:[38]

> Regularly-maintained business records are admissible in evidence as an exception to the hearsay rule because the circumstance that they are regularly-maintained records upon which the organization relies in conducting its business assures accuracy not likely to be enhanced by introducing into evidence the original documents upon which the records are based.

2.1. Original Records

There are, however, circumstances when an original, paper record may be mandated by statute or regulation.

§ 673.32 Fiscal procedures and records

(e) *Retention of records*

$$* \; * \; * \; * \; *$$

---

37 Older, superseded laws specifically mandated paper records or bound books. Very few laws now mandate specific forms of records, although some may restrict the type of reproduction technologies that may be used.

38 *United States v. De Georgia*, 420 F.2d 889, 893 (9th Cir. 1969).

(3) *Loan records.*

* * * * *

(iv) An institution shall keep the original promissory notes and repayment schedules in a locked, fireproof container until the loan obligations are satisfied. The institution shall then return the original notes to the borrower marked "paid in full" . . . [39]

When the law specifies original records, preservation of duplicates instead of originals may subject the organization to fines, penalties and loss of rights. The records management program must clearly identify when originals must be preserved.

Courts have addressed questions involving the admissibility in litigation of records created and stored on various media. In addition to paper records, courts have admitted records stored on microfiche, [40] and microfilm.[41] Records stored on microfilm or microfiche may be subject to extensive technical requirements promulgated by state and federal regulatory agencies.

The Uniform Preservation of Private Business Records Act[42] states that maintaining duplicate records constitutes compliance with state laws that require records to be maintained. The Uniform Photographic Copies of Business and Public Records as Evidence Act[43] permits duplicates to be used "to the same extent as the originals" in any "judicial or administrative proceeding" unless the law requires that originals be preserved or, by implication, the law permits originals to be destroyed after duplication provided that specific regulatory requirements have been met.

Records created and maintained on computers and similar equipment are equally acceptable to the courts. In early cases involving the question of admissibility of computer records,[44] the courts explicitly recognized the necessity for courts to keep pace

---

39   34 C.F.R. § 673.32. This is a regulation regarding student loan programs prepared by the Office of Postsecondary Education, U.S. Department of Education.

40   *Rudo v. Karp*, 564 A.2d 100 (Md.Ct.App. 1989); *State v. Hunnicut*, 261 S.E.2d 682 (N.C.Ct.App. 1980).

41   *Neier v. United States*, 127 Bankr. 669 (D.Kan. 1991).

42   *Infra. See also* Appendix A for the text of this uniform law.

43   *Infra. See also* Appendix A for the text of this uniform law.

44   *See *King v. State ex rel. Murdock Acceptance Corp.* 222 So.2d 393 (Miss. 1969).

with technological advancement in information storage in the business world. One court also noted that the general reliability of computers is undisputed in the business world, and concluded that, so long as the computer-generated records met criteria of reliability and trustworthiness, they were admissible into evidence.[45] A long line of cases establishes beyond dispute the acceptability of computerized recordkeeping.[46]

2.2. Duplicate Records

Legal acceptance of duplicate records has been equally pragmatic, and has been codified in a number of jurisdictions that have adopted various uniform or model acts. The Uniform Preservation of Private Business Records Act[47] states:

> If in the regular course of business a person makes reproductions of original business records, the preservation of such reproductions constitutes compliance with any laws of this state requiring that business records be kept or preserved.

The Uniform Photographic Copies of Business and Public Records as Evidence Act[48] states:

---

45 It is beyond the scope of this book to address the specific legal requirements for electronic records. *See* Donald S. Skupsky, *Legal Requirements for Microfilm, Computer and Optical Disk Records*, Information Requirements Clearinghouse (1994).

46 *See, e.g., *United States v. Linn*, 880 F.2d 209 (9th Cir. 1989); *United States v. Catabran*, 836 F.2d 453 (9th Cir. 1988); *United States v. Russo*, 480 F.2d 1228 (6th Cir. 1973); *Grand Liquor Co., Inc. v. Department of Revenue*, 367 N.E.2d 1238 (Ill. 1977); *People v. Bovio*, 455 N.E.2d 829 (Ill.Ct.App. 1983); *King v. State ex rel. Murdock Acceptance Corp.*, 222 So.2d 393 (Miss. 1969); *Missouri Valley Walnut Co. v. Snyder*, 569 S.W.2d 324 (Mo.Ct.App. 1978); *Transport Indemnity Co. v. Seib*, 132 N.W.2d 871 (Neb. 1965); *State v. Kane*, 594 P.2d 1357 (Wash.Ct.App. 1979).

47 The Uniform Preservation of Private Business Records Act has been adopted in Colorado, Georgia, Illinois, Maryland, New Hampshire, Oklahoma and Texas.

48 The Uniform Photographic Copies of Business and Public Records as Evidence Act has been adopted in Alabama, Alaska, California, Colorado, Connecticut, Georgia, Idaho, Iowa, Kansas, Kentucky, Maine, Massachusetts, Michigan, Minnesota, Missouri, Nebraska, New Hampshire, New Jersey, New York, North Carolina, North Dakota, Pennsylvania, Rhode Island, South Carolina, South, South Dakota, Tennessee, United States, Utah, Vermont, Virgin Island, Virginia, Washington, West Virginia, Wisconsin.

If any business, institution, member of a profession or
calling, or any department or agency of government, in the
regular course of business or activity has kept or recorded
any memorandum, writing, entry, print, representation or
combination thereof, of any act, transaction, occurrence or
event, and in the regular course of business has caused
any or all of the same to be recorded, copied or reproduced
by any photographic, photostatic, microfilm, microcard,
miniature photographic or other process which accurately
reproduces or forms a durable medium for so reproducing
the original, the original may be destroyed in the regular
course of business unless held in a custodial or fiduciary
capacity or unless its preservation is required by law. Such
reproduction, when satisfactorily identified, is as admissible in evidence as the original itself in any judicial or
administrative proceeding whether the original is in existence or not, and an enlargement or facsimile of such
reproduction is likewise admissible in evidence if the
original reproduction is in existence and available for
inspection under direction of court. The introduction of a
reproduced record, enlargement or facsimile, does not
preclude admission of the original.

The Uniform Rules of Evidence also permit the admission of
duplicate records:

Rule 1003. Admissibility of duplicates.[49]

A duplicate is admissible to the same extent as an original
unless (1) a genuine question is raised as to the authenticity of the original or (2) in the circumstances it would
be unfair to admit the duplicate in lieu of the original.

The Uniform Rules of Evidence do not explicitly permit the
destruction of original records. Instead, it eliminates the need to
admit original records if the originals are destroyed without bad
faith, and permits the admission of other evidence of the contents
— such as a duplicate:

---

49 *See* Fed.R.Evid. 1003. The Uniform Rules of Evidence, similar to the Federal Rules
of Evidence have been adopted in whole or in part in Alaska, Arizona, Arkansas,
Colorado, Delaware, Florida, Hawaii, Iowa, Maine, Michigan, Minnesota,
Mississippi, Montana, Nebraska, Nevada, New Jersey, New Mexico, North Carolina,
North Dakota, Ohio, Oklahoma, Oregon, Puerto Rico, Rhode Island, South Dakota,
Tennessee, Texas, Utah, Vermont, Washington, West Virginia, Wisconsin, Wyoming.

Rule 1004. Admissibility of other evidence of contents.[50]

The original is not required, and other evidence of the contents of a writing, recording, or photograph is admissible if:

(1) Original is lost or destroyed. All originals are lost or have been destroyed, unless the proponent lost or destroyed them in bad faith; or

(2) Original not obtainable. No original can be obtained by any judicial process or procedure; or

(3) Original in possession of opponent. At a time when an original was under the control of the party against whom offered, that party was put on notice, by pleadings or otherwise, that the contents would be a subject of proof at the hearing, and that party does not produce the original at the hearing . . .

These provisions focus judicial inquiry into questions of trustworthiness, rather than on philosophical questions regarding "originals" or "duplicates," or similar discussions concerning particular technologies.

For computer records, the rules of evidence even blur the distinction between "original" and "duplicate".

An "original" of a writing or recording is the writing or recording itself or any counterpart intended to have the same effect by a person executing or issuing it. An "original" of a photograph includes the negative or any print therefrom. If data are stored in a computer or similar device, any printout or other output readable by sight, shown to reflect the data accurately, is an "original".[51]

The court in *In re Gulph Woods Corp.*[52] concluded that a computerized business record, prepared simultaneously or within a reasonable time period of the written record, and containing the same or similar information, is an original. Courts have concluded

---

50 *See* Fed.R.Evid. 1004.
51 Fed.R.Evid. 1001(3).
52 *In re Gulph Woods Corp.*, 82 Bankr. 373 (B.E.D.Pa. 1988).

that there is no basis for sanctions if companies destroy original documents, but retain copies. *Kansas-Nebraska Natural Gas Co. v. Marathon Oil Co.,*[53] is illustrative. The plaintiff moved for sanctions on the grounds that the defendant destroyed certain documents relevant to the issues pending before the court. While declining to impose sanctions, the court noted that there was no evidence that the defendant tampered with any of the destroyed documents or that the copies made available to counsel differed in any way. In the absence of such evidence, the court could not speculate that the duplicates sent to the plaintiff were not true duplicates.

Similarly, in *Joba Construction Co. v. Burns & Rowe,*[54] the court, citing Michigan Rules 1003 and 1004, dismissed, virtually without comment, an objection to the admission of photostatic copies of the minutes of a meeting. The court's conclusion was based solely upon a showing that the originals had been destroyed and a lack of evidence of bad faith in the destruction.

In *Pittman v. Dixie Ornamental Iron Co.,*[55] the court, construing Georgia Code § 38-702, concluded that photostatic copies of checks, apparently made from microfilm copies kept at the bank, were improperly excluded by the trial court. The court concluded that:

> [I]t makes no difference how many copies of the original
> are made, any copy of the original identified as a correct
> copy is admissible in evidence in lieu of the original.[56]

Other courts addressing the question of duplicate records have reached similar results in the absence of genuine questions about the accuracy of the reproductions.[57]

Reproduction of records on newer media such as electronic imaging systems using optical disk has yet to be subject to judicial

---

53 *Kansas-Nebraska Natural Gas Co. v. Marathon Oil Co.,* 109 F.R.D. 12 (D.Neb. 1983).
54 *Joba Construction Co. v. Burns & Rowe, Inc.,* 329 N.W.2d 760 (Mich.Ct.App. 1982).
55 *Pittman v. Dixie Ornamental Iron Co.,* 177 S.E.2d 167 (Ga.Ct.App. 1970).
56 *Id.* at 169.
57 *See *Hertz Corp. v. McCray,* 402 S.E.2d 298 (Ga.Ct.App. 1991); **Anametrics Services, Inc. v. Clifford A. Botway, Inc.,* 552 N.Y.App.Div.2d 238 (1990); **Vaught v. Nationwide Mutual Ins. Co.,* 156 S.E.2d 627 (S.C. 1967).

review. However, prior court decisions addressing computer-generated records are directly applicable to optical or other advanced
storage methods. As observed by the court in *United States v.
Vela*,[58] "computer data compilations . . . should be treated as any
other record of regularly conducted activity." [59] Further, the *Vela*
court defined the issue as whether the records are sufficiently
trustworthy to "be relied on by the company in conducting its
day-to-day business affairs." Precisely the same factors govern
acceptability of electronic imaging systems and optical disk
records.

Most statutes and regulations affecting business records do not
explicitly mention optical disk storage technology. A few statutes
and regulations explicitly limit the use of optical disk technology
to WORM (write once read many times) or other non-erasable
technology.[60]

Judicial review will not likely add to limitations on reproduction technology, other than reiterate those specified by statute or
regulation. Recent computer cases that have eliminated the need
to provide additional or extraordinary foundational testimony will
likely be applied to electronic imaging technology and optical disk
records. Thus, if an organization demonstrates that its optical disk
records meet the requirements established for admissibility of
paper or computer records, the records will likely be admitted.
Factors facilitating admissibility include evidence that the optical
disk records were prepared as part of a regularly conducted business activity, and are relied upon by the organization in conducting
its daily affairs.[61]

---

[58] *United States v. Vela*, 673 F.2d 86 (5th Cir. 1982).
[59] *Id.* at 90 (quoting **Rosenberg v. Collins*, 624 F.2d 659, 665 (5th Cir. 1980)).
[60] *See* 17 C.F.R. §§ 1.31 and 1.35 for regulations of the Commodity Futures Trading
      Commission that specifies WORM·technology must be used for maintaining required
      reports electronically instead of on paper or microfilm. This regulation, however, does
      not address maintaining reproductions of original records in electronic form.
[61] *See* Donald S. Skupsky, *Legal Requirements for Microfilm, Computer and Optical
      Disk Records*, Information Requirements Clearinghouse, Denver, CO (1994) for
      further analysis plus the text of statutes and regulations affecting microfilm,
      computer and optical disk records.

Part II. Business Records in Litigation

The role of those records admitted at trial is obvious — they will be used to bolster the contentions of the party that advocated their admission. Since the custodian of the records has a clear and compelling interest in proving its own contentions in a legal dispute, an important function of the records management program is to ensure that those records necessary to prevail in legal disputes are preserved, available, and, if need be, admissible at trial.

Chapter 3.   Admitting Records in Evidence

3.1. Hearsay Defined

> A "statement" is (1) an oral or written assertion or (2) non-verbal conduct of a person, if it is intended by him to be communicative. . . . "Hearsay" is a statement other than one made by the declarant while testifying at the trial or hearing, offering evidence to prove the truth of the matter asserted.[62]

> Hearsay is not admissible except as provided by law or [by the rules of evidence].[63]

Records or documents are "statements" made out of court. Records are hearsay if produced at trial with the intent of proving the truth of matters set forth in the document's contents. Records or documents will be inadmissible unless they qualify under one of the prescribed exceptions to the hearsay rule.

---

[62]   Fed.R.Evid. 801(a) and (c).
[63]   Fed.R.Evid. 802.

3.2. The Business Record Exception to the Hearsay Rule

At common law, hearsay was not admissible at trial. However, over time, a number of exceptions to the hearsay rule developed. These exceptions were ultimately codified in the Federal Rules of Evidence and in the Uniform Rules of Evidence.

Business records will not be excluded by the hearsay rule, even though the declarant[64] is unavailable as a witness if they qualify under one of these exceptions to the hearsay rule:

> *Records of regularly conducted business activity.* A memorandum, report, record, or data compilation, in any form, of acts, events, conditions, opinions, or diagnoses, made at or near the time, by, or from information transmitted by, a person with knowledge, if kept in the course of a regularly conducted business activity, and if it was the regular practice of that business activity to make the memorandum, report, record, or data compilation, all as shown by the testimony of the custodian or other qualified witness, unless the source of information or method or circumstances of preparation indicate lack of trustworthiness. The term "business" as used in this paragraph includes business, institution, association, profession, occupation, and calling of every kind, whether or not conducted for profit.[65]

> *Absence of entry in records kept in accordance with the provisions of [the above paragraph].* Evidence that a matter is not included in the memoranda, reports, records, or data compilations, in any form, kept in accordance with the provisions of [the above paragraph], to prove the nonoccurrence or nonexistence of the matter, if the matter was of a kind of which a memorandum, report, record, or data compilation was regularly made and preserved, unless the sources of information or other circumstances indicate a lack of trustworthiness.[66]

These provisions form the basis for the admissibility of business records at trial. It is when admission is sought under these provi-

---

64 In the case of a business record, the person who created the record.
65 Fed.R.Evid. 803(6).
66 Fed.R.Evid. 803(7).

sions that a document's status as a business record, as defined *infra*, must be established.

If the declarant is unavailable,[67] and the records do not meet the legal definition of business record, they may still be admissible under the following provision:

> *Statements for purposes of medical diagnosis or treatment.* Statements made for purposes of medical diagnosis or treatment and describing medical history, or past or present symptoms, pain, or sensations, or the inception or general character of the cause or external source thereof insofar as reasonably pertinent to medical diagnosis or treatment.[68]

If the declarant is available as a witness, a document or data compilation may still be admissible:

> *Recorded recollection.* A memorandum or record concerning a matter about which a witness once had knowledge but now has insufficient recollection to enable him to testify fully and accurately, shown to have been made or adopted by the witness when the matter was fresh in his memory and to reflect that knowledge correctly. If admitted, the memorandum or record may be read into evidence but may not itself be received as an exhibit unless offered by an adverse party.[69]

In addition to the above exceptions, there are a variety of other exceptions for public documents, treatises, historical documents, and other written hearsay. A residual hearsay exception for documents which fit none of the other categories allows some other records to be admitted if they contain:

> Equivalent circumstantial guarantees of trustworthiness [as compared with the other hearsay exceptions] if the court determines that (A) the statement is offered as evidence of a material fact; (B) the statement is more probative on the point for which it is offered than any other evidence which the proponent can procure through rea-

---

67 *See* Fed.R.Evid. 804(a) for circumstances defined as "unavailable".
68 Fed.R.Evid. 803(4).
69 Fed.R.Evid. 803(5).

sonable efforts; and (C) the general purposes of these rules
and the interests of justice will best be served by admission of the statement into evidence.[70]

This provision also contains provisions requiring that notice,
and certain information, be given the other party so that they have
a fair opportunity to prepare.

Certain types of documents with high intrinsic levels of reliability may, at least in theory, be admitted under this hearsay
exception, if the proponent is unable to establish any of the prerequisites necessary for admission under another hearsay
exception.

If the creator of the document included information detrimental
to the creator's interests, the document may be admissible without
meeting any of the above criteria.

> Statement against interest. A statement which was at the
> time of its making so far contrary to the declarant's pecuniary or proprietary interest, or so far tended to subject
> him to civil or criminal liability, or to render invalid a claim
> by him against another, that a reasonable man in his
> position would not have made the statement unless he
> believed it to be true. A statement tending to expose the
> declarant to criminal liability and offered to exculpate the
> accused is not admissible unless corroborating circumstances clearly indicate the trustworthiness of the statement.[71]

The statement against interest exception to the hearsay rule is
applied to admit records that contain information that is highly
contrary to the declarant's own interest. The exception may allow
a record produced by a third party to be introduced into evidence,
that might otherwise not be admissible.

---

70   Fed.R.Evid. 803(24).
71   Fed.R.Evid. 804(b)(3).

3.3. Admitting Records That Are Not Hearsay

However, records are not hearsay, and are admissible, if they contain statements or admissions made by the party opponent:

> A statement is not hearsay if —
>
> * * * * *
>
> Admission by party opponent. The statement is offered against a party and is (A) his own statement, in either his individual or a representative capacity or (B) a statement of which he has manifested his adoption or belief in its truth, or (C) a statement by a person authorized him to make a statement concerning the subject or (D) a statement by his agent or servant concerning the matter within the scope of his agency or employment, made during the existence of the relationship or (E) a statement made by a co-conspirator of a party during the course and in furtherance of the conspiracy.[72]

This broad language allows the admission of virtually any statement made by a party, if it is beneficial to the opponent's case, including virtually any document created by the party. This has two implications for the records management program: anything it maintains in its files which was created by a party opponent is admissible into evidence without the necessity of overcoming a hearsay objection. However, the party opponent may also delve into that same record system, and if it discovers anything there that is useful to its case, that material is also admissible without the necessity of overcoming a hearsay objection.

Such documents are deemed reliable because of the information which is adverse to the declarant's position. The law presumes that the declarant would not have recorded such adverse information, had it not been true.

Due consideration should be given to the effect of Fed.R.Evid. 801(d)(2) on electronic mail.[73] The admission by a party opponent rule gives an opponent a virtually unlimited ability to admit this

---

72 Fed.R.Evid. 801(d)(2).
73 Electronic mail is common referred to as "E-mail."

type of information into evidence. The organization's records management program must therefore take active control of these records, as well as of paper records. Employees throughout the organization should be informed that any record of any type that they create is likely to be admissible by an opponent in litigation if the opponent deems that information beneficial to its case.

While it is not an appropriate goal of a records management system to hide relevant information from opposing litigants, neither is an organization required to create evidence for opponents, absent a legal mandate to do so. The organization and its employees should bear these considerations in mind at all stages of the information creation process. Employees should refrain from creating documents that are not adequately researched for factual accuracy, that do not accurately reflect organizational policy, that state the author's unofficial, personal views as those of the organization, or that are created under circumstances, such as anger, that have a high likelihood of causing other problems.

In conjunction with this, the organization and its employees should bear in mind that E-mail and similar documents will be viewed long after the fact when the author may not be available, or the author's memory of the events has faded. In such a case, the organization will be unable to offer any mitigating explanation for damaging statements contained in the records.

The organization may find itself faced by the very worst of those documents in court. Opponents may selectively use those documents, picking among the available documents and arranging them in order to maximize their evidentiary impact. Yet, because of the higher barriers placed on documents which are not admissions of a party opponent, the organization may be unable to admit its own documents which would tend to explain the damaging ones.

3.4. Admitting Records Produced by Third Parties

The fact that something maintained in a business's files is used as a business record does not guarantee its acceptance as a business record at trial. As observed earlier, a document that qualifies as a business record must be:

- Made at or near the time of the event that it records;

- Made based on information by or from a person with knowledge;

- Made in the course of a regularly conducted business activity;

- Made as a regular practice of that business activity; and

- Shown to fulfill the above criteria by a competent witness.

In the case of documents created by third parties, and then retained in the recipient's files — letters, memoranda, invoices, bills, etc. — the recipient may be unable to establish the prerequisites necessary for qualification as a business record. For example, the records manager from the recipient organization will probably be unable to testify as to the circumstances of the creation of a letter or invoice — whether it was made by or from information transmitted by a person with knowledge, or whether it was made at or near the time of the event that it records. The inability to establish such documents as business records may be problematic in the event such documents are needed in litigation.

Many organizations retain large numbers of such documents, and, in many cases, rely upon them as the primary record for various kinds of transactions. To the business personnel who routinely rely on the accuracy of such records, formalistic objections to their qualifications as business records may seem absurd. Nonetheless, it is prudent to conclude and expect that courts will reject the offer of such third party documents as business records.

Some courts have had little trouble accepting documents produced by third parties as business records of the custodian. In *Harris v. State*,[74] the defendant was charged with unauthorized use of a motor vehicle. As proof of ownership of the vehicle by a vehicle dealer, the State introduced into evidence a certificate prepared by the manufacturer, transferring the vehicle to the dealer. On *voir dire*, the defense established that the dealership employee establishing the foundation for the record had no knowledge of whether the employee of the manufacturer who signed the

---

[74] *Harris v. State*, 846 S.W.2d 960 (Tex.Ct.App. 1993).

certificate had personal information of the information contained in the certificate. The certificate was admitted over defense objections. The appellate court concluded that the certificate was properly admissible as a business record of the dealership:[75]

> The test of whether such records should be admitted rests upon their reliability. Here the test of reliability is met. Automobile manufacturers have a great interest in assuring that the vehicle information number (VIN) on their products correspond with the appropriate invoices, since reliable identification procedures are an economic necessity for their business.

For this court, the formal requirements of the business records exception can be eliminated when a document has a high degree of intrinsic reliability. That reliability need not be established by a foundation witness, but can apparently be established from the nature of the record itself and from the presumed reliability of its source. The only requirement left is that the record be *maintained* in the regular course of business. But, this is not a universal view.

In *United States v. Pelullo*[76] the defendant was charged with wire fraud and racketeering. The government introduced a number of wire transfer records taken from both the defendant's businesses and several banks. On appeal, the defendant contended that the documents were inadmissible hearsay. The government first contended that the documents were admissions of the defendant, since they were records of the corporations controlled by him. The court rejected this argument, observing that the records were made by banks, and not by the defendant or corporations controlled by him. Further, the court noted that the defendant neither directed nor authorized the creation of the records.

The government also asserted that the documents were admissible under the business records exception. Acknowledging that no

---

75 *See also *United States v. Hines*, 564 F.2d 925, 928 (10th Cir. 1977), aff'd, 434 U.S. 1022 (1978). The defendant was charged with selling stolen vehicles. A witness referred to an invoice she alleged to have received when she purchased the car. The defendant objected, claiming that the invoice was inadmissible as a business record, because the witness had not prepared the invoice herself. The court concluded that the document was admissible as a business record.

76 *United States v. Pelullo*, 964 F.2d 193 (3rd Cir. 1992).

records custodian had provided foundation for their admission, the government nonetheless contended that sufficient indicia of reliability were evident because (1) the records were obtained in response to grand jury subpoenas directed to the corporations and their banks; (2) testimony of witnesses involved in the transactions corroborated the information in the records; and (3) defendant pointed to no reason why the records would not be reliable.

The court rejected this argument. Although noting that a wide variety of testimony and evidence may qualify a record as a business record, the court nonetheless concluded there is no authority for the proposition that documents containing hearsay are admissible simply because there are some indicia of trustworthiness to the statements. The court concluded that, even though a non-custodial witness such as a government agency, or even documentary evidence, may be used to lay the foundation required under the business records exception:

> [T]hat witness or those documents must still demonstrate that the records were made contemporaneously with the act the documents purport to record by someone with knowledge of the subject matter, that they were made in the regular course of business, and that such records were regularly kept by the business. [citations omitted]

The court then observed that the government agent used to qualify the records did not purport to have familiarity with the recordkeeping system of the banks, nor did he attest to any of the other requirements under the business records exception. Thus, the court concluded, an adequate foundation for admission of the records had not been laid.

Presumably, the wire transfer records in *Pelullo* had as great, or nearly as great, an inherent degree of reliability as the motor vehicle certificate and invoice in *Harris v. State* and *United States v. Hines*. The difference appears to have been more in the court's willingness to do away with the formal requirements of the business records exception, than with the intrinsic reliability of the documents in question. Other courts faced with similar situations have produced a variety of results, and a general rule is difficult to perceive. This is particularly so in cases where the documents are not intrinsically reliable.

In *Hamilton Music v. York,*[77] the plaintiff attempted to introduce into evidence a computer printout created by and received from a third party. The appellate court concluded that the printout's mere presence in the plaintiff's files did not render it admissible as a business record of the plaintiff. Since the plaintiff had met none of the requisites for admission of the printout as a business record under the business records exception to the hearsay rule, the court concluded that the trial court properly rejected the printout.

However, the plaintiff in *Hamilton* could have qualified the printout as a business record with appropriate preparation. The plaintiff was not prepared to demonstrate that the printout met the formal requisites of the business records exception to the hearsay rule — it was made in the regular course of business, at or near the time of the act or event it recorded, and that the method and time of preparation were such as to justify its admission.[78] Had the plaintiff introduced evidence such as placing an employee of the third party with knowledge of the method of preparation of the record on the stand, the printout undoubtedly could have been admitted into evidence. Although the printout was not a business record of the plaintiff, it would have been viewed by the court as a business record of the third party. Once admitted, this distinction would have had little impact on the use of the printout at trial.[79]

> Documents may be admitted under 803(6) even though they are records of a business entity other than the proponent . . . .[80]

In *River Dock & Pile v. O&G Industries,*[81] the court examined whether letters sent by third parties and maintained in the recipient's files are business records of the recipient. After noting that the business record exception is predicated upon the entrant having a business duty to report, and noting that the foundation

---

77 *Hamilton Music, Inc. v. York*, 565 S.W.2d 838 (Mo.Ct.App. 1978).
78 Fed.R.Evid. 803(6).
79 The prosecution in *Pelullo* could also have employed a similar technique.
80 **Baxter Health Care Corp. v. Healthdyne, Inc.*, 944 F.2d 1573, 1577 (11th Cir. 1991).
    See also United States v. Vela, 673 F.2d 86 (5th Cir. 1982); **United States v. De Georgia*, 420 F.2d 889 (9th Cir. 1969).
81 *River Dock & Pile, Inc. v. O&G Industries, Inc.*, 595 A.2d 839 (Conn. 1991).

witness testified only that the letter was received in the ordinary course of business, the court concluded that:

> The mere fact that [the recipient] received this letter in the ordinary course of business and included the document in its files tells us nothing about the motivation of the maker, and therefore would not ordinarily satisfy the requirements of [the business records exception].[82]

After noting that the foundation witness might be able to establish that the letter was a business record of the third party, the court further concluded:

> We emphasize, however, that the mere receipt of documents in the ordinary course of business, in the absence of any duty owed by the entrant to the business to prepare the record, would not ordinarily establish such documents as business records.[83]

A similar conclusion was reached in *United States v. Rosenstein*.[84] The court concluded:

> Some of the Liechtenstein documents were letters from third parties who were not working for CTI. They "were not made in the regular course of the business of the company in whose files they were found . . . . "[citations omitted] The requirements of the Business Records Rule are not fulfilled by a showing that the addressee routinely kept a file of such correspondence. It must appear that the letter was written in the regular course of its author's business.

United States v. Rosenstein suggests that such documents may be admissible either as business records of the person who wrote them, or, if written under a duty to the addressee, as business records of the addressee. In either case, the proponent must be prepared to establish either such basis by an adequate foundation.

Under certain circumstances, records prepared by third parties may qualify as business records of the litigant introducing them

---

82 *Id.* at 847.
83 *Id.*
84 *United States v. Rosenstein*, 474 F.2d 705, 710 (2nd Cir. 1973).

into evidence. The court in *River Dock & Pile v. O&G Industries,* *supra,* concluded that, under Connecticut law, there is no requirement that a business record be prepared by an organization itself in order to be admissible as a business record of that organization. If the organization does not prepare the records itself, the creator must have had a duty to the organization to prepare the records for it. The court concluded that, under the particular facts of that case, an inadequate foundation had been laid for the admission of the report in question, and thus its admission was reversible error. But the court noted that on retrial it might be possible to satisfy the foundational requirements and properly admit the report.

A similar conclusion was reached in *Argueta v. Baltimore and Ohio Chicago Terminal Railroad Co.*[85] The court distinguished a number of prior Illinois cases where documents prepared by third parties were inadmissible, noting that in those cases the documents were not commissioned by the business seeking to introduce them into evidence, even though the documents were retained in that business's files. The court then concluded that test reports on parts of a collapsed crane, commissioned from an independent laboratory by the defendant, should have been admitted as business records of the defendant. The court noted that the key consideration in a situation such as this is the authority of the third party to act on behalf of the business.[86]

> Where a third party is authorized by a business to generate the record at issue, the record is of no use to the business unless it is accurate and, therefore, the record bears sufficient indicia of reliability to qualify as a business record under the hearsay rule.[87]

---

[85] *Argueta v. Baltimore and Ohio Chicago Terminal Railroad Co.,* 586 N.E.2d 386 (Ill.Ct.App. 1991).

[86] *See also United States v. Childs,* 5 F.3d 1328 (9th Cir. 1993) (records prepared under contract by private motor club admissible as business records of the Alberta, Canada, department of motor vehicles). *But see Paddack v. Dave Christensen, Inc.,* 745 F.2d 1254 (9th Cir. 1984), wherein the court rejected the contention that an audit of a pension fund, conducted by an outside accountant for the trustees of the fund, was admissible as a business record. The court reasoned that, because the audit was a special audit, ordered after irregularities were suspected, it was a document prepared in anticipation of litigation, and was thus inadmissible.

[87] *Argueta v. Baltimore and Ohio Chicago Terminal Railroad Co.,* 586 N.E.2d 386, 392 (Ill.Ct.App. 1991).

There may be circumstances in which third party documents are admissible as business records of their ultimate custodian, even though the maker of the records had no duty to the custodian to make them. In *GT & MC v. Texas City Refining, Inc.*,[88] the plaintiff kept invoices from outside vendors as part of its business records. In a suit over the collapse of an oil tank, the plaintiff sought to introduce these invoices as part of its business records.

The court noted that although the documents were initially authored by outside vendors, employees of the plaintiff placed markings on the invoices after receipt including the date, identity of the recipient, approval for payment and other information. By these acts, the invoices became the plaintiff's primary record of information about the underlying transaction and, thus, the plaintiff's business records. The court explicitly declined to conclude that the word "made" as used in Rule 803(6) was synonymous with the words "authored by".

An organization cannot assume that documents prepared by third parties and retained in its files will be admissible at trial as the organization's business records. If the organization determines that it maintains large numbers of records which do not meet the requirements for admission as business records, and the information contained on them is likely to be relevant for litigation, it may be worthwhile to determine if the information can be maintained so that records can be admitted under the business records exception to the hearsay rule.

The precise strategy for incorporating these third party documents into an organization's business records will depend upon a variety of factors, including the nature of the records themselves, as well as court decisions in the jurisdiction whose law controls.

As indicated in *GT & MC v. Texas City Refining*, it may be possible to incorporate the original third party documents into an organization's business by routine use and reliance. As observed by the *GT & MC* court, such routine use and reliance can be indicated by adding information to the records, which has the

---

[88] *GT & MC, Inc. v. Texas City Refining, Inc.*, 822 S.W.2d 252 (Tex.Ct.App. 1991).

additional effect of making the document more than just some-thing received from a third party.

This area should, however, be approached with some caution. The records custodian may not be able to avoid the hearsay problem by the simple strategy of incorporating the hearsay state-ments made by third parties into documents created by the organi-zation. Hearsay statements contained within an organization's business records must themselves be admissible under one of the hearsay exceptions if those statements are to be admissible. Courts do not ignore this issue:

> Hearsay included within hearsay is not excluded under the hearsay rule if each part of the combined statements conforms to an exception of the hearsay rule provided in these rules.[89]

As observed by the court in *River Dock & Pile v. O&G Industries:*[90]

> [T]he information contained in [a record] must be based on the entrant's own observation or on information of others whose business duty it was to transmit it to the entrant. If the information does not have such a basis, it adds another level of hearsay to the [record] which neces-sitates a separate exception to the hearsay rule in order to justify its admission. [citation omitted]
>
> Documents may be admitted under 803(6) even though they are records of a business entity other than the pro-ponent, and there is no requirement that the person whose firsthand knowledge was the basis of the entry be identi-fied, so long as it was the recording entity's business practice to obtain such information from persons with firsthand knowledge.

As stated by another court:

> Rule 803(6) does not eliminate a double hearsay problem unless the informant's statement also conforms to one of the exceptions to the rule against hearsay. "Each partici-pant in the chain producing the record — from the initial

---

89 Fed.R.Evid. 805.
90 *River Dock & Pile, Inc. v. O&G Industries, Inc.*, 595 A.2d 839, 844 (Conn. 1991).

observer-reporter to the final entrant — must be acting in
the course of this regularly conducted business, or must
meet the test of some other hearsay exception." [citations
omitted].[91]

An alternative approach is to maximize the number of circumstances under which third party documents are created under a
duty to the recipient. This can be achieved by inserting language
into contracts or requiring the periodic submission of invoices or
bills, transforming these documents into a legal obligation between the parties. These documents then have two indicia of
reliability — the recipient's reliance upon the accuracy of the documents in the conduct of its business affairs and a legal duty on the
part of the third party to create and submit these documents.

This approach may also prove effective for those documents
produced through less automatic or routine procedures than invoices. Reports, memoranda, and correspondences can also be
produced by third parties under a business duty, if the relevant
contract is structured appropriately to require their preparation
and submission when a certain type of problem, special event or
other specified circumstance occurs.

But, other parties may not be willing to agree to contract
provisions which place a duty on them to produce accurate, periodic
records for the benefit of the recipient, even if their customary
practice already conforms to that requirement. Regardless, a contract cannot predict all types of potentially relevant documents
produced by third parties and many will, therefore, be produced
without a duty.

The overall approach to third-party documents must therefore
be multifaceted and proactive. Long in advance of litigation, at the
time such documents are received by the custodian, at least the
following steps should be taken:

- Controlling law should be carefully reviewed to determine the
  extent to which third party documents will be considered as
  business records of the custodian.

---

91   *Baxter Health Care Corp. v. Healthdyne, Inc., 944 F.2d 1573, 1577 (11th Cir. 1991).

- The third party records should be maintained and used in a way that conforms with requirements stated in controlling decisions.

- If third party records cannot be incorporated into the custodian's record system, and to the extent allowed by Fed.R.Evid. Rule 805 and controlling decisions, additional pertinent information should be added to the records received by third parties or on new records created by the custodian.

- Those documents created by a third party under a duty such as a contract should be clearly so designated to facilitate their admissibility at trial.

- In those cases where none of the above can be achieved, the third party can provide a witness to establish that it was a business record of that party.

These steps will not guarantee the admission of every record prepared by a third party, but they do create the greatest likelihood of getting such documents admitted. In some cases, these steps may get records admitted into evidence which otherwise would not have been admitted.

For those documents that do not qualify as business records, it may be possible to admit them under the residual hearsay exception.[92] At least one case has suggested that bank documents and similar kinds of records possess sufficient indicia of reliability to justify admission under the residual exception.[93]

The conclusion changes when the records to be admitted into evidence were created by the party opponent. Under Fed.R.Evid. 801(d)(2), virtually anything created by an opponent is admissible. However, an organization cannot always anticipate which records received from another will become material in future litigation. Thus, procedures should attempt to maximize the admissibility of all documents, rather than assuming that they will be admissible under Fed.R.Evid. 804(b)(3) or Fed.R.Evid. 801(d)(2).

---

[92] Fed.R.Evid. 803(24).

[93] *United States v. Pelullo*, 964 F.2d 193 (3rd Cir. 1992). The bank records in that case were not admitted under the residual exception, because the government had failed to follow the procedural steps outlined in the residual exception.

3.5. Records Created for Litigation

The basis for the admissibility of business records is the reliance of the organization on them for the conduct of its everyday affairs, and the necessary accuracy that reliance implies. A corollary of this is that records created for purposes other than everyday business use may not be sufficiently reliable to justify their admission at trial. This is true of records prepared and maintained specifically for litigation, where the temptation to create misleading or inaccurate documents is obvious.[94]

The prohibition against the admission of records created for litigation is not necessarily universal. The court in *River Dock & Pile* stated the following:

> We have stated that "documents prepared for litigation are excluded, not on a per se basis, but rather upon an inquiry into whether such documents bear circumstantial indicia of lack of trustworthiness. In the exercise of appropriate discretion, courts may exclude such records where they are self serving and a motive for falsification can be demonstrated."[95]

Even courts which may allow admission of documents created for litigation will expect a high degree of intrinsic reliability from such documents. If use of such documents and files in litigation is considered a possibility, prepare them with great care, so that the court will be able to accurately judge their reliability.

For those business records whose business use is not obvious, and which might appear to have been created solely for the purpose of litigation, the business use must be carefully documented, so that, should the documents be needed in litigation, they will be able to meet any challenge based upon a contention that they are untrustworthy.

---

[94] *See, e.g.,* *United States v. Sanders*, 749 F.2d 195 (5th Cir. 1984); *River Dock & Pile, Inc. v. O&G Industries, Inc.*, 595 A.2d 839, 846 (Conn. 1991). *See also* *United States v. Fendley*, 522 F.2d 181, 184 (5th Cir. 1975). (Business records must be created for motives that would tend to assure accuracy; preparation for litigation is not such a motive.)

[95] *River Dock & Pile, Inc. v. O&G Industries, Inc.*, 595 A.2d 839, 846 (Conn. 1991).

Chapter 4.   Laying the Foundation for Admitting Records in Evidence

Unless the parties stipulate to the admissibility of records at trial, they may only be admitted into evidence after laying of an adequate foundation. In the case of a document, foundation is simply testimony which identifies the document, shows that it is what its proponent purports it to be, and demonstrates that it meets the formal prerequisites to admission as evidence.

4.1. Witness Used to Lay Foundation

An organization wishing to admit a document under the business records exception to the hearsay rule must first produce a witness to lay a proper foundation for that record. The witness must identify the document as having come from the files or records of the organization, and provide formal proof that the document is a business record worthy of admission under the business records exception.

There is no requirement that the party offering a business record produce the author of the item.[96] Foundation under the

---

96   *FDIC v. Staudinger*, 797 F.2d 908 (10th Cir. 1986).

business records exception to the hearsay rule may be supplied by a custodian of records or other qualified witness who has no personal knowledge regarding creation of the document.[97] A witness need not even know who actually recorded the information,[98] nor must the proponent of the record demonstrate a chain of custody.[99] Rather, the hearsay exception is satisfied if the custodian demonstrates that a document has been prepared and kept in the course of a regularly conducted business activity.[100] However, the testimony of a qualified witness is essential. A writing is not admissible merely because it may appear on its face to be a record made in the regular course of business.[101]

The witness need not be a records manager. Anyone with the requisite basic information can testify:

> While the most commonly encountered witness today may be a person in authority of the recordkeeping department of the business, he or she is not the only witness who can provide the necessary foundation for admission of a business record. This foundation can be established by anyone who possesses, with respect to the particular document in question the knowledge of the . . . [required foundational elements]. [brackets in original] This could be the entrant, the entrant's supervisor, co-workers, a records custodian or any other such person. What we demand is not a witness with a formalistic title but one with a functional understanding of the record-keeping process of the business with respect to the specific entry, transaction or declaration contained in a document.[102]

Although fulfillment of the above formal requirements will lead to admission of an organization's documents as business records in most cases, the ultimate question facing the court is whether the records are sufficiently trustworthy to be admitted into evi-

---

97 *United States v. Kail*, 804 F.2d 441, 448 (8th Cir. 1986); *United States v. Pfeiffer*, 539 F.2d 668, 670 (8th Cir. 1976); *United States v. Page*, 544 F.2d 982, 986 (8th Cir. 1976).

98 *United States v. Keplinger*, 776 F.2d 678, 693 (7th Cir. 1985).

99 *In re Thirtyacre*, 154 B.R. 497 (C.D.Ill. 1993).

100 *United States v. Franks*, 939 F.2d 600 (8th Cir. 1991); *United States v. Pfeiffer*, 539 F.2d 668 (8th Cir. 1976).

101 *Belber v. Lipson*, 905 F.2d 549 (1st Cir. 1990).

102 *Cobb v. State*, 585 N.E.2d 40, 43 (Ind.Ct.App. 1992).

dence. Notwithstanding the fact that the foundation for admission of a record may meet all of the above requirements, there may be circumstances which call into question its trustworthiness. If so, it may not be admitted into evidence. For example, in *Woolner Theaters v. Paramount Pictures Corp.*,[103] the court refused to receive the plaintiff's business records into evidence, after evidence adduced at trial indicated that they had been fraudulently altered and rewritten as part of a scheme to defraud the defendants out of motion picture royalties. The court concluded that, in such circumstances, the records were not business records within the meaning of the Federal Business Records Act.[104]

4.2. Establishing the Foundation for Computer Records

Records prepared or maintained on computers or other electronic equipment are admissible as business records. Although all such records must meet the requirements of Fed.R.Evid. 803(6), courts have on occasion imposed foundational requirements unique to electronic records. Many of these cases date from the 1960's and 1970's, long prior to the current, ubiquitous use of computers in business and commerce. Recent cases gloss over the additional requirements imposed by earlier cases and appear to accept the reliability of computerized recordkeeping systems virtually without question.

However, unless the earlier requirement has been explicitly repudiated in the jurisdiction which initially imposed it, it still stands as at least a theoretical barrier to admission of a computer-generated record. Thus, the proponent of a computer-generated record should be prepared, as part of its foundation, as well as in its substantive testimony concerning the record, to meet issues raised concerning the unique circumstances of computerized recordkeeping. This consideration applies even more forcefully to records stored on optical disk or other very new technologies. These systems have not received the repeated, explicit approval from the courts that computerized systems have received, and thus a party

---

[103] *Woolner Theaters, Inc. v. Paramount Pictures Corp.*, 333 F.Supp. 658 (E.D.La. 1970).
[104] 28 U.S.C.A. § 1732.

opposing the admission of records stored on such systems may raise questions as to the adequacy of the foundation laid for the admission of such records. The foundation witness should also be fully prepared to address questions concerning the reliability of the underlying technology used to produce the records.

Courts have held that computer evidence is not intrinsically unreliable.[105] Further, a computer system need not be shown to be completely error free in order to justify admission of records stored on it.[106] However, in *People v. Bovio*,[107] the court concluded that an inadequate foundation had been laid for admission of computerized records. Although the foundation witness testified that other banks used similar systems and computers, the appellate court concluded that such general testimony was insufficient to prove that the particular equipment it used to prepare the statement in question was standard and accurate. The court also criticized the lack of testimony describing how transaction information was entered into and processed through the computer system at the data center, which would verify the accuracy of the output. Further, no testimony established that the computer program at the data center was standard, unmodified, and operated according to its instructions. The court also noted that computer systems which perform calculations must be scrutinized more thoroughly than those systems which merely retrieve information.[108] Other courts, similarly concerned with the effect of nonstandard equipment or improper operation, have required a showing that the computer equipment must be standard, unmodified, and operated according to instructions,[109] or that the foundation witness testify to the accuracy and reliability of the computer.[110]

---

[105] *United States v. Vela*, 673 F.2d 86 (5th Cir. 1982); *United States v. Scholle*, 553 F.2d 1109 (8th Cir. 1977).

[106] *United States v. Catabran*, 836 F.2d 453 (9th Cir. 1988).

[107] *People v. Bovio*, 455 N.E.2d 829 (Ill.App 1983).

[108] *Id.* at 833.

[109] *People v. Boyd*, 384 N.E.2d 414 (Ill.Ct.App. 1987); *King v. State ex rel. Murdock Acceptance Corp.*, 222 So.2d 393 (Miss. 1969); *Missouri Valley Walnut Co. v. Snyder*, 569 S.W.2d 324 (Mo.Ct.App. 1978).

[110] *See Monarch Federal Savings and Loan Assn. v. Genser*, 383 A.2d 475 (1977). *But see* *State v. Swed*, 604 A.2d 978 (1992), calling into question some of the reasoning of *Monarch* and noting that, in the 15 years since that opinion was issued, substantial changes have occurred in computer technology, and in society's trust in the reliability of that technology.

In contrast to *People v. Bovio*, the court in *United States v. Vela*,[111] concluded that the failure to certify the brand or proper operating condition of computer equipment did not betray a circumstance of preparation indicating any lack of trustworthiness under Fed.R.Evid. 803(6). Other courts have shown a similar lack of concern about purported weaknesses in technical foundation, concluding that the foundation witness need not be the person who entered the data into the computer,[112] and that the foundation witness need not be a computer expert. [113]

Although computer records may not be admissible if prepared specifically for trial,[114] courts have generally concluded that printouts made long after the original data entry, including printouts made specifically for trial, are admissible.[115] However, at least one court has required verification of the accuracy of the printout as a prerequisite to its admission at trial.[116] Another court has concluded that, although printouts made long after the data entry and in the regular course of business, are admissible, printouts made specifically in preparation for trial are not made in the regular course of business, and are not admissible.[117]

Since foundation requirements vary from case to case, prior to seeking admissibility of computer records, the proponent should consult case law in the controlling jurisdiction in order to ensure that an adequate foundation is laid. The possibility that some of the older, seemingly outmoded, requirements for introduction of computer records will be raised is not entirely theoretical. In a later case, *State v. Ford*,[118] the defendant objected to the admission of computer records because the foundation witness did not have a degree in computer science or other technical engineering background, enabling the witness to testify with respect to various

---

111 *United States v. Vela*, 673 F.2d 86 (5th Cir. 1982).
112 **United States v. Hutson*, 821 F.2d 1015 (5th Cir. 1987).
113 **United States v. Linn*, 880 F.2d 209 (9th Cir. 1989).
114 **United States v. Sanders*, 749 F.2d 195 (5th Cir. 1984); **United States v. Fendley*, 522 F.2d 181 (5th Cir. 1975).
115 **United States v. Hutson*, 821 F.2d 1015 (5th Cir. 1987); **United States v. Sanders*, supra; *United States v. Russo*, 480 F.2d 1228 (6th Cir. 1973); *Transport Indemnity Co. v. Seib*, 132 N.W.2d 871 (Neb. 1965).
116 *People v. Boyd*, 384 N.E.2d 414 (1987).
117 *Monarch Federal Savings & Loan Assn. v. Genser*, 383 A.2d 475 (1977).
118 *State v. Ford*, 501 N.W.2d 318 (Neb.Ct.App. 1993).

technical aspects of the computer's design, and was only able to testify as to its business operation. The defendant also cited *People v. Bovio* to show that a necessary part of the foundation is proof that the computer equipment is standard within the industry. The court rejected these contentions, observing:

> As new technologies develop and win acceptance, courts move in the direction of taking judicial notice of the validity of the underlying scientific principle. Radar is a case in point . . . . Similarly, the principles of electronic data processing are now a proper subject of judicial notice and should not require proof.[119]

Nonetheless, these contentions were considered meritorious enough to address, and the opposing party was required to spend time, effort, and money opposing them. It is also possible that a court may agree with such contentions.

Therefore, a conservative approach should be taken in the laying of a foundation, including testimony in those areas discussed above which caused concern for appellate courts. While in most cases, laying of an extensive technical foundation for routine business records may seem unnecessary, it is likely to be worth the small extra price paid in order to avoid challenges. Employees of the proponent are undoubtedly already in possession of all of the requisite information. Preparation for the additional foundation will consist largely of speaking with employees and preparing a series of questions based upon their knowledge of the computer system. Since the custodian of the computer records may well be computer literate, this process may not even entail the preparation of an additional foundation witness, and preparation of extensive foundation may well preclude a challenge to the records. In addition, an extensive foundation for the computer records is likely to enhance their credibility with the judge or jury.

---

[119] *Id.* at 322.

4.3. Records Management Impact on Admissibility of Records

The key to admissibility of business records at trial is preparation of the proper foundation for admission. The record should be prepared and maintained in a manner which meets the formal requisites of Fed.R.Evid. 803(6). In addition, the witness who gives foundation testimony should be thoroughly familiar with the recordkeeping system that produced the document. The witness should be prepared to testify concerning the steps that went into preparation of the document, procedures used to ensure accuracy of the systems of records involved, reliance by the organization on records such as the one in question in the conduct of its everyday affairs, and any special foundation requirements that the courts have established for the particular type of record in question.

Most routine business records, such as ledgers, balance sheets, and the like, will be admitted without serious challenge, frequently by stipulation. However, a variety of documents — letters, memoranda, files apparently created specifically for litigation, and other documents of a less obvious routine nature — are subject to the real possibility of successful challenge. The key to establishing admissibility as business records is to integrate their creation and maintenance into the records management program prior to the initiation of any litigation. The controlled creation and retention of documents for business purposes is what makes them admissible business records, and it is the records management program which demonstrates controlled creation and retention.

Part III. The Legal Duties Regarding Records

Chapter 5.   The Duty to Create Records

Statutes and regulations promulgated by government regulatory agencies impose thousands of legally-enforceable duties on organizations to create and maintain records.[120]

The duty to create records may arise from other sources. A party may be bound by a contractual relationship to create certain kinds of records.[121] Court imposed recordkeeping requirements may also be found in consent decrees. [122]

5.1. Breach of the Duty to Create Records

Breach of the duty to create records is punishable by a wide variety of sanctions. Statutes or regulations imposing such a duty often contain their own sanctions for its breach, in the form of fines or criminal prosecution. If the matter for which there is a duty to keep records reaches litigation, the party which failed to keep the records may find that judicial relief is unavailable. Thus, a bankrupt which fails to keep financial records may find itself unable to

---

120 *See Legal Requirements for Business Records*, Information Requirements Clearinghouse (1994).

121 *See, e.g., Burchfield v. United States Fidelity and Guarantee Co.*, 118 So.2d 767 (Miss. 1960) (Insurance contract required business to maintain books of account).

122 *See Equal Employment Opportunity Commission v. C.W. Transport, Inc.*, 658 F.Supp. 1278 (W.D. Wisc. 1987) (Defendant required by consent decree to maintain records concerning job applications.).

obtain a discharge in bankruptcy.[123] In tax cases, tax deductions may be disallowed[124] or the government's method of computing tax, rather than the taxpayer's, may be used by the court to determine tax liability.[125] In contract cases, the party failing to keep records may find itself in breach of contract, and thus unable to enforce its own rights under the contract.[126]

5.2. When No Duty to Create Records Exists

In the absence of a duty to create a record, there is no basis for sanctioning a party's failure to create records. But, once a record *has* been created, a duty to preserve it may subsequently arise.[127]

In *Soria v. Ozinga Brothers,*[128] the plaintiff filed an employment discrimination suit against the defendant. A key issue in the suit was whether the defendant's disciplinary policies were impartially administered. A large part of the defendant organization's employee discipline policy was informal and no records were kept of informal disciplinary actions. The plaintiff sought the sanction of an evidentiary presumption against the defendant for failure to keep such records. However, distinguishing other cases in which companies destroyed records which already existed, the court concluded that it would be unfair to create such a presumption in the absence of a duty to create records in the first place.[129]

---

123 *See, e.g., *In re Delancey Co.,* 58 B.R. 762 (Bkrtcy.S.D.N.Y. 1986); *In re Hyder,* 38 B.R. 467, (Bkrtcy.D.Mass. 1984); *In the matter of Silverman,* 10 B.R. 727 (Bkrtcy.S.D.N.Y. 1981).

124 *See Vogler v. Commissioner,* 34 TCM 1550 (1975).

125 *See, e.g., *Estate of Curry,* 23 T. C. 305 (1954); *Moore v. Commissioner of Internal Revenue,* 37 B.T.A. 378 (1938); *Torridge Corp. v. Commissioner of Revenue,* 506 P.2d 354 (N.M. 1972); *Hennekens v. State Tax Commission,* 494 N.Y.2d 208 (S.Ct. 1985); *In the matter of W.T. Grant Co.,* 159 N.Y.2d 150 (App.Div. 1957); *Russo v. Donahue,* 226 N.E.2d 747 (Ohio 1967); *Hylton v. State,* 665 S.W.2d 571 (Tex.Ct.App. 1984).

126 *See Burchfield v. United States Fidelity and Guarantee Co.,* 118 So.2d 767 (Miss. 1960). The plaintiff was denied recovery on an insurance policy since pertinent business books, required by the policy, had been destroyed by fire. The contract required that certain business books be maintained in a safe and secure location. The same result would undoubtedly have been reached had the plaintiff failed to make the records in the first place, since the insurance policy required both creation and maintenance as a condition of recovery.

127 *See* Chapter 9, *infra.*

128 *Soria v. Ozinga Brothers Inc.,* 704 F.2d 990 (7th Cir. 1983).

129 *Id.* at 996 fn 7.

In *Galyon v. Stutts,*[130] the plaintiffs bought a business, based partially on defendant's representations of the volume of sales. At trial the plaintiff subpoenaed defendant's tax and accounting records to confirm that they had been misled. The undisputed evidence was that the defendant had not kept copies of income tax returns, ledgers, journals, or other business records, and that the only records he had kept, cash register receipts, had been eaten by rats. Finding a duty to preserve these records and produce them for inspection, the trial court found the defendant in contempt.

On appeal, the Supreme Court concluded that, since there were no records with which to comply with the trial court order, it was error to find the defendant in contempt. The defendant's failure to maintain copies of tax returns and business records for tax purposes was undoubtedly in violation of a statutory mandate that he keep such records, and thus exposed him to the risk of severe consequences in the event of tax audit. Failure to keep such records was arguably indicative of the defendant's awareness of his own culpability and could have raised an inference or presumption that the records, if preserved, would have been favorable to the plaintiffs. However, the court apparently concluded that although a duty existed to keep records for tax purposes, the duty did not apply to other litigation, such as that arising from the sale of a business. Since the defendant had not failed in a duty to preserve records, he could not be held in contempt.

The outcome differs once a legal duty exists to keep records for reasons related to the litigation. In *Valcin v. Public Health Trust of Dade County,*[131] the court found that the hospital had a statutory duty to preserve records and negligently failed to make them at the time of treatment. Because it failed in its statutory duty, the burden of proof shifted to the hospital to prove that it performed the treatment in a proper or non-negligent manner.

---

130 *Galyon v. Stutts,* 84 S.E.2d 822 (1954).
131 *Valcin v. Public Health Trust of Dade County,* 473 So.2d 1297 (Fla.Ct.App. 1984).

Chapter 6.   The Duty to Preserve Records

The duty to preserve records arises from the same sources as the duty to create them: statute, regulation, and contract. When the records relate to litigation or potential litigation an additional duty arises to preserve relevant material. Once records become relevant to a legal dispute, the fact that there was no duty to have created them in the first place becomes irrelevant.

6.1. Notice to Preserve Records

In the absence of some other duty to preserve records, there is no duty to preserve them merely because they may some day become relevant in litigation. The organization must be given some notice that records are relevant in litigation. In the absence of such notice, they need not be preserved. In *Moore v. General Motors Corp.*,[132] certain payroll and overtime records were discarded by the defendant as part of its normal business practices, prior to initiation of the lawsuit by the plaintiff. The court concluded:

> There is no evidence that at [the time the records were thrown out] defendant had any knowledge that it was

---

[132] *Moore v. General Motors Corp.*, 558 S.W.2d 720, 735 (Mo.Ct.App. 1977). *See also Schroedl v. McTague*, 129 N.W.2d 19 (Iowa 1964).

facing litigation so that it was put on notice that it should not pursue its customary practice of destroying these records. Anyone knowledgeable of business practices and the cost of storing records in these times would find it reasonable and not smacking of fraud for the defendant, with no knowledge of pending litigation, to follow its customary practice.

The court in *INA Aviation Corp. v. United States*[133] viewed the principle of notice differently — the party must be placed on notice sufficient to reasonably determine that records are relevant to the litigation and should be maintained. The plaintiff sued over allegedly negligent weather information provided by the Federal Aviation Administration, resulting in an airplane crash. Although plaintiff's counsel had issued a general request that weather records relevant to an aircraft accident be retained, certain records from weather instruments, known as traces, were destroyed after 30 days. The court concluded that as a matter of law, the plaintiff's request for the retention of pertinent documents did not provide specific notice that the traces should be retained.

INA Aviation Corp. might be criticized because the defendant should have reasonably concluded that the trace records were relevant, even though they were not specifically requested. Others in a similar situation might conclude that the risk is too great to destroy even marginally relevant records, even if they have not been specifically requested. However, while the conclusion in *INA Aviation Corp.* is arguable, the principle of law remains: there is no duty to preserve records for litigation in the absence of reasonable notice to an organization that records are relevant.

These two cases confirm that courts do not expect organizations to preserve every record indefinitely, because there exists a possibility that some party may file a future lawsuit to which the records pertain. Courts understand the economic issues related to records retention and destruction. They demand suspension of normal records destruction practices only when the organization is aware of some set of facts which should reasonably lead it to believe that the records have or will become pertinent to a lawsuit.

---

133 *INA Aviation Corp. v. United States*, 468 F.Supp. 695 (E.D.N.Y. 1979).

In addition, courts do not require that, once a lawsuit is filed, every record generated by the organization must be retained until the lawsuit is resolved. Courts only expect retention of records that can be reasonably expected to be relevant to the lawsuit.

In the absence of specific facts requiring their continued retention, records need not be retained for production in some future, hypothetical dispute. Companies will not be penalized by the courts if they have not been placed on notice of such facts and destroy old records in the normal course of business. The question then becomes: what facts constitute notice to preserve records?

6.2. When The Duty to Preserve Records Arises

6.2.1. Litigation in Progress or Imminent

Although courts require notice prior to the imposition of a duty to preserve records, they have differed as to what constitutes notice and when the duty to preserve records arises. Not surprisingly, once litigation has been initiated, courts impose a duty to preserve existing records during the pendency of that litigation, and breach of that duty is viewed with the gravest suspicion.

> [A] party is on notice once it has received a discovery request. Beyond that, the complaint itself may alert a party that certain information is relevant and likely to be sought in discovery. Finally, the obligation to preserve evidence even arises prior to the filing of a complaint where a party is on notice that litigation is likely to be commenced. [citations omitted] [134]

In the absence of a compelling explanation for the destruction of records, courts will likely conclude that the destruction was an attempt to destroy relevant, damaging evidence, often resulting in an adverse inference or presumption.[135] Juries may also review evidence of destruction to determine whether to reach adverse

---

[134] *Turner v. Hudson Transit Lines, Inc.*, 142 F.R.D. 68, 73 (S.D.N.Y. 1991).

[135] *See* **Griffith v. Gardner*, 217 S.W.2d 519 (Mo. 1949). Defendant railroad's destruction of relevant train movement records four months after initiation of a personal injury lawsuit by one of its employees justified imposition of an adverse inference.

conclusions,[136] or whether to shift the other party's burden of proof with respect to issues covered by the destroyed records and deem those issues established without further proof.[137]

The duty to preserve records during the pendency of litigation overrides any business procedures that may be in place for destruction of records, including otherwise appropriate destruction under a records retention program. Once the duty to preserve is in effect, a duty also arises to notify appropriate organization personnel of the need to preserve relevant records.

> This obligation [runs] first to counsel, who [has] a duty to advise his client of the type of information potentially relevant to the lawsuit and of the necessity of preventing its destruction. Similarly . . . corporate managers [are] responsible for conveying this information to the relevant employees. [citation omitted]
>
> It is no defense to suggest . . . that particular employees were not on notice. To hold otherwise would permit an agency, corporate officer, or legal department to shield itself from discovery obligations by keeping its employees ignorant. The obligation to retain discoverable materials is an affirmative one; it requires that the agency or corporate officers having notice of discovery obligations communicate those obligations to employees in possession of discoverable materials.[138]

On occasion, courts have excused negligent destruction of records because records management personnel were not notified to stop routine destruction.[139] Other courts have rejected contentions that destruction according to regular business practice or an

---

136 *See Brown and Williamson Tobacco Corp. v. Jacobson*, 644 F.Supp. 1240 (N.D.Ill. 1986).

137 *See Rogers v. Chicago Park District*, 89 F.R.D. 716 (N.D.Ill. 1981).

138 *Turner v. Hudson Transit Lines, Inc.*, 142 F.R.D. 68, 73 (S.D.N.Y. 1991).

139 *See Jackson v. Harvard University*, 721 F.Supp. 1397 (D.Mass. 1989). The court declined to impose an evidentiary presumption on the defendant for the negligent destruction of relevant personnel records after the institution of litigation, due to communication errors between counsel, the defendant business school, and the university records management center. *See also Kansas-Nebraska Natural Gas Co. v. Marathon Oil Co.* 109 F.R.D. 12 (D.Neb. 1983).

established retention schedule is an adequate excuse when the destruction occurred after litigation was pending.[140]

In *William T. Thompson Co. v. General Nutrition Corp.*,[141] the court stated:

> Sanctions may be imposed against a litigant who is on notice that documents and information in its possession are relevant to litigation, or potential litigation, or are reasonably calculated to lead to the discovery of admissible evidence, and destroys such documents and information. While a litigant is under no duty to keep or retain every document in its possession once a complaint is filed, it is under a duty to preserve what it knows, or reasonably should know, is relevant to the action, is reasonably calculated to lead to the discovery of admissible evidence, is reasonably likely to be requested during the discovery, and/or is the subject of a pending discovery request.

In *Telectron v. Overhead Door Corp.*,[142] the court concluded that the defendant improperly destroyed records in a series of antitrust lawsuits. Even before the start of this lawsuit, the defendant participated in a series of antitrust lawsuits. Within months of concluding the previous lawsuits, the defendant's corporate counsel instructed employees to systematically destroy documents and files related to those suits.

Approximately a month later, and four days after the records destruction concluded, another antitrust action was brought against the defendant. On the same day the plaintiff filed this new suit, defendant's corporate counsel initiated a destruction program for relevant sales-related documents that were over two years old in the business's various locations. Corporate counsel did not intercede nor suspend this policy even after being served with a complaint and discovery requests. Many relevant records were destroyed while the lawsuit was in progress.

---

140 See *Turner v. Hudson Transit Lines, Inc.*, *supra*; **T.P. Orthodontics, Inc. v. Professional Positioners, Inc.*, 17 U.S.P.Q.2d 1497 (E.D.Wisc. 1990); **Griffith v. Gardner*, 217 S.W.2d 519 (Mo. 1949).

141 *William T. Thompson Co. v. General Nutrition Corp.*, 593 F.Supp. 1443, 1455 (C.D.Cal. 1984).

142 *Telectron, Inc. v. Overhead Door Corp.*, 116 F.R.D. 107 (S.D.Fla. 1987).

Seventeen months after the complaint was filed, the corporation finally sent out a memo suspending the normal document destruction program, and ordering employees to maintain old documents. Apparently not all employees received this memo. As a result, records continued to be destroyed, including certain records maintained by at least one high ranking official.

The plaintiff claimed to operate a document destruction program and claimed that the destruction of records described above took place under that program. The program called for the destruction of records at the end of each year. However, an organization official could not provide any information or detail about the program, did not think the program had been formalized and did not know if anyone was in charge of it.

Predictably, the court found fault with the records destruction practices and concluded that the organization engaged in egregious bad faith. Due to the previous history of antitrust litigation, the defendant could have reasonably expected another suit. The court applied an inference that the documents would have been adverse to the defendant's case had they been produced, concluded that the damage done to the plaintiff's case was irreparable, and entered a default judgment on behalf of the plaintiff.

The court did not apply sanctions for the mere absence of records. Rather, it concluded the pattern of records destruction constituted a clear and willful attempt to destroy evidence and a grossly negligent failure to preserve relevant evidence for other litigation that seemed likely in the near future.

Cases such as *Telectron* raise the question: does a duty exist to maintain records in case of future litigation? In *Telectron*, the court concluded that a duty existed to preserve records because other lawsuits had either previously been initiated or could reasonably be expected. In other situations, when only a single lawsuit has been filed and no future lawsuits could reasonably be anticipated, the courts may not impose a similar duty. As discussed below, the question may hinge on whether future lawsuits are reasonably foreseeable, rather than just theoretically possible.

6.2.2. Litigation Foreseeable

The duty to preserve evidence for litigation may arise before a complaint is filed. In *Lewy v. Remington Arms Co.,*[143] the court remanded to the trial court to determine whether the defendant's document retention policies were reasonable considering the facts and circumstances surrounding the relevant documents:

> For example, if the corporation knew or should have known that the documents would become material at some point in the future, then such documents should have been preserved.

A standard such as "would have become material at some point" offers little in the way of guidance for those seeking to conform their document retention practices. But other courts have similarly concluded that knowledge of future or potential litigation gives rise to a duty to preserve relevant documents.[144]

In *Telectron*, the defendant had just concluded a series of antitrust lawsuits. At a time when it could reasonably anticipate further lawsuits, the defendant nonetheless destroyed records. The court concluded that more lawsuits were foreseeable and a duty arose to preserve the records.

In *Carlucci v. Piper Aircraft Corp.,*[145] the defendant engaged in the practice of selectively destroying certain types of engineering records that might become detrimental in the event of a future lawsuit. The court imposed sanctions, based primarily upon the "bad faith" shown by selectively identifying potentially harmful records and destroying them, rather than actually determining that this activity harmed a future litigant. Realistically, the organization could not determine precisely which records might be relevant, until the event leading to a lawsuit actually occurred and the organization received the exact document production requests.

---

143 *Lewy v. Remington Arms Co., Inc.*, 836 F.2d 1104, 1112 (8th Cir. 1988).
144 *See Capellupo v. F.M.C. Corp.*, 126 F.R.D. 545 (D.Minn. 1989); *National Association of Radiation Survivors v. Turnage*, 115 F.R.D. 543 (N.D.Cal. 1987); *Struthers Patent Corp. v. Nestle Co., Inc.*, 558 F.Supp. 747 (D.N.J. 1981).
145 *Carlucci v. Piper Aircraft Corp.*, 102 F.R.D. 472 (S.D.Fla. 1984).

The court in *Carlucci*, nonetheless, concluded that "potential litigation" need not be a particular lawsuit nor a particular incident. The court entered a default judgment based, in part, upon its conclusion that engineering documents were selectively destroyed, not in response to this lawsuit, but with the intention of preventing them from being available in future lawsuits.

Under *Carlucci*, motive is of primary importance. Even in the absence of a known dispute, *any* document destruction, particularly selective document destruction, is forbidden, if the motive for destruction is to eliminate evidence which may become relevant in a lawsuit. The degree of suspicion which attaches to such destruction is related to the type of documents destroyed. In *Carlucci*, the documents selectively destroyed were critical engineering documents, of obvious utility to future plaintiffs.

Thus, Carlucci indicates a stricter rule than *Telectron*, since the defendant in *Telectron* had recently concluded a series of antitrust lawsuits, and could reasonably anticipate further lawsuits. *Carlucci* stands for the principle that the duty to refrain from "bad faith" destruction of records arises well before the party becomes aware of a particular lawsuit.

Anticipating a future duty to preserve records, such as a the duty imposed in *Telectron*, *Lewy* and *Carlucci*, depends on the particular industry and type of records involved. For industries or activities where litigation is common or routine, such as hazardous substances and product liability,[146] the courts may expect that records be preserved, even if when no particular litigation is currently anticipated. Manufacturers may elect to maintain records related to product design, customer complaints, or other areas likely to be crucial to a lawsuit. Other documents, without obvious relevance in litigation, may be destroyed after shorter retention periods.

---

[146] Plaintiffs in product liability cases rarely have documentation related to design, testing, quality control, manufacturing, distribution, customer complaints or other aspects of the development and manufacturing processes. Without records from the manufacturer, plaintiffs would rarely be able to pursue their product liability claims. This may partially explain the court attitudes in *Lewy* and *Carlucci* since both companies were manufacturers of potentially dangerous products, subject to likely litigation.

Litigants should be aware, however, that the precise time at which a duty to preserve records arises may be viewed differently by the courts, depending upon the jurisdiction. Thus, in situations where this timing is important, the controlling jurisdiction's decisions on the subject must be examined.

Once notice has been given, and the duty to preserve records arises, that duty may continue for a considerable period of time, even if there is no further indication that the dispute is being pursued by the other party. In *Fowler v. Blue Bell*,[147] the Equal Employment Opportunity Commission informed the defendant organization that it was investigating civil rights allegations against the defendant. Under EEOC regulations, a duty to preserve relevant employment records arose at that point. A year later, having heard nothing from the EEOC, the defendant concluded that the allegations were no longer being pursued, and destroyed the records. Nearly three years later, the EEOC decided not to pursue the matter. It informed the complaining party of this decision, and that party commenced suit against the defendant.

The defendant asserted that the passage of time and the destruction of records prejudiced its ability to present a defense to the charges. The court rejected this contention, observing that the EEOC had informed the defendant of the investigation, and that the defendant would be notified as soon as a determination was made. Thus, concluded the court, the defendant was on notice of the need to preserve the records, and any prejudice was the result of its own negligence in destroying them in spite of that need.

If, between the time a party receives notification of the need to preserve records and subsequent initiation of litigation, there are unusual intervening events, the duty to preserve records may be relieved. In *Equal Employment Opportunity Commission v. Liberty Loan Corp.*[148] the EEOC initiated an investigation against the defendant, and then waited four and one-half years before filing suit. In the interim, the company underwent a drastic economic

---

147 *Fowler v. Blue Bell, Inc.*, 596 F.2d 1276 (5th Cir. 1979).
148 *Equal Employment Opportunity Commission v. Liberty Loan Corp.*, 584 F.2d 853 (8th Cir. 1978).

reversal, closing eight of nine branch offices, dismissing 140 of 145 employees, and transferring to new management. In the course of this drastic reorganization, records were consolidated, moved and, in some cases, lost.

The defendant asserted laches,[149] and cited the absence of relevant records as justification. The court concluded that no set length of delay was per se unreasonable, but concluded that, on the facts of this case, the defendant was severely prejudiced, and it affirmed the district court's dismissal of the lawsuit.

The mere fact that a government agency has the authority to bring suit against a business does not constitute notice to that business of a duty to preserve records. In *Equal Employment Opportunity Commission v. Dresser Industries*,[150] the EEOC prosecuted a discrimination suit against the defendant. When first filed, the suit alleged discrimination against a single individual and, pursuant to EEOC's regulations, requested that all "records relevant to the charge" be preserved. EEOC later filed a class-action suit, at which time it discovered that records relevant to the class-action suit, but not the original action, had been destroyed according to routine practice. EEOC then argued that the employer should have known that EEOC's ability to bring a class-action suit put it on notice of a need to preserve the records.

The court noted that the records had been kept for the period required by law, and that the employer had kept all further records relative to any charges of which the employer had notice. Thus, the court rejected the EEOC's argument that destruction of the records violated a duty to preserve. The court in *Equal Employment Opportunity Commission v. M.D. Pneumatics, Inc.*,[151] faced with a nearly identical fact pattern, rejected precisely the same argument, and refused to allow the EEOC to amend its complaint to allege violation of agency-imposed recordkeeping requirements.

---

149 Delay such as to preclude a court from arriving at a safe conclusion as to the truth. Black's 4th Ed. citing *Grant v. Hart*, 14 S.E.2d 860, 869.

150 *Equal Employment Opportunity Commission v. Dresser Industries*, 668 F.2d 1199, 1203 (11th Cir. 1982).

151 *Equal Employment Opportunity Commission v. M.D. Pneumatics*, 31 Empl.Pract.Dec. (CCH) 33, 459 (W.D.Mo. 1983).

6.3. The Duty to Preserve Records in a Specific Form

Regulatory agencies may prepare opinion letters or other informal communications stating requirements related to the retention of originals or "recommended" retention periods, not otherwise required by statutes or administrative regulations. In this situation, the organization must balance the cost savings incurred in not preserving paper originals against the possibility that the agency opinion may be legally enforceable. Failure to comply might also strain relations with the agency or create problems in other areas in which the agency has discretionary powers.

Promulgation of rules governing the conduct of the public by administrative agencies is, in most jurisdictions, governed by the Administrative Procedure Act.[152] Before an agency can impose a requirement, such as a recordkeeping requirement, upon the public, it must engage in a formal promulgation process whereby the proposed rule is published, the regulated public is given an opportunity to comment upon the proposed rule, and the final rule is then adopted and published after consideration of the public comments. Agency actions purporting to affect the rights of the general regulated public, which have not been subjected to this process, may not be binding.[153]

---

[152] Adopted by the United States and the following 31 states: Alabama, Alaska, Arizona, Connecticut, District of Columbia, Georgia, Hawaii, Idaho, Illinois, Iowa, Louisiana, Maine, Maryland, Michigan, Mississippi, Missouri, Montana, Nebraska, New Hampshire, Nevada, New York, Oklahoma, Oregon, Rhode Island, South Dakota, Tennessee, Vermont, Washington, West Virginia, Wisconsin, Wyoming.

[153] *See, e.g.*, *American Paper Institute, Inc. v. United States Environmental Protection Agency*, 882 F.2d 287 (7th Cir. 1989) (where the court concluded that policies, statements, and guidelines not published in the *Federal Register* or codified in the *Code of Federal Regulations* had no legal effect, and thus could not render conduct unlawful); *Fears v. Iowa Department of Human Services*, 382 N.W.2d 473 (Iowa App. 1985) (overruling the denial of Medicaid benefits because the agency based its decision upon provisions contained in a providers' manual that were not duly promulgated according to the provisions of the Administrative Procedure Act since the manual set forth a policy of general applicability which would substantially effect the public); *Ohio State Chiropractic Ass'n. v. Ohio Bureau of Workers Compensation*, unpublished option, (Ohio App. 1993) (where the court concluded that the provisions contained in a provider billing and reimbursement manual were invalid and not binding on the public because they were adopted in violation of the rulemaking procedures of chapter 119 of the Ohio Code).

Courts typically grant administrative agencies considerable deference to interpret the enabling legislation that grants authority to the agency and to promulgate rules that implement the legislation. Further, the courts regard administrative agencies as having considerable expertise in making technical and administrative determinations in their area of regulation.[154] While courts may conclude that agency opinions are not validly promulgated regulations, and thus do not have the force of law, a court may nonetheless conclude that the position taken by the agency with respect to the preservation of original records is reasonable:

> We consider that the rulings, interpretations and opinions of the Administrator under this Act, while not controlling upon the courts by reason of their authority, do constitute a body of experience and informed judgment to which courts and litigants may properly resort for guidance.[155]

The decision to comply with informally promulgated agency requirements may come down to cost and risk. If the agency imposes an onerous burden, the organization may challenge that position in court, even at the risk of damaging relationships with the agency. But if the agency imposes only a slight burden, acquiescence may prove more prudent, particularly if the agency licenses the activity or the organization needs agency cooperation.

6.4. Responding to the Duty to Preserve Records

In order to comply with a duty to preserve records, an organization must first identify all applicable duties to create and preserve records, including pending, imminent and foreseeable litigation. Procedures can then be developed and implemented

---

154 *See, e.g., *Forse v. Director, Office of Workers Compensation Programs, Department of Labor*, 938 F.2d 981, 984 (9th Cir. 1991) (explaining "[w]e accord 'considerable weight' to the construction of the statute urged by the Director of the Office of Workers Compensation Programs, as he is charged with administering it"); *Duffy v. Oele*, 274 F.Supp. 307, 310 (W.D.Mich. 1967) (stating "interpretive bulletins and rulings of the Administrator of the Wage and Hour Division of the Department of Labor are not binding on the courts. They are entitled, however, to careful consideration.").

155 *Duffy v. Oele*, 274 F.Supp. at 310 (quoting *Skidmore v. Swift and Co.*, 323 U.S. 134, 140, 65 S.Ct. 161, 89 L.E.2d 124 (1944)).

which will preserve those records until that duty is discharged. Some factors that should be addressed include:

- Identifying the source of the duty to create records and which records must be created and preserved in order to comply.

- Determining which records are needed for business purposes.

- Identifying laws applicable to the business including statutes, regulations, revenue rulings, and no-action letters.

- Identifying when the duty to create and preserve records arises from unique or specific circumstances, e.g., a contractual relationship, a consent decree, a court order, or litigation.

- Establishing the records management program procedures to alert the group or individuals affected by a duty to create or preserve records so they can respond in the fastest possible time, and, yet, still respond to the business needs of the organization. Effective indexing, filing, tracking and other records management techniques facilitate this process.

Certain classes of records with clear implications for litigation, such as customer complaint files and incident reports, demand careful treatment in the records management program. Early or inconsistent destruction may later be viewed with some suspicion, even if records were destroyed at a time when no litigation was pending or likely. If litigation does ultimately arise, the records may be deemed relevant. If they have been destroyed, the court can easily impose sanctions, concluding that the organization should have known they would become relevant.

6.5. Implementing the Duty to Preserve Records

The economic value gained from destroying records must be carefully weighed against their possible relevance in future litigation. Controlling law may identify a duty to preserve records in advance of an actual dispute. Retention decisions for these types of records will be scrutinized after the fact. Thus, even after the fact, they must be reasonable and defensible decisions in light of information that may not be known at the time the retention decision was made.

The key to demonstrating reasonableness in this case is conducting sufficient legal research prior to making the retention
decisions. Adequate legal research will provide the organization
with a base of knowledge upon which to support its retention
decisions. Thus, the likelihood of an erroneous decision will be
drastically reduced. Should any retention decisions subsequently
be challenged, adequate legal research and documentation of the
legal research and analysis process provides a tangible and objective basis for claims that the retention periods were reasonable
and made in good faith. Even if that research ultimately proves to
be incomplete, incorrect or subject to a different interpretation, the
organization can still demonstrate that it made a reasonable
attempt to comply with the law.

Courts are fully aware of the imperfections in statutory and
regulatory compilations and case law reporters, and the attendant
difficulties in doing legal research. They are aware that, notwithstanding the most diligent efforts, it is possible and even likely that
a relevant statute, regulation, or case may not be reviewed, particularly if the necessary research is extensive. Instead, the courts
expect to see a reasonably diligent attempt to understand the
appropriate law and comply with it.

A second key aspect is communicating the legal research to the
appropriate personnel. This does not mean that every records
manager or file clerk in the organization should be required to read
the relevant statutes, regulations, and cases. Policies and procedures must incorporate these principles of law. Training should
then inform and educate personnel of their responsibilities.

All personnel involved in the records management process
must be aware of when a duty to preserve records in connection
with litigation arises. There must be effective lines of communication between legal counsel and the records management staff, to
ensure that notice communicated to counsel is effectively communicated to those in records management.

This communication is perhaps the key element in meeting the
duty to preserve records for litigation. Some cases, in which records
subject to a duty to preserve were destroyed, raised the fact that
the need to preserve the records was never effectively communi-

cated from legal counsel to records management staff. Unfortunately, no matter how understandable such a failure may be in a large corporation with widely scattered personnel and large volumes of records, it is unlikely to prevail as an excuse. Legal counsel and records management staff are agents of the same principle — the corporation that employs them. From a judicial perspective, notice to one agent, legal counsel, is notice to all.

Chapter 7. Discovery — The Duty to Disclose Information

The role of discovery[156] has been summarized as follows:

> The purposes of litigation are best served when each party
> knows as much about the controversy as is reasonably
> practical. The objectives of the pretrial discovery are to
> enhance the truth-seeking process, to enable attorneys to
> better prepare and evaluate cases, to eliminate surprises,
> and to insure that judgments rest on the merits and not
> upon the skillful maneuvering of counsel. Discovery is not
> a tactical game. Pretrial discovery presupposes a wide
> range of relevance and materiality which includes not only
> what is admissible at trial but also that which leads to
> what is admissible at trial.[157] [citations omitted.]

The courts impose an affirmative obligation upon the parties
to a dispute to make relevant information available to the other
party. Information traditionally has been obtained from an opposing party by depositions, production of documents or other relevant
things, permission to enter upon land or other property, physical
and mental examinations, and requests for admissions.[158]

---

156 This book reviews the issues of discovery in civil cases. Discovery in criminal case is
substantially different. However, an organization should not establish a records and
information program in contemplation of criminal activity or prosecution.

157 *Cole Taylor Bank v. Corrigan*, 595 N.E.2d 177, 180 (Ill.App.Ct. 1992).

158 Fed.R.Civ.P. 26(a).

7.1. The Duty to Disclose Under Fed.R.Civ.P. Rule 26

Fed.R.Civ.P. 26 traditionally made no distinction between records maintained because of a legal duty or for other reasons:

> Parties may obtain discovery regarding any matter, not privileged, which is relevant to the subject matter involved in the pending action, whether it relates to the claim or defense of the party seeking discovery or to the claim or defense of any other party, including the existence, description, nature, custody, condition and location of any books, documents, or other tangible things and the identity and location of persons having knowledge of any discoverable matter. It is not ground for objection that the information sought will be inadmissible at the trial if the information sought appears reasonably calculated to lead to the discovery of admissible evidence.[159]

On December 1, 1993, the Supreme Court revised Rule 26 of the Federal Rules of Civil Procedure to create a new affirmative duty to identify and preserve records subject to litigation:[160]

> Rule 26. General Provisions Governing Discovery; Duty of Disclosure.[161]
>
> (a) *Required Disclosures to Discover Additional Matter.*
>
> (1) *Initial Disclosures.* Except to the extent otherwise stipulated or directed by order or local rule, a party shall, without awaiting a discovery request, provide to other parties:
>
> (A) the name and, if known, the address and telephone number of each individual likely to have discoverable information relevant to disputed facts alleged with particularity in the pleadings, identifying the subjects of the information;

---

159 Former Fed.R.Civ.P. 26(b)(1), superseded on December 1, 1993.

160 Some states that have adopted rules of civil procedure patterned after the federal rules may incorporate provisions similar to those found in Rule 26. *But see* Mark Hansen, *Early Discovery Hits Snag*, 80 A.B.A.J. 35 (1994), citing research performed by the Federal Judicial Center as of February 23, 1994. Of the 94 federal district courts, 32 have adopted the rule verbatim, 31 have adopted the rule with modifications, 23 have opted out of the rule and 8 give individual judges authority to require early discovery.

161 Fed.R.Civ.P. Rule 26, adopted December 1, 1993.

(B) a copy of, or a description by category and location of, all documents, data compilations, and tangible things in the possession, custody, or control of the party that are relevant to disputed facts alleged with particularity in the pleadings;

(C) a computation of any category of damages claimed by the disclosing party, making available for inspection and copying as under Rule 34 the documents or other evidentiary material, not privileged or protected from disclosure, on which such computation is based, including materials bearing on the nature and extent of injuries suffered; and

(D) for inspection and copying as under Rule 34 any insurance agreement under which any person carrying on an insurance business may be liable to satisfy part or all of a judgment which may be entered in the action or to indemnify or reimburse for payments made to satisfy the judgment.

Unless otherwise stipulated or directed by the court, these disclosures shall be made at or within 10 days after the meeting of the parties under subdivision (f). A party shall make its initial disclosures based on the information then reasonably available to it and is not excused from making its disclosures because it has not fully completed its investigation of the case or because it challenges the sufficiency of another party's disclosures or because another party has not made its disclosure.

* * * * *

(3) *Pretrial Disclosures.* In addition to the disclosures required in the preceding paragraphs, a party shall provide to other parties the following information regarding the evidence that it may present at trial other than solely for impeachment purposes:

(A) the name and, if not previously provided, the address and telephone number of each witness, separately identifying those whom the party expects to present and those whom the party may call if the need arises.

(B) the designation of those witnesses whose testimony is expected to be presented by means of a deposition and, if not taken stenographically, a transcript of the pertinent portions of the deposition testimony; and

(C) an appropriate identification of each document or other exhibit, excluding summaries of other evidence, separately identifying those which the party expects to offer and those which the party may offer if the need arises.

Unless otherwise directed by the court, these disclosures shall be made at least 30 days before trial. Within 14 days thereafter, unless a different time is specified by the court, a party may serve and file a list disclosing (i) any objections to the use under Rule 32(a) of a deposition designated by another party under subparagraph (B) and (ii) any objection, together with the grounds therefor, that may be made to the admissibility of materials identified under subparagraph (C). Objections not so disclosed, other than objections under Rules 402 and 403 of the Federal Rules of Evidence, shall be deemed waived unless excused by the court for good cause shown.

(4) *Form of Disclosures; Filing.* Unless otherwise directed by order or local rule, all disclosures under paragraphs (1) through (3) shall be made in writing, signed, served, and promptly filed with the court.

(5) *Methods to Discover Additional Matter.* Parties may obtain discovery by one or more of the following methods: depositions upon oral examination or written questions; written interrogatories; production of documents or things or permission to enter upon land or other property under Rule 34 or 45 (a)(1)(C), for inspection and other purposes; physical and mental examinations; and requests for admission.

* * * * *

The new rule specifies that each party shall provide to the other, *without waiting for discovery requests*, a copy of the description of all records that are relevant to disputed facts. The information must be provided, unless otherwise stipulated or directed by the court, within ten days after the meeting specified in subdivision (f) — a meeting which normally takes place 14 days before the scheduling conference. In cases where no scheduling conference is held, this means that the prescribed meeting must ordinarily be held within 75 days after the defendant first appears (and files an answer) in the case. In the worst case scenario, the initial disclosures related to records specified in the rule would generally be due no later than 85 days after the defendant's first appearance.

The rule states that each party makes its initial disclosure "based on the information then reasonably available to it." Each party must review the pleadings filed by the others and determine what records would reasonably be relevant. To facilitate this process, the pre-trial conference should clarify the issues. Each party will also have an on-going responsibility to disclose subsequent information as it becomes clear that additional issues become relevant to the matter. Neither party is excused from its affirmative duty even if the other party fails to comply with the rule.

The changes to Rule 26 affect an organization's records management program. The burdens formerly placed on the records management program to produce information for opponents in litigation remain intact. Now, the records program must facilitate rapid and complete identification of relevant information. Indexes must be sufficiently detailed to enable researchers to identify information, even without the specific guidance previously found in discovery requests.

The rule may cause courts to judge the adequacy of a records management program. Without recognized records management program standards, this might be difficult and quite subjective.[162]

When information under Rule 26 appears complete and without obvious inconsistency, the court may not pursue the issue further. If parties identify only limited information or fail to reveal typical or expected information, then the court may review the adequacy of the procedures and systems implemented by the party. Failure to find relevant information due to a poor filing system is a basis for adverse judgments and sanctions.[163]

---

[162] ARMA International, Prairie Village, KS, the association for records managers and administrators, and the Association for Information and Image Management, the association for image managers (e.g., microfilm and electronic imaging technology) have published standards and guidelines for components of records and information management programs. The Institute of Certified Records Managers (administered by ARMA International) provides a certification program for records managers. However, no recognized certification program exists to evaluate a records management program nor determine its adequacy.

[163] *See* Chapter 10, generally.

7.2. Sanctions

If a party fails to respond to its discovery obligations, or its response is evasive or incomplete, the party's opponent may motion the court for an order compelling discovery.[164] If the response is still inadequate, the court is empowered to make such orders in regard to the failure as are just, including the following:

> An order that the matters regarding which the order was made or any other designated facts shall be taken to be established for the purposes of the action in accordance with the claim of the party obtaining the order;

> An order refusing to allow the disobedient party to support or oppose designated claims or defenses, or prohibiting that party from introducing designated matters into evidence;

> An order striking out pleadings or parts thereof, or staying further proceedings until the order is obeyed, or dismissing the action or proceeding or any part thereof, or rendering a judgment by default against the disobedient party;

> In lieu of any of the foregoing orders or in addition thereto, an order treating as a contempt of court the failure to obey any orders except an order to submit to a physical or mental examination;

> * * * * *

> In lieu of any of the foregoing orders or in addition thereto, the court shall require the party failing to obey the order or the attorney advising that party or both to pay the reasonable expenses, including attorney's fees, caused by the failure, unless the court finds that the failure was substantially justified or that other circumstances make an award of expenses unjust.[165]

Some actions appear so suspicious that the imposition of sanctions seems virtually automatic. In *In re South Florida Title, Inc.,*[166] a witness observed a party systematically removing books and records in trash sacks from a business office, immediately

---

164 Fed.R.Civ.P. 37(a).
165 Fed.R.Civ.P. 37(b)(2)(A), (B), (C), (D) and (E).
166 *In re South Florida Title, Inc.,* 102 Bankr. 266 (Bkrtcy. S.D. Fla. 1989).

prior to a bankruptcy receiver taking possession of the premises. The court unsurprisingly found this to be grounds for denial of a discharge in bankruptcy.

Similarly, in *Dow Chemical Co. (U.K.) Ltd. v. S.S. Giovannella D'Amico*,[167] a party conducted an extensive series of tests on a contaminated shipment and then destroyed the test results while the suit was pending. The court viewed this with suspicion.

The duty to preserve and disclose information for litigation is, however, much broader than merely avoiding flagrant acts of destruction. Sanctions may be imposed in instances of lesser misconduct.

7.2.1. Power to Impose Sanctions

A trial court's power to impose such sanctions has been affirmed at the highest levels of the judicial system. In *Societe Internationale Pour Participations Industrielles et Commerciales, S.A. v. Rogers*,[168] the Supreme Court reaffirmed the ability of a trial court to impose sanctions for failure to comply with discovery, and implicitly approved of application of those sanctions in cases where a party's inability to meets its obligations during discovery is caused by its own conduct.

The plaintiff's complaint in that case was dismissed because it was unable to produce a number of documents stored in Switzerland, due to that country's laws, which forbade the production of these records. Although the Supreme Court struck down the lower court's ruling, it did so on the basis of findings that the plaintiff had made good faith efforts to comply with discovery, and that the failure to satisfy the requirements of the production order were due to inability fostered neither by its own conduct nor by circumstances within its control.[169]

---

[167] *Dow Chemical Co. (U.K.) Ltd. v. S.S. Giovannella D'Amico*, 297 F.Supp. 699 (S.D.N.Y 1969).

[168] *Societe Internationale Pour Participations Industrielles et Commerciales, S.A. v. Rogers*, 357 U.S. 197, 78 S.Ct. 1087 (1958).

[169] *Id.* at 211, 78 S.Ct. at 1095.

Societe Internationale places minimal limitations on a court's power to impose sanctions for noncompliance. It limits the court's power only in circumstances where the sanctioned party has made extensive, good faith efforts at compliance, and is thwarted by circumstances beyond its control. Indeed, the court was careful to distinguish the unique circumstances of this case, including the fact that mere production of the requested documents would violate penal laws of a foreign sovereign. This contrasts with other situations where production might put the custodian at risk, such as when compliance would reveal facts which might prove the basis for prosecution under a foreign law. The power of a court to impose sanctions for noncompliance in other than an extraordinary situation remains untouched by the court's ruling. Rulings by lower courts have affirmed the power of a court to impose sanctions for noncompliance with discovery.

7.2.2. Sanctions for Delays in Responding to Discovery Requests

A party cannot delay production of relevant, unprivileged material by interposing bad faith objections to discovery requests, and such behavior is sanctionable when it occurs. Payment of the other party's costs, including attorney fees, deposition costs, and similar expenses is a commonly imposed sanction.

In re Air Crash Disaster near Chicago, Illinois, on May 25, 1979,[170] the defendant objected to requests for the production of certain documents, claiming that they were privileged. The court ordered the production of the allegedly privileged documents *in camera*. The defendant not only failed to comply, but also failed to inform the court that certain records subject to discovery had been destroyed. The court concluded that the allegedly privileged documents were not privileged, and that the defendant's objections were not in good faith. The court further cited the fact that the defendant had ignored orders compelling the production of the documents, and that the defendant had not informed the court of

---

[170] *In re Air Crash Disaster near Chicago, Illinois, on May 25, 1979*, 90 F.R.D. 613 (N.D.Ill. 1981).

the destruction of documents. The court then awarded the plaintiffs all costs and fees related to all depositions, court appearances, or motions arising out of the sanctioned conduct.

7.2.3. Severe Sanctions for Bad Faith

If a court concludes that a failure to comply with discovery is severe, drastic penalties may be imposed.[171] The fact that the stakes may be very high has not prevented courts from imposing severe sanctions for failing to meet discovery obligations. In *United Nuclear Corp. v. General Atomic Co.*,[172] the defendant engaged in an ongoing pattern of obstructing discovery, including shipping and storing documents out of the country so that they would be unavailable for the litigation. Based solely upon the defendant's discovery abuses, the trial court struck the defendant's pleadings and entered judgment for nearly $25 million, required specific performance of a contract for the supply of five million pounds of uranium and voided other contracts requiring supply of several million pounds of uranium to the defendants. The New Mexico Supreme Court concluded that the trial court's actions were proper under the circumstances and upheld the entire judgment.

United Nuclear Corp. v. General Atomic Co. presented a unique and particularly egregious set of circumstances. Other courts have been willing to find bad faith in less egregious circumstances. In *Georges v. Insurance Technicians*[173] the plaintiffs filed requests for the production of documents. On the last day of the time for production, the defendant filed a motion for a 90 day extension. The motion was granted, but the additional time went by without any production or a motion for extension. The trial court then gave the defendants an additional ten days within which to produce.

---

171 *See, e.g., *National Hockey League v. Metropolitan Hockey Club, Inc.*, 427 U.S. 639, 96 S.Ct. 2778, 49 L.Ed.2d 747 (1976). Interrogatories were not answered for 17 months and when finally submitted were found to be evasive and unresponsive. The United States Supreme Court reversed the Court of Appeals and upheld a district court ruling dismissing the plaintiff's antitrust action, concluding that dismissal was justified under the circumstances because of "flagrant bad faith" and counsel's "callous disregard" of their responsibilities.

172 *United Nuclear Corp. v. General Atomic Co.*, 692 P.2d 231 (N.M. 1980).

173 *Georges v. Insurance Technicians, Inc.*, 448 So.2d 1185 (Fla.Ct.App. 1984).

Following a hearing on a motion for sanctions, the court entered a default judgment on behalf of the plaintiffs, concluding that the defendant had embarked upon a path of intentional delay and abuse of the system. Other courts have also been willing to enter a default judgment for failure to produce records.[174]

A sanctioned party should not assume that an extreme sanction will be overturned on appeal:

> Although the severest of the sanctions should be imposed only in extreme circumstances, "in this day of burgeoning, costly and protracted litigation courts should not shrink from imposing harsh sanctions where, as in this case, they are clearly warranted." As one court stated: [W]hen a defendant demonstrates flagrant bad faith and callous disregard of its responsibilities, the district court's choice of the extreme sanction is not an abuse of discretion. It is not our responsibility as a reviewing court to say whether we would have chosen a more moderate sanction.[175]

7.2.4. Sanctions for Negligent or Careless Conduct

Intentional conduct is not required in order for the court to impose sanctions. In *Petroleum Insurance Agency v. Hartford Accident and Indemnity Co.,*[176] the plaintiff failed to produce certain documents, and answered certain interrogatory questions in a careless and incomplete fashion. The court concluded that the plaintiff's actions did not amount to "failing to file a response" within the meaning of Fed.R.Civ.P. 37(e), and further concluded that the plaintiff's behavior did not amount to willful or vexatious

---

174 See *Carlucci v. Piper Aircraft Corp.*, 102 F.R.D. 472 (S.D.Fla. 1984); *Poleo v. Grandview Equities, Ltd.*, 629 P.2d 309 (Ariz.Ct.App. 1984) (reversed for failure to hold a hearing to determine the appropriate measure of damages); **Agencias Maritimas Nicaraguenses, S.A. v. Usatorres*, 435 So.2d 247 (Fla.Ct.App. 1983); *Universal Film Exchanges, Inc. v. Benbar Cinema Corp.*, 370 N.Y.S. 311, (S.Ct. 1975); *American Blue Stone Corp. v. Cohn Cut Stone Co.*, 164 N.Y. 506 (S.Ct. 1917); *Edison Electric Light Co. v. Tipless Lamp Co.*, 130 N.Y. 1089 (S.Ct. 1911).

175 *United Nuclear Corp. v. General Atomic Co.*, 629 P.2d 231, 315 (N.M. 1980), quoting **Cine 42nd Street Theatre v. Allied Artists*, 602 F.2d 1062, 1068 (2nd Cir. 1979) and **Emerick v. Fenick Industries, Inc.*, 539 F.2d 1376, 1381 (1976).

176 *Petroleum Insurance Agency, Inc. v. Hartford Accident and Indemnity Co.*, 106 F.R.D. 59 (D.Mass. 1985).

refusal to comply with discovery. The court did, however, conclude that the plaintiff's actions were negligent and careless, and that the court had the inherent power to impose sanctions for such conduct. The court then required the plaintiff to pay all costs incurred by the defendant arising out of this negligent behavior.

7.2.5. Other Types of Sanctions

A wide variety of other sanctions are available for failure to produce documents. For example, in *LeMaster v. Chicago Rock Island and Pacific Railroad Co.*, [177] the court concluded that the trial court properly allowed plaintiff's counsel to cross-examine a witness concerning certain records under the defendant's control and to argue to the jury that the defendant did not produce all of the relevant documents in its possession, notwithstanding defendant's contention that it had complied completely.

In *Alliance to End Repression v. Rochford*,[178] the court concluded that the appropriate sanction for discovery abuses was to enjoin the defendants from later introducing certain allegedly destroyed documents in their own behalf, and in addition deemed the plaintiffs to have made a *prima facie* showing of causation in fact regarding certain allegations in their complaint.

The nature of the sanction ultimately imposed depends on the egregiousness of the conduct being sanctioned and the degree of injury or prejudice to the other party. Courts attempting to balance these two considerations often attempt to arrive at a sanction which, in effect, eliminates any advantage gained by or prejudice caused by the sanctioned conduct.

In *Equal Employment Opportunity Commission v. Jacksonville Shipyards*,[179] the court concluded that sanctions were appropriate

---

[177] *LeMaster v. Chicago Rock Island and Pacific Railroad Co.*, 343 N.E.2d 65 (Ill.Ct.App. 1976). *See also Hunt v. Sanders*, 232 S.W. 456 (Mo. 1921), wherein the presumption arising out of destruction of records was deemed a question for the jury, rather than a proper subject for a jury instruction requiring a presumption.

[178] *Alliance to End Repression v. Rochford*, 75 F.R.D. 438 (N.Dist.Ill. 1976).

[179] *Equal Employment Opportunity Commission v. Jacksonville Shipyards*, 690 F.Supp. 995 (M.D.Fla. 1988).

for the destruction of records relevant to a lawsuit. However, the court reserved judgment on the precise nature of the sanctions, because some of the records could be reconstructed from other sources. The court thus concluded that, until the precise degree of prejudice could be fully determined, the nature of the sanction would remain undecided.[180]

7.2.6. Sanctions For Punitive Purposes

The court's temperament, and its degree of exasperation with the sanctioned party also come into play in the imposition of sanctions. In such cases, the punitive aspect of the sanction may well be more prominent in the court's mind than an attempt to correct the damage done by the sanctioned conduct. In imposing default judgment upon the defendant, the court in *Carlucci v. Piper Aircraft Corp.*[181] made the following observations:

> When a party has consistently disobeyed orders, obstructed discovery, delayed proceedings and made misrepresentations to the court, an extreme sanction is warranted. When a party engaging in such conduct has previously been sanctioned by the court and yet continues the same pattern of conduct, the ultimate sanction is warranted.
>
> This is a case where the defendant has demonstrated flagrant bad faith and callous disregard for its responsibility . . . . [The defendant's] conduct has been reprehensible and intolerable. [citation omitted]
>
> It is not the court's function to drag a party kicking and screaming through discovery. That is what the defendant required in this case and such conduct must be deterred if the courts are to perform their intended functions . . .[182]

Companies must assume that courts will vigorously enforce the duty to disclose information to opposing parties.

---

180 *See also Veeder v. Trustees of Boston College*, 85 F.R.D. 13 (D.Mass. 1979) (sanction for deliberate destruction of records limited to attorney fees where plaintiff failed to destroy all copies, and defendant's prejudice was limited to extra expenses resulting from attempted destruction.)

181 *Carlucci v. Piper Aircraft Corp.*, 102 F.R.D. 472 (S.D.Fla. 1984).

182 *Id.* at 488, 489.

7.3. Inferences and Presumptions

When courts find that records are missing or destroyed in breach of a duty to preserve them, and the contents would have shed light on a legal controversy, they may attempt to fill the void in the evidence created by destruction of the relevant records. This is typically done through inferences and presumptions that make assumptions about what the contents of the documents would have been if they had been available.

7.3.1 Inference

An inference is:

> [A] truth or proposition drawn from another which is supposed or admitted to be true. A process of reasoning by which a fact or proposition sought to be established is deduced as a logical consequence from other facts, or a state of facts, already proved or admitted.[183]

Thus, an inference provides the missing facts. The contents of the records may be inferred solely from the absence of those records in breach of a duty to preserve them.

7.3.2 Presumption

A presumption of fact is:

> An inference affirmative or disaffirmative of the truth or falsehood of any proposition or fact drawn by a process of probable reasoning in the absence of actual certainty of its truth or falsehood, or until such certainty can be ascertained.[184]

A presumption of law is:

---

[183] *Black's Law Dictionary*, 917 (4th Ed. 1968).
[184] *Id.* at 1349.

> A rule of law that courts and judges shall draw a particular
> inference from a particular fact, or from particular evi-
> dence, unless and until the truth of such inference is
> disproved. [. . . A] rule which in certain cases, either forbids
> or dispenses with any ulterior inquiry[185]

From evidence related to the missing records, a presumption
draws a certain conclusion about what they would have contained,
and requires the use of that conclusion in place of any evidence
concerning their contents.

Presumptions may be rebuttable or irrebuttable. A rebuttable
presumption establishes a *prima facie* case regarding the presumed facts. The presumption is taken to be true unless and until
evidence is presented which is sufficient to rebut it. If evidence
which contradicts the presumption is presented, it may overcome
the presumption, if strong enough. An irrebuttable presumption
precludes the use of contradictory evidence. The statement of facts
presumed to be true cannot be contradicted, and must be taken as
true by the finder of fact.

7.3.3 Operation of Inferences And Presumptions

The line between inferences and presumptions is often impre-
cise. The presumption may be established by the court and then
presented to the jury as an established fact, or it may be a factual
question on which evidence is presented by one or both side, and
then argued to the jury. However, the mere destruction of something, somewhere, does not give rise to any of these scenarios.

> Before a jury may be permitted to draw an inference adverse
> to the defendant, plaintiffs must establish, at a minimum,
> that relevant evidence existed, that it was within the ability
> of the defendant to produce it, and that it has not been
> produced due to the actions of the defendant.[186]

---

[185] *Id.*
[186] *Friends For All Children, Inc. v. Lockheed Aircraft Corp.*, 587 F.Supp. 180, 189 (D.D.C. 1984).

In addition, the party seeking the inference may be required to show that its case has been prejudiced.[187] The court in *Nation-wide Check Corp. v. Forest Hills Distributors*, Inc.[188] stated:

> The adverse inference is based on two rationales, one evidentiary and one not. The evidentiary rationale is nothing more than the common sense observation that a party who has notice that a document is relevant to litigation and who proceeds to destroy the document is more likely to have been threatened by the document than is a party in the same position who does not destroy the document. The fact of destruction satisfies the minimum requirement of relevance: it has some tendency, however small, to make the existence of a fact at issue more probable than it would otherwise be. *See* Fed.R.Evid. 401. Precisely how the document might have aided the party's adversary, and what evidentiary shortfalls its destruction may be taken to redeem, will depend upon the particular facts of each case, but the general evidentiary rationale for the inference is clear.

> The other rationale for the inference has to do with its prophylactic and punitive effects. Allowing the trier of fact to draw the inference presumably deters parties from destroying relevant evidence before it can be introduced at trial. The inference also serves as a penalty, placing the risk of an erroneous judgment on the party that wrongfully created the risk. In McCormick's words, "the real underpinning of the rule of admissibility [may be] a desire to impose swift punishment, with a certain poetic justice, rather than concern over niceties of proof."

The court, citing *Wigmore*, further concluded:

> The failure or refusal to produce a relevant document, or the destruction of it, is evidence *from which alone* its contents may be inferred to be unfavorable to the possessor, provided the opponent, when the identity of the document is disputed, first introduces some evidence tending to show that the document actually destroyed or withheld is the one as to whose contents it is desired to draw an inference.[189]

---

[187] *New Hampshire Insurance Co. v. Royal Insurance Co.*, 559 So.2d 102 (Fla.Ct.App. 1990).

[188] *Nation-wide Check Corp. v. Forest Hills Distributors*, Inc., 692 F.2d 214, 218 (1st Cir. 1982).

[189] *Id.* at 217, 218.

Courts vary widely in their views as to exactly what may be inferred by the absence or destruction of relevant records. In *The Bermuda's Claimants v. United States*,[190] the court examined the question in the context of the destruction of the ship's logs and papers of an alleged blockade runner seized during the Civil War, and whose ownership was at issue. The court stated that:

> This spoliation was one of unusual aggravation, and warrants the most unfavorable inferences as to ownership, employment and destination.
>
> * * * * *
>
> The spoliation makes the conclusion of ownership out of *Haigh* and in *John Frazier and Co.* well nigh irresistible.[191]

Other courts are willing to make far-reaching presumptions from the destruction of records:

> Missouri . . . has followed the spoliation rule that the destruction of written evidence without a satisfactory explanation gives rise to an inference unfavorable to the spoliator, and he who destroys such evidence is thereby held to admit the truth of the allegations of the opposing party.[192]

Florida uses either of two presumptions, depending on the level of culpability arising out of the absence of the documentary evidence. In *Valcin v. Public Health Trust of Dade County*,[193] plaintiff sued defendant hospital over a surgical procedure alleged to be negligent. Certain critical records were lost or destroyed, thus prejudicing the plaintiff's ability to prove her case. The Court of Appeals remanded the case for determination of the circumstances concerning the loss or destruction of the records, stating:

---

[190] *The Bermuda's Claimants v. United States*, 70 U.S. 514 (1866).

[191] *Id*. at 550.

[192] *Moore v. General Motors Corp.*, 558 S.W.2d 720, 733 (mo. 1977). *See also Furlong v. Stokes*, 427 S.W.2d 513 (Mo. 1968); *Tracy v. Buchanan*, 151 S.W. 747, 748 (Mo.Ct.App. 1912). "To permit the despoiler to dispute his adversary's statement of the contents of the destroyed document would be to permit him to profit by his own wrong — to gain the very advantage his lawless act was designed to secure."

[193] *Valcin v. Public Health Trust of Dade County*, 473 So.2d 1297 (Fla.Ct.App. 1984).

If the fact-finder, under appropriate instructions, determines that the hospital had sustained its burden of showing that Dr. Shroder did not deliberately omit making an operative report or, if one was made, that the hospital did not deliberately remove or destroy the report, then the fact that the record is missing will merely raise a presumption that the surgical procedure was negligently performed, which presumption may be rebutted by the hospital by the greater weight of the evidence. However, if the fact-finder is not satisfied that the records are missing due to inadvertence or negligence, then a conclusive, irrebuttable presumption that the surgical procedure was negligently performed will arise, and judgment as to liability shall be entered in favor of Valcin.[194]

Other courts have stated the nature of the inference far less precisely. The court in *Trupiano v. Cully*[195] formulated the presumption as follows:

At best, in the event the jury found destruction of records with an intent to suppress the truth, defendant was entitled to an inference that the original records, if available, would not prove favorable to plaintiff.

While some courts will impose an inference or presumption based upon a finding of negligence,[196] other courts will not impose an adverse inference or presumption in the absence of bad faith. In *Vick v. Texas Employment Commission*,[197] the court quoting *McCormick on Evidence*, stated:

[T]he circumstances of the act must manifest bad faith. Mere negligence is not enough, for it does not sustain an inference of consciousness of a weak case.

---

[194] *Id.* at 1306.

[195] *Trupiano v. Cully*, 84 N.W.2d 747, 748 (Mich. 1957).

[196] *See, e.g., Yoffe v. United States*, 153 F.2d 570 (1st Cir. 1946); *INA Aviation Corp. v. United States*, 468 F.Supp. 695 (E.D.N.Y. 1979); **Equitable Trust Co. v. Gallagher*, 77 A.2d 548 (Del. 1950).

[197] *Vick v. Texas Employment Commission*, 514 F.2d 734, 737 (5th Cir. 1975).

Other courts have used a variety of formulations for determining the circumstances under which an inference or presumption is appropriate, and the precise nature of the inference.[198]

The court in *Battocchi v. Washington Hospital Center*[199] concluded that, under Maryland and D.C. Circuit law, a rebuttable presumption of negligence and causation was unavailable to the plaintiffs as a sanction for the apparent loss of records created by emergency room personnel. The court ruled that an inference that the document would have been unfavorable to the party responsible for its destruction was only available in the case of deliberate, bad faith destruction. When the loss or destruction is not intentional or reckless, the court concluded that the fact-finder may draw an inference adverse to the party who fails to preserve the relevant evidence within his exclusive control.[200] This distinction appears to be similar to that in *Valcin* — the more culpable the behavior, the stronger and more precise the inference to be drawn.

---

198 *See Akiona v. United States*, 938 F.2d 158 (9th Cir. 1991) (concluding that a rebuttable presumption was inappropriate); *Synanon Church v. United States*, 820 F.2d 421, 428 (D.C.Cir 1980) ("The occurrence of a cover-up raises the presumption that disclosure of the material would be damaging.") *Rogers v. Exxon Research and Engineering Co.*, 550 F.2d 834 (3rd Cir. 1977) (The inference to be drawn from the destruction of records was a matter for argument to the jury.); *Commercial Insurance Co. of Newark, New Jersey v. Gonzalez*, 512 F.2d 1307 (1st Cir. 1975) (failure to produce a document warrants an inference that the document would have been unfavorable); *Brown and Williamson Tobacco Corp. v. Jacobson*, 644 F.Supp. 1240, (N.D.Ill. 1986) (bad faith required in order to draw an adverse inference); *Carr v. St. Paul Fire and Marine Insurance Co.*, 384 F.Supp 821 (W.D.Ark. 1974), (the court approved of the trial court's actions in allowing evidence and argument concerning destroyed hospital records, apparently using Arkansas law); *Dollison v. Chicago, Rock Island & Pacific R. Co.*, 355 N.E.2d 588 (Ill.Ct.App. 1976) (once a prima facie case is established by a plaintiff, the trier of fact may infer that available evidence which is not produced would be unfavorable to the defendant); *Reo Movers, Inc. v. Industrial Commission*, 589 N.E.2d 704 (Ill.Ct.App. 1992) (where a party fails to produce evidence his control, the presumption arises that the evidence would be adverse to that party.); *Prudential Insurance Co. of America v. Lawnsdail*, 15 N.W.2d 880, 883 (Iowa 1944), (destruction of insurance records by the insurance company, after having knowledge that a dispute had arisen, "authorizes an inference which tends to corroborate the evidence adduced by appellant."); *Garrett v. Terminal R. Ass'n of St. Louis*, 259 S.W.2d 807 (Mo. 1953) (where a party is guilty of spoliation of documentary evidence, he is held to admit the truth of the allegation of the opposing party); *Tracy v. Buchanan*, 151 S.W. 747 (Mo.Ct.App. 1912) (intentional destruction of documentary evidence proved plaintiff's assertions and disproved defendant's); *Fuller v. Preston State Bank*, 667 S.W.2d 214 (Tex. Ct. App. 1983) (the destruction of relevant evidence raises a presumption that the evidence would have been unfavorable to the spoliator).

199 *Battocchi v. Washington Hospital Center*, 581 A.2d 759 (D.C.Ct.App. 1990).

200 *Id.* at 765-766.

The court in *May v. Moore*,[201] concluded that:

> Proof may be made concerning a party purposefully and wrongfully destroying a document which he knew was supportive of the interest of his opponent, whether or not an action involving such interest was pending at the time of the destruction. Additionally, the spoliation, or attempt to suppress material evidence by a party to the suit, favorable to an adversary, is sufficient foundation for an inference of his guilt or negligence. [citation omitted]

A number of other courts have also come to the conclusion that bad faith is a prerequisite for the imposition of an inference, presumption, or similar sanctions for destruction of records.[202]

7.4. Bad Faith

Courts vary widely in the extent and circumstances when they will apply inferences or presumptions to supply the contents of missing documents. A majority of jurisdictions either require bad faith or impose a harsher penalty for bad faith than for negligence. Effective records retention procedures control and document the destruction of records and may preclude a court from concluding bad faith by inference.[203]

Even with good procedures, good faith delays caused by the need to search large numbers of documents, or mere human error in preparing, storing or producing could still result in sanctions. Many courts have been unwilling to impose sanctions in the absence of bad faith. But the precise conduct constituting bad faith, and the quantum of evidence required as proof, varies with the facts of each case. Courts recognize that "bad faith" is difficult to

---

201 *May v. Moore,* 424 So.2d 596, 603 (Ala. 1982).
202 *See Eaton Corp. v. Appliance Valves Corp.*, 790 F.2d 874 (Fed. Cir. 1986); *Jackson v. Harvard University*, 721 F.Supp. 1397 (D.Mass. 1989); *Independent Petrochemical Corp. v. Aetna Casualty and Surety Co.*, 654 F.Supp. 1334 (D.D.C. 1986); *United States v. Ungar*, 648 F.Supp. 1329 (E.D.N.Y. 1986); *Britt v. Block*, 636 F.Supp. 596 (D.Vt. 1986); *Kansas-Nebraska Natural Gas Co. v. Marathon Oil Co.*, 109 F.R.D. 12 (D.Neb. 1985); *Bowmar Instruments Corp. v. Texas Instruments, Inc.*, 196 U.S.P.Q. 199 (N.D.Ind. 1977)
203 *See* Chapter 9, *infra.*

quantify, and may not be a meaningful standard. In *Nation-wide Check Corp. v. Forest Hills Distributors*,[204] the court observed:

> The [trial] court's reluctance to label Gordon's conduct as "bad faith" is not dispositive: "bad faith" is not a talisman, as [prior case] itself made clear when it stated that the adverse inference "ordinarily" depended on a showing of bad faith. Indeed, the "bad faith" label is more useful to summarize the conclusion that an adverse inference is permissible than it is actually to reach the conclusion.

Other courts have explicitly rejected the concept of bad faith:

> [An adverse inference] should be available even for the negligent destruction of documents if that is necessary to further the remedial purpose of the inference. It makes little difference to the party victimized by the destruction of evidence whether that act was done willfully or negligently. The adverse inference provides the necessary mechanism for restoring the evidentiary balance. The inference is *adverse* to the destroyer not because of any finding of moral culpability, but because the risk that the evidence would have been detrimental rather than favorable should fall on the party responsible for its loss.[205]

In those jurisdictions where a determination of bad faith is required, a court may readily conclude bad faith whenever a litigant is unable to produce documentary evidence without some reasonable explanation. Direct evidence of obstructionist behavior is unnecessary. While flagrant misconduct, such as destruction of relevant documents during the pendency of litigation, is evidence of bad faith, such evidence is not necessary. Bad faith is a factual question, to be determined from the totality of the circumstances.[206] Bad faith may be found even in the absence of a provably improper motive for the sanctioned conduct.[207] The circumstances surrounding the sanctionable conduct may justify an inference of bad faith in the absence of concrete evidence of willful or contumacious behavior.

---

[204] *Nation-wide Check Corp. v. Forest Hills Distributors, Inc.*, 692 F.2d 214, 219 (1st Cir. 1982).

[205] *Turner v. Hudson Transit Lines, Inc.*, 142 F.R.D. 68, 75 (S.D.N.Y. 1991).

[206] *Brown and Williamson Tobacco Corp. v. Jacobson*, 644 F.Supp. 1240 (N.D.Ill. 1986).

[207] *Nation-wide Check Corp. v. Forest Hills Distributors, Inc.*, 692 F.2d 214 (1st Cir. 1982).

A mere lack of effort may be viewed as bad faith. In *P Stone v. Koppers Co.*,[208] the court dismissed a complaint for failure to comply with discovery, in the express absence of a finding of willful behavior. The plaintiff failed to produce certain relevant documents and plaintiff's attorney represented to the court that diligent inquiry had been made, but failed to turn up the documents. The documents suddenly appeared nearly two years later, and inquiry by the court determined that a simple inquiry to their custodian would have produced them; plaintiff and its attorney had simply failed to make the diligent search promised.

A partial, but inadequate, response to discovery may be viewed as bad faith. The court in *International Mining Co. v. Allen & Co.*,[209] faced with a series of very inadequate responses to the defendant's discovery requests, concluded that the plaintiff was at least negligent, and possibly willful, and dismissed the complaint.

The lack of effort may have occurred in advance of litigation. In *United States v. ABC Sales & Service*,[210] the court sanctioned the defendant for, *inter alia*, a poorly managed records system:

> [A] business which generates millions of files cannot frustrate discovery by creating an inadequate filing system so that individual files cannot readily be located.

The court in *Alliance to End Repression v. Rochford*,[211] expressed similar sentiments:

> To allow a defendant whose business generates massive records to frustrate discovery by creating an inadequate filing system, and then claiming undue burden, would defeat the purposes of discovery rules.

In both cases, the courts concluded that the appropriate sanction was to deem the facts allegedly contained in the missing documents to be as claimed by the plaintiffs.

---

208 *P Stone, Inc. v. Koppers Co., Inc.*, 94 F.R.D. 662 (M.D.Penn. 1982).
209 *International Mining Co. v. Allen & Co.*, 567 F.Supp. 777 (1983).
210 *United States v. ABC Sales & Service, Inc.*, 95 F.R.D. 316, 318 (D.Ariz. 1982).
211 *Alliance to End Repression v. Rochford*, 75 F.R.D. 441, 447 (N.D.Ill. 1977) (quoting *Kozlowski v. Sears Roebuck & Co.*, 73 F.R.D. 73, 76 (1978)).

Inability to locate records may by itself be taken as proof of bad faith. In *Paytes v. Kost*,[212] the plaintiffs were injured by a driver insured by the defendant insurance company. The defendant at first could not produce the insurance policy in question, and ultimately produced a partial copy. In concluding that the defendant acted in bad faith, the court stated:

> The most basic document governing the relations between an insurance company and its client is the insurance policy. It strains credibility to believe that a company with the experience of Nation-wide cannot produce such a document on immediate demand or that partial policy documents comprise the entire contractual relationship between itself and its insured.

Courts have imposed sanctions for obvious outrageous conduct or bad faith. But, some courts have imposed sanctions for poor recordkeeping practices, practices that could not be explained or practices that just "looked bad." The costs of a records management program to resolve these deficiencies is small compared to the risks, costs and adverse consequences associated with the imposition of sanctions in litigation.

---

212 *Paytes v. Kost*, 482 N.W.2d 130, 133 (Wis.Ct.App. 1992).

Chapter 8.   The Absence of Records

The duty to produce records and documents for litigation is linked to the duties to create and preserve them. In circumstances where a court or opposing party demands production of records that do not exist, the question may arise whether a duty existed to create the record. If a duty existed to create the records, the court will explore whether a duty existed to preserve the records.

Sanctions punish offending parties for failure to produce requested records without a justifiable excuse and to deter others from abusing discovery. Since sanctions cannot extract records that do not exist, the court may attempt to either prevent the offending party from benefiting from the abuse of discovery or create a "fiction" by allowing into evidence information that would presumably have been derived from the records. The circumstances surrounding the unavailability of records determines of the remedial measures the courts will impose.

Even when sanctions are not imposed, the absence of records that ought to exist is likely to create problems for the offending party. In *Cecil Corley Motor Co. v. General Motors Corp.*,[213] the plaintiff destroyed business records while contemplating the filing of the suit, and after the filing of the complaint. After losing a jury verdict, the defendant sought a judgment notwithstanding the

---

[213] *Cecil Corley Motor Co. v. General Motors Corp.*, 380 F.Supp. 819 (M.D.Tenn. 1974)

verdict. The court rejected the motion, observing that the burden
was on the plaintiff to produce the best evidence available and that
the defendant ought not to be penalized for plaintiff's actions.[214]

8.1. Missing Records

Sometimes a party responding to discovery determines that
pertinent records simply cannot be found. Nobody appears to know
what happened to the records and why they are missing.[215]

When this occurs, a court orders the party to make a diligent
search for the missing records. If they still cannot be found, the
court will then order the party to make a diligent inquiry to
determine what happened to the records.[216]

The consequences of missing records will depend on two factors:
(1) the controlling law in the jurisdiction and (2) the court's assessment of the party's diligence in searching for the missing records
and in inquiring as to the circumstances leading to their unavailability. The court may inquire into the procedures followed to
maintain the records and the circumstances surrounding their
ultimate disappearance. If negligence or willful behavior led to the
problem, sanctions may be imposed for higher levels of culpability.

The court may also determine whether a party is actually
responsible for the loss of the records. Unless the loss can be
attributed to a particular party with some certainty, no sanctions
may be imposed even when the records are missing under highly
suspicious circumstances.[217]

---

[214] *See also WASCO, Inc. v. Economic Development Unit*, 461 So.2d 1055 (La.Ct.App.
1984). In contrast, where the party which seeks the records can show no prejudice,
and there is a reasonable explanation for the absence of the records, sanctions will
likely not be imposed. *See Pressey v. Patterson*, 898 F.2d 1018 (5th Cir. 1990).

[215] *See Battocchi v. Washington Hospital Center*, 581 A.2d 759 (D.C.App.Ct. 1990) (Note
contained in medical chart apparently misplaced.).

[216] *See Turner v. Hudson Transit Lines, Inc.*, 142 F.R.D. 68 (D.S.N.Y. 1991).

[217] *See In the Matter of Grace Line, Inc.*, 397 F.Supp.1258 (S.D.N.Y. 1973). A salvage crew
sent to recover the deck logs and course recorder tape of a ship discovered that the
tape had been ripped out intentionally, and the logs were missing. Since there was
no way to determine whether the tape had been ripped out by agents of the shipping
line, or by the pilot or his cohorts, the court declined to impose an adverse inference.

8.1.1. Inability to Find Recent Records

Courts reject assertions that records which ought to exist, cannot be located. In *United States v. ABC Sales & Service*,[218] the court rejected the defendant's assertion that certain potentially relevant files could not be located among several million other files.

Although courts may accept a variety of legitimate reasons for not being able to locate records, the courts consistently expect that a party can find reasonably current business records without excessive difficulty. A party claiming the inability to find missing records because it does not maintain a file management system or maintains a poor system will probably not prevail.[219] Absence of records which under reasonable practice would have existed is enough to allow a court to conclude that the absence is due to improper motives.[220] This is true even if there is no direct evidence of improper motive.

Even if the records turn up at a later time, the offending party may still be penalized. In *Davis v. Johns Hopkins Hospital*,[221] the defendant claimed to be unable to locate vital medical records for several years and then located them after only a 45-minute search on the day before a deposition to inquire about the records was scheduled. The court of appeals concluded that under Maryland law, this raised a jury question whether the defendant had incurred liability for withholding the medical records.

---

[218] *United States v. ABC Sales & Service, Inc.*, 95 F.R.D. 316, 318 (D.Ariz. 1982).

[219] *See also Alliance to End Repression v. Rochford*, 75 F.R.D. 441 (N.D.Ill. 1977); *Kozlowski v. Sears Roebuck & Co.*, 73 F.R.D. 73 (D.Mass. 1976).

[220] *See, e.g., Moore v. Jackson Tube Co.*, 86 N.Y.2d 488 (S.Ct. 1949) (two years worth of sales records for a large corporation apparently vanished without a trace); *Paytes v. Kost*, 482 N.W.2d 130 (Wisc.Ct.App. 1992) (insurance company unable to produce copy of current insurance policy, and ultimately able to produce only a partial copy); *May v. Moore*, 424 So.2d 596 (Ala. 1982) (treatment records of deceased infant vanished without explanation, and testimony indicated that, in the past, records of other patients of defendant doctor had similarly vanished without explanation).

[221] *Davis v. Johns Hopkins Hospital*, 585 A.2d 841 (Md.Ct.App. 1991).

8.1.2. Inability to Find Older Records

When the records were created long before the litigation, the party's diligence in maintaining the records, searching for them, and other circumstances surrounding their disappearance, become relevant. In *Addeo Loan Co. v. Manocchio*,[222] the defendant entered into a series of mortgages with the plaintiff twenty years earlier. Although the parties had nearly one and one-half years to prepare, the defendant was unable to produce relevant business records for the trial. The court entered judgment for the plaintiff. The defendant moved for a new trial, asserting that a long period of time had elapsed since execution of the mortgages, that many of his business records had been stolen, and that the premises where the records had been kept had been foreclosed upon subsequent to the filing of the action. Following the entry of judgment, a new search had turned up many of the missing records.

In denying the motion for a new trial, the court noted that the missing records had been discovered within ten days of the entry of judgment and that the defendant had nearly one and one-half years to prepare the case. The court concluded that the defendant had not exercised due diligence in searching for the missing records prior to trial. It specifically rejected the proposition that the mere passage of nearly twenty years justified the need to exercise due diligence when searching for records.

8.1.3. Prejudice Resulting from Loss of Own Record

A party claiming prejudice to its case due to the loss of its own records in circumstances beyond its control has the burden of proving that the loss of records materially prejudiced its case. In *Equal Employment Opportunity Commission v. C.W. Transport*,[223] the defendant asserted the defense of laches,[224] due to the loss of large quantities of records from flooding in the records storage

---

222 *Addeo Loan Co., Inc. v. Manocchio*, 313 A.2d 649 (R.I. 1974).
223 *Equal Employment Opportunity Commission v. C.W. Transport, Inc.*, 658 F.Supp. 1278, 1296 (W.D.Wisc. 1987).
224 "Delay such as to preclude the court from arriving at a safe conclusion as to truth," *Black's Law Dictionary*, 4th Ed. 1968, citing *Grant v. Hart*, 14 S.E.2d 860 (1941).

rooms, a tornado, employee pilfering, and misplacement. The court rejected the defendant's contention that it had been substantially prejudiced by the loss of records because it could not precisely catalog what had been destroyed or lost:

> Laches is an affirmative defense, on which the defendant bears the burden of proof. It is CWT's burden to establish that the loss of records from natural disasters and the normal course of business loss will prejudice its defense of this lawsuit. The burden cannot be met merely by showing that some unspecified records have been destroyed or misplaced during some occurrences at some facilities. Despite its claim that it cannot catalog precisely what records are missing, the organization should know generally what records it maintained and, to some level of specificity, what records remain after the various natural disasters and other events. It does not seem unreasonable to require CWT to establish with more specificity what records are missing and why the loss of these records will materially prejudice its defense of this enforcement action.

Parties asserting laches when the loss of records was due to their own actions, will likely find the court even less sympathetic when they reasonably should have anticipated litigation concerning the records. In *Equal Employment Opportunity Commission v. Jacksonville Shipyards, Inc.*,[225] the E.E.O.C. served the defendant with a Notice of Charge and a copy of charge, and then did not file suit for nearly six years. In the interim, the defendant destroyed certain records to which the charges pertained. The defendant then asserted the defense of laches, claiming to be prejudiced and unable to defend its case due to the long period of time which had passed since the initial Notice Of Charge and its inability to now find the relevant records. The court rejected this contention, concluding that:

> A party cannot assert the defense of laches merely because it has failed to preserve evidence despite knowledge of a pending claim.[226]

---

225 *Equal Employment Opportunity Commission v. Jacksonville Shipyards, Inc.*, 690 F.Supp. 995 (M.D.Fla. 1988).
226 *Id*. at 1001.

8.1.4. The Adverse Inference When Records Are Missing Under Suspicious Circumstances

If a party claims records are missing under suspicious circumstances, the court may apply an adverse inference or presumption related to the missing records. In *DeLaughter v. Lawrence County Hospital*,[227] a decedent's family sued the defendant hospital over alleged improper treatment resulting in the decedent's death. The hospital refused to voluntarily release the decedent's medical records. When ordered to release the records by the court, the defendant purportedly discovered that the records were missing.

The appellate court ruled that the trial court correctly instructed the jury that if a party caused the records to be destroyed, misplaced, or unavailable, the jury could infer that the records would be unfavorable to that party. However, the trial court failed to instruct the jury that the defendant hospital had the burden of proving that it did not destroy or misplace the records in order to rebut that presumption. The appellate court concluded that the error in instructing on the rebuttable presumption and burden of proof was not a harmless error, and reversed and remanded for a new trial.

In *Bihun v. AT&T Information Systems, Inc.*,[228] the plaintiff alleged sexual harassment by the plaintiff's supervisor, an employee of the defendant. When the plaintiff sought discovery of the supervisor's personnel file, defendant's attorney objected claiming privacy, even though he had never seen the file. In fact, the attorney had been informed by the defendant several months earlier that the supervisor's file could not be located. The attorney did not advise the court and the plaintiff that the file was missing until the plaintiff renewed her demand for production during trial.

The judge instructed the jury that it could find that the defendant willfully suppressed the personnel file and that it could draw an inference that there was something damaging to the defendant's case in that file.

---

[227] *DeLaughter v. Lawrence County Hospital*, 601 So.2d 818 (Miss. 1992).
[228] *Bihun v. AT&T Information Systems, Inc.*, 16 Cal.Rptr. 2d 787 (Cal.Ct.App. 1993).

In concluding that the jury was properly instructed, the appellate court found the following facts persuasive:

- Although they resigned within a few months of each other, the supervisor's personnel file could not be found, even though the plaintiff's file existed.

- The disappearance of the supervisor's file was covered up by the defendant.

- The defendant's rules required maintenance of resigned employees' personnel files if the matter is in litigation.

- It was reasonably probable that the supervisor's performance evaluations and any complaints of sexual harassment would be in the personnel file.[229]

In *Paytes v. Kost*,[230] the plaintiffs were injured by a vehicle insured by the defendant insurance company. During discovery, the defendant asserted that it could not find the relevant policy, and ultimately produced only parts of it. The court concluded that the defendant exhibited bad faith and egregious conduct in its handling of the discovery request:

> The most basic document governing relations between an insurance company and its client is the insurance policy. It strains credibility to believe that a company with the experience of Nation-wide cannot produce such a document on immediate demand or that partial policy documents comprise the entire contractual relationship between itself and its insured.[231]

Cases such as these mandate the necessity for adequate physical control of records. Records must be stored in locations and environments which are safe from disasters such as fire or flood and the program must ensure an appropriate level of security. Some records and information management design considerations include:

---

229 *Id.*
230 *Paytes v. Kost*, 482 N W 2d 130 (Wisc. 1992).
231 *Id.* at 133

• Limiting access to records areas to authorized persons.

• Designating an authorized person or custodian to be responsible for records.

• Documenting records that are lost, destroyed, or damaged due to circumstances beyond the organization's control

• Making a reasonable attempt to salvage damaged records.

• Determining what records were lost or destroyed and, if possible, reconstructing them.

8.1.5. Reconstructing Missing Records

Sometimes, lost or destroyed records may be reconstructed from other information or copies obtained from other sources. In egregious cases, courts often preclude the offending party from attempting to reconstruct lost information from other sources.[232] However, in cases of inadvertent or negligent destruction, where the court can be persuaded that prejudice to the other party can be fully remedied by reconstruction of the records from other sources, only limited sanctions may be imposed or no sanctions imposed at all. For example, in *Equal Employment Opportunity Commission v. Jacksonville Shipyards*,[233] the court concluded that if the defendant could adequately reconstruct lost records, the appropriate sanction would be to require the defendant to bear the cost and burden of reconstructing the records.

Even when lost or destroyed evidence cannot be found or reconstructed, the court may not impose sanctions if the innocent party is not significantly prejudiced. In *Hernandez v. Pino*,[234] the plaintiff's attorney in a dental malpractice case lost or destroyed x-rays that had been provided by the defendant. But, prior to giving

---

[232] Fed.R.Evid. 1004(1) "Secondary evidence of the contents of destroyed writings prohibited where the proponent lost or destroyed them in bad faith". *See also Telectron, Inc. v. Overhead Door Corp.*, 116 F.R.D. 107 (S.D.Fla. 1987).

[233] *See Equal Employment Opportunity Commission v. Jacksonville Shipyards, Inc.*, 690 F.Supp. 995 (M.D.Fla. 1988).

[234] *Hernandez v. Pino*, 482 So.2d 450 (Fla.Ct.App. 1986)

them to the plaintiff, defendant and his expert witness reviewed the x-rays and made notations about them. The court concluded that sanctions were not appropriate for the loss since the defendant could adequately introduce evidence concerning the x-rays from information obtained during the earlier review.

8.1.6. Informing the Court About Missing Records

Besides creating legal problems for the party responsible for missing records, questionable conduct regarding missing records may expose individual participants to personal liability. The attorney in *Bihun v. AT&T Information Systems* asserted a privilege based on privacy for a personnel file that he had never seen. This ethical violation exposed him to possible professional discipline.[235]

In *Telectron*, the defendant's in-house counsel initiated a widespread document destruction program in order to prevent the records from being used in antitrust litigation. This program continued even after the plaintiff filed the lawsuit and demanded documents that fell under the destruction program. When challenged, in-house counsel claimed to be unable to remember key aspects of this document destruction program. Not only did this attorney commit fraud on the court, contempt of court, and probably perjury, he also exposed himself to possible suspension or disbarment.

In *Bihun v. AT&T Information Systems*, *DeLaughter v. Lawrence County Hospital*, and *Paytes v. Kost* there was no direct evidence that the defendants had improperly destroyed records. However, in all three cases, records that should have existed were

---

[235] *See also* *Chicago Park District v. Chicago and Northwestern Transportation Co.*, 607 N.E.2d 1300 (Ill.Ct.App. 1992). A Park District employee discovered that certain documents relative to a personal injury suit were missing and tried to cover up the problem by executing crude forgeries. During the trial, the Park District's attorney learned that the documents were forged, but failed to inform either the court or opposing counsel. The plaintiff's lawyer conclusively demonstrated at trial that the documents were forged. The employee committing the forgeries committed perjury by lying about them to the court. He also risked disciplinary action from his organization. The attorney subjected himself to possible disciplinary action or disbarment by failing to inform the court or opposing counsel when he first learned the documents were forged.

missing and the party's behavior with respect to the missing records could reasonably be viewed by a court or jury as an attempt to hide something. The combination of factors allowed a conclusion that impropriety was involved in the absence of the records.

Parties which discover that important documentary evidence is missing should be aware of the pitfalls surrounding attempts to equivocate to the court. Care should be taken to avoid suspicious or questionable behavior regarding the circumstances surrounding missing records or subsequent actions taken once the records cannot be found. No party enjoys going to court and admitting that highly relevant documentary evidence is missing, especially when no satisfactory explanation can be provided.

But, it is far better to voluntarily inform the court about missing records at an early stage of the proceeding. Courts frown upon parties misrepresenting the truth about missing records, revealing the correct information at a late stage of the proceedings, or revealing information about the missing records under circumstances which appear as though the party is attempting to defraud the court.

8.2. Records Stored In Foreign Countries

Companies that store records in foreign countries face a legal dilemma and potential liability if those records become relevant in a lawsuit filed in the United States. Records stored in foreign jurisdictions are discoverable in the same manner as records stored in the United States, and failure to produce them may subject the party to sanctions. Foreign law, however, may forbid the disclosure of certain information or require that the records remain in the country.

Companies may face sanctions in the United States for failure to produce records and sanctions in the foreign country if the records are produced outside that country. In evaluating this dilemma, courts will review the reasons for storing the records in the foreign country and whether the organization made a good faith effort to comply with the court order.

8.2.1. Good Faith Effort to Produce Records

The United States Supreme Court addressed this issue in *Societe Internationale Pour Participations Industrielles et Commerciales, S.A. v. Rogers.*[236] The plaintiff, a Swiss holding company, sued the United States Attorney General to recover property seized under the Trading With the Enemy Act during World War II. During discovery, the government moved for an order requiring the plaintiff to make a large number of Swiss banking documents available for inspection. After the district court concluded that the plaintiff controlled the documents, the plaintiff moved to dismiss the production order on the ground that disclosure of the required documents would violate Swiss penal laws. At the same time, the government moved to dismiss the complaint due to noncompliance with the production order. To further complicate the issue, the Swiss Federal Attorney soon confiscated the records to prevent a violation of Swiss law by preventing their disclosure.

The matter was referred to a Special Master who concluded that the Swiss government acted in accordance with its own law by confiscating the records. There was no evidence of collusion between the plaintiff and the Swiss government to interfere with the production of documents. Finally, the plaintiff showed good faith in attempting to comply with the production order and did everything which a reasonable man would have undertaken in these circumstances to comply with the order. These findings were confirmed by the District Court.

Nonetheless, the District Court dismissed the complaint, concluding that the plaintiff had control over the records, the records might prove crucial in the outcome of the lawsuit, and that Swiss law did not furnish an adequate excuse for the plaintiff's failure to comply with the production order. Following entry of this order, the Swiss government agreed to release some of the records. However, full compliance and production ultimately proved impossible, and the court dismissed the case. This dismissal was affirmed by the Court of Appeals.

---

[236] *Societe Internationale Pour Participations Industrielles et Commerciales, S.A. v. Rogers,* 357 U.S. 197, 78 S.Ct. 1087, 2 L.Ed.2d 1255 (1958).

The Supreme Court reversed. The court first noted that the confiscation of the records was not the central issue, since the threat of criminal sanctions existed prior to the confiscation. Also, the Swiss government did not actually physically remove the records, it only prohibited the plaintiff from removing the records from the country.

The court next addressed Fed.R.Civ.P. Rule 37, which authorizes the imposition of sanctions against a party who "refuses to obey" an order to produce documents or other evidence for inspection. The court concluded that a party "refuses to obey" simply by failing to comply with an order.

The court then reviewed the plaintiff's extensive good faith efforts to comply with the order. Although the Supreme Court struck down the lower court's ruling, it did so on the basis of findings that the plaintiff had made good faith efforts to comply with discovery, and that the failure to satisfy the requirements of the production order were due to inability fostered neither by its own conduct nor by circumstances within its control.[237]

The court also noted that the plaintiff had sought no special privileges because of its foreign citizenship which were not accorded domestic litigants. The plaintiff explicitly recognized that it was subject to the procedural rules of United States courts and had made full efforts to comply with those rules. In light of the plaintiff's actions and of due process concerns under the Fifth Amendment, the court concluded that Fed.R.Civ.P. Rule 37 did not authorize dismissal of the complaint for noncompliance.

The court did note that the plaintiff still carried the ultimate burden of proof on its claims, and that the defendant would also be handicapped by the lack of records. The court further noted that circumstances might justify drawing an adverse inference against the plaintiff due to nonproduction.[238]

---

[237] *Id.*, 357 U.S. at 211, 78 S.Ct. at 1095, 2 L.Ed.2d at 1266.
[238] *Id.*, 357 U.S. at 212-213, 78 S.Ct. at 1095-1096, 2 L.Ed.2d at 1267-1268.

8.2.2. Circumventing the Discovery Process

Courts respond differently when parties do not make good faith attempts to comply, or use foreign law to circumvent the discovery process. In *General Atomic Co. v. Exxon Nuclear Co.*,[239] plaintiff sued defendant to enforce a uranium supply contract. The defendant sought discovery of documents pertaining to the activities of an international uranium cartel.

The plaintiff asserted Canadian laws prohibiting the removal of the records from Canada. The plaintiff nonetheless made several good faith attempts to overcome the prohibitions in the Canadian regulations, including hiring a Canadian law firm and meeting with the Canadian Minister of Energy and Mines. However, evidence indicated that soon after the plaintiff began participating in the international cartel, it established a policy requiring cartel-related documents to be stored in Canada. This policy intentionally prevented production of these documents in United States litigation affecting the cartel.

The court found that the plaintiff's inability to produce the documents resulted from a deliberate strategy of concealment. Storing the documents in Canada amounted to knowingly taking advantage of Canadian law to interfere with the judicial process in the United States. The court concluded that the plaintiff's failure to produce the documents had prejudiced the defendant and deprived it of a full and fair trial. Sanctions included rebuttable presumptions rendering defendant counterclaims true, precluding evidence in support of affirmative defenses to these counterclaims, considering certain documents to be admitted in evidence, and requiring payment of attorney fees and expenses incurred in connection with the motion for sanctions.

A related case, *United Nuclear Corp. v. General Atomic Co.*,[240] produced an even harsher result. The plaintiff in *General Atomic Co. v. Exxon Nuclear Co.* was the defendant in this case. The plaintiff sought a declaratory judgment that two contracts requir-

---

239 *General Atomic Co. v. Exxon Nuclear Co., Inc.*, 90 F.R.D. 290 (S.D.Cal. 1981).
240 *United Nuclear Corp. v. General Atomic Co.*, 629 P.2d 231 (N.M. 1980).

ing it to supply 27 million pounds of uranium to the defendant were unenforceable. Again, the court concluded that the defendant had housed cartel documents in Canada in order to prevent their production in litigation in the United States. In addition, the court concluded that the defendant had engaged in a pattern of obstructing discovery and acted in bad faith and in callous disregard of its responsibilities. The New Mexico Supreme Court upheld this award in its entirety, recounting the defendant's actions at length, and concluding that:

> When a party has displayed a willful, bad faith approach to discovery, it is not only proper, but imperative that severe sanctions be imposed to preserve the integrity of the judicial process and the due process rights of the other litigants.[241]

8.2.3. Records in Foreign Countries

The court in *Societe Nationale Industrielle Aerospatiale v. United States District Court*[242] reinforced the conclusions reached in the uranium cases:

> [I]t is well settled that such [foreign] statutes do not deprive an American court of the power to order a party subject to its jurisdiction to produce evidence even though the act of producing may violate that statute.

The court adopted the following balancing test to decide whether foreign law excuses noncompliance with discovery orders:

- The importance of the documents or other information requested to the investigation or litigation.

- The degree of specificity for documents in the request.

- Whether the information originated in the United States.

---

[241] *Id.* 629 P.2d at 317.
[242] *Societe Nationale Industrielle Aerospatiale v. United States District Court*, 482 U.S. 522, 544, 107 S.Ct. 2542, 96 L.Ed.2d 461 (1987) n. 29.

• The availability of alternative means to secure the information.

• The extent to which compliance with the request would undermine important interests of the United States, or compliance
with the request would undermine important interests of the
country where the information is located.[243]

The court noted that this list of factors was not exhaustive.
Subsequent cases have considered such factors as:

• The extent and the nature of the hardship that inconsistent
enforcement would impose upon the person.

• The extent to which enforcement by action of either country can
reasonably be expected to achieve compliance with the rule prescribed by that country.[244]

The test developed by the court in *Societe Nationale Industrielle
Aerospatiale v. United States District Court* was used in *Richmark
Corp. v. Timber Falling Consultants (TFC)*.[245] TFC procured timber for plaintiff and then sold it to Ever Bright Industrial Co., a
corporation and arm of government organized under the laws of
the People's Republic of China. When the contract with Ever Bright
fell through, plaintiff sued TFC and TFC filed a cross-claim against
Ever Bright. TFC obtained a judgment against Ever Bright, and
then served Ever Bright with discovery requests and interrogatories to identify Ever Bright's assets for the purpose of collecting on
the judgment.

In response, Ever Bright asserted that "state secrecy laws" of
the People's Republic of China prohibited it from disclosing the
requested information. After considering the factors set forth by
the Supreme Court in *Societe Nationale Industrielle Aerospatiale
v. United States District Court*, the court concluded that the balance tipped in favor of TFC. The United States' interest in enforcing judgments outweighed the People's Republic of China's interest
in confidentiality. The information sought was vital and could not

---

243 *Id.*, at 544 n. 28.
244 *United States v. Vetco Inc.*, 691 F.2d 1281, 1288 (9th Cir. 1981), *cert. denied* 454 U.S.
1098, 102 S.Ct. 671, 70 L.Ed.2d 639.
245 *Richmark Corp. v. Timber Falling Consultants*, 959 F.2d 1468 (9th Cir. 1992).

could not be obtained elsewhere. In addition, the court concluded that Ever Bright could alleviate any hardship itself and avoid having to produce the documents by either posting a bond or letter of credit to stay the execution of the judgment pending appeal, or simply paying the judgment.

In light of these cases, companies storing records in countries which may prohibit their production in litigation outside of that country should carefully determine the existence and scope of such laws prior to litigation. Although the courts employ balancing tests and other devices to weigh the competing interests, a party storing records in a foreign country is likely to discover that the balance tends to favor production. Courts perceive the need to produce these documents for United States litigation as being an important interest, even when the records custodian faces the possibility of criminal sanctions in the foreign country.

Income tax issues provided a different and unique situation in *William E. Powe Trust v. Commissioner.*[246] The Internal Revenue Service denied capital loss carryovers claimed by the plaintiff as a result of the seizure and expropriation of business assets by the Cuban government. The petitioner testified that the books relating to the business assets were unavailable in Cuba making it impossible for him to establish the precise amount of these carryovers.

The Tax Court agreed that the records were unobtainable through reasonable means and also overturned the IRS's denial of the carryover loss. It concluded that an approximation of the value of the assets could still be established through testimony and other evidence, rather than the unavailable records.

8.3. Altered Records

Alteration of records is analogous to the destruction of records in that the original informational content of the records is obliterated and rendered unavailable for future use.

---

[246] *William A. Powe Trust v. Commissioner*, 44 T.C.M. 933 (1982).

The court may inquire into the motives for the alteration. The motives may be established either by circumstantial evidence,[247] or by direct testimony.[248] If the party satisfactorily explains the alterations, the court may not impose sanctions.

In *United States v. S.S. Soya Atlantic*,[249] officers erased and rewrote entries in the deck log of a ship involved in a collision. The officers who made the erasures indicated that the original entries would not fit into the allotted space and that the informational content of the erased material had not changed. The court believed that the party's explanation and did not impose sanctions.

In contrast, courts impose harsh penalties the alteration of records manifesting an intent to hide or destroy evidence. In *Professional Seminar Consultants v. Sino American Technology Exchange Counsel*,[250] defendant converted $120,000 to its own use. At trial, the defendant produced documents, including photocopies of canceled checks, which purported to show that the money had been passed to the appropriate party. The trial court concluded that the documents were false and entered default judgment under Fed.R.Civ.P. 37(b). The court of appeals, under a plain error standard, upheld the trial court's actions.

In *Skibs Aktieselskapet Orenor v. The Audrey*,[251] the plaintiff removed pages from the ship's log and replaced them with pages containing falsified entries. The court concluded that:

> The authorities are legion to the effect that intentional falsification of material records presumptively destroys the weight of the offender's evidence as to the entire case.

Circumstances leading a court to conclude that records are fraudulent may lead the court to exclude them from trial entirely.

---

[247] *See May v. Moore*, 424 So.2d 596, 603 (Ala. 1982).

[248] *See United States v. S.S. Soya Atlantic*, 213 F.Supp. 7 (D.Md. 1963).

[249] *Id.*

[250] *Professional Seminar Consultants, Inc. v. Sino American Technology Exchange Counsel, Inc.*, 727 F.2d 1470 (9th Cir. 1984).

[251] *Skibs Aktieselskapet Orenor v. The Audrey*, 181 F.Supp. 697, 701 (E.D.Va. 1960). *See also Villaneuva Compania Naviera, S.A. v. S.S. Matilde Corrado*, 211 F.Supp. 930 (E.D.Va. 1962)

In *Woolner Theaters v. Paramount Pictures Corp.*,[252] the plaintiffs admitted defrauding the defendants out of royalties due them by means of a scheme involving fraudulent alterations in the plaintiff's books. Nonetheless, the plaintiffs sought to have the books admitted as business records in the antitrust action, arguing that the records contained accurate numbers related to the antitrust action, even though the plaintiff did perpetrate the scheme to defraud the defendants out of royalties. The court concluded that the fraudulently rewritten records were inadmissible as business records under the Federal Business Records Act.[253] A court may also allow evidence of the falsification to be presented to the fact finder, and adverse inferences to be drawn from the falsification.[254]

8.4. Destruction by Third Parties

Relevant records may be destroyed by third parties not directly involved in litigation. Whether the court imputes responsibility for destruction of records by third parties to a litigant may depend upon the relationship between the third party and the litigant, and on the type of records involved.

In *Friends for All Children, Inc. v. Lockheed Aircraft Corp.*,[255] the plaintiff sought an adverse inference against defendant based upon the destruction of investigation records arising out of an airplane crash. The plaintiff established that the United States Air Force had destroyed many accident investigation records while the litigation was pending, after the records had been the subject of discovery requests, and in violation of its own regulations. The Air Force then misrepresented the matter to the court and the plaintiff for several years. The court nonetheless declined to hold the defendant accountable for this misconduct for the purpose of an adverse inference, even though the defendant and the Air Force had cooperated closely in the course of the investigation.

---

252 *Woolner Theaters, Inc. v. Paramount Pictures Corp.*, 333 F.Supp. 658 (E.D.La. 1970).
253 28 U.S.C. § 1732.
254 See *May v. Moore, supra.*
255 *Friends for All Children, Inc. v. Lockheed Aircraft Corp.*, 587 F.Supp. 180 (D.D.C. 1984).

In *Breeden v. Weinberger*,[256] the court ruled in favor of a claimant seeking to establish eligibility for social security benefits. The court declined to consider the fact that previous employers whose records presumably would have demonstrated the claimant's eligibility had either gone out of business or had destroyed the relevant records. It also declined to rule against the claimant even though the Social Security Administration's records failed to show covered employment during periods when the claimant claimed to have worked. Instead, the court allowed the claimant to establish her eligibility through affidavits and other testimony.

A different position was taken in *Stouman v. Commissioner of Internal Revenue*.[257] The managing partner was entirely responsible for managing partnership books, while the other knew nothing of the financial affairs of the partnership. The managing partner engaged in a scheme to defraud the government of taxes, destroyed most of the partnership books and then committed suicide. The Commissioner of Internal Revenue Service concluded that, without records to the contrary, all money in certain bank accounts would be considered partnership income for tax purposes and assessed the surviving partner with one-half of the amount due for taxes. The court concluded that the Commissioners properly assessed taxes under the relevant sections of the tax code, regardless of the party's innocence either in the scheme to defraud the government or in the destruction of the records.

Even if the records are lost by a third party with a more distant relationship to the litigant, sanctions are still possible. In *Florida Mortgage Financing, Inc. v. Kassner*,[258] a dispute arose over precisely what documents were submitted to the defendant mortgage broker. The defendant had forwarded the loan documents to an institutional lender, who lost them. The defendant was ordered to produce the documents, and when it could not, was prohibited from producing them at a later date for use at trial. Thus, its ability to challenge the plaintiff's version of the document submittal was severely curtailed, if not entirely eliminated.

---

[256] *Breeden v. Weinberger*, 493 F.2d 1002 (4th Cir. 1974).
[257] *Stouman v. Commissioner of Internal Revenue*, 208 F.2d 903 (3rd Cir. 1953).
[258] *Florida Mortgage Financing, Inc. v. Kassner*, 317 So.2d 112 (Fla.Ct.App. 1987).

Part IV. Records and Information Management Programs

Chapter 9.   Destruction of Records Under a Records Retention Program

A records retention program provides for the orderly, legal destruction of valueless records. The program balances the duty to preserve evidence with the organization's need for eliminating valueless records, reducing space requirements, improving access to valuable information and reducing costs.

A court could impose sanctions if it concludes that records destruction occurred under circumstances manifesting bad faith or an attempt to circumvent the judicial process. The circumstances surrounding the destruction of records present a factual question. The records and information management procedures implemented, as shown by documentation and testimony about the system, represent evidence relevant to that question.

Court decisions provide guidance regarding practices that they have consistently approved or disapproved. Records destruction undertaken in a manner consistent with prior court decisions provides a firm legal basis for limiting exposure in litigation.

As a general rule, courts will accept the proper destruction of valueless records under a records retention program as a legitimate excuse for nonproduction of records. The courts will rarely try to second-guess an organization's decision regarding how long to keep records. Instead, they look to consistency in developing and implementing the program. A records retention program that reflects consistent procedures based on business needs will generally be legally acceptable. Inconsistent procedures may be viewed as attempts to destroy evidence and circumvent justice. Improper destruction of records "looks bad" and raises judicial concern about possible evil intent or wrongdoing.

9.1. The Legal Basis for a Records Retention Program

The duty to preserve records includes a duty not to destroy those records for the period the duty is in effect. When no duty is in effect, records may be destroyed to meet other business needs.

The courts have exhaustively defined when a duty exists.[259] It is the responsibility of each organization to determine when the duty no longer exists. Typically this analysis will include the following:

- Conducting adequate legal research to determine minimum legal requirements stated in statutes or regulations, and

- Determining whether litigation is pending, imminent, or, in some cases, foreseeable.

Even when the duty to preserve records no longer exists, the records can be safely destroyed only under procedures established by the records retention program. Destruction of records under a records retention program demonstrates the intent of the organization to systematically destroy records at a time when no duty to preserve records exists, the records are no longer needed for organizational needs, and the organizational needs can best be met by destruction of valueless records.[260]

---

[259] *See* Chapter 9, generally.
[260] *See* Chapter 2. Benefits of a Records and Information Management Program.

9.2. Records Retention Program Upheld

Court decisions confirm that records may be destroyed under a records retention program. An organization that demonstrates destruction of records for legitimate business purposes, as evidenced by a records retention program, will likely prevail.

In *Vick v. Texas Employment Commission*,[261] the plaintiff contended that the adverse inference rule should be applied against the defendant for the improper destruction of records. In denying the claim, the court said:

> TEC [Texas Employment Commission] records on Vick were destroyed before trial, apparently pursuant to Commission regulations governing disposal of inactive records . . . . The adverse inference to be drawn from destruction of records is predicated on bad conduct of the defendant . . . . There was indication here that the records were destroyed under routine procedures without bad faith and well in advance of Vick's service of interrogatories. Certainly, there were sufficient grounds for the trial court to so conclude.

In *Telectron v. Overhead Door Corp.*, the court approved the destruction of records for one party but not the other. The defendant filed a motion for sanctions against the plaintiff, claiming the plaintiff destroyed relevant records as well. The court declined to impose sanctions against the plaintiff, noting that the plaintiff had destroyed the records pursuant to a preexisting records retention policy, after preserving them for seven years in compliance with Internal Revenue Service requirements, and after reviewing the records prior to destruction to make sure that relevant documents were not destroyed. This contrasts with the court's harsh treatment of the defendant, resulting from the inappropriate destruction of records and the lack of a systematic records retention program.[262]

In declining to impose sanctions against the plaintiff, the court did not approve of the chosen retention period for the records, the

---

261 *Vick v. Texas Employment Commission*, 514 F.2d 734 (5th Cir. 1975).
262 *Telectron, Inc. v. Overhead Door Corp.*, 116 F.R.D. 107 (S.D.Fla. 1987).

details of the records retention program, nor the review process prior to destruction. Rather, the court simply concluded that these factors demonstrated that the destruction of records lacked bad faith.

The court in *Moore v. General Motors Corp.*[263] observed:

> Absent any evidence that the defendant was put on notice by the plaintiff that these records were essential to the preservation of his case, or a court order that these records not be destroyed, we see no evidence of fraud or bad faith in a corporation destroying records it is no longer required by law to keep and which are destroyed in accord with its regular practices. As we have previously observed, storage of records for big or small businesses is a costly item and destruction of records no longer required is not in and of itself evidence of spoliation.

Courts have imposed sanctions on parties claiming to have destroyed records pursuant to records retention programs when the claim could not be sustained, the destruction took place when a duty to preserve records existed or the courts determined that the destruction of records occurred to prevent unfavorable information from being considered in the case.[264]

But, in the absence of a duty to preserve records, courts have consistently refused to sanction parties who have destroyed records pursuant to a records retention program.[265]

---

263 *Moore v. General Motors Corp.*, 558 S.W.2d 720, 737 (Mo.Ct.App. 1977).

264 *See e.g., Id.; Carlucci v. Piper Aircraft Corp.*, 102 F.R.D. 472 (S.D.Fla. 1984); *National Association of Radiation Survivors v. Turnage*, 115 F.R.D. 543 (N.D.Cal. 1987).

265 *See e.g., Akiona v. United States*, 938 F.2d 158 (9th Cir. 1991); *Valentino v. United States Postal Service*, 674 F.2d 56 (D.C. Cir. 1982); *Vick v. Texas Employment Commission*, 514 F.2d 734 (5th Cir. 1975); *Britt v. Block*, 636 F.Supp. 596 (D.Vt. 1986); *Piechalak v. Liberty Trucking Co.*, 208 N.E.2d 379 (Ill.Ct.App. 1965); *Coates v. Johnson & Johnson*, 756 F.2d 524 (7th.Cir. 1985).

9.3. Records Retention Periods

Records retention periods generally will be based on several factors:

- *Operational / Record User Needs* — retention periods based upon an organization's need to preserve records to protect the organization's rights, conduct business, or facilitate research.

- *Legal Requirements* — retention periods stated in statutes, regulations and rules establishing legal minimum periods for maintaining records. These periods can be enforced by government by subjecting the party to fines, penalties and loss of rights.

- *Legal Considerations* — retention periods based on other legal issues such as statutes of limitation or a legal duty to preserve records for future or current litigation, tax or other audit.

- *Historical* — retention periods to preserve records for public historical or research needs or as part of internal organizational archives.

Courts will generally not attempt to impose their view of what the records retention periods should be. Records must generally be kept for mandated periods — the legal requirements period found in statutes, regulations and rules. Records must also be kept for the legal considerations period during which a court-defined legal duty may exist to preserve them. Otherwise, an organization can select any longer retention period that meets its needs.

Court decisions focus on the reasonableness of the records destruction decision, based upon the particular facts and circumstances of the case. If records were destroyed under a records retention schedule prior to litigation, the details of the retention periods will rarely be reviewed.[266]

---

[266] *But see Carlucci v. Piper Aircraft Corp.*, 102 F.R.D. 472 (S.D.Fla. 1984) (Records claimed to be destroyed under a records retention program found to be selectively destroyed in anticipation of future litigation); *Lewy v. Remington Arms Co.*, 836 F.2d 1104 (8th Cir. 1988) (Even though records properly destroyed under a records retention program, court remanded case to trial court for review of reasonableness of records retention period, considering the likelihood of future litigation involving the records)

9.3.1. Judicial Review of Retention Periods

Courts may inquire into whether the retention periods chosen were reasonable, based on the nature of the documents, normal business needs, and industry practice. In *Valentino v. United States Postal Service*,[267] the court accepted as reasonable the destruction of postal service employment promotion records after five years or less of retention. In *Piechalak v. Liberty Trucking Co.*,[268] the court accepted a three-year retention period for vehicle maintenance records. In *Moore v. General Motors Corp.*,[269] the court concluded that two- and five-year retention periods, based upon federal requirements, were reasonable for automobile inspection records created by the manufacturer.

The court in *Akiona v. United States*[270] approved of a retention period for hand-grenade records of two years after disposition to third parties. Considering the dangerous nature of the product and the likelihood of litigation in case of injury, this case firmly establishes the conclusion that courts will not likely second-guess a retention period, provided that the period was established as part of a records retention program.

Courts have focused on the motives to destroy records and the existence of a legitimate records retention program. When records are destroyed outside this context, the courts have expressed concern. An organization that reasonably creates a records retention program and establishes reasonable records retention periods demonstrates good faith.

Nonetheless, in some circumstances, the specific retention period may still be closely scrutinized. In *Lewy v. Remington Arms Co.*,[271] the plaintiffs sued the defendant arms manufacturer over an allegedly defective rifle. The defendant asserted that certain complaint files and other records had been destroyed pursuant to an existing document retention policy. Plaintiff responded with

---

267 *Valentino v. United States Postal Service*, 674 F.2d 56 (D.C.Cir. 1982).
268 *Piechalak v. Liberty Trucking Co.*, 208 N.E.2d 379 (Ill.Ct.App. 1965).
269 *Moore v. General Motors Corp.*, 558 S.W.2d 720 (Mo.Ct.App. 1977).
270 *Akiona v. United States*, 938 F.2d 158 (9th Cir. 1991).
271 *Lewy v. Remington Arms Co.*, 836 F.2d 1104, 1112 (8th Cir. 1988).

evidence of the company's records retention program, which authorized the destruction of complaint files after three years. The Appellate Court remanded the case for findings on the document retention policy, stating:

> We are unable to decide, based on the record we have before us, whether it was error for the trial court to give this instruction. On remand, if the trial court is called upon to again instruct the jury regarding failure to produce evidence, the court should consider the following factors before deciding whether to give the instruction to the jury. First, the court should determine whether Remington's record retention policy is reasonable considering the facts and circumstances surrounding the relevant documents. For example, the court should determine whether a three year retention policy is reasonable given the particular document. A three year retention policy may be sufficient for documents such as appointment books or telephone messages, but inadequate for documents such as customer complaints. Second, in making this determination the court may also consider whether lawsuits concerning the complaint or related complaints have been filed, the frequency of such complaints, and the magnitude of the complaints. Finally, the court should determine whether the document retention policy was instituted in bad faith.

The records retention period must reflect such practical factors as legally mandated periods, customer expectation, industry practice, the nature of the records and the likelihood that the record might be needed in pending or future litigation.

The court in *Peskin v. Liberty Mutual Insurance Co.*[272] also questioned the retention periods. As in *Lewy,* the court remanded the case back to the trial court for express findings on the issues of whether the retention periods were reasonable based on the nature of the records, business needs and business practices. As in *Lewy,* the court did not reject the retention periods, but, rather, did not have enough information to determine whether the retention periods in question were reasonable.

---

[272] *Peskin v. Liberty Mutual Insurance Co.*, 530 A.2d 822 (N.J.Supr. 1987).

Lewy and *Peskin* reinforce the importance of documenting the basis for records retention decisions so that they can be explained later. While it is unlikely that a court will question a specific retention period, an organization should be prepared to demonstrate the procedures followed for developing the records retention program and the reasonableness of the records retention periods selected.[273]

9.3.2. Retention for Mandated Legal Periods

Courts may inquire whether the retention periods meet minimum legal requirements. Failure to preserve records when the law establishes a legal duty to preserve them evokes a strong suspicion that records were destroyed in bad faith.

Even good faith destruction under a program, made in ignorance of applicable law, may create problems. Everyone is presumed to know the law. This is particularly true for large, sophisticated organizations who face significant regulation and who employ legal counsel to ensure legal compliance.

In *United States v. ABC Sales & Service, Inc.*,[274] the United States filed suit against the defendant based upon a series of consumer complaints. The defendants failed to respond to discovery, asserting, *inter alia*, that many of the files had been destroyed after two years, because they were kept only as "space allows." The court observed that the defendants maintained offices in California, and that under California law, the files were required to be preserved for four years:

> ... [A]ny destruction of files of named complaining debtors appears to have been motivated more from an attempt to suppress evidence than from the need of additional filing space for new files. Three of defendants' offices are in California and defendants admit in their answers to interrogatories that debt collectors in that state are required

---

273 *See* Donald S. Skupsky, *Records Retention Procedures*, Information Requirements Clearinghouse (1991) for systematic procedures for developing and documenting a records retention program.

274 *United States v. ABC Sales & Service, Inc.*, 95 F.R.D. 316, 318 (D.Ariz. 1982).

to maintain collection files for a period of at least four years. The defendants were given notice that many of the named debtors were complaining to the Federal Trade Commission or had complained to lawyers regarding the conduct of defendants' employees. Given that notice, one would reasonably think that the defendants would have taken steps to preserve the files relating to those complaining debtors if there were any information in the files which would tend to refute the complaints.

When an organization disposes of records after retaining them for a legally mandated period of time, courts appear reluctant to impose sanctions for the destruction of the records. In two cases, *Equal Employment Opportunity Commission v. Dresser Industries*,[275] and *Equal Employment Opportunity Commission v. M.D. Pneumatics, Inc.*[276] the EEOC sought sanctions against employers who had destroyed business records at the end of a legally mandated retention period, when the employer had no notice that the records destroyed were needed for any litigation or other pending matter.

The EEOC argued that a pending action concerning an individual employee, combined with the employer's knowledge that the EEOC could bring a suit involving other employees at any time, required the employer to retain *all* employment records past the legally mandated minimums. In both cases, the EEOC's position was rejected, the courts reasoning that an employer should not be punished for failing to exceed standards promulgated by the very agency which was seeking the sanctions.

Other courts have similarly rejected requests for sanctions for records destroyed after the legally-mandated period, in the absence of some notice and a duty to preserve them.[277]

---

275 *Equal Employment Opportunity Commission v. Dresser Industries, Inc.*, 668 F.2d 1199 (11th Cir. 1982).

276 *Equal Employment Opportunity Commission v. M.D. Pneumatics, Inc.*, 31 Emp.Prac.Dec. (CCH) 33, 459 (W.D.Mo. 1983).

277 *See, e.g., Vick v. Texas Employment Commission*, 514 F.2d 734 (5th Cir. 1975), (no sanctions warranted where state agency destroyed inactive records pursuant to its own regulations concerning management of inactive records); *Moore v. General Motors Corp.*, 558 S.W.2d 720 (Mo.Ct.App. 1977), (automobile manufacturer's defect repair inspection tickets destroyed at the end of federally-mandated retention period).

In the absence of a duty to preserve them for a longer period, due to litigation, extension of a tax audit, or government investigation, records destruction after the legally mandated period and under the records retention program is likely to be viewed as reasonable and done in good faith.

9.3.3. Retention After Mandated Legal Periods

The question then becomes how long past the mandated legal requirements periods should records be kept. The decision will be based on a number of factors:

- *Legal considerations.* Will a court likely impose a duty to keep the records longer due to the likelihood of litigation? Will the organization need the records to protect its rights? For example, will contract records be needed to enforce or defend claims throughout the statute of limitations period? Alternatively, could the records be used effectively by adverse parties to frivolous litigation to gain a competitive advantage, create a nuisance or force an unfavorable settlement?

- *Business needs.* Are the records needed for any other business purposes, such as reference?

- *Cost.* Does the cost of maintaining the records outweigh the value of maintaining the records?

Can government regulatory agencies review records after mandated legal requirements periods? Many statutes or regulations that impose a recordkeeping requirement on businesses place no time limit on when an agency may inspect the records. Rather, they allow inspection by the appropriate authority at any time, similar to this typical unemployment compensation statute:

> Each employing unit shall keep true and accurate work records of all workers employed by it . . . . Such records shall be open for inspection and subject to being copied by the Secretary or his authorized representatives at any reasonable time and as often as necessary.[278]

---

278 Kentucky Revised Statutes, 27 KRSA 341.190

The statute sets no limitation on the period during which the records may be inspected. In the absence of any other duty to preserve records, the records can be inspected at any time.

In *United States v. Powell*,[279] the Internal Revenue Service (I.R.S.) sought access to a taxpayer's records after the statute of limitations barring assessment of taxes had expired, and after having once examined the taxpayer's records. The I.R.S. suspected fraud and asserted that further examination and assessment would not be barred by the statute of limitations. The taxpayer contended that, before he could be forced to produce the records, the I.R.S. had to demonstrate some ground for suspecting fraud.

Reversing the Court of Appeals, the Supreme Court concluded that the I.R.S. did not need to show probable cause to suspect fraud in order to investigate a taxpayer. A taxpayer could raise a substantial question of abuse of process, but it would have to be based on more than a second examination and the running of the statute of limitations on ordinary tax liability.[280]

The court did not base its conclusion on whether or not the statute of limitation had run. Rather, the I.R.S. must simply show that the statutory grounds for issuance of a summons have been met: the investigation is for a legitimate purpose, the inquiry may be relevant to the purpose, the information sought is not already within the I.R.S.'s possession, and the administrative steps required have been followed.

In *Phillips Petroleum v. Lujan*,[281] the Department of the Interior sought access to oil and gas lease records maintained by Phillips Petroleum. Phillips resisted production of the records, asserting that the statutory period for maintenance of the records had expired, as had the statute of limitations for filing suit on the matters covered by the records. The trial court granted Phillips' motion for summary judgment, concluding that the Department's request for records was untimely.

---

[279] *United States v. Powell*, 379 U.S.48, 85 S.Ct. 248, 13 L.Ed.2d 112 (1964).
[280] *Id.*, 379 U.S. at 51, 85 S.Ct. at 251, 13 L.Ed.2d at 115.
[281] *Phillips Petroleum v. Lujan*, unpublished opinion (10th Cir. 1991).

The Court of Appeals reversed, concluding that neither the lease agreements which were the subject of the dispute nor the statutes and regulations governing the leases placed any time limitation upon the inspection of records. These records would also be discoverable in ordinary civil litigation. Although Phillips had a right to destroy the records after the mandated legal retention period, it chose instead to keep them.

The court confirmed that administrative agencies possess broad investigatory powers, even if the investigation consists of a "fishing expedition" with no concrete evidence to support the demand for production. Because the records existed, the Department could still examine them. But since the mandated retention period and the statute of limitation had ended, the Department could not impose any fines or penalties based on its findings.

Phillips extends the *Powell* doctrine by confirming that administrative agencies may inspect records *at any time*, even without suspicion of fraud or specific wrongdoing. Both parties could have destroyed the records after the legally mandated period. But since the records still existed, they could be inspected by the administrative agencies.[282]

At least one state has taken a contrary position. In *Cascio v. Beam*,[283] the State Department of Revenue sought production of taxpayer's books and records after the expiration of a legally-mandated two-year retention period. In contrast to *Powell*, no allegation of fraud was made. The Department of Revenue, citing *Powell*, asserted that neither the statute imposing the recordkeeping requirement, nor the applicable statute of limitations, placed a limit upon the Department's ability to inspect records kept past the legally-mandated retention period.

The Missouri Supreme Court rejected this contention, and upheld a trial court injunction denying access to the records.

---

[282] Because of the unique statute of limitations for fraud in tax matters compared to normal statutes of limitation, the I.R.S. could impose fines and penalties at any time in cases of suspected fraud. The Department of the Interior in *Phillips* could not impose additional fines and penalties after the prescribed period.

[283] *Cascio v. Beam*, 594 S.W.2d 942 (Mo. 1980).

Adopting the taxpayer's reasoning that tax statutes must be strictly construed in favor of the taxpayer, the court concluded that the legislature had not intended to grant the agency the powers of the United States Internal Revenue Service. Thus, the Department of Revenue must make a showing of a legitimate purpose for its investigation in order to gain access to the records from the distant past.

Cascio v. Beam may afford little protection to an organization which retains records past legally-mandated minimums. The court in *Cascio v. Beam* concluded that the relevant state statute did not grant government the right to review the records after the mandated legal period. But, the federal government, as well as the states, prepares a large number of statutory and regulatory record-keeping laws in areas such as tax, employment, environment and health and safety. Even if a state court concludes that records will not be available to state agencies, they remain available to federal agencies.

Regardless, retention mandates impose requirements on affected entities, rather than limiting the power of administrative agencies. Many courts take a strict approach to construction of statutes and will not construe phrases such as "records will be available for inspection at any time" to mean a limited period of time. Unless the legislature has specifically established limits on the investigative authority of the state administrative agencies, it is doubtful that such a court would take it upon itself to establish such limits. Thus, records will probably remain available for inspection by government agencies as long as they are in existence.

Records retained after the expiration of legal retention periods are also subject to discovery during litigation. In *Bubrick v. Northern Illinois Gas Co.*,[284] the defendant asserted the expiration of legal retention periods as a justification for nonproduction of documents, notwithstanding that testimony from its own employees indicated that the records still existed. The court rejected that contention, and concluded that an adverse inference instruction based upon the nonproduction was appropriate.

---

[284] *Bubrick v. Northern Illinois Gas Co.*, 264 N.E.2d 560 (Ill.App.Ct. 1970)

9.3.4. Inconsistent Retention Periods

Courts evaluating whether records destruction occurred under a retention program may examine the consistency of the program. When organizations destroy comparable records at the same or similar time, it appears more likely that the destruction took place under a retention program. However, when records are selectively destroyed or similar records are destroyed at different times, the program appears suspicious.

In *Interstate Electric Co. v. Interstate Electric Co. of Shreveport, Inc.*,[285] the plaintiff claimed to have destroyed vouchers, checks and other records according to its custom of periodic destruction and requested that secondary evidence of these records be admitted, instead. The court rejected this claim after it found inconsistencies in the plaintiff's destruction practices since older checks and vouchers existed and had been introduced into evidence:

> The doubt cast upon plaintiff's explanation, and the acceptance thereof as a foundation for the introduction of secondary evidence, is further emphasized by the fact that other checks and vouchers bearing upon matters involved in this litigation, older in point of time, were produced and introduced in evidence. This circumstance clearly indicates that plaintiffs failed in their attempt to show such an enduring custom of periodic destruction of records as would justify the acceptance of secondary evidence.[286]

Evidence in both *Telectron* and *Carlucci* conclusively showed selective destruction of records. Other courts have reached similar conclusions based on much less conclusive evidence.[287] Selective destruction of records in any form may be viewed as "bad faith" and may preclude a finding that records were destroyed under a records retention program.

---

[285] *Interstate Electric Co. v. Interstate Electric Co. of Shreveport, Inc.*, 33 So.2d 779 (La.Ct.App. 1948).

[286] *Id.* at 782.

[287] *See, e.g., Bihun v. AT&T Information Systems, Inc.*, 16 Cal.Rptr.2d 787 (Cal.Ct.App. 1993) (defendant unable to produce employment file of supervisor alleged to have engaged in sexual harassment); *Paytes v. Kost*, 482 N.W.2d 130 (Wisc.Ct.App. 1992) (defendant insurance company unable to locate current insurance policy issued to plaintiff).

9.4. Components of a Legally-Acceptable Records Retention Program

If an organization's records retention decisions are challenged in court, the mere assertion that the records were destroyed pursuant to a records retention program is unlikely to survive the challenge. The defendants in both *Telectron v. Overhead Door Corp.* and *Carlucci v. Piper Aircraft Corp.* asserted the existence of records retention programs as the justification for the destruction of relevant documents. Courts rejected those contentions in both cases and entered default judgments against the offending party. Together, these two decisions provide useful guidance regarding how to develop a legally-acceptable program:

- No records retention schedule or procedure manual existed to support the claim that a records retention program existed.

- No documentation existed of the records destruction — what records were destroyed, when, and by whom?

- No person appeared to be responsible for the records retention program and the destruction of records.

- Claims that records were destroyed under a program came late in the proceeding, after long delays and numerous excuses.

- Records appeared to be selectively destroyed under suspicious circumstances.

A records retention program must avoid both actions and appearance demonstrating intent to deprive opponents in litigation of relevant records. To achieve this goal, an organization should:[288]

- Define what materials are official records (versus unofficial records or non-record material) of the organization.

- Identify records subject to a legal duty to create, preserve and disclose.

---

[288] The detailed procedures for establishing a records retention program is beyond the scope of this book. See Donald S. Skupsky, *Records Retention Procedures*, Information Requirements Clearinghouse (1991).

- Determine the retention period for records based on a legal duty and legitimate business needs.

- Retain similar records for the same or substantially similar retention periods.

- Retain records until the destruction date authorized in the records retention program and not destroy them *before* that date for any reason.

- Change the retention schedule, following approved procedures, when legitimate business or legal considerations, such as a duty to preserve records caused by litigation, justify shortening (or lengthening) the records retention period.

- Destroy records only under the records retention program.

- Maintain documentation of the records retention program including records retention schedules, procedures, audits, approvals, program development and proof of destruction.

9.5. Documentation of the Records Retention Program

A litigant claiming proper destruction of records under a records retention program must provide sufficient information to support its claim. The fact of destruction can be established by showing that the records were destroyed as part of a regular records retention program and that the program results in accurate destruction of records.[289] Normally, documentation of the retention schedule, procedures and destruction, introduced by the records manager or other qualified person, will suffice.[290]

Without adequate documentation it may be difficult to show the existence and adequacy of the records retention program. An unsupported assertion that a records retention program existed, and that records were destroyed under it, provides some evidence

---

[289] See Fed.R.Evid. 901(b)(9) under which evidence can be authenticated and identified by "evidence describing a process or system and showing that the process or system produces an accurate result."

[290] Fed.R.Evid. 803(6).

that the program possibly existed. However, in light of judicial concern related to the duty to preserve records and destruction of records with bad intent, such an assertion alone is likely to not be persuasive. The nonexistence of documentation may even be viewed as evidence that there was no records retention program. In either situation — an unsupported and unpersuasive assertion that records were destroyed under a retention program or the court construing the absence of documentation as evidence that no program existed — a court could easily conclude that records destruction was negligent or in bad faith, and impose sanctions.

In both *Carlucci v. Piper Aircraft*,[291] and *Telectron, Inc. v. Overhead Door Corp.*,[292] the parties claimed that records had been destroyed under a records retention program but never provided supporting documentation. A similar fact pattern emerged:

- A company official asserted from the witness stand that a records retention program existed.

- The official could provide little or no detail concerning the program or its implementation.

- The company could not produce a records retention schedule, policy and procedures manual, or other documentation of destruction to support its claims.

The courts concluded that the unsupported assertion of the existence of a records retention program lacked credibility in light of the size and sophistication of the companies and the allegedly company-wide nature of the programs. Since insufficient evidence existed to support the claims, both courts imposed sanctions.[293]

The lack of reasonable documentation related to destruction of records creates suspicion that records were destroyed for with bad intent — to eliminate potentially harmful evidence from being

---

[291] *Carlucci v. Piper Aircraft Corp.*, 102 F.R.D. 472 (S.D.Fla. 1984).

[292] *Telectron, Inc. v. Overhead Door Corp.*, 116 F.R.D. 107 (S.D.Fla. 1987).

[293] *See also Laing v. Liberty Loan Co.*, 264 S.E.2d 381 (N.C.Ct.App. 1980). The court rejected an unsupported assertion that relevant records had been destroyed when the assertion was made after the party had ignored previous court orders to produce the records.

uncovered in litigation. Courts in *Paytes v. Kost*[294] and *DeLaughter v. Lawrence County Hospital*,[295] suspected impropriety and imposed sanctions when the parties failed to adequately explain why certain records were missing and also imposed sanctions.

In both cases, the records disappeared without explanation and may have just been inadvertently destroyed. Documentation of the records retention program might have shown that the companies regularly operated a records retention program and regularly documented destruction. If reasonable procedures existed and documentation confirmed that they were consistently followed — a sign of good intent related to records destruction — the parties could have demonstrated that the missing records disappeared due to human error, rather than evil intent. The documentation might have provided information about what happened to the records.

When a litigant adequately proves, through documentation and live testimony, that records were destroyed under a records retention program, courts consistently accept records destruction without imposing sanctions.[296]

No court decision specifies what type and how much documentation would be adequate to support a conclusion that records were destroyed under a records retention program. The following documentation seems to be customary and appropriate:

- *Procedures Followed to Develop the Records Retention Program and Program Procedures.* To prove the existence of a records retention program, documentation must first be introduced into evidence. Fed.R.Evid. 901(b)(9) supports a conclusion that the evidence of authentication and identification of the documentation must be "sufficient to support a finding that the matter in question is what its proponents claim." It might be necessary to show that even the retention procedures and schedules were

---

294 *Paytes v. Kost*, 482 N.W.2d 130 (Wisc.App. 1992).
295 *DeLaughter v. Lawrence County Hospital*, 601 So. 2d 818 (Miss. 1992).
296 *See e.g.*, *Akiona v. United States*, 938 F.2d 158 (9th Cir. 1991); *Valentino v. United States Postal Service*, 674 F.2d 56 (D.C. Cir. 1982); *Vick v. Texas Employment Commission*, 514 F.2d 734 (5th Cir. 1975); *Britt v. Block*, 636 F.Supp. 596 (D.Vt. 1986); *Piechalak v. Liberty Trucking Co.*, 208 N.E.2d 379 (Ill.Ct.App. 1965); *Coates v. Johnson & Johnson*, 756 F.2d 524 (7th.Cir. 1985).

themselves systematically developed. Appropriate documentation of development of the retention program could include legal research and analysis, interviews with record users to determine business requirements, reviews and revisions of draft documents, and final, signed approval of the entire program.

- *The Records Retention Schedule and Procedures.* In order to prove that records were destroyed under the records retention program, it will first be necessary to show that a program existed. Since the program will be modified over time, each set of different schedules and procedures should be retained for the likely period the destruction of records could be challenged in court.

- *Destruction of Records.* Typically, a certification of destruction form is prepared for every batch of records destroyed under the records retention schedule. It is neither practical nor necessary to provide detailed descriptions of all records, every file or every document destroyed. Instead, the documentation of destruction of records should generally identify the content of boxes or groups of records destroyed — e.g., canceled checks (1981), time sheets (1982-83), terminated contracts (prior to 1980).

- *Audit of Records Retention Program.* The audit of the records retention program is an independent, statistically valid sampling of program activities to confirm accuracy of the program. At least once each year, the auditors can review program documentation, records destruction and records still in existence to confirm that the records retention program is being followed.

Similarly, no court decision indicates how detailed the documentation should be and how long records retention documentation should be kept. Since it is impossible, for practical reasons, to maintain sufficiently detailed documentation to "prove" that certain documents were destroyed, the goal must be to prove that records were destroyed under the records retention program and the program produces accurate results. The statistically-valid audit confirms that records that should have been destroyed under the program were destroyed, and that records that should still be in existence are still in existence.

The record retention documentation should be kept for the likely period it will be needed to support a claim that records were destroyed under the records retention program — e.g., 10 years.

Chapter 10. Filing Systems and Indexes

Some cases resulting in sanctions for failure to respond to discovery point to problems in the recordkeeping practices; others do not explicitly state that poor practices resulted in sanctions. Courts may become suspicious when a party claims to be unable to locate documents, without a satisfactory explanation, even with the threat of sanctions looming as a real possibility.

10.1. Ineffective Recordkeeping Systems

Courts reject contentions that the duty to provide records to other litigants or to the court is excused by poor, ineffective records organization or other similar problems. In *Alliance to End Repression v. Rochford*,[297] the court rejected an objection to discovery requests on the grounds that production of the information would be unduly burdensome because the materials were not in an organized filing system:

The court further concluded that:

> To allow a defendant whose business generates massive records to frustrate discovery by creating an inadequate

---

[297] *Alliance to End Repression v. Rochford*, 75 F.R.D. 441, 447 (N.D.Ill. 1977).

filing system, and then claiming undue burden, would defeat the purposes of discovery rules.[298]

Courts do not tolerate situations in which litigants organize records in a fashion intended to hide information from opponents. In *Shatzkamer v. Eskind*,[299] the law required the City of New York to keep records of notices it received of defects in roads and sidewalks, so that injured parties could determine whether the city had prior notice of the defect. The indexing system for these notices was so ineffective that it prevented plaintiffs from finding information that would prove that the city had prior notice of defects. In authorizing sanctions against the City, the court noted:

> While the defendant was not required to use any particular system of indexing under [the applicable law], it could not and cannot choose to index notices of defect . . . in so scattered and Byzantine a fashion as to deprive those with legitimate claims against the city of the right to maintain civil actions for damages because prior notice of defects that exist cannot be found, either by the city or by the plaintiff.[300]

10.2. Records Neglected Over Time

Courts also will not excuse poor recordkeeping practices that may be due to a long passage of time. In *Addeo Loan Co. v. Manocchio*,[301] the defendant was sued on promissory notes executed over 16 years prior to the filing of suit. In the interim, the defendant closed his business and stored records in a basement. Over time, the records became disorganized and some were lost. After entry of an adverse judgment, the defendant found some of the missing records. The court refused to reopen the judgment, concluding that, with due diligence, the records could have been located prior to trial.

---

298 *Id.*, quoting *Kozlowski v. Sears Roebuck & Co.*, 73 F.R.D. 73, 76 (1976). *See also United States v. ABC Sales & Services, Inc.*, 95 F.R.D. 316 (D.Ariz. 1982).
299 *Shatzkamer v. Eskind*, 528 N.Y.S.2d 968 (N.Y. City Civ.Ct. 1988).
300 *Id.* at 972
301 *Addeo Loan Co. v. Manocchio*, 313 A.2d 649 (R.I. 1974).

But at least one case indicates a party need not reorganize records maintained in a particular form for several years. In *Evangelos v. Dachiel*,[302] the plaintiff sought production of every record made by two defunct corporations over a period of several years. The defendant produced thirty boxes, in the form that they had been kept in the record center. The trial court struck the defendant's answer for, among other things, failure to reorganize the records for the plaintiff's benefit. The court of appeals reversed, concluding that producing the records as they had been kept in the regular course of business constituted compliance with the court order and that the plaintiff was not entitled to have them reorganized for its benefit.

10.3. Records Missing Due to No Fault of Party

Courts may be sympathetic when records cannot be located due to acts of nature such as floods, hurricanes, tornadoes and fires. But a party may still be held responsible if its records deteriorate due to circumstances beyond its control. In *Equal Employment Opportunity Commission v. C.W. Transport*,[303] the defendant asserted that it would be unable to properly defend the lawsuit because it could not find the necessary records. The evidence indicated that the records became lost or unavailable due to a series of unexpected events including employee pilfering, fires, floods, and tornadoes, as well as the transfer of records between various company facilities.

The court concluded that the defendant might be able to prove that it was materially prejudiced due to the lost and missing records. It still placed the burden on the defendant to establish what records were missing and why the loss would materially prejudice its defense.

---

[302] *Evangelos v. Dachiel*, 553 So.2d 245 (Fla.Ct.App. 1989)
[303] *Equal Employment Opportunity Commission v. C.W. Transport, Inc.*, 658 F.Supp. 1278 (W.D.Wisc. 1987).

10.4. Inadvertent Loss of Records

In some cases, the party simply could not locate the documents, in spite of good faith efforts to do so. Inadvertent loss of records may be viewed more harshly or result in more severe consequences if it involved documents critical to the case. A party could became the victim of its own poor records management practices.[304]

Careful physical control of records ensures that critical records are available when needed. Even when ineffective recordkeeping practices do not justify sanctions, the organization may still find itself severely disadvantaged by its inability to produce evidence for its own case. Besides reducing the organization's efficiency, poor recordkeeping practices may lead to future litigation because the organization may not know its legal obligations.

10.5. Filing System Requirements Under Fed.R.Civ.P. Rule 26

The new Rule 26[305] imposes fundamental new requirements on litigation in the federal courts. Previously, the requesting party had to request basic information through depositions and interrogatories, identify relevant records, request the relevant records and, finally, in some cases, obtain a subpoena to compel the other party to turn over those records. If the discovery request did not specify certain records, the receiving party had no legal obligation to produce those records or identify the omission.

Rule 26 now eliminates the arduous procedures previously imposed on the requesting party. Instead, near the beginning of each federal lawsuit (generally within 85 days), each party now has an affirmative duty to identify relevant records and make information about those records available to the other party. Each party can then request actual copies of records.

---

304 *See, e.g. Bihun v. AT&T Information Systems, Inc.*, 16 Cal.Rp.2d 787 (1993) (missing employment files); *Battocchi v. Washington Hospital Center*, 581 A.2d 759 (D.C.Ct.App. 1990) (patient treatment records lost or destroyed); *Valcin v. Public Health Trust of Dade County*, 473 So.2d 1297 (Fla.Ct.App. 1984) (patient treatment records lost or destroyed); *Paytes v. Kost*, 482 N.W.2d 130 (Wisc.Ct.App. 1992) (defendant insurance company unable to produce policy).

305 Fed.R.Civ.P. Rule 26.

Although we still lack experience with the new rule, the courts will probably expect that each party make a full disclosure at the early stages of the case. Failure to provide information on relevant records will probably be the basis for court-imposed sanctions.

The courts have previously dealt with excuses for failure to comply with discovery requests, including the issue of "the inability to find records." In *United States v. ABC Sales & Service*,[306] the court ruled that "a business which generates millions of files cannot frustrate discovery by creating an inadequate filing system so that individual files cannot readily be located."[307] A poor records management program will therefore not serve as a excuse for an organization's failure to respond to Rule 26.

Prior to implementation of the rule, the Senate Judiciary Committee conducted hearings. Fierce opposition arose from groups representing larger corporations and defendant interests, complaining about the potential burden that this rule would place on their constituency. The rule still went into effect, indicating that the Senate and the Supreme Court will not tolerate excuses for abuse of discovery, regardless of the burdens. Since the disclosures related to records must take place within 85 days of the defendant's first appearance and subsequent disclosures completed within 90 days before trial, organizations subject to federal discovery procedures must organize their records in advance to comply within the time period. A period of 90 days is not sufficient time to adequately search the records of a major organization. This is especially true if the organization has undertaken mergers and acquisitions, resulting in thousands of boxes of records that have yet to be examined.

In order to fully comply with Rule 26, the records program must meet the following criteria:

---

[306] *United States v. ABC Sales & Service Inc.*, 95 F.R.D. 316 (1982).

[307] *See also Kozlowski v. Sears Roebuck & Co.*, 73 F.R.D. 73 (1976) ("to allow a defendant whose business generates massive records to frustrate discovery by creating an inadequate filing system, and then claiming undue burden, would defeat the purpose of discovery rules.").

- Identify all records, including active and inactive records, within the organization at all locations.

- Identify records that have been destroyed by the organization.

- Demonstrate the accuracy and reliability of the records program.

A records management program achieves these three objectives. An appropriately designed active and inactive records program, including a file and box tracking system, enables the organization to quickly identify records throughout the organization. The records retention program enables the organization to systematically destroy records and to identify those records that have been destroyed under the program. Finally, when the records management program includes documentation, training and audit, the organization can confirm the accuracy of its procedures, including indexing and destruction.

Appendix A. Uniform Laws and Rules of Evidence

The following Uniform Laws were prepared by the National Conference of Commissioners on Uniform State Laws. Differences may exist between the original versions and the versions finally adopted by the states.

Uniform Business Records as Evidence Act.

§ 1. "Business" defined.

The term "business" shall include every kind of business, profession, occupation, calling or operation of institutions, whether carried on for profit or not.

§ 2. Business records as evidence.

A record of an act, condition or event, shall in so far as relevant, be competent evidence if the custodian or other qualified witness testifies to its identity and the mode of its preparation, and if it was made in the regular course of business, at or near the time of the act, condition or event, and if, in the opinion of the court, the sources of information, method and time of preparation were such as to justify its admission.

§ 3. Construction.

This chapter shall be so interpreted and construed as to effectuate its general purpose to make uniform the law of those states which enact it.

§ 4. Short title.

This chapter may be cited as the "Uniform Business Records as Evidence Act".

The following jurisdictions have adopted this provision:

Arizona
California
Connecticut
Idaho
Minnesota
Missouri
New Jersey
New York
North Dakota
Ohio
Pennsylvania
Rhode Island
South Carolina
Tennessee
Vermont
Washington

Uniform Preservation of Private Business Records Act.

§ 1. Definitions.

As used in this Act:

"Business" includes every kind of private business, profession, occupation, calling or operation of private institutions, whether carried on for profit or not.

"Person" means an individual, partnership, corporation, or any other association.

"Records" or "Business Records" include books of account, vouchers, documents, canceled checks, payrolls, correspondence, records of sales, personnel, equipment and production, reports relating to any or all of such records, and other business papers.

"Reproduction" means a reproduction or durable medium for making a reproduction obtained by any photographic, photostatic, microfilm, micro-card, miniature photographic or other process which accurately reproduces or forms a durable medium for so reproducing the original.

§ 2. Period of preservation.

Unless a specific period is designated by law for their preservation, business records which persons by the laws of this state are required to keep or preserve may be destroyed after the expiration of three years from the making of such records without constituting an offense under such laws. [This section does not apply to minute books of corporations nor to records of sales or other transactions involving weapons, poisons or other dangerous articles or substances capable of use in the commission of crimes.]

§ 3. Preservation of reproductions.

If in the regular course of business a person makes reproductions of original business records, the preservation of such reproductions constitutes compliance with any laws of this State requiring that business records be kept or preserved.

§ 4. Destruction of records by state officers.

Nothing in this Act shall be construed to diminish the authority of an officer of this State under existing law to permit the destruction of business records.

§ 5. Uniformity of interpretation.

This Act shall be so interpreted and construed as to effectuate its general purpose to make uniform the law of those states which enact it.

The following jurisdictions have adopted this provision

Colorado
Georgia
Illinois
Maryland
New Hampshire
Oklahoma
Texas

Uniform Photographic Copies of Business and Public Records as Evidence Act

§ 1. Admissibility of reproduced records in evidence.

If any business, institution, member of a profession or calling, or any department or agency of government, in the regular course of business or activity has kept or recorded any memorandum, writing, entry, print, representation or combination thereof, of any act, transaction, occurrence or event, and in the regular course of business has caused any or all of the same to be recorded, copied or reproduced by any photographic, photostatic, microfilm, micro-card, miniature photographic, or other process which accurately reproduces or forms a durable medium for so reproducing the original, the original may be destroyed in the regular course of business unless held in a custodial or fiduciary capacity or unless its preservation is required by law. Such reproduction, when satisfactorily identified, is as admissible in evidence as the original itself in any judicial or administrative proceeding whether the original is in existence or not and an enlargement or fac-simile of such reproduction is likewise admissible in evidence if the original repro-duction is in existence and available for in-spection under direction of court. The introduction of a reproduced record, enlarge-ment or facsimile, does not preclude admis-sion of the original.

§ 2. Interpretation.

This act shall be so interpreted and construed as to effectuate its general purpose of making uniform the law of those states which enact it.

§ 3. Short title.

This act may be cited as the "Uniform Pho-tographic Copies of Business and Public Records as Evidence Act."

The following jurisdictions have adopted this provision

Alabama
Arkansas
California
Colorado
Connecticut
Georgia
Idaho
Iowa
Kansas
Kentucky
Maine
Maryland
Massachusetts
Michigan
Minnesota
Nebraska
New Hampshire
New Jersey
New York
North Carolina
North Dakota
Pennsylvania
Rhode Island
South Carolina
South Dakota
Tennessee
United States
Utah
Vermont
Virgin Islands
Virginia
Washington
West Virginia
Wisconsin

Uniform Rules of Evidence.

Article VIII. Hearsay.

Rule 801. Definitions.

The following definitions apply under this article:

(a) Statement. A "statement" is (1) an oral or written assertion or (2) nonverbal conduct of a person, if it is intended by him to be communi-cative.

(b) Declarant. A "declarant" is a person who makes a statement.

(c) Hearsay. "Hearsay" is a statement other than one made by the declarant while testify-ing at the trial or hearing, offered in evidence to prove the truth of the matter asserted.

(d) Statements which are not hearsay.

* * * * *

(2) Admission by party-opponent. The statement is offered against a party and is (A) his own statement in either his individual or a representative capacity or (B) a statement of which he has manifested his adoption or belief in its truth, or (C) a statement by a person authorized by him to make a state-ment concerning the subject, or (D) a state-ment by his agent or servant concerning a matter within the scope of his agency or employment, made during the existence of the relationship, or (E) a statement by a co-conspirator of the party during the course and in furtherance of the conspiracy.

Rule 802. Hearsay rule.

Hearsay is not admissible except as provided by law or by these rules.

Rule 803. Hearsay exceptions; availability of declarant immaterial.

The following are not excluded by the hear-say rule, even though the declarant is avail-able as a witness:

* * * * *

(5) Recorded recollection. A memorandum or record concerning a matter about which a witness once had knowledge but now has insufficient recollection to enable him to testify fully and accurately, shown to have been made or adopted by the witness when the matter was fresh in his memory and to reflect that knowledge correctly. If admitted, the memorandum or record may be read into evidence but may not itself be received as an exhibit unless offered by an adverse party.

(6) Records of regularly conducted business activity. A memorandum, report, record, or data compilation, in any form, of acts, events, conditions, opinions, or diagnoses, made at or near the time by, or from information transmitted by, a person with knowledge, if kept in the course of a regularly conducted business activity, and if it was the regular practice of that business activity to make the memorandum, report, record, or data compilation, all as shown by the testimony of the custodian or other qualified witness, unless the source of information or the method or circumstances of preparation indicate lack of trustworthiness. The term "business" as used in this paragraph includes business, institution, association, profession, occupation, and calling of every kind, whether or not conducted for profit.

(7) Absence of entry in records kept in accordance with the provisions of paragraph (6). Evidence that a matter is not included in the memoranda, reports, records, or data compilations, in any form, kept in accordance with the provisions or paragraph (6), to prove the nonoccurrence or nonexistence of the matter, if the matter was of a kind of which a memorandum, report, record, or data compilation was regularly made and preserved, unless the sources of information or other circumstances indicate lack of trustworthiness.

(8) Public records and reports. To the extent not otherwise provided in this paragraph, records, reports, statements, or data compilations in any form of a public office or agency setting forth its regularly conducted and regularly recorded activities, or matters observed pursuant to duty imposed by law and as to which there was a duty to report, or factual findings resulting from an investigation made pursuant to authority granted by law. The following are not within this exception to the hearsay rule: (i) investigative reports by police and other law enforcement personnel; (ii) investigative reports prepared by or for a government, a public office, or an agency when offered by it in a case in which it is a party; (iii) factual findings offered by the government in criminal cases; (iv) factual findings resulting from special investigation of a particular complaint, case, or incident; and (v) any matter as to which the sources of information or other circumstances indicate lack of trustworthiness.

(9) Records of vital statistics. Records or data compilations, in any form, of births, fetal deaths, deaths, or marriages, if the report thereof was made to a public office pursuant to requirements of law.

(10) Absence of public record or entry. To prove the absence of a record, report, statement, or data compilation, in any form, or the nonoccurrence or nonexistence of a matter of which a record, report, statement, or data compilation, in any form, was regularly made and preserved by a public office or agency, evidence in the form of a certification in accordance with Rule 902, or testimony, that diligent search failed to disclose the record, report, statement, or data compilation, or entry.

(11) Records of religious organizations. Statements of births, marriages, divorces, death, legitimacy, ancestry, relationship by blood or marriage, or other similar facts of personal or family history, contained in a regularly kept record of a religious organization.

(12) Marriage, baptismal, and similar certificates. Statements of fact contained in a certificate that the maker performed a marriage or other ceremony or administered a sacrament, made by a clergyman, public official, or other person authorized by the rules or practices of a religious organization or by law to perform the act certified, and purporting to have been issued at the time of the act or within a reasonable time thereafter.

(13) Family records. Statements of fact concerning personal or family history contained in family Bibles, genealogies, charts, engravings on rings, inscriptions on family portraits, engravings on urns, crypts, or tombstones, or the like.

(14) Records of documents affecting an interest in property. The record of a document purporting to establish or affect an interest in property, as proof of the content of the original recorded document and its execution and delivery by each person by whom it purports to have been executed, if the record is a record of a public office and an applicable statute authorizes the recording of documents of that kind in that office.

(15) Statements in documents affecting an interest in property. A statement contained in a document purporting to establish or affect an interest in property if the matter stated was relevant to the purpose of the document, unless dealings with the property since the document was made have been inconsistent with the truth of the statement or the purport of the document.

(16) Statements in ancient documents. Statements in a document in existence twenty years or more the authenticity of which is established.

(17) Market reports, commercial publications. Market quotations, tabulations, lists, directories, or other published compilations, generally used and relied upon by the public or by persons in particular occupations.

(18) Learned treatises. To the extent called to the attention of an expert witness upon cross-examination or relied upon by him in direct examination, statements contained in published treatises, periodicals, or pamphlets on a subject of history, medicine, or other science or art, established as a reliable authority by testimony or admission of the witness or by other expert testimony or by judicial notice. If admitted, the statements may be read into evidence but may not be received as exhibits.

* * * * *

(24) Other Exceptions. A statement not specifically covered by any of the foregoing exceptions but having equivalent circumstantial guarantees of trustworthiness, if the court determines that (A) the statement is offered as evidence of a material fact; (B) the statement is more probative on the point for which it is offered than any other evidence which the proponent can procure through reasonable efforts; and (C) the general purposes of these rules and the interests of justice will best be served by admission of the statement into evidence. However, a statement may not be admitted under this exception unless the proponent of it makes known to the adverse party sufficiently in advance of the trial or hearing to provide the adverse party with a fair opportunity to prepare to meet it, his intention to offer the statement and the particulars of it, including the name and address of the declarant.

Rule 804. Hearsay Exceptions; Declarant Unavailable.

* * * * *

(b) Hearsay exceptions.***

* * * * *

(3) Statement against interest. A statement which was at the time of its making so far contrary to the declarant's pecuniary or proprietary interest, or so far intended to subject him to civil or criminal liability, or to render invalid a claim by him against another, that a reasonable man in his position would not have made the statement unless he believed it to be true. A statement tending to expose the declarant to criminal liability and offered to exculpate the accused is not admissible unless corroborating circumstances clearly indicate the trustworthiness of the statement.

* * * * *

(5) Other exceptions. A statement not specifically covered by any of the foregoing exceptions but having equivalent circumstantial guarantees of trustworthiness, if the court determines that (A) the statement is offered as evidence of a material fact; (B) the statement is more probative on the point for which it is offered than any other evidence which the proponent can procure through reasonable efforts; and (C) the general purposes of these rules and the interests of justice will best be served by admission of the statement into evidence. However, a statement may not be admitted under this exception unless the proponent of it makes known to the adverse party sufficiently in advance of the trial or hearing to provide the adverse party with a fair opportunity to prepare to meet it, his intention to offer the statement and the particulars of it, including the name and address of the declarant.

Article IX. Authentication and Identification.

Rule 901. Requirements of Authentication or Identification.

(a) General provision. The requirement of authentication or identification as a condition precedent to admissibility is satisfied by evidence sufficient to support a finding that the matter in question is what its proponent claims.

(b) Illustrations. By way of illustration only, and not by way of limitation, the following are examples of authentication or identification conforming with the requirements of this rule:

* * * * *

(7) Public records or reports. Evidence that a writing authorized by law to be recorded or filed and in fact recorded or filed in a public office, or a purported public record, report, statement, or data compilation, in any form, is from the public office where items of this nature are kept.

(8) Ancient documents or data compilation. Evidence that a document or data compilation, in any form, (A) is in such condition as to create no suspicion concerning its authenticity, (B) was in a place where it, if authentic, would likely be, and (C) has been in existence 20 years or more at the time it is offered.

(9) Process or system. Evidence describing a process or system used to produce a result and showing that the process or system produces an accurate result.

Rule 902. Self-authentication.

Extrinsic evidence of authenticity as a condition precedent to admissibility is not required with respect to the following:

(1) Domestic public documents under seal. A document bearing a seal purporting to be that of the United States, or of any State, district, Commonwealth, territory, or insular possession thereof, or the Panama Canal Zone, or the Trust Territory of the Pacific Islands, or of a political subdivision, department, officer, or agency thereof, and a signature purporting to be an attestation or execution.

(2) Domestic public documents not under seal. A document purporting to bear the signature in his official capacity of an officer or employee of any entity included in paragraph (1) hereof, having no seal, if a public officer having a seal and having official duties in the district or political subdivision of the officer or employee certifies under seal that the signer has the official capacity and that the signature is genuine.

(3) Foreign public documents. A document purporting to be executed or attested in his official capacity by a person authorized by the laws of a foreign country to make the execution or attestation, and accompanied by a final certification as to the genuineness of the signature and official position (A) of the executing or attesting person, or (B) of any foreign official whose certificate of genuineness of signature and official position relates to the execution or attestation or is in a chain of certificates of genuineness of signature and official position relating to the execution or attestation. A final certification may be made by a secretary of embassy or legation, consul general, consul, vice consul, or consular agent of the United States, or a diplomatic or consular official of the foreign country assigned or accredited to the United States. If reasonable opportunity has been given to all parties to investigate the authenticity and accuracy of official documents, the court may, for good cause shown, order that they be treated as presumptively authentic without final certification or permit them to be evidenced by an attested summary with or without final certification.

(4) Certified copies of public records. A copy of an official record or report or entry therein, or of a document authorized by law to be recorded or filed and actually recorded or filed in a public office, including data compilations in any form, certified as correct by the custodian or other person authorized to make the certification, by certificate complying with paragraph (1), (2), or (3) of this rule or complying with paragraph (1), (2), or (3) of this rule or complying with any Act of Congress or rule prescribed by the Supreme Court pursuant to statutory authority.

(5) Official publications. Books, pamphlets, or other publications purporting to be issued by public authority.

(6) Newspapers and periodicals. Printed materials purporting to be newspapers or periodicals.

(7) Trade inscriptions and the like. Inscriptions, signs, tags, or labels purporting to have been affixed in the course of business and indicating ownership control, or origin.

(8) Acknowledged documents. Documents accompanied by a certificate of acknowledgment executed in the manner provided by law by a notary public or other officer authorized by law to take acknowledgments.

(9) Commercial paper and related documents. Commercial paper, signatures thereon, and documents relating thereto to the extent provided by general commercial law.

(10) Presumptions under Acts of Congress. Any signature, document or other matter declared by Act of Congress to be presumptively or prima facie genuine or authentic.

Article X. Contents of Writings, Recordings, and Photographs.

Rule 1001. Definitions.

For purposes of this Article the following definitions are applicable:

(1) Writings and recordings. "Writings" and "recordings" consist of letters, words, sounds, or numbers, or their equivalent, set down by handwriting, typewriting, printing, photostating, photographing, magnetic impulse, mechanical or electronic recording, or other form of data compilation.

(2) Photographs. "Photographs" include still photographs, X-ray films, video tapes, and motion pictures.

(3) Original. An "original" of a writing or recording is the writing or recording itself or any counterpart intended to have the same effect by a person executing or issuing it. An "original" of a photograph includes the negative or any print therefrom. If data are stored in a computer or similar device, any printout or other output readable by sight, shown to reflect the data accurately, is an "original."

(4) Duplicate. A "duplicate" is a counterpart produced by the same impression as the original, or from the same matrix, or by means of photography, including enlargements and miniatures, or by mechanical or electronic rerecording, or by chemical reproduction, or by other equivalent techniques which accurately reproduces the original.

Rule 1002. Requirement of original.

To prove the content of a writing, recording, or photograph, the original writing, recording, or photograph is required, except as otherwise provided in these rules or by [rules adopted by the Supreme Court of this State or by] statute.

Rule 1003. Admissibility of duplicates.

A duplicate is admissible to the same extent as an original unless (1) a genuine question is raised as to the authenticity or continuing effectiveness of the original or (2) in the circumstances it would be unfair to admit the duplicate in lieu of the original.

Rule 1004. Admissibility of other evidence of contents.

The original is not required, and other evidence of the contents of a writing, recording, or photograph is admissible if:

(1) Originals lost or destroyed. All originals are lost or have been destroyed, unless the proponent lost or destroyed them in bad faith; or

(2) Original not obtainable. No original can be obtained by any available judicial process or procedure; or

(3) Original in possession of opponent. At a time when an original was under the control of the party against whom offered, he was put on notice, by the pleadings or otherwise, that the contents would be a subject of proof at the hearing, and he does not produce the original at the hearing; or

(4) Collateral matters. The writing, recording, or photograph is not closely related to a controlling issue.

Rule 1005. Public records.

The contents of an official record, or of a document authorized to be recorded or filed and actually recorded or filed, including data compilations in any form, if otherwise admissible, may be proved by copy, certified as correct in accordance with Rule 902 or testified to be correct by a witness who has compared it with the original. If a copy complying with the foregoing cannot be obtained by the exercise of reasonable diligence, other evidence of the contents may be admitted.

Rule 1006. Summaries.

The contents of voluminous writings, recordings, or photographs which cannot conveniently be examined in court may be presented in the form of a chart, summary, or calculation. The originals, or duplicates, shall be made available for examination or copying, or both, by other parties at a reasonable time and place. The court may order that they be produced in court.

The following jurisdictions have adopted this provision

Alaska
Arizona
Arkansas
Colorado
Delaware
Florida
Hawaii
Iowa
Maine
Michigan
Minnesota
Mississippi
Montana
Nebraska
Nevada
New Jersey
New Mexico
North Carolina
North Dakota
Ohio
Oklahoma
Oregon
Puerto Rico
Rhode Island
South Dakota
Tennessee
Texas
United States
Utah
Vermont
Washington
West Virginia
Wisconsin
Wyoming

Appendix B. Federal Rules of Civil Procedure

Rule 26. General Provisions Governing Discovery; Duty of Disclosure.

(a) Required Disclosures to Discover Additional Matter.

(1) Initial Disclosures. Except to the extent otherwise stipulated or directed by order or local rule, a party shall, without awaiting a discovery request, provide to other parties:

(A) the name and, if known, the address and telephone number of each individual likely to have discoverable information relevant to disputed facts alleged with particularity in the pleadings, identifying the subjects of the information;

(B) a copy of, or a description by category and location of, all documents, data compilations, and tangible things in the possession, custody, or control of the party that are relevant to disputed facts alleged with particularity in the pleadings;

(C) a computation of any category of damages claimed by the disclosing party, making available for inspection and copying as under Rule 34 the documents or other evidentiary material, not privileged or protected from disclosure, on which such computation is based, including materials bearing on the nature and extent of injuries suffered; and

(D) for inspection and copying as under Rule 34 any insurance agreement under which any person carrying on an insurance business may be liable to satisfy part of all of a judgment which may be entered in the action or to indemnify or reimburse for payments made to satisfy the judgment.

Unless otherwise stipulated or directed by the court, these disclosures shall be made at or within 10 days after the meeting of the parties under subdivision (f). A party shall make its initial disclosures based on the information then reasonably available to it and is not excused from making its disclosures because it has not fully completed its investigation of the case or because it challenges the sufficiency of another party's disclosures or because another party has not made its disclosure.

* * * * *

(3) Pretrial Disclosures. In addition to the disclosures required in the preceding paragraphs, a party shall provide to other parties the following information regarding the evidence that it may present at trial other than solely for impeachment purposes:

(A) the name and, if not previously provided, the address and telephone number of each witness, separately identifying those whom the party expects to present and those whom the party may call if the need arises.

(B) the designation of those witnesses whose testimony is expected to be presented by means of a deposition and, if not taken stenographically, a transcript of the pertinent portions of the deposition testimony; and

(C) an appropriate identification of each document or other exhibit, excluding summaries of other evidence, separately identifying those which the party expects to offer and those which the party may offer if the need arises.

Unless otherwise directed by the court, these disclosures shall be made at least 30 days before trial. Within 14 days thereafter, unless a different time is specified by the court, a party may serve and file a list disclosing (i) any objections to the use under Rule 32(a) of a deposition designated by another party under subparagraph (B) and (ii) any objection, together with the grounds therefor, that may be made to the admissibility of materials identified under subparagraph (C). Objections not so disclosed, other than objections under Rules 402 and 403 of the Federal Rules of Evidence, shall be deemed waived unless excused by the court for good cause shown.

(4) **Form of Disclosures; Filing.** Unless otherwise directed by order or local rule, all disclosures under paragraphs (1) through (3) shall be made in writing, signed, served, and promptly filed with the court.

(5) **Methods to Discover Additional Matter.** Parties may obtain discovery by one or more of the following methods: depositions upon oral examination or written questions; written interrogatories; production of documents or things or permission to enter upon land or other property under Rule 34 or 45 (a)(1)(C), for inspection and other purposes; physical and mental examinations; and requests for admission.

* * * * *

Rule 37. Failure to Make or Cooperate in Discovery; Sanctions

(a) **Motion for Order Compelling Discovery.** A party, upon reasonable notice to other parties and all persons affected thereby, may apply for an order compelling discovery as follows:

(1) **Appropriate Court.** An application for an order to a party may be made to the court in which the action is pending, or, on matters relating to a deposition, to the court in the district where the deposition is being taken. An application for an order to a deponent who is not a party shall be made to the court in the district where the deposition is being taken.

(2) **Motion.** If a deponent fails to answer a question propounded or submitted under Rules 30 or 31, or a corporation or other entity fails to make a designation under Rule 30(b)(6) or 31(a), or a party fails to answer an interrogatory submitted under Rule 33, or if a party, in response to a request for inspection submitted under Rule 34, fails to respond that inspection will be permitted as requested or fails to permit inspection as requested, the discovering party may move for an order compelling an answer, or a designation, or an order compelling inspection in accordance with the request. When taking a deposition on oral examination, the proponent of the question may complete or adjourn the examination before applying for an order.

If the court denies the motion in whole or in part, it may make such protective order as it would have been empowered to make on a motion made pursuant to Rule 26(c).

(3) **Evasive or Incomplete Answer.** For purposes of this subdivision an evasive or incomplete answer is to be treated as a failure to answer.

(4) **Award of Expenses Motion.** If the motion is granted, the court shall, after opportunity for hearing, require the party or deponent whose conduct necessitated the motion or the party or attorney advising such conduct or both of them to pay to the moving party the reasonable expenses incurred in obtaining the order, including attorney's fees, unless the court finds that the opposition to the motion was substantially justified or that other circumstances make an award of expenses unjust.

If the motion is denied, the court shall, after opportunity for hearing, require the moving party or the attorney advising the motion or both of them to pay to the party or deponent who opposed the motion the reasonable expenses incurred in opposing the motion, including attorney's fees, unless the court finds that the making of the motion was substantially justified or that other circumstances make an award of expenses unjust.

If the motion is granted in part and denied in part, the court may apportion the reasonable expenses incurred in relation to the motion among the parties and persons in a just manner.

(b) Failure to Comply with Order.

(1) Sanctions by Court in District Where Deposition is Taken. If a deponent fails to be sworn or to answer a question after being directed to do so by the court in the district in which the deposition is being taken, the failure may be considered a contempt of that court.

(2) Sanctions by Court in Which Action is Pending. If a party or an officer, director, or managing agent of a party of a person designated under Rule 30(b)(6) or 31(a) to testify on behalf of a party fails to obey an order to provide or permit discovery, including an order made under subdivision (a) of this rule or Rule 35, or if a party fails to obey an order entered under Rule 26(f), the court in which the action is pending may make such orders in regard to the failure as are just, and among others the following:

(A) An order that the matters regarding which the order was made or any other designated facts shall be taken to be established for the purposes of the action in accordance with the claim of the party obtaining the order;

(B) An order refusing to allow the disobedient party to support or oppose designated claims or defenses, or prohibiting that party from introducing designated matters in evidence;

(C) An order striking out pleadings or parts thereof, or staying further proceedings until the order is obeyed, or dismissing the action or proceeding or any part thereof, or rendering a judgment by default against the disobedient party;

(D) In lieu of any of the foregoing orders or in addition thereto, an order treating as a contempt of court the failure to obey any orders except an order to submit a physical or mental examination;

(E) Where a party has failed to comply with an order under Rule 35(a) requiring that party to produce another for examination, such orders as are listed in paragraphs (A), (B), and (C) of this subdivision, unless the party failing to comply shows that that party is unable to produce such person for examination.

In lieu of any of the foregoing orders or in addition thereto, the court shall require the party failing to obey the order or the attorney advising that party or both to pay the reasonable expenses, including attorney's fees, caused by that failure, unless the court finds that the failure was substantially justified or that other circumstances make an award of expenses unjust.

(c) Expenses on Failure to Admit. If a party fails to admit the genuineness of any document or the truth of any matter as requested under Rule 36, and if the party requesting the admissions thereafter proves the genuineness of the document or the truth of the matter, the requesting party may apply to the court for an order requiring the other party to pay the reasonable expenses incurred in making that proof, including reasonable attorney's fees. The court shall make the order unless it finds that (1) the request was held objectionable pursuant to Rule 36(a), or (2) the admission sought was of no substantial importance, or (3) the party failing to admit had reasonable ground to believe that the party might prevail on the matter, or (4) there was other good reason for the failure to admit.

(d) Failure of Party to Attend at Own Deposition or Serve Answers to Interrogatories or Respond to Request for Inspection. If a party or an officer, director, or managing agent of a party or a person designated under Rule 30(b)(6) or 31(a) to testify on behalf of a party fails (1) to appear before the officer who is to take the deposition, after being served with a proper notice, or (2) to serve answers or objections to interrogatories submitted under Rule 33, after proper service of the interrogatories, or (3) to serve a written response to a request for inspection submitted under Rule 34, after proper service of the request, the court in which the action is pending on motion may make such orders in regard to the failure as are just, and among others it may take any action authorized under paragraphs (A), (B), and (C) of subdivision (b)(2) of this rule. In lieu of any order or in addition thereto, the court shall require the party failing to act or the attorney advising that party or both to pay the reasonable expenses, including attorney's fees, caused by the failure, unless the court finds that the failure was substantially justified or that other circumstances make an award of expenses unjust.

The failure to act described in this subdivision may not be excused on the ground that the discovery sought is objectionable unless the party failing to act has applied for a protective order as provided by Rule 26(c).

Appendix C. Court Cases

ADDEO LOAN COMPANY, INC. v. Pasquale MANOCCHIO, alias Pasco Manochio, alias d/b/a Knight Motors

313 A.2d 649

Supreme Court of Rhode Island
January 11, 1974

* * * * *

On October 19, 1968, the plaintiff brought this civil action to recover the unpaid balance alleged to be due on six promissory notes made by the defendant and payable to the plaintiff. The case was heard in April 1970, before a justice of the Superior Court without a jury and resulted in a decision for the plaintiff. After entry of judgment on April 27, 1970, the defendant, on May 7, 1970, filed a Super.R.Civ.P. 59 motion for a new trial on the ground of newly discovered evidence. The trial justice denied this motion and defendant then filed the instant appeal.

The following facts are undisputed. Prior to 1952 plaintiff and defendant entered into an arrangement under which plaintiff financed or floor planned defendant's automobile business. The defendant would borrow money from plaintiff for the purchase of motor vehicles for sale in his business. The defendant would give plaintiff a promissory note for the amount borrowed on each case. Each note was secured by a chattel mortgage on the car to be purchased.

* * * * *

In commenting on defendant's testimony, the trial justice observed that in his opinion defendant never kept any reasonable records concerning his indebtedness to plaintiff; that defendant in 1952 probably did not know what he owed, and he certainly did not know then what he owed plaintiff; that defendant's evidence regarding the balance due and the amount of the loans is really not of any great value, because he never kept track of what he paid; and that defendant simply made payments to plaintiff and expected that plaintiff would give him appropriate credit.

* * * * *

In the affidavit in support of his motion for a new trial, defendant alleges that after the commencement of this action he diligently searched for any canceled checks and/or records which pertained to this action but was unable to find or locate pertinent records for the defense of this action for the following reasons: (1) the long period of time which had clapsed since the execution of the notes; (2) the theft of many of his records from his former place of business; (3) the destruction of many of his records during the course of the operation of his business; and (4) the termination of his business in 1967.

As further reasons for his inability to find or locate such records defendant alleges in the affidavit accompanying his motion (1) that immediately after the commencement of this action a mortgage on his real estate and place of business was foreclosed; (2) that any other records which may have been in existence were in the foreclosed premises; (3) that he did not have access to those premises after the foreclosure; and (4) that since the foreclosure a new tenant occupied the premises.

The defendant then asserts in his affidavit that he prevailed upon the new tenant to search the premises in an attempt to locate any tangible evidence which would affect the adjudication of this action; that he has successfully located a canceled check in the amount of $1,187 which was given to plaintiff in full payment for one of the notes involved in the instant action; that at the trial of this action he did not know of the existence of the check; and that he was unable to locate the same after diligent search prior to and during the trial.

The defendant concluded his affidavit by claiming that it was his belief that the discovery of the canceled check would change the result of his action. The plaintiff then filed and affidavit which contradicted the material allegations of the defendant's affidavit.

* * * * *

In his decision denying defendant's motion for a new trial, the trial justice referred to the trial on the merits and to his feeling then that plaintiff's records were reliable and persuasive. He also noted that the defendant at the time had little or no recollection and even fewer records to support his position. After further discussing the events which transpired at the trial, the trial justice found (1) that defendant had not exercised due diligence in searching for the documents prior to or at the time of the trial; (2) that the documents referred to in defendant's affidavit were not relevant to the six notes on which this action was based; and (3) that the alleged

new evidence would not cause a change in result. In making these findings he said:

"Now, apparently after the trial was ended, the defendant began a meticulous preparation of his case, which apparently he had not bothered to do prior to the trial itself. In going over the affidavits, the Court is of the opinion that what the defendant is doing here is attempting to throw up a great mass of transactions in the hope that some of them may fall into the right place. In looking over the affidavit and the matters alleged therein, the Court is of the opinion that there is nothing contained herein that could not have been presented with reasonable diligence at the time of the trial. There was ample time for preparation. The Court had not denied anyone continuance or request to produce further evidence.

"Now, this question of going back and finding other checks in a place of business that was certainly as available prior to the trial as it was after the trial, is not in the opinion of the Court persuasive, and even assuming that some of these materials would not have been readily available, I can't say they wouldn't have been available. It just may not have been convenient for the defendant to go to the effort he later did go to.

"The Court is of the opinion that the same questions are unanswered by the affidavit as were unanswered during the course of the trial. The Court is of the opinion that the defendant doesn't demonstrate by his affidavit that he is any better equipped with precision to relate his payments to the obligations specifically that were outstanding now than he was then. The Court does not feel that justice would serve by starting all over again and coming to what the Court believes is the same result. For the reasons given, the motion for new trial is hereby denied."

* * * * *

As Professor Kent points out in 1 Kent, R.I.Civ.Prac. § 59.5 at 442 (1969), certain conditions must be met before newly discovered evidence may constitute grounds for a new trial. To constitute grounds for a new trial, newly discovered evidence must be material, and due diligence must be shown. *Zoglio v. T.W. Waterman Co.*, 39 R.I 396 , 98 A. 280 (1916). Evidence, which through ordinary diligence would have been available at the trial, does not justify a new trial on the ground it has been newly discovered. *Levy v. Equitable Fire & Marine Ins. Co.*, 88 R.I. 252, 146 A.2d 231 (1958). Nor should a new trial be granted unless newly discovered evidence is of such a character as would probably affect the verdict. *Carmara v. Rodriques*, 74 R.I. 161, 59 A.2d 354 (1948). If the newly discovered evidence would be likely to change the verdict, a new trial should be granted, even though the evidence might be merely cumulative, *Zoglio v. T.W. Waterman Co.*, *supra.*

With these guidelines in mind we address ourselves to the defendant's first question. As we have pointed out above, the trial justice, after examining the affidavits, found that there was nothing contained therein that could not have been presented with reasonable diligence at the time of the trial and that there was ample time for preparation. He also found that the documents referred to in the affidavits were just as available prior to the trial as they were after the trial, but that it just may not have been convenient for defendant "to go to the effort he later did go to."

The defendant contends that the trial justice erred in finding a lack of due diligence. He argues that he used due diligence to gather all evidence known to him or discoverable by him prior to trial, and discovery of this new evidence was in no way the result of any lack of ordinary diligence on his part. The defendant further contends that we should consider the fact that he had neither possession nor knowledge of the newly discovered evidence nor access to it even if he knew of the existence. Finally, he argues that we should relax the standard of ordinary diligence required because nearly twenty years had elapsed between the transactions involved and the entry of judgment.

We find no merit in defendant's argument on this issue. The fact that nearly twenty years had elapsed between the transactions and entry of judgment is no reason for relaxing the rule that evidence which by the use of ordinary diligence is available at the trial cannot be called newly discovered. *Levy v. Equitable Fire & Marine Ins. Co.*, *supra.*

In passing on the question of due diligence the trial justice considered all of the factors now advanced by defendant and came to the conclusion that defendant had not exercised due diligence prior to or at the time of the trial to locate the alleged newly discovered evidence. He found in substance that by the use of due diligence the evidence would have been available at the trial. Although the transactions on which this action is based took place in 1951–1952 and the action was commenced in October, 1968, the trial did not take place until April, 1970.

The defendant had ample time to look for and locate records which could have helped him defend this action. He knew since 1952 that balances were outstanding on these six notes and in October, 1968, he knew that plaintiff was suing him to recover balances which it claimed were due on those very notes. How can it reasonably be said that defendant acted with due diligence when he was unable to locate the records during the period between October 19, 1968 (the date of commencement of trial) and yet was able to locate them within ten days after the judgment was entered against him?

Under our cases evidence which through ordinary diligence would have been available at the trial is not newly discovered evidence and does not justify a new trial on the ground that it has been newly discovered. *Levy v. Equitable Fire & Marine Ins. Co.*, *supra.* On this record we cannot say that the trial justice erred in finding a lack of due diligence on the defendants part. Since this finding is dispositive of this appeal it is unnecessary to consider or answer the defendant's remaining questions.

The defendant's appeal is denied and dismissed, the judgment appealed from is affirmed, and the case is remanded to Superior Court for further proceedings.

AIR CRASH DISASTER NEAR CHICAGO, ILLINOIS ON MAY 25, 1979

90 F.R.D. 613

United States District Court, N.D. Illinois, E.D.
June 23, 1981

Plaintiffs' Committee for Liability Discovery has moved for sanctions against American Airlines, Inc. (American). They contend that American has obstructed and abused the discovery process throughout this action, and has ignored or disobeyed discovery orders of this court. Defendant American denies that any of its actions was improper, and requests costs and fees for responding to this motion. For the reasons hereinafter stated, plaintiffs' motion will be granted in part and denied in part. Defendant American's motion for costs and fees will be denied.

This action was consolidated in this court by the Judicial Panel for Multidistrict Litigation for coordinated pretrial proceedings of the claims of persons killed or injured in the May 25, 1979, American Airlines DC–10 crash near O'Hare Airport. After initial efforts to avoid a liability trial appeared to be unsuccessful, the court permitted liability discovery to begin in April, 1980. Plaintiffs selected a discovery committee to coordinate all their liability discovery. This discovery committee served both defendants with requests for production, requests for admissions, interrogatories, and disposition notices. The parties and the court worked out a procedure for handling the discovery. Pretrial Order No. 8, Practice and Procedure Order. The court contemplated that all liability discovery, including dispositions would be completed by September, 1980.

Liability discovery became necessary when many plaintiffs rejected defendants' offered stipulation. The stipulation provided that each signing plaintiff would waive any claim for punitive damages and defendants would not contest their liability. The majority of plaintiffs, concerned with the wording of the stipulation or the possible availability of punitive damages, refused to stipulate. In their briefs, the parties

expend great effort attacking or defending the stipulation. It is clear that whether or not the stipulation was a delaying tactic or a sincere good faith effort is irrelevant. While other factors may have played a role in the decision not to sign the stipulation, the major concern clearly was a reluctance to waive possible discovery of punitive damages.

On May 29, 1980, after extensive briefing of the issue, we held that punitive damages might be asserted against defendant McDonnell Douglas Corporation, but not against defendant American Airlines. 500 F.Supp. 1044. On January 5, 1981, the Court of Appeals for the Seventh Circuit reversed that decision as to McDonnell Douglas and affirmed as to American holding that, under the controlling Illinois law, neither defendant could be sued for punitive damages in a wrongful death action. 644 F.2d 594. Several plaintiffs have filed a petition for a writ of certiorari from that holding to the United States Supreme Court, which is currently pending.

From April to January, 1981, plaintiffs' committee conducted it own discovery and participated in depositions and discovery noticed by the defendants. Plaintiffs contend that American's actions throughout this period caused needless discovery costs and expenses so that all of the expenses for this period should be charged to American. Primarily, plaintiffs' claims are based on three matters: 1) that American's destruction of the "Eastburn report," and its actions to conceal that destruction, directly and indirectly imposed excessive and unnecessary costs on plaintiffs; 2) that American's failure to properly produce documents, as requested, and admit items requested in the plaintiff's request to admit further directly and indirectly imposed unnecessary costs on plaintiffs; 3) that American's general failure to participate in good faith in discovery proceedings directly and indirectly led to additional unnecessary costs and delays.

American denies that any of its actions during discovery violated or contravened any court orders, or that it acted in any improper manner throughout these proceedings. American suggests that the motion is so frivolous and baseless that cost sanctions should be imposed on plaintiffs.

Scope of Sanctions

Plaintiffs' Committee has requested that American be required to pay all fees and expenses incurred by the discovery committee. American, on the other hand, contends that all these fees and expenses are unrelated to its conduct. It is clear that some of these expenses and fees are unrelated to any conduct of defendant American in this litigation. It is also clear, however, that *some* of these fees and expenses resulted solely from American's conduct in certain phases of the litigation.

The plaintiffs' committee incurred costs and fees in the appeals to the Seventh Circuit Court of Appeals of this court's decisions on punitive damages and prejudgment interest. The fees and expenses related to those appeals clearly could bear no casual relation to American's conduct in discovery. Similarly, plaintiffs incurred expenses, and request fees, for depositions of McDonnell Douglas, NTSB, and FAA personnel. Again, these costs and whatever fees are associated with them bear no apparent relation to American's conduct.

The more difficult question relates to depositions of American employees, court appearances, conferences, and other costs related to motions to compel testimony and production by American, as well as appearances and conferences, redepositions and motions associated therewith. After review of the record in this action, it is apparent that many of these costs were incurred or increased due to American's conduct.

In order to ascertain which costs and fees are properly assessable against American, the conduct of the discovery of this action, and American's role in that process must be considered.

Discovery Proceedings in MDL 391

In addition to reviewing the history of American's actions in the Eastburn matter it is also relevant to consider the actions and statements of American counsel at hearings in this court. On May 29, 1979, Judge Gilberto of the Circuit Court of Cook County, Illinois, entered an order directing the preservation of all records of MDC and American relating to, or which might be relevant to the May 25, DC–10 accident. A few days later, on plaintiffs' motion for a similar order in the District Court for the Northern District of Illinois, counsel for American advised Judge Hoffman of the existence of the state protective order, and agreed that American would destroy no documents that plaintiffs might attempt to obtain through discovery. Accordingly, no federal court preservation was entered. At numerous times, in this court, when liability discovery was discussed, counsel and the court relied upon the Circuit Court preservation order.

On April 20, 1980, counsel for American stated in open court that they had complied with plaintiffs' request for documents except where objections to the production would be made. Objections, primarily that the request called for post–accident remedial measures, were made in May, 1980, and motion to compel production was filed May 22, 1980. After briefing of this issue, the court, during the September 23, 1980, pre–trial conference, overruled the objections except as to possible attorney–client and work product privilege. The court directed that any documents for which a privilege claim was being made be submitted *in camera.* The written order directing that submission was signed October 8, 1980. On November 6, 1980, MDC brought a motion to compel production. The court again directed American to submit all "privileged" documents *in camera* by November 13, 1980. The court cautioned American to review the documents to make sure a colorable claim of privilege existed. On November 13, 1980, American submitted documents *in camera.* The documents and the "list" accompanying them reveal the following:

1. The list did not identify which documents had been requested by plaintiffs, which by McDonnell Douglas Corporation or both, nor did it identify the basis for the claim of privilege.

2. Thirty–three documents on the list had

either author or addressee or the date of the document, or all three listed as "unknown."

3. Four additional documents identified the author or addressee only by their initials.

4. No information accompanied the list as to the identity, position, or responsibility of most of the persons named therein. Neither did the list indicate who had received copies of the documents, even where this appeared on the document itself.

5. The "documents" included a letter from a court reporting company correcting testimony (Document 46); a cover letter stating that enclosed are the records requested by FAA (Document 1); letters merely transmitting final replies by American to outside agencies and companies (Documents 2, 10); a letter transmitting notices of depositions (Document 12).

6. The list included duplicates of documents with different descriptions for identical documents. Item 47 was listed as being authorized by Randall Craft (although the addressee was "unknown"). Document 82, an identical document, was listed with both author and addressee "unknown."

7. Additional duplicates were found upon examination of the documents. For example, the following documents were either wholly identical or parts of each other: Documents 17, 26, and 52; Documents 8 and 32; Documents 39, 40, 41, and 163; Documents 28 and 66; Documents 87 and 38; Document 97 and 98; Documents 111 and 108; Documents 62 and 128; Documents 137 and 138; Documents 8 and 150; Documents 30 and 151; Documents 68 and 152; Documents 142 and 153; Documents 143 and 154; Documents 141 and 155; Documents 156 and 132; Documents 77 and 167. In many cases, the description on the list did not disclose this duplication. For example, in some cases, each "description" listed different authors or addresses for identical documents (Documents 8 and 32; Documents 29, 41, and 163; Documents 143 and 154; Documents 77 and 167).

8. Twelve documents were listed but were not actually included in the submission.

9. Minutes of Board of Directors meetings were submitted, but the attachments, which apparently were reports delivered at those meetings, were not included, (i.e., Attachment E to September, 1979, Board Meeting).

On the day the documents were submitted, American filed a motion "to deny production and not read documents." American contended that a review of the documents "in camera" would prejudice the court against their cause, and the court should either deny the request to produce or refer the matter to a magistrate. In support of this motion, American attached the affidavit of Gregory Long, one of American's California counsel, who stated that "Each (document) was either drafted by the attorney representing American in an attorney–client context or was drafted by employees of American or its attorneys at the request of American's attorneys." The court denied this motion. It is quite clear that the assertion under oath that each document was prepared by or for counsel is inconsistent with the failure to identify the author of a large proportion of the documents. It also is inconsistent with the substance of many of the documents. See, e.g., documents referred to in paragraph 5 hereof. American has offered no explanation for this inconsistency.

The first occasion on which the so–called "Eastburn report" was mentioned to the court was on November 6, 1980. McDonnell Douglas Corporation (MDC) filed a motion to compel the production of various documents. Among the documents requested was "Mac Eastburn's report, notes, drafts, etc." In that motion, MDC noted that, although American's attorneys advised them no written report was ever prepared, testimony from American employees indicated that some form of report had been prepared. The motion to compel production was granted. On November 7, and 12, 1980, MDC held 12(d) conferences with American attorneys relative to the request for and the order directing production. During the first conference, attorney Christensen of Overton, Lyman (American's California counsel) stated "[T]here seems to be an assumption on your part that there is a written Mac Eastburn report." Upon MDC stating they intended to apply for sanctions, Christensen replied, "You can't get sanctions for a report that doesn't exist. I'm making a statement to you now that this written report does not exist." During the November 12, conference, attorney Long (also of Overton, Lyman) stated, "[t]here are not such documents" referring to the Eastburn report. After a certain amount of discussion, attorney Guerin of MDC suggested American clarify whether it was their position that the document never existed or that it did exist at some point but had been destroyed. Long stated, "it does not exist period." Alpert, counsel for Aviation Underwriters, stated that MDC was not entitled to ask whether the report had existed or not, and that the attorneys were not there to answer questions concerning the existence or nonexistence of documents. MDC then filed a motion for a rule to show cause why American should not be held in contempt. On November 20, 1980, MDC's motion came on for hearing. Haley, one of American Airlines' counsel, stated he had been informed that there was no Eastburn report, whether regarding the probable cause of the crash or otherwise, that anyone had been able to discover. The court asked whether semantic games were being played. Haley stated he certainly believed this was not the case. Haley suggested, and the court agreed, that MDC could finally ascertain whether the report existed or not during the Eastburn deposition scheduled to begin shortly.

On February 23, 1981, American filed a motion for an order to protect American employees from undue annoyance, oppression, and burden in reference to deposition notices served by MDC. Attached to that motion was an affidavit from Malahowski stating that "to the best of my recollection, all information . . . received by me with respect to the Chicago Air Crash . . . has been received in my capacity as a counsel for American." Attorney Alpert filed an identical affidavit. MDC filed their response on February 26, 1981. That response noted that the affidavits of Alpert and Malahowski apparently contended that the privilege applied to any instructions concerning the Eastburn investigation, or the destruction of the report. MDC strongly disagreed with the apparent contention.

On February 26, 1981, at the regularly scheduled pretrial conference in this cause, the question was discussed. Mr. Allen, another of American's counsel, suggested that the question of deposing the attorneys wait until after the Lloyd–Jones deposition. Judge Will, after noting that Lloyd–Jones was not going to produce the report either, rejected that suggestion. Allen then stated the attorneys did not advise that the report itself be destroyed, and there was nothing in the motion to indicate to the contrary. Judge Will noted that Mr. Allen could not testify as to what other lawyers had or had not said.

In response to questioning from Judge Will, Mr. Alpert stated that he had never seen anything called the "Eastburn report," and that he gave no instructions to anyone with respect to that report or any other reports or copies of reports. If any such instructions were given, he stated, they were given without his knowledge, and his first knowledge of any such instructions came at the time of Eastburn's deposition. He first learned of the Eastburn report when MDC filed their motion to compel production. (Tr. 58). Although he did know earlier that Eastburn was conducting an investigation as to some aspect of the accident he never found out what the Eastburn report covered. He further stated that someone (unidentified) informed him that American Airlines was involved in a Maintenance Action Program to correct certain aspects of DC–10 aircraft maintenance but that Eastburn's report would not involve any aspects of the probable cause of the accident or anything relating to it. (Tr. 59). Mr. Alpert also stated that no one had submitted any testimony to the court from any of the people who reviewed the Eastburn report that it in any way came within the ambit of the Circuit Court preservation order. (Tr. 65). The court denied American's motion and ordered the disposition to proceed.

On March 13, 1981, during the deposition of Donald Lloyd–Jones, Senior Vice–President of American, the parties requested a telephone conference with the court regarding certain claims of privilege. Upon hearing the arguments, Judge Robson indicated it was his reaction that the questions fell squarely within Judge Will's earlier comments as not privileged. The parties requested briefing on the issue. American's position was that, although the activities of Eastburn's audit were not privileged, the role of counsel concerning advice on the destruction of documents was.

On March 23, 1981, the court overruled American's objections to most of the questions, and granted the motion to compel. The court's opinion stated that post–destruction advice on the legal consequences of destruction was the limit of any privilege in this area, and that advice to destroy was not privileged. Lloyd–Jones deposition then continued. Lloyd–Jones testified that Eastburn informed him in late August, 1979, that he had been instructed by counsel not to retain copies of notes or drafts of the report. He testified that some time in September, 1979, he confirmed with Malahowski, in–house counsel for American, that Malahowski had given such instructions to Eastburn. Some months later, he stated, Eastburn informed him that he had not retained any notes or drafts. He estimated that would have occurred in January, 1980. Lloyd–Jones testified that he is not certain he was aware at the time of his June, 1980, deposition either of the existence of the preservation order or that all copies of the Eastburn report were destroyed. Lloyd–Jones stated that at the time he discarded his copy of the report, he was not aware that it was the sole remaining copy, but that Malahowski informed him that no copies remained some time in the summer, 1980.

American's Position re Eastburn Report

American's position, once it acknowledged that a report had in fact been written at some time and, together with all notes, drafts and copies, had been destroyed on the advice of counsel, became that the Eastburn report was fully incorporated into the Maintenance and Engineering Action plan prepared by Schaefer. American now contends that the full contents of the Eastburn report are known and need not be the subject of speculation. American further contends that the Eastburn report was not subject to the Circuit Court protective order, and, since it was destroyed prior to MDC and the plaintiffs' request for

its production, there was nothing improper about the advice to destroy or the fact of destruction of the report.

During the period April, 1980, to January 5, 1981, (when the plaintiffs' committee ceased their discovery efforts), plaintiffs' counsel attended and took depositions, reviewed documents and other materials, and appeared at pretrial conferences, all under the mistaken belief that all relevant reports had been released or were being submitted for a ruling on possible privilege. As indicated, American contends that the Eastburn report was not within the scope of the preservation order, and, because it was destroyed before discovery requests were filed, sanctions should not be ordered. This contention is untenable. A party may not destroy documents where a preservation order has been entered, conceal that destruction for almost one year, then claim that the preservation order never applied, and contend that, since the document no longer exists, it cannot be determined to have been within the ambit of the preservation order. Moreover, it is inconceivable that the Eastburn report did not deal with matters relevant to the issue of liability and the cause of the May 25, accident.

Eastburn Report History

Documents produced by American indicate that on July 17, 1979, Lloyd–Jones directed Mac Eastburn, Senior Director of Safety for American to prepare an investigation and report on the facts, circumstances, and cause of the May 25, 1979, DC–10 accident. The investigation, as originally conceived, clearly included the probable cause of the accident. Eastburn and Lloyd– Jones testified that sometime around the NTSB hearings, or shortly thereafter, the scope of the investigation was altered to exclude all matters relating to the crash itself, and the report/audit was to constitute a review of practices and procedures used in American's DC–10 operations. Eastburn and Lloyd–Jones both testified that neither contacted other American personnel who had been notified of the original investigation to inform them of any change.

During September, 1979, two in–house briefings were held by American regarding the Eastburn report. Prior to this time, Eastburn had instructed his "teams" that only the team chiefs were to keep notes, that these notes were to be delivered to him, and that no copies of such notes were to be made. Eastburn testified at his deposition that he prepared his draft report, and destroyed the notes of the team chiefs. He stated that these actions were taken on the advice of house counsel for American, Richard Malahowski. Eastburn testified that, following the second briefing, he made final corrections and sent the sole copy of the report to Lloyd–Jones. He stated he also either sent a copy to legal counsel or informed them that the sole copy had gone to Lloyd–Jones. Eastburn had earlier testified that he had notified Lloyd–Jones of his instructions from Malahowski, and had been advised to follow those instructions.

Lloyd–Jones testified at his second deposition in March, 1981, that he had "discarded" the Eastburn report. He stated that he compared the Eastburn report with the Maintenance and Engineering Action Plant (M & E plan) prepared by Schaefer of American. He was satisfied that the matters discussed in the Eastburn report were covered by the M & E plan. He testified he therefore wrote "superseded" on the Eastburn report, and threw it in his wastebasket. Lloyd–Jones testified that he earlier either gave the report to Schaefer or had caused Schaefer to receive a copy of the report so that he could include it in the M & E plan.

Schaefer testified that after the second briefing, he asked Eastburn for a copy of the report to compare it with his M & E plan, then in draft form. He testified Eastburn gave him the draft, but instructed him to make no copies, and to return the draft to Eastburn when he was through. Schaefer testified that he made four copies, showed the report to certain members of his staff, and compared it with his M & E plan. Schaefer did not testify that either Eastburn or Lloyd–Jones, or any other American employee requested that he make the comparison.

Eastburn, moreover, could not recall the number of pages in his report. He testified that it was more than ten but less than fifty.

Lloyd–Jones testified that it was twenty pages long. Schafer testified it was between twenty–five and fifty pages. When questioned regarding the contents of the M & E plan, Schaefer stated it was difficult to determine which elements came from the Eastburn materials, reports prepared by NTSB, FAA and others, or which were generated by his own personnel. Eastburn similarly could not recall what specific areas were reviewed in formulating Schaefer's recommendations. On many items, Eastburn could not recall whether the matter was discussed in his report or not. Lloyd–Jones, during his March, 1981, deposition, also experienced difficulty in remembering more than whether or not an item might have been in the report. On some items, Eastburn's testimony and that of Lloyd–Jones varied on whether or not certain items were discussed: Items 8 & 9, development of standard training requirements, (Eastburn, yes, Lloyd–Jones no); Item 13, reorganizing the general technical manual (Eastburn, yes, Lloyd–Jones, no); Item 25, procedures for prototype requirements on Fleet Campaign Directives (Eastburn yes, Lloyd–Jones no); Items 37, 42, 43, 44, ground equipment fueling procedures, maintenance training, technical support, preventative maintenance on jacks, (Eastburn yes, Lloyd–Jones no). On others, neither Lloyd–Jones nor Eastburn could recall whether the item was in the Eastburn report: Item 21, revising work card development; Item 22, revising maintenance work release procedure; Item 29, release of MWR to FAA; Items 34, 35, 36, updating reliability document, developing improved pilot report of discrepancies system. In any case, it is clear that neither Lloyd–Jones nor Eastburn apparently could give any useful description of the items covered in the Eastburn report, the manner in which they were covered, the reports by the team members or the operations or offices they examined.

American's contention that the contents of the Eastburn report are known and need not be a matter of speculation is clearly incorrect. The American employees most responsible for the report could not agree even on the *number of pages* in that report much less its content.

Rule 37(a)

Production of documents upon request is governed by Rule 34 of the Federal Rules of Civil Procedure, F.R.C.P. 34. That rule provides in part: "If objection is made to part of an item or category, the part shall be specified." The party submitting the request may move for an order under Rule 37(a) with respect to any object to or *other failure to respond to the request . . . "* F.R.C.P. 34(b). Rule 37(a) provides, in part: "A party . . . may apply for an order compelling discovery." Rule 37(a)(4) provides that upon granting of the motion, the court shall require the party whose conduct necessitated the motion or the attorney to pay the reasonable expenses incurred in obtaining the order including fees unless the refusal was substantially justified. The costs and fees which are to be awarded on this motion include costs for 12(d) or other conferences, preparation of motions and court time. *Aerway Laboratories v. Arco Polymers, Inc.,* 80 C 2327 (N.D.ILL. filed May 28, 1981) (Shadur, J.); *Persson v. Faestel Investments, Inc.,* 88 F.R.D. 668 (N.D.Ill. 1980) (Shadur, J.); *See also* Schaefer, *Sanctions under Rule 37(a); The Old Order Changeth,* 62 Chi.B.Rec. 168 (Jan.–Feb., 1981).

In this action, American's objection to plaintiff's request for production of documents were not substantially justified. The first set of objections, post–accident remedial measures, was clearly incorrect. The privileged documents are, to a large extent, clearly not privileged. It appears therefore, that costs and fees associated with the motions to compel, including 12(d) conferences, should be awarded to plaintiffs.

Additionally, American's failure to produce the documents *in camera* after the September 28, 1980, direction and the October 8, 1980, order was a clear failure to respond. Therefore, it appears that costs and fees regarding the "privilege" objections, including 12(d) conferences and court appearances should be awarded to plaintiffs.

Additionally, American's failure to produce the Eastburn report due to its undisclosed

destruction of that report was also a "failure to respond" within the context of Rule 34(b).

Rule 37(b)

On September 28, 1980, the court overruled American's objections to production of documents. On April 20, 1980, American had told the court that other than those objections, all requested documents had been produced. Not until March, 1981, did it become clear to the court that the Eastburn report, and all copies, drafts and notes of that report, had been destroyed by American. During the intervening months, plaintiffs and McDonnell Douglas noticed and attended depositions of American employees. Rule 37(b) provides that upon failure to comply with an order of court relating to discovery, the court *shall require the party "failing to obey the order or the attorney advising him or both to pay the reasonable expenses, including attorney's fees, caused by the failure,* unless the court finds the failure to obey *substantially justified.*

Like Rule 37(a) Section b requires that costs be assessed unless the failure to obey the order was *substantially justified.* Contrary to American's assertions, there have been at least two failures to obey orders of court. First, American failed to obey the October 8, 1980, order to submit the "privileged" documents *in camera* until after another court order in November, 1980. The fact that the court permitted the filing at that time does not relieve American from assessment of costs and fees for the failure to obey the first direction. Similarly, the fact that the first order did not specify a date by which the documents must be submitted is irrelevant. Court orders are effective when entered. American was ordered to submit the documents as of October 8, 1980. Plaintiffs are entitled to costs and fees, if any, incurred as a result of the failure to obey the first direction to submit the documents.

Second, and more seriously, American ignored the court order directing that the answers to the request for production be filed within a certain time, ignored the order compelling production and overruling objections in September, 1980, ignored the order in

November 6, 1980, to produce the documents to plaintiffs and to MDC. American failed to produce the Eastburn report or report its destruction until depositions of American employees completely revealed that destruction. American failed to advise the court that the document had been destroyed on the *advice of American's counsel.*

American's sole defense to these repeated refusals to reveal the existence and destruction of the Eastburn report is that destruction was complete by the time discovery was commenced. American's sole defense to the charge that they violated the Circuit Court preservation order and their preservation stipulation in this court is their self–serving assertion that the document was not subject to the preservation order or stipulation.

The parties expend much time and effort in discussing the "adverse inference" rule, and its application to the presumptions of the contents of the report. Plaintiffs contend that application of this rule, and other evidence, indicate that the Eastburn report showed that American knew of the crack in engine N110 prior to the accident. American refutes this suggestion with the assertion that the contents of the report are known, that the other evidence is contradicted by deposition testimony, and that the "adverse inference" rule does not require or support the contention of American's prior knowledge, or that such information was contained in the Eastburn report. Both plaintiffs and American miss the point. This is not a trial on liability, and the court is not required to find whether or not American knew of the crack. The purpose of this motion is to determine what, if any, costs and fees were caused by American's conduct.

The "adverse inference" rule does not apply to this motion, however. That rule basically holds that upon a party's willful failure to produce evidence, there is a presumption that the evidence would have been unfavorable to that party. American has not produced the Eastburn report. Its inability to do so is self–inflicted. It cannot be determined with mathematical certainty which depositions, motions, or court appearances would have been avoided had American produced the

report as requested in April, 1980. The proper "adverse inference" is that to the extent that depositions, court appearances, or motions may or were related to the apparent subject matter of the Eastburn report, i.e., the probable causes of the accident and recommendations for future procedures to avoid further similar accidents and to the extent that American cannot produce competent evidence to the contrary, American must reimburse plaintiffs for costs and fees related to all depositions, court appearances, or motions dealing with the Eastburn report or which might have been unnecessary had the Eastburn report not been destroyed.

* * * * *

Aaron K. AKIONA; Adam Baker; Bonnie Baker; Edward W. Moore, III v. UNITED STATES of America; Secretary of Defense

938 F.2d 158

United States Court of Appeals, Ninth Circuit
July 9, 1991

On June 1, 1985, Dennis Keliinui Kaululaau threw a hand grenade in the parking lot of a restaurant in Honolulu. The grenade exploded and injured plaintiffs Aaron Akiona, Adam Baker, and Edward Moore, who were nearby. Kaululaau was convicted of attempted murder and is currently in prison.

Investigation showed that the grenade had been part of one of two lots of grenades manufactured for the United States government. One lot, consisting of 30,000 grenades was shipped to Iowa. The other lot was shipped to Japan (700 grenades), Germany (12,557 grenades), and Hawaii (11,450 grenades). These shipments took place between 1967 and 1969.

The government has no record of what happened to the grenades after these shipments. It has a policy of destroying records pertaining to grenades two years after the grenades are disposed of. Kaululaau maintains his innocence, so he has provided no information about how he got the grenade. The parties stipulated, however, that he had the grenade unlawfully without the knowledge or consent of the government.

Akiona, Baker, and Moore, along with Baker's wife, Bonnie, filed suit under the Federal Tort Claims Act against the United States, alleging that the government was negligent in letting the grenade fall into Kaululaau's hands. The district court held a nonjury trial based on stipulated facts and stipulated testimony. It concluded that the government owed a duty to the plaintiffs to safeguard its grenades, and it found, despite any direct evidence of negligence that the government has been negligent in failing to keep the grenade out of unauthorized hands and awarded damages to the plaintiffs. *Akiona v. United States*, 732 F.Supp. 1064 (D.Haw.1990). The district court reached its decision by applying *res ipsa loquitur* to infer that the injuries would not have happened if the government had not been negligent in maintaining the grenade and by shifting the burden of proof to the government based on its destruction of records.

The government appeals, challenging the finding of liability, and the plaintiffs cross–appeal, challenging the sufficiency of the damages awarded.

* * * * *

In order for *res ipsa loquitur* to apply in this case, the plaintiffs must first prove that the government had exclusive control and management of the grenade at the time of the negligence. *Jenkins v. Whittaker Corp.*, 785 F.2d 720, 730 (9th Cir.) (applying Hawaii law), *cert. denied*, 479 U.S. 918, 107 S.Ct. 324, 93 L.Ed.2d 296 (1986). The plaintiffs therefore must show that the government had exclusive control over the grenade at the time it was allowed to get into unauthorized hands.

The evidence establishes that the grenade was initially in the possession of the government because it was stipulated that the grenade was manufactured for and delivered to the government. However, the plaintiffs have presented no evidence that the grenade stayed in the possession of the government.

The government's expert witness testified that, to the contrary, the grenade could have been transferred to another country or used in Vietnam. Indeed, a significant number of grenades in the relevant lots were shipped out of the country. Even if this grenade had gone to Hawaii, almost twenty years passed between the time when it was clear that the government possessed the grenade and the time when the grenade was used to harm the plaintiffs. During that period, it could have been used or transferred to others, removing it from the control of the government without any negligence. With this much uncertainty, it was error to find that the government had exclusive control over the grenade, and the district court therefore erred in applying *res ipsa loquitur*.

The government also argues that the second prong of the *res ipsa loquitur* test is not satisfied because the occurrence is not of the sort that ordinarily does not happen without someone's negligence. We need not reach that issue because, without a showing of exclusive control, *res ipsa loquitur* does not apply.

The district court also facilitated its finding of liability by shifting the burden of proof to the government because of the government's destruction of records pertaining to the grenade. Generally, a trier of fact may draw an adverse inference from the destruction of evidence relevant to a case. *Welsh v. United States*, 844 F.2d 1239, 1246 (6th Cir.1988).

The adverse inference is based on two rationales, one evidentiary and one not. The evidentiary rationale is nothing more than the common sense observation that a party who has notice that a document is relevant to litigation and who proceeds to destroy the document is more likely to have been threatened by the document than a party in the same position who does not destroy the document . . .

The other rationale for the inference has nothing to do with its prophylactic and punitive effects. Allowing the trier of fact to draw the inference presumably deters parties from destroying relevant evidence before it can be introduced at trial.

Nation–Wide Check Corp. v. Forest Hills Distribs., Inc., 692 F.2d 214, 218 (1st Cir.1982). The evidentiary rationale does not apply here. Nothing in the record indicates that the government destroyed the records pertaining to the grenade in response to this litigation. Thus, its destruction of the records does not suggest that the records would have been threatening to the defense of the case, and it is therefore not relevant in an evidentiary sense.

The deterrence rationale similarly does not apply. A party should only be penalized for destroying documents if it was wrong to do so, and that requires, at a minimum, some notice that the documents are potentially relevant. *See id.* at 218 ("The inference depends, of course, on a showing that the party had notice that the documents were relevant . . ."); *id.* at 219 (indicating that this "minimum link of relevance" is required before deterrence rationale would justify shifting burden of proof); *see also Vick v. Texas Employment Comm'n*, 514 F.2d 734, 737 (5th Cir. 1975) (requiring showing of bad faith). Here, the plaintiffs have not shown any bad faith in the destruction of the records, nor even that the government was on notice that the records had potential relevance to litigation. Nothing in the record indicates that the government destroyed the grenade records with the intent of covering up information.

Indeed, the government may have destroyed the records pursuant to its policy of destroying documents regarding grenades two years after their disposition. Unlike *Welsh,* 844 F.2d 1239, in which the destruction of medical evidence clearly violated a hospital policy, the destruction of the records in this case could have been entirely consistent with the government's document retention policies. If the government had disposed of the grenade (for example, by transferring it to another country), it would not suggest any irregularity or unreasonableness to have destroyed the documents because the government would not expect to be held liable for misuse of the grenade after it left its hands. Because the government's destruction of records is neither relevant nor indicative of bad faith, the district court erred in shifting the burden of proof to the government.

We conclude that the district court erred by applying *res ipsa loquitur* and by shifting the burden of proof to the government, and we therefore reverse the district court's judgment as to liability to the extent that it relied on these principles.

* * * * *

ALLIANCE TO END REPRESSION et al. v. James ROCHFORD et al., AMERICAN CIVIL LIBERTIES UNION et al. v. CITY OF CHICAGO et al., CHICAGO LAWYERS COMMITTEE FOR CIVIL RIGHTS UNDER LAW v. CITY OF CHICAGO et al

75 F.R.D. 441

United States District Court, N.D. Illinois, E.D.
June 7, 1977

Defendants' Objections To Discovery

Pursuant to Paragraph 7 of Pretrial Order Number 6, defendants are required to file memoranda in support of objections to discovery requests. Federal defendants object to plaintiffs' first set of document requests on the grounds that: (1) certain information in the files of named plaintiffs is not relevant to the named plaintiff who is the subject of the file; (2) certain information is not relevant to issues raised in the Complaint; (3) certain information is privileged from disclosure for the protection of confidential informants; (4) certain information is so sensitive that disclosure could jeopardize or obviate the effectiveness of F.B.I. operations in furtherance of its investigative responsibilities; (5) certain information could jeopardize an ongoing investigation; and (6) certain documents are internal memoranda containing suggestions or recommendations rather than factual material. This court considers defendants' relevancy objections first, then each of the defendants' other arguments.

* * * * *

C. Defendants' Claim of Undue Burden

Defendants finally object to certain discovery on the grounds that production of such information would be unduly burdensome. This motion primarily seeks to withhold from discovery materials which would be difficult to produce because these materials are not stored in any organized filing system. Defendants' objection is totally without merit. This court agrees with the reasoning of the district court in *Kozlowski v. Sears, Roebuck and Company*, 73 F.R.D. 73 (1976):

> To allow a defendant whose business generates massive records to frustrate discovery by creating an inadequate filing system, and then claiming undue burden, would defeat the purposes of discovery rules. (*Id.* at 76.)

Accordingly, Federal defendants' objection to discovery on grounds of undue burden is overruled.

AMERICAN BLUE STONE CO. v. COHN CUT STONE CO.

164 N.Y.S. 506

Supreme Court, Special Term, Erie County
January 1917

Action by the American Blue Stone Company against the Cohn Cut Stone Company. On motion to punish defendant company and Joseph M. Cohn, its secretary, for contempt in failing to produce books and papers, and Joseph M. Cohn for refusing to sign his deposition after it had been made. Defendant Cohn adjudged guilty of contempt of court, and fined not exceeding the amount of the complainant's costs and expenses, and to stand committed until such costs, expenses, and fine are paid, and defendant Cohn Cut Stone Company adjudged guilty of contempt, and fined $250, and its answer stricken, and complainant allowed to proceeds as upon a default.

This action was brought to recover upon a guaranty of the payment of a bond and mort-

gage caused to be transferred by the defendant to plaintiff to apply upon an indebtedness for stone sold to the defendant.

The complaint alleges that the guaranty was executed by the defendant December 10, 1908, under its corporate seal, and signed by Joseph M. Cohn, president, guaranteeing "the payment of the full amount of the principal and interest of said bond and mortgage at the time and in the manner provided in and by said bond and mortgage," that the bond and mortgage became due in 1911, and that no part has been paid, except one year's interest. The defendant by its amended answer puts in issue every allegation of the complaint and interposes several defenses, one of which is "that the alleged agreement of guaranty purported to have been made and executed by the defendant, as described * * * in the complaint, was not executed with the consent of or by the defendant or by any officer thereof duly authorized and empowered to execute or deliver the same," and that the act was ultra vires. The plaintiff, in preparing to establish its cause of action, served upon the defendant and upon said Joseph M. Cohn, admitted to be its secretary, an order for examination before trial and for the production upon such examinations of —

"any and all books kept by the secretary of said defendant in the years 1907, 1908, and 1909; all books kept by the defendant or its secretary during those years, showing the election of directors and officers of said corporation defendant; the stock books or books of said corporation, showing the amount of stock issued by said corporation and the names of the stockholders therein in the years 1907, 1908, and 1909; the books of account of the defendant, showing its account with the plaintiff in the years 1908 and 1909; all letters written by defendant to plaintiff, and from plaintiff to defendant, in the years 1908, 1909, and 1910, concerning the bond and mortgage, or either of them, described in the complaint herein, and in the possession of defendant; and all letterpress or other copies kept by defendant, and in its possession, of all letters so written by defendant to plaintiff."

A perusal of the record of the proceedings before the referee pursuant to the order discloses a course of conduct on the part of Joseph M. Cohn, representing the defendant, which must be characterized as evasive, disingenuous, and contemptuous, plainly indicating the intention of an unscrupulous mind, guided by a shrewd attorney, to defeat and evade the purpose and object of the order made by the court pursuant to the provisions of the statute providing for an examination before trial, and having the effect to defeat, impede, impair, and prejudice the rights and remedies of the plaintiff. The defendant failed to produce a single one of the books and papers it was ordered to produce, and Joseph M. Cohn, its secretary, gave an explanation of the failure to do so that is wholly unsatisfactory and is unbelievable. He also refused to subscribe the deposition he had already made, unless certain answers to material questions which gave some useful information to the plaintiff were stricken out, on the ground that these answers might tend to incriminate him.

It appears from the records that the defendant company was organized in October, 1907; that the original stockholders were said Joseph M. Cohn, Minnie B. Cohn, his wife, and one Joseph Jervitz. Asked if he was its first president, he answered, "I don't remember, unless I have something to refresh my memory." The original guaranty, a copy of which is set forth in the complaint, was then shown to the witness, and he was asked if the signature thereto was his.

"A. I believe it is; yes. Q. And the words 'Cohn Cut Stone Company, Joseph M. Cohn, President,' are in your handwriting? A. I think so. Q. Now, that you wrote in the 10th of December, 1908, didn't you? A. I think so; yes. Q. And at that time you were the president of this company, were you not? A. I cannot answer that without consulting my attorney. Q. You know, at the time that you signed your name as president, whether you were the president of the company, don't you? A. I will not answer, unless I consult my attorney."

The record proceeds:

"Witness has consulted his attorney, Mr. Spigelgass, and his attorney advises him that he may decline to answer on the ground that it might tend to incriminate him. A. I refuse to answer the question upon the ground stated by my counsel."

Throughout the examination he professes not to be able to remember much of anything without referring to the books; that he could not remember who the stockholders of the company were without the books; that he could not remember when he was president; and, being shown certain letters, he testified that he could not remember writing them, and could not tell whether they were written from the defendant's office. He testified that they kept carbon copies of letter, and, being asked if the defendant company received letters from the plaintiff in the fall of 1908, he answered that he presumed they did, and when asked where those letters were his first answer was:

"Destroyed in the fire. Q. You say they were destroyed? A. I believe they were. Q. Can you swear to that? A. No; I cannot swear to that. They are not in the office. Q. Did you look anywhere else? A. No."

And in reply to his own counsel he testified:

"Q. Did you have those letters at the time of the fire? A. Yes. Q. Copies of the letters sent by you? A. Yes. Q. Are those the letters that might possibly have been destroyed in the fire? A. They are."

He testified that he could not say, without seeing the books, whether the defendant charged up to the plaintiff anything on account of the guaranteed mortgage which was turned over to the plaintiff in payment for stone sold to the defendant. As one time he testified that the office was destroyed by fire, but that the contents of the safe, which did not include the books and papers ordered to be produced, were not destroyed. and that he did not know whether these books and papers were burned, but they might have been, and, further, that he did not know whether the insurance company took them. It is incredible that all of the books of account, the stockbook, the secretary's book, the stock certificate book, and all the letters and copies of letters of this company should be destroyed by fire or otherwise lost, and that Joseph M. Cohn, who had been its president, and closely interested in its affairs from the time of its incorporation, and who is at the present time its secretary, and has had charge of the company's office, should not know whether these books and papers were burned or destroyed or where they are. He evades the direct question, and places himself in a position where he could afterwards produce the books, if he desired to do so.

Throughout the examination there is evident a persistent attempt to evade answers to material and proper questions, and while at the beginning some important information was elicited from the witness without any claim of immunity on his part, after the stenographer's minutes had been written out, and it could be seen that there was some evidence adduced which would be material for the use of the plaintiff, the witness refused to subscribe the deposition, unless the material questions and answers were stricken out, and the plaintiff thus deprived of practically all of the benefits derived from the examination.

* * * * *

Joseph M. Cohn is adjudged guilty of contempt of court, and a fine is imposed upon him, not exceeding the amount of complainant's costs and expenses, the amount to be determined upon settlement of the order; he to stand committed until such costs and expenses and fines are paid.

The defendant Cohn Cut Stone Company is also adjudged guilty of contempt of court, and so fined the sum of $250, and in addition thereto, because of its failure to produce, when ordered to do so, the books and papers containing material evidence for the plaintiff, the answer of the defendant will be stricken out, and the plaintiff may proceed as upon a default in pleading, with $10 costs of this motion. *Edison Electric Light Co. v. Tipless Lamp Co.*, 72 Misc. Rep. 116, 130 N.Y.Supp. 1089.

Ordered accordingly.

Frank ARGUETA and Barton KOHL, Plaintiffs–Appellees, v. BALTIMORE & OHIO CHICAGO TERMINAL RAILROAD COMPANY, Defendant–Appellant, and PARSEC, INC., and TRANSPERSONNEL, INC., Defendants/Third–Party Plaintiffs–Appellees, Separate Appellants, v. PACECO, INC., Third–Party Defendants, Separate Appellee.

586 N.E.2d 386

Appellate Court of Illinois, First District,
Fourth Division
December 19, 1991

The plaintiffs, Frank Argueta and Barton Kohl, employed as carmen by the Baltimore & Ohio Chicago Terminal Railroad (B&OCT), were injured on the job while riding in the cab of a gantry crane when a spindle pin attaching one of the crane's wheels fractured, causing the wheel to snap off and the crane to collapse.

The plaintiffs brought an action against B&OCT under the Federal Employers' Liability Act (FELA) *(45 U.S.C. § 51 et seq.)* alleging that B&OCT failed to provide a safe work place. The plaintiffs also sued Parsec, Inc., whose employee was operating the crane at the time of the accident.

The plaintiffs settled with Calumet Machine, Inc. the manufacturer of the spindle pin, before trial. The plaintiffs also sued Transpersonnel, Inc., who supplied crane operators to Parsec, Inc. Transpersonnel was granted a directed verdict after a finding that Transpersonnel had no control of the crane operators once they were employed by Parsec.

B&OCT filed a cross–complaint against Parsec, Inc., for contribution and contractual indemnity. Parsec, Inc., filed a third–party action under the Contribution Among Joint Tortfeasors Act (Ill. Rev. Stat. 1985, ch. 70, par. 301 et seq.) against Paceco, Inc., the manufacturer of the crane.

The jury found that B&OCT and Parsec were both negligent and awarded $269,591.38 to Kohl and $1,986,246.59 to Argueta. During jury deliberation, but before the jury returned its verdict, Parsec settled with both plaintiffs for $150,000. After the verdict, the court entered judgment solely against B&OCT and denied B&OCT's motion to enter judgment against Parsec pursuant to the contractual indemnity agreement.

After all of the evidence had been presented, the court severed the closing arguments and jury deliberation in the third–party action from the main action. Accordingly, the jury returned a separate verdict and found Paceco not liable to Parsec for contribution.

* * * * *

II. Evidentiary Issues

B&OCT further contends that the trial court erred in refusing several pieces of proffered evidence. The first challenge pertains to ultrasonic test reports of the spindle pins. Prior to the accident, Calumet Testing Services, Inc. and Conam Inspection performed the tests at the request of B&OCT as a part of B&OCT's routine testing of the spindle pins. Calumet and Conam recorded their findings and submitted the reports to B&OCT. The trial court refused to admit the reports under the business record exception to the hearsay rule, reasoning that the reports were generated by the third parties, Calumet Testing Services, Inc., and Conam, and therefore, were not B&OCT's business records.

B&OCT argues that the failure of the trial court to admit the reports into evidence allowed the jury to assume that B&OCT was negligent in failing to test the spindle pins and prevented B&OCT from defending its action on the basis that it took reasonable steps to provide a safe place to work.

Supreme Court Rule 236 provides for the admission of business records "made in the regular course of any business" as an exception to the hearsay rule. (Ill. Rev. Stat. 1985, ch. 110A, par. 236(a).) At issue is under what circumstances does a document,

produced by a third party, become a business record of the party seeking to introduce it.

A number of Illinois cases have held that documents produced by third parties were inadmissible as business records. In each of these cases, the documents were not commissioned by the business seeking to introduce them into evidence, albeit the documents were retained in the business files. *International Harvester Credit Corp., v. Helland (1986), 151 Ill. App. 3d 848, 503 N.E.2d 548)* (minutes of board of director's meeting of a company were not the business records of a second company); *Pell v. Victor J. Andrew High School (1984), 124 Ill. App. 3d 423, 462 N.E.2d 858)* (letter from a manufacturer was not the business record of a second manufacturer); *Benford v. Chicago Transit Authority (1973), 9 Ill. App. 3d 294 N.E.2d 496)* (a note made by employee's private physician was not the business record of employer).

By contrast, a business report generated by a third party has been held to be admissible when it was commissioned in the regular course of business of the party seeking to introduce it. *Birch v. Township of Drummer (1985), 139 Ill. App. 3d 397, 487 N.E.2d 798 (survey of an engineering firm commissioned by county admissible as business record of the county).*

The key consideration is the authority of the third party to act on the business' behalf. Where a third party is authorized by a business to generate the record at issue, the record is of no use to the business unless it is accurate and, therefore, the record bears sufficient indicia of reliability to qualify as a business record under the hearsay rule. See also *N.L.R.B. v. First Termite Control Co., Inc., (9th Cir. 1981), 646 F.2d 424*; Fed. R. Evid. 803(6); M. Graham, Cleary & Graham's Handbook of Illinois Evidence § 803.10, at 647 (5th ed. 1990).

Accordingly, we find that the trial court erred in its ruling that the ultrasonic test reports were inadmissible. The reports were the business records of B&OCT. Although the reports were generated by Calumet & Conam, the tests were performed at the direction of the railroad in the regular course of its business.

However, we believe that the failure to admit the ultrasonic testing reports was harmless error. The jury heard sufficient other testimony that the spindle pins were regularly tested at the direction of the railroad. B&OCT's assistant foreman testified to the frequent inspection of the cranes and spindle pins. The railroad's mechanical superintendent testified that the pins were ultrasonically tested at three–month intervals. Thus, the ultrasonic testing reports would have merely been cumulative evidence on the issue of B&OCT's negligence.

* * * * *

ARMSTRONG, et al. v. EXECUTIVE OFFICE OF THE PRESIDENT

1 F.3d 127

United States Court of Appeals, District of
Columbia Circuit
August 13, 1993

Before MIKVA, Chief Judge; WALD and HENDERSON, Circuit Judges.

Opinion for the Court filed Per Curiam.

PER CURIAM: This consolidated appeal presents us with important questions of federal agencies' statutory obligations to manage electronic questions of federal agencies' statutory obligations to manage electronic records as well as issues related to the appropriate use of the civil contempt power to coerce conformity with district court orders.

In the flagship portion of the appeal, defendants–appellants — the Executive Office of the President ("EOP"), the Office of Administration, the National Security Council ("NSC"), the White House Communications Agency, and Trudy Peterson, Acting Archivist of the United States — challenge the district court's conclusion that EOP and NSC guidelines for managing electronic documents do not comport with Federal Records

Act ("FRA" or the "Act") requirements. More specifically, these government agencies and officials contend that, contrary to the court's ruling, they have, in the past, reasonably discharged their FRA obligations by instructing employees to print out a paper version of any electronic communications that falls within the statutory definition of a "record" by managing the "hard–copy" documents so produced in accordance with the Act. We reject the government's argument on this score. The government's basic position is flawed because the hard–copy print–outs that the agencies preserve may omit fundamental pieces of information which are an integral part of the original electronic records, such as the identity of the sender and/or recipient and the time of receipt.

The defendants also appeal the district court's order holding them in civil contempt of its prior order enjoining the Archivist to "take all necessary steps" to preserve federal records and requiring the defendant agencies not to remove, alter, or delete any information until the Archivist takes action to prevent the destruction of federal records. More specifically, they contest that (1) the defendant agencies failed to issue adequate record-keeping instructions to employees in the four months after their former guidelines were held invalid and (2) the transfer of nearly 6,000 backup tapes to the Archivist "adversely affected" those tapes. Because the district court orders on which the contempt citation rests did not specify that the defendants had an affirmative duty to create new guidelines by a certain date, the district court abused its discretion in holding the defendants in contempt at least in part because of their failure to issue such guidelines within four months. We remand to allow the district court to determine whether, in light of the tapes, its second ground, the failure to preserve these tapes, by itself, justifies a contempt citation.

Finally, we are presented with a cross–appeal. The plaintiffs–cross–appellants — Scott Armstrong, the National Security Archive, and several other researchers and nonprofit organizations — take issue with the district court's conclusion that federal courts have no authority to review NSC and Office of Science and Technology Policy ("OSTP") guidelines differentiating federal records subject to the FRA from presidential records subject to the President Records Act ("PRA"), 44 U.S.C. s 2201 et. seq. Contrary to the district court, we conclude that the PRA allows limited review to assure that guidelines defining presidential records do not improperly sweep in nonpresidential records. Accordingly, we remand to the district court to determine whether the relevant NSC and OSTP directives categorize non-presidential records as subject to the PRA.

I. Background

A. Statutory Framework

Federal agencies' records creation, management, and disposal duties are set out in a collection of statutes known collectively as the Federal Records Act. See 44 U.S.C. ss 2101 et seq., 2901 et seq., 3101 et seq., 3301 et seq. The FRA, Congress informs, is intended to assure, among other things, "[a]ccurate and complete documentation of the policies and transactions of the Federal Government," "[c]ontrol of the quantity and quality of records produced by the Federal Government," and "[j]udicious preservation and disposal of records." 44 U.S.C. s 2902(1), (2), (5); see also *Armstrong v. Bush*, 924 F.2d 282, 292 (D.C.Cir.1991) ("Armstrong I") (the FRA is intended to guarantee that agencies' records management programs "strike a balance 'between developing efficient and effective records management, and the substantive need for Federal records'") (quoting S. REP. NO. 1326, 94th Cong., 2d Sess. 2 (1976)). To achieve those ends, the FRA burdens the heads of federal agencies with several obligations. Most basically, each agency head must "make and preserve records containing adequate and proper documentation of the organization, functions, policies, decisions, procedures and essential transactions of the agency and designed to furnish the information necessary to protect the legal and financial rights of the Government and of persons directly affected by the agency's activities." 44 U.S.C. s 3101. Moreover, under the Act,

agency chiefs must also "establish and maintain an active, continuing program for . . . economical and efficient [records] management," id. s 3102, and "establish safeguards against the removal or loss of records [the agency head] determines to be necessary and required by regulations of the Archivist." Id. s 3105; see also Armstrong I, 924 F.2d at 293 (noting that these provisions, as well as others furnished "law to apply" under the Administrative Procedure Act ("APA"), see 5 U.S.C. s 701(a)(2), and thus permitted judicial review of agency recordkeeping guidelines' conformity with the FRA).

Besides assigning specific duties to agency heads, the FRA prescribes the exclusive mechanism for disposal of federal records. See 44 U.S.C. s 3314 (no records may be "alienated or destroyed" except in accordance with the FRA's provisions). For these purposes, "records" are defined as

all books, papers, maps, photographs, machine readable [i.e., electronic] materials, or other documentary materials, regardless of physical form or characteristics, made or received by an agency of the United States Government under Federal law or in connection with the transaction or public business and preserved or appropriate for preservation by that agency . . . as evidence of the organization, functions, policies, decisions, procedures, operations, or other activities of the Government or because of the informational value of data in them. Library and museum material made or acquired and preserved solely for reference or exhibition purposes, extra copies of documents preserved only for convenience of reference, and stocks of publications and of processed documents are not included.

Id. s 3301. If a document qualifies as a record, the FRA prohibits an agency from discarding it by fiat. See *American Friends Service Committee v. Webster*, 720 F.2d 29 62 (D.C.Cir.1983) ("Congress did not intend to grant [the agency] . . . a blank check for records disposal."). Instead, the FRA requires the agency to procure the approval of the Archivist before disposing of any record. Cf. id. at 63.

Normally, that approval may be obtained in one of two ways. First, an agency may submit a schedule of records sought to be discarded to the Archivist, who will sign off on the records' destruction only if she concludes that they do not "have sufficient administrative, legal, research, or other value to warrant their continued preservation." 44 U.S.C. s 3303a(a). Second, the agency may jettison certain common types of records pursuant to disposal schedules promulgated in advance by the Archivist (the disposal schedules are, of course, designed to take into account the FRA's goal of preserving documents of "administrative, legal, research, or other value"). Id. s 3303a(d).

Under the FRA, the Archivist's duties are not limited to judging the suitability of records for disposal. In addition, the Archivist must provide guidance and assistance to Federal agencies with respect to ensuring adequate and proper documentation of the policies and transactions of the Federal Government and ensuring proper records disposition," id. s 2904(a), "promulgate standards, procedures, and guidelines with respect to records management," id. s 2904(c)(1), and "conduct inspections or surveys of the records and the records management programs and practices within and between Federal agencies." Id. s 2904(c)(7). The Archivist also plays a key role in the FRA's enforcement scheme. If the Archivist discovers that an FRA provision has been or is being breached, the Archivist must (1) inform the agency head of the violation and suggest corrections and (2) if ameliorative measures are not undertaken with reasonable time, submit a written report to Congress and the President. Id. s 2115(b). Also, should the Archivist become aware of any "actual, impending, or threatened unlawful removal, defacing, alteration, or destruction of records in the custody of [an] agency," she must notify the agency head of the problem and assist the agency head in initiating an action through the Attorney General for the recovery of wrongfully removed records or for other legal redress. Id. s 2905(a); see also id. s 3106 (requiring agency heads to notify the Archivist of any unlawful destruction or removal of records and placing upon them an independent duty to seek legal action

through the Attorney General to recover the records). If the agency head is recalcitrant in pursuing legal remedies, the Archivist herself is to (1) request the Attorney General to initiate action and (2) inform Congress that she has made that request. Id. s 2905(a); see also Armstrong I, 924 F.2d at 295 (holding that "if the agency head or Archivist does nothing while an agency official destroys or removes records in contravention of agency guidelines and directives, private litigants may bring suit to require the agency head and Archivist to fulfill their statutory duty to notify Congress and ask the Attorney General to initiate legal action").

B. The NSC and EOP Electronic Communications Systems

Since the mid–1980s, the NSC and the EOP have utilized electronic communications systems to improve their operational efficiency. These systems allow employees to create and share electronic appointment calendars as well as to transfer and edit word processing documents, but it is their electronic mail (or "e–mail") capacity that has racked up the most mileage. The 1,300 federal employees with access to the EOP and NSC electronic mail systems can, and apparently do, utilize them to relay lengthy substantive — even classified — "notes" that, in content, are often indistinguishable from letters or memoranda. But, in contrast to its paper cousin, e–mail can be delivered nearly instantaneously at any time of the day or week. And, in contrast to telephone conversations, e–mail automatically creates a complete record of the exact information users send and receive.

Other attributes of the EOP and NSC electronic mail systems are also relevant here. First, these systems give recipients the option of storing notes in their personal electronic "log." After receiving a message, a user may instruct the computer to delete the note; otherwise, it will be stored in her log for later use. Second, both the recipient and the author of a note can print out a "hard copy" of the electronic message containing essentially all the information displayed on the computer screen. That paper rendering will not, however, necessarily include all the information held in the computer memory as part of the electronic document. Directories, distribution lists, acknowledgments of receipts and similar materials do not appear on the computer screen — and thus are not reproduced when users print out the information that appears on the screen. Without this "non-screen" information, a later reader may not be able to glean from the hard copy such basic facts as who sent or received a particular message or when it was received. For example, if a note is sent to individuals on a distribution list already in the computer, the hard copy may well include only a generic reference to the distribution list (e.g., "List A", not the names of the individuals on the list who received the document. Consequently, if only the hard copy is preserved in such situations, essential transmittal information relevant to a fuller understanding of the context and import of an electronic communication will simply vanish. A final relevant fact here is that the individual note logs are not the only electronic repositories for information on the e-mail system. The defendant agencies periodically create backup tapes — snapshots of all the material stored on these electronic communications systems at a given time — that can be used later for retrieval purposes.

C. Procedural History

On January 19, 1989, the final day of the Reagan Presidency, the National Security Archive filed several freedom of Information Act ("FOIA"), 5 U.S.C. s 552, requests for all the material stored on the EOP and NSC electronic communications systems from their installation in the mid-1980s up to that time. Simultaneously, the plaintiffs filed this suit for a declaration that the electronic documents contained on the NSC and EOP electronic communication systems and backup tapes were federal and presidential records and an injunction prohibiting those documents' destruction. After agreeing to preserve the electronic tapes, the defendants filed a motion in the district court for dismissal or, in the alternative, for summary judgment. After that motion was denied, see *Armstrong v. Bush*, 721 F.Supp. 343

(D.D.C.1989), this court, on the interlocutory appeal, settled several threshold issues in the litigation. Specifically, we held that the plaintiffs had standing to assert these claims because they were within the zone of interests of the records management provisions of the PRA and the FRA, see Armstrong I, 924 F.2d at 287–88, but that the President was not an agency under the APA and that the PRA impliedly precluded judicial review of the President's record creation, management, and disposal decisions under that statute. See id. at 288–91. We said, however, that the plaintiffs could seek judicial review of (1) agency guidelines' conformity to the FRA and (2) the agency heads' and Archivist's discharge or removal of federal records. See id. at 291–96. We then remanded the case to allow for supplementation of the records as to the precise guidance — written and oral — that the defendant agencies had given employees. See id. at 296–97.

On remand, the parties developed an extensive record, including a Joint Statement of Facts (the "Joint Statement"), and, on January 6, 1993, the district court issued its ruling on all the FRA issues raised by the plaintiffs (the FOIA claims remain undecided). See *Armstrong v. Executive Office of the President*, 810 F.Supp. 335 (D.D.C.1993). In that ruling, the district court first addressed whether the communications stored in these electronic communications systems constituted federal records. Because the FRA's definition of "records" includes material "regardless of physical form or characteristics," the court concluded that substantive communications otherwise meeting the definition of federal "records" that had been saved on the electronic mail came within the FRS's purview. See id. at 340–41.

The court then found that the defendant's current practices for electronic records management were deficient in two key respects. First, assuming arguendo that the defendant agencies unequivocally informed their staffs to print out all on-screen information of any electronic note that qualified as a federal record (an assumption that the plaintiffs have vigorously contested throughout this litigation), that instruction was not adequate to meet the FRA's requirements because the "electronic material . . . [is] qualitatively different than a copy printed out in paper form." Id. at 341. The district court emphasized that unless employees also printed out the transmittal information stored in the computer but not appearing on screen, the hard copies preserved in the paper files would not necessarily contain all the important items retained in the electronic system. See id. ("A paper copy of the electronic material does not contain all of the information included in the electronic version."); see also Appellants' Brief at 22 ("[The defendant agencies] do not require that all information related to an electronic message be preserved, but only that information that is captured when the message screen is printed or incorporated into a written memorandum."). Specifically, data "regarding who has received the information and when the information was received" might well be omitted from the paper versions. 810 F.Supp. at 341; see also id. at 346–47 (discussing NSC guidance).

The court found a second flaw in the agencies' records management practices: they failed to provide for any supervision of agency employees' electronic recordkeeping practices. Noting that (1) the National Archives Records Management Handbook provided that only "records officers" should determine the status of FRA records and (2) the defendant agencies supervise staffers' management of paper, but not electronic records, the court concluded that the defendants' failure to supervise employees' electronic recordkeeping was arbitrary and capricious. See id. at 343; see also id. at 347 (discussing NSC guidance).

Finally, the district court refused to adjudicate plaintiffs' claim that the NSC guidelines did not adequately distinguish between federal and presidential records. The court found that our holding in Armstrong I precluded judicial review of any guideline affecting the status of a presidential record. See id. at 347–48.

To implement its decision, the district court issued a multi–part declaratory and injunctive order. The order, as amended, first de-

clared that the defendant agencies' current guidelines were arbitrary and capricious and contrary to law. See Amended Order, *Armstrong v. Executive Office of the President*, No. 89–142 (D.D.C. Jan. 11, 1993). Second, it enjoined the Archivist to "seek the assistance of the Attorney General with notice to Congress, and take all necessary steps to preserve, without erasure, all electronic Federal Records generated at the defendant Agencies." Id. Finally, it enjoined all the defendants "from removing, deleting, or altering information on their electronic communications systems until such time as the Archivist takes action . . . to prevent the destruction of federal records, including those records saved on backup tapes." Id. In response to an emergency motion by the defendants, this court stayed this last requirement to the extent of allowing the agencies to "remove, delete, or alter" information so long as it was preserved elsewhere in identical form. See *Armstrong v. Executive Office of the President*, No. 93–5002 (D.D.Cir. Jan. 15, 1993).

On May 21, 1993, on petition of the plaintiffs, the district court found the defendants in civil contempt. See *Armstrong v. Executive Office of the President*, No. 89–142 (D.D.C. May 21, 1993). First, it found that interim guidance issued by the defendants in the wake of the court's invalidation of their old guidelines was inadequate. Accordingly, the court reasoned, the defendants were in contempt for not substantially complying with its orders requiring the agencies to preserve all records. See id., slip opinion ("slip op.") at 5–13. Second, the court held that the conditions surrounding the January 19, 1993, inauguration–eve transfer of backup tapes from the White House to the National Archives, as well as the Archivist's subsequent failure to recopy Reagan–era backup tapes nearing the end of their natural lifespan, violated the court's order requiring preservation of the tapes. This treatment of the backup tapes, including the failure to recopy deteriorating tapes, thus furnished an additional basis for the contempt citation. See id. at 17–21. The court then set out a list of specific acts that the defendants were required to undertake by June 21, 1993 to purge themselves of contempt; if the defendants failed to accomplish them, fines of $50,000 a day would be doubled in subsequent weeks, would be imposed until the defendants cleansed themselves of their contempt. See Order, *Armstrong v. Executive Office of the President*, No. 89–142 (D.D.C. May 21, 1993).

Following oral argument on June 15, 1993, this court stayed the district court's contempt sanctions pending the outcome of this appeal. See *Armstrong v. Executive Office of the President*, No. 93–5002, et al. (D.C.Cir. June 15, 1993).

The Validity of Current NSC and EOP Guidelines

A. The Instruction to Print "Hard–Copy" Paper Versions

We first address appellants' contention that the district court erred in finding that their pre–January–order instruction to print on-screen information from electronic federal records was inconsistent with the FRA. This question implicates two parts of this case. First, if the agencies' policy of printing on-screen information did not result in "papering" all federal records material, then at least some federal records will be permanently lost or destroyed unless the electronic backup records, currently being retained pursuant to the district court's orders, are preserved. This circumstance alone creates the predicate for an order requiring the Archivist and the relevant agency heads to take the statutorily prescribed steps to prevent the destruction of those tapes. Second, if this "print screen" policy — which was still in effect at the time the district court ruled in January — is inadequate under the FRA, then the district court appropriately issued a declaratory judgment invalidating its future use.

In proceeding to the decision on this point, we adopt the district courts' assumption, based on the appellants' submissions, that both the EOP and the NSC have consistently instructed employees, either orally or in writing, that when any electronic document meets the definition of a federal record, the employee should either print out the information that appears on her computer screen

or incorporate that material into a written memorandum. See Appellants' Brief at 7–8; see also id. at 22 ("[The agencies] do not require that all information related to an electronic message be preserved, but only that information that is captured when the message screen is printed or incorporated into a written memorandum.").

Accepting appellants' factual predicate, however, does not lead us to their legal conclusion that such an approach satisfied the Act. Our analysis is a straightforward one. We begin with the apparently undisputed proposition that the EOP and NSC electronic communications systems can create, and have created, documents that constitute federal records under the FRA. The FRA contemplates that documents qualifying as records may be stripped of that status only if they are "extra copies of documents preserved only for convenience of reference." 44 U.S.C. s 3301. Applied to this case, that means that the mere existence of the paper print–outs does not affect the record status of the electronic materials unless the paper versions include all significant material contained in the electronic records. Otherwise, the two documents cannot accurately be termed "copies" — identical twins — but are, at most, "kissing cousins." Since the record shows that the two versions of the documents may frequently be only cousins — perhaps distant ones at that — the electronic documents retain their status as federal records after the creation of the paper print–outs, and all of the FRA obligations concerning the management and preservation of records still apply. See, e.g., id. s 3105 (requiring agency heads to "establish safeguards against the removal or loss" of "records"); id. s 3314 (stating that "records" may only be "alienated or destroyed" in accordance with FRA provisions, i.e., with the approval of the Archivist).

To qualify as a record under the FRA, a document must satisfy a two–pronged test. It must be (1) "made or received by an agency of the United States Government under Federal law or in connection with the transaction of public business" and (2) "preserved or appropriate for preservation by that agency . . . as evidence of the organization, functions, policies, decisions, procedures, operations, or other activities of the Government or because of the informational value of data in [it]." Id. s 3301. The appellants do not contest the fact that many, if not all, of the communications relayed over the electronic system satisfy the "public transaction" element of this test. At oral argument, the government appeared to acknowledge that the "preserved or appropriate for preservation" criterion was satisfied as well for some documents on the system.

To the extent that any question remains, we reject the appellants' argument, on brief, that agency head have sweeping discretion to decide which documents are "appropriate for preservation" (since we reject this contention, we do not consider whether the disputed documents have also been "preserved"). The appellants have stipulated that the electronic communications systems "contain information on the organization, functions, policies, decisions, procedures, operations, and other activities" of the agencies. Joint Statement P. 64. Such documents could only fail to qualify as records if, despite their content, the agency has the inherent discretion to consider them en masse as not "appropriate for preservation . . . as evident of [the government's] organizations, functions, policies, decisions, procedures, operations or other activities." 44 U.S.C. s 3301 (emphasis added), an odd proposition to assert in this case since the agency heads admit they have never surveyed the contents of the electronic systems. See Joint Statement P 67 ("neither the EOP nor the NSC ha[s] conducted any formal examination, inspection, or survey to determine the types of communications recorded on the system, or the amount of information on the organization, functions, policies, decisions, procedures or other activities of the EOP or NSC recorded in [electronic] files."); cf. American Friends, 720 F.2d at 65. In any case, while the agency undoubtedly does have some discretion to decide if a particular document satisfied the statutory definition of a record, see Armstrong I, 924 F.2d at 297, n.14, the statute surely cannot be read to allow the agency by fiat to declare "inappro-

priate for preservation" an entire set of substantive e–mail documents generated by two administrations over a seven–year period. Cf. American Friends, 720 F.2d at 41 ("Congress was certainly aware that agencies, left to themselves, have a built–in incentive to dispose of records relating to [their] 'mistakes' . . . ."). Indeed, to conclude that agencies have broad discretion to exempt seven years of substantive documents from record status would flout our prior holding in Armstrong I that the FRA furnishes sufficient "law to apply" to permit judicial review of agency guidelines relating to the management of federal records. See Armstrong I, 924 F.2d at 293 (noting that the FRA contains a "detailed definition of the 'records' that agencies must preserve") (emphasis added); see also id. ("although the FRA understandably leaves the details of records management to the discretion of individual agency heads, it does contain several specific requirements . . . ").

Having established that the electronic communications systems contain preservable records, we turn finally to the question of whether the government has the discretion to convert only part of the electronic records to paper and then manage only the partial paper records in accordance with the FRA and the Archivist's regulations. The question answers itself. Only one FRA provision exists that would even arguable sanction a document, once denominated a federal record, shedding that appellation at a later point. That provision states that "extra copies of documents preserved only for convenience of reference" are not "records." 44 U.S.C. s 3301. But it is too tight a fit for the government to shoehorn the electronic records at issue here into that exception. Even assuming, without of course deciding, that one set of parallel documents retained in a different records system in a different medium than another set may be classified as a "cop[y]" under the FRA and thus subject to unobstructed destruction, the electronic records would still not qualify as "full reproduction[s] or transcription[s]; imitation[s] of a prototype; . . . duplicate[s]," WEBSTER'S NEW UNIVERSAL UNABRIDGED DICTIONARY 404 (2d ed.1979), of the paper print–outs. This is because important information present in the e–mail system, such as who sent a document, who received it, and when that person received it, will not always appear on the computer screen and so will not be preserved on the paper print–out. See Joint Statement P 46 ("When printed on paper, a[n] [e–mail] will not always identify the sender(s) and recipient(s) of a note by name. Instead, the sender(s) or recipient(s) may be identified only by (a) userid [i.e., user identification]; (b) nickname; or (c) the title given to a distribution list identifying several individuals. Identifying the names of the sender(s) or recipient(s) for such notes requires reference to the distribution lists or directories maintained only in electronic form." (emphasis added; record citations omitted); see also id. at P 47 ("If requested, [the electronic communications system] will provide the sender of a note with a confirmation that it has been received, called an 'acknowledgment.' The acknowledgment records the date and time the addressee of the note opened his or her electronic mail. This information on the date and time the note is received does not appear on the paper copy of the notes when it is printed–out.") (record citations omitted). Since employees had never been — at least until the time of the district court's January order — instructed to include these integral parts of the electronic record in any paper print–out, there is no way we can conclude that the original electronic records are mere "extra copies" of the paper print–outs. Cf. National Archives and Records Administration, Managing Electronic Records 19 (1990) ("Most agencies have decided to meet their record-keeping requirements for documents that are created by using word processing or electronic mail or messaging by printing those documents in hard copy. The success of this approach depends upon a clear understanding by all employees of the obligation to print and file all record material." (emphasis added).

Our refusal to agree with the government that electronic records are merely "extra copies" of the paper versions amounts to far more than judicial nitpicking. Without the missing information, the paper print–outs — akin to traditional memoranda with the "to" and "from" cut off and even the "received" stamp pruned away — are dismembered documents indeed. Texts alone may be of quite limited utility to researchers and investigators studying the formulation and dissemination of significant policy initiatives at the highest reaches of our government. See 810 F.Supp. at 341 (noting that the omitted information may be "of tremendous historical value in demonstrating what agency personnel were involved in making a particular policy decision and what officials knew, and when they knew it"). The "[t]omorrow, and tomorrow, and tomorrow" of government will be allowed to "creep in [their] petty pace from day to day" without benefit of the "last syllable of recorded time." WILLIAM SHAKESPEARE, MACBETH, Act V, scene v, line 19. In our view, as well as the district judge's, the practice of retaining only the amputated paper print–outs is flatly inconsistent with Congress' evident concern with preserving a complete record of government activity for historical and other uses. See 44 U.S.C. s 2902(1) (listing first among the Act's goals the "[a]ccurate and complete documentation of the policies and transactions of the Federal Government"); see also Armstrong I, 924 F.2d at 288 (noting the "expressed statutory goal of preserving records for historical purposes"); American Friends, 720 F.2d at 57 (describing the FRA's legislative history as demonstrating that "Congress intended, expected, and positively desired private researchers . . . to have access to the documentary history of the federal government"); cf. 36 C.F.R. s 1222.38 ("Agency recordkeeping requirements shall prescribe the creation and maintenance of records of the transaction of agency business that are sufficient to: . . . (e) Document the formulation and execution of basic policies and decisions and the taking of necessary actions, including all significant decisions and commitments reached orally (person to person, by telecommunications, or in conference)."). Perhaps that is why, in this court, the appellants seem to have abandoned their former heavy reliance on this theory.

Before us they plead an alternative, related, but no more compelling theory of statutory compliance: "that the extra information that plaintiffs argue must be preserved in fact not always 'appropriate for preservation' as evidence of an agency's essential transactions, and that printing the actual message text on the computer screen is normally sufficient for adequate documentation of the agency's business. Since the printed copy is identical to what is on the computer screen, the electronic version of the message that remains is a copy that is nonrecord within the meaning of the statute." Reply Brief for Appellants at 9. In other words, the appellants content that given the broad discretion vested in the agencies by the FRA, they may reasonably determine that some parts of a record document — the so–called "extra information" — are not "appropriate for preservation"; thus, after the creation of the paper records, the electronic version is a "copy" because the paper record contains all the material worth preserving from the electronic files.

This appeal to discretion, however, relies in the main on snippets of language from different parts of the FRA pasted together in ways incompatible with the overall design of the Act. As noted above, the "appropriate for preservation" phrase in the definition of "records" at most allows the agency some discretion in deciding whether a document meets that definition in the first place. See 44 U.S.C. s 3301 (providing that federal "records" must be, inter alia, "preserved or appropriate for preservation by that agency . . . as evidence of the organization, functions, policies, decisions, procedures, operations, or other activities of the Government or because of the informational value of data in them"). It does not, as appellants imply, grant agencies the discretion to automatically lop off a predesignated part of a whole series of documents that qualify as records (nor would it allow the wholesale destruction of the directories and similar materials if they were perceived to be independent records, see supra note 8). In substance the appellants are claiming that it satisfies the Act to preserve a second version of a record that is an approximation of the first version if it includes all the material that, in their view, is "appropriate for preservation." Even if this argument made sense with respect to a par-

ticular document, it cannot be accepted across the board for seven years of records documenting high–level government decisionmaking. Further, as our discussion above makes clear, it cannot be squared with the FRA's "extra copies" provision. The Act explicitly provides an "out" of the system for a federal record only when a second version is identical to — i.e., an "extra copy" of — the first. There is no provision accepting abbreviated or summary versions of the original as the only record if the summary contains all material deemed "appropriate for preservation."

Equally unconvincing is the appellants' suggestion that Congress' directive to preserve "adequate documentation" of agencies' "essential transactions" justifies their practice of retaining only the "substantive information" displayed on the computer screen. The phrases "adequate documentation" and "essential transactions" are lifted from 44 U.S.C. s 3101, which states: "The head of each Federal agency shall make and preserve records containing adequate and proper documentation of the organization, functions, policies, decisions, procedures and essential transactions of the agency and designed to furnish the information necessary to protect the legal and financial rights of the Government and of persons directly affected by the agency's activities." The purpose of this provision, by its own terms, is to place a general obligation on agency leaders to create and then retain a baseline inventory of "essential" records. See American Friends, 720 F.2d at 54; see also id. at 56 (summarizing legislative history of this provision and concluding that it provided an enforceable "across–the–board requirement" that agencies retain certain types of records); S. REP. NO. 2140, 81st Cong., 2d Sess. 15 (1950) (this provision "provides a general declaration by the Congress [to maintain adequate records]". Other parts of the FRA, however, go on to prescribe more particularized duties for agency head that reach beyond their general obligation to "adequately document" core agency functions. In particular, the Act includes (1) a separate definition of the term "records" that the appellants acknowledge sweeps in many of the electronic communications at issue here — whether or not preservation of those documents is necessary to maintain "adequate documentation" of "essential transactions" — and (2) other statutory provisions that mandate that all records — again, whether or not related to "adequate documentation" of "essential transactions" — be managed and retained in accordance with explicit statutory directives. See 44 U.S.C. s 3314 ("[R]ecords . . . may not be alienated or destroyed except under this chapter.") (emphasis added); see also id. s 3105 (agency heads must "establish safeguards against the removal or loss of records") (emphasis added). In sum, appellants' arguments fail to detour us from the analytical path we started down and now come close to finishing: (1) substantive e–mail communications satisfy the FRA definition of "records"; (2) the lone FRA provision for terminating their status as such requires that they be merely "extra copies" of other documents preserved elsewhere; and (3) since there are often fundamental and meaningful differences in content between paper and electronic versions of these documents, the electronic versions do not lose their status as records and must be managed and preserved in accordance with the FRA.

Contrary to appellants' assertions, the conclusion that agencies must retain and manage these electronic documents in no way collides with Congress' oft–expressed intent to balance complete documentation with efficient, streamlined recordkeeping. See, e.g., S. REP. NO. 2140, 81st Cong. 2d Sess. 4 (1950) ("It is well to emphasize that records come into existence, or should do so, not in order to . . . satisfy the archival needs of this and future generations, but first of all to serve the administrative and executive purposes of the organization that creates them."). Our decision does not require that agencies, in appellants' words, save "every scrap of paper" they create. Not all scribbles and off–the–cuff comments will qualify as federal records. Nor do we saddle agencies with any new obligations to make additional documents in order to satisfy the needs of researchers or investigators. Cf. Armstrong I, 924 F.2d at 288 ("[P]laintiffs do not seek the

creation of any new records, but rather ask only that the records already created be appropriately classified and disposed of . . . ."); S. REP. NO. 1326, 94th Cong., 2d Sess. 8 (1976) (emphasizing the need for economy in records creation because that is where 80% of total recordkeeping costs are incurred). Finally, our decision leaves undisturbed the agencies' ability to purge identical electronic records from their files by acting, with the Archivist's approval, to dispose of those documents that lack "sufficient administrative, legal, research, or other value to warrant their continued preservation." 44 U.S.C. s 3303(a); see also Fed.Reg. 19,216 (1990) (Archivist notes that the burden of managing electronic records "can be reduced significantly by promptly scheduling all electronic records, thus limiting the application of [regulatory] requirements to the very small percentage of records that are scheduled as permanent").

In sum, we find that the district court was fully justified in concluding that appellants' recordkeeping guidance was not in conformity with the Act.

B. Supervision of Electronic Recordkeeping Practices

Appellants also dispute the district court's finding that their records management practices were arbitrary and capricious in failing to provide for supervision or auditing of employees' electronic recordkeeping practices by knowledgeable records management personnel. Specifically, appellants contend that they reasonably discharged their obligation to "safeguard" federal records by assigning records managers the task of providing oral and written guidance to agency personnel and making those recordkeeping experts available for resolution of specific problems.

The FRA explicitly requires each agency head to establish such safeguards against the removal or loss of federal records as she "determines to be necessary and required by regulations of the Archivist." 44 U.S.C. s 3105; see also 36 C.F.R. s 1220.2 ("Federal agency records management programs must be in compliance with regulations promulgated by [the Archivist].”). In this case, the agency heads clearly failed to discharge this obligation.

The Archivist's regulations provide:

The head of each Federal agency shall ensure that the management of electronic records incorporates the following elements: . . .

(1) Reviewing electronic records systems periodically for conformance to established agency procedures, standards, and policies . . . The review should determine if the records have been properly identified and described, and whether the schedule descriptions and retention periods reflect the current information content and use . . . .

Id. s 1234.10 (emphasis added). The Archivist has defined an “electronic records system” as “any information system that produces, manipulates, or stores Federal records by using a computer.” Id. s 1234.2 (emphasis added). As previously discussed, the electronic communication systems used by the EOP and the NSC do produce federal records, and it follows that agencies have an obligation under the Archivist's guidelines to undertake periodic reviews to assure that “established agency procedures, standards, and policies,” including instructions as to what constitutes a record, are being adhered to. Moreover, the relevant regulations make clear that they apply to all electronic systems used by agency employees to create electronic records, not just, as appellants suggest, to “official” agency electronic records systems. See id. s 1234.1 (“Unless otherwise noted, [this section's] requirements apply to all electronic records systems, whether on microcomputers, minicomputers, or mainframe computers, regardless of storage media, in network or stand–alone configurations.”); cf. id. s 1234.22 (listing specific requirements for electronic records systems “that maintain the official file copy of text documents on electronic media”). Moreover, to the extent there is any residual doubt on this question, we think that the agencies' own action in undertaking some review of employees' paper records before those employees exit government service

and the common sense insight that an adequate program for ensuring records preservation must include some ongoing inspections and evaluations tip that balance against the government and lead to the conclusion that oversight is necessary as part of “an agency-wide program for the management of all records created, received, maintained, used or stored on electronic media.” Id. s 1234.10(a).

On that basis, we affirm the district court's holding that the defendant agencies must undertake some periodic review of their employees' electronic recordkeeping practices.

III. The District Court's Civil Contempt Order

Next, the appellants appeal from the district court's May 21, 1993 civil contempt order. The district court found that the appellants “in contempt of this Court's Orders of January 6 and 11, 1993, and the Order of the United States Court of Appeals for the District of Columbia dated January 15, 1993” in two respects: (1) “for failing to promulgate new, appropriate, and proper recordkeeping regulations for electronic federal records to replace those regulations struck down by this Court on January 6, 1993” and (2) ”because the transfer of 5,839 tapes from the Defendant agencies to the Archivist has adversely affected the condition of the tapes and the information stored therein” which was “contrary to this Court's Orders to preserve the tapes and federal records contained on them.” Order, *Armstrong v. Bush*, No. 89–142 (D.D.C. May 21, 1992). The court further ordered that, unless the appellants should “purge themselves of this finding of contempt” by “tak[ing] appropriate action by 4:00 p.m. on June 21, 1993,” they would be subject to a fine of $50,000 for each day of noncompliance during the first week, to be doubled to $100,000 per day the second week and $200,000 per day the third week, “with increases in such sanctions reserved thereafter for any further noncompliance with Court Orders.” id. at 2–3. The appellants assert that the contempt finding must be reversed because, inter alia, the district court's first ground, the failure to promulgate new regulations, was not a violation of the cited orders and therefore cannot support civil contempt. "The standard of review on an appeal from a finding of contempt is whether the District Court abused its discretion." *International Ass'n of Machinists and Aerospace Workers v. Eastern Airlines, Inc.*, 849 F.2d 1481, 1486 (D.D.Cir.1988). We agree with the appellants that the contempt finding, as articulated, was an abuse of discretion because it rests in part on an impermissible ground.

As a preliminary matter, we reject the appellee's jurisdictional argument that the May 21, 1993 order is not an appealable one because it "imposes only a conditional sanction for failure to comply with a preexisting order." See Appellees' Contempt Brief at 13. As both the Eleventh Circuit and the Second Circuit have concluded, "'Being placed under the threat of future sanction is a present sanction'" and an order so threatening "'imposes a present remedy and hence is appealable.'" *United States v. O'Rourke*, 943 F.2d 180, 186 (2d Cir.1991) (quoting *Sizzler Family Steak House v. Western Sizzler Steak House, Inc.*, 793 F.2d 1529, 1533 n.2 (11th Cir.1986)) (emphasis in original). We agree and therefore proceed to the merits of the contempt appeal.

"There can be no question that courts have inherent power to enforce compliance with their lawful orders through civil contempt." *Shillitani v. United States*, 384 U.S. 364, 370 (1966). Nevertheless, "civil contempt will lie only if the putative contemnor has violated an order that is clear and unambiguous," *Project B.A.S.I.C. v. Kemp*, 947 F.2d 11, 16 (1st Cir.1991), and the violation must be proved by "clear and convincing evidence. *Washington–Baltimore Newspaper Guild, Local 35 v. Washington Post Co.*, 626 F.2d 1029, 1031 (D.C.Cir.1980). The district court's first ground for its contempt findings, however, did not involve violation of any court order. The district court's January 11, 1993 order did not expressly direct the appellants to promulgate new regulations, but merely issued "a Declaratory Judgment that the guidelines issued by and at the direction of the Defendant Agencies are inadequate

and not reasonable and are arbitrary and capricious and contrary to law in that they permit the destruction of records contrary to the Federal Records Act." Amended Order, *Armstrong v. Bush*, 89–142 (D.D.C. Jan. 11, 1993). As the Supreme Court has observed: "[E]ven through a declaratory judgment has 'the force and effect of a final judgment,' 28 U.S.C. s 2201, it is a much milder form of relief than an injunction. Though it may be persuasive, it is not ultimately coercive; non-compliance with it may be inappropriate, but is not contempt." *Steffel v. Thompson*, 415 U.S. 452, 471 (1974) (quoting *Perez v. Ledesma*, 401 U.S. 82, 125–26 (1971) (Brennan, J., concurring)). Thus, because the appellants were never directly ordered to promulgate new regulations, we must reverse the district court's contempt finding which was based in part on their failure to do so. Cf. *Spallone v. United States*, 492 U.S. 265, 276–77 (1990) (reversing contempt finding against individual city councilmembers for city's violation of consent decree where "the individual city councilmembers . . . were not parties to the action" and "although the injunctive portion of that decree was directed not only to the city but to 'its officers, agents, employees, successors and all persons in active concert with any of them,' . . . the remaining parts of the decree ordering affirmative steps were directly only to the city"); *International Longshoremen's Ass'n, Local 1291 v. Philadelphia Marine Trade Ass'n*, 389 U.S. 64, 76 (1967) (reversing opinion upholding contempt finding for violating order that "did not state in 'specific . . . terms' that the acts that it required or prohibited") (quoting FED. R. CIV. P. 65(d)). Accordingly, we vacate the contempt order and remand to the district court to consider whether its second ground, the failure to preserve the tapes, by itself, justifies a finding of contempt, taking into account all efforts that have or will then have been made to assure the tapes' integrity.

* * * * *

Conclusion

To recap: We affirm the district court's decision that the EOP and NSC electronic records management guidelines violate the FRA, reverse the district court's civil contempt finding, and remand to allow the district court to determine whether the challenged NSC and OSTP guidelines inaccurately classify some documents as presidential records.

So ordered.

**Raymond D. BATTOCCHI, et al. v.
WASHINGTON HOSPITAL CENTER,
et al**

581 A.2d 759

District of Columbia Court of Appeals
October 16, 1990

Raymond D. Battocchi and Kathleen A. Buck appeal from a judgment in favor of Washington Hospital Center (the hospital) and Dr. Douglas Brady (an employee of the hospital at the relevant time) in a medical malpractice action arising from injuries — including permanent brain damage — to their son Adam allegedly caused by the use of obstetrical forceps during his delivery. Dr. Brady, then a third–year resident, used the forceps to effect the delivery after the attempts of Dr. Cohn, Ms. Buck's attending physician, also using forceps, had failed. Dr. Cohn settled before trial and was not a party to the instant suit.

Appellants raise several challenges to the conduct of the trial, foremost of which is the judge's refusal to give a missing evidence instruction as a sanction for the hospital's failure to preserve a note written by an attending nurse shortly after the delivery. We conclude that a remand of the record is necessary for an express finding central to resolution of that issue. Appellants' remaining arguments provide no basis for reversing the jury's determination.

I. The Delivery

Ms. Buck entered the Washington Medical Center Hospital at 11:15 a.m. on April 2,

1982, after her amniotic membranes had ruptured spontaneously earlier that morning. At about 12:00 noon, mild contractions began. From about 1:00 p.m. until 6:30 p.m., a drug was administered to stimulate contractions, and thereafter various measures were taken to combat abnormal labor. At 1:30 a.m. on April 3, the attending physician, Dr. Cohn, diagnosed the position of the baby as left occiput posterior (face–down). In fact, the baby's position was occuput anterior (face–up). At about 3:59 a.m., after some fifteen hours of labor, Ms. Buck was brought into the delivery room in an exhausted condition. Dr. Cohn decided to attempt a vaginal delivery using obstetrical forceps. The forceps slipped off the baby's head at least twice, perhaps several times, requiring reinsertion. Ultimately Dr. Cohn's attempts were unsuccessful. Dr. Brady was called in and, using the forceps, delivery the baby at 4:50 a.m.

Adam was born with a fracture at the base of the skull, small linear fractures of the right and left parietal bones (located on the upper sides of the skull), intracranial hemorrhaging, shock from low blood volume (hypovelemic shock), and seizures. He spent the next thirteen days in the neonatal intensive care unit. He now suffers from mild cerebral palsy and related permanent motor and perceptual dysfunctions.

The parties appear to agree that the most significant of Adam's injuries resulted from the compressional force exerted on the skull required to move his head through the opening in the pelvic bone. There is sharp disagreement, however, as to whether Dr. Cohn or Dr. Brady, or both, exerted this considerable degree of force. Dr. Brady testified that, when he entered the delivery room, the baby's head had already passed through the pelvic opening and that the delivery was accomplished easily in a single contraction. He contended that the crushing injury occurred during Dr. Cohn's attempts, when the forceps slipped off and the baby's head was squeezed between the tips of the instrument. Plaintiffs maintained that, although the forceps may have slipped off during Dr. Cohn's attempts, causing some superficial injuries, Dr. Brady failed to examine the mother to ascertain the position of the baby, which did not permit safe use of forceps, and his use of the forceps to bring the baby through the pelvic opening caused the more serious injuries.

II. The Nurse's Missing Note

A. Factual background

Marlene Aretino, a registered nurse, was present in the delivery room during the events in question. Because she resided in New Mexico and was unable to testify at trial, the court admitted her videotaped deposition in evidence. Aretino testified that, shortly after the birth, although not required to do so, she wrote a nurse's note:

> [b]ecause I felt, after I left that room, that I needed to write my side of what I had observed . . . Because of what went on in there with the forceps and the way they slipped off when and then were reapplied, and what I anticipated, possibly, the condition of the baby might be . . . [I] wrote a log. I tried to document times, forceps applied, condition of the mother, condition of the baby, when Doctor Brady came in. I tried to document as much as I could remember. I remember having difficulty remembering times because — yes, the clock was there and all I had to do was glance at it, but so many things were going on, "Go get another pair of forceps; check the monitor; listen to the fetal heart tone;" that I really didn't have time, at the Delivery Room, to write everything down chronologically . . .

> [W]hen I left the Delivery Room, I was very upset, just very upset with the way things had turned out. [Not so much upset with the doctors, but] more upset for the family, okay . . .

> Around the corner from the nurse's station there's a little quiet area. I wanted to make note here that when I did [the] chart, my intent was not to incriminate anyone or lay blame anywhere; I just wanted to write what I had seen, as I had seen it, as accurately as possible.

Aretino further testified that she wrote the note, about 1 1/3 pages long, on a blank for entitled "Progress Notes" obtained from the nurse's station, and placed it in the medical chart. She said that it should have appeared after other progress notes she made prior to delivery (the last at 3:50 a.m.), but when she reviewed the copy of the chart produced in discovery in preparation for her deposition, the note was not there.

To ascertain what may have become of the note, plaintiffs deposed Michael Anthony Forte, Director of Washington Medical Center. Forte testified that standard procedure in the records department was to retain original charts in active status there for eighteen months after the last activity. Following that, they would be sent to a firm in Baltimore to be microfilmed. Ms. Buck's record should have been retained in original, hard copy form until October of 1983, and then sent to be microfilmed; but after investigating the matter, Forte concluded that the chart had never been sent for microfilming.

Forte acknowledged that on May 26, 1983, the medical records department had received a request for Ms. Buck's chart from Truman Haskell, then Risk Manager for the Washington Hospital Center. The original chart was transmitted to Haskell's office, and a departmental form indicating this fact was placed in Buck's file folder in lieu of the record. Haskell was among the few hospital personnel permitted to review a chart outside the medical records department, a privilege not enjoyed even by physicians. Forte testified that, after his internal investigation to ascertain whether the chart had been misfiled, he determined that "subsequent to Mr. Haskell's request of May 26th, 1983, the original copy . . . ha[d] not been returned to the [medical records] Department." When asked what he thought had happened to the chart, Forte said:

> We suspected that at some point after 1983 — some point in time after May 26, 1983 when the chart was initially signed out to Mr. Haskell and subsequent to his physical move from one office building to another office building[,] the

medical record may have been misplaced or that he may have given it to someone, whereabouts currently unknown.

* * * * *

We had a reorganization. Truman Haskell was reassigned and I'm hoping this is accurate, to the corporate office. A Risk Management Department was established with Marilyn Owens assuming some of the responsibilities that Truman Haskell had. Subsequently, Linda Jones. Therefore, I am surmising that they would have shared information in those files.

* * * * *

I think when Truman Haskell moved to the corporate office, which is on campus, a separate building, the subsequent reassignment of responsibilities, the fact that legal also moved about the same time, there was some involvement on their part, I'm sure. The fact that Marilyn Owens' files were subsequently moved even though this was after the fact, much after the fact, it probably was misfiled or has yet to be located somewhere between the move and where they currently are.

Forte acknowledged that Haskell's job included reviewing charts in anticipation of litigation. At trial, as part of plaintiff's proffer on the "missing evidence" issue, the court permitted a neonatologist, Dr. Cherian, to testify out of the jury's presence that the current practice for Risk Management to be informed whenever an infant was born with birth trauma. It was his understanding that the same rule obtained in 1982 when Adam was born, but he did not know personally whether Risk Management had been informed in this case. He noted that the standard procedure was for the attending neonatologist or nurse to note on the chart that Risk Management had been contacted, but that there was not such notation on the charts in this case.

At trial, plaintiffs sought to have the judge instruct the jury that it could infer from the defendants' failure to preserve and produce Nurse Aretino's note that it would have harmed their case. The court analogizing to "missing witness" cases, observed that those

decisions: support[] my inclination that the Court of Appeals looks with disfavor on creating evidence out of no evidence, which, of course, is what the missing evidence inference does.

The court noted that, "[u]nlike the missing witness inference where a witness if floating around somewhere who is peculiarly available to a part, and the party fails to call the witness," the missing evidence situation is "a little different because its more like, a failure to preserve than a failure to produce . . . [T]he [missing evidence] inference really is an illogical inference because . . . the failure to preserve really doesn't in any logical way give rise to an inference that what was not preserved would have been unfavorable to the party who failed to preserve it." Plaintiffs' counsel responded that the inference might indeed not be logical in circumstances where, at the time the records were lost, the party failing to preserve them had no knowledge of a reason (such as of the possibility of a lawsuit) to preserve them, but that if the plaintiff could prove the defendant had such knowledge and exclusive control over the records, "the law has got to give the party damaged by the loss of the record some small advantage."

The court concluded:

Well, I understand your point and I think it's a good one. Part of my problem with your approach, all along, has been that the statement of the problem assumes the answer. We don't know that you're the party that's been damaged by the loss. For all I know, the hospital records in this case, just as one example, would show Cohen [*sic*] did this, Cohen did that, Cohen did the other thing and Brady did nothing, and since Cohen is not a party to this trial, that's Mr. Barse's [the hospital's] point. He may have been damaged by the loss of these records . . .

Ultimately, after considering the standards developed by this court in the area of "missing evidence" and in the analogous (criminal) context of failure of the government to preserve evidence, the judge refused to instruct the jury they could infer from the failure to preserve the note that it would be unfavorable to either the hospital or Brady. Accordingly, neither Forte nor Dr. Cherian was allowed to testify before the jury on the circumstances surrounding the loss of the note or the role of Risk Management.

B. Legal discussion

Appellants contend that Nurse Artino's missing note "was a crucial piece of evidence which would shed great light on whether Dr. Cohn or Dr. Brady was responsible for causing the injuries at issue." They argue that their proffer — including the deposition of Forte and Dr. Cherian's testimony warranted the conclusion that the hospital negligently, even intentionally, allowed the note to be destroyed and that the trial court erred in refusing to let the jury hear evidence of the loss and draw inferences adverse to the hospital under an appropriate "missing evidence" instruction.

1. Rebuttal presumption

Appellants first assert, relying on *Welsh v. United States*, 844 F.2d 1239 (6th Cir.1988), that the jury should have been instructed that it could *presume* negligence and causation from the fact of the missing note, thus shifting the burden of disproving all aspects of liability to the defendants. In *Welsh*, the court held that "[t]wo acts by the hospital surgeons in this case create a rebuttal presumption of negligence and proximate causation against the defendant — the negligent destruction of a skull bone flap after the second [of two] operation[s], and the consequent failure at that time to undertake a pathological examination of this evidence . . . " *Id.* at 1239–40. Although the court characterized the presumption of negligence and causation as "rebuttal," its discussion makes clear that it concluded a *shift in the burden of persuasion* to the defendants was an appropriate sanction for negligent loss of evidence. *Id.* at 1246–49.

We find no error in the trial court's refusal to give the requested instruction. In some jurisdictions, a presumption from destruction of evidence can substitute for a lack of affirmative proof on an essential element of a

party's prima facie case. *See, e.g., id.* at 1248; C. McCORMICK, McCORMICK ON EVIDENCE § 273, at 810 & n. 20 (3d ed. 1984). Decisions in this jurisdiction, however, do not appear to support his view. In *Tendler v. Jaffe*, 92 U.S. App.D.C. 2, 7, 203 F.2d 14, *cert. denied*, 346 U.S. 817, 74 S.Ct. 29, 98 L.Ed 344 (1953), our Circuit Court analyzed the problem of allocation of burden of proof of the plaintiff's violation of the Emergency Price Control Act, which the counterclaiming defendant alleged to be a fact peculiarly within the knowledge of the plaintiff. The court stated in dictum:

> There is a further rule that the omission by a party to produce relevant and important evidence of which he has knowledge, and which is peculiarly within his control, raises the presumption that if produced the evidence would be unfavorable to his case . . . Such presumption *aids the case of an opposite party having the burden of proof . . . This rule, however, is not one which determines who bears the burden of proof* and, therefore, is not strictly pertinent to our present inquiry.

Id. at 7, 203 F.2d at 19 (citations omitted; emphasis added). In *Aetna Casualty & Sur. Co. v. Smith*, 127 A.2d 556 (D.C.1956), our predecessor court pointed out that the inference is "merely another factor which may be given consideration by the trier of the facts when weighing the evidence and determining the credibility of witnesses." *Id.* at 559. This perspective is consistent with the rule prevailing in Maryland, to whose common law we look for guidance. *See Burkowske v. Church Hosp. Corp.*, 50 Md.App. 515, 521, 439 A.2d 40, 45 (1982), *quoting Maszczenski v. Meyers*, 212 Md. 346, 355, 129 A.2d 109, 114 (1957) (well settled "that this inference does not amount to substantive proof and cannot take the place of proof of fact necessary to the other party's case"). This court has cautioned against overuse of the missing witness inference and "the dangers inherent in creating evidence from nonevidence." *Stager v. Schneider*, 494 A.2d 1307, 1313 (D.C.1985). It would, we conclude, be inconsistent with our decisions to allow an inference appropriate in limited circumstances to be converted to a burden–shifting presumption, and we find no abuse of discretion in the judge's failure to give that instruction.

2. Missing evidence instruction

Still relying on *Welsh* and the authorities it considered persuasive, appellants contend that the judge erred in refusing to instruct the jury "that, if it found that the Hospital's loss of the note was merely negligent (or grossly negligent), it . . . could draw the inference that the evidence was adverse to the Hospital." Appellants appear to hold in other words, that a missing evidence instruction is mandatory once negligence is apparent, and that it is for the jury, as the trier of fact, to weigh the circumstances concerning the loss of the evidence and draw an adverse inference accordingly. The trial judge concluded, to the contrary, that our decisions leave a trial court broad discretion on whether to give or withhold an instruction that inherently risks "creating evidence from nonevidence." *Stager, supra.* We agree, and hold that in a civil case the judge may decline to submit to the jury an issue of loss of evidence — and to instruct on missing evidence — when the conduct of the party causing the loss does not rise to the level of reckless disregard for the relevance of the evidence to a potential lawsuit.

(a) The Law of "Spoliation" of Evidence

The doctrine of what has been termed spoliation of evidence includes two sub–categories of behavior, the deliberate destruction of evidence and the simple failure to preserve evidence. It is well settled that a party's bad faith destruction of a document relevant to proof of an issue at trial gives rise to a strong inference that production of the document would have been unfavorable to the party responsible for its destruction. *Brown v. Williamson Tobacco Corp. v. Jacobson*, 827 F.2d 1119, 1134 (7th Cir.1987); *Vick v. Texas Employment Comm'n*, 514 F.2d 734, 737 (5th Cir.1975); *Friends for All Children, Inc. v. Lockheed Aircraft Corp.*, 587 F.Supp. 180, 190 (D.D.C.) *modified*, 593 F.Supp. 388, *Aff'd.* 241 U.S.App.D.C. 83, 746, F.2d 816 (1984). Adverse inferences from the destruc-

tion of document have both an evidentiary and a punitive rationale.

The evidentiary rationale is nothing more than the common sense observation that a party who has notice that a document is relevant to litigation and who proceeds to destroy the document is more likely to have been threatened by the document than is a party in the same position who does not destroy the document.

Nation–wide Check Corp. v. Forest Hills Distributors, 692 F.2d 214, 218 (1st Dir.1982). In essence, the inference is akin to an admission by conduct of the weakness of one's own case. *See C. McCORMICK, supra*, § 273, at 808. The other rationale for the inference "has to do with its prophylactic and punitive effects. Allowing the trier of fact to draw the inference presumably deters parties from destroying relevant evidence before it can be introduced at trial." *Nation–wide Check Corp., supra*, 692 F.2d at 218.

The prevailing rule is that, to justify the inference, "the circumstances of the [destruction] must manifest bad faith. Mere negligence is not enough, for it does not sustain the inference of consciousness of a weak case." C. McCORMICK, *supra*, § 273, at 800. Even courts eschewing that the destruction must transcend ordinary negligence, and evince at least knowing disregard of the importance of the document to an opposing litigant's claim. *See Allen Pen Co. v. Springfield Photo Mount Co.*, 653 F.2d 17, 23–24 (1st Cir.1981) (inference ordinarily improper unless documents destroyed "in bad faith" or from "consciousness of a weak case"); *Nation–wide Check Corp., supra*, 692 F.2d at 219. Where proffered evidence demonstrates that documents were concealed or destroyed in bad faith either deliberately or with reckless disregard for their relevance — a trial court may well abuse its discretion by refusing to allow factual inferences adverse to the culpable party to be suggested to the jury through an instruction or argument of counsel. *See Alexander v. Nat'l Farmers Org.*, 687 F.2d 1173, 1205–06 (8th Cir.1982), *cert. denied*, 461 U.S. 937, 103 S.Ct. 2108, 77 L.Ed.2d 313 (1983).

When the loss or destruction of evidence is not intentional or reckless, by contrast, the issue is not strictly "spoliation" but rather a failure to preserve evidence. The rule that a fact–finder may draw an inference adverse to a party who fails to preserve relevant evidence within his exclusive control is well established in this jurisdiction. *Aetna Casualty & Sur. Co. v. Smith, supra*, 127 A.2d at 559. *Hartman v. Lubar*, 49 A.2d 553, 556 (D.C.1946); *Tendler v. Jaffe, supra*, 92 U.S.App.D.C. at 7, 203 F.2d at 19; *Washington Gas Light Co. v. Biancaniello*, 87 U.S.App.D.C. 164, 167, 183 F.2d 982, 985 (1950); *Fidelity & Deposit Co. v. Helverina*, 72 App.D.C. 120, 126, 112 F.2d 205, 211 (1940). Like the spoliation rule, it derives from the common sense notion that if the evidence was favorable to the non–producing party's case, it would have taken pains to preserve and come forward with it. *International Union (UAW) v. NLRB*, 148 U.S.App.D.C. 305, 311–12, 314, 459 F.2d 1329, 1335–36, 1338 (1972); *Washington Gas Light Co. v Biancaniello, supra*, 87 U.S.App.D.C. at 167, 183 F.2d at 985.

As the trial judge recognized, in recent years this court has dealt with the issue of failure to preserve evidence almost entirely in the criminal context of evidence the government is required to produce under the Jencks Act, 18 U.S.C. § 3500, or Super.Ct.Crim.R. 16. The court has made clear that, "[a]bsent an abuse of discretion, the decision of what sanctions, *if any*, to impose [for loss of evidence] is committed to the trial court," *Cotton v. United States*, 388 A.2d 865, 869 (D.C.1978) (emphasis in original), and that at least where the failure to preserve evidence is merely negligent, "nothing in the decision of this jurisdiction requires that sanctions be automatically imposed." *Id.* at 870. *See also Gibson v. United States*, 536 A.2d 78, 84 (D.C.1987); *Bartley v. United States*, 530 A.2d 692, 697 (D.C.1987); *Wiggins v. United States*, 521 A.2d 1146, 1148 (D.C.1987). It is also chiefly in the criminal cases that the court has expressed skepticism about the missing witness/evidence doctrine and underscored the discretion which the trial judge retains to deny the instruction even when its prerequisites have been met. *See Thomas v.*

United States, 447 A.2d 52, 58 (D.C.1982); *see also Stager v. Scheider, supra*, 494 A.2d at 1313 (applying same rule to civil cases, and stating that "it seldom will constitute error to deny the missing witness instruction or to prohibit argument of the missing witness inference").

These principles, in our judgment, compel rejection of a rule that a party's failure in a civil case to preserve evidence regardless of degree of fault requires the court to instruct the jury on the missing evidence inference. Rather, as in criminal cases, the trial judge has discretion to withhold the issue from the jury after considering factors such as the degree of negligence or bad faith involved, the importance of the bad faith involved, the importance of the evidence lost to the issues at hand, and the availability of other proof enabling the party deprived of the evidence to make the same point. *Cf. Cotton v. United States, supra*, 388 A.2d at 869. We hold that, upon a finding of gross indifference to or reckless disregard for the relevance of the evidence to a possible claim, the trial court must submit the issue of lost evidence to the trier of fact with corresponding instructions allowing an adverse inference. Short of that finding, however, a refusal to instruct on missing evidence is not error unless we can say that the trial court, in all of the circumstances, abused its discretion.

(b) Application to This Case

Appellants maintain that their proffer of evidence established that the hospital intentionally, or at least recklessly, allowed the Aretino note to be destroyed. They point to the facts that (1) the Risk Management division likely had been informed of Adam's injury near the time of his birth; (2) the hospital anticipated litigation as of May 26, 1983, because the records were transmitted to Risk Management on that date; (3) the last person known to have custody of the original records was Mr. Haskell of Risk Management; (4) Haskell never returned the original records to the medical records department; and (5) after May 26, the hospital was only able to produce copies of the records which did not include the Aretino note.

Were this the sort of issue this court decides *de novo*, we might well agree with appellants that the evidence demonstrated at least reckless disregard by the hospital for the likely relevance of the note to a malpractice claim. But we do not decide the issue afresh. In the analogous criminal context, we have made clear that a finding by the trial court as to the degree of fault of a party in failing to produce or preserve evidence will not be disturbed unless clearly erroneous. *E.g., United States v. Jackson*, 450 A.2d 419, 426 (D.C.1982); *Johnson v. United States*, 336 A.2d 545, 547 (D.C.1975), *cert. denied*, 423 U.S. 1058, 96 S.Ct. 793, 46 L.Ed 648 (1976), citing *Campbell v. United States*, 373 U.S. 487, 493–95, 83 S.Ct. 1356, 136–62, 10 L.Ed.2d 501 (1963). *Cf. Simpson v. Chesapeake & Potomac Tel. Co., 522 A.2d 880, 885 (D.C.1987)* (trial court's implied finding of bad faith for purpose of Rule II sanctions reviewed for clear error). The fact that the file containing the nurse's note was called for and last in the possession of a hospital official responsible for reviewing documents in anticipation of litigation supports, but certainly does not compel, a conclusion of recklessness on the hospital's part. Forte's explanation in his deposition points to an inadvertent loss of the records during a reorganization and physical move of the Risk Management division, testimony the trial judge was free to credit. Moreover, the record indicates that, contrary to appellant's suggestion that only the Aretino was missing from the copies of the medical records produced in discovery, Adam's footprint record and several unspecified laboratory reports also could not be located. The record, in short, does not yield a conclusion as a matter of law that the defendants acted recklessly (or worse) in permitting the loss or destruction of the note.

The problem is that we lack an express finding by the trial judge on either side of the issue: recklessness or mere negligence. The judge recited from the bench the principles generally governing the decision whether to impose sanctions for destruction or loss of evidence, including the gradations of culpability affecting the decision. In ultimately declining the request for an instruction, however, he merely stated that he had "considered the issue many times and read the deposition of Mr. Forte and the relevant portions of Dr. Cohn's deposition." Although we have often sustained rulings of the trial court on the basis of implied findings, we conclude that an express finding on the issue of fault is necessary in this case. First, as discussed above, the issue of the degree of fault is a close one. *See Spellman v. American Security Bank*, 579 A.2d 151, 156 (D.C.1990) ("the closeness of the fee [sanction] issue here dictates that we have the benefit of the judge's express findings in light of the applicable standard"). Moreover, as the trial judge himself recognized, the "applicable standard" governing loss of evidence in a civil case has not been set forth explicitly in our decisions until now, and thus we cannot be certain that the judge recognized that he was required to give a missing evidence instruction in the event he found that the hospital's loss of the record resulted from "gross indifference to or reckless disregard for the relevance of the evidence to a possible claim . . ." *Supra*, at 767. Without implying any view on the issue, therefore, we think it prudent to remand the record to the judge for an express finding on the degree of fault underlying the hospital's loss of the note, and for a corresponding application of law. Our further analysis of the matter will await that determination.

* * * * *

The record is remanded in accordance with part II of this opinion.

So ordered.

THE BERMUDA'S CLAIMANTS v. THE UNITED STATES

70 U.S. 200

Supreme Court of the United States
March 12, 1866

* * * * *

If the Bermuda were on a voyage at the time of her capture, from the port of Bermuda, a neutral port, to the port of Nassau, another neutral port, being a British vessel and owned by British subjects, she was not liable to capture.

In order to render her so liable to capture under these circumstances, she must have been actually on voyage to Charleston or some other blockaded port of the southern states, with an intent to run the blockade.

There can be no legal blockade by a belligerent of any other than a hostile port. There can be none of a neutral port. The Bermuda was therefore at perfect liberty to navigate to and from among the British West India islands, so far as the question of blockade is concerned, unless she were actually on a voyage to a blockaded port of our country.

There can be no proper legal assertion of a continued voyage of which Nassau was but an intermediate port, unless the evidence shows (which it does not) that the Bermuda was on her way to a blockaded port, *via* Nassau. Every voyage must have a *terminus a quo* and a *terminus ad quem*.

What the voyage of the Bermuda was, is a question of fact to be deduced from all the evidence in the cause. The shipping articles which describe it with particularity, are persuasive evidence of the voyage on which the Bermuda started from Liverpool. The letter of instructions to the captain at that place is in accordance with the shipping articles. The legal construction of those documents is, that the violation of the blockade was not embraced by them; and that if, after arriving at Bermuda, the ship should be ordered to a port of the United States, some open port and not a blockaded port must have been intended.

British merchants as neutrals, in our present war, had a perfect right to trade even in military stores, between their own ports and to sell, at any one of them, even to an enemy of the United States, goods of all sorts, although with the knowledge that the purchaser bought them with the view of employing them afterwards out of the neutral territory in war against us.

A neutral may sell in his own territory, to either belligerent, munitions of war.

The question of contraband of war cannot arise with any respect to any portion of the Bermuda's cargo unless she were on a voyage to a blockaded port.

On a proper construction of the evidence, the control which John Fraser & Co., of Charleston, had over the voyage of the ship, did not clothe them with any ownership, even in a prize court.

The power of attorney from Edwin Haigh, registered in the Liverpool custom–house, was not accompanied with any interest. Any sale under it must have been for the use of the principal, and all money received under it would have been the funds of the principal.

Spoliation of papers is cause for condemnation, and excludes further proof only as against the parties committing it, if interested in the vessel or cargo. Against a party not committing the spoliation and not authorizing it nor interested in the act, it neither excludes further proof nor is it damnatory, where other circumstances are clear.

There is no proof in the cause that any spoliation of papers was authorized by Mr. Haigh, or conducted to his benefit as owner of the ship; nor is there any evidence of the spoliation of any papers which might properly be considered as proprietary documents.

* * * * *

At the time of capture, two small boxes and a package, supposed to contain postage stamps, were thrown overboard, and a bag, understood to contain letters was burned. The bag was burned by the captain's brother, and under the orders of the captain, after the vessel had been boarded by the captors. Deposition of C.V. B. Westendorff, record 16. It was burnt, as Westendorff says, in pursuance of his instructions. Record, 12. One of the passengers also burned a number of letters, which, he says, were private. Deposition of Huger, record, 17.

The instructions, in pursuance of which this destruction of papers was made, are not produced; nor is any explanation of this spoliation offered. The instructions were, doubtless, given by John Fraser & Co., in view of the contingency of capture, and were in accordance with the suggestion of Fraser, Trenholm, & Co.'s letter of the 28th February, that the most certain measures should be adopted to prevent any of the bills of lading or invoices falling into improper hands. They, doubtless, included directions for the destruction of all compromising papers, and among them of the instructions themselves. If they had been preserved and produced, it is not unlikely that they would have disclosed the real ownership of the vessel, the true nature of her employment, and the actual destination of both ship and cargo.

This spoliation was one of unusual aggravation, and warrants the most unfavorable inferences as to ownership, employment and destination.

All these transactions, prior to capture, and at the time of capture, repel the conclusion that Haigh was owner. Not a document taken on the ship shows ownership in him except the shipping articles, and these were false in putting upon the crew list employees of the rebel government and enemy passengers — the last under assumed names. He was permitted to put into the cause his original declaration of ownership of August 1, 1861, by way of further proof; but we cannot give much weight to this, in view of the "certificate of transaction subsequent to registry," which shows his execution of the power of sale to Hanckel & Trenholm. After giving that power, there is no indication that he performed a single act of ownership. No letter alluded to him as owner. No direction relative to vessel or cargo recognized him as owner. All the papers and all the circumstances indicate rather that a sale was made in Charleston under the power by which the beneficial control and real ownership were transferred to John Fraser & Co. while the apparent title, by the British papers, was suffered to remain in Haigh as a cover.

The spoliation makes the conclusion of ownership out of Haigh and in John Fraser & Co. well nigh irresistible. Would the master have obeyed such instructions from John Fraser &

Co. if he had been really appointed by Haigh, and was really responsible to him as owner?

We are obliged to think that the ownership of Haigh was a pretense, and that the vessel was rightly condemned as enemy property.

*****

Our conclusion is that both vessel and cargo even if both were neutral, were rightly condemned; and on every ground, *the decree of the District Court for the Eastern District of Pennsylvania must be affirmed.*

Oksana R. BIHUN, Plaintiff and Respondent, v. AT&T INFORMATION SYSTEMS, INC., Defendant and Appellant.

16 Cal.Rptr.2d 787

Court of Appeal of California, Second Appellate District, Division Seven

Defendant, AT&T Information Systems, appeals from a judgment in favor of Oksana Bihun, a former employee, in her suit for damages arising from sexual harassment by one of defendant's senior officials. We affirm.

Facts and Proceedings Below

Ms. Bihun worked for defendant or one of its predecessors from 1977 to 1985. Ms. Bihun became an area personnel manager in 1983. Her immediate supervisor was Ms. Jimetta Moore, the district personnel manager. Ms. Bihun received a "number one" staff rating and was eligible for promotion to the next level of management in January 1984.

In March 1984, Peter Fellows, a longtime employee of defendant, was transferred from Denver to Los Angeles as area vice–president. Fellows's sexual harassment of Ms. Bihun began almost immediately.

On their first meeting, Fellows winked at Ms. Bihun and lightly brushed his hand against hers. Later that month while Ms. Bihun and Ms. Moore were working after hours in Ms.

Moore's office, Fellows walked in with his shirt unbuttoned and his pants unzipped. He pressed his body against Ms. Bihun's right shoulder. Ms. Bihun jumped up and left Ms. Moore's office. As she retreated down the hall she heard Fellows softly calling her name, "Oksana." Again in March, at a birthday luncheon for Ms. Moore, Fellows sat down next to Ms. Bihun and started rubbing her leg with his foot. When she kicked his leg away, Fellows stood up and thrust his groin at her. He pointed to his groin area and told Ms. Bihun there was a food spot there and asked her to rub it off. Later that day, Fellows summoned Ms. Bihun to his office. When she arrived he asked her to have dinner with him that evening. She declined. Fellows then asked her to go to the beach with him the following Saturday. Again, she declined. Fellows then leaned back in his chair revealing his open fly.

The week after these events took place Fellows walked into Ms. Bihun's office, closed the door, and told her they were having dinner together that evening. Ms. Bihun said "No," but Fellows insisted, stating that it was "strictly business" to discuss his staff and job–related matters. Ms. Bihun felt threatened and not at liberty to refuse. They drove to the restaurant in separate cars. When they arrived Fellows presented Ms. Bihun with a bouquet of flowers. After they were seated Fellows began telling Ms. Bihun about his unsatisfactory sex life with his wife and his need for extramarital affairs. Then he told her a major reorganization of the company was going to take place soon and if she "played her cards right" she could have any job she wanted. He asked her if she would like Ms. Moore's job and remarked Ms. Moore could be made to disappear. Fellows than leaned across the table and began playing with her earring. He told her she looked like a gypsy and asked her to have an affair with him. He went on to say he did pretty much what he wanted in the company and no one questioned him. For example, he told her, he once hired a waitress from a restaurant to be his secretary because of her large breasts.

The next day, Ms. Bihun told Ms. Moore what had happened at the restaurant. Ms. Moore went to Fellows and complained about his treatment of Ms. Bihun. Fellows told Ms. Moore it was none of her business. After that, the incidents of direct sexual harassment by Fellows became less frequent. Once, while they were passing in the hall, Fellows cupped his hand on her breast. On another occasion Fellows asked Ms. Bihun if she had "softened up yet." And, in November 1984, Fellows asked her "Have you changed your mind?"

Fellows retaliated against Ms. Bihun for rejecting his advances. Her budgetary responsibilities were taken away from her and branch managers stopped dealing with her and took their work to another personnel manager on the same level as Ms. Bihun. A few months later, Fellows accused Ms. Bihun of forging her supervisor's signature on a memo. All her responsibilities were taken away from her; she had nothing to do.

In December 1984, Ms. Bihun went on disability leave. Her doctor diagnosed her as suffering from an "adjustment disorder" coupled with anxiety and depression. He attributed this to what had occurred at work.

Although Ms. Bihun made numerous complaints about Fellows to defendant's supervisory personnel, no one ever contacted her or Ms. Moore regarding these complaints. While she was on disability leave, Fellows resigned.

The day before Ms. Bihun was to return to work she was told not to come back for another week because there was no job for her. When she did return she was demoted two levels and placed in sales where she had no background or skills. Shortly thereafter Ms. Bihun resigned.

When Ms. Bihun took disability leave and sought psychological help she suffered from headaches, dizziness, vomiting, diarrhea, weight loss, sleep disturbances, teeth grinding, a facial twitch, crying spells and depression. Her psychologist testified that, in his opinion, the incidents of sexual harassment would continue to "affect her in the future." At the time of trial, Ms. Bihun was employed as an attorney with the Los Angeles County Public Defender.

The case went to the jury on Ms. Bihun's claims of sexual harassment and subsequent retaliation for complaining about the harassment in violation of California's Fair Employment and Housing Act (FEHA). The jury awarded Ms. Bihun compensatory damages of $1.5 million and $500,000 in punitive damages. The trial court added $893.698 in prejudgment interest, $151,468 in attorney fees plus costs and interest from the date of the verdict. The total judgment against defendant was for $3,057,369.34.

Government Code section 12940 declares it an unlawful employment practice for an employer: to sexually harass an employee (subd. (h)), to discharge, expel, or otherwise discriminate against any person because the person has opposed any practices forbidden [by FEHA] (subd. (f)); or "to fail to take all reasonable steps necessary to prevent [sexual] harassment for occurring" (subd. (i)).

* * * * *

II. The Jury Was Properly Instructed On Wilful Suppression Of Evidence

In February 1990, three months before trial, plaintiff served on defendant a demand that it produce Fellows's personnel file at trial. (Code Civ. Proc., § 1987, subd. (c).) Defendant filed a objection to this demand on the ground production of Fellows's personnel file would violate his right to privacy and there was nothing in Fellows's file relevant to this litigation. Plaintiff did not seek and order for the production of the file.

Code of Civil Procedure section 1987, subdivision (c) provides that within 20 days before trial a party may request an opposing party to bring to trial "books, documents or other things." Within five days thereafter, the party of whom the request is made "may serve written objections to the request or any part thereof, with a statement of grounds." Thereafter, on noticed motion and a showing of good cause, "the court may order production of items to which objection was made. . .."

At the time defense counsel filed the objection to the production of the file on grounds

of privacy and relevancy, he had never seen Fellows's personnel file. In fact, he had been informed by defendant several months earlier Fellows's personnel file could not be located. Defense counsel never advised the court or plaintiff the file was missing until, during trial, plaintiff renewed her demand for the production of the file. Then, for the first time, defense counsel informed the court and plaintiff: "Attempts have been made to locate Mr. Fellows's file. It cannot be located."

AT&T argues on appeal the trial court "plainly misunderstood the nature and workings of Code of Civil Procedure section 1987, subdivision (c)" in using counsel's failure to disclose the fact the file was missing as a basis for the wilful suppression of evidence instruction. Defense counsel, Mr. Gartner argued below and continues to insist on appeal he had no duty to disclose the fact the file was missing because no such duty is specifically imposed by Code of Civil Procedure section 1987, subdivision (c). He notes, in contrast, that under Code of Civil Procedure section 2031, subdivision (f)(2) a party unable to comply with an inspection demand during discovery must state the reason, e.g. "the item . . . has never existed, has been destroyed . . . lost . . . misplaced or stolen . . .."

This argument totally ignores the fact that when he objected to the request to produce the file on the grounds of privacy and relevancy he acted in bad faith (Code Civ. Proc., § 128.5) and, in our view, in violation of the ethical duty of an attorney "[t]o employ . . . such means only as are consistent with truth . . .." (Bus. & Prof. Code § 6068, subd. (d).) Attorney Gartner admitted at trial he had never seen Fellows's personnel file and he knew it could not be located at the time he responded to plaintiff's request for production. Nevertheless he asserted to plaintiff disclosure of the contents of the file would violate Fellows's right of privacy and the contents of the file were "irrelevant to the instant case." Although these were legal conclusions they carried with them an implicit factual assertion. The implicit assertion of fact was Mr. Gartner had reviewed the contents of the file. There is no other way he could make a meritorious claim the contents were irrelevant to the action or that their production would invade Fellows's privacy. It turns out, however, this assertion of fact was false. Therefore, his opposition to the request to produce was "totally and completely without merit." (Code. Civ. Proc., § 128.5, subds. (a), (b).) More serious, Mr. Gartner employed a dishonest means of avoiding production of the requested file. Rather than tell the truth, that the file had been lost or destroyed, he asserted, without any factual basis, that the file contained nothing relevant to this action and production of the file would violate Fellows's right of privacy. Business and Professional Code section 6068, subdivision (d) states it is the duty of an attorney, "To employ, for the purposes of maintaining the causes confided to him or her such means only as are consistent with truth, and never to seek to mislead the judge or any judicial officer by an artifice or false statement of fact or law." Although counsel for plaintiff was entitled to challenge the asserted grounds for refusing to produce the file, he was also entitled to rely on defense counsel's good faith and truthfulness in not challenging the asserted grounds for refusing to produce the file. (Cf. *Drociak v. State Bar (1991) 52 Cal.3d 1085, 1088 [278 Cal.Rptr. 86, 804 P.2d 711].*) Of course, had he known the truth, that the file could not be located, he could have taken steps to assure himself a diligent search had been made or requested other files that might contain the same or similar information as contained in the missing personnel file.

At plaintiff's request, the trial court gave the jury the following instruction on wilful suppression of evidence:

"If you find that defendant AT&T Information Systems, Inc. wilfully suppressed the personnel file of Peter Fellows, you may draw an inference that there was something damaging to defendant's case contained in that personnel file. Such an inference may be regarded by you as reflecting defendant's recognition of the strength of plaintiff's case generally and/or the weakness of its own case. The weight to be given such circumstance is a matter for your determination."

Defendant contends there was no evidence to support this instruction and the instruction misstates the law. We reject both these contentions.

The substantial evidence test applies to jury instructions as well as judgment (*Barry v. Raskov (1991) 232 Cal.App.3d 447, 458 [283 Cal.Rptr. 463]*), and it is prejudicial error to instruct the jury on wilful suppression of evidence when there is no evidence to support the instruction. (*County of Contra Costa v. Nulty (1965) 237 Cal.App.2d 593, 598 [47 Cal.Rptr. 109].*) However, contrary to defendant's position, a wilful suppression instruction does not require direct evidence of fraud.

Defendant relies principally on *Thor v. Boska (1974) 38 Cal.App.3d 558 [113 Cal.Rptr. 296]*, a case which did not involve an instruction on wilful suppression of evidence. Thor was a medical malpractice case in which defendant admitted during discovery he was unable to produce his original clinical records concerning his treatment of plaintiff. He "assume[d] that they were thrown away." (at pp. 560–561.) Defendant claimed, however, he had verbatim copies of the records. This claim was later called into question because plaintiff testified that when she first showed defendant the lump on her breast he drew a diagram showing its location. No such diagram appeared in the copies of the lost original records. (at p. 561.) Prior to trial, defendant admitted he had been negligent at some point in his treatment of plaintiff and on strength of that admission obtained a ruling from the trial court that any reference to the unavailability of his original records would be unduly prejudicial. (Ibid.)

In reversing judgment for the defendant in Thor the appellate court found defendant's admission of negligence was "ephemeral" at best and did not justify exclusion of evidence of the missing files. The trial court's error was prejudicial because: "The fact that defendant was unable to produce his original clinical record concerning his treatment of plaintiff after he had been charged with malpractice, created a strong inference of consciousness of guilt on his part. He apparently claimed to have an innocent explanation: exact copying to make the records more legible and inadvertent loss of the originals. On that issue, at least, plaintiff's testimony that he did not copy the diagram drawn in 19656 would have been of relevance. The issue was, however, never tried. The court apparently felt that even if the jury did not accept the explanation — which, if believed, would have made the suppressed evidence irrelevant (Evid. Code, § 403) — the prejudicial effect would outweigh the probative value because negligence was admitted." (*38 Cal.App.3d at pp. 565–566.*)

Thor is clearly distinguishable from the case before us. Thor did not involve an instruction on wilful suppression of evidence and, therefore, did not address the showing necessary for such an instruction. The case certainly does not stand for the proposition asserted by defendant: that a wilful suppression instruction is only proper where the party proposing the instruction can point to some direct evidence the opposing party deliberately destroyed a specific piece of material evidence.

Thor is distinguishable from the present case in another important way. In Thor, the court held the fact the defendant was unable to produce his original clinical records after he had been sued for malpractice, "created a strong inference of consciousness of guilt on his part." (*38 Cal.App.3d at p. 565.*) But at least, in Thor, the defendant admitted up front the records had been lost or destroyed. In our case the defendant not only was unable to produce records it clearly could anticipate would be requested after it was sued, when those records were requested it covered up the fact the records had been lost or destroyed and did not reveal this fact until forced to do so in the middle of trial. Arguably, the facts in the present case raise an even stronger inference of consciousness of guilt on defendant's part than the facts in Thor.

In the present case, the following facts provided sufficient circumstantial evidence of wilful suppression for the issue to go to the jury: (1) Although they resigned within a few months of each other, Fellows's personnel file could not be located but Ms. Bihun's file

was found; (2) the disappearance of Fellows's file was covered up by the defendant; (3) defendant's rules require maintenance of resigned employees' personnel files if a matter is in litigation; (4) it was reasonably probable Fellows's performance evaluations and any complaints of sexual harassment would be in his personnel file. Considering the evidence in the light most favorable to respondent (*County of Contra Costa v. Nulty, supra, 237 Cal.App.2d at p. 594*), we find no error in giving the jury an instruction on wilful suppression of evidence.

Defendant contends the instruction the trial court gave misstated the law because it told jurors if they found the file was wilfully suppressed they could draw an inference the file contained something damaging to defendant's case and such inference could be regarded as reflecting defendant's recognition of the strength of plaintiff's case generally or the weakness of defendant's case or both.

It is true the instruction the trial court gave goes beyond the language of BAJI No. 2.03 and Evidence Code section 413. It is, however, a correct statement of the law. Code of Civil Procedure former section 1963, subdivision 5, permitted the jury to infer "That evidence wilfully suppressed would be adverse if produced." Evidence Code section 413 was not intended as a change in the law. Rather, "[s]ection 413, taken together with section 412, restates in substance the meaning that had been given to the presumptions appearing in subdivisions 5 and 6 of Code of Civil Procedure Section 1963." (Cal. Law Revision Com. co., West's Ann. Evid. Code (1966 ed.) § 412, p. 295.) Furthermore, although *Thor v. Boska, supra*, did not involve an instruction on wilful suppression of evidence, the court did discuss the effect to be given to evidence of spoliation. The court stated the proponent of such evidence "should be entitled to an instruction that 'the adversary's conduct may be considered as tending to corroborate the proponent's case generally, and as tending to discredit the adversary's case generally.' (*38 Cal.App.3d at p. 567*, quoting McCormick on Evidence (2d ed. 1972) § 273, p. 661 (italics added by the court).)

2.03 provides: "If you find that a party wilfully suppressed evidence in order to prevent its being presented at this trial, you may consider that fact in determining what inferences to draw from the evidence."

Evidence Code section 413 provides: "In determining what inferences to draw from the evidence or facts in the case against a party, the trier of fact may consider, among other things, the party's failure to explain or to deny by his testimony such evidence or facts in the case against him, or the wilful suppression of evidence relating thereto . . . .."

BOWMAR INSTRUMENT CORP., et al. v. TEXAS INSTRUMENTS INCORPORATED

196 U.S.P.Q. 199

District Court, N.C. Indiana, Fort Wayne Div.
May 2, 1977

Defendant's Motion to compel compliance with a subpoena duces tecum will be considered at the outset. In this motion, the defendant seeks to compel the production of a large body of documents in the possession of John Young, an attorney who was employed by plaintiffs prior to and during the earlier period of this litigation. Young interposed two personal objections to the subpoena duces tecum. The first objection was that the documents were subject to Young's attorney's lien, enforceable against the defendant. At a hearing on this question on April 7, 1977, Mr. Young was personally present and informed the court that a bond having been obtained securing his legal fees he no longer had any objection to production based upon the lien. The attorney's lien issue therefore appears to be moot. Also moot is Young's second objection, based upon an order of a bankruptcy judge placing certain of these document under seal. It was represented to the court at the hearing that the seal placed upon certain of the documents no longer poses an obstacle to their production. The

plaintiffs have offered as an exhibit an order of the bankruptcy judge to this effect dated March 17, 1977.

The only remaining issues are those posed by the plaintiffs' invocation, through Mr. Young, of the attorney–client and work product privileges. Questions related to production by Young came before the court for a hearing on June 15, 1976. At that hearing the plaintiffs agreed to produce the documents sought by defendant in its February 23, 1976 motion to compel; the court entered an order to this effect on June 18, 1976. The significance of this order and the significance of the plaintiffs' agreement to produce the documents sought in 1976 have become issues in the present proceedings.

In its "Second Motion to Compel Production," filed February 23, 1976, the defendant sought the following:

files containing the correspondence and other communications between Plaintiff and its patent attorneys, John A. Young and the firm of [Gust, Irish, Jeffers & Rickert], and/or by and between said attorneys, relating to Bowmar's Patents Nos. 3,781,852 and 3,755,806, the patentability of the alleged inventions covered thereby, and the prosecution in the Patent Office of the applications for said patents, production of which has been requested by Defendant and refused by Plaintiff on the basis of a claimed attorney–client privilege.

Clearly, the documents sought were with respect to an alleged fraud on the Patent Office in prosecuting these patents. This is also made clear in defendant's supporting memorandum of February 23, 1976. In its reply to plaintiffs' memorandum in opposition to the second motion to compel, dated April 21, 1976, defendant stated that its request for production was "clearly limited" to files containing correspondence between and among "plaintiff" and its patent attorneys relating to . . . patentability." and "the prosecution in the Patent Office of the applications for said patents . . . " The defendant continued

It is with respect to these specific matters that Defendant charges the fraud was committed, and it is only these specific files by and between Bowmar and the designated patent attorneys that Defendant seeks to examine. It is definitely *not* our intent or desire to challenge or undermine the attorney–client privilege generally. (original emphasis).

This was the posture of the case at the June 15, 1976 hearing. The defendant made a showing on its claim that the attorney–client privilege had been vitiated by fraud. During the hearing, the plaintiffs agreed to make production and the court, in its order of June 18, 1976, ordered production of these items.

The defendant argues that the plaintiffs, in agreeing to make production, have waived any privilege with respect to a larger category of documents in the possession of Attorney Young, including documents generated after the commencement of this lawsuit on December 3, 1974. As acknowledged by defendant's counsel at the hearing on this matter, the present motion goes beyond the June 18, 1976 order in several respects. The defendant now seeks not only "communications" between attorneys and client, but "notes, memos, file memos, things that would normally constitute an attorney's work product." Moreover, the defendant also seeks Young documents related to the interference and other "post–lawsuit" documents. That is, the defendant now seeks documents generated after December 3, 1974.

The defendant seeks to pierce any privileges pertaining to these documents. First, the defendant argues that the plaintiffs' voluntary production in June of 1976 constitutes a waiver of the privileges. The general rule that a partial waiver of the attorney–client privilege constitutes a waiver as to the entire subject matter of the waiver. The court has no difficulty in concluding that the plaintiffs' production, in June, 1976, of certain documents related to the prosecution of the patent constitutes a waiver of the attorney–client privilege with respect to all documents related to prosecution of the patent. With respect to prosecution of the patent and the claim of fraud, the files of plaintiffs' counsel

are very much in issue. This renders all of John Young's files with respect to the prosecution of the patent discoverable, despite the fact that they may constitute "work product." see 4 J. Moore, Federal Practice (188) 26.64[4] (2d ed. 1975). Hence, as to Young's files relating to the prosecution of the patent, the attorney–client and work product privileges have no bearing, and to the extent that any such documents are sought, the defendant's motion to compel will be granted.

The defendant apparently also seeks a further category of "pre–lawsuit" documents in Young's possession. As set forth by defendant's counsel on February 11, 1977, in "Defendant's Report of Meeting of Counsel:"

" . . . TI is claiming not only that Bowmar and Young perpetrated a fraud on the Patent Office during prosecution of the '852 Patent, but that after the patent had issued, and after Bowmar and Young had full knowledge of facts indicating that the patent was invalid, Bowmar and Young had asserted the patent against TI and other calculator manufacturers, charging infringement and threatening suit, and that this was a continuation of the original fraud and an attempt to use an invalid patent to obtain an illegal monopoly."

With respect to these documents, the issue is whether they are related to the subject matter of the June, 1976 waiver. The court concludes that the alleged "abuse" of a patent obtained through fraud is sufficiently closely related to the original allegation of "fraud" that the waiver in June of 1976 must apply to any documents in Young's files which pertain to the alleged abuse. For reasons that will be discussed below, however, the court concludes that no documents generated after the commencement of this lawsuit must be produced. To the extent that defendant seeks documents in Young's possession generated prior to December 3, 1974, which may relate to an alleged abuse of the '852 patent, the defendant's motion will be granted.

Among the post–lawsuit documents sought are those related to the plaintiffs' defense of the interference action and the issues in the present lawsuit. The court concludes that the June, 1976 waiver did not constitute a waiver as to these matters. The alleged fraud on the Patent Office, on the one hand, and the defense of the interference and the prosecution of this lawsuit, on the other, are distinct matters, both temporally and substantively. The plaintiffs' waiver as to the former cannot be viewed as a waiver of the attorney–client privilege with respect to all patent documents of whatever kind or character.

Nor has the defendant raised such grave doubts as to the good faith of plaintiffs' counsel in the interference and in this action so as to pierce the privilege asserted. The defendant has not shown that the behavior of plaintiffs' counsel since December 3, 1974, has been so extraordinary as to justify their inquiry into their motives and their litigation strategies. Hence, the defendant's motion will be denied insofar as it seeks documents in Young's possession related to the interference and to this proceeding.

Furthermore, the court concludes that the date of December 3, 1974, should, as the plaintiffs contend, be used as a benchmark in resolving this motion. Documents with respect to interference and this lawsuit were generated after that date. Although the court has concluded that no privilege attaches to documents concerning the alleged "abuse" of the patent, production of any documents related to this subject matter generated after December 3, 1974 might result in an invasion of the privilege which exists with respect to the interference and this litigation. Furthermore, resolution of this protracted discovery problem will be expedited by the invocation of an objective measure of the scope of the plaintiffs' privileges — the day on which this suit was filed.

* * * * *

Plaintiffs' First Motion for Sanctions

The plaintiffs, Bowmar and Bowmar/AKI, request that the court impose sanctions against the defendant for an alleged suppression and destruction of evidence. An evidentiary hearing was held to consider this matter on April 7, 1977.

The plaintiffs' principal charge is an extremely serious one. It is alleged that in the spring and summer of 1974, with knowledge that the present lawsuit would be filed, the defendant engaged in the wholesale destruction of documents relevant to this case.

The defendant contends that this charge is legally insufficient to form a basis for sanctions. The most extreme legal position taken by the defendant is that the court is powerless to punish the wholesale, willful destruction of relevant evidence where the destruction takes place prior to a specific court order for their production. Surely this proposition must be rejected. The plaintiffs are correct that such a rule would mean the demise of the real meaning and intent of the discovery process provided by the Federal Rules of Civil Procedure.

It has long been recognized that sanctions may be proper where a party, before a lawsuit is instituted, willfully places himself in such a position that he is unable to comply with a subsequent discovery order. Cf., e.g., *Societe Internationale v. Rogers*, 357 U.S. 197, 208–09 (1958). Although a potential litigant is under no obligation to preserve every document in its possession, whatever its degree of relevance, prior to the commencement of a lawsuit, see *United States v. International Business Machines Corp.*, 66 F.R.D. 189, 194 (S.D.N.Y. 1974), some duty must be imposed in circumstances such as these lest the fact–finding process in our courts be reduced to a mockery.

The proper inquiry here is whether the defendant, with knowledge that this lawsuit would be filed, willfully destroyed documents which it knew or should have known would constitute evidence relevant to this case. Since the plaintiffs have not convincingly demonstrated that this took place, the court will deny the first motion for sanctions.

The plaintiffs' contentions regarding destruction of evidence are based entirely upon certain exhibits and deposition testimony. The defendant concedes that "in the spring and summer of 1974 transcripts of recorded telephone conversations were destroyed at the direction and under the supervision of defendant's Legal Department." The critical question is when the threat of litigation first became known to Texas Instruments Legal Department. Without a clear showing of this knowledge, it is quite impossible to find that the defendant's actions constituted the willful destruction of evidence.

The plaintiffs relied on certain exhibits to establish this crucial point. Only two items seem relevant. First, there is the deposition testimony of Leonard J. Donahoe, Manager of the defendant's Component Design Department for Calculators, that he had heard rumors since 1972 that Bowmar intended to sue. Second, there was the testimony of John Brougher that he had learned that TI employee Chris Graham had visited Bowmar in early 1974, and had reportedly been told by Ed White, President of Bowmar, that Bowmar planned to file suit against TI.

This is not convincing evidence that those responsible for the document destruction were aware at the time it took place that this litigation was a serious threat. No attempt was made to show when the threat of litigation became known to the Legal Department. The plaintiffs' evidence at best shows that a rumor circulated in the offices of a large corporation. This is too slim a reed to support the plaintiffs' charges.

The "Project Red Tag" materials, apparently offered by the plaintiffs to show TI's concern over potential litigation, are extremely ambiguous. Documents such as these and the "Beach–Kapp" telephone transcript would require this court to rely on innuendo to reach the conclusions advanced by the plaintiffs.

As this court made clear at the hearing, the involvement of the TI Legal Department in document destruction in 1974, according to the plaintiffs, the first such involvement, aroused considerable concern. However, the testimony of William Roche, General Counsel for TI, adequately refuted any malevolent implication. It was Roche's testimony that the destruction of telephone transcripts after a limited period of time was long–standing policy; that the Legal Department has long been assigned the task of "following up" on implementation of this policy; that in May of 1974 the Legal Depart-

ment was again requested to see that the procedure was followed; and that the Legal Department did so. Most significantly, Roche testified that at the time of the destruction he had no knowledge of a threatened suit by Bowmar. On cross–examination it was established only that at the time Roche ordered enforcement of the transcripts policy was he aware of a suit pending against TI and Burroughs by the Master Calculator Company. The significance of this fact has never been adequately explained by the plaintiffs. The issue before the court is whether the defendant willfully destroyed documents which it knew might constitute evidence relevant to *this* case. Even if it were established that the defendants willfully destroyed evidence relevant to the Master Calculator litigation, something which has not been established, this would not lead to a conclusion that evidence relevant to the present case was willfully destroyed.

The evidence with respect to the telephone transcripts demonstrates only that any destruction was pursuant to a long–standing company policy. The plaintiffs have failed to prove that relevant evidence was willfully and knowingly destroyed by the defendant. The other alleged grounds for sanctions have not been pressed forcefully by the plaintiffs. The controversy with respect to the "Canadian document" was not pursued at the hearing. Plaintiffs fail to mention it in the supplemental memorandum. The court has no basis for considering this issue.

The plaintiffs also failed to offer further evidence or argument with respect to certain documents from the files of J. Fred Bucy and Morris Chang of TI which were routinely destroyed by the respective secretaries shortly after this suit was instituted. There is no assertion that this constituted a willful act of destruction. Nor does the evidence support such an inference. At most, there may have been a lack of diligence on the part of the Legal Department. Even assuming that this were established, this would not provide a basis for sanctions. Since the plaintiffs have failed to show that evidence was willfully destroyed or suppressed, their first motion for sanctions will be denied.

* * * * *

Minnie Florence BREEDEN v. Caspar W. WEINBERGER, Secretary Health, Education, and Welfare

493 F.2d 1002

United States Court of Appeals, Fourth Circuit
March 19, 1974

* * * * *

Appellant Minnie Breeden was declared ineligible for Social Security disability benefits because Social Security Administration Credited her for 18 quarters of covered employment in the ten years preceding her disability, instead of the 20 quarters required for coverage under 42 U.S.C. § 423 (c)(1) (1970). Mrs. Breeden attempted to prove that she had actually earned wages during quarters for which the secretary's records showed none, but she encountered an administrative requirement that she prove her case "clearly and convincingly."

* * * * *

Mrs. Breeden filed an application for disability benefits in 1969. Upon discovering that her Social Security wages records showed a deficit covered quarters, she began trying to prove that she had earned wages between 1957 and 1963 in addition to those that appeared on her record. Several of the employees had since gone out of business; others had discarded records that would prove or disprove Mrs. Breenden's claims. Consequently, her supporting evidence was limited to affidavits and testimony of people who had known her during the periods in question. Most of her witnesses were relatives, some were friends, others were coworkers and acquaintances, and one was the wife of a former employer. If any substantial part of their testimony were accepted it would establish coverage for more than the two quarters that Mrs. Breeden lacked. But the administrative law judge rejected all the testimony, including Mrs. Breeden's own account of her work history. He indicated distrust for the testimony of "friends and kinfolk." He complained repeatedly that none of the witnesses produced written records and that much of their testimony was inexact. And he insisted

that Mrs. Breeden prove her case "clearly and convincingly." On this ground he concluded that she had not carried her burden of proof. The appeals counsel adopted his findings and conclusions, and Mrs. Breeden petitioned the district court for review. The district judge remanded the case for more evidence, indicating that the denial of benefits was not supported by substantial evidence. On remand, the appeals council accepted several pieces of documentary evidence that Mrs. Breeden's attorney offered, but reaffirmed the original decision without convening another hearing. Taking the case a second time on substantially the same records as before, the district judge held that Mrs. Breeden had the burden of proving coverage by "clear and convincing evidence." On a survey of the record he concluded that her evidence did not meet that standard and that the administrative decision was therefore based on substantial evidence. We reverse.

* * * * *

The Progression of evidentiary value embodied in the Social Security Act — evidence, presumptive evidence, and conclusive effect — suggests that the provision concerning blank wage records reflects congressional sensitivity to need to balance two somewhat conflicting purposes. One purpose, akin to the supposed rationale for statues of limitation, is to guard against false claims after contradictory evidence is unavailable. But Congress did not write a statue of limitations for contradicting blank wage records, as it did for self–employment income reports. The different treatment afforded to blank wage records suggests a second purpose — that Congress intended not to penalize wage earners for the carelessness or dishonesty of their employers. A requirement of proof by clear and convincing evidence would all but destroy this secondary congressional intent. Applying the preponderance standard to the claimant's evidence affords the government reasonable protection against spurious claims and also makes it possible to establish valid ones. We hold that the claimant need not persuade the administrative law judge by any standard of "high probability"; she need only persuade him that it is more probable than not that she received the wages she claims. This is the meaning of the rubric common in jury trails: "satisfied by the greater weight of the evidence." See McCormick. *supra*, § 339, at 794–95.

* * * * *

Unlike the statute in *Del Vecchio*, which creates certain presumptions "in the absence of substantial evidence to the contrary," 33 U.S.C. § 920 (1970), the Social Security Act provides that the absence of a record entry shall be "presumptive evidence" that no wages were paid — whether or not there is other evidence. We think the Congress did not intend the presumption to evaporate when the contrary evidence is introduced. Instead, we hold this presumption survives the offering of contradictory evidence and thereafter may itself constitute substantial evidence that no wages were paid.

* * * * *

[However, [i]f reliance on the presumption is arbitrary or if it is not "justified by a fair estimate of the worth of the testimony of the witnesses" who support the claimant, [citation omitted] we must conclude that the administrative decision is not supported by substantial evidence.

* * * * *

Carl T. BRITT v. John R. BLOCK, Secretary, U.S. Dept. of Agriculture; Bruce Watson, U.S. Dept. of Agriculture, S.C.S.; Robert Shaw, U.S. Dept. of Agriculture, S.C.S.; Richard Babcock, U.S. Dept. of Agriculture, S.C.S.

636 F.Supp. 596

United States District Court, D. Vermont
April 4, 1986

Destruction of Records

At the threshold of consideration of the merits of this controversy, the court is confronted with the charge by the plaintiff that SCS representatives engaged in bad faith destruction of pertinent documents. Evidence on this point was pre-

sented by two witnesses called by the defendant. This contention has been strenuously pursued by the plaintiff throughout the extensive discovery process. The claim has been opposed with equal vigor by the Secretary in pretrial hearings conducted and reported by the United States Magistrate and the court as well. The court will not repeat the considerations and ruling written in denying the plaintiff's motion to impose the extreme sanction of default for willful destruction of documents requested by the plaintiff. (Civil Action No. 82–279, Opinion filed October 16, 1985.) This aspect of the controversy was revised and revisited at the trial.

The plaintiff's complaint centers on destruction of personnel and work records of various white employees that the plaintiff sought to use as a basis of comparison to support the contention that racial discrimination was a factor in the plaintiff's delayed advancement, particularly in his being passed over for the Rutland vacancy. To refute this untoward inference, the defendant summoned two SCS employees concerned with the responsibility of preservation and destruction of related documents.

After the plaintiff's EEO complaint was initiated, and the extensive investigation undertaken by the general counsel's office of the Department, the plaintiff's personnel records were preserved. However, the retention did not include all of such records of other persons in SCS that might shed some light on the racial preference issue. The defendant's witness, Karen Davignon, testified that the disposition made of the documents sought by the plaintiff was dictated by guidelines established by the SCS. The policy practice and rules of the agency directed that employees' performance evaluations and appraisals be routinely destroyed three years after the date the supervisory officials had prepared and filed them. In keeping with this practice, the personnel records of other employees for the years 1978 and before were destroyed by 1981. Apparently John Pratt's appraisal summaries for 1977 and 1978 and his standard of performance dated October 28, 1976, were preserved since his promotion was implicated in the EEO complaint. (Pltf's Ex. 34, 35, 36). In any event the court finds that the witness Davignon was not advised of the relevancy or expediency for retaining the records of other employees. She was neither advised nor directed by any employee of the SCS to retain or destroy the documents in question. Her acts in this regard were performed in good faith. The destruction was prompted entirely by her understanding of the applicable agency directives.

A further shortage claimed by the plaintiff concerned the working papers, including field notes, daily diary sheets and time attendance records prepared by soil scientists in the performance of their assigned duties in Vermont. Ms. Ferrier served in the accounting section of the SCS during the time under investigation. The daily records were submitted and retained as financial documentation of a variety of related expenses and disbursements at the Winooski office of SCS. She was not aware of the plaintiff's EEO complaint. She disposed of the field notes and time sheet records pursuant to her understanding of the agency rules. In this function she received no instructions from her supervisors concerning the preservation or destruction of the records of which the plaintiff complains. In consequence, those documents were preserved for a three year period and then routinely destroyed.

The plaintiff urges that failure of the defendant to call other witnesses who had higher responsibility for record maintenance creates and adverse inference that the destruction of records was wrongful.

The record does not bear this out. Numerous witnesses of higher rank in the SCS were available and cross examined by counsel. The list includes John Titchner, the present State Conservationist who served as assistant to Robert P. Shaw, his predecessor in office at the time the Rutland selection was made. As noted earlier, Dunton resides in Florida after retiring in 1982.

To be sure, the destruction of personnel and daily work records might arouse suspicion. However, in the context of the evidence at hand, it does not prove bad faith on the part of those responsible for the agency records.

Destruction of records through misunderstanding or negligence is not sufficient to supply evidence or recast the burden of proof. *See Coates v. Johnson & Johnson*, 756 F.2d 524, 551 (7th Cir.1985); *Valentino v. U.S. Postal Service*, 674 F.2d 56, 73 n. 31 (D.C.Cir. 1975).

BROWN & WILLIAMSON TOBACCO CORPORATION v. Walter JACOBSON and CBS, INC.

644 F.Supp. 1240

United States District Court (N.D.Ill. 1986)
August 7, 1986

Defendants Walter Jacobson and CBS, Inc. move to vacate the judgment entered against them and to enter judgment in their favor notwithstanding the verdicts or, in the alternative, for a substantial remittitur of damages or a new trial.

The complaint upon which this case was tried was initially dismissed. On appeal it was upheld and the case was remanded for trial. *Brown & Williamson Tobacco Corp. v. Jacobson*, 713 F.2d 262 (7th Cir. 1983). The Court of Appeals upheld that a television broadcast stating that advertising designed to attract children to smoke by associating smoking with pleasure illicit activity — pot, wine, beer and sex — was libelous per se because it accused plaintiff Brown & Williamson Tobacco Co. ("B & W") of immoral conduct.

The Court of Appeals accurately described the nature of this case (as shown by the evidence at trial) as follows:

In 1975, Ted Bates, the advertising agency that had the Viceroy account, hired the Kennan market–research firm to help develop a new advertising strategy for Viceroy. Kennan submitted a report which stated that for "the younger smoker," "a cigarette, and the whole smoking process, is part of the illicit pleasure category . . . In the young smoker's mind a cigarette falls into the same category with wine, beer, shaving, wearing a bra (or purposely not wearing one), declaration of independence and striving for self–identity. For the young starter, a cigarette is associated with introduction to sex life, with courtship, with smoking 'pot' and keeping studying hours . . ." The report recommended, therefore, the following pitches to "young smokers, starters": "Present the cigarette as part of the illicit pleasure category of products and activities . . . To the best of your ability, (considering some legal constraints), relate the cigarette to 'pot', wine, beer, sex, etc. *Don't communicate health or health–related points.*" Ted Bates forwarded the report to Brown & Williamson. . . . Brown & Williamson rejected the "illicit pleasure strategy" proposed in the report, and fired Ted Bates primarily because of displeasure with the proposed strategy.

Years later the Federal Trade Commission conducted an investigation of cigarette advertising, and in May 1981 it published a report of its staff on the investigation. The FTC staff report discusses the Kennan report, correctly dates it to May 1975, and after quoting from it the passages we have quoted states that "B & W adopted many of the ideas contained in this report in the development of a Viceroy advertising campaign." In support of this assertion the staff report quotes an internal Brown & Williamson document on "Viceroy Strategy," dated 1976, which states, "The marketing efforts must cope with consumers' attitudes about smoking and health, either providing them a *rationale* for smoking a full flavor VICEROY or providing a means of *repressing* their concerns about smoking a full flavor VICEROY." The staff report then quotes a description of three advertising strategies. Although the description contains no reference to young smokers or to 'starters,' the staff report states: "B & W documents also show that it translated the advice [presumably from the Kennan report] on how to attract young 'starters' into an advertising campaign featuring young adults in situations that the vast majority of young people probably would experience and in situations demonstrating adherence to a 'free and easy, hedonistic lifestyle.'" The interior quotation is from another 1976 Brown & Williamson document on advertising strategy.

On November 4, 1981, a reporter for WBBM–TV called Brown & Williamson headquarters and was put in touch with a Mr. Humber in the corporate affairs department. The reporter told Mr. Humber that he was preparing a story on the tobacco industry for Walter Jacobson's "Perspective" program and asked him about the part of the FTC staff report that dealt with the Viceroy advertising strategy. Humber replied that Brown & Williamson had rejected the proposal and had fired Ted Bates in part because of dissatisfaction with those proposals.

Walter Jacobson's "Perspective" on the tobacco industry was broadcast on November 11 and rebroadcast on November 12 and again on March 5, 1982. In the broadcast, Jacobson, after stating that "pushing cigarettes on television is prohibited," announces his theme: "Television is off limits to cigarettes and so the business, the killer business has gone to the ad business in New York for help, to the slicksters on Madison Avenue with a billion dollars a year for bigger and better ways to sell cigarettes. Go for the youth of America, go get 'em guys . . . Hook 'em while they are young, make 'em start now — just think how many cigarettes they'll be smoking when they grow up." Various examples of how cigarette marketing attempts "to addict the children to poison" are given. The last and longest concerns Viceroy.

The cigarette business insists, in fact, it will swear up and down in public, it is now selling cigarettes to children, that if children are smoking, which they are, more than ever before, it's not the fault of the cigarette business. That's what Viceroy is saying, "Who knows whose fault it is that children are smoking? It's not ours."

Well, there is a confidential report on cigarette advertising in the files of the Federal Government right now, a Viceroy advertising, the Viceroy strategy for attracting young people, starters they are called, to smoking — FOR THE YOUNG SMOKER . . . A CIGARETTE FALLS INTO THE SAME CATEGORY WITH WINE, BEER, SHAVING OR WEARING A BRA . . ." says the Viceroy strategy — "A DECLARATION OF

INDEPENDENCE AND STRIVING FOR SELF–IDENTITY." Therefore, an attempt should be made, says Viceroy to " . . . PRESENT THE CIGARETTE AS AN INITIATION INTO THE ADULT WORLD," TO " . . . PRESENT THE CIGARETTE AS AN ILLICIT PLEASURE . . . A BASIC SYMBOL OF THE GROWING–UP, MATURING PROCESS." An attempt should be made, says the Viceroy slicksters, "TO RELATE THE CIGARETTE TO 'POT', WINE, BEER, SEX. DO NOT COMMUNICATE HEALTH OR HEALTH–RELATED POINTS." That's the strategy of the cigarette slicksters, the cigarette business which is insisting in public, "we are not selling cigarettes to children."

They're not slicksters, they're liars.

id. at 266.

The liability and damage issues were bifurcated with the same jury hearing the evidence on both liability and damages. Pursuant to Rule 49(a) of the Federal Rules of Civil Procedures, the jury made separate findings on the liability issues. The jury found that: (1) plaintiff proved by a preponderance of evidence that defendants' broadcast was "of and concerning" B & W; (2) plaintiff proved by a preponderance of evidence that defendants' broadcast was substantially false; (3) plaintiff proved by clear and convincing evidence that defendants knew the broadcast was false or recklessly disregarded whether or not the broadcast was false; and (4) defendants did not prove by a preponderance of the evidence that the broadcast was a "fair summary" of portions of a government report. After hearing evidence with respect to damages the jury awarded B & W $3 million in general damages, $2 million in punitive damages from CBS, and $50,000 in punitive damages from Jacobson.

Defendants contend that they are entitled to post–trial relief because the jury's findings and verdicts are against the manifest weight of the evidence, evidence offered by plaintiff was improperly received or evidence offered by defendants was improperly excluded; instructions tendered were improperly given or refused; defendants were precluded from asserting to the jury the defense opinion; punitive damages are unconstitutional; and the amount of compensatory and punitive damages was excessive. Defendants request in the alternative that the court order a remittitur.

* * * * *

Actual Malice

* * * * *

Radutzky also conducted an unsuccessful search to locate Viceroy advertising that reflected the "pot, wine, beer and sex" strategy. Radutzky stated that he specifically noted this failure to find such ads when he submitted a sample script to Jacobson (Tr. 631–32, 667–68, 691). Jacobson specifically directed Radutzky to find such ads (Tr. 707–08). Unable to find any such ads, defendants illustrated the broadcast with, among other things, an ad showing a pack of Viceroy cigarettes next to two golf clubs and a golf ball (Tr. 708–09). The jury could have regarded defendants' failure to find any ads corroborating the "Viceroy strategy," after inquiry and active attempts to do so, as evidence either that they knew Viceroy never adopted such a strategy or as evidence which would show reckless disregard of the truth.

There was also testimony that Radutzky destroyed parts of certain relevant research and script documents. Radutzky testified he threw away that part of his copy of the FTC Staff Report with handwritten notes relating to B & W (Tr. 602), portions of his outline (Tr. 603), his copy, Jacobson's copy and several other copies of his sample script (Tr. 684), and his contemporaneous notes of interviews with people regarding Viceroy (Tr. 560–61).

The destruction of documents while a litigation is pending can be "an admission that the introduction of such evidence would be damaging to the party not producing it." *A.C. Becken Co. v. Gemex Corp.,* 314 F.2d 839, 841 (7th Cir.), *cert. denied,* 375 U.S. 816, 84 S.Ct. 68, 11 L.Ed.2d 51 (1963). Radutzky's selective description of documents, containing substantial notes reflecting his research and thinking prior to the broadcast, could have led the jury to conclude that he knew the statements made in the broadcast were false or had doubts as to their truth.

Defendants argue that the selective document destruction evidence should not have been admitted because B & W failed to show as a preliminary matter that the destruction was in bad faith. *See Coates v. Johnson & Johnson,* 756 F.2d 524, 550–51 (7th Cir. 1985); *S.C. Johnson & Son, Inc. v. Louisville & Nashville Railroad Co.,* 695 F.2d 253, 258–59, (7th Cir.1982). The Seventh Circuit stated the general rule in *S.C. Johnson*:

> It is elementary that if a party has evidence . . . in its control and fails to produce it, an inference may be warranted that the document would have been unfavorable. *However . . . it must appear that the party had some reasons to suppose that nonproduction would justify the inference . . . the totality of the circumstances must bring home to the nonproducing party notice that the inference must be drawn.*

695 F.2d at 259 (quoting *Commercial Insurance Co. of Newark v. Gonzalez,* 512 F.2d 1307, 1314 (1st Cir.), *cert. denied,* 423 U.S. 838, 96 S.Ct. 65, 46 L.Ed.2d 57 (1975) (emphasis added by Seventh Circuit)). Thus the "totality of the circumstances" must demonstrate that Radutzky destroyed his notes and other documents in bad faith.

Radutzky knew that the present case had been brought against CBS and Jacobson. He learned of the lawsuit in March, 1982, shortly after it was filed. CBS had a retention policy that provided:

> Once the station is notified of a claim pertaining to any of the following material, the litigation section of the Law Department should be notified and any and all related materials should be retained until specifically released.

> Some materials are retained indefinitely on a selected basis. Our policy is to review the files in January to determine what

should be selectively retained. Obviously if there is a . . . pending legal action, our policy if to retain all pertinent materials unless specifically released by the Law Department.

Radutzky testified that he was kept informed about the case by lawyers (Tr. 558) and that he only destroyed the documents when he heard the case was dismissed (Tr. 623); that he did not know that the dismissal was being appealed (Tr. 624); and that he was only housecleaning when he threw those documents away (Tr. 758–59).

However, Radutzky admitted he was not given permission by the CBS attorneys to destroy documents (Tr. 560). The notice of appeal from the dismissal was filed only six days after the motion to dismiss was granted. Although Radutzky denied knowing about CBS's retention policy, his emphasis on destroying the documents only after learning of the dismissal would indicate he understood that documents should not be destroyed while litigation is pending.

Radutzky testified he "gathered up the notes that [he] had taken on the cigarette series as well as a bunch of other notes . . . and [he] used that opportunity to just clean house, as it were, and relieve overflowing files." (Tr. 758–59). This explanation implies a wholesale, nonselective process. But only part of the copy of the FTC report with Radutzky's handwritten notes in the margins was destroyed the first five of ten pages were destroyed and the others were not (Tr. 586–87, 591).

Radutzky made an original and six or seven copies of his "sample script," one of the documents destroyed, and distributed them to Jacobson and other CBS executives (Tr. 685–86). Yet not one of these copies could be found, and Radutzky did not claim to destroy documents in the possession of anyone other than Jacobson and himself.

The jury could reasonably find, based on the totality of the circumstances, that Radutzky's destruction of documents was in bad faith, justifying an inference that the documents were damaging to defendants' case. The jury could conclude that the contents of these documents would indicate serious doubt, or more, on the part of Radutzky, as to the truth of the broadcast.

* * * * *

Steve C. BUBRICK, Jr., and Mae E. Bubrick v. NORTHERN ILLINOIS GAS COMPANY, a corporation

264 N.E.2d 560

Appellate Court of Illinois First District, Fourth Division
September 23, 1970

Plaintiffs brought an action for property damage to their home and personal belongings by the alleged negligence of defendant in causing a fire. Defendant appeals from a judgment in favor of plaintiffs, in the amount of $22,114.00. Defendant contends that the trial court permitted prejudicial error by allowing certain instructions to be submitted to the jury, thus entitling defendant to a new trial.

Plaintiffs moved into their home in July, 1959, and remained in residence until January 24, 1961, when it was extensively damaged by fire. The fire originated in a small enclosure attached to the rear of the house. This enclosure was described as a shed, cubicle, cabinet or box and in appearance was similar to a dog house. It was of wood construction, 4 feet high, 3 1/2 to 4 feet long and 3 1/2 feet in width with a concrete foundation.

This enclosure contained a water pipe, gas meter and regulator and an electrical switch that actuated the water pump which was located in a well 75 to 80 feet from the house.

* * * * *

Joseph W. Lynch, was called as an adverse witness and testified:

He is manager of Maintenance and Construction for defendant and was operating superintendent at the time of the fire. He was in charge of the construction of gas mains, services, installing meters, regulators, maintenance of pressure and underground facilities and servicing of equipment.

Gas is purchased at 700 lbs. pressure per square inch and is reduced to 150 lbs. p.s.i. and thus forced into the mains. In the cities the pressure is reduced to between 20 to 60 lbs. p.s.i. where it is distributed in mains. The gas main near plaintiff's home was 60 lbs. p.s.i. and the line leading into their regulator was about the same. Defendant has records of the main but not the services. The company maintains records showing when the pipe was installed, but the witness did not remember when the gas service line was put in from the main to plaintiff's home; although he had looked at the records after the fire and the day he testified, he forgot the date of installation. Records of mapping of mains and dates of installation are at the Crystal Lake office. Practically every one of defendant's lines has anodes but this would depend on when the pipe was installed and ground conditions, because some soil is more corrosive to pipe than others. Defendant keeps a record of lines which have anodes and the record would show if the line to plaintiff's home was equipped with anodes.

The witness had never seen these records but believed they are also at Crystal Lake. The meters are read every month, or at least every two months, but the witness did not believe the records were kept after billing the customer. A record is maintained by defendant on service calls, but this witness did not know if there was a record of a service call from July, 1959, to January, 1961, regarding plaintiff's home. There was no service call for one year previous to the fire. A search of the records which are retained from a year to 18 months indicated there was no call at plaintiff's home. When asked as to the whereabouts of these records, this witness responded that they have either been destroyed or would be at the Aurora office of defendant. He made no personal search but relied upon a clerk whose name he could not remember, so that the witness personally did not know if a service call had been made.

About 30,000 service calls a year are made by

defendant. Defendant has a regular maintenance policy regarding its underground systems and keeps a record of maintenance, but he did not know the last time the main near plaintiff's home was inspected. The lines are checked every five years and an instrument is used on the surface to detect underground leaks. A record of this practice is maintained and may be at Crystal Lake or in general storage at Aurora, but he had never seen it.

* * * * *

He was not present when the meter and regulator were removed, but the record of when it was done would probably be kept in general files in Aurora. The presence of a quantity of gas removes oxygen and this could cause vegetation to "brown out."

* * * * *

The first instruction complained of by defendant is Illinois Pattern Instruction No. 5.01 which permits an unfavorable inference if a party, without reasonable excuse, fails to produce evidence under his control. Defendants contend that the records concerning installation, maintenance and inspection of its lines and equipment were not material under plaintiff's theory and that in any event, many of the records were unobtainable having since been destroyed.

Since these records pertain to the construction and maintenance of the defendant's lines, allegedly the cause of the conflagration, we find these records to be particularly material to plaintiff's theory of the case. We also note that defendant's employee Lynch testified to checking some of these records after the conflagration. Therefore, even defendant attached sufficient interest in these records that warrant their examination demonstrating their materiality and relevancy.

Defendant in an endeavor to show a reasonable excuse for the absence or lack of records, introduced into evidence Illinois Commerce Commission regulations which provide for mandatory retention of records of general inspections, tests, meter repairs, customer services and reports of complaints for two or three year periods. However, these regulations do not prohibit the retention of records beyond the specified intervals. In light of the testimony of Lynch, we assume that some of these records were still available. However, defendant offers no reasonable explanation for their non–production. It is also difficult to discern which of the records were in existence and which had been destroyed.

Defendant cites *Piechalak v. Liberty Trucking Co.*, 58 Ill.App.2d 289, 208 N.E. 2d 379 (1965) wherein a minor plaintiff was struck down by defendant's truck as she ran across the street. The plaintiff subpoenaed the truck maintenance records of a year previous to the accident, but they were unavailable because they had been destroyed in the regular course of business. The court permitted plaintiff to comment on the unavailability of the records, but refused to give the instruction complained of in the case at bar.

In the case at bar plaintiff pursued and was awarded a verdict on the theory that defendant's negligence in the maintenance and operation of its property caused the fire. In *Piechalak*, there was no suggestion that the condition of the truck caused or contributed to the accident and it was firmly established that the records in that case had been destroyed in the ordinary course of business.

Therefore, we find no error in submitting this instruction to the jury.

* * * * *

A. E. BURCHFIELD, d/b/a Burchfield Grocery v. UNITED STATES FIDELITY AND GUARANTY COMPANY

118 So.2d 767

Supreme Court of Mississippi
March 14, 1960

This suit was brought by A.E. Burchfield, doing business as Burchfield Grocery, against the United States Fidelity and Guaranty Company for recovery on a fire insurance policy for $1,000 on his merchandise and stock of goods situated in a one–story, frame, metal roofed building occupied as a grocer store situated about six miles west from Duncan on the south side of the Duncan–Round Lake Road in Bolivar County, Mississippi.

This policy contained the usual Iron Safe Clause which is as follows:

* * * * *

The insured will keep a set of books, which shall clearly and plainly present a complete record of business transacted, including all purchases, sales and shipments, both for cash and credit, from date of inventory, as provided for in first section of this clause, and during the continuance of this policy.

* * * * *

In the event of failure to produce such set of books and inventories for the inspection of this Company, this policy shall become null and void, and such failure shall constitute a perpetual bar to any recovery thereon.

The appellee pleaded the Iron Safe Clause and pleaded that it had been violated, and that a violation thereof forfeited all rights under the policy. At the trial the lower court granted a peremptory instruction in favor of the appellee from which Mr. Burchfield appeals.

* * * * *

In 29A Am.Jur., Insurance Section 9 at page 137, it is said: "The destruction or theft of books and papers required by policy of insurance to be kept or produced will excuse a noncompliance with requirement if due to no fault or design of the insured. If, however, the destruction of such papers is due to the negligent failure of the insured to preserve them as required by this policy, his failure to produce them in accordance with the requirement of the policy will preclude any recovery thereon." In the footnote to this statement there is again cited the said case of *Joffe v. Niagara Fire Insurance Company*, supra. "Furthermore, if no such books and inventories are kept as are required by a fire insurance policy, the loss of those which were kept will not excuse the failure of the insured to meet the requirement."

We are of the opinion that the trial court was correct in granting a peremptory instruction for the appellee and that for this reason the judgment of the lower court should be and it is hereby affirmed.

Joan CAPELLUPO, et al. v. FMC CORPORATION

126 F.R.D. 545

United States District Court, D. Minnesota, Fourth Division
June 19, 1989

Plaintiffs claim that defendant FMC and, in particular, its Northern Ordnance Division (FMC/NOD) engaged in intentional destruction of evidence. Plaintiffs seek sanctions against defendant for the conduct alleged. The Court heard evidence concerning the charges on May 1 and 2, 1989.

Having heard and considered the evidence, the Court finds that the defendant and its agents have ordered and participated in the knowing and intentional destruction of documents and evidence. This conduct commenced in October, 1983, and was part of a premeditated effort to subvert the proceedings in the present case. The Court further finds that thereafter, and continuing to and until May 3, 1989, the defendant and its agents have engaged in a conspiracy to lie and disseminate knowing half–truths in an effort to disguise and secrete their wrongful acts. To this end they have twisted and tortured the truth both in depositions and in the proceedings before this Court.

The penalties for these acts will be considered hereafter.

Facts

This case arises out of a complaint of employment–related gender discrimination at FMC/NOD. The case was initially commenced by plaintiff Kathy Smith who was thereafter joined by co–plaintiff Joan Capellupo.

During Summer 1983, Smith advised Barbara Jabr, the FMC/NOD Equal Employment Opportunity Manager, that she was "fed–up" with FMC/NOD's gender–based treatment and she was contemplating bringing a class action gender discrimination charge against the company, based upon her experience and observations. It is clear from the evidence in the hearing that Jabr communicated the information to co–worker Don Bauer at FMC/NOD in Minnesota. She also informed Messrs. Nick Derrough and James Renfroe at FMC's corporate headquarters. The information was made known in late August and early September, 1983.

Bauer is an employee at FMC/NOD where he specializes in industrial relations. In 1983, Bauer was manager of employee relations. Derrough is the corporation's coordinator of Equal Employment Opportunity/Affirmative Action (EEO/AA) at FMC's corporate headquarters in Chicago, Illinois. Renfroe is presently retired, but at the time of these events he was a member of the general counsel's staff. Until his retirement in 1986, Renfroe was engaged in corporate labor matters as corporate labor counsel.

This evidence demonstrates that Jabr's concerns about NOD's employment practices were intensified by Smith's threatened employment discrimination complaint. To this end, Jabr directed a memorandum to Renfroe, dated August 30, 1983, which concluded "My largest concern goes beyond all that I have recounted above. It is the possible filing of a class action lawsuit by Paul Sprenger on behalf of Northern Ordnance women." Plaintiffs' exhibit 5.

This concern was particularly acute in light of FMC's recent experience in another gender–based discrimination class action lawsuit in San Jose, California. Derrough and Renfroe were involved in the San Jose litigation. Renfroe testified that the San Jose experience was instructive on the issue of document retention.

The hearing evidence indicated that Jabr's memorandum of August 30, 1983, and its expressed concerns were forwarded through the FMC hierarchy. On September 6, 1983, Renfroe of the Chicago legal department sent

a confidential memo to FMC's general counsel, P. J. Head, referring to "Sex Discrimination Charges." That his memo refers to the Northern Ordnance Division is clear from the fact that the memo bears a handwritten note from Tom Epley, a vice president and general manager at FMC/ORD. Plaintiffs' exhibit 30. Further confirmation of the extent of FMC's concern is exemplified by General Counsel Head's September 6, 1983, calendar notation in which he wrote "NOD sex discrimination claim. Renfroe checking up." Plaintiffs' exhibit 18.

A follow–up entry in Head's calendar, dated September 27, 1983, notes, "Day thinks task force has been set up." Plaintiffs' exhibit 18. The meaning of the entry was clarified in Head's deposition (plaintiffs' exhibit 46, p. 23, ff. 7–10) in which he made clear the reference is to one Mr. Day, an associate general counsel.

On October 3, 1983, Derrough, Chicago's EEO/AA supervisor, along with labor counsel Renfroe, arrived in Minnesota for a meeting at FMC/NOD the next day, October 4, 1983. Smith's complaints were discussed at the meeting. The meeting was initially attended by Renfroe, Bauer, and a Mr. Johnson, a new employee from FMC corporate. Later, the attendees were joined by Jabr. Still later, and either during the meeting or just subsequent to it, Derrough and Renfroe met with Mark DelVecchio. DelVecchio was, at the time, employed at FMC/NOD as an associate employee relations representative.

The Court finds that during, or very shortly after, the October 4, 1983, meeting, Derrough and Renfroe made the decision to systematically destroy FMC/NOD's documents relating to NOD's employment practices and the employee relations department's personally–held records relating to equal employment opportunity and employee complaints of discrimination. While Bauer does not recall a direct instruction to destroy documents at this October 4, 1983, meeting, he testified to his recollection of speaking of Kathy Smith at least in general. He further indicated he recalled discussing getting rid of documents which were not required to be maintained.

Under oath, both Derrough and Renfroe denied making or implementing the document destruction decision at this meeting. The Court finds their denials to be inherently unbelievable. In making this finding, the Court has specifically considered each man's credibility based on the Court's observation of their mien and manner while on the witness stand, the believability of their statements, the array of oral and physical evidence in opposition to their testimony, and the course of events which took place thereafter. With these considerations in mind, the Court rejects their denials.

DelVecchio testified that he met with Derrough and Renfroe on or about October 4, 1983. DelVecchio recalls being instructed by Derrough or Renfroe that he was to collect and destroy FMC/NOD's records relating to EEO/AA. Derrough's recall in this area is instructive and indicative of the studied deception in which he engaged; he claims he did not tell DelVecchio to destroy documents, *per se*, rather, he wanted DelVecchio to see that some documents were retained and others disposed of. DelVecchio is clear in his recollection that the instruction did not come from Bauer, one of the other attendees, but at the same time it is clear, as will be set forth below, that Bauer was well familiar with the document destruction decision.

The October 4, 1983, oral destruction order to DelVecchio was confirmed in writing shortly thereafter by Derrough, who sent a memorandum to DelVecchio designating the documents to be destroyed. Neither Derrough nor DelVecchio, according to the evidence, has retained a copy of this directive. Apparently no copy exists today. DelVecchio recalls, however, that he was to collect and destroy any affirmative action plans and personnel documents personally held in the hands of NOD division heads.

The timing of these events is of significance. DelVecchio met with Derrough and Renfroe on October 4, 1983. He testified that he received the written instruction via Federal Express from Derrough in Chicago. This implies a sense of urgency regarding the commencement of disposal. Derrough does not deny that he sent such instructions, but his files contain no copy of the instructions, a portion of which were hand–written. DelVecchio testified, and the Court finds, that the actual destruction began a few days later. Those days between October 4, 1983, and the commencement of destruction are of import because during their span, FMC's knowledge and understanding of Smith's sex discrimination claim increased.

On October 6, 1983, Bauer wrote a memo under the name of Kathy Smith, mentioning the name of the law firm of "Springer [sic] Olson & Shuts [sic]" and designating "class action." Plaintiffs' exhibit 14. The memo, or at least its content, were known by FMC's higher management. It was acknowledged by Derrough and Renfroe. Head's handwritten diary–calendar note for October 6, 1983, (plaintiffs' exhibit 17) alludes to this communication. In deposition testimony concerning the diary note, he stated "[t]hat would either reference a phone call, which it may have been, that there were sex discrimination complaints or claims that might be made." Dep., p. 24, ff. 17–20. By October 10, 1983, Head's calendar note is specific: "Charge filed by Sprenger firm." Plaintiffs exhibit 17.

DelVecchio's destruction work was not accomplished without difficulty. In fact, he had trouble on his first stop, at the office of one William Patterson: when asked for the personal records concerning EEO/AA, Patterson stated he would not comply with this irregular request, saying "this is out of the ordinary." Patterson refused to provide the documents. The logjam was broken when DelVecchio applied to employment relations manager Bauer for help. Bauer, under cross–examination, admitted that after DelVecchio's request for assistance, he spoke to Patterson, who expressed his concerns. Bauer told Patterson that DelVecchio was proceeding under Renfroe's instruction and Patterson could give up the documents for destruction. With this instruction, and Bauer's promise to contact the other division directors, DelVecchio visited not fewer than ten department heads. *See* plaintiffs' exhibit 8. From each he obtained personal office files concerning sex discrimination matters and

affirmative action plans. After dutifully removing paper clips and staples, every document was shredded. There is no exact record
of what was taken, which precludes meaningful document reconstruction.

The hearing's testimony indicated, and the
Court finds, that *at a minimum* FMC destroyed a) historically important affirmative
action plans, b) personally–maintained files
concerning employee discrimination claims,
c) files concerning personal investigations of
complaints of discrimination, d) personal
records of cases individually and informally
conciliated, and e) records of terminations
and employee interviews (including resumes). The evidence indicated that many
"document boxes" of items were destroyed.

Document destruction continued from early October, 1983, through all of 1984, and beyond. In
particular, at a meeting held on or about February
14, 1984, at FMC/NOD, Renfroe instructed Derrough, Epley, and Jabr to destroy documents,
including unofficial internal investigation information. All four of these individuals certainly
had extensive knowledge of the class action suit
by that time. There is no indication that Renfroe's
directive was not carried out.

While the vast bulk of document destruction
took place in the last quarter of 1983, this
behavior continued until the arrival of
George Trumble, a new corporate counsel, in
March or April of 1985, almost 18 months
later. When Trumble arrived, he directed that
there be no more document destruction.

FMC, while weaving a fabric of lies concerning its effort to destroy documents, makes a
second defense: FMC suggests that while it
may have thought Smith would file a gender
discrimination complaint, it did not really
know this until mid–November, 1983, when
FMC actually received Smith's EEOC complaint. Defendant's exhibit 29. Or, as a further fallback, perhaps FMC did not know
until it received Capellupo's complaint in
December, 1983. Defendant's exhibit 28.
Upon this slippery foundation, FMC constructs the argument that, without the class
action pleadings in hand, document destruction was permissible.

The Court rejects this formulation. The Court
finds that FMC, from its highest corporate
offices down through the entire NOD employee relations department, knew of
Smith's claim as well as the fact that she fully
intended to assert a class action as early as
October 1, 1983.

The Court has delineated, above, facts which
conclusively demonstrate that FMC was
acutely aware of the prospect of this case on
October 6, 1983. Further, FMC general counsel Head's calendar–diary, in an entry dated
October 10, 1983, indicated: "NOD sex discrimination, Kathy Smith, complaint filed
with State on class basis — informed supervisor, Eric Olson, Sprenger firm." A later
entry, on the same day, reads as follows:
"Kathy Smith — filed with EEO who will
defer to State, Right to sue letter — 90
days; change suggested class, Rule 23."
Plaintiffs' exhibit 26.

The Court finds this last entry not only indicates knowledge of an impending class action suit, but further determines the
testimony of Renfroe. By his own admission,
Renfroe, a general counsel staff lawyer, was
the information conduit to Head, the general
counsel. At the evidentiary hearing, Renfroe
testified he did not know the case would be
a class action, but the Head calendar diary
notes make clear the class action information
had been conveyed to Head. Lastly, the
words "Rule 23" most strongly suggest that
the information was conveyed by a lawyer.
Renfroe admitted he was experienced in Title
VII cases, and testified that he knew
Sprenger was a Title VII class action lawyer.

Derrough began his own investigation of the
claim no later than October 12, 1983. Plaintiffs' exhibit 12. In a memo dated October 18,
1983 (plaintiffs' exhibit 7), he reported his
efforts to deal with the Smith case.

It is clear Jabr was actively seeking counsel
for the defense of the impending suit. Telephone logs, dated September 29,1983, and
October 18, 1983, (plaintiffs' exhibit 53),
were maintained by Carolyn Chalmers, one
of FMC's outside counsel. The Jabr–Chalmers calls elicited a proposal letter, dated

October 20, 1983, from Chalmers' firm, then Pepin, Dayton, Herman, Graham & Getts, alluding to FMC's "need for representation in potential class action employment discrimination litigation," and specifically noting its relationship with the Sprenger, Olson and Schutes law firm. Plaintiffs' exhibit 24.

The Court finds that not later than October 1, 1983, FMC knew well that the Smith case was pending and that it was a matter of great consequence. Further, the Court rejects the sophistry that it was not until the December 28, 1983, charge (defendants' exhibit 30) that defendants knew this was to be a class action and that they could, therefore, destroy documents regarding these matters with impunity.

I. Propriety of Sanctions

The first determination this Court must make is whether sanctions are warranted. It is axiomatic that the imposition of sanctions for destruction of documents is within the trial court's discretion. *Perkinson v. Gilbert/Robinson, Inc.*, 821 F.2d 686, 689 (D.C.Cir.1987); *Alexander v. National Farmers Organization*, 687 F.2d 1173, 1205–06 (8th Cir.1982), *cert. denied*, 461 U.S. 937, 103 S.Ct. 2108, 77 L.Ed.2d 313 (1983); *Telectron, Inc., v. Overhead Door Corp.*, 116 F.R.D. 107, 126 (S.D.Fla.1987). In matters such as this — which lie beyond the scope of Rule 37, Federal Rules of Civil Procedure (Fed.R.Civ.P.) — the Court relies on its inherent power to regulate litigation, preserve and protect the integrity of proceedings before it, and sanction parties for abusive practices. *Roadway Express, Inc. v. Piper*, 447 U.S. 752, 764–67, 100 S.Ct. 2455, 2463–65, 65 L.Ed.2d 488 (1980); *EEOC v. Jacksonville Shipyards, Inc.*, 690 F.Supp. 995, 997, (M.D.Fla.1988); *Telectron*, 116 F.R.D. at 126; *National Ass'n of Radiation Survivors v. Turnage*, 115 F.R.D. 543, 556 (N.D.Cal.1987); *Independent Petrochemical Corp. v. Aetna Casualty and Surety Co.*, 654 F.Supp. 1334, 1363 (D.D.C.1986); *Wm. T. Thompson Co., v. General Nutrition Corp.*, 593 F.Supp. 1443, 1455 (D.C.Cal.1984).

Purposeful impairment of the opposing party's ability to discover information justifies invocation of these powers. Willful transgressions of discovery procedures, such as this case's document destruction, warrant imposition of sanctions. *Coleman v. Smith.* 814 F.2d 1142, 1145–46 (7th Cir.1987); *Independent Petrochemical*, 654 F.Supp. at 1364; *Wm. T. Thompson Co.*, 593 F.Supp. at 1456; *Carlucci v. Piper Aircraft Corp.*, 102 F.R.D. 472. 486 (S.D.Fla.1984) *as modified*, 775 F.2d 1440, 1449–54 (11th Cir.1985).

Sanctions are appropriately levied against a party responsible for causing prejudice when the party knew or should have known that the destroyed documents were relevant to pending or potential litigation. *National Ass'n of Radiation Survivors.* 115 F.R.D. at 557, *Wm. T. Thompson Co.*, 593 F.Supp. at 1455; *Struthers Patent Corp. v. Nestle Co., Inc.*, 558 F.Supp. 747, 765 (D.N.J.1981); *Bowmar Instrument Corp. v. Texas Instruments, Inc.*, 25 Fed.R.Serv.2d 423, 427 (N.D.Ind. 1977). This tenet is particularly applicable when a party is on notice that documents in its possession are relevant to existing or future litigation, but still abrogates its duty of preservation. *EEOC*, 690 F.Supp. at 998; *Wm. T. Thompson Co.*, 593 F.Supp. at 1455.

The Court finds sanctions to be absolutely appropriate in this case. The conduct of defendant's officers and employees, both in the destruction of documents and in their efforts to disguise their wrongful acts, are charitably described as "outrageous." *Alexander*, 687 F.2d 1205. They have demonstrated a "deliberate, willful and contumacious disregard of the judicial process and the rights of [the] opposing part[y]." *Carlucci*. 102 F.R.D. at 486. Having destroyed a significant quantity of documents, the exact extent of which is now indeterminable, defendant cannot now claim that the information contained is irrelevant and unimportant. *Alexander*, 687 F.2d at 1205–06. The Court has found, *supra*, that defendant cannot claim its actions were so far in advance of the first word of a potential lawsuit by Smith as to be excusable. *See Struthers Patent Corp.*, 558 F.Supp. at 765.

Defendant's purge was intentionally tailored to make forever unavailable records and documents which defendant knew or should have known would be pertinent to this gender discrimination lawsuit. The Court holds that defendant's senior officials and senior employees were on notice of this potential lawsuit and were acutely aware of its subject. Those individuals reacted by instituting a broad program of document destruction. Given these facts, sanctions are more than appropriate. 690 F. Supp. at 998. The sanctioning power is discretionary. *Davis v. American Jet Leasing, Inc.*, 864 F.2d 612, 614 (8th Cir. 1988); *Alexander*, 687 F.2d at 1205–06; *see Hazen v. Pasley*, 768 F.2d 226, 229 (8th Cir.1985); *Fox v. Studebaker–Worthington, Inc.*, 516 F.2d 989, 993 (8th Cir1975). Within the Court's grasp is a "spectrum of sanctions," from which the most appropriate may be selected. *National Hockey League v. Metropolitan Hockey Club, Inc.*, 427 U.S. 639, 644, 96 S.Ct. 2778, 49 L.Ed 747 (1976).

The most severe sanction available to the Court is default and dismissal. This is an extreme measure, reserved only for the most egregious offenses against an opposing party or a court. The Court must consider default and dismissal as a last resort if no alternative remedy by way of a lesser, but equally efficient, sanction is available. *See Perkins*, 821 F.2d at 691; *Adolph Coors Co., v. Movement Against Racism and the Klan*, 777 F.2d 1538, 1542–43 (11th Cir.1985); *Alexander*, 687 F.2d at 1205–06; *Fox*, 516 F.2d at 993; *EEOC*, 690 F.Supp. at 998; *Carlucci*, 102 F.R.D. at 486.

Before a sanction of default and dismissal may be entered, this Court must at least find that (1) defendant acted willfully or in bad faith, (2) plaintiffs were prejudiced by defendant's actions, and (3) alternative sanctions would fail to adequately punish defendant and deter future discovery violations. *Telectron*, 116 F.R.D. at 131. The Court finds that the first two elements of this test have been satisfied: defendant's officers and employees acted intentionally and plaintiffs have been deprived of significant amounts of potentially helpful information. An analysis of alternative sanctions applicable to this matter is necessary before a decision can be made as to the third prong of the test.

Courts have considered and imposed a variety of alternatives to the ultimate sanction of dismissal:

1. A number of courts have incorporated a party's destruction of documents into trial proceedings. Courts have permitted the fact-finder to draw inferences adverse to the document–destroying party. *Alexander*, 687 F.2d at 1205–06; *National Ass'n of Radiation Survivors*, 115 F.R.D. at 557. Similar to this sanction is an adjustment of the level of proof required of the aggrieved party. *EEOC*, 690 F.Supp. at 999; *see Hicks v. Gates Rubber Co.*, 833 F.2d 1406, 1418–19 (10th Cir.1987).

2. Another common remedy utilized by courts to punish and deter discovery abuse is imposition of monetary sanctions. Not surprisingly, an award of attorneys' fees and costs is frequently invoked to reimburse an aggrieved party of the price of investigating and litigating document destruction. Parties liable for document destruction have been assessed their opponents' fees and costs for investigating, researching, preparing, and arguing evidentiary motions and motions for sanctions. *National Ass'n of Radiation Survivors*, 115 F.R.D. at 558; *Alexander v. National Farmers' Organization*, 614 F.Supp. 745, 757, (W.D.Mo.1985); *see Perkinson*, 821 F.2d at 689.

3. A party which has destroyed documents may also be held accountable for the fees and costs of depositions, interrogatories, and supplemental discovery costs associated with willful concealment. *National Ass'n of Radiation Survivors*, 115 F.R.D. at 558.

4. A court may also impose monetary sanctions to rectify unnecessary consumption of its time and resources. *Id.* at 559; *see Olga's Kitchen of Hayward, Inc. v. Papo*, 108 F.R.D. 695, 711 (E.D. Mich.1985); *Itel Containers Int'l Corp. v. Puerto Rico Marine Management, Inc.*, 108 F.R.D. at 96 106 (D.N.J.1985).

After considering the available alternatives, the Court declines to summarily enter default judgment. This is a significant case and there remains other evidence concerning FMC's liability, if any. Notwithstanding defendant's document destruction, it appears plaintiffs have not been wholly deprived of the means to attempt their proof.

Defendant, however, will not be allowed to escape unpunished. The actions of defendant's officers and employees have imposed an enormous burden on counsel for plaintiffs. Had defendant not destroyed the records at issue, counsel for plaintiffs could have focused their efforts on their case in chief. Defendant's actions, however, have erected a formidable obstacle to that pursuit.

As such, the Court finds that plaintiffs are entitled to be reimbursed for all expenditures resulting from defendant's document destruction. Defendant, therefore, shall pay to plaintiffs all attorneys' fees and costs incurred in investigating, researching, preparing, arguing, and presenting all motions touching upon the issue of document destruction. This amount shall include all fees and costs associated with discovery of information concerning document destruction, including, but not exclusively, depositions, interrogatories, and document inspection.

The Court is not persuaded, however, that this amount alone will fully compensate plaintiffs for the harm done to them. Nor will it adequately punish defendant and deter future transgressions. *See National Hockey League*, 427 U.S. at 644, 96 S.Ct. at 2781. The Court, therefore, determines that it is appropriate to multiply plaintiffs' fees and costs by a factor of two. The multiplier is unquestionably justified given defendant's continued attempted deception of opposing counsel and this Court.

Consideration of document reconstruction or any further penalties will be difficult absent a common framework. To that end, within 20 days of this order, plaintiffs shall prepare and submit to the Court and opposing counsel a comprehensive list of documents they believe were destroyed by defendant. This list, which may be further supplemented as information comes to light, shall be utilized by both parties and the Court to delineate those further steps necessary to remedy the injustices arising out of defendant's actions.

Defendant argues that much of the information destroyed can be duplicated. Defendant suggests that a special master should be appointed to identify documents which were destroyed and the content of such documents. The Court presently declines to accept this suggestion, and instead directs counsel for both parties to prepare and submit brief and trenchant memoranda addressing possible resolutions to problems caused by defendant's document destruction. Defendant shall bear all of plaintiffs' attorneys' fees and costs expended in the preparation of these memoranda, document lists, and any hearings before the Court.

Defendant, further, shall forthwith pay to the Clerk of this Court the sum of $1,432.00 for consumption of the Court's time in hearing and considering this motion. This sum shall be deemed to reimburse the United States Courts for two days of otherwise unnecessary expense.

This court is intended to define, but not limit, the universe of penalties ultimately to be imposed. After consideration of the proposals and thoughts of counsel, the Court will render its final document–remedy order.

Accordingly, IT IS ORDERED that:

1. Plaintiffs' motion for sanctions is granted.

2. Upon approval of the Court, defendant shall pay to plaintiffs an amount twice that of all attorneys' fees and costs of investigating, researching, preparing, and arguing all motions touching upon document destruction and sanctions.

3. Plaintiffs shall submit their list of destroyed documents within 20 days of this order. The parties shall, not later than 30 days from the date of this order, simultaneously propose steps to be taken to identify and possibly replicate those documents which were destroyed.

4. All plaintiffs' costs and fees incurred in complying with this order shall be borne by defendant.

5. Defendant shall pay, forthwith, the sum of $1,432.00 to the Clerk of this Court.

Clara CARLUCCI, etc. v. PIPER
AIRCRAFT CORPORATION

102 F.R.D. 472

United States District Court, S.D. Florida
March 30, 1984

Memorandum Opinion and Order

William J. Campbell, Senior District Judge.

On January 20, 1984, plaintiffs filed their Third Motion to Strike Answer and Motion for Attorneys' Fees and Costs. The court granted their initial extension of time for the defendant to reply and at the conference held on January 27, 1984 granted an additional extension for a response. At that conference, I stated:

> "I have reviewed Plaintiffs' third motion for sanctions and the matters raised therein cause me great concern. Very serious claims are made regarding the unexplained disappearance of some of Piper's documents, which coincidentally are the records dealing with the testing and development of the specific component claimed to be defective in this case.
>
> Defendant has not yet responded to that motion and I have decided to grant Piper's motion for an extension of time to respond to it. But I expect and hereby direct Piper to prepare a comprehensive response addressing each set of documents not produced, detailing by affidavit or otherwise the past custody of those documents and the efforts it has made to locate them." Tr. pp. 12–13.

I also denied Piper (as well as the plaintiffs) leave to seek discovery on the issue of destruction of documents pending its response, since the issue at the time was Piper's good faith, i.e., what it knew about the missing documents and what it had done to find them. In any event, it later became apparent that the witnesses Piper wished to depose had been previously interrogated by it on numerous occasions regarding the same matter.

Therefore, I granted an additional extension of time to the defendant to respond on February 27, 1984, approximately five weeks after the motion was filed, defendant's response was filed. Only one affidavit was submitted and it did not detail the efforts Piper had made to locate the missing documents nor did it provide information regarding the past custody of the documents. Therefore, I ordered an evidentiary hearing on the motion to develop the record and to provide an additional opportunity for the defendant to present this information. It again failed to do so. At the conclusion of the hearing the parties were given ten days to file simultaneous briefs. Upon review of the briefs, the record in this cause, and the evidence presented at the hearing, I hereby grant the plaintiffs' Motion to Strike Defendant's Answer and enter a finding of liability against the defendant in this case.

The complaints in these actions sought damages for the deaths of three men who perished in a crash of a Piper Cheyenne II at Shannon, Ireland on November 12, 1976. The pilot took off in low visibility conditions and soon thereafter lost control of the plane and it crashed into the ground killing all five aboard. The plaintiffs allegedly various design defects relating to the longitudinal stability of the aircraft including that the plane was not aerodynamically sound, that its Stability Augmentation System (SAS) was dangerous and that the maximum weight and center of gravity (c.g.) specifications were misleading and inadequate. The complaint sought relief under numerous legal theories: negligence, express and implied warranties, strict liability, and wrongful death.

The following is a chronological summary of the significant events in this cause:

11/9/78 Complaints filed in the three cases.

12/22/78 Joint stipulation for consolidation of the three cases for purposes of discovery.

12/31/81 In response to discovery dispute arising from plaintiffs' request for production of documents, Judge Paine orders parties to confer in good faith to resolve discovery disputes. Order includes list of categories of documents which are legitimate subjects of discovery.

3/5/82 As the result of the failure of the parties to resolve discovery dispute, Judge Paine orders hearing for April 2, 1982. (Subsequently, hearing is reset for May 18, 1982.)

5/18/82 Discovery hearing held. Judge Paine directs that production occur in Lock Haven, Pennsylvania (Piper's factory).

6/11/82 Judge Paine enters order discussed at discovery hearing listing documents to be produced by defendant. The list of documents is identical to the one contained in the order of December 31, 1981; the only modification is the requirement that originals be produced. The order specifically provides that the production session shall continue until all documents are produced and identified.

6/14/82 Document production session held in Lock Haven with Richard Reeder as deponent. Proceedings unilaterally terminated after one day by Mr. Anania.

7/15/82 Plaintiffs file Motion to Strike Pleadings, etc., seeking sanctions for defendant's conduct at Lock Haven session.

7/21/82 Defendant files status report regarding discovery proceedings.

7/27/82 Defendant files Response to Plaintiffs' Motion to Strike Pleadings, etc.

11/17/83 Judge Paine enters order with memorandum finding Piper and its counsel, Mr. Anania, in bad faith for violating the court's order of June 11, 1982 in five respects at Lock Haven session, assesses fees and costs incurred by plaintiffs as sanction against Piper as well as requiring the documents to be produced at plaintiffs' counsel's office.

11/29/83 Defendant files Motion for Rehearing of Judge Paine's order and Motion for Protective Order seeking to postpone document production session and to have it occur at Lock Haven.

11/30/83 In Judge Paine's absence and with his authority, Judge Campbell denies defendant's Motion for Rehearing and Motion for Protective Order but grants relief to the extent that the document session is postponed until December 5, 1983.

12/1/83 Defendant files Motion for Stay and Motion for Rehearing; hearing held in West Palm Beach before judge Campbell and the motions are denied in open court on that day.

12/2/83 Defendant files Petition for Mandamus with Court of Appeals and Motion for Stay is granted by the Court of Appeals.

12/5/83 Court of Appeals denies Petition for Writ of Mandamus, vacates stay and denies Petition for Rehearing.

12/6–20/83 Document production session occurs at plaintiffs' counsel's office in Chicago with Richard Reeder as deponent. Session unilaterally terminated by defendant.

12/7/83 Parties appear for hearing before Judge Prentice Marshall of the Northern District of Illinois in Chicago.

12/11/83 Cause referred to Judge Campbell by Judge Paine for all pending and future pretrial matters.

12/21/83 Plaintiffs appear before Judge Marshall for hearing.

12/22/83 Judge Campbell enters memorandum denying defendant's Motion for Sanctions and noting further delaying tactics by the defendant.

12/28/83 Pretrial status conference held before Judge Campbell in West Palm Beach.

12/29/83 Judge James R. Knott appointed as Special Master to preside over all discovery proceedings.

1/3/84 Plaintiffs file Second Motion to Strike Answer, etc. arising out of defendant's conduct in Chicago.

1/4–10/84 Document production session

continues in West Palm Beach before Judge Knott with Richard Reeder as deponent.

1/20/84 Plaintiffs file Third Motion to Strike Answer, etc., raising issue of missing documents.

1/27/84 Conference with parties and Judge Campbell in Chambers which briefing schedule is set for plaintiffs' Third Motion to Strike Answer, etc. The Court orders that no discovery regarding alleged destruction of documents will be permitted until defendant's response is filed.

2/27/84 Special Master enters written discovery order. Defendant files Response to Third Motion to Strike, etc.

2/29/84 Judge Campbell schedules evidentiary hearing on plaintiffs' Third Motion to Strike Answer and sets it for March 8, 1984.

3/7/84 Special Master files the interim report and describes defendant as having "demonstrated an attitude of indifference in responding to requirements in the discovery process."

3/8–9/84 Evidentiary hearing on Third Motion to Strike held in West Palm Beach before Judge Campbell. At conclusion of hearing Court orders simultaneous briefs to be filed by March 19, 1984.

3/19/84 Simultaneous briefs filed by parties on plaintiffs' Third Motion to Strike Answer.

This cause was referred to me by Judge Paine on December 11, 1983. I reviewed the record and came to the conclusion, as did Judge Marshall of Chicago, see December 7, 1983, Tr. pp. 5–6, that the case was shocking. The defendant had delayed and obstructed discovery to the extent that the case was five years old and nowhere near ready for trial.

Judge Paine's order of November 17, 1983 found the defendant and its counsel to have acted in bad faith for violating his June 11, 1982 order regarding discovery. Judge Paine detailed the numerous instances of discovery misconduct and concluded:

"In the instant litigation, the defendant has shown a chronic, obstructionist attitude toward a production of the materials being sought by plaintiffs, even in the face of a Court order compelling production." P. 16.

He warned defendant:

"Such behavior sorely tests the limits of tolerance and defendant is hereby instructed that further obstruction of the discovery phase shall be met with appropriate sanctions." P. 17.

One of the sanctions Judge Paine imposed was that:

Defendant is further instructed to produce forthwith all materials which fall within the confines and categories of the court's June 11 order in original form at a location and time convenient to plaintiffs, with costs for copying or reproduction to be borne by defendant." P. 17.

The document production session commenced in Chicago on December 6, 1983. On December 8, 1983, defendant filed a Motion for Protective Order to suspend the proceedings so that its lead counsel could attend the depositions in Ireland. On December 9, 1983, I denied that motion. On December 19, 1983, defendant filed another Motion for Protection order claiming that plaintiffs' counsel were engaging in "harassing, oppressive and dilatory tactics." Without awaiting a ruling by the Court, defendant unilaterally terminated the document production session. Thereafter, plaintiffs filed their Second Motion for Sanctions alleging continued misconduct on the part of defendant and its counsel.

At the status conference on December 28, 1983, I indicated that I would take under advisement the issue of sanctions, noting specifically, however, my concern regarding defendant's unilateral termination of the production session in violation of Judge Paine's order. But my immediate concern was to recommence discovery and to complete it expeditiously so the case could be tried on April 16, 1984. Because the personal animosity between the lawyers had reached a point where unsupervised discovery was impractical, I appointed a Special Master to oversee all discovery proceedings. I intended to proceed with a clean slate:

"When I consider the matter [sanctions], I will consider your conduct from here henceforward, and advise defense counsel, who has already been held in bad faith, that they may purge themselves of the necessity for further sanctions. I'll decide that when I see how you cooperate in the discovery process from now on." Tr. p. 6.

I was disappointed to find, however, that the defendant was not going to be cooperative. The Special Master, who bore the brunt of the hardship, entered an Interim Report on March 7, 1984 stating:

"[D]efendant has demonstrated an attitude of indifference in responding to requirements in the discovery process." P. 4.

The Special Master supported his assessment with specific examples of misconduct. My review of the record confirms Judge Knott's conclusion and I describe some additional examples of obstruction and delay in the "Discovery Misconduct" section, *infra.*

Additionally, plaintiffs' Third Motion to Strike Answer, etc. raises the issue of defendant's alleged destruction of documents. The section immediately following discusses certain types of documents which were not produced by the defendant. The categories of documents discussed are not intended to be exhaustive as there are other groups of documents which were not fully produced, i.e., modification sheets and data regarding the rigging of the SAS system, etc. I address those categories of documents which highlight defendant's pattern of conduct and which provide a background for the "Destruction of Documents" section which follows. The discussion of "Discovery Misconduct" is separate because that is an additional basis, independent of the destruction of documents, for the entry of a default as a sanction.

Documents Relating to Irish Crash

On September 4, 1981, plaintiffs filed a request for production of documents which included in paragraph 12 the following request:

"All documents relating to the investigation of the crash complained of, to the site or investigation thereof, to the wreckage or parts therefrom, or to persons having knowledge of any of the foregoing (including witnesses)."

Defendant requested and received from the court an extension of time to respond to the plaintiffs' discovery request. On October 20, 1981, defendant filed its objections to the document production request, stating in response to paragraph 12:

"The defendant objects to this request on the grounds that it is work product; privileged; overbroad and burdensome; unlimited as to time and scope."

On December 31, 1981, Judge Paine specifically noted that the production of the crash investigative data was a legitimate subject of discovery. At the hearing on May 18, 1982, Judge Paine specifically asked counsel for Piper:

"Now, have you produced the accident investigation reports, item 5 in the order I entered back in December — accident investigation reports?" Tr. p. 14.

Mr. Anania responded:

"Your Honor, I haven't produced any of the documents, because I was told such production would be unacceptable; and Your Honor, I saw no practical reason to proceed with the compilation of all these documents if at some future time plaintiff was going to reject it, and Your Honor was going to say go back and do it all over again." Tr. p. 14.

Thereafter, at the document production session which occurred at Lock Haven, Mr. Reeder testified that the only document he had in his possession was the published version of the Irish government crash report and that he had not asked anyone else at Piper whether they had any documents or information relating to the crash, Tr. p. 152. The Irish report specifically states in the synopsis that Piper participated in the investigation and it is undisputed that Calvin Wilson, Jr., the Director of Piper's Engineering Department, flew to Ireland for the purpose of participating in the Irish investigation. Also, at the Lock Haven production session, Mr. Anania stated:

> "We will attempt to determine the existence of any reports which were not contained in Mr. Reeder's file. If there are such reports, we will make them available to you." Tr. p. 153.

Subsequently, in its status report filed on July 21, 1982, the defendant asked:

> "Although Mr. Reeder made it very clear in his deposition, defendant will reiterate that Piper has no documents relating to the investigation of the subject accident, other than the Irish report and associated papers, all of which are in the possession of the Plaintiff." p. 9.

(In his order of November 17, 1983, Judge Paine noted the conflicting representations by the defendant as a matter of concern, see pages 9 through 10.)

At the evidentiary hearing conducted on March 8, 1984, plaintiffs produced, as Exhibit 3, a copy of a two–page letter dated January 19, 1978 on Piper stationary from Mr. Donald P. Zurfluh, Assistant Chief Engineer at Piper, to Mr. Paul Alexander of the National Transportation Safety Board (NTSB), in which he answered specific questions prepounded by the Irish government which related only to the subject crash. I noted that the letter indicates on its face that the NTSB had previously sent a letter to Piper requesting this information. Mr. Wilson was unable to explain why that document was not produced in this case, see Tr. p. 40, but subsequently admitted that Mr. Zurfluh

was still employed at Piper and was under his direction and control, see Tr. p. 70.

There are only two possible explanations for this series of events. One is that Piper possessed documents relating to the crash at the time the objection was made to plaintiffs' request for production and that it subsequently disposed of them. It is now undisputed that Piper had such documents in its possession at one time and the only conclusion is that they were either disposed of in some manner or intentionally withheld. The fact that Mr. Reeder and Mr. Anania had apparently failed to make any search for these documents even after Piper was ordered to produce them at Lock Haven must be considered in this regard.

The only other possible explanation for these events is that when Piper filed its objection to plaintiffs' discovery request its attorney made no inquiry regarding the existence of such documents (despite having sought an extension of time to respond) and he filed the objection without any factual basis whatsoever. This type of conduct can only be construed as improper and misleading. The objection filed by the defendant implied the existence of documents other than the Irish report since that document was already a part of the record, see Request for Admission, October 2, 1981, and was a government document to which none of the objections could apply. Furthermore, under this possible explanation, counsel for Piper deliberately misled Judge Paine at the hearing on May 18, 1982 regarding the existence of such documents.

Under either of the explanations discussed above, Piper has engaged in discovery misconduct which warrants sanctions. While Judge Paine did impose a sanction against Piper for its deceptive conduct in his November 17, 1983 order, there was no evidence at that time to indicate that any documents other than the Irish report were ever possessed by Piper. Such evidence was revealed at the hearing on March 8, 1984 and the fact is now undisputed. The revelation casts a different light on the situation and supports the imposition of more severe sanctions.

Calspan Report Documents

On October 1, 1981, plaintiffs filed a request for production of documents which included in paragraph 3 the following request:

"All flight test data or documents give [sic] Calspan Corporation by PAC [Piper] and all data or flight test data developed in connection with the Calspan Corporation report commissioned by the NTSB after the crash of a PA–31T aircraft at Bressler, Pennsylvania, and all documents relating in any manner to the study undertaken by Calspan Corporation which resulted in said report, or to the preparation or initiation of said study."

Defendant filed its objection to that request on October 30, 1981 stating:

"The Defendant objects to this Request on the grounds that it is irrelevant and immaterial to the issues raised herein; beyond the scope of reasonable discovery contemplated by the Federal Rules of Civil Procedure; overly broad and burdensome; vague and ambiguous; unlimited as to time and scope."

The Court notes that the Calspan report was commissioned by the NTSB in conjunction with its investigation of the Bressler accident. That accident involved a Cheyenne II crashing soon after takeoff and the Calspan report was intended to assess the longitudinal flying qualities of that aircraft at various c.g. locations. The study was critical of the plane's handling characteristics, see Report p. 12, and it is undisputed that Piper conducted flight tests for the study, see Report p. 2.

Judge Paine's orders of December 31, 1981 and June 11, 1982 directed the production of all flight test data. Furthermore, in his November 17, 1983 order, Judge Paine specifically noted the defendant's failure to produce the documents relating to the Calspan report as a violation of his previous order. At the document production session in West Palm Beach on January 6, 1984, Richard Reeder stated that Piper had no other documents in its possession other than the Calspan report itself:

"Just the Calspan report is all we have, and that has been produced. I think we went through that in Chicago." Tr. p. 77.

Mr. Reeder's statement was subsequently reaffirmed by defense counsel, Tr. p. 77. However, on January 9, 1984, certain flight tests relating to the Calspan study were produced by Piper, having allegedly been produced but mislabeled in Chicago. Upon reference to the Calspan report it was demonstrated that the data from these reports was found by Calspan to be unsatisfactory and it was not utilized. Subsequent flight tests were conducted by Piper for Calspan and that data was utilized, see Report, Appendix I–1, but those reports were never produced by Piper, January 9, 1984 Tr. pp. 317–320.

This is another example of defendant's pattern of discovery conduct. In its objections to the plaintiffs' document request, the defendant did not state that it did not possess any of the requested documents, which would, of course, have been a valid objection. Instead, it provided numerous objections including that production would be burdensome, which implied that such documents did exist and were in Piper's possession. However, it did not produce any of these documents at the Lock Haven production session and Judge Paine specifically noted this deficiency in his November 17, 1983 order, p. 7. Thereafter, Piper denied the existence of any of the documents until January 9, 1984. At that time it identified certain documents as being within the category requested by the plaintiffs but, as discussed above, the documents produced were of no value. Furthermore, with respect to the alleged destruction of documents, Piper has made no effort to explain why it retained the unacceptable and useless flight test reports and apparently disposed of the subsequently generated acceptable flight test report.

Certification Photographs

Judge Paine's order of December 31, 1981 suggested, and his order of June 11, 1982 directed, the production of all FAA certification documents. As a prerequisite for FAA certification, it is required that certain takeoff and landing tests be performed and documented with stop–action photography. Such tests were performed by Piper with a 8,500 lb. Cheyenne prototype (which was never certified) and subsequently with a 9,000 lb. Cheyenne prototype (which was eventually certified). These latter tests were performed in April 1973 in preparation for the 1974 certification of the PA–31T.

At the Chicago document production session, Piper produced photographs relating to the 8,500 lb. prototype but has never produced those relating to the 9,000 lb. prototype. Richard Reeder stated at the document production session in West Palm Beach on January 6, 1984 that Piper permanently retained documents relating to FAA certification and that these photographs were within that category. Tr. pp. Procedures Manual, p. 011–2. Piper has provided no explanation why it retained the older and seemingly useless 8,500 lb. photos and apparently disposed of the subsequently generated photographs relating to the 9,000 lb. prototype. In Piper's initial reply to plaintiffs' Third Motion to Strike Answer it claims that the photos are irrelevant, but that objection is clearly untimely at this stage of the discovery process. Furthermore, it appears obvious that the photographs are relevant since the Irish accident occurred soon after takeoff and involved the same model airplane. The plaintiffs have also noted in their brief Piper documents that suggest that the SAS system was removed from the 9,000 lb. prototype for the photography tests. Mr. Weil, a former FAA official, stated at the evidentiary hearing on March 9, 1984 that such conduct would have been improper and, thus, the photographs could be relevant to the punitive damage claim.

Product Condition Reports

On September 14, 1981, plaintiffs requested that documents relating to failed parts of the SAS system be produced. Judge Paine indicated in his December 31, 1981 order that production documents and documents relating to quality control and testing were legitimate subjects of discovery. His June 11, 1982 order required the production of the originals of those documents. Only copies were produced at the Lock Haven production session and at subsequent sessions only copies were produced for the period 1979–1981. Piper Engineering Procedures Manual provides for the retention of originals of these documents for two years, see p. 011–2. Thus, at the time Judge Paine entered his June 11, 1982 order, the originals for the period 1980–81 should have been retained by Piper. However, Piper has admitted that it destroyed those original documents, January 10, 1984 Tr. pp. 404–405, and Mr. Reeder admitted that he took no steps to preserve those documents, March 9, 1984 Tr. p. 230.

Furthermore, with reference to Product Condition Reports prior to 1979, Piper did not produce any documents at all. While originals of those documents may have been disposed of pursuant to Piper's document retention policy, it is clear that defendant's search for copies was not extensive. Mr. Reeder testified that he only contacted the service department in search of those documents even though the Product Condition Reports were multiple forms which indicated on their face that copies were also sent to numerous other departments, January 6, 1984 Tr. pp. 62–64.

Flight Test Data

On December 31, 1981, Judge Paine suggested, and on June 11, 1982 he ordered, that Piper produce flight test data for the Cheyenne aircraft. At the West Palm Beach document production session, Piper produced originals of certain flight test documents relating to the development of the Cheyenne from 1969 to 1971. The documents were contained in a black looseleaf notebook and were consecutively numbered. In their initial memorandum in support of their motion, plaintiffs noted that five flight test reports and their corresponding data sheets were missing from the notebook and all of them involved either longitudinal stability or flight characteristics at aft c.g. loading (defendant did produce a copy of one of the reports). Defendant did not offer any explanation for the missing documents except to say that it has not intentionally destroyed or withheld any documents from the plaintiffs.

In its initial memorandum in response to plaintiffs' motion, Piper admitted its failure to produce numerous pre–1972 flight test documents but claimed it had made complete production regarding the Cheyenne as certified in 1974. This was subsequently proven to be false. At the hearing on March 9, 1984, the plaintiffs introduced evidence showing that flight test data for 526 test flights was not produced in either original or copy form, see Exhibit 10. Plaintiffs also demonstrated defendant's failure to produce numerous other documents relating to flight test data, see Exhibits 7 and 8. The vast majority of FAA flight test data and approximately two–thirds of the flight test documents relating to longitudinal stability were not produced. At the evidentiary hearing, Mr. Calvin Wilson, Piper's Director of Engineering, testified that there was no central file for flight test data and that the missing documents could be explained by the lack of an official document retention policy in the engineering department until 1974. The issue, however, is not whether Piper had an official document retention policy prior to 1974, but whether it did in fact retain these documents during that period.

Two of plaintiffs' witnesses, David Lister and James Wrisley, testified regarding the retention of records in the flight test department in the period from 1969–1979. Mr. Wrisley stated that he had worked in the flight test department from 1969 to 1971 and that one of his responsibilities was the maintenance of flight test records, Tr. p. 84. He testified that, other than the documents which were intentionally destroyed, see discussion *infra*, there were records kept in that department regarding every flight test made, Tr. pp. 80–81, 84. David Lister was also a flight test engineer whose responsibilities included the maintenance and organization of the files, Tr. p. 184. He worked in that department from 1969 through 1979. He testified that, other than the documents which were intentionally destroyed, see discussion *infra*, the flight test department kept a copy or an original of each flight test data sheet and report for every flight it made, Tr. p. 183.

The testimony of Lister and Wrisley is corroborated by the testimony of J. Arlington Myers, a former flight test supervisor for

Piper, given in the case of *Dedman v. Piper Aircraft Corp.*, (No.Dist. of Ohio, C76–168), p. 30. Furthermore, the existence of the black notebook containing the originals of flight test documents, consecutively numbered, also supports their testimony.

Wrisley, Lister, and Myers, who were all intimately involved with the flight test records, stated that the flight test department retained its records in an orderly manner. Thus, when the document retention policy regarding engineering documents was promulgated in 1974, those documents should have been retained until two years "after [the] developing airplane is no longer under engineering control," Engineering Procedures Manual 011–2. Richard Reeder testified that the aircraft in issue in this case was still under engineering control, January 6, 1984 Tr. p. 28, and that the provision of the document retention guidelines quoted above has been effective since the inception of the official policy, Tr. p. 115.

Therefore, I find that the defendant's explanation for its failure to produce these documents is not credible. Further discussion regarding the non–production of flight test documents is contained in the "Destruction of Documents" section, *infra*.

Destruction Of Documents

On the issue of the destruction of documents, the plaintiffs presented the testimony of former Piper employees, David Lister and James Wrisley. While I rely primarily on their live testimony before me, numerous transcripts of depositions of Mr. Lister, Mr. Wrisley and J. Myers, another Piper employee, taken in cases in which Piper was a party, have been submitted for consideration without any objection.

As noted previously, both Wrisley and Lister had worked as flight test engineers for Piper and were directly responsible for the maintenance of records in the flight test department. Their testimony before me regarding the defendant's policy and practice of destroying documents was remarkably consistent. This policy was initiated in the late 1960's or early 1970's when they received the instruction from J. Myers, the flight test supervisor and their direct superior, to "purge" the department's files, Tr. pp. 84–87, 179–184. The stated purpose of the destruction of records was the elimination of documents that might be detrimental to Piper in a law suit, Tr. pp. 85, 181. Wrisley and Lister were delegated the discretion to determine which documents were to be destroyed, Tr. pp. 85, 181, 204. The initial purging involved hundreds of flight test department documents, Tr. pp. 87, 182. They were also directed to retrieve copies of the detrimental documents from other departments, Tr. pp. 90, 182. Thereafter, the destruction of all potentially harmful documents was an ongoing process, Tr. pp. 83, 186.

Certain physical evidence corroborates the testimony of Wrisley and Lister. The black notebook containing flight test documents, discussed *supra*, had specific flight documents missing, thus supporting their statements that documents were selectively disposed of by Piper employees. The internal memorandum authored by Calvin Wilson entitled "PA–31T Pt6–28 Engine Problem," Exhibit 13, was not produced in this case. Lister testified that copies of the memorandum were retrieved for destruction soon after it had been issued but that he retained a copy. The contents of that document are clearly detrimental to Piper, making it a prime candidate for destruction under the guidelines described by Lister and Wrisley.

Wrisley's and Lister's testimony was also consistent with regard to other misconduct in the engineering department. They both testified that data on flight test documents they had prepared were altered by other Piper employees to make the results of the tests appear to satisfy the required criteria, Tr. pp. 83–84, 185–186. This testimony is corroborated by the FAA decision to restrict Piper's Delegation of Authority as the result of the company's presentation of biased data, Tr. pp. 66–67. This evidence, of course, established an additional motivation for Piper to destroy flight test documents.

The testimony of J. Myers in the deposition in the *Dedman* case corroborates the testimony of Lister and Wrisley. His rendition of the facts is consistent with theirs as to the time frame of the initial instructions and the employees directed to carry out the initial purging, i.e., Lister and Wrisley, Dep. p. 26. He also testified that his instruction to them was to destroy any documents that would be detrimental to Piper in a law suit and that beyond that direction he delegated the selection of documents to Lister and Wrisley, Dep. p. 32. I note that the other deposition testimony submitted is generally consistent with respect to the destruction of documents.

Lister was an employee of Piper until 1979 (after the inception of this law suit) and stated that the policy and practice of destroying detrimental documents was still in effect at that time. Certain physical evidence confirms his testimony. Plaintiffs submitted a copy of a Piper memo dated October 17, 1979 which relates to the PA–31T, Exhibit H. Typed in capital letters at the conclusion of the memo are the words "DO NOT FILE — DESTROY COPY". Obviously, this indicates that normally the document would have been filed and retained but that for some reason this document was to be treated differently, i.e., destroyed. At the evidentiary hearing before me, plaintiffs submitted as Exhibit 2 a copy of a four–page internal memo, dated May 24, 1974, titled "Proposal to Install PA–31T horizontal tail on PA–31P" (a subject admittedly related to longitudinal stability). Stamped on the memo is a control number and the date showing that the document was produced by the defendant in the *Buzzard v. Piper Aircraft Corp.*, case in May 1981. The defendant has not explained why that document was not produced in this case despite its assertion that it has produced all internal memos relating to the PA–31 in its possession. Additionally, plaintiffs' Exhibit No. 3 at the evidentiary hearing was the letter from Mr. Zurfluh regarding the Irish crash, which was dated January 19, 1978. Piper's document retention policy for the engineering department provides that correspondence should be retained for two years. Thus, under its own internal regulations, that letter should have been retained until at least 1980 at which time this suit was pending. Piper has not explained why that document was not produced. The fact that Piper has not produced a single document (other than the official report) relating to its involvement in the Irish investigation is very damaging in view of defense counsel's representation to Judge Paine on May 18, 1982 that such documents existed. Furthermore, defendant has admitted that it destroyed the originals of the Product Condition Reports from the period 1980–1981 despite Judge Paine's order requiring their production.

Defendants did not impeach either Wrisley or Lister in any significant manner. In its supplemental memorandum Piper notes that Lister's testimony has differed regarding whether Calvin Wilson personally gave him instructions to destroy documents. This is not, of course, a crucial fact and it is somewhat understandable that Lister might be uncertain given the lapse of time and the circumstances. Wilson was the direct supervisor of J. Myers who gave Wrisley and Lister the instructions to destroy the documents, Tr. pp. 79, 178. He was also the direct superior of the subsequent flight test supervisors who continued the document destruction program, Tr. p. 178. Both Wrisley and Lister indicated that, based on their experience at Piper and their understanding of the organization, that kind of instruction would not have originated with Myers, Tr. pp. 83, 184. This is consistent with J. Myers' testimony that he was given the instruction by a Mr. McNary in Calvin Wilson's presence, Dep. p. 27. Furthermore, many of the copies that Lister and Wrisley were directed to retrieve were from Calvin Wilson's department, Tr. p. 90. Thus, Calvin Wilson was not a stranger to Piper's practice of destroying documents and, therefore, Lister's uncertainty as to whether Wilson personally instructed him to destroy documents does not render his testimony unacceptable.

Defendant's principal witness to rebut the testimony of Wrisley and Lister regarding the destruction of documents was Calvin Wilson, Jr. I was not impressed with the credibility of Mr. Wilson who appeared to me to be a classic "company man," who would color his testimony in favor of his employer. He has been an employee of Piper for twenty-five years and has worked his way up through

the Engineering Department to his present position of Director of Engineering.

On February 27, 1984, Piper filed Mr. Wilson's affidavit in support of its response to plaintiffs' Third Motion to Strike Answer, etc. He stated in that affidavit that he had personally assisted with the compilation of documents for production. Paragraph 4 of the affidavit reads:

"Affiant has read the response of Piper to plaintiffs' Motion to Strike and states that to the best of his knowledge all factual information contained in Section 1–14 thereof are true and correct."

Mr. Wilson reaffirmed this statement under oath at the evidentiary hearing on March 8, 1984, Tr. p. 9. In Section 1 of defendant's memorandum is stated:

"it is most significant to note that even counsel for plaintiffs has acknowledged that each and every flight test data sheet, flight test report and modification sheet relating to the Cheyenne aircraft, as certified in 1974, has been produced by Piper." P.71.

No citation to the record is mentioned and, indeed, the existence of such an acknowledgment by plaintiffs is unlikely. Plaintiffs demonstrated at the evidentiary hearing that defendant failed to produce any flight test documents for approximately 320 Cheyenne flight tests for the period 1973–1974, see Exhibit 10, and failed to produce numerous other documents for that period, see Exhibits 7 and 8. Defendant did not challenge the accuracy of plaintiffs' showing either at the hearing or in its supplemental memorandum. In fact, Calvin Wilson had no difficulty accepting and explaining the defendant's failure to produce those documents, Tr. p. 50. Thus, the falsity of the statement in defendant's response regarding the alleged production of complete records is obvious.

Also in Section 1 of its response, Piper stated with regard to the five missing sets of flight test documents noted by plaintiffs in their initial motion:

"It is clear that the flight test reports which plaintiffs disingenuously describe as "key" documents do not even relate to the aircraft which is the subject of this law suit."

This factual statement is misleading. The Cheyenne was originally certified in 1972 and the flights noted above occurred prior to that certification. Piper chose not to market that mode, rather it continued developing the aircraft further and had it certified again in 1974. However, the 1972 and 1974 models were very similar, being in actuality variations of the same plane. Mr. Wilson admitted at the evidentiary hearing that some of the data gathered in testing the first model was relied upon in the Type Inspection Report for the 1974 model, Tr. p. 65. Furthermore, he admitted that the basic physical change in the aircraft between 1972 and 1974 was the installation of the SAS system, one of the alleged design defects in this suit. It is undisputed that the SAS system is directly related to the longitudinal stability of the aircraft. Therefore, to say that the missing flight data noted above which involved the longitudinal stability of the 1972 Cheyenne is unrelated to the aircraft in issue can only be perceived as an attempt to mislead the court.

In Section 12 of its response, Piper stated with regard to the Bressler documents:

"Even though Piper was not required to produce documents relating to the Bressler crash, even though all depositions and answers to interrogatories were readily available to plaintiffs from a variety of sources, Piper has voluntarily produced numerous documents including depositions, answers to interrogatories and the investigative report relating to the Bressler crash."

However, as discussed *infra*, defendant was ordered by the Special Master to produce the documents and that order was appealed to me on February 7, 1984. Calvin Wilson, Jr. was present at that hearing as Piper's representative. Tr. p. 4. The Special Master's order and my order were made clear in his presence, Tr. p. 28–31. Furthermore, the issue was extensively discussed on numerous occasions during his deposition in West Palm Beach at which

time production of some of the documents was eventually made. Thus, again his affidavit blatantly misrepresents the true facts.

Additionally, I note that at the evidentiary hearing Mr. Wilson refused to describe the FAA airworthiness standards as minimum standards despite the clarity of such description in the FAA statues, see 49 U.S.C. § 1412(a)(1), and FAA Designated Engineering Representative Guidance Handbook, Chapter 2, § 7a. This statement is clearly evasive since, as Mr. Wilson must be aware, the applicable regulations are clear and not reasonably subject to alternative interpretation.

My perception of Mr. Wilson as a "company man" is further buttressed by a review of the two internal memos authored by him which have been submitted to me, Exhibit A to plaintiffs' Third Motion to Strike Answer, Exhibit 13 from the evidentiary hearing. (I note that defendant has not challenged the authenticity of these documents.) Those memos reveal a man whose overriding interest is the sale of aircraft and the financial success of the company. Based on my observation of Mr. Wilson and the records in this case, I conclude that that interest has adversely affected the truthfulness of his testimony before this court.

Additionally, I note another consideration regarding Wilson's credibility. As discussed previously, Wilson is implicated by Wrisley, Lister and Myers in the document destruction campaign. He is also implicated by Wrisley in the alteration of flight test data. Thus, he has an additional personal interest in denying the allegations in order to protect his own reputation and integrity.

With respect to the destruction of documents, Mr. Wilson's testimony was not convincing. He stated:

"[T]he destruction or retention of documents was strictly on the basis of our procedures that we have." Tr. p. 19.

Certain uncontroverted facts contradict this statement. Richard Reeder testified on January 6, 1984 that Piper's document retention policy required permanent retention of documents relating to FAA certification, Tr. p. 90. He also made it clear that the stop–action photographs were considered to be in that category, Tr. p. 91. Yet, those documents were never produced and no explanation has been provided. Furthermore, the defendant has not explained why the useless 8,500 lb. model photographs were retained. Piper has also not explained why, under its document retention program, it retained the unacceptable flight test documents from the Calspan study and disposed of the subsequently generated acceptable flight test documents.

Defendant's other witnesses were Richard Reeder, Piper's legal coordinator, and Mr. Bleck, its president. Mr. Reeder denied the improper destruction of any documents by Piper and claimed to have made an effort to locate and produce all documents required in this case, Tr. p. 228. However, it is undisputed that he did not preserve the originals of the Production Condition Reports, as required by Judge Paine's order of June 11, 1982. Furthermore, he provided no explanation for the defendant's failure to produce the internal memorandum, Exhibit 2, which had been produced in the Buzzard case. Mr. Reeder did not give any testimony regarding the document retention practices of the engineering department and, thus, his testimony did not rebut, in any manner, Wrisley's or Lister's testimony on that subject.

Mr. Bleck testified regarding the instructions he gave his employees upon being informed of the court's orders requiring the production of documents in Chicago, Tr. p. 117–119. That testimony is not directly responsive to the issues raised in plaintiffs' motion. Mr. Bleck also testified that Piper's policy is to cooperate in litigation and to fully disclose documents in compliance with court orders, Tr. p. 119–120.

Piper has utterly failed to demonstrate that its document retention policy is actually implemented in any consistent manner. The defendant included with its initial response to plaintiffs' motion a copy of a portion of the Corporate Procedures Manual addressing document retention. At the evidentiary hear-

ing, I relied on that document to inquire of Mr. Wilson regarding Piper's means of authorizing and documenting the disposal of records, Tr. p. 71–74. He was unable to answer my questions and it has become apparent that the documents submitted to me is virtually irrelevant to the issues before this court. The relevant documents retention procedures are contained in the Engineering Procedures Manual which the defendant never introduced into evidence or submitted to the court. The plaintiffs submitted a copy of the relevant provisions in their appendix with the supplemental memorandum. The court obtained the original by examining the boxes of documents which have been kept in the custody of the Clerk's Office since the documents production session.

Piper presented no evidence to substantiate Mr. Wilson's claim that the document retention procedures are strictly complied with by Piper's employees. In fact, with the exception of the improper destruction of the Product Condition Reports, discussed *supra*, the defendant did not provide any evidence that the procedures are ever complied with by its personnel. This is particularly shocking in the light of my instruction on January 27, 1984 to Piper to detail for me its means of retaining and disposing of documents. My questions at the evidentiary hearing further indicated my concern. Piper's absolute failure to provide any evidence on this issue must be construed as a tacit admission that the policy is a sham.

The plaintiffs had the burden of proving the factual allegations underlying their Third Motion to Strike Answer, etc.: that the defendant had failed to produce the documents and that the defendant intentionally destroyed documents to prevent them from being produced. It is undisputed that the documents in issue were not produced. As to the destruction of documents, the plaintiffs have presented convincing and consistent testimony from two former Piper employees who were responsible for the relevant documents. From my observation of those witnesses, I found them to be credible. Their testimony was corroborated by the physical evidence and the testimony of J. Myers. Furthermore, those witnesses were not impeached in any material way. My observation of the only significant rebuttal witness, Mr. Wilson, indicated he was not credible and my analysis of his testimony in this case reinforces that determination. His suggestion that the documents may have been lost in the flood of 1972 was effectively rebutted by Mr. Lister's testimony, Tr. pp. 189–190, 192.

Therefore, I conclude that the defendant engaged in a practice of destroying engineering documents with the intention of preventing them from being introduced in law suits. Furthermore, I find that this practice continued after the commencement of this law suit and that documents relevant to this law suit were intentionally destroyed. I would note that I am not the first fact finder to conclude that Piper has intentionally destroyed documents, *see Piper Aircraft Corp. v. Coulter*, 426 So.2d 1108, 1110 (Fla. 4 DCA 1983).

I am not holding that the good faith disposal of documents pursuant to a *bona fide*, consistent and reasonable document retention policy can not be a valid justification for failure to produce documents in discovery. That issue never crystallized in this case because Piper has utterly failed to provide credible evidence that such a policy or practice existed.

Having determined that Piper intentionally destroyed documents to prevent their production, the entry of a default is the appropriate sanction. Deliberate, willful and contumacious disregard of the judicial process and the rights of opposing parties justifies the most severe sanction, *see, National Hockey League v. Metropolitan Hockey Club*, 429 U.S. 874, 97 S.Ct. 197, 50 L.Ed.2d 158 (1976). The policy of resolving lawsuits on their merits must yield when a party has intentionally prevented the fair adjudication of the case. By deliberately destroying documents, the defendant has eliminated the plaintiffs' right to have their cases decided on the merits. Accordingly, the entry of a default is the only means of effectively sanctioning the defendant and remedying the wrong.

Discovery Misconduct

On January 27, 1984, defendant was ordered by the Special Master to produce by February 6, 1984 documents and depositions from the Bressler case. The documents were not produced by that date. On February 7, 1984, the defendant appealed the Special Master's order to me, raising only a frivolous argument. I rejected it and the defendant was still, at that time, unprepared to comply. Furthermore, it engaged in deceptive conduct by producing some depositions and claiming to have made full production. Subsequently, it was demonstrated that it had not made full production, see February 7, 1984 Tr. pp. 324–334. The additional depositions were eventually produced but various attached exhibits were not produced until even later.

Defendant's explanation for this conduct was nonsensical:

> "Even though Piper was not required to produce documents relating to the Bressler crash, and even though all depositions and answers to interrogatories were readily available to plaintiffs from a variety of sources, Piper has voluntarily produced numerous documents including depositions, answers to interrogatories and the investigative report relating to the Bressler crash." Defendant's Response to Plaintiffs' Third Motion to Strike Answer, pp. 13–14.

(It was clearly demonstrated, however, that some of the depositions were not readily available to the plaintiffs since they were not filed in the Bressler case by agreement of the parties in that case.) Such representations are clearly false and are contemptuous of the orders of this Court.

On January 27, 1984, Judge Knott ordered the defendant to file by February 6, 1984 an answer to plaintiffs' interrogatory regarding changes made in the longitudinal control system in the PA–31T. The defendant did not answer the interrogatory by that deadline but on February 7, 1984 the defendant appealed Judge Knott's decision to me, claiming only that the interrogatory was too burdensome to answer. I granted temporary relief from that order of Judge Knott and granted the parties leave to discuss the matter in their briefs on the Third Motion for Sanctions. On February 14, 1984, plaintiffs limited the scope of the interrogatory in response to defendant's objection and filed a motion to compel a response. Defendant did not file a timely response to that motion, i.e., within five days, see Local Rule 10C, but eventually filed a response on February 24, 1984 in Miami, said pleading not being received in West Palm Beach until February 29, 1984. On February 24, 1984, Judge Knott entered a written discovery order requiring *inter alia* that the new interrogatory be answered by the defendant by March 5, 1984. No answer was ever provided nor has the defendant ever appealed that decision to me.

On March 23, 1984, four days after the deadline for filing briefs, defendant sent to my chambers, a copy of an affidavit of Calvin Wilson, Jr. which addressed the alleged burden involved in satisfying the discovery request. No explanation was offered why the affidavit was untimely filed nor why Judge Knott's order of February 24, 1984 was ignored.

During the deposition of Calvin Wilson, Jr. on February 7, 1984, plaintiffs' attorney asked certain questions regarding the incidence angle of the horizontal stabilizer on certain aircraft. Due to problems in immediately obtaining the necessary documents, defense counsel suggested that the answer be provided through an interrogatory, Tr. p. 401. The exact language of the interrogatory was then agreed upon and the Special Master directed the defendant to file an answer by February 20, 1984. On February 29, 1984, plaintiffs filed a Motion for Rule to Show Cause noting defendant's failure to answer the interrogatory. Defendant filed an answer to the interrogatory on March 6, 1984 but did not respond to plaintiffs' motion until March 19, 1984. In its response defendant suggests that the delay was due to plaintiffs' alleged lack of diligence in filing the written interrogatories (they were served on defendant on February 13, 1984), the illness of Mr. Anania, and the burden of responding to other discovery requests. These explanations are clearly

insufficient. The exact language of the interrogatory was agreed to and put on the record on February 7, 1984, thus, there was no reason why the defendant could not prepare forthwith to obey the Special Master's order. The other explanations are also unpersuasive since, even assuming they had merit, an extension of time should have been requested.

On March 19, 1984, defendant filed a Notice of Taking Depositions of "plaintiffs' experts," David Lister, William Kelly and J. Wrisley, for Thursday, March 22, 1984, at 9:30 a.m., in defense counsel's West Palm Beach office. On March 21, 1984, plaintiffs filed an Emergency Motion for Protective Order with respect to that notice. At no time did defense counsel contact Judge Knott to inform him of these depositions. Judge Knott was first informed of this development when the Court, after receiving plaintiffs' motion, contacted him late in the afternoon on March 21st to inquire whether he was aware of this discovery dispute.

This action by defense counsel violates this Court's previous orders. I stated in open court on December 28, 1983:

> "The discovery from here on, in view of the contemptuous conduct thus far in this case, will be before a Special Master of this court who will preside at all hearings starting with the first hearing next Wednesday, January 3rd." Tr. p. 9.

A written order to this effect was entered by me on December 29, 1983. Subsequently, on January 4, 1984, at the first document production session in West Palm Beach, I stated in the presence of all parties:

> "Gentlemen, this is Judge Knott, formerly Chief Circuit Judge of Palm Beach County, Florida; and he is the Special Master whom I have appointed to preside over your further discovery and to take whatever testimony is going to be offered by way of deposition or otherwise." Tr. pp. 4–5.

Since that time, all discovery has been conducted in accordance with those orders. Judge Knott has presided at all testimonial discovery sessions and the scheduling has always been arranged through him. Thus, defense counsel's tactics can only be construed as contemptuous of this Court's orders.

Furthermore, the harassing nature of the notice is obvious from a review of the record. Plaintiffs' notices of filing expert resumes was not filed until March 20, 1984. Of the three persons named in defendant's notice, only David Lister is named as an expert for the plaintiffs. Also, it is obvious that the notice gave plaintiffs very little time to bring these witnesses to West Palm Beach. As the testimony indicated at the hearing before me on March 8th and 9th, David Lister resides in Ontario, Canada and J. Wrisley resides in Pennsylvania. The defendant's urgent need to depose them is somewhat questionable in view of the fact that it interrogated them extensively at the evidentiary hearing and has deposed them numerous times in other similar cases.

On March 23, 1984, the Court received a letter from defense counsel which attempted to explain his conduct in this matter. He stated that after reviewing the Notice of Depositions, "I found that Judge Knott did not receive a copy of this notice as he should have." Even assuming that this omission was inadvertent, this explanation is insufficient. Merely sending a copy to Judge Knott would have presumed his availability for the three consecutive depositions and placed the burden on him to arrange his schedule accordingly. Furthermore, the Notice of Depositions set the depositions at defense counsel's local office despite the fact that all testimonial discovery proceedings before the Special Master have been held in West Palm Beach Courthouse. Defense counsel's suggestion that plaintiffs' attorneys were at fault for not conferring in good faith with him regarding this discovery dispute is also unpersuasive. As I have made clear, the Special Master is in charge of discovery and the parties in this case do not have the authority, by agreement or otherwise, to schedule discovery hearings in this matter without his participation.

This description of defendant's misconduct is not intended to be exhaustive. There are other examples of defendant's delaying tactics, obstruction, and deception noted elsewhere in this opinion. The Special Master also describes certain actions of the defendant which demonstrate its contemptuous pattern of conduct. Furthermore, a review of the record will reveal other incidents which support this characterization, *see e.g.*, Judge Paine's order of July 17, 1982 and my memorandum of December 22, 1983. This pattern of conduct warrants the imposition of serious sanctions.

The entry of a default against a party as a Rule 37 sanction should be rarely utilized, but the court must be able to enforce its orders and to maintain control over discovery. When a party has consistently disobeyed orders, obstructed discovery, delayed proceedings and made misrepresentations to the court, an extreme sanction is warranted. When a party engaging in such conduct has been previously sanctioned by the court and yet continues the same pattern of conduct, the ultimate sanction is warranted. This is such a case.

The use of a default as a Rule 37 sanction is controlled by the same guidelines as the use of a dismissal order, *United Artists Corporation v. Freeman*, 605 F.2d 854, 856–857 (5th Cir.1979). In *Marshall v. Segona*, 621 F.2d 763, 768 (5th Cir.1980), the Court discussed the appropriate standards:

> "First, dismissal is to be sparingly used and only in situations where its deterrent value cannot be substantially achieved by use of less drastic sanctions. Whether the other party's preparation for trial was substantially prejudiced is a consideration. 'Dismissal is generally inappropriate and lesser sanctions are favored where neglect is plainly attributable to an attorney rather than to his blameless client.' Nor does a party's simple negligence, grounded in confusion or sincere misunderstanding of the Court's orders, warrant dismissal. Finally, the Rule 'should not be construed to authorize dismissal . . . when it has been established that failure to comply has been due to inability . . . ,' " *National Hockey League supra*, 427 U.S. at 640, 96 S.Ct. at 2779, 49 L.Ed.2d at 749. [Footnotes deleted]

In this case the deterrent value of a default cannot be achieved by other means. The defendant and its counsel have already been found to have acted in bad faith for violations of a court order. The defendant was sanctioned in two ways: It was required to pay certain fees and costs of the plaintiffs and to produce the required documents at its own expense and at plaintiffs' convenience. The Court reserved ruling on the issue of sanctions against Mr. Anania. The defendant has been repeatedly threatened with sanctions since that time. Judge Paine warned the defendant in his order of November 17, 1983. On January 27, 1984, I stated at a hearing:

"As I said, the charges made in plaintiffs' motion are very serious and, considering the sanctions imposed to date in this law suit, if I find that Piper has engaged in any additional discovery misconduct, I do not see how I would have any other choice but to enter a default against it on the issue of liability." Tr. pp. 13–14.

Nonetheless, the pattern of conduct continued.

The entry of a default is also appropriate because the plaintiffs' case has been severely prejudiced by the inordinate delay in getting this case to trial. Defendant's failure to produce certain documents, regardless of whether they were destroyed or not, has hampered plaintiffs' preparation and the plaintiffs' attempts to obtain this information by other means has been thwarted by defendant's obstruction.

This is not a case in which the client is blameless and the attorney is solely responsible for the discovery violations. Piper has already been found to have acted in bad faith and its discovery misconduct has continued. Furthermore, to the extent any discovery violations are attributable to its counsel, Piper was put on notice regarding its pattern of conduct by Judge Paine's order of November 17, 1983.

Piper's discovery violations cannot be attributed to negligence or confusion. Deadlines were clearly set and the requirements of discovery were obvious. Additionally, the close supervision of the case by Judge Knott and myself provided ample opportunity for clarification.

Neither can defendant's failure to comply with court orders be attributed to inability. When the defendant demonstrated inability to comply with a discovery order, I granted appropriate relief, *see e.g.*, February 7, 1984 Tr. p. 22.

This is a case where the defendant has demonstrated flagrant bad faith and callous disregard for its responsibility, *see Emerick v. Fenick Industries, Inc.*, 539 F.2d 1379, 1381 (5th Cir.1976). Piper's conduct has been reprehensible and intolerable. Chief Justice Warren E. Berger recently spoke at the Mid–Year Meeting of the American Bar Association and discussed the problem of discovery abuse. He described it as "a breakdown in the professional standards of the entire profession," and noted that some lawyers have exploited pretrial discovery "with at least an excess of adversary zeal." That is what occurred in this case and the defendant supported and actively participated in that conduct.

Even with the constant supervision of the Special Master and myself, the requisite discovery has not been completed so that the parties can be adequately prepared for trial. Had this case remained on the overburdened docket of Judge Paine, or any of the overworked judges in this district, the supervision required would have made it impossible to maintain an efficient calendar. It is not the court's function to drag a party kicking and screaming through discovery. That is what the defendant required in this case and such conduct must be deterred if courts are to perform their intended function, *see e.g., National Hockey League v. Metropolitan Hockey Club*, 427 U.S. 639, 643, 96 S.Ct. 2778, 2781, 49 L.Ed.2d 747 (1976).

For each of the two reasons discussed above, the Court grants plaintiff's Third Motion to Strike Answer. The Court hereby strikes defendant's pleadings and enters a finding of liability. The case will proceed to trial on April 16, 1984 solely on the issue of damages. Additionally, the Court will assess against the defendant fees and costs of the Special Master and the amount stated in his Interim Report shall be paid by defendant within ten (10) days. The remainder of the Special Master's fees and costs shall be assessed against defendant by further order of this court.

So ordered.

Jewel Louise CARR, Administratrix of the Estate of Carlos Carr, Deceased, v. ST. PAUL FIRE & MARINE INSURANCE COMPANY

384 F.Supp. 821

United States District Court, W.D. Arkansas, Fayetteville Division
November 19, 1974

* * * * *

This case was commenced May 20, 1972, when plaintiff, a citizen and resident of the State of Arkansas, filed her complaint against defendant, a foreign corporation authorized to do and in fact doing business in the State of Arkansas, to recover damages for alleged negligence on the part of Washington General Hospital and its employees in the treatment and failure to treat the decedent, Carlos Carr, who had been received in the emergency room of said hospital during the evening of January 8, 1972.

Washington General Hospital is owned and operated by Washington County, Arkansas, and is not subject to suit for damages under the laws of the State of Arkansas. The defendant, St. Paul Fire and Marine Insurance Company, is the insurer of said hospital under Ark. Stat.Ann., § 66–3240 (1966 Repl.), is subject to suit for the recovery of damages caused by the negligence of the insured.

The plaintiff alleged that, relying on the practice and custom of the hospital which operated an emergency service and facilities, plaintiff's decedent, Carlos Carr, went to the hospital and "was refused treatment by the agent, employee and servant in charge after a superficial examination of the decedent; that said agent, employee and servant refused to call a physician or make any effort to have plaintiff's decedent examined by a qualified medical practitioner." That the hospital's employees failed to render to the decedent the necessary attention and service that his physical condition at the time required, and he was permitted to return to his home in Fayetteville, and died before or about midnight January 8, 1972, after leaving the hospital. It is further alleged that the decedent

was permanently disabled and died as a result of the negligence of the hospital as set forth in the complaint.

After removal of the case to the U.S. District Court for the Western District of Arkansas, Fayetteville, Division, the defendant filed its answer on June 12, 1972, in which it denied that the hospital was negligent in the treatment of failure to treat the decedent.

* * * * *

In contention G the defendant contends that the court erred in allowing testimony as to changes in hospital procedures subsequent to the death of Carlos Carr. The objection is based on the evidence which discloses that the emergency room employees destroyed the record after he had died. The defendant contends that the testimony should not have been admitted since it implies that the hospital changed its procedure as a result of the incident after Carlos Carr died. The court does not know why the record was destroyed, but does know that the plaintiff was greatly hampered in proving just what was done by the employees and what their examination disclosed, and the jury had a right to consider the effect that such destruction had in determining the actual facts. It seems highly unreasonable that the findings of the physical condition of a person examined by the emergency room employees would be destroyed. No one knows the effect that such action had on the jury, but the jury certainly had a right to infer that the record had it been retained would have shown that a medical emergency existed and that a doctor should have been called and that more attention should have been given him than was given.

The court is convinced that the facts and circumstances and evidence are substantial when considered in the light most favorable to the plaintiff and are ample under the applicable law to sustain the verdict.

Therefore, the defendant's motion for judgment notwithstanding the verdict should be overruled.

The motion in the alternative for a new trial has been considered, and the court finds that since no material error was committed during that trial that the same should be denied.

Judgment in accordance with the above is being entered today.

Ben CASCIO, d/b/a Cascio's Food Market v. Ronald BEAM et al.

594 SW 2nd 942

Supreme Court of Missouri, En Banc
March 11, 1980

* * * * *

Respondent conducts a retail sales business known as Cascio's Food Market and Cascio's Delicatessen. On January 20, 1977, the director of revenue issued a summons to the respondent which called for production of various books and records pertaining to the business for the period from January 1, 1970, through December 31, 1973. The records demanded by the summons included general ledgers, all journals, retained copies of Missouri State Sales Tax returns, and retained copies of Federal and State withholding tax reports, monthly and yearly profit and loss statements, all payroll ledgers, any records of daily sales (*i.e.,* cash register tapes or daily summaries), and all bank statements and canceled checks. The summons was allegedly issued pursuant to § 144.330, RSMo 1969, which authorizes examination of records for the purpose of ascertaining the correctness of any tax return or for the purpose of determining the amount of tax due. The printed form summons did not recite a specific purpose other than disclosing that it concerned the tax liability of respondent and that respondent was summoned and required to appear before appellant, Ronald G. Beam to give testimony relating to respondent's tax liability of the collection thereof.

* * * * *

Respondent contends that the statutes such as this one providing for inspection of business records are to be construed strictly against the state and liberally in favor of the taxpayers. Respondent argues that construing the statutes so as to limit the right of inspection is in keeping with public policy interests which are furthered by statutes of limitation and the doctrine of repose. He contends that when § § 144.320 and 144.330, RSMo 1969, are read together and construed in this fashion, the director's power to examine a taxpayer's books and records is limited to that period during which preservation of the records is mandated. Respondent argues that since the keeping of the records is required for only two years, it is reasonable to infer that the legislature intended to limit the director's right to investigate such records to two years. We agree.

* * * * *

The object and the purpose of § 144.330, RSMo 1969, is clearly stated in that section. The object is to permit the director to have access to records relating to certain sales. The purpose is to ascertain the correctness of returns or to determine amounts of taxes due. Respondent could not be liable for taxes for sales recorded in the materials summoned absent fraud or failure to file a return. § 144.220, RSMo 1969. We do not reach the question of what records may be subject to investigation under § 144.330, RSMo 1969, in a case involving fraud, because the director of revenue in this case has neither alleged such fraud as would remove the statute of limitations bar to tax liability for the years in question, nor has he alleged reasonable grounds to suspect such fraud. In the light of the object and purpose of § 144.330, we do not believe that the legislature intended to give the director the unfettered authority he now asserts.

Appellants argue that the use of a summons such as that involved herein is reasonably necessary for the director of revenue to implement and enforce the provisions of the Sales Tax Act. We may take notice of the fact that the department of revenue has agents in every area of the state for the purpose of collecting sales tax and that these agents are permitted by § 144.320, RSMo 1969, to look at and inspect any taxpayer's business records at any time during business hours. We also take notice of the fact that the director of revenue has for several years had access to federal tax returns for the specific purpose of comparing them with state tax returns. The director of revenue is not without the means to discover fraud, nor is he presently without the necessary tools to enforce the Sales Tax Act. There is no reason to think that customary methods of discovery would not be available to the director for all the years in question in a suit or prosecution for fraud. Approval of a summons that reaches back for records older than two years would place in the director's hands the means to conduct fishing expeditions and to harass taxpayers. We find nothing in § 144.330, RSMo 1969, that authorizes the issuance of such a summons by the director of revenue or his agents.

Appellants contend that the right of the director to examine books and records is not limited by either the two year period for preserving records prescribed in § 144.320, RSMo 1969, or the two year limitation period provided by § 144.220, RSMo 1969, for additional assessments. Appellants urge that we adopt the reasoning of the United States Supreme Court in *United States v. Powell*, 379 U.S. 48, 85 S. Ct. 248, 13 L. Ed. 2d 112 (1964). In *Powell*, the Court permitted the Commissioner of Revenue under § 7602(2)[6] of the Internal Revenue Code of 1954 to summon a taxpayer in March of 1963 to appear and produce his records pertaining to 1958 and 1959 tax returns of the company of which he was president. The taxpayer contended that the commissioner was not authorized to summon the records in the absence of a showing of probable cause to suspect fraud, because the three year statute of limitations on ordinary tax liability had run and because the commissioner has already had the one examination of records permitted by the statute. The court of appeals upheld the taxpayer's contentions, reasoning that since the returns in question could only be reopened for fraud, re–examination of the records sought would constitute an "unnecessary examination" forbidden by 26 U.S.C. § 7605(b) unless the commissioner showed that he had a reasonable suspicion that the returns for an otherwise closed year were fraudulent. The Supreme Court reversed and held that

the Government need make no showing of probable cause to suspect fraud unless the taxpayers raises a substantial question that judicial enforcement of the administrative summons would be an abusive use of the court's process, predicated on more than the fact of re–examination and the running of the statute of limitations on ordinary tax liability.

Id. at 51, 85 S.Ct. at 251. The Court also stated:

We are asked to read § 7605(b) together with the limitations sections in such a way as to impose a probable cause standard upon the Commissioner from the expiration date of the ordinary limitations period forward. Without some solid indication in the legislative history that such a gloss was intended, we find it unacceptable.

Id. at 56, 85 S.Ct. at 254.

Appellants' attempt to draw an analogy between the investigatory powers of the Commissioner of Internal Revenue and those of the Director of Revenue of the State of Missouri is misdirected. We do not believe that the legislature of this state intended to make the department of revenue into an investigatory bureaucracy as powerful as the Internal Revenue Service of the federal government. Appellants disregard those safeguards that are built into the federal system by statute and case decision. The federal statutes expressly provide, in 26 U.S.C. § 7605(b) (1976):

No taxpayer shall be subjected to unnecessary examination or investigations, and only one inspection of a taxpayer's books of account shall be made for each taxable year unless the taxpayer requests otherwise or unless the Secretary or his delegate, after investigation, notifies the taxpayer in writing that an additional inspection is necessary.

Although in *Powell*, the United States Supreme Court construed § 7605(b) not to require the government to show "probable cause to suspect fraud" in order to enforce a summons to produce documents relating to periods on which the statute of limitations on ordinary tax liability had run, the court outlined a panoply of restrictions on the use of investigatory power which the government would be required to observe:

[The commissioner] must show cause that the investigation will be conducted pursuant to a legitimate purpose, that the inquiry may be relevant to the purpose, that the information sought is not already within the Commissioner's possession, and that the administrative steps required by the Code have been followed — in particular, that the "Secretary or his delegate," after investigation, has determined the further examination to be necessary and has notified the taxpayer in writing to that effect. This does not make meaningless the adversary hearing to which the taxpayer is entitled before enforcement is ordered. At the hearing he "may challenge the summons on any appropriate ground," *Reisman v. Caplin,* 375 U.S. 440, at 449, [84 S.Ct. 508, at 513, 11 L.Ed.2d 459]. Nor does our reading of the statutes mean that under no circumstances may the court inquire into the underlying reasons for the examination. It is the court's process which is invoked to enforce the administrative summons and a court may not permit its process to be abused. 379 U.S. at 57–58, 85 S.Ct. at 255. Appellants would have this court impose no similar restrictions on the director's use of the power in § 144.330, RSMo 1969.

A court should inquire into the reasons for which the examination of records is sought in order to guard against abuse of the court's process. The director has not shown that the investigation is for a legitimate purpose, despite the fact that he had free access to the records for two years and now seeks to inquire into records of the distant past. A court must do more than summarily affix its stamp of approval to administrative action before it permits enforcement of the director's summons.

For the foregoing reasons, we affirm the judgment of the trial court, permanently enjoining enforcement of the summons in this case.

6 § 7602 authorizes the commissioner to summon persons and examine records "[f]or the purpose of ascertaining the correctness of any return, making a return where none has been made, determining the liability of any person for any internal revenue tax . . . or collecting any such liability."

CECIL CORLEY MOTOR COMPANY, INC. and Cecil Corley, Jr. v. GENERAL MOTORS CORPORATION and Paul Porter

380 F.Supp. 819

United States District Court, M.D. Tennessee, Nashville Division
July 17, 1974

After jury trial and verdict in favor of the corporate plaintiff, Cecil Corley Motor Company, Inc., but not for the individual plaintiff, Cecil Corley, Jr., this civil private antitrust, breach of contract and Dealers Day in Court action is now before the Court on General Motors' motion for judgment notwithstanding the verdict under Fed.Rules Civ.Proc. 50(b), or a new trial, Fed.Rules Civ.Proc. 59.

* * * * *

From 1957 to January 19, 1966, Cecil Corley, Jr. operated an automobile dealership in Galatin, Tennessee (about 30 miles from Nashville) as a sole proprietorship, under franchise agreements issued separately from time to time by Oldsmobile, Pontiac and GMC Truck Divisions of General Motors Corporation, and by American Motors Corporation. On January 19, 1966, Cecil Corley, Jr., caused the business to be incorporated as Cecil Corley Motor Company, Inc. and this corporation continued to operate as an American Motors dealer until sometime in 1967, when it voluntarily terminated its contract with American Motors Corporation, and as an Oldsmobile, Pontiac and GMC Truck dealer of General Motors until April 1, 1970, when it again voluntarily terminated its contracts with General Motors, sold its assets, and went out of the automobile business.

Cecil Corley, Jr. had discussed incorporation with General Motors in 1965, requesting that the existing Franchise Agreements be terminated and that new Agreements be executed with the proposed corporation. Pontiac Motor Division of General Motors would not agree to the granting of an Agreement to the proposed corporation unless Cecil Corley, Jr. executed a general release in Pontiac's favor. Before trial, Cecil Corley, Jr., having admitted to executing a general release (except for antitrust claims) in favor of Pontiac Motor Division as consideration for the granting of an Agreement to the plaintiff corporation, this Court granted General Motors' motion for partial summary judgment with respect to any breach of contract claims asserted by the individual plaintiff, Cecil Corley, Jr.

From 1948 until October 1968, defendant, Paul Porter, was a partner with his father, B.A. Porter, in a Pontiac dealership known as Broadway Motor Company in Hartsville, Tennessee, some 16 miles northwest of Nashville. (B.A. Porter had obtained his first Agreement with Pontiac in Hartsville in 1935.) In October 1968, Broadway Motor Company terminated its Dealer Selling Agreement with Pontiac Motor Division and moved to Lebanon, Tennessee. A new entity, Porter Pontiac, Inc. obtained Pontiac and GMC Truck Franchise Agreements for Lebanon in October 1968.

* * * * *

Summary of Evidence

The evidence developed in this case underscores the importance of the law's requirement that legal injury be proved and not simply assumed, for neither the testimony nor the documentary evidence in this record supported the jury verdict. Plaintiff introduced no basic dealership records in support of its contentions. Records of vehicle orders and preference lists submitted to Pontiac Motor Division and monthly distribution reports received from Pontiac were all destroyed or otherwise not available. The evidence is that destruction of important dealership records took place while plaintiff contemplated litigation and even after this litigation has commenced. Certainly, Pon-

tiac Motor Division cannot be penalized for plaintiff's destruction or failure to keep essential records. See *Associated Press v. Taft–Ingalls Corp.*, 340 F.2d 753, 765–766 (6th Cir. 1965). This Court agrees with the Court in *Woolner Theatres, Inc. v. Paramount Picture Corp.*, 333 F.Supp. 658, 661 (E.D.La.1970) when it noted:

> "It is inconceivable that those records would have been destroyed after the suit was filed, or even after the decision was made to file the suit, if they would not indict plaintiffs."

Where the requisite evidentiary tests are lacking, such as in this case, because plaintiff destroyed its records (even after litigation commenced) or chose not to produce such records, "heed must be given to the burden of proof." *Shapleigh v. Mier*, 299 U.S. 468, 475, 57 S.Ct. 261, 264, 81 L.Ed. 355 (1937), Cardozo, J.). Plaintiff "must always produce all the evidence he can" and "the best available evidence." *William Goldman Theatres, Inc. v. Loews, Inc.*, 69 F.Supp. 103, 106 (E.D. Pa.1946), aff'd per curiam, 164 F.2d 1021 (3rd Cir.), cert. denied, 334 U.S. 811, 68 S.Ct. 1016, 92 L.Ed. 1742 (1948);*Riss & Co. v. Association of American Railroads*, 190 F.Supp. 10, 18 (D.D.C.1960), aff'd, 112 U.S.App.D.C. 49, 299 F.2d 133, 136 (1962). The law requires that where a party attempts to show injury by reason of lost sales or profits, it must present direct evidence of such losses caused by the alleged unlawful conduct. *Dantzler v. Dictograph Prods., Inc.*, 309.F.2d 326, 329 (4th Cir.1962), cert. denied, 372 U.S. 970, 88 S.Ct. 1097, 10 L.Ed.2d 133 (1963); *Herman Schwabe, Inc. v. United Shoe Mach. Corp.*, 297 F.2d 906, 913 (2d Cir.), cert. denied, 369 U.S. 865, 82 S.Ct. 1031, 8 L.Ed.2d 85 (1962); *American Sea Green Slate Co. v. O'Halloran*, 229 F. 77, 81 (2d Cir. 1915).

* * * * *

Wesley COATES, individually and on behalf of all others similarly situated and Equal Employment Opportunity Commission v. JOHNSON & JOHNSON, et al.

756 F.2d 524

United States Court of Appeals, Seventh Circuit
March 4, 1985

* * * * *

On April 23, 1975, the company discharged plaintiff Wesley Coates, a wage employee who had survived his probationary period by two months, for sleeping on the job. This incident occurred on day after Coates had been reinstated from a suspension for damaging company property while driving a forklift truck. The company decided not to lessen the punishment because an undercover investigative agent working inside the plant reported that Coates was selling drugs on company property.

Coates filed a charge with the EEOC and about three years later brought this suit. The complaint was amended to allege Title VII class discrimination and to add a count alleging individual and class discrimination under 42 U.S.C. § 1981 (1976). Coates contended that he and more than 200 other blacks were discharged "as consequence of a uniform policy and practice to reduce black employment and discriminatorily discharge black employees at defendants' plant." He alleged that defendants maintained a continuing policy and practice of discriminatorily discharging black employees through (1) an articulated plan to reduce the representation of blacks at the plant and (2) a highly discretionary discipline–discharge–reinstatement system under which blacks were treated less favorably than whites. The district court certified the class on May 29, 1981 and Coates, a somewhat less than exemplary employee, became the named class representative.

After extensive discovery and a thirteen–day bench trial, the district court ruled for defendants on both the class and individual claims. The court found that plaintiffs' statistical and nonstatistical evidence was adequately rebutted by defendants, and that plaintiffs failed to meet their burden of persuasion. It is from this ruling that plaintiff Coates, individually and on behalf of the class, and the EEOC appeal. Although there are some questionable and close aspects, they do not, in the context of this case, result in reversible error. We affirm.

* * * * *

VI. Evidentiary Issues

A. Admission of Employee Disciplinary Records and Summaries

Plaintiffs maintain that the disciplinary memoranda that defendants' lawyers' paralegal used in preparing the summaries, as well as the summaries themselves, should not have been admitted into evidence. Plaintiffs argue that the disciplinary memoranda are hearsay and do not fall within any of the exceptions, such as the business records exception provided by Rule 803(6) of the Federal Rules of Evidence. In addition, plaintiffs contend that the summaries were in any event inadmissible under Rule 1006 because they were inaccurate and because they were produced too late. The district court has broad discretion in admitting evidence under Rules 803(6) and 1006, and we will not disturb its decision unless there has been an abuse of that discretion.

Rule 803(6), the business records exception to the hearsay rule, was intended to permit the admission of records maintained in the regular course of business, unless "the source of information or the method or circumstances of preparation indicate a lack of trustworthiness." *United States v. Chappell*, 698 F.2d 308, 311 (7th Cir.), *cert. denied*, 461 U.S. 931, 103 S.Ct. 2095, 77 L.Ed.2d 304 (1983). Plaintiffs argued that the disciplinary memoranda were prepared and kept primarily for use by the grievance procedures, and that consequently there is a high risk that the versions of the rule violations represented by the memoranda are biased. They compare the memoranda to company reports about accidents, * * *

* * * * *

Next, plaintiffs argue that even if the disciplinary records themselves were admissible, the summaries of those records prepared by defendants' counsels' paralegal were not admissible as summaries under Rule 1006.[24] Plaintiffs maintain that the admission of the summaries was inappropriate because they were not made available to plaintiffs at a reasonable time and place and because they are inaccurate. As defendants correctly point out, however, only the underlying documents, and not the summaries, must be made available to the opposing party so as to give them a reasonable time to respond, *United States v. Foley*, 598 F.2d 1323, 1338 (4th Cir.1979), *cert. denied*, 444 U.S. 1043, 100 S.Ct. 727, 62 L.Ed.2d 728 (1980), and there is no question that the underlying personnel records here were made available to plaintiffs well before trial. In addition, we find nothing wrong with the district court's acceptance of the summaries as basically accurate. The trial court heard testimony as to specific incidents of misconduct and had no trouble finding the summaries reliable. Had we been conducting the trial we may have permitted plaintiffs more time to respond to defendants' summaries than they were given by the district court, but we cannot say that the district court abused its discretion in admitting the summaries.

B. Destruction of Departmental Files

Plaintiffs also argue that they should have had the benefit of an evidentiary presumption because certain documents were destroyed by defendants during the closing of the plant. One group of documents destroyed was the departmental files, which were maintained plant–wide, beginning in 1976 and contained duplicates of all disciplinary documents. Although only the personnel files were relied on by defendants in considering discharge decisions, the departmental files were allegedly important to plaintiffs' case because they allegedly contained the only record of oral counseling given to employees, which plaintiffs contended were given to white employees in situations in which blacks were issued written warnings. Plaintiffs argue that because of defendants' spoliation of this evidence, plaintiffs were entitled to an evidentiary presumption that the records of the oral reprimands would corroborate plaintiffs' testimonial evidence that blacks were "written up" in situations in which whites were not. In addition, defendants' manager of labor relations, Thomas Rochon, destroyed a small group of disciplinary letters that were in his possession at the plant closing. These letters had been removed from some personnel files after March, 1978, in connection with an agreement with the union that disciplinary letters more than three years old would be removed. Plaintiffs maintain the presumption should also have applied to these letters.

The prevailing rule is that bad faith destruction of a document relevant to proof of an issue at trial gives rise to a strong inference that production of the document would have been unfavorable to the party responsible for its destruction. *S.C. Johnson & Son, Inc. v. Louisville & Nashville Railroad*, 695 F.2d 253, 258–59 (7th Cir.1982); *Vick v. Texas Employment Commission*, 514 F.2d 734, 737 (5th Cir.1975). However, considering the circumstances surrounding the destruction of the documents in this case, nothing gives rise to an inference of bad faith by defendants. The district court accepted the testimony of Williams, the black plant manager, that the personnel files were destroyed only after he consulted with the EEOC/Affirmative Action coordinator regarding which files needed to be maintained in light of the pending class action. Williams was told that these files, in view of the closing of the plant, did not have to be kept. He then decided that they could be destroyed considering that (1) the departmental files were not official records and the management had agreed with the union not to rely on them in issuing discipline, and that (2) to Williams' knowledge, the departmental files included only incomplete duplications of documents kept in the official files and were not well maintained. Similarly, the district court found that Rochon was unaware at the time he destroyed the disciplinary letters that there was any pending litigation regarding defendants' disciplinary policies, although Rochon was aware that one employee had filed a suit regarding his discharge. These circumstances suggest that the documents were destroyed under routine procedures, not in bad faith, and thus cannot sustain the inference that defendants' agents were conscious of a weak case.

* * * * *

[24] Rule 1006 provides: The contents of voluminous writings, recordings, or photographs which cannot conveniently be examined in court may be presented in the form of a chart, summary, or calculation. The originals, or duplicates, shall be made available for examination or copying, or both, by other parties at reasonable time and place. The court may order that they be produced in court.

Frank Augustus COBB, Jr., Appellant–Defendant v. STATE OF INDIANA, Appellee–Plaintiff

585 N.E.2d 40

Court of Appeals of Indiana, Third District
January 29,1992

I. Facts and Procedural History

This is an appeal from a jury verdict and judgment in a criminal case in which the defendant was found guilty of conspiracy to commit theft, conspiracy to commit fraud on a financial institution, and fraud on a financial institution. We affirm.

On January 16, 1991, an information and a probable cause affidavit were filed against defendant Frank A. Cobb (Cobb), Jr. The information contained four counts:

1. Count I charged Cobb with conspiracy to commit theft, a class D felony;

2. Count II charged Cobb with conspiracy to commit fraud on a financial institution, a class C felony;

3. Count III charged Cobb with theft, a class D felony; and

4. Count IV charge Cobb with fraud on a financial institution, a class C felony.

The State alleged that Cobb and an accomplice, Rosita Collazo (Collazo), stole checks from the Lake County Clerk's Office, forged signatures on those checks, and deposited them into a business account established by Cobb and Collazo.

Both Cobb and the State set forth basically the same set of facts:

Collazo was employed as a deputy clerk for the Circuit Court Clerk Robert Antich. During her employment, Cobb and Collazo lived together. Cobb suggested that Collazo take some blank checks from the Clerk's Office so that the two of them could start a business. In June of 1990, Collazo took six checks from the Clerk's Office and gave them to Cobb.

Cobb and Collazo established a business known as R & J Data Processing (R & J) in the early spring of 1990. Cobb told Collazo how to set up a bank account in the name of R & J at the Mercantile National Bank (Bank) in Hammond, Indiana. At Cobb's suggestion, Collazo used fictitious names for the two of them in setting up the account.

Cobb typed in R & J as the payee on the checks Collazo obtained from the Clerk's Office. He signed the names of the Clerk and another employee of the Clerk's Office to the checks, endorsed the checks, and deposited them into the R & J account. Collazo and Cobb made withdrawals by using R & J checks signed in their fictitious names. After four checks from the Clerk's Office were forged and deposited, Collazo and Cobb were arrested.

Pursuant to a plea agreement with the State, Collazo pled guilty to theft. Her sentencing was continued. The plea agreement provided that the State would recommend to the court that Collazo receive probation if she fully cooperated with the State.

The case proceeded to trial on May 13, 1991, in the Lake County Superior Court. During trial, Collazo identified various checks and deposit slips related to the crimes charged. When the State offered the documents into evidence, Cobb objected, noting that the documents constituted hearsay which rendered the documents inadmissible without proper authentication. The trial court agreed and sustained Cobb's objection, noting that the State could enter the records into evidence through the proper Bank representative.

On the following day of trial, the State called Arthur King (King), a vice president and internal auditor of the Bank, through which Group Exhibit JJ, photocopies of checks and deposit tickets relating to the alleged crimes and which had been previously marked as exhibits at trial, were offered for admission. Cobb objected to admission of the records on the basis that an improper foundation had been laid. Initially, the court sustained his objection, noting that King had failed to testify that he was the keeper of the records. After the State elicited testimony from King that he was the recordkeeper, Cobb took King on voir dire, and King stated that he did not actually work in the record–keeping department, but that he was the record–keeper for purposes of trial and as department head of investigations within the auditing department. Cobb once again objected to lack of foundation for admission of the documents. However, the trial court overruled Cobb's objection and admitted the documents. On May 14, 1991, a jury returned a verdict against Cobb, finding him guilty on counts I, II, and IV, and not guilty as to count III.

Cobb now appeals alleging that the documents showing deposits into the R & J account and withdrawals from the account were admitted in violation of the hearsay rule because the State failed to lay a proper foundation for the records under the business record exception.

II. Issue

The issue on appeal is whether the trial court properly allowed admission of the copies of checks and deposit slips into evidence via the business record exception to the hearsay rule through King, a Bank officer and auditor, who at trial stated he was familiar with the Bank's record keeping procedures in general and the copies at issue in particular, even though King did not actually prepare the records or their contents or work in or supervise the record keeping department of the Bank.

Cobb also alleges that the state did not show that the documents were placed in the record by an authorized person, that such person had personal knowledge of the transaction represented by the documents at the time of entry, and that the records were kept in the routine course of business of the Bank. However, King, in fact, did testify as to these matters (see R. pp. 253–255). While his testimony may have been in the form of conclusory answers to foundational questions posed by his counsel, we find that it was sufficient to satisfy the requisite foundational elements. Cobb also failed to present any evidence or elicit any testimony to the effect that King did not, in fact, have personal knowledge of the foundational elements. It is well settled that, absent evidence to the contrary, courts may presume entries in business records were made by a person who had a duty to make the record and may presume that person had personal knowledge of the transaction presented by the record. *Lyons v. State (1987), Ind., 506 N.E.2d 813, 817*; Accord *Knuckles v. State (1990), Ind. App., 549 N.E.2d 85, 87. We find no error in regard to these issues.*

III. Discussion and Decision

Cobb asserts that King was not the proper recordkeeper to authenticate the business records at issue in this case. He claims the trial court erred by allowing the documents into evidence under the business record exception of the hearsay rule. We disagree.

Generally, the sufficiency of an evidentiary foundation is a matter left to the trial court's discretion. We will reverse only upon a showing of an abuse of discretion by the court. *Sutton v. State (1981), Ind. App., 422 N.E.2d 430, 432*. We find that the trial court committed no error in finding that a sufficient foundation had been laid for the admission of the copies of checks and deposit slips into evidence.

As both the State and Cobb point out, we have recently set for the necessary foundational elements of the business records exception to the hearsay rule as follows:

The business records exception to the hearsay rule permits the admission of documentary evidence if it is identified by its entrant or one under whose supervision it is kept and shown to be an original or first permanent entry, made in the routine course of business, at or near the time of the recorded transaction, by one having a duty to so record and personal knowledge of the transaction represented by the entry.

Getha v. State (1988), Ind. App., 524 N.E.2d 325, 327.

Cobb's primary contention is that King was not the proper party to authenticate the records because he was not the entrant or supervisor of the entrant, and was not involved in the Bank's general keeping of the records. Cobb argues that King's familiarity with the Bank's record–keeping practices as an officer and auditor in the Bank is not enough to qualify him as a proper sponsor of the records. We disagree.

While in Getha the foundational requirement that the record be identified by "its entrant or one under whose supervision it is kept," reflects the common practice of the records being identified at trial by their entrant or a supervisor of the entrant, we have previously held that the requirement should not be misinterpreted to mean that only an entrant or his supervisor can identify the records at trial. Specifically, we noted:

While the most commonly encountered witness today may be a person in authority of the record–keeping department of the business, he or she is not the only witness who can provide the necessary foundation for admission of a business record. This foundation can be established by anyone who possesses, with respect to the particular document in question the knowledge of the . . . [required foundational elements]. This could be the entrant, the entrant's supervisor, co–workers, a records custodian or any other such person. What we demand is not a witness with a formalistic title but one with a functional understanding of the record–keeping process of the business with respect to the specific entry, transaction or declaration contained in the document.

Baker v. Wagers (1984), Ind. App., 472 N.E.2d 218, 221, trans. denied; See also, *Cardin v. State (1989), Ind. App. 540 N.E.2d 51, 55*, trans. denied; *Hatton v. State (1986), Ind. App., 498 N.E.2d 398, 401; Jackson v. Russell (1986), Ind. App., 498 N.E.2d 22, 37*, trans denied; *Wilson v. Jenga Corp. (1986), Ind. App., 490 N.E.2d 375, 377.*

The key requirement is that the witness through which a business record is to be admitted must have personal knowledge of the various elements of the foundation. Id. A sponsor of the exhibit need not have made the entry, filed it, or have first hand knowledge of the transaction represented at the time of the entry. Instead, he or she need only show that it is a part of the records kept in the routine course of business and placed in the record by one authorized to do so, who had personal knowledge of the transaction represented at the time of entry. *Getha, 524 N.E.2d at 327*. Therefore, the foundational elements that a witness through which a business record is to be admitted must have personal knowledge of are as follows:

1) That the record is the original or first permanent entry;

2) That it was made in the ordinary course of business;

3) That it was made at or near the time of the occurrence recorded,

4) By a person with personal knowledge of the matters recorded, and

5) A business duty to record them.

Wilson, 490 N.E.2d at 376. Accordingly, we clarify and modify the foundational requirements as they were listed in Getha to the extent they are inconsistent with this holding, and reaffirm our listing of the requirements as stated in Wilson.

A review of the cases discussing the foundational elements of the business records exception to the hearsay rule reveals a lack of unanimity in Indiana as to the necessary elements. For example, our courts have included as a foundational element in some decisions the common law requirements that "the witness who had knowledge of the facts must be unavailable." *Smith v. State (1983), Ind., 455 N.E.2d 606, 261 N.E. 865;* see also *Bryce v. State (1989), Ind. App., 545 N.E.2d 1094*, trans. denied (supervisor of department of toxicology who reviewed and signed off on test results, but who did not conduct the test and was not the records custodian, was not the proper party to identify records at trial where the state did not show that a witness who had knowledge of the tests was unavailable to testify). However, other decisions have failed to address the unavailability issue and have excluded the unavailability element when listing the necessary foundational elements of the business record exception. See e.g., *Perry v. State (1989), Ind., 541 N.E.2d 913, 918; Smith v. State (1983), Ind. 455 N.E.2d 346, 353. Thompson v. State (1979), 270 Ind. 442, 386 N.E.2d 682 684; Crosson v. State (1978), 268 Ind. 511, 376 N.E.2d 1136, 1141.* Therefore, it is unclear whether unavailability is a necessary element to establish a foundation for the business record exception to the hearsay rule. Some commentators in Indiana have concluded that there is no requirement that the sponsor of a business record prove the actual entrant to be unavailable. See Tanford & Quinlan, Indiana Trial Evidence Manual § 20.3 (2d ed. 1991 supp.); But see Miller, Indiana Evidence § 803.106, p. 189 (1984) (listing unavailability as an element, but stating that it has been virtually eliminated as an element by *Wells, 261 N.E.2d at 865*, in which the Indiana Supreme Court recognized that the unavailability requirement is satisfied if the witness is present and unable to recall the facts sufficiently to testify from memory). Furthermore, although finding the unavailability element met by the facts of the case, Judge Ratliff recently noted that unavailability could be met by a minimal showing and that it is not a crucial element under the business record exception to the hearsay rule because the "heart of the rule . . . is the requirement that the

observation, reporting, and the recording of the facts all be made by someone in the regular course of the business". *Jones v. Marengo State Bank (1988), Ind. App., 526 N.E.2d 709, 715*, quoting *Wells, 261 N.E.2d at 870*. We also believe that the unavailability element of the business record exception, especially in the absence of evidence tending to show that the record is not authentic. As one commentator has noted, "today, the inconvenience of calling those with firsthand knowledge and the unlikelihood of their remembering accurately the details of specific transactions convincingly demonstrate the need for recourse to their written records, without regard to physical unavailability". McCormick on Evidence § 306, p. 720 (2d ed. 1972). We also note that the Federal Rules of Evidence no longer contain unavailability as a requirement. See Fed.R.Evid. 803(6). However, while we do not list it as a required element under the business records exception in this case, we do recognize that our supreme court has not expressly abolished the requirement. In the case at bar, Cobb did not make a specific objection regarding unavailability at trial or raise or argue the issue on appeal. Therefore, regardless of its status, the unavailability element does not affect the outcome of this case.

In this case, the record reveals testimony by King that he was familiar with the Bank's operations and record–keeping system (R. p. 249). At trial, he identified Group Exhibit JJ which consisted of copies of the checks and deposit tickets that had been previously marked as exhibits for trial. King stated he had seen the records before in the course of his involvement with investigations at the Bank, and that he recognized the documents within the group exhibit as statements and copies of checks and deposit slips that were posted to the R & J account (R. p. 252). He also testified that the Bank kept records of the checks at issue and the transactions involving the R & J account (R. p. 252). Furthermore, King testified that the copies of the checks and deposit slips were true and exact copies obtained from the Bank's film records of the originals, that they were kept in the course of regularly conducted business activity at the bank, that they were made by a person with knowledge of or made from information transmitted by a person with knowledge of the acts and events appearing on them, and that the records were made at or near the time of the acts and events appearing on them (R. p. 253–255). King also testified that as an officer of the Bank he appears in court proceedings regarding Bank records and, as head of his auditing department, he oversees the records that his department keeps concerning the Bank's investigations (R. p. 257). Finally, the record reveals that as an auditor of the Bank, King is responsible for internal controls, procedures, and seeing that other systems within the Bank are maintained and are working properly. (R. p. 272).

Accordingly, we find that King was a proper sponsor of the records, although he was not the entrant of the records or the entrant's immediate supervisor. The evidence reflects that he had sufficient knowledge of the Bank's record keeping procedures and business practices in general, and in regard to the documents at issue in particular, to satisfy the required foundational elements of the business record exception to the hearsay rule.

The trial court's judgment is affirmed.

James Robert DAVIS, III, et al. v. JOHNS HOPKINS HOSPITAL

585 A.2d 841

Court of Special Appeals of Maryland
February 13, 1991

* * * * *

Bobby was born on December 12, 1979. At about eight months old, Hopkins diagnosed that Bobby suffered from status epilepticus, a disorder in which the victim sustains a series of prolonged seizures accompanied by difficulty in breathing. If not treated properly, a seizure could result in brain damage or death due to lack of oxygen. Bobby also suffered from status asthmaticus (long, unremitting asthma attacks) and cerebral palsy.

Bobby was a patient of Hopkins since these conditions were first diagnosed.

Because Bobby lived with his family in Anne Arundel County, whenever Bobby would have an attack, emergency medical assistance was provided initially by paramedics of the Anne Arundel Fire Department (AAFD). AAFD protocol required that a patient in a seizure and in need of hospitalization would be taken to the nearest hospital which, in Bobby's case, was North Arundel County Hospital (NACH). On one occasion, while receiving emergency treatment for a seizure, Bobby went into respiratory arrest at NACH. On another occasion, treatment was delayed because a staff member at NACH was unfamiliar with one of Bobby's medications. Concerned that Bobby's condition was too complex for NACH staff, Mr. Davis sought to have Bobby transported directly to Hopkins for treatment of future seizures. In order to deviate from its protocol, AAFD officials told Mr. Davis that a letter was required from Hopkins stating that it was medically acceptable to transport Bobby directly to Hopkins.

After Mr. Davis conferred with Dr. Shlomo Skinnar, one of Bobby's neurologists at Hopkins, the following letter was prepared on the Hopkins' letterhead, signed by Dr. Shinnar and his superior, Dr. John M. Freeman:

February 9, 1981

Department of Neurology
Chief Roger C. Simonds
Emergency Medical Service Care
Division
Anne Arundel County Fire Department
P. O. Box 276
Route 3
Millersville, MD 21108

Dear Chief Simonds:

Re: James Davis

I am writing to you concerning special transportation arrangements for James Davis. James is a one year old child with a complex seizure disorder who is followed by us at the Pediatric Neurology clinic at Johns Hopkins. He is currently on multiple medications including phenobarbital, clonazepam and valproate. When James goes into status epilepticus, which he does frequently with high fevers, he is difficult to manage. In the past he has required transfer to the Johns Hopkins Pediatric Intensive Care Unit or the Pediatric Neurology ward each time. Initial management at the outlying hospital was at times delayed secondary to lack of familiarity with James' complex seizure disorder. I feel that in view of these problems it would be better to transport James directly to the Johns Hopkins Pediatric Emergency Room with advance warning by radio to the ER and pediatric neurology. There are always risks in transporting a seizing child, but I feel that they are in this case justified. These risks have been explained to James' parents who understand and support this decision. I will be glad to provide more details on request.

Sincerely,

Shlomo Shinnar, M.D., Ph.D.
Department of Pediatric
Neurology

John M. Freeman, M.D.
Director Pediatric Neurology
Department

In the event Bobby could not be treated at Hopkins, Dr. Shinnar and other Hopkins physicians provided the Davises with "To Whom It May Concern" letters that listed the dosages of his current medication, the medication necessary to stop his seizures and other instructions how to manage his condition. As Bobby's condition and thus his treatment changed, the letters were updated. Seven letters were drafted and delivered to the Davises. The Davises always carried a copy of the latest letter with them. In August 1982, Bobby was taken to the Medical College of Virginia Hospitals because he began seizing while at Kings Dominion, an amusement park nearby. Through the use of the latest letter the paramedics and the doctor at the hospital properly treated Bobby.

Based on the receipt of the February 9, 1981

letter, Chief Simonds of the AAFD directed the paramedic units to transport Bobby directly to Hopkins. As a result, from February 9, 1981, until July 1982, Bobby was transported to Hopkins nine times by ambulance and twice by helicopter. Hopkins never designated which method of transportation was preferable. In July 1982, the AAFD decided always to transport Bobby by helicopter, weather permitting. An AAFD mobile paramedic unit would take Bobby to a rendezvous point where a waiting helicopter would transport him to Hopkins. Between July 1982 and March 2, 1983, Bobby was transported to Hopkins eight times by helicopter and once by ambulance because of fog. By ambulance, the trip from the Davis' home to Hopkins took approximately thirty five minutes. By helicopter, the same trip took approximately twelve minutes plus a few minutes for the time to travel by ambulance from the Davis' home to the rendezvous point.

Bobby's mode of transportation determined the unit at Hopkins to which he was delivered. When brought by ambulance, he arrived at the Pediatric Emergency Room located on the first floor. When brought by helicopter, he was landed on the roof of the Children's Center (14th floor) and than taken to the Pediatric Intensive Car Unit (PICU) located on the 7th floor.

The PICU at Hopkins is part of the Maryland Institute for Emergency Medical Services System (MIEMS). See Md. Education Code Ann. § 13–103 (1989). The MIEMS System is designed to provide emergency care to persons throughout Maryland and Washington, D.C. Involved are hospitals, state and county agencies that provide treatment and transportation to the hospitals, and a communications network that coordinates the process.

At times, the demand on the PICU staff and facilities is so great that it cannot accept additional patients without risking the health of the new patients or those already in PICU. This is never the case with the Pediatrics Emergency Room. When the PICU is in a non–accepting condition, it notifies the MIEMS Systems that it is to be placed on "fly–by" status which means that patients who are to arrive by hospital to the PICU are directed, at the time of the initial radio contact, to the next comparable unit in the MIEMS Systems which in this case was the Children's Hospital in Washington, D.C. The helicopter trip from the Davis' home to Children's Hospital was approximately eighteen minutes, six minutes more than the trip to Hopkins.

Even when the PICU was on fly–by status, it received calls through the MIEMS System communication network. On occasion the paramedics at the scene were able to convince the physician in charge of the PICU to accept a patient even though the PICU was on fly–by status. On other occasions, the physician in charge would not make an exception. At times, even when it was on fly–by status, the PICU provided consultation to paramedics on the scene, though the patient was to be flown to another hospital. The Davises were not informed of the possibility that the PICU might go on fly–by status and, as a result, refuse to accept Bobby when transported by helicopter.

In the early morning hours of March 2, 1983, three year old Bobby began seizing at home. Mrs. Davis called the paramedics who arrived at the Davis' home, loaded Bobby, accompanied by his father, into the ambulance and drove to the rendezvous with the waiting helicopter. Paramedic Calvin Cavey, the ambulance driver, called Hopkins to advise that Bobby was seizing and that he was to be flown by helicopter to the PICU. The call was patched through to both the PICU and the emergency room. Dr. Morrow, a resident physician in the PICU, responded that the PICU was on fly–by status and therefore Bobby should be taken to NACH, the nearest hospital. This was refused. Dr. Morrow then said Bobby would be flown to Children's Hospital in Washington, D.C. This procedure was also refused. Mr. Cavey read the February 9, 1981 letter to Dr. Morrow. At about the same time, Trooper Deal, the medical observer on the helicopter, entered the conversation and demanded admission to Hopkins for Bobby. Dr. Nancy Setzer, Dr. Morrow's supervisor, was contacted by Dr. Morrow and advised of the situation. Dr. Setzer authorized Bobby's admission to the PICU. Dr. Morrow relayed this to Mr. Cavey. This admission discussed lasted between ten and fourteen minutes. Bobby accompanied by his father, was then loaded into the helicopter and flown to Hopkins. The flight took thirteen minutes. During the flight, a patient was moved out of the PICU to make room for Bobby.

Bobby required ventilation during transportation from his house to Hopkins. He was ventilated in the ambulance with an "airway" which held down his tongue to ensure good air passage into his lungs. A pediatric airbag with pure oxygen was then placed over Bobby's mouth and squeezed to force oxygen into his lungs. Bobby was being ventilated in this manner from the time he was loaded in the ambulance until he was loaded in the helicopter, after the discussion between Mr. Cavey and Dr. Morrow. During the helicopter flight, Bobby retained the "airway" in his mouth, but Trooper Deal was not able to use the pediatric airbag to force oxygen into Bobby's lungs. Instead, Trooper Deal used a non–rebreather mask, a soft, clear plastic mask connected by a tube to a cylinder of oxygen which fits over the patient's mouth and nose.

Bobby was landed on the roof the Children's Center at Hopkins and immediately treated. Bobby suffered severe brain damage due to the events of March 2, 1983.

1. Medical Records

In October 1983, Mr. Davis and his counsel went to Hopkins to review and copy Bobby's records and were told that volumes containing records of admissions from late 1980 through 1982 were missing. All other records were reproduced. Lisa Cowalt, the Senior Claims Coordinator for Hopkins, as well as other Hopkins personnel, periodically searched for the records in the various clinics and in–patient areas where Bobby was treated. In February, 1986, a Request for Production of Documents, filed by Davises' counsel, demanded all medical records for Bobby. The records for 1981 were produced in April 1987. In August 1989, counsel for the Davises noted the deposition of Lottie

Cole, head of the Medical Records Department of Hopkins, to determine the whereabouts of the missing 1980 and 1982 records. On the business day before the deposition, Ms. Cowalt asked the Medical Records Department to search for the missing records. Forty–five minutes later the records were located. The records were produced the following business day, less than one month before the trial. Ms. Cowalt testified that no one at Hopkins ever withheld any medical records from the appellants and that both counsel received the same records at the same time.

* * * * *

Md. Health–General Code Ann. § 4–302(d)(2) imposed liability on a hospital which "refuses to disclose a medical record within a reasonable time" after request by or on behalf of a patient. We have determined "refuse" within the meaning of the statute to be "intentional, as opposed to negligent or contractual, conduct." *Laubach v. Franklin Square Hospital*, 79 Md.App. 203, 218, 556 A.2d 682 (1989), *aff'd*, 318 Md. 615, 569 A.2d 693 (1990).

In *Laubach*, Timothy and Nancy Laubach (Laubachs) sued Franklin Square Hospital (hospital) for violation of Health–General § 4–302 which arose out of a separate medical malpractice action. The Laubachs contended that the hospital violated the statute by not producing fetal monitoring tracings (tracings). The hospital countered with a two–fold argument; that it did not refuse to produce the tracings because it did not "*mentally* determine[] not to comply," 79 Md.App. at 219, 556 A.2d 682 (emphasis in original), and that the tracings were not medical records. *Id.* at 225, 556 A.2d 682. The court denied cross–motions for summary judgment and the issue proceeded to trial before a jury, at the conclusion of which, a verdict was entered in favor of the Laubachs. The jury assessed damages at one million dollars.

The hospital appealed arguing that the record was devoid of any evidence of a refusal. We rejected this argument finding sufficient evidence to send the issue to the jury. "Whether,

as the hospital has recognized, and, indeed, argued below, the hospital merely failed to comply or, by an act of volition, refused to comply is a question to be answered by the jury after proper instructions." *Id.* at 221, 556 A.2d 682. In addition, we found sufficient evidence to uphold the jury's verdict, stating:

> There was evidence in the record that counsel for appellants in communications with counsel for the hospital, in connection with a malpractice action filed by appellants against the hospital and others, specifically requested that the fetal heart monitoring tracings be produced. This request was made in connection with appellants' medical malpractice action against the hospital and others. Moreover, the appellants' counsel testified that that was not the first discussion he had had with the hospital concerning appellants' need for the tracings. This is confirmed, it appears, by a letter, dated September 7, 1984, from appellee Gately to the chairman of the Health Claims Arbitration panel. In that letter, Gately reported, based on conversations with appellee Rifkin and hospital personnel, that a prior investigation to locate the tracings had failed to turn them up; he concluded that they were not available. In addition to the evidence that appellants requested fetal monitoring tracings, there is evidence in the record that the hospital was on notice as to appellants' need for, and desire to have, them.

Id. at 224, 556 A.2d 682.

In affirming the decision of this Court, the Court of Appeals held, "To achieve these purposes, no more than a mere refusal to disclose within a reasonable time, upon proper request, whether done maliciously or not, results in liability for punitive damages in addition to actual damages." *Laubach*, 318 Md. at 622, 569 A.2d 693.

As noted in the facts, *supra*, the 1981 medical records were not produced until over a year after they were due to be produced and the 1982 records were not produced until almost three and one–half years after they were due. The 1982 records were located forty–five minutes after Ms. Cowalt requested the Medical Records Department to search for them on the business day before Lottie Cole was to be deposed to explain their absence. The long delay in producing these records followed by their sudden disclosure combined with the fact that these were records at the center of the appellants' case against Hopkins is sufficient evidence to survive a motion for judgment and submit this issue to the jury. That Ms. Cowalt testified to the contrary does not alter our conclusion since the evidence is to be viewed in the light most favorable to appellants. The credibility of the witnesses and the weight of the evidence are for the jury. *Thodos*, 75 Md. App. at 713–14, 542 A.2d 1307.

Finally, appellee contends that the medical records claim is barred by the statute of limitations. Since there is no statute of limitations specified in the Health–General § 4–302, the general three year statute of limitations applies. Md.Cts. & Jud.Proc. Code Ann. § 5–101 (1989). Appellee asserts that Mr. Davis knew that medical records were not going to be produced in October 1983 when, upon his request for production, he and his attorney were told that the 1980–82 records were missing. The court rejected this contention in denying the appellee's motion for summary judgment on the medical records claim and did not address the statute of limitations issue in granting appellee's motion for judgment at the close of appellants' case.

Under Cts. & Jud.Proc. § 5–101, an action must be filed within three years of the date that it "accrues". The question of when a cause of action accrues is left to judicial determination. *Booth Glass Co. v. Huntingfield Corp.*, 304 Md. 615, 619, 500 A.2d 641 (1985) *citing Pierce v. Johns–Manville Sales Corp.*, 296 Md. 656, 664, 464 A.2d 1020 (1983); *Harig v. Johns–Manville*, 284 Md. 70, 75, 394 A.2d 299 (1978).

The test to be utilized in fixing the accrual date of a cause of action calls for a determination of the time the action became vested and enforceable, *Vincent v. Palmer*, 179 Md. 365, 19 A.2d 183 (1941), *i.e.*, when the plaintiff could have maintained his action to a successful result. *James v. Weisheit*, 279 Md. 41, 367 A.2d 482 (1977); *W., B., & A. Elec. R.R. Co. v. Moss*, 130 Md. 198, 100 A. 86 (1917).

Goldstein v. Potomac Elec. Power Co., 285 Md. 673, 684, 404 A.2d 1064 (1979). Further, the discovery rule is applicable generally to all actions and the cause of action accrues when the claimant in fact knew or should have known of the wrong. *Poffenberger v. Risser*, 631, 636, 431 A.2d 677 (1981).

For appellants to have a "vested and enforceable" claim, under Health–General § 4–302, they must wait for passage of a reasonable amount of time. Thus, the statute of limitations would not begin to run in October 1983 at Mr. Davis's initial notice that the medical records were missing.

The general rule seems also settled in the computation of the statutory period, in cases where there is an undertaking which requires a continuation of services, or the party's right depends upon the happening of an event in the future, the statute begins to run only from the time the services can be completed or from the time the event happens.

Waldman v. Rohrbaugh 241 Md. 137, 141–2, 215 A.2d 825 (1966) *quoting Moss*, 130 Md. at 204–05, 100 A. 86.

Appellants filed their medical records claim as part of their Amended Complaint in May 1988. The statute of limitations then would extend back to May 1985. Given the size of Hopkins' facilities, the total number of pages of records maintained, the number of pages and records requested, the fact that the initial request was oral and not written, and that many requested records were produced by Hopkins, even if we were to consider appellee's inability to produce Bobby's medical records upon request in October 1983 a refusal, we do not believe that the delay of nineteen months to be so inherently unreasonable under the circumstances as to charge appellants with knowledge of a vested and enforceable claim for violation of Health–General § 4–302. It was not until 1986 that appellant made a formal written request for these records in claimants' First Request for

Production of Documents. Although a response was due in March 1986, appellee did not respond until September 1986 that it would produce the records. In fact, appellee did not produce the records at that time. It was at this point that appellants should have known that appellee was in violation of Health–General § 4–302. The May 1988 filing was within the three year statute of limitations.

Robbie DeLAUGHTER v. LAWRENCE COUNTY HOSPITAL & ROGER COLLINS, M.D.

601 So. 2d 818

Supreme Court of Mississippi
April 22, 1992

On the morning of Saturday, February 2, 1985, seventy (70) year old Tera Lambert was taken by ambulance from her home to the Lawrence County Hospital (hereinafter "the Hospital"), seen by the emergency room physician, Dr. Roger Collins, and admitted to the Intensive Care Unit. Ms. Lambert's regular physician, Dr. Brantley Pace, examined her Sunday afternoon; she was stable. At approximately 10:00 p.m. Sunday evening, the ICU nurse, who had just come on shift, observed that Ms. Lambert's blood pressure was elevated, she was confused, her speech was non–intelligible, and she was having an abnormal heart rhythm. The nurse notified Dr. Collins who, without assessing the patient, told the nurse to continue Ms. Lambert's present treatment.

At approximately 8:00 a.m. on Monday morning, Ms. Lambert had a grand mal seizure. As a result of the seizure, Ms. Lambert became comatose. She was transferred to St. Dominic Hospital in Jackson, Mississippi, upon the orders of Dr. Pace. A CT scan was performed which indicated that Ms. Lambert had a subarachnoid aneurysm, which had hemorrhaged. Ten days later the aneurysm ruptured and Ms. Lambert died.

Robbie DeLaughter, one of Ms. Lambert's eight (8) children, filed suit on behalf of all the children against Lawrence County Hospital, Dr. Collins and Dr. Pace in January, 1987, alleging wrongful death resulting from failure to diagnose and negligence in destruction of hospital records. Following discovery, Dr. Pace was dismissed from the suit. After five (5) days of trial, the jury returned a 9–3 verdict in favor of the Hospital and Dr. Collins. DeLaughter filed a Motion for a New Trial, which the trial court overruled. Aggrieved, DeLaughter timely perfected appeal to this Court raising three assignments of error. Finding merit on two assignments of error, we reverse and remand for a new trial on the merits as to Lawrence County Hospital.

* * * * *

DeLaughter next argues that the trial court erred by refusing three (3) jury instructions concerning the failure of the Hospital to maintain accurate and detailed medical records as required to be kept by every hospital on its patients. Miss. Code Ann. § 41–9–63 (1972), and § 41–9–69 (Supp. 1990). The patient's hospital record, an integral component in any malpractice action against the hospital, contains information impossible to adequately reconstruct from memory. In this case, however, a reconstructed medical record was presented.

The evidence in this case shows that the Hospital refused to release Ms. Lambert's medical records to her family without proper authorization. On March 5, 1985, after the death of Ms. Lambert, the Director of Nurses at Lawrence County Hospital instructed the records custodian to lock up Ms. Lambert's record so that the family could not get them. When the records custodian attempted to comply with the instruction, she discovered that Ms. Lambert's hospital records were missing.

The records had last been seen at the Hospital two or three days prior to March 5, 1985, sitting in Dr. Pace's box awaiting dictation of Ms. Lambert's discharge summary. Upon discovery that the chart was missing, the Hospital set about reconstructing the file by gathering copies of items from the various medical departments within the Hospital. When reconstructed, the chart was incomplete, lacking the medical history or physical assessment taken by Dr. Collins on Ms. Lambert's admission to the Hospital on February 2, and the "nurses' progress notes" compiled during Ms. Lambert's hospitalization from February 2 through the morning of February 4 when Ms. Lambert was transferred to St. Dominic Hospital. One of the "nurses' progress notes" contained the ICU nurse's observations of Ms. Lambert from 10:00 p.m. on February 3 until 1:30 a.m. on February 4.

This issue concerns what the jury was entitled to hear and what instruction should have been given regarding the reconstructed medical records. The jury was entitled to be told the original hospital record would not be produced in court, as that was a relevant fact. The hospital had the duty to give an adequate explanation for the absence of the original hospital record. Therefore, the jury was entitled to be told why the original hospital record was missing, also a relevant fact.

As with any other evidence, the explanation for the original record's absence may be fully satisfying either that it was lost through no fault of the hospital, that the hospital deliberately destroyed it, or as in most cases, somewhere in between, thereby making it a jury issue. For example, where the evidence is positive that the hospital had been destroyed by fire, such circumstances would adequately account for the loss of the original medical record without fault attributable to the hospital, and there would be no reason for the jury to be instructed on a presumption or inference arising from the loss.

On the other hand, where the evidence is positive that the hospital deliberately destroyed the original medical record or where a record required by law to be kept is unavailable due to negligence, an inference arises that the record contained information unfavorable to the hospital, and the jury should be so instructed. This is precisely the situation when a patient claims the medical privilege and prevents his physician from testifying in court. *Pittman v. Mendenhall–Mims Mitchell Funeral Home, Inc., 242 Miss. 877, 137 So.2d 518 (1962).* Likewise, where the evidence is somewhere in between such that the jury could find that the hospital either had or had not deliberately or negligently destroyed the

original medical record, the jury should be instructed to take this into account.

Thus, where the evidence regarding the missing original medical records is such that the jury is entitled to an instruction, the instruction should require the jury to first determine whether reasonable explanation for the loss of the missing original medical record has been presented by the hospital. Should the jury determine from the explanation provided that the loss of the original medical record was not in any way attributable to the deliberate or negligent actions of the hospital, the jury could not infer that the missing original medical record contained information unfavorable to the hospital. However, should the jury determine from the explanation provided that the loss of the original medical record was deliberately or negligently brought about by the actions of the hospital, the jury could infer that the missing original medical record contained information unfavorable to the hospital.

This Court has spoken rather clearly on this subject. In *Bott v. Wood, 56 Miss. 136 (1878),* we held:

The principle of the maxim omnia praesumuntur in odium spoliatoris, as applicable to the destruction or suppression of a written instrument, is that such destruction or suppression raises a presumption that the document would, if produced, militate against the party destroying or suppressing it, and that his conduct is attributable to this circumstance, and, therefore, slight evidence of the contents of the instrument will usually, in such a case, be carried too far. It cannot properly be pushed to the extent of dispensing with the necessity of other evidence; and should be regarded as "merely matter of inference, in weighing the effect of evidence in its own nature applicable to the subject in dispute. 2 Best on Ev., sec. 412 et seq.

The doctrine is, that unfavorable presumption and intendment shall be against the party who had destroyed an instrument which is the subject of inquiry, in order that he may not gain by his wrong. (Footnote omitted)

56 Miss. at 140–141. Where, as here, one is under a statutory obligation to maintain records and where one was negligent in failing to do so, the same analysis obtains.

The evidence in this case is such that De-Laughter was entitled to an instruction regarding the missing original medical records. In light of our analysis on this issue, we review each of DeLaughter's three (3) proposed instructions.

Instruction P–8 reads as follows:

The Court instructs you that if you find that the hospital records in this case were intentionally destroyed by the defendant hospital in the full amount of the plaintiff's damages.

This instruction creates an impermissible irrebuttable presumption of negligence. While the Court does not advocate destruction of evidence, we also do not irrevocably impose liability because of it. We find that the trial court did not err in refusing this instruction.

The trial court, also, did not err by refusing Instruction P–4. Instruction P–4 reads as follows:

If you find that the Defendant [hospital] negligently or intentionally failed to maintain the medical records of Tera Lambert and you further find that the failure to maintain such records proximately contributed to the failure of the Plaintiff to prove any essential element of her case, then you should return a verdict for the Plaintiff against the Defendant hospital in the full amount of the Plaintiff's damages.

This instruction is improper because negligent treatment is not inferred from the missing hospital record. The failure by the Hospital to show that it did not lose or destroy the missing record only creates a jury issue as to whether the Hospital rebutted the presumption that the missing information in the record would have been unfavorable to the Hospital. DeLaughter still was required to prove each element of her negligence action.

The court also should not have granted Instruction P–7. Instruction P–7 reads as follows:

If you find the Defendant Hospital negligently failed to maintain the hospital records, the burden of proving that the hospital was not negligent and that the hospital's negligence did not cause the death of Tera Lambert rests upon the Defendant Hospital and that if the Defendant Hospital does not prove beyond the preponderance of the evidence that it was not negligent and that such negligence did not cause the death of Tera Lambert then you should return a verdict for the plaintiff.

This instruction clearly would have shifted the burden of proof on the issue of negligence to the Hospital. The burden does not shift; DeLaughter was only entitled to have the jury presume the missing information in the Hospital record, which the Hospital did not show was favorable to the Hospital, was unfavorable to it.

Because DeLaughter did not submit a proper instruction, we find that the trial court did not err in refusing the submitted instructions. Had we found one of DeLaughter's instructions proper, we would have considered the Hospital's argument that instruction D–1–12, which was withdrawn at the request of both DeLaughter and Lawrence County Hospital, was a proper instruction.

Due to the absence of law on this issue, we will arguendo address this contention. Instruction D–1–12 reads in pertinent part:

The Court instructs the jury that if you determine by a preponderance of evidence that either the Plaintiff or the Defendants caused the original Lawrence County Hospital records of Tera Lambert to become either destroyed, misplaced, or unavailable then the jury may infer that such records, which are not a part of the recreated record would be unfavorable to such party, if any, determined to be the party responsible and the jury may give to such evidence whatever weight, worth and credibility the jury determines it is entitled.

This instruction correctly creates a rebuttable

presumption that the information contained in the missing documents was unfavorable to the party which the jury finds caused the loss of Ms. Lambert's hospital record. *Bott v. Wood, 56 Miss. 136, 140–41 (1878)* (all things are presumed against the spoliator). However, the instruction fails to inform the jury that the Hospital has the burden to show it did not destroy or misplace the hospital record. The party against whom the presumption operates must overcome the presumption; otherwise, the presumption operates against the party.

In sum, we find that the hospital chart was not fully reconstructed. We further find that the trial court erred in failing to place the burden of proof on the Hospital to show that the chart was not lost or destroyed by the Hospital. In addition, we find that the trial court erred in failing to give an instruction on the spoliation issue. We recognize that DeLaughter did not submit a proper instruction on this issue; however, based upon the record now before us, we cannot say that the error was harmless.

* * * * *

Stanley DOLLISON v. The CHICAGO, ROCK ISLAND & PACIFIC RAILROAD COMPANY, et al.

355 NE.2d 588

Appellate Court of Illinois, First District, First Division
September 7, 1976

* * * * *

Stanley Dollison brought an action based upon negligence and product liability against The Chicago, Rock Island & Pacific Railroad Company ("Rock Island"), the Penn–Central Railroad, and Unarco Industries, Inc. Dollison, a janitor for Campbell Soup Company, suffered injuries when he was struck by a 700 pound steel load divider door which fell from its attachment located beneath the ceiling of a railroad boxcar. The Rock Island is the owner of the boxcar; and the Penn–Central is the servicing railroad for the Campbell Soup

loading docks in Chicago. After a lengthy trial, the jury returned a verdict of $75,000 for the plaintiff against the Rock Island. defendants Unarco and Penn–Central received favorable verdicts. The trail court denied Rock Island's post–trial motion, and this appeal followed.

* * * * *

During one point of his direct examination, Salapatek testified that it was the Rock Island's intention to install the new doors at the Biddle Yards. At another point of his direct examination, Salapatek stated that he did not know if it was the custom and practice of the Rock Island to replace the new doors at the Biddle Yards. Salapatek was impeached on direct examination with his deposition testimony given prior to trial wherein he stated Rock Island employees would have installed the new doors as well as repaired the exterior damage of car 6407 at Biddle Yards.

Salapatek kept in his possession for one year a ledger book which contains a record of the movement of car 6407. Pursuant to instructions from the Rock Island, the ledger book and Salapatek's written order relating to repair instructions for car 6407 were destroyed at the Burr Oak Yards. Salapatek stated that he had no further knowledge of any record pertaining to the repair work conducted on car 6407. Salapatek did not testify that any other records maintained by the Rock Island at Biddle, Arkansas were destroyed. Salapatek's testimony does not indicate that it is the policy of the Rock Island to destroy all business records or certain types of repair records on a widespread basis at all company offices.

Salapatek further stated that all four load divider doors would be installed at one time as a unit. Never in Salapatek's 36 years of experience had he known of an instance when any other railroad other than the owner railroad would replace load divider doors in a boxcar. If an "on–line" railroad repaired a pivot bolt assembly in a carriage connection, a bill would be sent to the railroad which owned the repaired car as a matter of custom and practice. the replacement of a cotter pin or hex nut would trigger the billing process for labor and parts reimbursement. Salapatek knew of no bills sent to the Rock Island by any other railroad for repair work on car 6407.

At trial in September, 1973, the Rock Island stipulated that it did not possess any documents relating to the repair of car 6407 during times in which the car was located at the Burr Oak Yards in Blue Island or at the yards in Biddle, Arkansas. The Rock Island further stipulated that it did not possess any bills or documents indicating that any other person or any other railroad performed repair work on any part of car 6407. Moreover, the record indicates that the Rock Island never responded to plaintiff's discovery motion filed June 1, 1970, for production of documents relating to the inspection, maintenance or repair of the load divider doors in car 6407. On July 15, 1970, the Rock Island responded with the answer "unknown" to a plaintiff's interrogatory asking for the identity of the person who repaired or reinstalled the load divider doors in car 6407.

* * * * *

An unfavorable evidentiary presumption arises if a party, without reasonable excuse, fails to produce evidence which is under his control. (*Tepper v. Campo*, 398 Ill. 496, 76 N.E.2d 490, *Hudson. Hudson,* 287 Ill. 286, 122 N.E. 497) The presumption does not relieve the plaintiff from the burden of proving a prima facie case. (*Gage v. Parmelee,* 87 Ill. 329; *Walker v. Herke,* 20 Wash.2d 239, 147 P. 2d 255.) Once a prima facie case is established by a plaintiff, the trier of fact may infer that available evidence which is not produced would be unfavorable to the defendant. (*Beery v. Breed,* 311 Ill.App. 469, 36 N.E.2d 591.) Since the record before us does not include all jury instructions tendered, we are unable to determine if a relevant instruction was given (Illinois Pattern Instruction No. 5.01). However, defendant did not give any reasonable explanation for the failure to produce repair records kept at Biddle, Arkansas. We believe that the jury could reasonably infer that any record relating to the repair of car 6407 would adversely affect the Rock Island's interests. (*Bubrick v. Northern Ill. Gas,* 130 Ill.App.2d 99, 264 N.E.2d 560.) Moreover, it was entirely proper for plaintiff's counsel to argue to the jury that the Rock Island would have produced repair

documents if those documents were favorable. *LeMaster v. Chi. Rock Island & Pac. R.R.,* Ill.App.3d 1001, 343 N.E.2d 65.

* * * * *

DOW CHEMICAL CO. (U.K.) LTD. v. S.S. GIOVANNELLA D'AMICO, her engines, etc. and D'Amico Societa Di Naviganzione, S. p. A.

297 F.Supp. 699

United States District Court S.D. New York
March 31, 1969

The plaintiff seeks to recover the loss arising from damage to a cargo of styrene monomer carried in defendant's vessel from Canada to Europe. Plaintiff claims that it turned over to defendant approximately 1,006 tons of clear water–white styrene monomer and that defendant delivered the chemical at Rotterdam seriously discolored and 11 1/2 tons short of the shipped weight.

The plaintiff is Dow Chemical Company (United Kingdom), Ltd. (hereinafter Dow UK), a British corporation. The defendant is D'Amico Societa Di Navigazione, S.P.A. (hereinafter D'Amico), an Italian corporation, which owns the S/S "GIOVANNELLA D'AMICO". The impleaded defendant is Dow Chemical International Limited, S.A. (hereinafter Dow International), originally a Venezuelan corporation and now a Panamanian corporation; Dow International chartered a portion of the vessel for the shipment.

The subject of the suit, styrene monomer, is a petrochemical used in the manufacture of plastics. Dow Chemical Company of Canada (hereinafter Dow Canada) manufactured the styrene monomer in question at its plant in Sarnia, Ontario. Dow UK bought the styrene there and directed Dow International to ship it to London; later, Dow UK changed the destination to Rotterdam.

The cargo was loaded aboard the GIOVANNELLA on 7 November 1960 at Sarnia and the ship sailed the following day. After a stormy North Atlantic passage, the vessel arrived at Rotterdam on 25 November 1960.

The styrene monomer, as manufactured at Sarnia, was a clear water–white liquid. Plaintiff introduced documentary evidence at trial that the cargo was delivered to the ship at Sarnia in apparent good order and condition and that when delivered at Rotterdam it was a brownish yellow which materially impaired its value. Ordinarily, this would have been enough to establish a prima facie case, leaving the defendant, in order to avoid liability, with the necessity of proving that it exercised due diligence to make the ship seaworthy — that is, fit for the carriage of the cargo. *Schnell v. The Vallescura*, 293 U.S 296, 303–305, 55 S.Ct. 194, 79 L.Ed. 373 (1934).

However, where the cargo may contain a hidden defect or inherent vice present at the time of shipment and not readily discernible, then plaintiff must show delivery to the ship in actual good order and condition in order to establish its prima facie case. *Elia Salzman Tobacco Co. v. S.S. Mormacwind*, 371 F.2d 537, 539 (2d Cir. 1967); *The Niel Maersk*, 91 F.2d 932 (2d Cir.1937).

Dow Canada personnel and their independent cargo surveyor, the Saybolt Company, took numerous samples of the styrene monomer from the end of the loading line and a few samples from the GIOVAN-NELLA's tanks while the cargo was being put aboard. At least ten of these samples were subjected to more or less complete chemical analysis by a technician at Down Canada's Sarnia laboratory. However, the logbooks in which the technician's results were originally recorded were not introduced at trial, having been inexplicably destroyed by Dow Canada after the commencement of this litigation. The samples themselves were likewise inexplicably discarded after this controversy had arisen. Nor was the technician himself produced, despite the fact that he was still employed by Dow Canada well after the suit had begun.

Instead, plaintiff introduced at trial a summary table of the results of ten of the chemical analyses, with only four of these being reported in full. This table had been prepared by the supervisor of the Dow Canada laboratory five months after the cargo was loaded aboard the GIOVANNELLA. Plaintiff also introduced a memorandum prepared by this same supervisor shortly before this suit was commenced which set forth the same results in even more conclusory fashion. In addition, plaintiff introduced a letter, dated two weeks after the discoloration was discovered at Rotterdam, from a Dow Canada executive to a "Claims Agent" setting forth a single set of figures, evidently a composite of some sort of the analyses of eleven samples taken from the end of the loading line.

These documents, if credited, would tend to establish the actual good order and condition of the styrene monomer at loading. (A few of the samples taken from the ship's tanks showed some discoloration; these will be discussed further below.)

However, it is well settled that the intentional destruction of a document or object relevant to the proof of an issue on trial can give rise to a strong inference that its production would have been unfavorable to the spoliator. Richard on Evidence, § 91 at p.64 (9th ed. Prince 1964); Fisch on New York Evidence, § 1127 at p. 554 (1959). Moreover, where a witness is under the control of a party and could testify, if called, to material facts, the failure to call that witness can give rise to the strongest inference against that party which the opposing evidence permits. This is particularly true where the testimony would be important and where it can be inferred that the witness would ordinarily tend to be favorable to that party. Richardson on Evidence § 92 at pp. 64–65 (9th ed. Prince 1964); Fisch on New York Evidence, § 1126 at pp. 551–552 (1959); 1 Bender's New York Evidence, § 30 at pp. 443–444 (Frumer & Biskind 1968). See also *A.C. Becken Co. v. Gemex Corporation*, 314 F.2d 839, 841 (7th Cir. 1963); *Matter of Eno*, 196 App.Div. 131. 163, 187 N.Y.S. 756 (1st Dept. 1921).

* * * * *

At the close of plaintiff's case, defendant moved to dismiss for failure to establish a claim upon which relief could be granted.

The Court reserved decision and the defendant then went forward in the discharge of the burden cast upon it by the plaintiff's proofs. The evidentiary problems discussed above thereupon became largely academic on the evidence presented by defendant affirmatively establishing the actual cause of the damage to the cargo and defendant's freedom from negligence.

* * * * *

EATON CORPORATION v. APPLIANCE VALVE CORPORATION, Thomas R. Krzewina, William R. Donahue, Jr., David F. Miller, and Design & Manufacturing Corporation

790 F.2d 874

United States Court of Appeals
April 30, 1986

Briefly, defendants Krzewina, a sales engineer, and Donohue, a supervisory engineer, both left employment with Eaton in November, 1980, to form Appliance Valves Corporation (AVC), a defendant here.

In mid–1981, Eaton sued all three defendants in federal court because of diversity. Eaton's complaint contained three state law counts: 1) misappropriation of trade secrets; 2) breach of contract not to disclose trade secrets; and 3) conspiracy to misappropriate trade secrets.

The district court denied Eaton's motion for preliminary injunction and Eaton appealed. The United States Court of Appeals for the Seventh Circuit, in an unpublished opinion affirmed the denial of the injunction and remanded for further proceedings.

* * * * *

Regarding misappropriation of trade secrets and confidential information, the court concluded:

> The additional evidence presented at trial demonstrates that all Donohue removed from the Eaton files were clean copies of

patents, i.e., patent information readily available to the public. Moreover, the actual copies of the patents delivered to [one of defendants' attorneys] for evaluation are devoid of Eaton notations or Eaton summaries for five years and the notes on the patents were not made from Eaton files. This evidence simply does not support Eaton's allegation that Donohue inspected and copied patent materials from . . . Eaton.

* * * * *

On appeal, Eaton challenges each aspect of the judgment, asserting *inter alia* that reversal is required because the district court refused to draw an inference from a destruction of documents, and because the district court admitted into evidence a reference not noticed in accord with 35 U.S.C. § 282, third paragraph.

Issues

1) Whether the district court erred in concluding that a destruction of documents was harmless; and 2) whether the district court abused its discretion in admitting into evidence a prior art reference not explicitly noticed under 35 U.S.C. § 282.

* * * * *

Destruction of Documents During Discovery

The trial court correctly determined that Eaton did not carry its burden on the trade secret or confidential counts, because it did not prove that the property allegedly misappropriated was protectable either as a trade secret or as confidential. However, Eaton argues on appeal that AVC's destruction of documents raises an inference of guilt not overcome in this case by AVC.

The destruction of one or more documents was first brought to light by AVC's own counsel. In a September 16, 1981, letter to Eaton's counsel, AVC's counsel stated after some introductory remarks:

> As you know, the original of the January 23, 1980 quotations to Design & Manufacturing Corporation by Circle Plastics

Products, Inc. [(a potential manufacturer of the AVC valves)] were produced by Defendant Appliance Valves Corporation at the deposition of Thomas Krzewina on July 30, 1981, and were identified as Exhibit 13, pages 20 and 21. Copies of these documents in the Circle Plastics Products, Inc. file were improperly destroyed at the request of David Miller. Exhibit 98, which was produced at the time of the deposition of Dale Minor . . . was a created document which Circle Plastics Products, Inc. placed in its files. The destruction and creation was done without knowledge of counsel for Defendants.

The district court noted the incident in its opinion, having also been informed by AVC's counsel on September 16, 1981, and did not consider the document destruction dispositive on the issue of liability.

The law with respect to inferences to be drawn from a party's act of spoliation was enunciated in *S.C. Johnson & Son, Inc. v. Louisville & Nashville Railroad Co.,* 695 F.2d 253, 258–59 (7th Cir.1982). *See A.C. Becken Co. v. Gemex Corp.,* 314 F.2d 839, 841 (7th Cir.), *cert denied,* 375 U.S. 816, 84 S.Ct. 68, 11 L.Ed.2d 51 (1963). Eaton Points out that the test is whether the court could draw "from the fact that a party has destroyed evidence that the party did so in bad faith." 695 F.2d at 258. If a court finds that both conditions precedent, evidence destruction and bad faith, are met, it may then infer that the evidence would be unfavorable to the destroying party if introduced in court. However, Eaton fails to recognize that this test can not apply in the present case, where the evidence destroyed has been produced.

Eaton argues vigorously that intentional destruction of evidence mandates reversal, but we are satisfied that the trial court reasonably determined that the effect of the action was negligible, because the originals of the documents were, in fact, earlier produced by AVC during discovery. Eaton has not shown that the documents would have been critical or controlling on the issue of liability. We in no sense would condone the destruction of evidence, but we discern no error in the district court's conclusion that "Eaton has

prescribed no additional evidence of appreciable significance to support its contention as to trade secrets and confidential information." At 634 F.Supp. 986. We agree that the document destruction was in this case harmless.

* * * * *

EDISON ELECTRIC LIGHT CO. et al. v. TIPLESS LAMP CO.

130 N.Y.S. 1089

Supreme Court, Special Term
May, 1911

This action was brought to recover royalties alleged to be due from the defendant to the plaintiffs upon the lamps made and sold by the defendant under a license agreement. The amount of royalties being predicated upon the manufacture and sale by the defendant, the books of the defendant contained the evidence necessary to prove plaintiffs' cause of action. An order was granted for the examination before trial of the defendant by Herman J. Jaeger, its then president, and by Edward L. Crans, its then secretary, before a referee on the 27th day of June, 1910, and said defendant was further ordered to produce before said referee such of its books and papers covering the period specified in the complaint as contained entries showing the number of incandescent lamps of all classes sold and invoiced by it during said period or any part thereof, such production being for the purpose of aiding the memory and refreshing the recollection of said Jaeger and Crans, and not for any purpose except the use of said witnesses. This order was personally served upon the defendant company and Herman J. Jaeger. Mr. Jaeger appeared before the referee and submitted to an oral examination. When, however, questions were asked tending to show the sales made during the period covered by the complaint, he answered, "I do not remember," and stated he had not produced the books and that they might have been destroyed. He made no effort to find them. The defendant did not produce the books by any one else. It transpired that there had been a new board of directors elected, and that Jaeger was, at the time of the examination, the treasurer of the defendant and had access to the books, and that he had delivered the order for their production to the president of the company.

A motion was made for the punishment of the defendant and Jaeger for their contempt of court. The facts not being sufficiently before the court, a referee was ordered to take proof of the facts with respect to the failure of the defendant to produce such books and papers as ordered by the court, and as to their alleged destruction, and report to the court. The referee has found that the defendant and Herman J. Jaeger, its treasurer, failed and neglected to produce said books and papers as required by the said order; that the said books and papers required to be produced by said order were in the custody and control of the defendant and Herman J. Jaeger, its treasurer, shortly prior to the issuance and service of said order; that the defendant and its treasurer, Herman J. Jaeger, have not shown by competent common–law proof that the said books and papers have been destroyed, or that they are not under the control of the defendant, and were not in its possession or under its control at the time of the service of said order; that the failure of the defendant and Herman J. Jaeger to comply with said order did defeat, impede, impair, and prejudice the rights of the plaintiffs. An examination of the record before the referee shows that these findings are entirely justified by the evidence and that the failure of the defendant and its treasurer, Jaeger, to produce the books and papers in compliance with the order for examination did defeat, impede, impair, and prejudice the rights of the plaintiffs and resulted in substantial miscarriage of justice, and that the defendant and Jaeger are in contempt of court.

The matter now comes on for a hearing upon the referee's report and upon the original motion. The failure of the defendant and its treasurer, Jaeger, to produce these books and papers under the court's order and the subsequent failure to offer any satisfactory explanation for their nonproduction constitutes a contempt (*Holly Mfg. Co. v. Venner*, 74 Hun, 458, 26 N.Y.Supp. 581), the plaintiff having shown, beyond a reasonable doubt, that the defendant's failure to do so was a willful refusal to do as the court directed. Matter of Wegman's Sons, 40 App. Div. 632, 57 N.Y.Supp. 987.

The difficulty lies in fixing the appropriate penalty. § 874 of the Code of Civil Procedure provides:

> "If the party or person so served fails to obey the law, his attendance may be compelled, and he may be punished in like manner, and the proceedings thereon are the same, as if he failed to obey a subpoena, issued from the court, in which the action is pending."

§ 853 reads so far as material to the question under consideration:

> "A person so subpoenaed, * * * or a person who fails, without reasonable excuse, to obey an order, duly served upon him, made by the court, or a judge, in an action, before or after final judgment therein, requiring him to attend, and be examined, or so to attend, and bring with him a book or a paper, is liable, in addition to punishment for contempt, for the damages sustained by the party aggrieved in consequence of the failure, and fifty dollars in addition thereto. Those sums may be recovered in one action, or in separate actions. If he is a party to the action in which he was subpoenaed, the court may, as an additional punishment, strike out his pleading."

The imposition of a fine and the bringing of an action for the recovery of the damages sustained would be inadequate relief for the wrong done. The defendant has deprived the plaintiffs of the means of establishing their full damage by the destruction or concealment of the books which contain the entries upon which they are compelled to rely to prove the cause of action. The damages provable would be the expenses of the referee and the amount paid for counsel for services rendered necessary by the failure to produce the books. Plaintiffs would still be unable to prove their case; and defendant would thus be able, by the payment of a comparatively small sum, to escape its liability on plaintiffs' cause of action. That a party may not thus be allowed to defeat or impair the remedy to which the adverse party is entitled, the proper and adequate relief would be to strike out his answer and permit the plaintiff to obtain judgment for the amount demanded in the complaint as upon a default. The power of this court to so deal with a party in contempt has frequently been recognized and exercised in this state until questioned by the United States Supreme Court in *Hovey v. Elliott*, 167 U.S. 409, 17 Sup. Ct. 841, 42 L.Ed.215, which disapproved of *Walker v. Walker*, 82 N.Y. 260, the court saying:

"A more fundamental question yet remains to be determined; that is, whether a court possessing plenary power to punish for contempt, unlimited by statute, has the right to summon a defendant to answer, and then, after obtaining jurisdiction by summons, refuse to allow the party summoned to answer, or strike his answer from the files, suppress the testimony in his favor, and condemn him without consideration thereof, and without a hearing, on the theory that he has been guilty of contempt of court. The mere statement of this proposition would seem in reason and conscience to render imperative a negative answer. The fundamental conception of a court of justice is condemnation only after hearing. To say that courts have inherent power to deny all right to defend an action and to render decrees without any hearing whatever is, in the very nature of things, to convert the court exercising such an authority into an instrument of wrong and oppression, and hence to strip it of that attribute of justice upon which the exercise of judicial power necessarily depends." Page 414 of 167 U.S., page 843 of 17 Sup. Ct. (42 L.Ed. 215).

Since this decision the Appellate Division has in two cases felt itself compelled to follow it, as the final expression of the highest court upon a federal question (*Sibley v. Sibley*, 76 App. Div. 132, 78 N.Y.Supp. 743; *Harney v. Harney*, 110 App. Div. 20, 96 N.Y.Supp. 905), while the Court of Appeals does not seem to have so considered it

(*Devlin v. Hinman*, 161 N.Y. 115, 55 N.E. 386). We, however, are relieved from all embarrassment by the decision of the United States Supreme Court in *Hammond Packing Co. v. Arkansas*, 212 U.S. 322, 29 Sup. Ct. 370, 53 L.Ed. 530, in which an order striking out the answer of a corporation for a refusal to produce books and papers on an examination before trial and judgment entered thereon by default pursuant to a state statute were before the court for consideration and affirmed. The court thus distinguishes its former decision:

"*Hovey v. Elliott* involved a denial of all right to defend as a mere punishment. This case presents a failure by the defendant to produce what we must assume was material evidence in its possession, and a resulting striking out of the answer and a default. The proceeding here taken may, therefore, find its sanction in the undoubted right of the lawmaking power to create a presumption of fact as to the bad faith and untruth of an answer begotten from the suppression or failure to produce the proof ordered, when such proof concerns the rightful decision of the cause. In a sense, of course, the striking out of the answer and default was a punishment; but it was only remotely so, as the generating source of the power was to create a presumption from failure to produce. The difference between mere punishment, as illustrated in *Hovey v. Elliott*, and the power exerted in this, is as follows: In the former, due process of law was denied by the refusal to hear; in this, the preservation of due process was secured by the presumption that the refusal to produce evidence material to the administration of due process was but an admission of the want of merit in the asserted defense."

Whether this distinction of its former ruling is sound, it is not necessary to consider. As the last expression of its decision upon the power of the state court to deal with a particular offense involved in this application, and being in harmony with our decisions, it may safely be followed. In this case we do not have to assume, as it affirmatively appears, that the evidence which the defendant failed to produce was most material to the decision of the cause.

Herman H. Jaeger will be adjudged guilty of contempt of court and fined an amount equal to the expenses of the two referees, the amount to be determined on the settlement of the order. The defendant will be adjudged guilty of contempt of court and fined $250; and, in addition thereto, because of its failure to produce, when ordered so to do, the books and papers containing material evidence for the plaintiffs, the answer of the defendant will be stricken out, and the plaintiffs may proceed as upon a default in pleading with ten dollars costs of this motion. Settle order on notice.

Ordered accordingly.

EQUAL EMPLOYMENT OPPORTUNITY COMMISSION, Petitioner, v. CW TRANSPORT, INC., Respondent

658 F.Supp. 1278

United States District Court, W.D. Wisconsin
April 10, 1987

* * * * *

1. Background

This lawsuit was filed by the EEOC on September 15, 1986, to enforce a consent decree entered into by CW Transport and other trucking companies on March 20, 1974. On that date, the United States Attorney General commenced an action in the United States District Court for the District of Columbia against over 350 of the nation's largest trucking companies, the International Brotherhood of Teamsters, the International Association of Machinists and Aerospace Workers, and the trucking industry's national bargaining representative, Trucking Employers, Inc. (now Trucking Management, Inc.). Each of the trucking companies sued was a party to the National Master Freight Agreement, each employed at least 100 persons, and each had annual gross revenues of at least one million dollars. Together the defen-

dant companies embraced virtually the entire trucking industry. The trucking companies were sued as a defendant class.

The complaint in that case alleged that the companies' seniority system violated Title VII and Executive Order 11246; that the unions perpetuated the effect of the companies' discriminatory practices by entering into the National Master Freight Agreement; and that "the defendants had engaged in systematic discrimination against black and Spanish–surnamed employees and applicants, the most important relating to the separation of employees into two classes, 'over–the–road drivers' and 'city drivers.'"

A consent decree was negotiated between the United States Department of Justice and seven named company defendants, who denied that they were class representatives. The decree was filed on March 20, 1974 in the United States District Court for the District of Columbia. On May 22, 1974, the EEOC was substituted as a party plaintiff for the United States with regard to the Title VII aspects of the case.

2. The Consent Decree

The consent decree included eleven sections: a general resolution against employment discrimination; hiring goals and attainment levels; job standards and testing; recruitment; training; transfer; a monetary compensation procedure providing for backpay; records and reports; adjustment of deficiencies; compliance officials; and the retention of jurisdiction by the court. In one of the series of cases centering on the trucking companies, known collectively as the "TMI cases," the court struck the backpay and transfer provisions from the consent decree. *United States v. Trucking Management, Inc.*, 20 Fair Empl. Prac.Cas. (BNA) 342, 351 (D.D.C.1977), *aff'd*, 662 F.2d 36 (D.C.Cir.1981).

* * * * *

Section VIII of the decree concerns record–keeping and reporting requirements. In relevant part, the record–keeping requirements provide:

Each Defendant Employer shall maintain

records concerning all applications, hires by job classification, transfers under the terms of this Decree, disqualifications, and dismissals during the life of this Decree. The Defendant Employer shall also record on the application of each Black and Spanish–surnamed applicant for employment who was found not to be qualified or otherwise was not hired, the reason therefor. The Defendant Employer shall maintain all records on which each report required below is based.

The reporting requirements of Section VIII require the employers to submit semi–annual reports detailing the racial composition of the existing work force, applicants, and hires and fires for the previous reporting period.

* * * * *

4. Employee Turnover and Record Loss at CWT

The Chicago facility, CWT's largest terminal, has employed more than 500 workers at various times. Since 1974, the Chicago terminal has experienced considerable turnover in supervisory personnel due to resignations, deaths, terminations, retirements, and work force fluctuations. Company–wide, at least 96 supervisors have left CWT since 1974 due to resignation, termination, retirement or death. Each of these supervisors had hiring and firing authority for the positions under their supervision. Neither CWT's regional manager in charge of the Chicago terminal nor its vice president of personnel knows where most of these persons presently are located. The burden and expense of locating these persons would be great.

Since 1974, CWT has acquired three companies: Overland Transportation in 1975, Trans Illinois Express in 1979, and Blue Arrow/Arledge in 1983. Under the collective bargaining agreements, CWT was required to employ workers from these companies. Senior employees from these companies could bump junior employees of CWT, resulting in layoffs of CWT employees. CWT is obliged to rehire laid off workers before hiring new employees. Because of the acquisitions of other companies,

various terminals were acquired and closed. In addition, CWT has closed at least 18 terminals due to economic or other circumstances since the decree was signed.

The Chicago facility stored large volumes of old employment records in the basement. Sometime during the fall of 1979 or the spring of 1980, the Chicago terminal experienced severe flooding in its basement. In 1985, the basement flooded again as a result of construction on an adjoining street. In both floods, records were destroyed, although CWT cannot catalog precisely what records were lost. Since 1974, the Chicago terminal's personnel office has moved twice, once in 1979 and again in 1982. In each move, employment records were destroyed or stored, as well as lost or misplaced.

Records have been lost or destroyed by natural disasters at other facilities as well. In 1981, a tornado destroyed the storage area at the West Frankfurt, Illinois terminal. In 1984, a pipe froze and broke at the Richmond terminal, damaging records in a storage room. The damaged records were discarded, and exactly what was lost is not known. Also in 1984, CWT's office in Wisconsin Rapids moved from one location to another; several boxes of employment records were lost or misplaced in this move. In 1985, a terminal manager who left the Atlanta facility removed records when he left.

Bill Close, the regional manager in charge of the Chicago terminal, was unaware that the EEOC required employers who signed the consent decree to keep all applications. Close first learned of the EEOC's position during an on–site inspection at the Chicago facility in 1985. Prior to the on–site inspection in 1985, it was CWT's practice to purge job applications approximately every six months.

R.D. Newberry is vice–president of safety and personnel for CWT in Wisconsin Rapids, Wisconsin; he has held that position since 1971. Newberry is also CWT's corporate compliance officer under the consent decree. In that capacity, he is responsible for furnishing the government with the reports required by the decree. It has never been Newberry's understanding that

CWT was required to retain all applications for employment during the life of the decree. It is unlikely that the company retains employment applications for rejected applicants that pre–date the last quarter of 1984.

* * * * *

I. Laches

CWT's primary argument on its motion for summary judgment is that this enforcement petition is barred by laches. CWT contends that twelve and one half years elapsed between the signing of the consent decree and the filing of the enforcement petition, that this delay is unreasonable, and that the delay caused CWT to suffer all the classic elements of prejudice: unavailable witnesses, faded memories, and lost records. In opposition, the EEOC argues that the defense of laches is not applicable to a petition to enforce on–going violations under a consent decree. Alternatively, the EEOC contends that laches should not bar its entire claim, but only limit the time period for which relief can be obtained.

The consent decree entered into by CWT does not contain an express expiration date or any express limitation on the time in which the government may seek to enforce the decree. Nonetheless, in the absence of an expiration date or statute of limitations, the EEOC may be barred by laches from filing a petition "if it has delayed inexcusably and the defendant was materially prejudiced by its delay." *Equal Employment Opportunity Commission v. Massey–Ferguson, Inc.*, 622 F.2d 271, 275 (7th Cir.1980). The affirmative defense of laches "is appropriate only if the Commission has 'unduly,' 'inexcusably,' 'unreasonably' or 'inordinately' delayed in asserting a claim and that delay has 'substantially,' 'materially' or 'seriously' prejudiced the defendant's ability to conduct its defense." *Id.*

* * * * *

4. Loss of Records

CWT argues that it is materially prejudiced by the loss of records it would need to defend this enforcement action. CWT's loss of records has resulted from two distinct series of events. The first of these is CWT's systematic destruction of employment applications in accordance with its internal business records retention/destruction schedule. The second consists of a number of natural disasters and the normal loss of records in the course of business.

CWT contends that it is severely prejudiced in its defense because it did not retain employment applications for more than six months. Prior to the onsite inspection of the Chicago terminal in July of 1985, the company routinely destroyed job applications after six months, and both the Chicago terminal manager and the vice president of personnel attest that they did not know that job applications had to be retained indefinitely. Accordingly, CWT argues, it does not have the precise, detailed applicant data necessary to defend itself. The EEOC counters that the plain language of the consent decree requires the company to keep all job applications for the life of the decree. Consequently, the EEOC claims, any prejudice arising from the destruction of the job applications is the result of CWT's non–compliance with the decree and not the result of any delay in bringing an enforcement action.

Generally, consent decrees are viewed as contracts. *Firefighters Local 93 v. City of Cleveland*, — U.S. — , 106 S.Ct. 3063, 92 L.Ed.2d 405 (1986); *Kasper v. Hayes*, 814 F.2d 332, 338 (7th Cir.1987). In particular, a consent decree "is to be construed for enforcement purposes essentially like a contract; its meaning is to be sought within its 'four corners,' although aids to construction such as circumstances surrounding the formation of the order may appropriately be used to resolve ambiguities. A consent decree may be specifically enforced as written." *Jones v. Milwaukee County*, 574 F.Supp. at 503, relying on *United States v. ITT Continental Baking Co.*, 420 U.S. 223, 233–38, 95 S.Ct. 926, 932–35, 43 L.Ed.2d 148 (1975). *See also Kasper*, at 338 ("The source of the obligations in the decree is the parties' will . . . ."). The resolution of the parties' dispute that CWT was required to keep all job applications is governed by the consent decree.

The relevant portion of Section VIII of that decree provides that:

Each Defendant Employer shall maintain records concerning all applications, hires by job classification, transfers under the terms of this Decree, disqualifications, and dismissals during the life of this Decree. The Defendant Employer shall also record on the application of each Black and Spanish–surnamed applicant for employment who was found not to be qualified or otherwise was not hired, the reason therefor. The Defendant Employer shall maintain all records on which each report required below is based.

CWT contends that this language in the decree requires it to keep only "records concerning all applications," and note the actual applications themselves. I do not find this argument persuasive.

First, the consent decree requires CWT to record "on the application" of each minority applicant who was not hired the reason for the failure to hire. If CWT were required to record pertinent information on the fact of the applications, but then was permitted to discard the applications after six months, this requirement of the decree would be meaningless. If I accept CWT's construction of the decree, the decree requires the company to engage in superfluous activity with regard to each rejected job application, only to discard the information shortly thereafter. It is nonsensical to suppose that the consent decree was intended to require such meaningless activity on the part of CWT.

Second, the consent decree expressly requires CWT to "maintain all records on which each report required below is based." The reports required by the consent decree include information on the number of hires during and the number of minority applications pending at the end of each reporting period. It is difficult to understand CWT's argument that a report on the numbers of minority applications is not "based" on the applications received from members of minority groups, but only on the subsequent compilation of data from those applications.

CWT argues also that it simply is not practicable for it to have retained all job applications over the life of the consent decree. Whatever the merits of this contention might be, CWT bound itself to do exactly that when it entered in to the decree as written. If CWT were unable to comply with the terms of the decree, it could have sought a modification from the EEOC. As the consent decree now stands, however, it requires CWT to have retained all job applications since the decree was signed.

Accordingly, I cannot find that any prejudice attaches to CWT as a result of the loss of job applications through its normal practice of retaining and destroying records. Although a company's adherence to its routine schedule "does not impute any bad faith or consciousness of guilt," *Jeffries*, 770 F.2d at 681, here there were the supervening requirements of the consent decree. "A party cannot assert the defense of laches merely because it has failed to preserve evidence despite knowledge" — actual or imputed — that it was required to do so. *Bernard*, 596 F.2d at 1257. I conclude that the consent decree as written requires CWT to retain all job applications for the life of the decree, and that no material prejudice to CWT results from its own failure to observe that requirement.

In addition to the destruction of the job application records, CWT contends also that it has been prejudiced by the loss of records from other causes. One of these causes was natural disasters and similar circumstances. In 1979 and 1980, severe flooding at the Chicago terminal destroyed records stored in the basement. In 1985, another flood at Chicago caused by outside construction again destroyed records stored in the basement. A 1981 tornado destroyed the storage area of the Frankfurt, Illinois terminal. And in 1984 at the Richmond terminal, records were damaged when a pipe in a storage room froze and broke.

Other causes of record loss were mislaying of records and employee pilfering. The Chicago terminal personnel office moved in 1979 and again in 1982; in each move, employment records were lost or misplaced. In 1984, the main office in Wisconsin Rapids moved, and several boxes of employment records were lost or misplaced. A terminal manager who left the Atlanta facility in 1985 removed records when he left. In all these instances, CWT maintains that it cannot catalog what records were destroyed, lost, or misplaced.

Natural disasters and the loss of records in the ordinary course of business present situations different from the destruction of records that CWT was on notice that it should retain. However, on the record now before the court, I cannot say that CWT has suffered material prejudice from the natural disasters and other occurrences. CWT argues that because it cannot catalog precisely what records have been lost or destroyed, it has been substantially prejudiced in general because of record loss. Accepting this argument would require a presumption that the loss of any records creates prejudice with regard to the entire case. I am not persuaded that such a presumption is reasonable.

Laches is an affirmative defense, on which the defendant bears the burden of proof. It is CWT's burden to establish that the loss of records from natural disasters and the normal course of business loss will prejudice its defense of this lawsuit. The burden cannot be met merely by showing that some unspecified records have been destroyed or misplaced during some occurrences at some facilities. Despite its claim that it cannot catalog precisely what records are missing, the company should know generally what records it maintained and, to some level of specificity, what records remain after the various natural disasters and other events. It does not seem unreasonable to require CWT to establish with more specificity what records are missing and why the loss of these records will materially prejudice its defense of this enforcement action.

* * * * *

EQUAL EMPLOYMENT OPPORTUNITY COMMISSION v. JACKSONVILLE SHIPYARDS, INC.

690 F.Supp. 995

United States District Court, M.D. Florida, Jacksonville Division
June 23, 1988

Plaintiff Equal Employment Opportunity Commission ("EEOC") filed its Motion for Partial Summary Judgment on November 12, 1987. The motion seeks relief on two issues raised by defendant's affirmative defenses and one issue raised by the destruction of records relevant to this lawsuit. Defendant's memorandum in opposition to the motion, filed herein on November 27, 1987, concedes the two affirmative defense issues and proposes to withdraw those defenses. The Court therefore will enter partial summary judgment in favor of EEOC on those issues, establishing that the charges filed by charging parties Samuel Green ("Green") and James Crittenden ("Crittenden") were timely filed and that EEOC fulfilled its obligation to attempt conciliation of the charges prior to filing suit.

The parties vehemently dispute the appropriate resolution of the third issue, which concerns the consequences to be attached to defendant's destruction of certain records that defendant was required to maintain pursuant to 29 C.F.R. § 1602.14(a). EEOC characterizes the destruction of records as "willful" and seeks, as a sanction against defendant, summary judgment on the issue of liability for the period covered by the destroyed records. In response, defendant maintains that EEOC has no basis in fact to claim that the destruction of records was willful, that the destruction of records was in fact inadvertent, that the information contained in the destroyed records is available from other sources, and that EEOC's requested sanction has no basis in law. Defendant seeks sanctions against EEOC over the motion for summary judgment. The Court will resolve that motion separately, but the memoranda filed on that matter also informs the present determination on the motion for partial summary judgment.

The basic facts are not in dispute. On October 24, 1970, EEOC sent a Notice of Charge to defendant, with a copy of the charge, in the matter of charging party Crittenden. This Notice of Charge contained a prominent admonition regarding 29 C.F.R. § 1602.14, stating that the regulation "requires the preservation of all personnel records relevant to this charge until a final disposition of this charge is made . . . " This process was repeated on October 20, 1980, in the matter of charging party Green. According to the affidavit of John Stewart ("Stewart"), defendant's Manager of Industrial Relations, the records at issue, defendant's so-called Change of Status Sheets, were destroyed approximately four or five years following the filing of charges. Stewart also avers that the records were not destroyed in contemplation of the prospect of this lawsuit; rather, he believes that the destruction was inadvertent, in the course of making room for other records.

Defendant argues that loss of the Change of Status Sheets does not prejudice EEOC because the information can be reconstructed from other records. The Court's review of the relevant documents reveals that the Change of Status Sheets uniquely format certain information in a fashion that facilitates comparative analysis of trends in promotions. While other records contain the same factual material, reconstruction of the format would impose a burden on EEOC. Moreover, EEOC alleges — and defendant does not dispute — that significant gaps are present in the other records. The Court finds that EEOC is prejudiced by the destruction of the records. The question squarely presented is whether this prejudice warrants the ultimate sanction of directing summary judgment on the liability issue for the relevant time period.

* * * * *

Application of Rule 37 principles however, works in opposition to EEOC's motion for partial summary judgment. EEOC effectively seeks a limited default sanction to redress the loss of the Change of Status Sheets. The Court must decline to impose

this extreme sanction. The default sanction under Rule 37 is a last resort, to be ordered only if noncompliance is due to willful or bad faith disregard of court orders which cannot reasonably be expected to be remedied by lesser but equally effective sanctions. *Adolph Coors Co. v. Movement Against Racism & the Klan*, 777 F.2d 1538, 1542–43 (11th Cir. 1985); *Telectron, Inc.*, 116 F.R.D. at 134–37. Although the Court believes that failure to insure the preservation of records after receiving official notice is "willful" behavior, *cf. Wm. T. Thompson Co.*, 593 F.Supp. at 1455, the law of the Circuit demands a greater record of intransigence to justify the default sanction. *See Ford v. Fogarty Van Lines, Inc.*, 780 F.2d 1582, 1583 (11th Cir.1986) (clear record of delay or contumacious conduct by party necessary to justify dismissal or default sanction); *see also Cox v. American Case Iron Pipe Co.*, 784 F.2d 1546, 1566 (11th Cir.) (court must make finding of bad faith resistance to discovery orders and indicate on record that less severe sanction than dismissal were considered and rejected), *cert. denied*, — U.S. — , 107 S.Ct. 274, 93 L.Ed.2d 250 (1986). Additionally, the Court perceives that lesser sanctions may effectively remedy the prejudice suffered by EEOC. In particular, if defendant is correct in asserting that the lost records can be reconstructed, then the appropriate remedy is to require that the defendant bear the cost and burden of accurately reconstructing the records. *Cf. United States v. American Telephone & Telegraph Co.*, 86 F.R.D. 603, 657 (D.D.C.1980). Since some evidence is available on the relevant issue, the Court also could limit defendant's production of evidence in opposition to EEOC's presentation, *see EEOC v. Troy State University*, 693 F.2d 1353, 1358 (11th Cir.1982), *cert. denied*, 463 U.S. 1207, 103 S.Ct. 3538, 77 L.Ed.2d 1388 (1983), and equitably adjust the level of proof necessary to demonstrate discrimination, *Hicks v. Gates Rubber Co., 833 F.2d 1406, 1419 (10th Cir. 1987) (granting presumption to plaintiff that records destroyed in violation of 29 C.F.R. § 1602.14 would support her case).*

The Court need not decide precisely what sanction is appropriate at this time. If defendant does not come forward with an accurate re-construction of the destroyed records, then plaintiff may seek an appropriate sanction prior to trial. Accordingly, the Court will deny EEOC's motion for partial summary judgment without prejudice to a subsequent motion for a lesser sanction at a time nearer to the trial date.

* * * * *

EQUAL OPPORTUNITY COMMISSION v. M.D. PNEUMATICS, INC.

31 Emp. Prac. Dec. (CCH) 33, 459

United States District Court, Western District of Missouri, Southern Division
March 10, 1983

* * * * *

Plaintiff has moved to amend its complaint to add an allegation that defendant violated 28 C.F.R. § 1602.14, the EEOC's recordkeeping requirements. Evidence at trial established that defendant periodically purged from its files any employment applications over six months old. In February, 1978, the EEOC served a notice of charge upon defendant. The charge alleged that defendant intentionally discriminated against one individual, Ms. Betty Rader. The defendant retained Ms. Rader's employment application, but in April of 1978, in keeping with its regular practice, destroyed all other applications then on file. Defendant received no notice of the plaintiff's class action until plaintiff filed its complaint in July, 1979. Based upon these facts, the Court finds that defendant did not violate 29 C.F.R. § 1602.14. The defendant maintained the records relevant to Ms. Rader's individual claim. The routine destruction of other employment applications occurred prior to the filing of the class action. Therefore, defendant complied with relevant EEOC regulations. In making this finding, the Court adopts the reasoning set forth in *EEOC v. Dresser Industries, Inc.*, 668 F.2d 1199, 1203–1204 (11th Cir. 1982). Faced with virtually the identical factual setting now before this Court, the Eleventh Circuit in Dresser Stated

the following: The EEOC argues that [the employer] should have known of the Commission's ability to bring a class action suit, and suggests that all "records relevant to the charge" is synonymous with all employment records. We do not believe the regulation's language should be given such an expansive interpretation.

By the time the class action was filed, [the employer] had retained all records relating to Smalley's claim, but had destroyed other employment records pursuant to its policy to keep records for a five year period. The District Court determined that [the employers] had retained those records "relevant" to the Smalley charge, the only one of which [the employer] had notification, and had therefore satisfied the requirements of § 1602.14(a). We agree. Once defendant satisfy the EEOC's record retention requirement in Title VII enforcement actions, they should not be punished for failing to exceed standards mandated by the very Commission that promulgated them.

* * * * *

George EVANGELOS v. H.H. DACHIEL

553 So.2d 245

District Court of Appeal of Florida, Third District
November 21, 1989

George Evangelos, who was defendant below, appeals from a final judgment awarding damages to plaintiff following the striking of Evangelos' pleadings as a sanction for failure to comply with discovery orders. We reverse.

H.H. Dachiel brought suit against Evangelos, and two defunct corporation, Bio–Med Corp. and Bio–Nu Laboratories, Inc., alleging in essence that he had been bilked of his investment in the corporations. Dachiel had been secretary of the two corporations and Evangelos was president. Evangelos appeared pro se to defend against the action and filed a pro se counterclaim. The defunct corporations in effect elected not to defend and have not appealed the judgment entered against them.

Plaintiff Dachiel propounded a request for production of documents which asked for production of every book and record of the two corporations from 1980 onward. The request also asked for production of documents supporting the defendants' affirmative defenses and the documents supporting the allegations in the counterclaim. In response Evangelos invited Dachiel's counsel to Evangelos' offices where counsel was shown thirty boxes of documents which were in storage there.

Dachiel filed a motion to compel production of documents, in which he claimed that Evangelos had failed to produce the requested documents; that the documents were not properly organized; and that the working conditions in the storage room were unsuitable. The trial court granted the motion and ordered the defendants to "produce categorically" all records responsive to the request for production of documents, and to make production at the offices of plaintiff's counsel. This was error.

Rule 1.350(b), Florida Rules of Civil Procedure, provides in part, "When producing documents, the producing party shall either produce them as they are kept in the usual course of business or shall identify them to correspond with the categories in the request." In the present case the two corporations were defunct and the entirety of their records were kept in storage boxes. That is the way they were then kept in the usual course of business within the meaning of the Rule. The plaintiff had requested production of literally every scrap of paper pertaining to the two corporations for the period 1980–1988. Having requested a large volume of records, the plaintiff should not have been surprised when a large volume was produced. Since the records were produced as they were then kept, it was error to order the defendant to reorganize the documents so as to correspond to the categories employed by the plaintiff in his request.

It was also error for the trial court to order Evangelos to transport the thirty boxes of documents at his expense to the office of plaintiff's counsel. Evangelos had offered to allow plaintiff's counsel to set up a work station in the storage room where the boxes were kept and suggested that plaintiff's counsel bring a copying machine if he so desired. The plaintiff was entitled to ask the trial court to order production at a location with better working conditions, and the trial court had the discretion to grant the motion, but the expenses of transporting the records should have been borne by the requesting party — the plaintiff — not the party producing the records. *See Schering Corp. v. Thornton*, 280 So.2d 493, 494 (Fla. 4th DCA 1973); *Cooper v. Fulton*, 117 So.2d 33, 36 (Fla. 3d DCA 1960).

Subsequent to the entry of the discovery order, Evangelos did make efforts to contact plaintiff's counsel to try to reduce the amount of documents to be produced, and also requested consideration by the trial court on at least one occasion. These efforts were unavailing. A further compliance deadline was set for December 22, 1988. The day before the deadline, Evangelos obtained counsel who appeared and requested an extension of the court–ordered deadline. While courtesy would have suggested agreement to *some* extension of time for new counsel, plaintiff instead filed a motion to strike the defendant's pleadings, which was granted. A default was entered against Evangelos and his counterclaim was dismissed with prejudice. A bench trial was held on damages and judgment entered against Evangelos in the amount of $432,806.48. In the meantime interim sanctions of $500 had also been entered against Evangelos for failure to comply with earlier document production orders.

The sanctions entered by the trial court were excessive. Evangelos had, in the first instance, complied with the request for production of documents. Had plaintiff not insisted on relief to which he was in no way entitled — reorganization of the documents by defendant and transportation of the records to plaintiff's office at defendant's expense — the inspection would have been promptly accomplished. Although the defendant did not comply to the letter with the interim discovery orders, the record does reflect that he attempted to work with both the plaintiff and the court in an effort to reduce the burden to manageable proportions. Defendant's non–compliance with the interim discovery orders simply does not rise to that level of willfulness which would justify the severe sanctions of striking his pleadings, particularly in view of the fact that he had already produced the documents at the outset, that the interim discovery orders were erroneous, and that the plaintiff failed to extend the elementary courtesy of a short extension of time for counsel who had newly entered the case. *See Velazquez v. Gaitan*, 499 So.2d 66, 67 (Fla. 3d DCA 1986); *Summit Chase Condominiums Ass'n, Inc. v. Protean Investors, Inc.*, 421 So.2d 562, 564–65 (Fla. 3d DCA 1982) (majority and concurring opinions); *Beaver Crane Service, Inc. v. National Surety Corp.*, 373 So.2d 88, 89 (Fla. DCA 1979); *see also Mercer v. Raine*, 443 So.2d 944, 946 (Fla. 1983) ("the striking of pleadings or entering a default for noncompliance with an order compelling discovery is the most severe of all sanctions which should be employed only in extreme circumstances.")

We therefore reverse the final judgment against Evangelos, vacate the default and reinstate Evangelos' answer, affirmative defenses, and counterclaim. As Evangelos did fail, in part, to comply with the terms of the interim discovery orders (even though entered on an erroneous basis), the trial court's authority is more than amply vindicated by allowing the $500 monetary sanction to stand.

Reversed and remanded.

FLORIDA MORTGAGE FINANCING INC., a Florida Corporation v. Henry KASSNER, an individual

317 So.2d 112

District Court of Appeal of Florida, Third District
July 8, 1975

This is an appeal by the defendant below from an adverse summary final judgment in an action to recover a $5,000 deposit made pursuant to the terms of a loan commitment application.

The plaintiff, Henry Kassner, a developer of real estate projects, instituted this suit on November 21, 1973 against the defendant–appellant, a mortgage broker, averring that he (Kassner) had received a letter dated August 23, 1973 from the appellant advising him that the appellant could not comply with the terms of the commitment application.

Under the commitment application, Kassner was seeking a construction loan and permanent financing in the amount of $4,010,710.00. The application states that the appellant would have 45 working days in which to procure the loan. Together with its answer to the complaint, the appellant filed a counterclaim which basically alleged that Kassner was in breach of contract and prayed for damages of $40,107.10 (its one percent brokerage fee based on the principal amount of the loan sought), plus costs and attorney's fees.

Appellant has presented two points on appeal. First, it argues that there were genuine issues of material fact precluding entry of a summary judgment.

Secondly, appellant submits that the court committed error by imposing sanctions against it because of its inability to produce certain documents which the court previously had ordered the appellant to produce.

These documents were ordered to be produced because of the appellant's assertion that Kassner had not supplied all of the documents necessary for the appellant to successfully obtain a loan from institutional lenders.

In short, appellant was ordered to produce the documents which Kassner had supplied so that it might be determined which documents he had *not* supplied.

As it turned out, appellant did not produce the required documents because an institutional lender in New York allegedly had possession of them and was unable to locate the documents.

The sanctions which the court imposed were that the appellant could not produce the documents at a later date and use them for impeachment purposes. We hold that these sanctions were not too severe after the court had given the appellant a reasonable opportunity to produce the required documents; and no abuse of discretion has been shown. *See, Hurley v. Werly,* Fla. App.1967, 203 So.2d 530, 537; *City of Miami Beach v. Chadderton,* Fla.App.1975, 306 So.2d 558.

Further, it is our view that summary judgment was proper because appellant has not shown that there were genuine issues of material fact that it had performed in accordance with the terms of the commitment application and therefore was entitled to retain the $5,000 deposit.

Accordingly, the judgment appealed is affirmed.

Affirmed.

Marlon Louis FOWLER, Individually and on behalf of all others similarly situated, Plaintiffs–Appellants, v. BLUE BELL, INC., a corporation, et al., Defendants–Appellees.

596 F.2d. 1276

United States Court of Appeals, Fifth Circuit
June 15, 1979

Plaintiff Fowler applied for a job with defendant Blue Bell, Inc. in March and again in November, 1970. Defendant did not hire him. Fowler then filed a charge with the EEOC in December, 1970, alleging that Blue Bell had violated Title VII of the Civil Rights Act of 1964, 42 U.S.C. § 2000e *et seq.*, by refusing to hire him because of his race. The EEOC notified Blue Bell of the charge in July, 1971, and served its Field Director's Findings of Fact on the company in December, 1971. Blue Bell entered exceptions to these filings, but in June, 1972, the EEOC informed Blue Bell that the exceptions were "non–meritorious." At the invitation of the EEOC, *Blue Bell* agreed to participate in settlement discussions. Fowler, however, refused to participate. In July, 1972, the EEOC's Birmingham district office informed Blue Bell that Fowler "declined the Director's invitation to engage in settlement discussions. Accordingly, this office is forwarding the full investigation file to the Commission for determination as to reasonable cause. As soon as the determination is made, you will be notified." One year after it received this letter, having heard nothing else from the EEOC or Fowler, Blue Bell concluded "that the entire matter had been closed administratively by the EEOC" and destroyed all records relevant to Fowler's claim. Affidavit of Richard M. Warren, General Counsel to Blue Bell, Inc. The EEOC had not terminated its consideration, however, and issued a determination of reasonable cause in March, 1975. After further correspondence between the EEOC and Blue Bell, the EEOC decided not to file a civil action itself. It informed both Fowler and Blue Bell of this decision and sent Fowler a Notice of Right–to–Sue in January, 1976. Fowler filed this suit in March, 1976, within 90 days of receiving the EEOC Notice.

In *Bernard v. Gulf Oil, Inc.*, 596 F.2d 1249 (5 Cir. 1979), also decided today, we recognize that laches may apply to Title VII suits brought by private plaintiffs if the evidence indicates both that the plaintiff delayed inexcusably in bringing the suit and that this delay unduly prejudiced defendants. *Id.* at 1256. As in *Bernard*, we hold that the evidence before the court on this summary judgment does not allow a finding that either of these elements exist.

Blue Bell argues that this conclusion is improper. First, it asserts that after it presented affidavits in support of its summary judgment motion, Fowler had the duty of submitting contrary evidence in order to raise an issue of fact. Blue Bell argues that since its affidavits alleged delay and prejudice and Fowler failed to dispute these allegations, the summary judgment was proper. This argument is without merit. Fowler does not dispute that more than five years lapsed between the filing of his charge with the EEOC and the commencement of this suit. Nor does he disagree with Blue Bell's contention that it has lost personnel and destroyed records that would be helpful in deciding Fowler's claim. Fowler's argument is that these facts do not permit a finding of laches in this case. Therefore, his failure to submit controverting evidence to the trial court is irrelevant.

* * * * *

Blue Bell's contention that Fowler's delay seriously prejudiced its defense of the case is also without merit. Blue Bell asserts two sources of prejudice. First, it argues that the testimony of several past personnel and plant managers is essential to Blue Bell's defense of the case and that these managers are no longer employed by Blue Bell. The mere assertion that these persons are not presently with the company is insufficient to support a finding of prejudice. Blue Bell must also show that they are unavailable to testify. *Akers v. State Marine Lines, Inc.*, 344 F.2d 217, 221 (5 Cir. 1965). Blue Bell does allege that the personnel manager at the time Fowler filed his complaint is now unavailable. The primary reason Blue Bell alleges that this individual's personal testimony is necessary, however, is that he was the custodian of records relevant to Fowler's charge and Blue Bell has since destroyed those records. Blue Bell knew of Fowler's charge soon after it was filed. In July, 1972, the EEOC informed Blue Bell that it was considering Fowler's charge for a determination as to reasonable cause and told Blue Bell: "As soon as the determination is made, you will be notified." Despite this explicit statement, and without asking the EEOC about the status of the charge, Blue Bell concluded in 1973 that the EEOC was no longer pursuing Fowler's claim and destroyed all records relevant to the claim. Blue Bell's destruction of these records violated clear EEOC regulations. 31 Fed.Reg.

2833 (Feb. 17, 1966) (currently at 29 C.F.R. 1602.14 (1977)). Thus, any prejudice to Blue Bell was the result of its own negligence and disregard of administrative regulations rather than Fowler's delay. *Barnard* at 1256.

* * * * *

FRIENDS FOR ALL CHILDREN, INC., as legal guardian and next friend of the named 150 infant individuals, et al. v. LOCKHEED AIRCRAFT CORPORATION v. The UNITED STATES of America, Margali Jose Patricia MAUPOINT, etc. v. LOCKHEED AIRCRAFT CORPORATION v. The UNITED STATES of America

587 F.Supp. 180

United States District Court, District of Columbia
March 16, 1984

This litigation is before the Court on plaintiffs' motions for partial summary judgment and a preliminary injunction. The 70 or so plaintiffs are orphans who were aboard a Lockheed–built and Air Force–operated C–5A military transport plane when it crashed near Saigon, Vietnam, on April 5, 1975, and who were subsequently adopted by families in Europe and Canada. The first of these foreign infant cases, that of the French child Margaret Maupoint, is set for trial on April 3, 1984. Through their guardian *ad litem* and counsel, plaintiffs have now requested that the Court enter a partial summary judgment and preliminary injunction against the defendant that would require defendant to pay the large sum of $8,700,000.00 for guardian's fees, attorneys' fees, diagnostic examinations, medical treatment, and education services, pending the outcome of the 70–odd trials on the merits.

During an exhaustive hearing on these motions, plaintiff presented evidence and testimony to support their contention that at trials on the merit, juries should be permitted to draw inferences adverse to the defendant from the wholesale destruction of crash–related photographs, video tapes, and documents which occurred after this litigation commenced. Plaintiffs also argued that at a trial on the merits, defendant would be precluded by the collateral source rule from introducing evidence at trials that free or subsidized health care is available to these plaintiffs in the countries where they reside. These two issues of adverse inference and collateral source have been fully briefed in the *Maupoint* case and are ripe for decision.

* * * * *

Before a jury may be permitted to draw an inference adverse to the defendant, plaintiffs must establish, at a minimum, that relevant evidence existed, that it was within the ability of the defendant to produce it, and that it has not been produced due to the actions of the defendant. If the defendant in this litigation were the United States, plaintiffs would have succeeded in carrying this burden. The court finds from the testimony at the hearing and the entire record (s) that numerous photographs of the interior of the troop compartment were taken during the United States Air Force investigation of the crash; (b) that these photographs were the subject of discovery requests from the plaintiffs as early as 1975; (c) that Air Force regulations required Air Force personnel to preserve this kind of evidence, and make it accessible to persons allegedly injured in the crash without limiting privilege claim; (d) that many of these photographs along with voluminous other evidence were intentionally destroyed by the Air Force in 1977 or 1978; (e) that an attorney for the United States (who was present in December 1975 when Lockheed's counsel represented to the late Chief Judge William B. Jones that to his knowledge all documents had been preserved) learned of this destruction by May 1978 at the latest, appeared frequently before the Court thereafter, and nevertheless failed to inform the Court or the plaintiffs of this destruction until 1980; and (f) that, although copies of the destroyed photographs were later discovered and produced, other photographs, including some photographs of the interior of the troop compartment, still have not and can never be produced.

But however questionable its conduct, the United States is not the defendant in this litigation. Even if it was, the jury hearing the case against Lockheed would not be privileged to draw any adverse inference against that defendant because of the Air Force's misconduct. Plaintiffs have a more difficult burden in establishing the prerequisites of an adverse inference against Lockheed.

Plaintiffs have not adequately shown that autopsies of the infant or infants who died in the troop compartment were ever conducted, or that autopsy reports were prepared, or that those reports could ever have been produced by Lockheed.

Plaintiffs have adequately shown that photographs of the interior of the troop compartment existed that have not as yet been produced. In addition, they have shown that many, although not all, of such troop compartment photographs were taken by Lockheed employees who participated in the accident investigation. These photographs, as well as the photographs taken by Air Force participants in the accident investigation, were known to Lockheed through its close involvement in the accident investigation. Photographs taken by Lockheed employees were returned to the Air Force at the conclusion of the investigation. Lockheed and the United States cooperated throughout the investigation and have worked together through much of the defense of this litigation.

Plaintiffs have also convincingly demonstrated that, but for the action and inaction of Lockheed and its counsel, the missing photographs of the interior of the troop compartment would have been produced. Most significantly, on December 18, 1975, plaintiffs' counsel formally requested that Chief Judge Jones enter a protective order that would have preserved the photographs. In opposing the issuance of a protective order, Carroll Dubuc, counsel for Lockheed, represented to Chief Judge Jones that:

> any relevant documents known to [Lockheed] have been preserved . . .

(Tr. 12/18/75 at p. 83). Chief Judge Jones thereupon denied the motion for a protective order. There is abundant evidence in the records of cooperation between Lockheed and the Air Force from which to infer that, if, after Chief Judge Jones denied the motion in reliance in Lockheed's representation, Lockheed had requested the Air Force to preserve the photographs, the Air Force could and would have done so. Lockheed's attorney–client, work–product and "executive privilege" claims, of dubious merit, also contributed to the delay in production of the relevant photographs and the delay in discovering that relevant evidence had been destroyed.

It is therefore clear that relevant evidence had not been produced, that Lockheed could have taken actions to preserve this evidence after its presentation to Chief Judge Jones, and that, but for Lockheed's failure to take action, the relevant evidence would not have been destroyed. Were it up to this Court alone to create a standard for this Circuit, Lockheed might be held to a strict fiduciary obligation to make good on its representation to Chief Judge Jones and might be held subject to an adverse inference for the breach of the fiduciary obligation that it there assumed. Or Lockheed's representation to Chief Judge Jones might be held to estop it from later denying or equivocating about its control of the documents. Defendant has argued, however, that the evidence must show bad faith or evil intent on its part in the actual destruction of the photographs before an adverse inference instruction to the jury is appropriate. Defendant cites *Vick v. Texas Employment Commission*, 514 F.2d 734, 737 (5th Cir.1975), in support of this argument. Although it is unclear whether the bad faith standard announced in *Vick* has been or would be adopted in this Circuit, *Vick* is the existing authority and should be followed unless and until our Court of Appeals indicates a contrary intent.

Plaintiffs have adduced considerable probative evidence in the form of documents and live testimony by hostile Lockheed officials that Lockheed deliberately limited the records which it made and retained about the crash, that it made dubious privilege claims to delay discovery, and that it quickly shipped to the Air Force photographs and other discoverable evidence that it had with the expectation that the Air Force would further shield them by privilege claims. In doing so, Lockheed failed to take any precautions to assume that the evidence would be preserved. Nevertheless, the evidence is equivocal on the issue of whether Lockheed officials possessed evil intent or bad faith concerning the actual destruction of evidence by the Air Force. For that reason, the bad faith standard of *Vick, supra*, is not satisfied. Plaintiff Maupoint will therefore be precluded from introducing evidence at her trial and from attempting to persuade a jury to draw an inference adverse to the defendant from that destruction. This ruling and the findings thereupon which it is based apply only to this recently completed phase of the preliminary injunction hearing and to the *Maupoint* case. These findings are not intended to apply to the cases of other foreign infant plaintiffs.

There is a second ground for precluding application of the adverse inference rule under these circumstances. The Court had hoped that, if adverse inference claims were to be raised before a jury, the testimony, affidavits, and exhibits offered into evidence could be strictly contained within the narrow framework envisioned by the pretrial orders in *Kurth II*. *See Kurth v. Lockheed Aircraft Corporation*, No. 80–3223, Orders of February 1, 1983; July 1, 1983; and September 7, 1983. The *Kurth* orders contemplated that adverse inference might be drawn simply from proof of the original existence and destruction of photographs and of the fact that defendant had some responsibility for such items of evidence while engaged in or anticipating litigation about the crash. So constrained, the evidence concerning an adverse inference would have been more probative than prejudicial. The recent hearing indicates that if the plaintiffs have the burden of proving bad faith on the part of defendant, the focus of trial is likely to be disturbed by lengthy and inflammatory testimony about the propriety of Lockheed's conduct not only in this litigation, but also in activities ranging from bribery of foreign officials to destruction of computer data on U.S. Congressmen. As the Court originally concluded before the first *Kurth* trial, the litigation before a jury of the issue of whether Lockheed acted in bad faith in such circumstances would be more prejudicial than probative and would be likely to divert the jury's attention from the central issues in this case. Thus, if plaintiffs must prove defendant's bad faith before they can present the adverse inference issue to the jury, the risk of distortion of the trial precludes plaintiffs' opportunity to raise the adverse inference issue in the *Maupoint* trial.

* * * * *

Ethel D. FULLER, Individually and as Unqualified Community Administrator of the Estate of J.B. Fuller, Deceased v. PRESTON STATE BANK, James S. Chafin, and Donald C. McLeaish, Individually and d/b/a Commonwealth Land Title Company of Dallas and Commercial Title and Abstract Company

667 S.W.2d 214

Court of Appeals of Texas, Dallas
December 28, 1983

This suit concerns the validity of a vendor's deed of trust lien arising from the sale of a homestead. Ethel D. Fuller, individually and as community administratrix of the estate of J.B. Fuller, sued Preston State Bank to cancel the lien. She alleged that the conveyance by her and her late husband to their son and his wife was a simulated transaction made for the purpose of obtaining a loan from the bank and fixing a lien on the homestead, contrary to the prohibition in article XVI, section 50 of the Texas Constitution. She also sought damages from the bank, its loan officer, and a title company attorney under the Deceptive Trade Practices Act, TEX.BUS. & COM.CODE § § 17.41–17.45. (Vernon Supp.1982–1983). The trial court instructed a verdict for all defendants, and plaintiff appeals. We hold that the evidence raises fact issues as to whether the bank had knowledge or notice that the sale was simulated. We also hold that plaintiff was not a "consumer" with respect to the bank within the Deceptive Trade Practices Act and that she was not adversely affected by any alleged deceptive trade practice within the Act. Consequently,

we reverse the judgment insofar as it denies the claim for cancellation of the lien and remand that claim for trial, but otherwise we affirm. In view of another trial, we also rule on points complaining of the exclusion of certain evidence.

* * * * *

Evidence of Bank's Minutes

Ethel Fuller complains of exclusion of evidence tending to show that the bank destroyed its minutes of a meeting at which the Fuller loan application was considered. In the discovery process, Ethel's counsel requested production of the bank's business record concerning its loan to the Fullers. One of the documents produced by counsel for the bank was a letter from Judith Sinclair, the bank's in–house attorney, to one of the bank's trial counsel. The letter states that the minutes of the meeting at which the bank's loan committee had considered the Fuller loan had been destroyed. The bank asserts that the letter was a privileged communication and that it was included by mistake in the papers produced in response to that request. However, the record before us contains no evidence of mistake or inadvertence. In the absence of such evidence, the privilege was waived. *Eloise Bauer & Associates v. Electronic Realty Associates*, 621 S.W.2d 200, 204 (Tex.Civ.App. — Texarkana 1981, writ ref'd n.r.e.); *see also Bendele v. Tri–County Farmer's Coop*, 635 S.W.2d 459 (Tex.Civ.App. — San Antonio 1982) *modified on other grounds*, 641 S.W.2d 200, 208 (Tex.1982). On another trial this letter will be admissible unless proof of mistake is made.

A further problem is presented by the court's exclusion of Judith Sinclair's testimony that although she was not employed by the bank at the time of the transaction in question, she was the principal contact between the bank and its trial counsel, that she was asked to produce the loan committee meeting minutes for the period that would have included that transaction, and that she found out that these minutes had been destroyed. The bank objected to this testimony on the ground that it was within the attorney–client privilege. The admissibility of the testimony depends on whether the privilege was waived by production of the letter. A waiver with respect to the letter would constitute a waiver of the same information given to the bank's in–house attorney. *McClure v. Fall*, 42 S.W.2d 821, 824 (Tex.Civ.App. — Waco 1931, per Alexander, J.) *aff'd.* 67 S.W.2d 231 (Tex.1934); *but see West v. Solito*, 563 S.W.2d 240, 245, n. 3 (Tex.1978).

The bank argues that neither the letter nor the testimony was relevant to the issues in this case. A party is entitled to show that the opposing party had destroyed documents that would bear on a crucial issue in the case, since the destruction of relevant evidence raises a presumption that the evidence would have been unfavorable to the spoliator. *H.E. Butt Grocery Co. v. Bruner.* 530 S.W.2d 340, 344 (Tex.Civ.App. — Waco 1975, writ dism'd). The minutes of the bank's loan committee meeting might well contain evidence bearing on the question of whether the bank knew any facts indicating that the Fuller sale was simulated, particularly since the loan application showed that John and Brenda had only $200, none of the information on the application had been verified, and the loan was originally turned down. Consequently, the court erred in excluding evidence of the destruction of these minutes.

* * * * *

Byrd V. FURLONG and Helen Furlong v. Dr. James M. STOKES

427 S.W.2d 513

Supreme Court of Missouri, Division No. 2
May 13, 1968

This is an action brought by plaintiffs in two counts. Count I sought damages of $75,000 on behalf of Byrd V. Furlong (referred to herein as Furlong) for personal injuries, and in Count II Helen Furlong sought damages of $25,000 for injuries to her husband. At the close of the plaintiffs' case, the Trial Court sustained defendant's motion for a directed verdict, and, thereafter, plaintiffs' motion for a new trial was overruled. Plaintiffs, in their appeal, contend that there was substantial evidence of negligence and causation to submit both counts to the jury.

* * * * *

Plaintiffs allege in their petition that the defendant prescribed and performed a left femoral saphenous bypass for and on Furlong; that during the operation, defendant negligently allowed and permitted a hot lamp to shine on the inside of the left knee of Furlong, resulting in a burn about his left knee.

The operation was performed at Barnes Hospital by the defendant, a licensed doctor of medicine, specializing in surgery. He was assisted in the operation by Dr. Robert D. Kane, surgical resident, and Dr. Bernard Jaffee, intern. Also present during the operation were the anesthesiologist resident, the anesthesiologist, the circulating nurse and the scrub nurse.

* * * * *

Furlong was anesthetized for approximately five hours for the operation, which lasted for about four and one–half hours. Shortly after the operation commenced a portable lamp was brought into the operation room for additional illumination, and it remained in use until the operation was concluded. It is this portable lamp that Furlong claims caused the burn about his knee. The portable lamp was kept about five feet away from the operative site. Defendant, the operating surgeon, was working between the patient and the portable lamp. The lamp was placed on the side of the operating table over the shoulders of the operating team to allow illumination of the popliteal area. The defendant was at all times sterile, wearing gown and gloves, and he did not touch or handle the portable lamp which was not sterile. The operating room was air–conditioned and none of those present felt any increased heat or warmth during the operative procedure.

* * * * *

The evidence in regard to the condition of plaintiff's knee was as follows: Following the operation and in the recovery room, Dr. Kane noted that there was some erythema and mottling of the skin about the knee. The defendant at that time noticed that this skin was discolored, and he told Helen Furlong that the skin "was discolored, red, and it had the appearance as a burn." * * *

* * * * *

Plaintiffs' theory throughout this case is that Furlong's knee was burned by the portable lamp used by defendant during the operation because it was equipped with a stronger bulb than was called for by the manufacturer. Plaintiffs do not contend that the operation to correct the femoral artery occlusion was unsuccessful nor that the defendant failed to use the necessary skills required in its performance. This case, therefore, does not fall within the category of a malpractice action against a physician.

* * * * *

Plaintiffs have also contended in their appeal that defendant's spoliation of hospital records permits the inference that Furlong's knee was burnt by the operating room light, citing *Garrett v. Terminal Railroad Association of St. Louis*, Mo., 259 S.W. 2d 807, and Black's Law Dictionary, 4th Edition, page 1573. In *Garrett v. Terminal Railroad Association of St. Louis*, plaintiff, an employee, destroyed the original of an order made by defendant company. This court held that where a party to a suit has been guilty of spoliation of documentary evidence he is held to thereby admit the truth of the allegation of the opposite party. "Spoliation" as defined in Black's Law Dictionary is "Destruction of a thing by the act of a stranger, as the erasure or alteration of a writing by the act of a stranger." The hospital record made by Dr. Sasser, intern, on Furlong's readmission to the hospital for skin graft to the lesion on his knee showed "burn area, 3 ° LT Medial thigh (old)." Defendant wrote of this "ulcer of left knee, medial aspect." It is apparent that a change was made in the record, but it is not the same as destroying the record, or the same as alteration or erasure intended to obliterate completely that which was there before. This act, therefore, could not be characterized as spoliation. The result of the Garrett decision was that defendant was held to have admitted that the words "and flat wheels" were not on the original bad order card, not that the car had flat wheels. Here, at most, defendant would be held to admit that the record originally said "burn" rather than "ulcer," not that plaintiff Furlong actually had a burn. However, even with this admission by defendant, the plaintiffs have failed to carry the burden of making a submissible case for the jury.

Luther E. GALYON and Ollie May Brown Galyon v. Roy B. STUTTS and Vernelle A. Stutts

84 S.E.2d 822

Supreme Court of North Carolina
November 24, 1954

Contempt Proceedings in Civil Action for Rescission.

The defendant Roy B. Stutts (hereinafter referred to as the defendant) formerly operated a retail grocery business in the town of Liberty, North Carolina. In May, 1953, he sold the business, including stock in trade and fixtures, as a going concern to the plaintiffs. As part of the cash payment the plaintiffs conveyed to the defendant Stutts their home in Asheboro. The deferred balance of $13,000 was evidenced by note secured by chattel mortgage on the store fixtures and equipment.

In October, 1953, the plaintiffs, on allegations of fraud and deceit, instituted this action for the purpose of rescinding the contract of sale and all written instruments incident thereto, alleging in gist that the defendant fraudulently misrepresented the established character of the business as to its volume of sales and profits. The defendants answered denying all allegations of fraud.

After the complaint and answer were filed, the plaintiffs obtained orders of court directing the defendant to produce for inspection and copy certain books and records and requiring him to appear before a commissioner for adverse examination.

The defendant failed to produce any documents or records. However, he appeared on the appointed day before the commissioner and was examined adversely at length by counsel for the plaintiffs.

Following adjournment of the adverse examination the defendant was served with notice that the plaintiffs would move before the presiding Judge at the March 1954 Term of court for an order declaring the defendant to be in contempt of court for his failure to produce records as directed. The defendant also was served with notice that the plaintiffs, pursuant to G.S. § 1–568.19, would move before the presiding Judge for an order holding the defendant in contempt of court for his failure and refusal to answer questions asked on adverse examination.

When the cause came on for hearing, judgment was entered adjudging the defendant in willful contempt of court (1) for failure to produce the records as previously directed and (2) for refusal to answer questions propounded on adverse examination. He was ordered to pay the costs of the adverse examination and the further sum of $50. From the judgment so entered the defendant appealed, assigning errors.

* * * * *

1. *The Failure to Produce Records.* By order signed by Judge Martin the defendant was directed to produce "all the documents, ledgers, journals, inventories, records and books" of his grocery business for the years 1951, 1952, and 1953. The court below found and concluded that the defendant willfully failed and refused to comply with this order and that such failure and refusal amounted to contempt of court within the purview of G.S.§ 5–1(4). The record does not support the findings and adjudication.

While the defendant produced no documents or records in response to the order, he did appear on the appointed date before the commissioner for the adverse examination. He was examined at length by counsel for the plaintiffs. The examination, as reported in question and answer form, is brought forward on the appeal and covers more than 40 pages of the record. In response to questions propounded by plaintiffs' counsel, the defendant explained that he had no records or

documents with which to comply with the order of Judge Martin. By way of explanation, he said in substance that he retained no copies of his income tax returns and that he kept no ledgers, journals, or other like records in connection with the operation of the grocery business. His testimony discloses that the only business records kept by him were the "cash register receipts." As to these, he said they were stored in boxes in "the car house," and that "the rats ate them up, gnawed them up," to the extent they "were not fit to be salvaged and when he found them in that condition after sale of the business in 1953, he threw "them all out."

The record thus affirmatively disclosed — with nothing appearing contrary that the defendant had no books or records with which to comply with the order of Judge Martin. Therefore, the court below erred in finding and concluding that the defendant was in contempt within the purview of G.S. § 5–1(4) for noncompliance with the order.

* * * * *

GARRETT v. TERMINAL R. ASS'N OF ST. LOUIS

259 S.W.2d 807

Supreme Court of Missouri, Division No. 2
July 13, 1953

Action under Federal Employers' Liability Act by switchman against railroad for injuries received in alleged defective shelter cab on train. The Circuit Court of the City of St. Louis entered judgment on verdict as reduced by remittitur, and railroad appealed The Supreme Court, Tipton J., held that, where evidence did not satisfactorily explain why original bad order card was not produced by switchman except that switchman had intentionally destroyed card, switchman would be held, in law, to have admitted truth of railroad's contention that words "and flat wheels" were not on original bad order card even though they were on photostatic copy thereof which was admitted in evidence.

* * * * *

In the circuit court of the city of St. Louis, respondent brought this action under the Federal Employers' Liability Act, U.S.C.A. § 51 et seq. The jury returned verdict for $25,000, but that amount was reduced to $18,500 by a remittitur and a judgment was entered for that amount.

Respondent had been in appellants' employ for over 30 years as a switchman. His home station was the Bremen Avenue Yard in St. Louis, Missouri. On June 8, 1951, he assisted in taking a train across the Mississippi River to the Madison Yard, Illinois. He was the rear brakeman on that train. For this trip the crew was furnished a shelter cab, which is a cab carrier on a flat car. The car's number was 544. A shelter cab is about 6 feet long and the same width as a box car. Inside the cab are board seats, a stove and closet. There is one center plate bolted to the floor of the car. Another plate is bolted on the bottom of the cab and that plate fits into the center plate which is bolted to the floor of the car. These plates hold a center pin which, in turn, holds the car to the bolster. There was substantial evidence that there were bolts missing from each of the center plates.

Respondent testified that if bolts were missing, the center plates would be loose and this would cause vibration of the center pin that would make the car rock and bounce. He further testified that on the trip to the Madison Yard he noticed a lot of "jumping of the car," and "it is the roughest car in which I ever rode." He also testified that when the train arrived at the Madison Yard he walked around the car to bleed it and noticed a "bad order card" on the opposite side from which he boarded the train. He took this bad order card from the car. He then called the yardmaster and told him about it. The yardmaster told respondent that the crew would have to go back in the same car. He further testified that he did not read the bad order card until his train reached the Twenty-third Street Yard on its return from the Madison Yard. When he went home he took this bad order card with him.

When Bremen Avenue was reached it was respondent's duty to go to the back of the train to "show" himself to the men in the tower or to the yardmaster so if anything was wrong with the train a signal might be given him. Respondent testified that he rose from his seat to make this appearance but he was unable to do so as he was thrown backwards and fell in the corner of the seat he had been sitting on. He testified that he was knocked down by "the rough riding and jumping of the car," and struck the lower part of his spine or tail bone. He stated that when he regained consciousness he pulled himself back upon the seat and remained there until the train stopped in the Twenty–Third Street Yard. He then telephoned to Elwood Davis, one of appellant's superintendents, and told Davis how he had been hurt. Davis asked respondent to help bring the train back to the Breman Yard and he complied with this request. Respondent's tour of duty for that day was completed when the train was brought there. Was it error for the trial court to admit in evidence respondent's exhibit 1, which was a photostatic reproduction of what was purported to be a bad order card which respondent said he removed from the car in which he was riding on the day of his alleged injury?

This offer was objected to by appellant for the reason that it was not the best evidence. In other words, this exhibit was not the original bad order card but only a photostatic copy of the original.

In order to determine if the original of exhibit 1 was in existence at the time of the trial or if it had been destroyed, by whom and for what purpose, if any, we deem it necessary to extensively quote from the record. The record shows that the following occurred without the hearing of the jury:

"The Court: What do you mean, 'there is no better evidence'? Did you serve notice to produce the original?

"Mr. Sheppard: We haven't got it, we never heard of it.

"Mr. Boecker: Their testimony is there was no such card.

"The Court: Well, then, it is admitted that —

"Mr. Boecker: On deposition.

"The Court: All right, then I will overrule the objection.

"Mr. Sheppard: Plaintiff's counsel stated that he took his card off, plaintiff took it off and had it photostated. There isn't any evidence that anybody ever saw it before or afterwards, so it was in his possession.

"Mr. Boecker: It is for this witness to say.

"The Court: Where would the original be, are you going to explain that?

"Mr. Boecker: So far as I know it must have been destroyed.

"The Court: By whom?

"Mr. Boecker: I don't know.

"Mr. Sheppard: As far as this record shows, the last time it was heard of, it was in the plaintiff's hands.

"Mr. Boecker: That is what I have said.

"The Court: Is it or is it not in existence, that is what I have got to first decide, because a photostat would be competent until the original has been accounted for. If it isn't available, all well and good, but it has got to be accounted for. If it is still in existence, it should be produced.

"Mr. Boecker: To my knowledge it is not in existence.

"Mr. Sheppard: I want to see this original.

"Mr. Boecker: The testimony of the rip track foreman on this deposition was that the car had been bad ordered.

"The Court: What is your man going to testify?

"Mr. Boecker: That he sent it back to them.

"The Court: He is going to testify to that?

"Mr. Boecker: That is right.

"The Court: After he had this picture taken, he sent it back?

"Mr. Boecker: That is right.

"The Court: In what way?

"Mr. Boecker: I don't know about that.

"The Court: You better talk to him and let's find out, because I don't want to admit something in here and later on exclude it. What is the evidence going to show with reference to it?

"Mr. Sheppard: Just look at that with those numbers all written over.

"Mr. Boecker: That is a matter for cross–examination. He said that the original was destroyed.

"The Court: By whom?

"Mr. Boecker: By himself.

"The Court: You mean after he had the picture taken, he destroyed it?

"Mr. Boecker: After he had the picture taken, he destroyed it.

"Mr. Sheppard: I would like to cross–examine the gentlemen about that before this is put in evidence, because I think this is phony.

"Mr. Boecker: I submit it is not. I haven't had an opportunity to ask this witness if it refreshes his recollection. I think this witness is the proper one to relate.

"The Court: Under those circumstances I will overrule this objection. If that is going to be the testimony, of course, this is the next best evidence."

During the cross–examination of respondent about the original of exhibit 1, he testified as follows:

"Q. Who made that photostat of that card? A. Stobit.

"Q. Did you take it down there? A. No, sir, I didn't.

"Q. Who did? A. The wife.

"Q. Where had it been from June the 8th, 1951, until October or November, 1951? A. I had it in my possession.

"Q. You took it off of this caboose on June 8th, 1951, didn't you? A. Yes, sir.

"Q. And you said awhile ago that you took it off for fear it would get lost and the company wouldn't see it didn't you? A. Well, I taken it off for my own benefit. * * *

"Q. What did you do with it after you took it home? A. Well, I laid it away, I put it in my papers or something. I don't remember where it was laid until I just happened to think one day. It was in such bad condition I was going to try to get a photostat of it.

"Q. You realized it was of importance to you, didn't you? A. Well, that is the reason I taken it with that intention, yes, sir.

"Q. But you didn't know where you kept it? A. I kept it in my house.

"Q. I know, but where? A. Well, I would say it was in my paper bill book.

"Q. And where did you keep the bill book? A. Right in here where I have got this one.

"Q. In your pocket? A. Yes, sir.

"Q. So you carried it in your pocket every day, did you, from the time you took it off of the car until you had it photostated? A. I did.

"Q. You did? A. As far back as I can remember.

"Q. When you went back to work the next day over there, you had it in your pocket, did you? A. I wouldn't say that. I never carried my billfold with me when I was working.

"Q. Did you have it folded up? A. No.

"Q. Well, what did you mean by my billfold then? A. (Indicates.)

"Q. That is what you mean? A. Yes, sir, it lays right in it.

"Q. And you don't have to fold it? A. No, sir.

"Q. Is it in your billfold now? A. No, sir.

"Q. Where is it? A. I couldn't tell you. It was disposed of after the picture was made. I don't remember whether the wife ever brought it home or what. I had no more use for it after I had the photostat, that is all I wanted.

"Q. Well, you threw it away, in other words? A. As far as I know, yes, sir.

"Q. Or did you burn it up? A. I didn't burn it up, no.

"Q. You just let it alone and you didn't care what happened to it? A. That is true.

"Q. I see. Did you show it to anybody. A. No, sir.

"Q. At any time? A. No, sir.

"Q. What sort of shape was it in by November? Was it ragged, torn? A. It was in pretty bad condition, yes, sir.

"Q. Just — the edges were torn and rough and worn out, were they? A. Yes, sir.

"Q. And the corners torn off? A. It was.

"Q. And how many photostatic copies did you have made? A. Just one, I believe."

The above quoted admissions of respondent's attorney and respondent's testimony were inconsistent and unsatisfactory as to what became of the original of exhibit 1. The only conclusion that can be drawn from these admissions and testimony is that the respondent intentionally destroyed the bad order card, since there is not the slightest evidence he made any effort to produce it.

* * * * *

Under this record, we do think the trial court abused his discretion amounting to an error of law in admitting respondent's exhibit 1. If it were possible to conclude from the preliminary proof that the original was still in existence, then exhibit 1 was not admissible because respondent did not show any diligence in attempting to locate the original card. *Bullock v. E. B. Gee Land Co.*, 347 Mo. 721, 148 S.W.2d 565. However, as we have already said, the only reasonable conclusion to be drawn from the above quoted admissions and testimony from the preliminary proof is that respondent intentionally destroyed the original of exhibit 1.

Respondent's attorney admitted to the trial court that "after the (respondent) had the picture taken, he destroyed it." Respondent testified he could not tell where it was. "It was disposed of after the picture was made."

David Earl Smith, a witness for respondent, testified that he was a car inspector for appellant. When shown exhibit 1 he was asked if he could identify it. His answer was, "Photostat of a bad order card that I made out." Exhibit 1 was a photostat of a card, and across the top of it the words, "Bad Order," were printed in large type. Below that was printed the word, "Defect." Following that word, Smith had printed by hand the following, "Cotter Keys Missing in Pin Lifter Brackets A End & Flat Wheels," and it was signed by this witness.

While the appellant was introducing its evidence, Smith was called to clarify his previous testimony. He testified that he was asked to report to Mr. Klein, who was the head claim agent for appellant. When he reported to Klein's office he was asked to print "Cotter Keys Missing in Pin Lifter Brackets in A End & Flat Wheels," which he did. He was then asked to compare what he had just printed with the same words that were on exhibit 1. When he did so he discovered that "& Flat Wheels" was not his printing. He later was recalled by respondent in rebuttal and testified as follows:

"Q. Now, on that '& flat wheels' do you have any doubts about that or are you positive about that? A. No, sir, I did not write that.

"Q. Positive about that? A. Absolutely.

On behalf of appellant, George G. Swett testified that he was "an examiner of questioned documents, commonly referred to as a handwriting expert," and that, in his opinion, witness Smith did not print the words, "& Flat Wheels," that appeared on exhibit 1.

So, the issue in regard to exhibit 1 between the parties to this litigation is: Did the original bad order card have the words, '& Flat Wheels," on it?

The law is well settled that the destruction of written evidence without a unsatisfactory explanation gives rise to an inference unfavorable to the spoliator. *Weir v. Baker*, 357 Mo. 507, 209 S.W. 2d, 253; *Griffith v. Gardner*, 358 Mo. 859, 217 S.W. 2d 519. We had nothing in this record that satisfactorily explains why the original bad order card was not produced by respondent except that it had been intentionally destroyed by respondent. His testimony was very unsatisfactory in reference to the original card and what became of it. It is to be remembered that he testified, "I had no more use for it after I had the photostat, that is all I wanted."

"This court has several times given effect to the rule that where a party to a suit has been guilty of spoliation of documentary evidence, he is held thereby to admit the truth of the allegation of the opposite party, and this upon the ground that the law, in consequence of the spoliation, will presume that the evidence destroyed will establish the other party's demand to be just. *Pomeroy v. Benton*, 77 Mo. 64,85; *Hunt v. Sanders*, 288 Mo 337, 252, 232 S.W. 456; *Haid v. Prendiville*, 292 Mo. 552, 565, 238 S.W. 452. See, also, *Tracy v. Buchanan*, 167 Mo. App. [432], 434, 151 S.W. 747; *Stuckes v. National Candy Co.*, 158 Mo. [342], 359, 138 S.W. 352; *Shawhan v. [Shawhan] Distillery Co.*, 195 Mo. App. [445], 450, 197 S. W. 369, and *Shawhan v. [Shawhan] Distillery Co.*, 195 Mo. App. [492], 495, 197 S.W. 371." *Gaugh v. Gaugh*, 321 Mo. 414, 11 S.W2d 729, loc. cit. 748.

Under the law above quoted from the Gaugh case, we must hold under the facts in this record that respondent must, in law, admit to the truth of appellant's contention that the words, "& Flat Wheels," were not on the original bad order card.

* * * * *

GENERAL ATOMIC COMPANY, a partnership composed of Gulf Oil Corporation and Scallop Nuclear, Inc. v. EXXON NUCLEAR COMPANY, INC., a Delaware corporation; EXXON NUCLEAR COMPANY, INC., a corporation v. GENERAL ATOMIC COMPANY, and Gulf oil Corporation, a corporation, and Scallop Nuclear, Inc., a corporation

90 F.R.D. 290

United States District Court, S.D. California
April 23, 1981

* * * * *

This action was brought by General Atomic Company (GAC), a partnership composed of Gulf Oil Company (Gulf) and Scallop Nuclear, Inc. (Scallop) to enforce a uranium supply contract against Exxon Nuclear Company Inc. (ENC). As amended, GAC's complaint seeks a declaratory judgment that the contract under which ENC was to deliver six million pounds of uranium to Gulf is valid and binding. Plaintiff seeks specific performance and damages for breach in excess of $250,000,000.

As a defense, ENC asserts that the contract is null and void because it was made in violation of U.S. antitrust laws. ENC and its parent organization, Exxon Corporation (Exxon), have filed a counterclaim against GAC, Gulf and Scallop for antitrust damages under the Sherman Act, 15 U.S.C., Sections 1 and 2 declaratory relief, fraud, negligent misrepresentation, unfair competition, and intentional interference with a business expectancy. Counterclaim plaintiffs assert that Gulf secretly participated in an international uranium cartel beginning in 1971 until at least 1976, and that the uranium supply contract, executed in

1973, was part of Gulf's effort to gain control of a substantial portion of United States uranium for the purpose of furthering the uranium cartel's unlawful objectives and restricting the free market supply of uranium. Exxon seeks damages for injuries to its uranium business caused by Gulf's unlawful activities. The counterclaim defendants rely on various defenses including the act of state doctrine and sovereign compulsion.

The Gulf Uranium Organization

Gulf through its divisions, affiliates, and subsidiaries is in the business of exploring for, acquiring, mining, milling and processing, fabricating, purchasing, and selling uranium and nuclear fuel. It entered the business in 1967 by purchasing a company known as General Atomic which was a manufacturer of nuclear reactors. It operated as a Gulf subsidiary in San Diego, California under the name of Gulf General Atomic until it became part of a new division called Gulf Energy and Environmental Systems (Gulf Energy). This entity was involved in the marketing of uranium and the manufacturing and servicing of nuclear reactors.

In 1967 Gulf undertook the exploration and development of uranium ore bearing properties. A gulf division in Denver, Gulf Minerals Resources Company (Gulf Minerals) was assigned responsibility for this production function of Gulf's uranium business. In 1967 Gulf discovered massive deposits of uranium at Rabbit Lake in Saskatchewan. Pursuant to Canadian law, Gulf established a wholly owned subsidiary, Gulf Minerals Canada Limited (GMCL) headquartered in Toronto to develop the Rabbit Lake uranium project. Gulf Minerals in Denver had administrative responsibility to oversee GMCL's operations.

In addition to its Canadian uranium reserves, Gulf, through its division, Gulf Minerals, began to acquire substantial uranium reserves in the United States. In the early 1970's it acquired the Mt. Taylor property in New Mexico which contained the largest uranium ore deposit in the United States. Through Gulf Energy (San Diego), Gulf also engaged in the purchase of substantial quantities of uranium on the open market from other producers and middlemen such as Exxon and ENC.

The Gulf–Exxon Uranium Contract

During the summer of 1972, Gulf (through Gulf General Atomic) began negotiating with ENC, and in August, 1972, a Letter of intent for the purchase of six million pounds of uranium by Gulf was signed. Draft contracts were negotiated until May 11, 1973, when a final contract was signed wherein ENC agreed to sell and Gulf agreed to buy at certain prices six million pounds of uranium to be delivered at the rate of one million pounds per year beginning in 1979. The contract was assigned by Gulf in December, 1973 to the plaintiff, General Atomic Company, a newly formed partnership between Gulf and Scallop. In 1979, Gulf bought out Scallop and obtained the sole beneficial interest in the "uranium business" of the GAC partnership. The settlement provided, *inter alia,* that Gulf would indemnify the partnership for losses, damages and judgments arising from the uranium business as well as for any liabilities incurred in connection with Gulf's participation in the cartel.

In its counterclaim Exxon alleges that during the contract negotiations, Gulf representatives concealed the fact that Gulf was a member of a secret international uranium cartel that intended to restrict the uranium supply and increase uranium prices. During the five years following the contract, the price of uranium increased rapidly to about six times the contract price. Exxon eventually learned of the existence of the cartel and Gulf's participation therein. In 1978 it informed GAC that it considered the contract null and void and would not deliver the uranium, whereupon GAC instituted this litigation in April, 1978.

The International Uranium Cartel

The precise facts regarding the creation development, and operation of the cartel are not completely known because much evidence continues to be located in foreign countries.

However, several matters appear to be well established from the available evidence.

It is undisputed that from at least 1972 through 1975 there existed a uranium cartel consisting of various international uranium producers and foreign governments including Canada, South Africa, Australia, and France. The cartel members gathered at general cartel meetings throughout the world at places such as Johannesburg, Paris, Ottawa, Sydney, London, and Las Palmas. The cartel also had committees known as the Policy Committee and the Operating Committee which held meetings. In addition, the Canadian uranium producers met on a regular basis. From the available evidence, it appears there were at least 46 cartel meetings between February, 1972 and December, 1975. Partial minutes of eleven meetings were available.

The objectives of the cartel were evident from the Johannesburg Rules adopted in Johannesburg in late May of 1972 (DX 51b) and from available cartel minutes. The cartelists sought to restrict the supply of uranium, set minimum prices and conditions on the sale of uranium, and allocate the production and marketing of uranium among themselves. The members agreed that the existence and activities of the cartel were to be secret (DX 14b). The cover title of the organization was established as "Market Research Organization" for its dealing with the outside world (DX 1002c) (DX 51b). The organization was also referred to by its members as "The Club" and "SERU".

Gulf, acting through its Canadian subsidiary GMCL, became a member of the cartel at or before the Johannesburg meeting (May 28–June 2, 1972). In addition to the general manager of GMCL (Ediger of Toronto), three Gulf officials from the United States attended that meeting: Hoffman and Hunter from Gulf Energy (GAC's predecessor) and Roger Allen, a Gulf attorney from the Gulf Minerals in Denver. Earlier, GMCL had been invited by the Canadian government to attend a meeting of Canadian uranium producers in Ottawa in February 1972. Ediger of GMCL and S.A. Zagnoli, president of Gulf Minerals (Denver) attended.

A major issue regarding the cartel in this litigation is the relationship between the government participants and the uranium producers. Gulf contends that the uranium cartel was initiated, mandated and directed by foreign nations involved, and GMCL was compelled by Canada to comply with cartel terms.

A second area of major dispute is the scope of the cartel's activities. Although the Johannesburg Rules provided for exclusion of the United States domestic uranium market from its terms, later cartel activities. The minutes of September 5, 1972 cartel meeting reveal the prospect of taking anticompetitive actions against an American uranium producer:

There followed a general discussion of the impact of Westinghouse bidding in Europe.... Some members thought that Westinghouse should be approached directly, whereas other views were that it would be a dangerous move. The consensus finally reached was that if the club was to survive as a viable entity, it would be necessary to delineate where the competition was and the nature of its strength, as a prelude to eliminating it once and for all. (Emphasis added) (DX 97b)

II. The Foreign Law Impediment and Gulf's Efforts to Overcome It

Gulf's reason for failing to comply with the discovery orders of November 16, 1979 and January 14, 1980 regarding documents in the possession, custody, and control of its Canadian subsidiary (GMCL) is that production would violate the Canadian Uranium Information Security Regulations (hereafter "Security Regulations") thereby subjecting Gulf and its Canadian personnel to criminal penalties. The Security Regulations became law on September 23, 1976, approximately 18 1/2 months before GAC commenced this lawsuit. As amended, they provide that no person shall release any documents related to conversations, discussions, or meetings that took place between January 1, 1972 and December 31, 1975 involving the exporting from Canada or marketing for outside Canada of uranium or its derivatives[5]

It is undisputed that the Security Regulations apply to the documents being withheld, and that they prohibit Gulf from identifying as well as producing the regulated documents. Knowing consent or acquiescence to a violation of the Regulations could subject an individual or corporate entity to criminal prosecution (TR 61). Violation of the regulations is an offense punishable by imprisonment for up to five years and/or a fine not exceeding $10,000 (TR 58–59; G–6).

Gulf's position is that no Canadian documents are being withheld on the basis of any Canadian law other than the Security Regulations (Gulf's Post Sanctions Hearing Brief, p.28; TR 99). Prior to the passage of the Security Regulations on September 23, 1976, Gulf relied on the Ontario Business Records Protection Act of 1947 (hereafter "Ontario Act") as an excuse for non–production of Canadian documents in other litigation

The Ontario Act forbids the removal of any business records from Ontario pursuant to an order of a foreign court unless such removal is a part of a regular reporting practice by a subsidiary to a foreign parent. The Act has no penal sanctions and is not enforceable unless a provincial court issues an order prohibiting removal. Because no such order has been sought or issued, the Ontario Act is not, nor has it ever been, a legitimate impediment to production by Gulf. See *In re Uranium Antitrust Litigation,* 480 F.Supp. 1138, 1143 (N.D.Ill.1979); *United Nuclear Corporation v. General Atomic Company,* 629 P.2d 231, 293 (N.M. 1980) (DX 5145).

During the course of this lawsuit, Gulf has made several good faith attempts to overcome the prohibitions of the Security Regulations. A Canadian law firm was retained in August of 1978 to explore methods by which GMCL's documents could be made available to this and other courts (TR 64). In a letter to the Canadian Minister of Energy, Mines and Resources, a meeting was requested to discuss several proposals (G–16). The meeting was unproductive and Canadian government viewed the discovery requests as unacceptable (G–17). After the Canadian national election in May of 1979 resulted in a new government (Prime Minister Joseph Clark), Gulf counsel sent a letter dated September

12, 1979 to Prime Minister of Energy, Mines and Resources requesting a change of policy with regard to disclosure of information governed by the Security Regulations so that production could be made in U.S. litigation (G–19). The Canadian response was negative (G–19a; TR 76–77), but nevertheless another meeting was held in March, 1980 in which Gulf and GMCL unsuccessfully renewed their requests for relief from the Security Regulations. (TR 82–86; G–20).

In addition, Gulf petitioned the Canadian courts for relief. Letters rogatory were presented to the Supreme Court of Canada on January 15, 1980 and Gulf presented oral argument on February 20, 1980. The Supreme Court denied the relief sought in a written opinion on March 18, 1980 (G–21; TR 81–82).

While Gulf's efforts to overcome the Security Regulations constitute a *prima facie* showing of good faith to comply with the production orders, Gulf's conduct prior to the passage of the Security Regulations must also be evaluated to determine the appropriateness of sanctions.

III. Basis for Sanctions

Gulf contends that because Canadian law forbids production of the cartel documents in the custody of GMCL in Canada, its failure to produce them in this litigation is due to an innocent inability to comply, and in view of its good faith efforts to produce, there is no basis for the drastic sanctions of dismissal and default judgment.

The power of a court to impose the severe sanction of dismissal for a party's failure to produce documents located under its control in a foreign country where disclosure is forbidden by foreign law was addressed by the Supreme Court in *Societe International v. Rogers,* 357 U.S. 197, 78 S.Ct. 1087, 2 L.Ed.2d 1255 (1958). In that case a Swiss holding company brought suit against the Attorney General under the *Trading with the Enemy Act* for the return of property seized by the U.S. Government. Pursuant to discovery request, the District Court ordered Societe International to produce certain relevant records of its Swiss bank. The records were not produced on the grounds that production would violate Swiss secrecy laws which carried criminal penalties. The District Court ruled that unless full production was made, the complaint would be dismissed, but delayed dismissal while plaintiff attempted to negotiate with Swiss government for release of the records. Several thousand documents were produced as a result of this effort, but full compliance with the production order was never realized. The District Court found the missing records might be crucial to outcome of the litigation and dismissed the complaint even though it had concluded that plaintiff had shown good faith in its efforts to comply with the court's order. On appeal the Supreme Court held that the production order was justified notwithstanding the penal nondisclosure law but that a party's failure to fully comply with the production order "due to inability fostered neither by its own conduct nor by circumstances within its control" does not justify the sanction of dismissal. 357 U,S, at 211, 78 S.Ct. at 1095. However, the Court did not completely preclude the imposition of sanctions. Rather, it held that a mere failure to satisfy a production order was a basis for sanctions and that the reasons for noncompliance and the good faith of the non–producing party "are relevant only to the path which the District Court might follow in dealing with petitioner's failure to comply." 357 U.S. at 208, 78 SCt. at 1094. The Court stated that in the absence of completed disclosure, the district court possessed "wide discretion to proceed in whatever manner it deems most effective", 357 U.S. at 213, 78 S.Ct. at 1096, such as drawing inferences of fact unfavorable to the non–producing party as to particular events related to the withheld documents.

It is clear from *Societe* that where a party's failure to comply with a production order has been due it is "willfulness, bad faith, or any fault", 357 U.S. at 212, 78 S.Ct. at 1096, the sanction of dismissal is not precluded. In making this determination, it is relevant to consider conduct of the non–producing party which occurred prior to the commencement of the litigation in which the production orders are issued. In *Societe,* the Government contended that despite the plaintiff's diligent efforts to execute the production order, dismissal of the complaint was nevertheless justified because plaintiff took action in 1941 (seven years prior to suit) that caused its records to come within the Swiss secrecy laws, and thus stood in the position of one who "deliberately courted legal impediments to production... and who thus cannot now be heard to assert its good faith after this expectation was realized." Although the contention was unsupported by a factual basis in the record, the Court stated that "these contentions, if supported by facts, would have a vital bearing on the justification for dismissal of the action." 357 U.S at 208–209, 78 SCt. at 1094.

Like the government in *Societe,* Exxon contends that Gulf has "courted the legal impediments" to production of the cartel documents. In evaluating this contention, we consider not only Gulf's recent efforts to comply with the court's orders, but also Gulf's conduct prior to passage of the Canadian Security Regulations (September 23, 1976) including an inquiry as to how the withheld documents came to be located in Canada.

In order to prevail on its motion for dismissal and default judgment, Exxon must establish by preponderance of the evidence that: (1) the failure to fully comply with the production orders was caused by "willfulness, bad faith, or any fault" of Gulf; (2) the withheld documents may be crucial to the outcome of this litigation; (3) Exxon is prejudiced by the failure or discovery in the presentation of its case; and (4) the sanctions sought are commensurate with the prejudice to Exxon and the degree of fault attributable to Gulf.

IV. Gulf's Present Inability to Produce Has Been Fostered by Its Own Conduct

Exxon contends that any impediments to Gulf's present inability to comply with the production orders are attributable to Gulf's strategy of concealment. In support of this contention, Exxon claims that (1) Gulf housed its cartel documents in Canada in anticipation of uranium antitrust litigation, (2) Gulf failed to produce the cartel documents in other litigation prior to the passage

of the Security Regulations, and (3) Gulf destroyed cartel documents which had entered the United States.

Housing Documents in Canada

Soon after Gulf began its participation in the cartel in 1972, it established a policy of limited distribution of cartel–related documents by which such information would be housed in Canada, and transmittal to the United States would be avoided. Donald Hunter who was the director of Uranium Supply and Distribution at Gulf Energy in San Diego (GAC's predecessor) and attended the Johannesburg cartel meeting in late May of 1972 testified that

> there was a clear understanding that any documentation any notes, any correspondence relative to the workings of the international producers would be limited to Canadian, that there would be no flow of information or documentation from Canada to the U.S. (Deposition of Don Hunter, DX 5148, p.282–283) When Hunter returned from Johannesburg, he destroyed his working papers from the meetings as the result of instructions from his superiors (DX 4440, p. 805).

One month after Johannesburg, L. T. Gregg, a uranium market analyst employee under Hunter, was transferred by Gulf to GMCL in Toronto to serve as manager of international uranium sales. Gregg later became Gulf's representative on the cartel's Operating Committee. Although Gulf contends that the Gregg transfer to Toronto was for sound business reasons, there is evidence that the purpose of the transfer was to implement the cartel concealment policy. Hunter has testified that Gregg was transferred to Canada "because we did not want documentation relating to the cartel in San Diego, Gulf Energy and Environmental Systems files." (DX 4440, p. 784–5 citing DX 4393, p. 98). In his testimony, Gregg admitted that if he remained based in San Diego, cartel documentation in the United States could not have been avoided.

Q. . . . Now, if you had remained based in

San Diego, how in the world could you have avoided generating documents with regard to the activities of the uranium cartel? You couldn't, could you?

A. Sitting here today and trying to imagine a way to do it, no, I cannot. (TR 1179)

Gregg also testified that after arriving in Canada, he had an understanding with Ediger, the General Manager of GMCL, to avoid transmittal of documents reflecting cartel activities into the United States (TR 1016–1017) and that he "didn't send any club documents to anybody in the U.S." (TR 1041)

Instead, some cartel–related documents that had accumulated in the United States were sent to GMCL in Toronto. On October 6, 1972, Roger Allen, general counsel for Gulf Minerals shipped cartel–related documents from Denver to GMCL in Toronto. This shipment took place shortly after Allen had received the minutes of the Owatta cartel meeting of September 5, 1972 wherein the members reached the consensus that "if the club was to survive as a viable entity, it would be necessary to delineate where the competition was and the nature of its strength, as a prelude to eliminating it once and for all." (DX 97d). Allen testified that he could not remember what documents he sent to Toronto and that the purpose of the shipment was for legitimate business reasons pertaining to forthcoming arbitration negotiations with Gulf's partner, UCL in the Rabbit Lake uranium project. Mr. Allen did admit that the shipment consisted of "all of the important cartel documents" (TR 2284). Mr. Gregg of GMCL to whom the documents were sent testified that the purpose of Allen's shipment was to carry out the secrecy policy. (TR 1163–1164). It is significant that Allen neither listed nor copied the documents shipped (TR 2281) and that he knew that Ediger at GMCL already had copies of the cartel documents shipped to him (TR 2284).

Gulf contends that the limited distribution policy regarding cartel related documents was not adopted or followed in anticipation of litigation or to frustrate discovery. Frank O'Hara, a Gulf attorney testified that dissemination was limited for several legitimate reasons. First, wide dissemination would have been inconsistent with the Canadian Government's policy that documents referring to the cartel be accorded confidential treatment and the Government's express statement that information relating to the terms and conditions under which export permits would be granted would not be released since it was not in the public interest to do so (TR 1482). Second, the cartel and the Canadian Government's minimum pricing and quota allocation requirements applied only to GMCL, a separate Canadian corporation (TR 1492–83). Thus there was no business need for general dissemination to others within the Gulf organization (in the U.S. or elsewhere) of documents relating to the information or operation of the cartel. Third, since many cartel–related documents were considered by the Gulf Law Department to be subject to the attorney–client privilege, O'Hara was concerned that their circulation outside the "control group" might constitute a risk of waiver (TR 1483–84). Fourth, the wide dissemination of cartel–related documents in the United States was unnecessary and undesirable since the United States market was excluded from the cartel.

Gulf's argument that it was a legitimate business practice to avoid dissemination of cartel documents to its offices in the United States is not convincing. Although GMCL is headquartered in Canada, Many Gulf officials from the United States participated in meetings of the cartel (e.g. Zagnoli & Allen of Minerals and Hunter & Hoffman of Gulf Energy). At the important Johannesburg meeting in May 1972, three of Gulf's four attendees were from the United States. Moreover, Gulf attorney Frank O'Hara of Pittsburgh had been assigned the duty of monitoring cartel developments from an antitrust standpoint. (TR 2359) At a meeting in Toronto in July of 1972, attended by Zagnoli of Gulf Minerals, Ediger of GMCL and several Gulf attorneys, including O'HARA, it was decided that: Nevertheless, it will be advisable that Frank [O'Hara] be kept adequately and currently informed of significant developments which might affect Gulf's overall antitrust posture. (DX 74b)

Surely, normal business practice would have resulted in copies of cartel minutes being sent to O'Hara. But, O'Hara never received any cartel minutes after September 1972. (TR 1561, 1691)

Contrary to Gulf's position, there is substantial evidence that the policy of avoiding dissemination of cartel–related information to Gulf offices in the United States was motivated in large part by apprehension of antitrust litigation. Gregg testified that one of the reasons for the policy was that he and Ediger "had [an] awareness of the fact that there was a set of antitrust laws in existence in the United States under which the [cartel] activity might be construed as being illegal." (TR 1037) In his testimony before the Grand Jury in 1977, Gregg stated:

Q. The documents that you worked with in your capacity as Marketing Manager for Gulf Minerals Canada, Limited,—

A. Yes

Q. —were there any efforts on your part or other employees of Gulf to isolate them from other Gulf subsidiaries or the Gulf parent and did you make a conscious effort to keep them in Canada?

A. Yes

Q. Why is that?

A. We didn't feel they should be distributed either outside of our offices or outside of Canada.

Q. What was the basis for that decision?

A. Again, an apprehension that perhaps this might result in investigation under the antitrust laws, under the U.S. antitrust laws.

Q. Point of clarification. When you are talking about keeping documents in Canada, you are not talking about general documents related to your activities as marketing manager?

A. No

Q. You are talking specifically about documents relating to the operation, formation and activities of the club, is that correct?

A. That is right. We sent a large number of marketing–related documents to the States, to Denver and Pittsburgh, but not any that related to these club activities.

(Gregg; Grand Jury, 2/22/77 at 106–7 [emphasis supplied], admitted TR 1034–5, and Gregg deposition, DX 4472, p. 506–507.)

A few months after the limited dissemination policy was established, Gulf attorney O'Hara prepared a memorandum of law in November, 1972 dealing with the strategy of utilizing the Ontario Business Records Protection Act as a possible impediment to production of cartel–related documents housed in Canada. The preface of that memorandum provides:

The question of the authority of a United States court to require production of documents located in the office of a foreign subsidiary or affiliated company may well be of considerable importance in the event the United States Justice Department should become interested in investigating the activities of this organization. (DZ 1117a)

The memorandum analyzes the Ontario Act, its shortcomings as a discovery impediment because of the absence of criminal sanctions without prior Canadian government action, but O'Hara notes that "Presumably, the Canadian Government would object to any disclosure of the SERU documents..." (DX 1117a)

At the hearing, O'Hara admitted that he anticipated a Department of Justice antitrust investigation into the activities of the cartel when he prepared the memorandum. (TR 1567)

Anticipation or fear of civil antitrust litigation in the United States is expressed in GMCL memorandum prepared by Gregg, Ediger and Boyce in September 1973 in which they observed:

Any tampering with "the trade and com merce of the United States" whether it be solely concerned with uranium for U.S.

consumption or with a U.S company who is carrying on foreign operations, invites the hot breath of the Sherman Act. U.S. Case law abundantly proves that the arm is long and that treble damage litigants are often successful, both at home and abroad. GMCL, because of its parent corporation, is probably the most vulnerable to an antitrust action filed in the U.S., and likely would be the first target that a U.S. litigant would go after, whether or not GMCL had any dealings with that litigant or not. (DX 2756a, at B–17–18)

The evidence clearly supports a finding that Gulf followed a deliberate policy of storing cartel documents in Canada with the expectation that they would be unavailable for discovery in anticipated litigation in the United States. For this conduct to amount to "courting legal impediments" to production under *Societe, supra,* it is not required that the actual litigation in which the documents ate ultimately ordered produced must be either pending or specifically contemplated at the time the housing policy was initiated and followed. *United Nuclear Corporation v. General Atomic,* 629 P.2d 231, 308–309 (N.M.1980) (DX 5145).

Gulf's Failure to Produce the Cartel Documents in Other Litigation Prior to the Passage of the Security Regulations

Gulf's anticipation of litigation became a reality in late 1975 when it learned of a Department of Justice investigation into activities of the cartel and when the UNC case was filed in New Mexico. (*United Nuclear Corporation v. GAC*) (DX 5145) Discovery requests in the UNC case requiring GAC to produce documents including the Canadian cartel documents were issued in 1976 several months prior to the passage of the Security Regulations. GAC produced its business records in the summer of 1976 but did not produce the cartel documents. After September 23, 1976, GAC relied on the Regulations as an impediment to production. The trial judge ultimately imposed sanctions of default judgment against GAC in 1977 finding that GAC had acted in bad faith and had deliberately housed cartel documents in Can-

ada in an attempt to court legal impediments to their production.

On appeal, the New Mexico Supreme Court affirmed the decision stating:

Had GAC been more assiduous in its responsibility in discovery prior to September 23, 1976, Canadian cartel discovery could have been made without any serious foreign law entanglements. *Accord State of Ohio v. Crofters, Inc.,* [D.C.] *supra,* 75 F.R.D. [12] at 23. By failing to provide cartel information prior to the passage of the Canadian Uranium Information Security Regulations, and then relying on these Regulations as an excuse for nonproduction, GAC is "in the position of having slain [its] parents and then pleading for mercy on the ground that [it] is an orphan." *Life Music, Inc. v. Broadcast Music, Inc.,* [D.C.] *supra,* 41 F.R.D. [16] at 26, *Accord Shepard v. General Motors Corporation,* 42 F.R.D. 425, 427 (D.N.H.1967). (DX 5145, 629 P.2d at 293).

In addition to the *UNC* case, another uranium action entitled *GAC v. Ranchers Exploration & Development Corp., et al.* (New Mexico state court) was pending in early 1976 in which discovery requests sought production and identification of the Canadian documents. Interrogatories and document requests were served to GAC in May 1976 by Ranchers. (DX 5024, DX 5025). GAC's counsel then negotiated with Ranchers' counsel (Marshall Martin) to limit the scope of the discovery requests. In those negotiations, Gulf's counsel informed Ranchers' counsel that the Ontario Business Records Protection Act barred production of Canadian documents. As a result of that representation, counsel entered into a stipulated order (DX 5026) excluding Gulf's Canadian documents from discovery. Later, Ranchers' counsel learned that GAC's position regarding the Ontario Act was not accurate, and described his reaction as, "I thought I was had." (TR 636) (Deposition of Marshall Martin, DX 5143).

It is not the court's intention to speculate whether the Canadian documents should have been produced in the Ranchers' litigation. Indeed, no order to that effect was ever entered. The relevancy of the *Ranchers'* case to our proceedings is simply that (1) there was litigation pending (in addition to the *UNC* case) before the Security Regulations were passed in which Canadian uranium documents were sought and (2) Gulf again relied on the Ontario Act as a discovery impediment which Frank O'Hara analyzed in his 1972 memorandum.

Contemporaneous with the pendency of the *UNC* and *Ranchers* cases, Gulf became involved with a grand jury investigation. In June of 1975 Gulf learned of a Justice Department investigation into the cartel. (DX 4218a) (DX 4262a). On November 11, 1975, Gulf attorney Frank O'Hara met with a Justice Department attorney who told him that the Department suspected that "the increases in uranium prices are tied to the alleged meetings" of the cartel members and that "there is a possible CID in the air" (DX 4132). Gulf reacted to this warning by attempting to marshal evidence to support antitrust defenses of sovereign compulsion and act of state. On December 4, 1975 at Roger Allen's request, a GMCL employee in Toronto gathered Canadian government public statements relating to the uranium cartel. This collection of public statements was sent to O'Hara in Pittsburgh and Allen in Denver. (TR 2368–71, DX 1219) (TR 1759–1762)

On June 16, 1976, Gulf was served with a Grand Jury subpoena calling for production of cartel documents "wherever located." (DX 2915) Other Canadian cartel members were also served (DX 2903a). Gulf retained the law firm of Howry and Simon in Washington to represent it in connection with the Grand Jury subpoena. On June 23, 1976 attorney Allen sent a copy of the Ontario Business Records Protection Act to Jack Howry and O'Hara (DX 5155). O'Hara sent a copy of his 1972 memorandum dealing with the Ontario Act to Howry & Simon in preparation for a meeting to be held on July 1, 1976 in Washington.

On June 30, 1976, GMCL president, Andrew Janisch of Toronto called S.A. Zagnoli, president of Gulf Minerals in Denver and reported as follows:

Mr. Janisch has been advised by telephone by the Energy, Mines & Resources people that they are convening a meeting of Canadian producers on July 13 in Ottawa. Those invited are those who have received a subpoena from the Grand Jury. *He has been told (or has concluded) that the Canadian government may decide that Canadian producers will be prohibited from passing on any information concerning Canadian uranium operations and the functions of their control over the uranium industry.* (DX 2903a, emphasis supplied)

The next morning, Gulf Minerals attorney Allen and O'Hara met with Howry & Simon attorneys in Washington. They discussed the grand jury subpoena, and the Ontario Act as a possible impediment to production of documents from Canada (TR 1862–63; TR 1871–2; TR 1885). At the meeting, Allen conveyed the news from Zagnoli that the Canadian government may decide to prohibit the Canadian producers from disclosing any information in response to the subpoena concerning the uranium industry. (TR 1877) (DX 2930a) In July 1976, three news articles appeared in Toronto newspapers reporting the U.S. Justice Department's investigation into the uranium cartel and the resistance by Canadian government officials to the subpoena. (DX 4264, DX 4265, DX 4266).

A meeting of the Canadian government officials and Canadian uranium producers took place on July 13, 1976 (DX 2903a), but it is not known whether GMCL or Gulf personnel attended. On the same day five Gulf attorneys (O'Hara, Allen, Groves, Dotson, and Gidel) met in Pittsburgh to discuss the grand jury subpoena (DX 5154). Two weeks later, Gulf in-house lawyers O'Hara, Allen, Groves and Dotson met with Howry & Simon lawyers to discuss the "grand jury uranium investigation" (DX 2923a). The agenda of that meeting reflects that the lawyers discussed:

GMCL files in Toronto, status of review . . . Notice to Canadian Government before any Toronto files moved out of Canada (DX 5156).

Gulf personnel did not move files out of

Canada or duplicate the cartel–related documents for dissemination to the United States in preparation for compliance with the grand jury subpoena. However, they did prepare an inventory of the Canadian documents. In early July, Allen sent instructions to GMCL with a copy of the subpoena.

GMCL retained a Toronto law firm to conduct an inventory of its cartel documents. In August, Gulf attorneys Dotson and Gidel visited Toronto to assist in the project. They were instructed "not to bring back any documents." The Gulf attorneys returned from Toronto with inventory worksheets identifying 3,400 cartel documents (DX 2899) along with notes of Dotson (Dotson depo. DX 5083). O'Hara was told of the worksheets (DX 2899) and Dotson notes (DX 2898), but these items were never produced to the Grand Jury or to any litigant until June 1980, when they were produced in the Westinghouse case. (See, *In re Uranium Litigation, supra.*)

On September 9, 1976, a Howry & Simon lawyer (Melvin Halpern) drafted a memorandum of law dealing with the weakness of the Ontario Act as a discovery impediment. He pointed out that the Ontario Act was not self–enforcing and did not subject Gulf to criminal sanctions unless the Attorney General of Canada took action in a provincial court. He advised Gulf that one alternative would be to seek authority from the Canadian government for removal of documents thereby alerting them of the need for government action to make the Ontario Act an effective impediment (DX 5157). The Halpern memorandum of September 7th was sent to O'Hara the following week. Two days before the Halpern memo, Howry & Simon began producing Gulf documents to the Justice Department (DX 2945). No Canadian documents nor the Dotson worksheets were included in the production.

On September 23, 1976, the Uranium Information Security Regulations were promulgated by Canada (G–1). Four days later, a Howry & Simon attorney wrote to the Justice Department:

We would like to meet with you this week at your convenience to discuss the matter

of Canadian documents located in the offices of Gulf Minerals Canada, Ltd., in Toronto, Ontario . . .

bcc: Frank O'Hara
Roger Allen
Thomas Groves (DX 2946)

There is no direct evidence of collusion between Gulf and Canadian governmental officials in the months preceding the Security Regulations. It is not known whether Gulf contributed to the passage of the Security Regulations. It appears there was enough governmental self–interest manifested by the Canadian officials to promulgate the Regulations regardless of Gulf's interest. However, it is clear that since 1972, Gulf was prepared to rely on the Ontario Act as an impediment to production of cartel–related documents in Canada. The impediment could be realized if Canada took necessary court action to trigger its enforceability as discussed in the O'Hara memorandum of 1971 and the Halpern memorandum of 1976.

The New Mexico Supreme Court in *UNC v. GAC, supra,* held that the housing of documents in Canada with the expectation that the Ontario Act would serve as the impediment amounted to "courting legal impediments" to production.

Although the Uranium Information Security Regulations were not in effect during the period the cartel was apparently in existence, the Ontario Business Records Protection Act was in effect. Although that Act is not a significant impediment to discovery, it was relied on by GAC in the court below as a total bar to the discovery of cartel records. If documents were housed in Canada with the expectation that the Ontario Act would be applicable, it is largely immaterial that the expectation was later realized in the form of a different secrecy law. When a party places documents outside this country with the expectation that production of those documents will be frustrated in litigation here, the strong policy in favor of broad discovery dictates that the party bear the consequences of the dilemma created by the realization of its expectations.

* * * * *

We hold . . . that there is substantial evidence to support the court's findings that Gulf followed a deliberate policy of storing cartel documents in Canada, and that this policy amounted to courting legal impediments to their production. Under *Societe*, these findings alone may be the basis for the imposition of such a discovery sanction as a default judgment. *United Nuclear Corp. v. GAC, 629 P.2d 231, 308–309 (N.M.1980)(DX 5145)*

Prior to September 23, 1976, Gulf had the ability to produce the Canadian documents without subjecting itself or its personnel to criminal sanctions. Had Gulf complied with the Grand Jury subpoena, or at least removed copies of the documents to the United States in preparation for a good faith compliance, the withheld documents would be available for trial in this litigation. Instead, Gulf relied on the Ontario Act hoping Canada would perfect the legal impediment.

Destruction or Disappearance of Cartel Documents in the U.S.

In addition to charging that Roger Allen shipped cartel–related documents to Canada in 1972 to make them unavailable in anticipated litigation (*supra*, p. 297), Exxon further claims that Gulf destroyed or altered cartel documents which had entered the United States.

In early December 1975, William Dix, a marketing research analyst employed by GAC, had a conversation with Tom Groves, a GAC in–house attorney, who was later transferred to Gulf's headquarters in Pittsburgh. According to a memorandum later written by Dix, Groves requested him to:

> Peruse our files to see if there was any information on meetings Gulf Canada, Ltd. (GCL) may have held with other uranium products [sic] in Canada. He [Groves] indicated the Justice Department was looking at possible antitrust violations. At that time he also suggested I throw away any old files pertaining to GCL (Dix memo to file, DX 4164).

In January 1976, Dix found a "book, perhaps a half inch thick, filled with various memorandum [sic] of meetings" (Dix depo, DX 5086 at 37–38). The book dealt in part with a GMCL meeting in Ottawa and included memos written by Gulf personnel "about a meeting of Canadian uranium producers", which "appeared under a tab 'Paris Meeting'" (DX 4164). On February 12, 1976, Dix met with Groves at GA in San Diego and handed the book to Groves (DX 5086 at 40, 49–50). The exchange is described in Dix's memorandum as follows:

> Tom read the book. When he finished we had the following conversation as close as I can reconstruct it.
>
> Tom: I'll take this book and probably destroy it.
>
> Bill: If anyone asks me about it, I'll tell them I gave it to you.
>
> Tom: No, that won't be necessary. Just say you never saw it.
>
> Bill: No, I won't do that. I will always tell the truth.
>
> Tom took the book with him when he left.
>
> (Dix memo, DX 4164)

It is unknown what Groves did with the book. Gulf has not been able to locate a book meeting Dix's description, and Exxon asserts that the GAC cartel book has never been produced by Gulf.

Dix testified at the sanctions hearing that he prepared the memo (DX 4164) because he was disturbed by the conversation with Groves (TR 418). The memo was prepared on February 25, 1976 on the advice of a fellow employee. Although Dix's recollection has dimmed, he recalls being told by Groves that he (Dix) "should forget that I saw the documents" (TR 418–19). Groves denies destroying any documents. He denies the conversations with Dix that are memorialized in the Dix memo. (Groves video tape depo, G–635 at 118–122) However, Dix's monthly diaries corroborate the events described in his memo. His diaries for November and December of 1975 show that he met or talked with Groves on November 18, December 4 and 12, 19756 (TR 514–19). The entries for December 12 include "files for Groves". (DX 5090) Dix testified that this entry relates to the files Groves asked him to search regarding the Justice Department investigation (TR 519–20). The diary also contains entries showing that Dix "read files for Canadian info" and "call to Groves re above" (TR 520). The February 1976 diary contains an entry for February 12 as follows: "Give GCL book on U meeting Ottawa book to Groves." (DX 5092) (TR 525–26)

The credible evidence supports a finding that the GAC cartel book has been destroyed or concealed and that such action was motivated by the Justice Department investigation into the activities of the cartel. It is also significant that interrogatories requiring identification of cartel–related documents in GAC's files had been served on GAC in December 1975 in *United Nuclear v. GAC* pending in New Mexico state court. (DX 5145 at 93–96 & 111–12).

Exxon has alleged other instances of destruction or disappearance of documents in Gulf's domestic files (Exxon Post Hearing Brief, pp. 52–66) and one instance of an "altered" document (DX 1539). However, the evidence fails to establish that these instances were motivated by pending or anticipated litigation or done in bad faith.

Whether the destruction of the GAC "cartel book" is sufficient basis in and of itself for the imposition of serious sanctions, such as those sought by Exxon, is unclear. Although this lawsuit had not been filed and may not have been specifically anticipated at the time of the destruction, it is likely that the destruction was in bad faith to preclude discovery in other similar litigation pending. "Although, a potential litigant is under no obligation to preserve every document in its possession, whatever its degree of relevance, prior to the commencement of a lawsuit, . . . some duty must be imposed in circumstances such as these lest the fact–finding process in our

courts be reduced to a mockery." *Bowman Instrument Corp. v. Texas Instruments, Inc.*, 25 F.R.Serv.2d (N.D.Ind.1977). See also *Alliance to End Repression v. Rochford*, 75 F.R.D. 438 (N.D.Ill.1976).

The destruction or disappearance of the GAC cartel book when combined with Gulf's housing of documents in Canada constitutes a sufficient basis of fault under *Societe Internationale v. Rogers, supra*, to conclude that harsh sanctions against Gulf are not precluded.

V. The Withheld Documents Are Crucial to a Fair Trial

In determining what sanctions are appropriate, the needs of the discovering party must be evaluated as well as the fault of the non–producing party. Specifically, we must consider how the absence of the withheld documents impairs Exxon's ability to establish its claims or defenses. *Wilson v. Volkswagen of America, Inc.*, 561 F.2d 494, 505 (4th Cir. 1977). Gulf contends that the missing documents are not essential and are merely cumulative of the available cartel evidence. It argues that the available evidence, consisting of documents produced by Gulf from its U.S. files and the testimony of Gulf personnel who attended cartel meetings, provides a wealth of information on the cartel and GMCL's activities in connection therewith. It points to the Johannesburg Rules (G–51), the Rules for Orderly Marketing (DX 292b) and other documents as well as the testimony of Gregg, Allen and O'Hara in support of its contention.

The attorney inventory worksheets (DX 2899) and the Dotson notes (DX 2898) prepared in Canada and brought to Gulf's headquarters in the United States by Gulf attorneys Gidel and Dotson in August of 1976 are somewhat helpful in describing the nature of the withheld documents. The missing documents include minutes of cartel meetings, communications between the Canadian government and GMCL, and various copies of telexes from Andre Petit, the Cartel Secretariat in Paris, to Runnalls of the Canadian Department of Energy, Mines and Resources relating to bids and allocation of uranium sales. Some of these documents may be crucial to the outcome of this litigation. For example, an entry appearing on page 2 of the inventory shows that the London cartel meeting of October 6, 1973, members agreed to fix prices in the U.S. market: "agreement that no bids to U.S. markets would be made below club prices" (DX 2899 at 2). It would appear that a complete set of the London minutes is crucial to disprove Gulf's contention that cartel arrangement excluded the U.S. market. Gulf argues that Dotson may have mischaracterized the London document she was reviewing and inaccurately reported on its contents. Gulf points to available evidence to the contrary regarding the cartel and the U.S. market. Exxon replies by pointing to an O'Hara file memo of October 15, 1973 (DX 264) dealing with a telephone call about the London meeting which appears to be consistent with Dotson's description in the worksheets. This debate underscores the need for all the cartel–related documents in the search for truth.

The available evidence indicates that there were at least forty cartel meetings of international uranium producers between 1972 and 1975. (DX 5051a). Exxon has partial minutes for eleven of these meetings. The last meeting for which Gulf produced minutes from its domestic files was the Ottawa meeting of September 5, 1972 attended by Ediger, Gregg of GMCL and Zagnoli of Gulf Minerals. (DX 96b). Exxon does have parties minutes for two meetings in 1973 (London, October 5–9, 1973 and Las Palmas, November 21–23, 1973) which cannot be authenticated and may be inadmissible in evidence without stipulations. These documents (DX 474 and DX 273) were apparently stolen by an environmental group known as "Friends of the Earth" from an Australian uranium producer, Mary Kathleen Uranium Ltd., a cartel member. The withheld cartel minutes are particularly critical because it appears from the available evidence that the scope of the activities of the cartel may have changed after Johannesburg in 1972. The broadening of cartel activities after Johannesburg impacts on Gulf's defenses of sovereign compulsion and act of state. Did the cartel uranium producers exceed the involvement

or requirements of the Canadian government? It is impossible to determine the entire range of cartel activities without the withheld minutes and other documents listed in the worksheets. A comparison of the worksheets and Dotson notes with Gulf's "Chronological Index and Summary of Cartel–Related Documents Produced from Files of the Gulf Oil Corporation" (DX 2976a) shows that the withheld cartel documents are not merely cumulative of the available evidence as Gulf speculates.

The testimony of Gulf witnesses relying on their memories is no substitute for the withheld documentary evidence. Memories have faded and, in some cases, have become selective. Mr. Gregg cannot recall what is written in the withheld documents, nor can he remember what was said at the various cartel meetings from 1972–1975 without referring to the documents. The testimony of Gregg did disclose that there was an "Exxon file" at GMCL, but he cannot recall its contents (TR 1136). He admitted that at the Paris cartel meeting in April 1973, the subject of a proposed uranium purchase by Exxon from Nufcor (a South African uranium producer and cartel member) was discussed, but he could not remember anything further (TR 969). Gregg also recalls seeing some Canadian minutes in GMCL's files on the Las Palmas meeting in November 1973, where the cartelists discussed negotiations with uranium middlemen (TR 967–969).

Negotiations With Middlemen

It was agreed that nobody would enter into serious discussions with Westinghouse before coming back to the club. Denison and Nufcor have been approached by Exxon [ENC] (DX 273).

Since only a partial set of the Las Palmas minutes are available from "Friends of the Earth," it is unknown what steps, if any, were taken regarding Exxon and Westinghouse in 1973.

The withheld documents have previously been determined to be relevant and crucial to the issues raised by the pleadings. In a related case, *Uranium Antitrust Litigation*, MDL 342 (N.D. 342 (N.D.Ill.), Judge Marshall described the nature of cartel–related Canadian documents as follows:

> The second consideration is whether the requested documents are crucial to the determination of a key issue in the litigation. Plaintiffs' showing on this factor is simply overwhelming. All of the discovery requests now at issue are directly relevant to a number of fundamental issues in the complaint, answers, affirmative defenses and counterclaims in this litigation. Plaintiffs seek vital information relating to, among other things, the time period when the alleged conspiracy of uranium producers was carrying out its activities, defendants' alleged efforts to conceal their conspiracy, the impact of that alleged conspiracy on United States interstate and foreign commerce, the defendants' defenses of sovereign compulsion, and information on uranium sales and market conditions. Plaintiffs have submitted voluminous exhibits which give a sketchy picture strongly supporting their allegations in these areas but also suggesting that there are larger gaps in defendants' document production.

> * * * * *

> The inevitable inference is that the withheld information is likely to be the heart and soul of plaintiffs' case. 480 F.Supp.1154–5.

From a detailed examination of the available evidence, along with the worksheet descriptions of the withheld documents, it is clear that Gulf's failure to comply with the production orders has deprived and prejudiced Exxon of a full and fair opportunity to cross–examine Gulf's witnesses, to defend against GAC's Complaint, to present its claims pleaded in the Counterclaim, and to rebut Gulf's defenses to its antitrust claims.

VI. Summary of Findings

After considering the entire record of evidence and assessing the credibility of the witnesses, the court makes the following findings:

1. Gulf has sole beneficial ownership and control over the GAC–ENC uranium contract and of counterclaim defendants' other uranium business interests involved in this litigation.

2. Gulf has failed to fully comply with the production orders of November 16, 1979 and January 14, 1980.

3. Gulf is withholding approximately 14,000 documents in the possession, custody, and control of its wholly–owned subsidiary, Gulf Minerals Canada Limited (GMCL) on the grounds that production would violate Canadian penal law.

4. Production of the documents withheld at GMCL would violate the Canadian Uranium Information Security Regulations. Violation of the Regulations is punishable by imprisonment up to five years and a fine not exceeding $10,000.

5. During this lawsuit, Gulf has attempted to negotiate with the Canadian government for relaxation or waiver of the Security Regulations and has pursued the matter in Canadian courts. Gulf has taken every reasonable effort available to overcome the prohibitions of the Security Regulations.

6. Gulf's conduct prior to the passage of the Security Regulations is relevant to determine whether its failure to comply with the discovery orders is attributable to "willfulness, bad faith, or any fault" of Gulf.

7. Gulf's present inability to comply with the production orders was fostered by its own conduct and is attributable to a deliberate strategy of concealment.

8. Gulf housed cartel documents in Canada with the expectation that they would be unavailable for discovery in anticipated antitrust litigation in the United States.

9. Gulf destroyed or shipped cartel–related documents to Canada to make them unavailable for discovery in anticipated antitrust litigation.

10. Gulf's action of storing cartel documents in Canada amounts to a deliberate courting of the legal impediment to production of the documents.

11. Prior to promulgation of the Security Regulations, Gulf used the Ontario Business Records Act as a legal impediment to production of the withheld documents with respect to discovery requests in other litigation. Prior to September 23, 1976, there was no effective legal impediment which would have justifiably prevented production of the Canadian cartel documents in response to discovery requests.

12. Gulf is at fault in creating the dilemma of its present inability to fully comply with the discovery orders.

13. The withheld documents are relevant and crucial to a fair trial. Failure to produce the documents has deprived and prejudiced Exxon of a full and fair opportunity to cross–examine Gulf's witnesses; to defend against GAC's complaint; to present its claims pleaded in its Counterclaim; and to rebut the defenses to its antitrust claims, particularly the affirmative defenses of Act of State and Sovereign Compulsion.

VII. Choice of Sanctions

Where a party "fails" to comply with a discovery order, the court "may make such orders in regard to the failure as are just." Rule 37(b), F.R.Civ.P. A wide spectrum of sanctions are provided for in Rule 37 ranging from an order awarding expenses and attorney's fees to the harsh sanctions of dismissal and default judgment. Other remedies include striking out portions of the pleadings, prohibiting the introduction of evidence on particular issues, and finding designated facts established adversely to the non–producing party.

The choice of sanctions must be carefully tailored to each case and must depend upon an evaluation of the nature or prejudice to the discovering party and the degree of fault of the non–producing party. *Wilson v. Volkswagen, supra*, 561 F.2d at 505. Imposition of the severe sanctions such as dismissal or default judgment require a finding of willfulness, bad faith, or fault, whereas the lesser sanctions may be predicated on an innocent failure to produce. *Societe Internationale v. Rogers, supra.*

Although the drastic sanctions sought by Exxon are not precluded here in view of the court's findings, their imposition should be reserved for extreme situations where lesser sanctions would be ineffective to cure the consequences of the discovery failure. See *Jones v. Louisiana State Bar Assoc.*, 602 F.2d 94,97 (5th Cir. 1979). This approach is sound because dismissal and default judgment, the sanctions of last resort, run counter to the strong public policy of deciding cases on their merits and affording litigants their fair day in court. *Wilson v. Volkswagen, supra* at 504; *Richman v. General Motors*, 437 F.2d 196, 199 (1st Cir. 1971).

Upon a review of the entire record, the court concludes that dismissal of GAC's complaint and default judgment on Exxon's counterclaim is not appropriate because the court is able to fashion other sanctions and remedies to effectively redress the prejudice caused to Exxon by the absence of the withheld documents.

Designated Facts Presumed

Although there are several cartel–related documents available to Exxon in presenting its claims and defenses, there is no doubt that Exxon's ability to prove the allegations in its counterclaim regarding the activities of the cartel has been seriously impaired by the absence of the withheld documents. Although a court is empowered by Rule 37(b)(2)(A) to order that designated facts relating to the missing evidence "be taken to be established" thereby foreclosing the non–producing party from proving otherwise, this court chooses to follow an approach taken in the case of *Alliance to End Repression v. Rochford*, 75 F.R.D. 433 (N.D.Ill.1976); namely, to deem designated facts presumed established subject to rebuttal by Gulf. In applying this sanction, we attempt to closely tailor the presumed facts to the withheld information to the extent possible.

Preclusion of Evidence

The withheld documents relate intimately to Gulf's affirmation defenses of the act of state doctrine and sovereign compulsion. The available evidence on the issues raised by these affirmative defenses is conflicting and ambiguous. Gulf's early strategy when it participated in the cartel in 1972 was to establish "sovereign compulsion" as the "fountainhead" of its antitrust defense (See DX 5145 at page 55). It assembled a war chest of documentary evidence in support of its sovereign compulsion defense while Exxon's best rebuttal evidence is likely secured in Canada among the 14,000 withheld documents.

It is not possible to fairly litigate the issues raised by the act of state and sovereign compulsion defenses without the held cartel–related documents. A preclusion order prohibiting Gulf from supporting these affirmative defenses is commensurate with the nature of the prejudice to Exxon and appropriate in these circumstances. "[I]t is fundamental that a party that does not provide discovery cannot profit from its own failure. Thus Rule 37(b)(2)(C) recognizes that parties failing to comply with discovery requests may be estopped from 'support[ing] or oppos[ing] designated claims or defenses.'" *Dellums v. Powell*, 566 F.2d, 235 (D.C.Cir.1977). Preclusionary orders ensure that a party will not be able to profit from its own failure to comply. *Cine Forty–Second St. Theatre v. Allied Artists*, 602 F.2d 1062, 1066 (2nd Cir. 1979).

Other Sanctions

An important factor in declining to impose harsher sanctions is the consideration that Exxon has some evidence available to utilize in the presentation of its claims. Most of the available evidence has been produced by Gulf from its U.S. offices and will be received in evidence without objection.

In addition, Exxon has certain cartel–related documents which were obtained from "Friends of the Earth" which may not be *actually* available to Exxon because of evidentiary problems. An adequate showing of authenticity and other foundational require-

ments to overcome hearsay objections may not be possible. Gulf has not stipulated to admissibility and has preserved objections for trial. A particularly relevant F.O.E. documents is the partial set of minutes of the Las Palmas meeting which bears on the critical issue of whether the cartel applied its minimum prices to the U.S. uranium market. (DX 273). This and other "Friends of the Earth" documents must be made *effectively* available to Exxon by deeming them admissible in evidence as a partial remedy to overcome the prejudice caused by the absence of the withheld Canadian documents.

In addition to the foregoing sanctions, reasonable expenses and attorneys fees in connection with the instant motion shall be recoverable by Exxon pursuant to Rule 37(b)(2)(E), F.R.Civ.P.

VIII. Conclusion

Exxon's Motion for Dismissal of the Complaints and the Granting of a Default Judgment on Exxon's Counterclaim should be denied. However, sanctions pursuant to Rule 37(b), Federal Rules of Civil Procedures, are imposed against the counterclaim defendants as follows:

1. The following allegations in the Third Amended Counterclaims of Exxon shall be presumed true subject to rebuttal by counterclaim defendants: Count One, Paragraph 13(e)(f)(g)(h) and Paragraph 14 and Paragraph 15; Count Three, the portion of Paragraph 25(a) beginning on page 12 at line 2 through line 13. The counterclaim defendants shall have the burden to prove the non–existence of the above allegations;

2. Counterclaim defendants shall be precluded from presenting evidence at trial in support of the allegations contained in the 14th, 15th and 16th affirmative defenses (Paragraphs 63, 64 and 65) contained in the Answer of Gulf Oil Corporation to the Third Amended Counterclaims and Complaint. (Act of state and sovereign compulsion defenses).

3. The documents described as "Friends of the Earth" documents offered by Exxon in

support of its claims and defenses shall be received in evidence at trial. Lack of evidence of authenticity or foundation shall be considered only as affecting the weight of the evidence and shall not be a bar to the admissibility of said documents;

4. Costs and attorneys fees in connection with the instant motion are awarded to Exxon in an amount to be determined.

SO ORDERED.

[5] The Security Regulations provide, in relevant part: "No person who has in his possession or under his control any note, document or other written or printed material in any way related to conversations, discussions or meetings that took place between January 1, 1972 and December 31, 1975 involving that person or any government, crown corporation, agency or other organizations in respect of the production, import, export, transportation, refining, possession, ownership, use or sale of uranium or its derivatives or compounds, shall, (a) release any such note, document, or disclose or communicate the contents thereof to any person, (b) fail to guard against or take reasonable care to prevent the unauthorized release of any such note, document or material or disclosure or communication of the contents thereof."

James R. GEORGES and Karen Georges, etc., et al. v. INSURANCE TECHNICIANS, INC., a Florida Corporation

488 So.2d 1185

District Court of Appeal of Florida, Fourth District
April 18, 1984

Insurance agency filed motion for sanctions against insureds who had failed to comply with a request for production of documents in action brought by agency against the insureds for unpaid insurance premiums on policies procured for the insureds. The Circuit Court, Broward County, John G. Ferris, J., rendered an order striking the insureds' pleadings and entered a default judgment against them, and insureds filed motion for relief from the order and default judgment. Their motion was denied, and the insureds appealed. The District Court of Appeal, Downey, J., held that entry of default judgment was proper, based on trial court's findings that the insureds had not complied with two court orders for production of documents, had made misrepresentations to the court, had filed evasive and incomplete pleadings, and generally had failed to act in good faith.

Affirmed.

* * * * *

Appellee, Insured Technicians, Inc., sued appellants to recover the balance due from appellants for unpaid insurance premiums on insurance policies that appellee had procured for appellants. During the course of the litigation appellee filed a request for production of documents. On the last day of the time for production, appellants filed a motion for a ninety day extension within which to comply. After a hearing on said motion, the trial court granted appellants an additional thirty days to produce. The new time for production came and went without any production or additional extension of time. Appellees then filed a motion for sanctions, which was heard on February 24, 1983. The trial court gave appellants ten additional days to produce the subject material. When production was not timely forthcoming a new motion for sanctions was filed. At the hearing on said motion on March 16, 1988, counsel for appellee advised the court that appellants' counsel would not attend due to a conflict but that counsel objected to imposition of any sanctions. On March 18, 1983, the trial court entered an order in which it found that appellants had not complied with two court orders for production; that appellants had made misrepresentations to the court; and some pleadings were evasive and incomplete and generally there was an absence of good faith on the part of the appellants. In fact, the court found that "Defendants have embarked upon and traveled down a path of intentional delay and abuse of the system on clear violation of the Orders of this Court validly entered on December 21, 1982 and February 24, 1983."

We have seriously considered all of appellants' contentions relative to the March 16, 1983, hearing which they did not attend and find little support in the record for them. On the other hand, the carefully prepared order of the trial court granting sanctions and entering a default against appellants makes findings of fact that adequately support the action taken.

Accordingly, appellants have failed to demonstrate reversible error which requires that we affirm the order appealed from.

AFFIRMED.

In the Matter of GRACE LINE, INC. as Owner of the STEAMSHIP SANTA LEONOR. For Exoneration From or Limitation of Liability

397 F.Supp. 1258

United State District Court, S.D. New York
July 27, 1973

Grace Line Inc., as owner of the Steamship SANTA LEONOR filed on April 25, 1968, a petition for exoneration from or limitation of liability. The petition relates to the stranding and total loss of the SANTA LEONOR on March 31, 1968 in the Patagonian Channels, an inland waterway on the coast of Chile, north of the Straits of Magellan. The SANTA LEONOR was on a voyage from Rio de Janeiro to San Francisco with intermediate calls at various ports. Her last port of call prior to the accident was Buenos Aires, and her next stop was scheduled to be Valparaiso, Chile.

The petition alleges that at the time of the stranding the SANTA LEONOR had on board 50 crew members and 7 passengers, all of whom were rescued. The SANTA LEONOR had a quantity of general cargo on board. The ship and the cargo are a total loss.

* * * * *

The Log and Course Recorder

Cargo claimants have requested that a strong inference be drawn against Grace Line because of the unavailability or disappearance of the deck log book and course recorder.

The evidence from the vessel personnel is that they abandoned the ship an hour or so after the accident without recovering or taking with them the deck log, the course recorder tape or other navigational records which were on the bridge.

Grace Line hired a salvage expert, Martignoni, to go aboard the vessel. He arrived at the scene on April 7, 1968. However, he had not been instructed to search for navigational records and did not do so. It was subsequent to this that Grace Line's trial counsel, Messrs. Kirlin, Campbell and Keating, were brought into the case. Apparently at their instance search was made for the missing navigational records. This was done by Martignoni and divers in early May 1968.

The course recorder (an instrument designed to make a continuous record of the gyrocompass headings of a vessel) was found by Martignoni's men. However, the portion of the tape covering the period of at least 48 hours surrounding and including the time of the accident had been ripped out. This was clearly the intentional act of someone.

With regard to the deck log and other navigational records, search was made in the wheelhouse and nearby spaces. Parts of these areas were submerged and divers attempted to locate the records in the water. Some papers were recovered, but nothing of any use. The deck log was not found.

I cannot draw an inference against Grace Line unless I have reasonable ground to believe that Grace Line was responsible for the disappearance of the records. As to the course recorder tape (and the other records, to the extent they were stolen), there is simply no way to tell whether these items were removed by Grace Line, by cohorts of Pilot Ruiz, or by someone else.

Under these circumstance, I decline to draw any adverse inference against Grace Line from the disappearance of the records.

* * * * *

GT & MC, INC. f/k/a GRAVER TANK AND MANUFACTURING COMPANY, INC., A SUBSIDIARY TO AEROJET–GENERAL CORPORATION, Appellant v. TEXAS CITY REFINING, INC. Appellee

822 S.W.2d 252

Court of Appeals of Texas, First District, Houston
December 19, 1991

The issue in this case is whether a trial court may award consequential damages arising from breach of an express warranty for design requirements, when the contract in question limits the aggrieved party's damages to repair or replacement only for workmanship and materials defects. We hold that the trial court correctly interpreted and enforced the parties' agreement and, therefore, affirm.

This is an appeal from a lawsuit for damages arising out of the failure of an oil tank designed, manufactured, and installed by appellant, GT & MC, Inc. at the Texas City, Texas, facility of Appellee, Texas City Refining, Inc. ("TCR"). The tank, designated Tank 089, is 340 feet in diameter and 48 feet high, with a capacity of 750,000 barrels of oil. The critical feature of the tank, for purposes of this appeal, is the roof, a patented design called an "Everfloat" roof, designed to float on the surface of the oil in the tank. Floatation is provided by a circular segmented ring pontoon that forms the circumferential outer edge of the roof and by multiple pontoons of various sizes spread over the remaining area of the roof. When oil is added, the roof rises, and as oil is withdrawn, the roof lowers.

The cause of action was based on breach of warranty. Appellant expressly warranted the tank and roof to withstand a wind velocity of 125 miles per hour, and to further withstand 10 inches of rainfall in a 24 hour period, even when the roof drains were blocked.

On August 17 and 18, 1983, Hurricane Alicia struck the Texas coast. Testimony at trial established that winds during the storm did not exceed 125 miles per hour at the TCR facility and that the rainfall did not exceed the 10 inch per 24 hours period design limit. Nevertheless, during the hurricane, the Everfloat roof sank, resulting in a loss of approximately 38,754 barrels of crude oil. TCR established that it incurred expenses in repairing the tank and roof, renting substitute tank space during the repair period, and transferring the oil from Tank 089 to substitute tanks.

* * * * *

In point of error three, appellant complains that the trial court erred and abused its discretion in overruling defendant's objections and admitting TCR's damage evidence. Appellant contends that TCR's evidence was limited to hearsay documents improperly admitted over objections of appellant's counsel.

To obtain reversal of a judgment based on error in the admission or exclusion of evidence, an appellant must show that the trial court's ruling was in error and that the error was calculated to cause and probably did cause rendition of an improper judgment. *Harrison v. Texas Employers Ins. Ass'n, 747 S.W.2d 494, 498* (Tex. App.–Beaumont 1988, writ denied); *Texaco Inc. v. Pennzoil Co., 729 S.W.2d 768, 837* (Tex. App.–Houston [1st Dist.] 1987, writ ref'd n.r.e.),cert. denied, *485 U.S. 994 (1988).* Reversible error does not usually occur in connection with rulings on questions of evidence unless the appellant can demonstrate that the whole case turns on the particular evidence that was admitted or excluded. *Texaco, Inc., 729 S.W.2d at 837.*

Appellant maintains that TCR failed to effect strict compliance with rule 803(6) of the Texas Rules of Civil Evidence. This rule pertains to admission of business records and provides:

A memorandum, report, record, or data compilation, in any form, of acts, events, conditions, opinions, or diagnoses, made at or near the time by, or from a person with knowledge, if kept in the course of a regularly conducted business activity, and if it was the regular practice of that business activity to make the memorandum, report, record, or data compilation, all as shown by the testimony of the custodian or other qualified witness, or by affidavit that complies with Rule 902(10), unless the source of information or the method or circumstances of preparation indicate lack of trustworthiness . . ..

TEX. R. CIV. EVID. 803(6). Appellant points to invoices that TCR offered to prove up damages that were not "made" by TCR employees. The invoices were presented to TCR requesting payment for services rendered and facilities leased. Appellant notes that the records custodian of TCR should not have been allowed to testify about records sent by another entity and that TCR failed to establish that the invoices became TCR's business records.

Though hearsay evidence is not generally admissible, records of regularly conducted activities are an exception to the general rule. The predicate for admissibility under the business records exception is established if the party offering the evidence demonstrates that the records were created by or from information transmitted by a person with knowledge, at or near the time of the event. *Clark v. Walker–Kurth Lumber Co., 689 S.W.2d 275, 281* (Tex. App. – Houston [1st Dist.] 1985, writ ref'd n.r.e.). The items appellant claims are inadmissible are plaintiffs exhibits 103 through 109.

These exhibits include invoices that establish the cost of moving the oil that was kept in Tank 089 before Hurricane Alicia, invoices covering inspection services Marintech, Inc. provided to TCR during the process of moving oil from Tank 089 to other storage facilities, invoices regarding rental of substitute storage tank space for the oil that was kept in Tank 089, a TCR record indicating that an invoice in exhibit 105A was approved and paid, a TCR document that values the inventory in Tank 089 at the time of the tank failure, a computer–generated calculation of the value of the crude oil in Tank 089 for the month of the

tank failure, and a computer–generated worksheet containing information about various crudes contained in Tank 089. Joseph Stratman, custodian of records for TCR, testified that the invoices and documents were maintained by TCR in the regular and normal course of its business. Stratman testified, based on personal knowledge, about who generated the documents and about the manner in which these records were kept.

Appellant would urge this Court to adopt an interpretation of rule 803(6) that the term "made" means "authored by." We decline to do so. Though the documents in question were initially authored by outside vendors, employees of TCR placed numerous markings on the invoices after receipt by TCR. These markings indicated the date of receipt, identity of the recipient, whether the invoices were approved for payment, who approved the invoices for payment, and other information about how the invoices were processed. Thus, the invoices became TCR's primary record of information about the underlying transaction. Further, Stratman testified about the procedure by which the invoices became TCR's business records. The documents were stamped when received, initialed by a TCR employee, stamped as approved for payment, initialed again, and kept in the ordinary course of TCR's business. Stratman also testified that he had personal knowledge of the manner in which the records were kept, as contemplated by rule 803(6). *Seaside Indus., Inc. v. Cooper, 766 S.W.2d 566, 571* (Tex. App. – Dallas 1989, no writ); *Texon Energy Corp. v. Dow Chem. CO., 733 S.W.2d 328, 330* (Tex. App. – Houston [14th Dist.] 1987, writ ref'd n.r.e.).

Appellant also argues, for the first time on appeal, that plaintiff's exhibits 107 through 109 were not admissible as summaries of business records under Texas Rule of Civil Evidence 1006 and that the damages evidence contained in these exhibits should have been excluded as a sanction for an alleged discovery violation. This Court will not consider a basis for objection that was not raised at the trial court level. TEX. R. APP. P. 52(a).

We find that the trial court properly overruled

appellant's objections and admitted plaintiff's exhibits 103 through 109 under the business record exception to the hearsay rule. As we find no error in the trial court's admission of these exhibits, we overrule point of error three.

* * * * *

In re GULPH WOODS CORPORATION

82 B.R.373

United States Bankruptcy Court, E.D. Pennsylvania
February 8, 1988

At the close of eight days of testimony between October 19, 1987, and December 8, 1987, at a consolidated hearing on a Motion of Nassau Savings and Loan Association (hereinafter referred to as "Nassau") for Relief from Automatic Stay, for Adequate Protection, and for Other Relief; and Motions of the Debtor (1) to Sell Four Building Lots [the "T" lots] Free and Clear, (2) for Authority to Use Cash Collateral, and (3) to Borrow and Incur Debt Pursuant to Section 364(d), Nassau moved for the admission of certain exhibits. The Debtor objected to the admission of Exhibits N–30 and N–31 (State Ethics Commission Orders) and Exhibits N–45 and N–46 (Monthly Statements) into evidence. We find that the State Ethics Commission Orders are clearly admissible under Rule 803(8)(C) as public reports. The Monthly Statements are clearly admissible as business records under 803(6); however, there remains some doubt as to whether the requirements of the best evidence rule contained in Rule 1002 have been satisfied, which causes us to reserve our decision of their admissibility until we have the opportunity to review the transcript.

* * * * *

II. The Monthly Statements

Nassau also seeks to introduce N–45 and N–46, copies of Monthly Statements of the Debtor's loan account, into evidence to establish the amount of the Debtor's obligation to it as of the specific dates of the Statements. The debtor objects to the admission of these documents under F.R.E. 1006, since Nassau failed at any time to offer the original business records for inspection.

Computerized business records, like other written documents, are necessarily hearsay and may not be admitted into evidence to prove the truth of the matter asserted therein unless they fall within the hearsay exception of Rule 803(6). However, in addition, the admissibility of these records is subject to the best evidence rule.

Where a party attempts to prove the content of a writing, the best evidence rule requires the production of the original writing. F.R.E. 1002. F.R.E. 1001(3) defines an "original" to include "any counterpart intended to have the same effect by the person executing or issuing it." The rule also provides that "if data are stored into a computer . . . , any printout . . . shown to reflect the data accurately, is an 'original.'" F.R.E. 1001(3). Thus, a computerized record may be admitted into evidence as an "original" only after the court has made a fact–specific determination as to the intent of the drafters and the accuracy of the documents.

In today's commercial world, a single transaction often generates successive entries of the same information in separately prepared writings. Though the purposes of these separate records may be different, a computerized business record, prepared simultaneously with or within a reasonable time period of the written record, and containing the same or similar information, would appear to be no less an "original" than a handwritten record. *See* 5 LOUISELL & MUELLER, FEDERAL EVIDENCE, § 354, at 309–315 (1977). However, it seems equally clear that where a written record, prepared prior to the computer record, contains a more detailed and complete description of the transaction than that contained in the computer record, the proponent of the evidence should be required to produce the more detailed record, or account for its nonproduction under F.R.E. 1004. *Id.* Similarly, where a computerized record appears to be nothing more than a summary of a more detailed written record, the written record should be produced except where the requirements of F.R.E. 1006 have been satisfied.

It is necessary for this Court to turn to the record to determine whether the documents at issue constitute an original writing or a summary of an original writing. Based solely on the facts contained in the motion, it is clear that the monthly statements were made from information transmitted by person with knowledge and were prepared on a monthly basis. However, there is no indication as to whether the computer record was prepared within a reasonable time of the written record, or whether the written record, if any, contained more or less information than that in the computer record.

An examination of the documents themselves would appear to indicate that the documents are more than a mere summary. The Statements reflect a day–by–day account of the accrual of the interest upon the outstanding loan and appear to be a complete record of the transactions which occurred in the Debtor's account during the months stated. The documents involved thus appear to be similar to pages from the bank's ledger sheet, and thus should be admissible as "originals". However, without further indication in the record as to how these documents are prepared, we are hesitant to rule on whether Nassau has laid the foundation that these documents constitute original business records. Frankly, given the length of the record, we are at this point unable to recall whether the record contains such sufficient foundation until we review the completed transcript.

If the transcript shows that the monthly statements were prepared within a reasonable time of any written record, and reflect the transactions as they occurred, then these documents would constitute "originals" within the meaning of the best evidence rule. The fact that a party selects weaker competent evidence instead of stronger competent evidence should not be cause to deny the admission of such evidence under the best evidence rule. *See United States v. Russo,* 480 F.2d 1228, 1239–40 (6th Cir. 1973); and

Smith v. Bank of South, 141 Ga.App. 114, 232 S.E.2d 629, 630 (1977).

If, however, the transcripts show these documents to be inferior substitutes or summaries of more detailed written records, then admission of these documents may be denied on the basis of the requirements of both F.R.E. 1004 and 1006.

An Order consistent with our above–stated conclusions will be entered.

HAMILTON MUSIC, INC. v. Donald E. YORK and Ronald E. Mahan, d/b/a Don and Ron's Music Center,

565 SW.2d 838

Missouri Court of Appeals, Kansas City District
May 1, 1978.

Hamilton Music, Inc. (hereinafter plaintiff) filed a three count action against Donald E. York and Ronald E. Mahan, d/b/a Don & Ron's Music Center (hereinafter defendants), in the Circuit Court of Cole County, Missouri. The action was inspired by a franchise agreement to operate a retail music store in Jefferson City, Missouri, and related business dealings between the parties. Plaintiff was the franchiser and holder of a certain promissory note; defendants were the franchisee and makers of the promissory note. Court I of the plaintiff's petition was an action on the promissory note, Count II thereof was an action for royalties due and owing under the franchise agreement, and Count III thereof was an action for money owed on an open account. Defendants filed a counterclaim seeking damages for plaintiff's breach of the franchise agreement.

* * * * *

Plaintiff's final point, that the trial court erred in not admitting Exhibits No. 4, 5, 6 and 8 offered by plaintiff as "business records", is at best a bare bones compliance with Rule 84.04(d). Exhibits No. 4, 5 and 6, after being tersely identified as letters from plaintiff's files, were offered into evidence under the guise of constituting "business records" and, hence, admissible as exceptions to the hearsay rule. Defendants' objections to these exhibits were sustained by the trial court. Plaintiff at the time apparently concurred with the trial court's ruling because it made no offer of proof of any kind, and, more particularly, no offer of proof that so much as even hinted or suggested that the exhibits were prepared in such a manner as to fall within the purview of § § 490.660 to 490.690, commonly cited as "The Uniform Business Records As Evidence Law". As succinctly stated in *Hays v. Western Auto Supply Company*, 405 S.W.2d 877, 881 (Mo.1966), "[n]othing is preserved for appellate review when a court rejects evidence, in the absence of an offer or proof." This excerpt from *Hays* was cited with approval and relied on in *Tile–Craft Products Co., Inc. v. Colonial Properties, Inc.*, 498 S.W.2d 547, 549 (Mo.1973), wherein the court held that when a rejected exhibit purportedly constituting a business record was unaccompanied by an offer of proof, nothing was preserved for appellate review insofar as the rejected exhibit was concerned. Regarding plaintiff's Exhibit No. 8, it too was declared inadmissible by the trial court. However, as some semblance of an offer of proof was made by plaintiff when it was rejected to ostensibly warrant its admission, the ruling of the trial court thereon will be treated as preserved for purposes of appellate review. With respect to Exhibit No. 8 offered by plaintiff, an employee of plaintiff testified that it was a computer print–out prepared by Westinghouse Credit corporation, a stranger to the litigation. rather than by plaintiff. Plaintiff's emaciated offer of proof indicated that it received the computer print–out from Westinghouse Credit Corporation and retained the same in its files as part of its business records. Flying in the face of the plaintiff's claim of admissibility is the previously mentioned testimony from the plaintiff's employee that the exhibit in question was not prepared by an employee of plaintiff but that it was prepared by someone at Westinghouse Credit Corporation. A quick perusal of § 490.680, RSMo 1969, discloses that plaintiff's offer of proof and what little evidence there was of record failed to qualify plaintiff's Exhibit No. 8 for admission into evidence as a business record: "A record of an act, condition or event, shall, insofar as relevant, be competent evidence if the custodian or other qualified witness testifies to its identity and the mode of its preparation, and if it was made in the regular course of business, at or near the time of the act, condition or event, and if, in the opinion of the court, the sources of information, method and time of preparation were such as to justify its admission." By no stretch of legal imagination did the exhibit's mere presence in plaintiff's files render it admissible as a business record under § 490.680, supra. Not even generalities, much less particularities, as to the time, mode and manner of its preparation by its "custodian or other qualified witness" were ever broached or touched upon by the plaintiff's offer of proof. This alone sealed the fate of the controversial exhibit from being qualified for admission into evidence under § 490.680, supra. *Del Monte Corp. v. Stark & Son Wholesale, Inc.*, 474 S.W.2d 854, 857 (Mo.App.1971). In the same vein, when the status of the record is such that it discloses that an exhibit was not made in the ordinary course of the offeror's business but was instead prepared elsewhere and merely found in the offeror's files, it is inadmissible as a business record under § 490.680, supra. *State v. Anderson*, 413 S.W.2d 161, 165 (Mo.1967); and *Rodenberg v. Nickels*, 357 S.W.2d 551, 557 (Mo.App.1962). For reasons stated, the trial court did not err in rejecting Exhibits No. 4, 5, 6 and 8 offered by the plaintiff.

Richard Paige HARRIS, Appellant v. THE STATE OF TEXAS, Appellee

846 S.W.2d 960

Court of Appeals of Texas, First District, Houston
February 11, 1993

A jury found the appellant, Richard Paige Harris, guilty of unauthorized use of a motor vehicle. The trial court found an enhancement paragraph to be true and sentenced appellant to confinement of 15 years and one day. We affirm.

The appellant was indicted for the unauthorized use of a truck identified at trial as a white GMC Jimmy bearing the vehicle identification number (VIN) IGKCS13Z4N2512531. The Jimmy was actually owned by Lester Goodson Pontiac–Honda–GMC, but the indictment alleged the owner of the truck to be John Sorenson, Lester Goodson's inventory control manager.

* * * * *

In point of error two, the appellant contends that the trial court erred by allowing the State to enter into evidence the manufacturer's certificate of origin from General Motors Corporation as a business record of Lester Goodson Pontiac–Honda–GMC. Specifically, he argues that the State's exhibit one, the certificate of origin, does not comply with the requirements of TEX.R.CRIM.EVID. 803(6), and is therefore inadmissible hearsay.

Rule 803(6) provides that the following is not excluded by the hearsay rule:

Records of regularly conducted activity. A memorandum, report, record, or data compilation, in any form, of acts, events, conditions, opinions, or diagnoses, made at or near the time by, or from information transmitted by, a person with knowledge, if kept in the course of a regularly conducted business activity, and if it was the regular practice of that business activity to make the memorandum, report, record, or data compilation, all as shown by the testimony of the custodian or other qualified witness, or by affidavit that complies with Rule 902(10), unless the source of information or the method or circumstances of preparation indicate lack of trustworthiness.

The certificate of origin is signed by Sandra J. Donovan, the authorized representative of the "Truck and Bus Group, General Motors Corporation." The certificate provides in pertinent part:

I, the undersigned authorized representative of the company, firm or corporation named below, hereby certify that the new vehicle described above is the property of the said company, firm or corporation and is transferred on the above date and under the Invoice Number indicated to the following distributor or dealer.

The vehicle is described in the certificate as a 1992 GMC Jimmy, Vehicle Identification No. 1GKCS13Z4N2512531. The certificate indicates that the Jimmy was transferred to Goodson Pontiac–GMC–Honda on November 22, 1991.

The State asked Sorenson a series of questions to comply with the business records exception to the hearsay rule, and then offered the record. The appellant objected and took the witness on voir dire. On voir dire, defense counsel established that Sorenson did not know whether Sandra Donovan, the employee of General Motors who signed the certificate, had personal knowledge of the information contained in the certificate. The trial court overruled defense counsel's objection to the record and admitted the record into evidence.

The predicate for admissibility under the business records exception requires, among other things, that the party offering the evidence prove the record was made by, or from information transmitted by, a person with knowledge, or that the record be kept in the course of a regularly conducted business activity. See *Crane v. State*, 786 S.W.2d 338, 351 (Tex.Crim.App. 1990). The appellant contends the State was required to prove that each person who made any notation on the record had personal knowledge of each matter about which that person noted. We disagree.

The State's burden was to prove the records were the business records of Lester Goodson GMC; the State was not required to prove the records were the business records of General Motors. As the business records of Lester Goodson, they were admissible.

In *Cole v. State*, 839 S.W.2d 798 (Tex. Crim.App. 1990), a case that addressed the propriety of using TEX.R.CRIM.EVID, 803(6), the Court of Criminal Appeals reminded us that the Texas Rules of Criminal Evidence are patterned after the Federal Rules of Evidence. In *Cole*, the court told us, "Cases interpreting federal rules should be consulted for guidance as to their scope and applicability unless the Texas rule clearly departs from its federal counterpart." *Id.* at 801. Texas Criminal Rule of Evidence 803(6) is substantively the same as the federal rule. Because we can find no Texas cases involving records such as the document at issue in this case, we look to federal cases interpreting Federal Rule of Evidence 803(6) for guidance.

In *United States v. Hines*, 564 F.2d 925 (10th Cir. 1977), *aff'd*, 434 U.S. 1022 (1978), the court faced a situation remarkably similar to the one before this Court. In Hines, the defendant was convicted of selling stolen vehicles. *Id.* at 926. At trial, the owner of one of the cars referred to an invoice or bill of sale that she claimed to have received when she purchased the car. The defendant alleged that the evidence was inadmissible because the witness had not prepared the invoice herself. *Id* at 928. The court disagreed and stated:

> This testimony was a predicate to Ritchie's identification of the automobile's VIN. . . . Business records prepared in the regular course of business are admissible in evidence. Such documents possess a high degree of trustworthiness and the necessity of admitting them far outweighs the inconvenience that would result in having the person who prepared the document testify. The test of whether such records should be admitted rests upon their reliability. Here the test of reliability is met. Automobile manufacturers have a great interest in assuring that the VIN's on their products correspond with the appropriate invoices, for without careful, reliable identification procedures their business would greatly suffer or even fail. . . . We view the automobile invoice as admissible under [the] Federal Business Records Act and F.R.E. 803(6).

Id. (citations omitted, emphasis added); but see *United States v. Pellulo*, 964 F.2d 193, 201 (3rd Cir. 1992) (bank records not admissible under rule 803(6) simply because there is some indi-

cia of the trustworthiness of the statements; a witness or documentary evidence must lay the foundation required by the rule).

We find the reasoning in *Hines* persuasive. We further find that, for the reasons identified in *Hines*, State's exhibit one, the manufacturer's certificate of origin from General Motors Corporation, possesses a high degree of trustworthiness. Because the certificate possesses a high degree of trustworthiness and because Sorenson testified that the certificate was kept in the regular course of Lester Goodson's business, we hold that it was admissible under rule 803(6).

The State also argues that the document was admissible under TEX.R.CRIM.EVID. 803(15). We agree.

Rule 803(15) provides that the following is not excluded by the hearsay rule:

> Statements in documents in affecting an interest in property. A statement contained in a document purporting to establish or effect an interest in property if the matter stated was relevant to the purpose of the document, unless dealings with the property since the document was made have been inconsistent with the truth of the statement or the purport of the document.

The certificate of origin certifies that General Motors, the owner of the 1992 GMC Jimmy bearing vehicle identification number 1GKCS13Z4N2512531, transferred the Jimmy to Goodson Pontiac–GMC–Honda on November 22, 1991, and this transfer was the first such transfer of the vehicle in ordinary trade and commerce. Thus, the certificate clearly establishes Lester Goodson's interest in the Jimmy. The certificate was admitted to prove the Jimmy's vehicle identification number. The VIN established that Lester Goodson owned the Jimmy in which the appellant was seen immediately prior to his arrest. The VIN, which identified the vehicle being transferred from General Motors to the dealership, was obviously relevant to the purpose of the certificate. No evidence was introduced to indicate any inconsistency between the VIN on the Jimmy and the VIN on the certificate, nor was there evidence that the Jimmy was not the property of Lester Goodson at the time of the offense. We hold that the certificate of origin was admissible as a statement affecting an interest in property pursuant to rule 803(15). See *Madden v. State*, 799 S.W.2d 683, 698 (Tex.Crim.App. 1990) (handwritten list of murder victim's weapons and corresponding serial numbers admissible as a statement affecting an interest in property, even though it was not a legally executed document).

The trial court did not specify the reason it overruled defense counsel's objection to the certificate of origin. If a trial court's decision is correct on any theory of law applicable to the case, we will sustain it on appeal. *Romero v. State*, 800 S.W.2d 539, 543 (Tex.Crim.App.1990).

Guido HENNEKENS et al. v. STATE TAX COMMISSION of the STATE OF NEW YORK

494 N.Y.S. 2d 208

Supreme Court, Appellate Division, Third Department
October 17, 1985

* * * * *

Proceeding pursuant to CPLR article 78 (transferred to this court by order of the Supreme Court at Special Term, entered in Albany County) to review a determination of respondent which sustained personal income and unincorporated business tax assessments against petitioners for 1971, 1972 and 1973.

Following a field audit, the Audit Division of the Department of Taxation and Finance determined that petitioners had understated their income on their personal income and unincorporated business tax returns for the years 1971, 1972 and 1973 and assessed deficiencies, exclusive of penalties and interest, of approximately $15,730. It appears that in an audit of gasoline service station and auto repair business conducted by petitioner Guido Hennekens, the department's auditors found that petitioners had no books or records for the year

1971, and that those books and records produced for the years 1972 and 1973 disclosed voluminous unidentified bank transfers between many bank accounts. For these reasons, and because the auditors were unable to obtain additional information and records from petitioners, a net worth audit was performed to determine if petitioners had understated their taxable income. The net worth audits indicated additional unreported income of approximately $100,000, upon which penalties and interest were added resulting in a total assessment of $27,765.41. Petitioners did not attend the hearing upon their petition for redetermination and offered no testimony, relying solely upon post–hearing submissions of documents and records. Respondent, concluding that petitioners had failed to sustain their burden of proving that the assessments were incorrect and that the penalties for fraud should be eliminated because of the failure of the Department to sustain its burden of proof on that issue, otherwise sustained the deficiencies. This CPLR article 78 proceeding was commenced to challenge the determination.

* * * * *

The obvious distinction between this case and the *Chartair* line of cases is the type of tax being imposed. Those cases seek recovery under Tax Law § 1138 for sales and use taxes imposed directly upon verifiable receipts evidence by books and records, which vendors are required by statue to maintain (*see, Matter of Licata v. Chu*, 64 N.Y.2d 873, 874, 487 N.Y.2d 552, 476 N.E.2d 997), whereas, in the case at bar, the tax is imposed upon income, the receipt of which cannot easily be verified by reference to books and records. In other words, *Chartair* depends upon the existence of verifiable records, not here at present. This court has recently upheld the use of net worth audits by the Department in personal income tax and unincorporated business tax cases where the taxpayer's income was not accurately reflected in his books and records (*Matter of Checho v. State tax Commn. of State of New York*, 111 A.D.2d 470, 488 N.Y.S.2d 859, 860).

Moreover, the United Sates Supreme Court has approved the use of net worth analysis in the prosecution of Federal income tax evasion cases as a recognized and respected method of determining a taxpayer's income (*Holland v. United States,* 348 U.S. 121, 131, 75 S. Ct. 127, 133, 99 L.Ed. 150; *see also, People v. O'Connor,* 2nd Cir., 273 F.2d 358, 361; *People v. Costello,* 2nd Cir., 221 F.2d 668, 675 *affed* 350 U.S. 359, 76 S.Ct. 406, 100 L.Ed. 397). Under the prevailing circumstances, where the business records for 1971 were unavailable and numerous unidentified bank transfers were made, we find the Department's use of net worth audit entirely acceptable (*Matter of Checho v. State Tax Commn. of State of New York, supra*).

* * * * *

Cynthia Sue HENSE v. G.D. SEARLE & CO.

452 N.W.2d 440

Supreme Court of Iowa
March 21, 1990

This appeal and cross–appeal arise out of a product liability action brought against the manufacturer of an intrauterine contraception device. The controversy centers on the parties' dispute over the method by which plaintiff should conduct discovery of the corporate defendant's 750,000 product–related documents. The wrangling has resulted in six continuances of trial over the six–year life of the litigation.

* * * * *

In May 1982, plaintiff Cynthia Sue Hense filed this action against defendant G.D. Searle & Company (Searle) for personal injuries she attributed to the use of Searle's product, the "Copper–7" intrauterine contraceptive device (IUD). Her claimed injuries included pelvic inflammatory disease and resultant sterility. Subsequent amendments to the petition named two physicians involved in prescribing the IUD and thereafter treating Hense. Her claims against these individuals have been settled or otherwise dismissed and are not before us on appeal.

* * * * *

The discovery problem underlying the many delays centered on whether, as plaintiff claims, Searle has been deliberately unwilling to produce documents or, as Searle claims, Hense's discovery requests have been too broad and unspecific to be answered. In repeated response to nearly every document request, Searle asserted that because no master retrieval system to the "universe" of Copper–7 documents existed, the requests were as burdensome to Searle as to the plaintiff. As an alternative to production, Searle suggested that plaintiff visit its corporate headquarters and locate the documents herself. Plaintiff never availed herself of Searle's invitation to visit the document warehouse in Skokie, Illinois, nor was she ever directed to do so by court order.

This simmering discovery conflict boiled over in July 1987, when Searle inadvertently produced the "INDA Summary Index" in connection with its delivery of some 15,000 documents produced pursuant to one of plaintiff's successful motions to compel. The INDA Summary Index is a 136–page document that references a 12,000–page document called the Copper–7 Investigational New Drug Application (INDA), an application submitted to the Food and Drug Administration to gain approval for the testing of a new drug. To plaintiff, the existence of this index belied Searle's repeated assertion that it had no retrieval system with which to find documents.

When plaintiff found the index, she moved for sanctions, including default judgment, under Iowa Rule of Civil Procedure 134(b)(2). In her motion, plaintiff cited fifteen responses made by Searle that denied the existence of any index to the "New Drug Application" (a 45,000–page successor to the 12,000–page INDA) or to any other Copper–7 documents. Searle resisted the motion on three grounds: (1) the index was attorney work product, and hence, not discoverable, (2) the index referenced an insignificant portion of the mass of Copper–7 documents, and (3) the index was of recent vintage and so had not been available for production during much of the litigation.

On September 4, 1987, the trial court ruled

that the index, though labeled "Attorney Work Product–Confidential," displayed no other characteristics supporting its allegedly protected status. Moreover, the court ruled that rather than denying the summary's existence, Searle should have informed the court that it existed and sought a protective order, if necessary, based on an *in camera* inspection by the court. Searle's lack of candor prompted the court's finding that Searle "willfully failed to obey the previous court's order regarding discovery." The court imposed a sanction of $54,706.95 against Searle for its discovery abuse. Searle's cross–appeal challenges this monetary sanction.

* * * * *

Before the trial court ruled on the motion to compel, plaintiff learned of a second index which Searle had not earlier revealed. Hense applied to the court for an *in camera* review. This index, which the parties concede to be no more than a list of labels appearing on boxes of documents, was produced to plaintiff in early May 1988. Upon its receipt, plaintiff urged court to continue the August trial date on the ground that Searle's failure to produce the list earlier had prevented plaintiff from framing further document requests prior to the discovery deadline of May 1. The court summarily overruled plaintiff's motion.

* * * * *

It appears undisputed that Searle prepared the INDA summary in anticipation of nationwide litigation over the Copper–7 IUD, a circumstance which would ordinarily trigger the plaintiff's burden of showing substantial need and undue hardship. *See* Iowa R.Civ. P. 122(c). Plaintiff, however, never had the opportunity to make such a showing because Searle inadvertently divulged the document in the face of denials concerning its existence. Given this conduct, the trial court properly rested its ruling, not on the status of the documents, but on Searle's lack of candor.

The party asserting privilege has the burden of showing that the privilege exists and applies. *Hutchinson v. Smith Labs, Inc.*, 392 N.W.2d 139, 141 (Iowa 1986); *Agrivest Partnership v. Central Iowa Prod. Credit Ass'n*,

373 N.W.2d 479, 482 (Iowa 1985). In each of the cases cited by Searle for the proposition that it had not duty to produce the index because it was protected work product the attorney asserted the privilege. *See Schaffer v. Rogers*, 362 N.W.2d 552, 554 (Iowa 1985) (declining to produce documents on work product grounds); *Ashmead*, 336 N.W.2d at 199 (asserting privilege); *Shelton v. American Motors Corp.*, 805 F.2d 1323, 1325 (8th Cir.1987) (refusing to answer questions on work product grounds); *Sporck v. Peil*, 759 F.2d 312, 313 (3rd Cir.1985) ("there is no allegation in this case that defendants have improperly concealed or refused to produce required documents"); *Berkey Photo, Inc. v. Eastman Kodak Co.*, 74 F.R.D. 613, 614 (D.C.N.Y.1977) ("counsel claimed work product privilege"); *Garcia v. Peeples*, 734 S.W.2d 343, 348 (Tex. 1987); *Lone Star Dodge, Inc. v. Marshall*, 736 S.W.2d 184, 186 (Tex.App.1987). In no case cited did the attorney mislead opposing counsel and then, once the document surfaced, attempt to claim the privilege. Searle does not now attempt to repudiate its many denials that an index existed because it uses those same negative responses to support its fallback argument that it answered the discovery requests truthfully, *i.e.*, there was no index to the *entire universe* of Copper–7 documents. Since there was only an index to 12,000 of the documents, Searle argues that it has been erroneously accused of deceit. We think the disingenuousness of Searle's argument speaks for itself. The court found Searle playing "hide the ball" and imposed a penalty. We see no abuse of discretion in that judgment call.

* * * * *

Luis HERNANDEZ and Daisy Hernandez, his wife v. Angel PINO, D.D.S. and Federal Insurance Company, a foreign corporation doing business in Dade County, Florida,

482 So.2d 450

District Court of Appeal of Florida, Third District
January 14, 1986

Plaintiffs in a malpractice action appeal from a final summary judgment entered for defendant dentist where X–rays were lost after defendant released them to plaintiffs' former attorney. We reverse.

Plaintiff Luis Hernandez suffers from holes in his palate owing to a congenital defect. The holes were covered by a partial upper denture. In December 1978 Hernandez visited Dr. Pino complaining of loose bottom teeth. After an examination which included X–rays, Dr. Pino informed plaintiff that none of his teeth were good and that they should be extracted. In response to plaintiff's inquiry as to the necessity of extracting the upper teeth to which the partial denture was affixed, Dr. Pino gave assurances that even after the teeth were removed, the denture could be satisfactorily replaced. After the teeth were removed plaintiff experienced severe discomforts which included food leakage into the nasal canal while eating. Dr. Pino finally referred plaintiff to a Dr. Steven Holmes who performed two operations, one to seal the hole in the palate and another to reconstruct the jaw and gum using bone from the plaintiff's hip. Another dentist, Dr. William Schiff, fitted plaintiff with new dentures which he says will continue to fall out frequently owing to the still existent deformities.

Plaintiffs filed suit against Dr. Pino and his insurer alleging negligent treatment, specifically that (1) the dentist's treatment fell below the requisite standard in extracting all of plaintiff's teeth without a competent periodontal evaluation, and (2) the dentist failed to inform plaintiff that after removal of the teeth there could be a difficulty in constructing dentures which would fit properly, that he would have to undergo corrective surgery with only a small chance of success, and that he would suffer an aggravation of pre–existing speech impediment and difficulty in eating.

After commencement of the litigation, defendant's counsel released to plaintiffs' counsel a set of X–rays taken by Dr. Pino prior to the extractions. In exchange Dr. Pino was given "a hold harmless agreement." The X–rays had been examined by Dr. Schiff, the dentist who fitted plaintiff with new dentures. From the X–rays Dr. Schiff had measured the amount of bone available for the support of plaintiff's maxillary teeth as depicted on the X–rays, which information was preserved as notations in his treatment records. The record shows that Dr. Pino's attorney had also shown the X–rays to a dentist selected by the attorney, apparently in preparation for litigation, but that the attorney had not yet received an interpretation of the "anatomical structures depicted in the x–rays."

On September 24, 1981, plaintiffs hired a new attorney who sought unsuccessfully to obtain the X–rays from the first attorney and then requested that defendants produce the X–rays. Upon learning that the X–rays could not be located, defendants filed a motion to compel plaintiffs to produce them. When plaintiffs were unable to comply, the court imposed, as a sanction, that Dr. Pino's recollection of the matters would constitute established facts on the subject for purposes of the litigation, and further ruled that a more severe sanction would be imposed if it appeared from the deposition testimony of Dr. Schiff that his notations conflicted with Dr. Pino's recollections.

* * * * *

Ordinarily where a party in possession loses or destroys crucial record evidence a burden is imposed on that party to prove that the loss or destruction was not in bad faith. *See* § 90.954, Fla.Stat. (1983); *Valcin v. Public Health Trust of Dade County*, 473 So.2d 1297 (Fla. 3d DCA 1985). In this case plaintiff was given no opportunity to show that ordinary negligence rather than mischief was behind the disappearance of the X–rays; thus a summary judgment on that ground alone was premature. Assuming that the X–rays were not intentionally made unavailable, the next inquiry would be whether Dr. Pino will be unable to mount a defense without them.

If *DePuy* plaintiffs' counsel had not completed testing of the evidence before it was lost. In this case, Dr. Pino had given the X–rays to his own expert for examination before they were misplaced. There has been no showing by the defendant, and none is apparent from the record, that he is unable to defend against the claim for negligent treatment.

There was no basis for excluding the affidavit testimony of plaintiffs' expert witness which was submitted in opposition to the motion for summary judgment. Unlike *DuPuy*, in this case there was other admissible evidence available to defendant. Defendant himself is an expert in the subject area out of which the action arises. He reviewed the X–rays, made notations, and drew conclusions upon which he based his decision to extract all of plaintiff's teeth. In preparation for the litigation defendant then gave the X–rays to his own expert for review. The record is silent as to the availability of defendant's expert witness.

Section 90.952, Florida Statutes (1983) states the general rule that:

> Except as otherwise provided by statute, an original writing, recording, or photograph is required in order to prove the contents of the writing, recording, or photograph.

Defendants have presented no Florida authority, not a persuasive argument, that the X–rays are, or should be, excepted from the best evidence rule on the facts of this case. Both parties direct us to the sponsors' note to section 90.952:

> Although the admissibility of X–rays under the "best evidence" rule has apparently never been ruled on directly by Florida courts, the implication is that such materials would be admissible and an expert would be permitted to testify as to what they show, etc. [cites omitted]. Presumably, Florida fol-

lows the weight of authority in other jurisdictions requiring production of the original X–ray, if an expert is going to testify as to what the X–ray disclosed. *Daniels v. Iowa City*, 191 Iowa 811, 183 N.W. 415 (1921); *Patrick & Tillman v. Matkins*, [154 Okl. 232] 7 P.2d 414 (Okl.1932). However, it should be noted that under § 90.704 the basis of an expert's testimony does not have to be admissible.

On the present state of the record, the question is answered by the best evidence rule, section 90.954, Florida Statutes (1983), which provides:

> Admissibility of other evidence of contents. —

> The original of a writing, recording, or photograph is not required . . . and other evidence of its contents is admissible when:

> (1) All originals are lost or destroyed, unless the proponent lost or destroyed them in bad faith.

> * * * * *

> (3) An original was under the control of the party against whom offered at a time when he was put on notice by the pleadings or by written notice from the adverse party that the contents of such original would be subject to proof at the hearing, and such original is not produced at the hearing.

We hold that in the absence of evidence that an X–ray was intentionally lost or destroyed, and where the party seeking to exclude the opponent's testimonial evidence as to the contents of the X–ray has had the X–ray examined by his own experts who are able to form and express opinions regarding its contents, the best evidence rule will apply to admit the expert testimony of both parties' experts.

* * * * *

HERTZ CORPORATION v. McCRAY

402 S.E.2d 298

Court of Appeals of Georgia
February 4, 1991

* * * * *

Appellee rented a car from appellant, and elected to purchase an optional loss/damage waiver. This waiver, in effect, provided that appellant waive any claim against appellee for loss or damage to its rental car unless it results from, inter alia, "the use of the car, with [appellee's permission, by persons other than authorized operators."

Appellant brought suit against appellee for damages to the rental vehicle. Appellee admitted, during her testimony, that she loaned the car to Bobby C. Lampley who subsequently wrecked the car.

* * * * *

Appellant asserts that the trial court erred in not permitting appellant's witness to be questioned about the witness' qualifications to testify to the appellant's books and records.

During the course of the trial, appellant called as a witness the southeast regional damage appraiser for the Hertz Corporation and attempted through this witness to lay the foundation for the introduction of certain copies of documents alleged to be business records of Hertz. Although the witness testified initially that he was familiar with the method used by plaintiff in keeping books and records and with the records of Hertz of this particular transaction relating to the subject of the lawsuit, the trial court sustained several varying objections to the testimony of this witness concerning the type of business records maintained by Hertz in the ordinary course of business, and whether the entries on certain records were made at or near the time of the occurrence of the transaction to which they referred.

OCGA § 24–3–14 prescribes the statutory standard for the admission in evidence of records made in the regular course of business.

This Code section is to be liberally interpreted and applied. OCGA § 24–3–14(d).

The trial court stated that appellant must show the witness "keeps these records" and "they are kept under his control and supervision."

Before a writing or record is admissible, under OCGA § 24–3–14(b), a foundation must be laid through the testimony of a witness who is familiar with the *method* of keeping the records and who can testify thereto and to facts which show that the entry was made in the regular course of business at the time of the event or within a reasonable time thereafter. *Suarez v. Suarez*, 257 Ga. 102, 103(2), 355 S.E.2d 649. Copies of business records can be admitted without accounting for the absence of the originals once the above foundation has been laid; likewise photostatic reproductions or duplicate originals of any original business record or document are admissible in lieu of the original. *Wiggins v. State*, 249 Ga. 302, 305(2)(c), 290 S.E.2d 427; *Smith v. Smith*, 224 Ga. 442, 443(1), 162 S.E.2d 379. A witness identifying business records under OCGA § 4–3–13 does not have to have personal knowledge of the correctness of the records or have made the entry himself. *Davis v. State*, 194 Ga.App. 902, 904(2), 392 S.E.2d 827; *Whittington v. State*, 155 Ga.App. 667(2), 272 S.E.2d 532; see *Smith v. Bank of the South*, 141 Ga.App. 114, 232 S.E.2d 629 (lack of personal knowledge of making of business records affects weight of admissibility). Moreover, unlike the so–called "official records" exception of some jurisdictions, the Georgia Business Records does *not* require that the person laying the foundation for business records' admissibility be the custodian of the records, that he be the person who "keeps the records" under his "control and supervision." Thus, "[n]o particular person, such as a bookkeeper or salesman, is required to be called," rather, "[a]ny person who is familiar with the method of keeping the records and can identify them may lay the necessary foundation." (Green, Ga.Law of Evid. 3d ed.), Business Entries, § 313. It would appear that the necessary degree of familiarity could be obtained through a number of common business practices, such as being records custodian, making the entries during the usual course of employment, observing the method of records keeping through on–the–job training, experience or observation, or by attending courses of destruction sponsored by the business regarding the method of keeping the particular business records in question. The manner in which familiarity is obtained, like the question of whether the witness has personal knowledge of the particular business entry, goes only to weight and not to document of admissibility. Cf. *Smith*, supra. Thus, it is apparent the trial court required overly stringent foundation requirements as a prerequisite to document admissibility.

* * * * *

Robert G. HILL v. JOSEPH T. RYERSON & SON, INC., v. UNITED STATES STEEL CORPORATION

268 S.E.2d 296

Supreme Court of Appeals of West Virginia
May 6, 1980

A product liability action was filed against seller of steel pipe which split while under hydraulic pressure, causing eye injury to an employee of the buyer. Defendant impleaded the alleged manufacturer of the defective pipe as a third–party defendant.

* * * * *

U.S. Steel urges a final ground of error, that the court permitted the introduction of hearsay, and that such hearsay was the only evidence that identified the defective pipe as having been manufactured by U.S. Steel. Because of the rather fungible quality of the involved pipe, the point merits some attention. Initially, we note that the record does contain evidence independent of the claimed hearsay evidence which connects the defective pipe to U.S. Steel.

It was not disputed at trial that the pipe which injured the plaintiff was received by the plaintiff's employer, Superior Hydraulics, accom-

panied by a shipping bill from Ryerson dated October 15, 1973. The shop foreman at Superior Hydraulics testified that the pipe which injured Hill was cold–drawn steel tubing, having an outside diameter of 5 1/4 inches and a wall thickness of 1/2 inch. The pipe length was specified at random as between 17 and 24 feet and the pipe had a weight per foot of 25.379 pounds. The shipping bill was identified at trial by the shop foreman and introduced as Plaintiff's Exhibit 3.

Ryerson's evidence on identify was that it' had ordered similar pipe, along with pipe of other sizes, from U.S. Steel on a purchase order dated March 21, 1973, which purchase order was introduced as an exhibit. This same type of pipe is contained on an order acknowledgment form of U.S. Steel dated April 2, 1973, which form was also introduced into evidence. The same kind of pipe is shown on U.S. Steel's load tally sheets dated May 4, 1973, which accompanied pipe delivered by U.S. Steel to Ryerson's loading dock on May 9, 1973. The pipe delivered on May 4, 1973, was to fill Ryerson's March 21, 1973, purchase order.

Ryerson's stock inventory supervisor testified from business records kept by his department that when goods are received at the loading dock entries are made in a ledger book which include the date of receipt, the vendor's name, the shipment invoice number and a receiving ticket number. The receiving ticket number is an identifying number which Ryerson maintains chronologically in its ledger book. This identifying number is placed on the vendor's load tally sheets received with the product. This receiving ticket number is also painted on the bundle of goods received. One of the purposes of this system of placing the identifying number on the vendor's tally sheets and on the goods is to enable the goods to be removed from the loading dock into the warehouse without having to inventory them on the loading dock.

Ryerson's Exhibit 13 was introduced without objection. It consisted of the tally sheets listing the various pipe delivered by U.S. Steel to Ryerson on May 9, 1973. The tally sheets showed pipe of the same size, diameter and weight as that later sold by Ryerson to Superior Hydraulics. U.S. Steel's tally sheets carried the Ryerson receiving ticket number of RT 1419.

To this point in the chain of identification, U.S. Steel makes no serious objection to the proof of identity. We are not asked to determine whether this evidence is sufficient to submit to the jury the issue of identity of the manufacturer of this pipe. There was no attempt on the part of Ryerson to show that this was the only type of pipe that it bought from U.S. Steel. The reason there was no effort to develop the evidence in this direction was that the foreman at Superior Hydraulics testified that he had saved a portion of the very pipe that injured the plaintiff and this portion was available at the trial. It bore a paint mark of RT 1419, which was the same receiving ticket number shown on the U.S. Steel tally sheets which were received with the May 9, 1973, shipment.

There can be little question that the invoice of U.S. Steel to Ryerson and the subsequent invoice from Ryerson to Superior Hydraulics, which served to show the characteristics of the pipe to be the same as those of the pipe which caused plaintiff's injury, were admissible as business entries or records under the "shopbook" exception to the hearsay rule. In *Tedesco v. Weirton General Hospital*, W.Va., 235 S.E.2d 463 (1977), we discussed in considerable detail the law in this area. The basis of the shopbook exception is that notations or entries made routinely in the regular course of business at the time of the transaction or occurrence, or within a reasonable time thereafter, are trustworthy and reliable. *See* 5 J. Wigmore, *Evidence* §§ *1420–22 (Chadbourn Rev.1974); C. McCormick, Evidence* Ch. 31 (2d ed. 1972); D. Binder, *The Hearsay Handbook* 69–82 (1975); Note, *Business Records Rule: Repeated Target of Legal Reform*, 36 Brooklyn L.Rev. 241 (1970). It is not essential to the admissibility of a business record that the clerk who actually made the record be called to testify. Part of the basis of the modern business records is a recognition that the quantity of modern recordkeeping will often not permit the particular clerk who recorded an entry to be later identified, or, if identified, that he may not

recall making the particular entry. We expressed this point in *Tedesco* as "'commercial unavailability, that is, the entry is admissible where the commercial inconvenience in calling the witness outweighs its utility,'" quoting Nash, *The Law of Evidence, Virginia and West Virginia*, Section 150 (The Michie Co. 1954). [235 S.E.2d at 464]. *See* McCormick, *Evidence* § 312 (2d ed. 1972).

The trustworthiness of the record entry is established by the testimony of a custodial or supervisory official if he can adequately demonstrate the regularity of the particular recordkeeping as an established procedure within the business routine. *United States v. Jones*, 434 U.S. 866, 98 S.Ct. 202, 54 L.Ed.2d 142; *Rice v. United States*, 411 F.2d 485 (8th Cir. 1969); *United States v. Olivo*, 278 F.2d 415 (3d Cir. 1960); *Hale v. State*, 252 Ark. 1040, 483 S.W.2d 228 (1972); *People v. Kirtdoll*, 391 Mich. 370, 217 N.W.2d 37 (1974); *State v. Matousek*, 287 Minn. 344, 178 N.W.2d 604 (1970); *State v. Berns*, 502 S.W.2d 364 (Mo.1973); *State v. Springer*, 283 N.C. 627, 197 S.E.2d 530 (1973); *Tedesco v. Weirton General Hospital*, W.Va., 235 S.E.2d 463 (1977). The supervisor of Ryerson's stock inventory department was a proper official to establish the recordkeeping routine and the records in Ryerson's possession were thus properly admitted.

The complexity arises with matching with those records the portion of pipe sought to be introduced. There is no question that the purely physical characteristics of the pipe — dimensions, weight, shape, substance, texture — are proper considerations in linking the pipe to the items identified in the records as having been purchased from the defendant, U.S. Steel. The problem is that the pipe bore the descriptive label "RT 1419," which matches the receiving ticket 1419 on the business record. Since the receiving ticket number identifies the delivery as having been obtained from U.S. Steel, the matching paint mark, if admissible, strongly implicates U.S. Steel as the manufacturer. It is this matching number on the pipe that is the focal point of the claim of hearsay.

It is difficult to find an enlightened discussion

of a hearsay question relating to the problem of the identification of a manufacturer based on marks or labels placed on the product. Although the identity of the manufacturer is always an issue in a products liability suit, often this fact is obvious or admitted, and thus rarely litigated. *See* 63 Am.Jur.2d *Products Liability* § 5 (1972); Annot., *Products Liability: Necessity and Sufficiency of Identification of Defendant as Manufacturer or Seller of Product Alleged to Have Caused Injury*, 51 A.L.R.3d 1344, 1349 (1973).

In those cases where the identity of the manufacturer is a litigated issue, the hearsay character of the identifying marks, labels or serial numbers is seldom discussed. Product identification markings fall within the category of out–of–court statements, since they are introduced to establish the truth of the matter asserted. *See* McCormick, *Evidence* Ch. 24 92d ed. 1972); D. Binder, *The Hearsay Handbook* 3 (1975). The reason that the hearsay question in this context is frequently raised is that where the name of the manufacturer is cast or stamped on the product by him, this would constitute an admission that it was his mark or stamp, and would be sufficient to identify him as the maker of the product.

The paint mark in the present case is in a different category, since it was not affixed by the manufacturer. A substantial level of trustworthiness was nevertheless established by several factors.

First, the pipe with the markings remained after the accident in the possession of the plaintiff's employer, where the markings were discovered in an inspection by an attorney and officials of Babcock & Wilcox, a suspected manufacturer. Subsequent to this discovery, the marking "RT 1419" was matched to Ryerson's receiving ticket number 1419, a record with a product description that accurately coincides with the pipe in question and which thus serves to support the authenticity of the label.

Second, the pipe itself corresponds in weight, diameter, and wall thickness to the U.S. Steel pipe described in its order acknowledgment form and shipping tallies which accompanied the pipe to Ryerson.

Third, there is no evidence in the record to suggest there was an alteration or fabrication of the paint mark. Finally, U.S. Steel's own examination of the pipe compelled the admission that the pipe is consistent with a U.S. Steel product, points to the conclusion that U.S. Steel manufactured the pipe.

Several criminal cases demonstrate the extent to which some courts have applied the business record exception to the hearsay rule. In *Rice v. United States*, 411 F.2d 485 (8th Cir. 1969), involving prosecution for interstate theft, the court considered the admissibility as business records of a luggage tag and corresponding claim check. The luggage tag was originally attached to a suitcase in Los Angeles by a Greyhound Bus employee. The ultimate destination of the suitcase was a city in Indiana. The court permitted a Greyhound Bus employee in St. Louis to identify the luggage tag and claim check as a part of Greyhound's regular business records and allowed them to be introduced for the purpose of establishing the fact that the suitcase had traveled in interstate commerce. Essential reliance was placed on the routine recordmaking within the regular course of business when the tag was prepared by Greyhound in Los Angeles. The person who prepared the tag did not testify and neither document was retained in the custody of Greyhound.

In *United States v. Flom*, 558 F.2d 1179 (5th Cir. 1977), involving prosecution for violation of the Sherman Act, the court considered the admissibility as business records of documents held by one company, but prepared and shipped by another. The court found the records to be admissible despite the fact that they were not retained in the custody of the company that prepared them.

Rice, *Flom* and our own *Tedesco* opinion stand for the proposition that the key to admissibility is the regularity and trustworthiness of the business recordkeeping and entries, rather than the method of storage or retention by the maker of the records. It is significant that both *Rice* and *Flom* were criminal prosecutions where the burden of proof upon the state is substantially higher than in a civil trial. A hearsay statement of a type that is trustworthy enough to be received by a jury in a criminal prosecution is even more appropriately admitted in a civil case.

Consequently, we hold that where, in the course of a business enterprise, systematic recordkeeping and product labeling are routinely conducted as a part of the business methods of the enterprise, the records and product identification fall within the business record exception to the hearsay rule. An employee who is knowledgeable as to the recordkeeping and product identification process can testify to that process and thus lay the foundation for the admission into evidence of a properly marked or labeled product. The fact that the product has passed into the hands of a consumer or user will not defeat its admissibility as a business record.

The trial court here was, therefore, correct in admitting the pipe bearing the paint mark "RT 1419."

Based upon the foregoing legal principles, we find that no error was committed by the trial court, and the judgment against U.S. Steel is therefore affirmed.

Affirmed.

HUNT v. SANDERS

232 S.W. 456

Supreme Court of Missouri, Division No. 1
June 6, 1921

Appeal from the circuit court of Jasper county. The plaintiff sued the defendant to recover the amount she paid him for certain forged negotiable notes, purporting to be secured by certain deeds of trust, also forgeries, which she claims defendant sold her, and which notes and mortgages, the petition alleges, "purported to be, and what defendant then warranted to be, and plaintiff relying on such warranty believed to be, good" and valid securities, but which were forgeries, and plaintiff lost her entire investment.

There were five counts in the petition, each arising out of the purchase of one of such notes.

The answer was a general denial.

That the notes and deeds of trust were forgeries was not seriously contested by defendant at the trial.

The plaintiff's evidence tended to prove the allegations in the petition, and to show that the plaintiff herself took no part in the purchase of the notes, but that her husband purchased them from defendant, representing plaintiff as her agent.

Plaintiff's husband testified that defendant showed him the real estate, which was all in the city of Joplin, by which the notes purchased purported to be secured by deeds of trust, and that witness said to defendant, before he purchased the notes, that he did not know whether the papers were all right or not, and that, if defendant knew they were all right, he would take the loans, but if they were not he did not want them; that defendant said, "I know the papers are absolutely good, and that you (plaintiff's husband) need not be worried a moment about it;" thereupon, and relying upon defendant's statement, the plaintiff's husband gave the defendant checks payable to defendant for the full amount of the notes, and received the notes and deeds of trust and abstract of the property from the defendant; that defendant said nothing about representing A. B. Wilgus, Jr., that witness asked defendant whether he had better get an attorney to examine the papers, and he said it was not necessary, they were absolutely good. The notes and deeds of trust purported to be made by different parties to the order of different parties, including two to said Wilgus, and the notes not made to him purported to be endorsed by the payees without recourse, and all the notes were endorsed in blank by said Wilgus, without recourse.

There was an opinion of an attorney attached to each abstract, which plaintiff's husband said was addressed to said defendant, but which defendant said was addressed to said Wilgus. This opinion plaintiff's husband stated he destroyed long before the suit was brought and before the forgeries were known, thinking it of no further consequence. The evidence of both parties tended to show that said opinions simply referred to the title to the real estate and said nothing about the genuineness of the notes or deed of trust.

* * * * *

The court gave the following instructions at the request of the defendant:

* * * * *

"C. The court instructs the jury that if they find and believe from the evidence that the plaintiff or her husband, who was acting for her, destroyed any document relating to the transactions in question, that the presumption is that if said document were produced and offered in evidence it would be against the interest of the plaintiff."

* * * * *

The jury found a verdict for the defendant, and judgment was entered accordingly. The plaintiff filed a motion for a new trial, but, being overruled, plaintiff appealed to this court.

* * * * *

Instruction C, given for the defendant was erroneous. It is true that willfully despoiling a document would justify a presumption of law against the despoiler; that the contents of the document were not as stated by him, but as by his adversary. *Pomeroy v. Benton*, 77 Mo. 87; *Tracy v. Buchanan*, 167 Mo. App. 438, 151 S.W. 747. In this case the only dispute between the parties was as to whether the destroyed opinions were addressed to said Wilgus or to the defendant. There was no dispute as to their contents. Had they been willfully destroyed by the plaintiff or her husband, the only legitimate inference, as a matter of law, against the plaintiff would have been that they were addressed to Wilgus, and not that they contained any other matter detrimental to plaintiff's case, which it is not claimed they did contain. If the said instruction was proper at all, it should have been limited to creating a presumption against plaintiff that the opinions were addressed to Wilgus, as claimed by defen-

dant, and should not have broadly stated, that if said documents had been produced they would have been against the interests of the plaintiff. But, we think, in this case, where the explanation of the destruction of the opinions by the plaintiff's husband, testified to by him, if true, shows that they were not destroyed willfully to suppress evidence, it would be error for the court to declare, in an instruction to the jury, that there was any presumption of law with reference thereto, because, when the facts and circumstances appear, and conflicting inferences may arise therefrom, presumptions of law disappear, and it is for the jury to pass on the weight of the evidence and credibility of the witnesses, in view of all the facts and circumstances in the case, without any suggestion or comment by the court in its instructions as to any such presumptions. *Mockowik v. R.R.*, 196 Mo. 550, 94 S.W. 256; *Guthrie v. Holmes*, 272 Mo. 215, 198 S.W. 854, Ann. Cas. 1918D, 1123; *Brunswick v. Ins. Co.*, 278 Mo. 154, 213 S.W. 45, 7 A.L.R. 1213; *Prentiss v. Ins. Co.*, 225 S.W. 701.

* * * * *

Let the case be reversed and remanded for a new trial in accordance with the views herein expressed. It is so ordered.

Volney R. HYLTON, Jr. v. The STATE of Texas, Austin

665 S.W.2d 571

Court of Appeals of Texas, Austin
January 25, 1984

* * * * *

During the period for which appellees sought taxes (October 1, 1973 through June 30, 1977), appellant was in the business of hauling and selling sand, gravel, and clay. In 1977 the Comptroller notified appellant that his account had been selected for routine sales tax audit. The Comptroller requested that appellant furnish records which would substantiate information reflected in appellant's sales tax returns. Thereafter, appellant burned his business records to prevent federal agents (attempting to enforce the Mining Safety Act) from inspecting them.

In 1979 the Comptroller issued a delinquency certificate stating that appellant owed approximately $153,000 on sales taxes, penalties, and interest. The taxes had been computed based upon the presumption that appellant's gross sales, as reflected on his sales tax returns, were subject to taxation.

In 1982 appellant's attorney reconstructed part of the burned records (from records of some purchasers) and submitted them to Comptroller. An updated delinquency certificate was issued reflecting that approximately $140,000 was owed. Some of the reconstructed records were rejected because they did not conform to regulations promulgated by the Comptroller.

The trial court rendered judgment against appellant for the amount reflected in the second delinquency certificate is presumed correct and that in order to overcome this presumption appellant must conclusively establish that he owes no taxes.

* * * * *

Appellant's evidence consisted primarily of the testimony of himself and his wife. They testified that they charged and remitted to the Comptroller a sales tax on all sales wherein the purchaser did not produce a "tax exemption." It is not clear from their testimony whether they procured from their customers a "resale certificate," and if so whether it complied with the Comptroller's requirements. Appellant does not challenge the trial court's findings that the records reconstructed by appellant and rejected by the Comptroller were unacceptable; such records were introduced into evidence.

Appellant's accountants testified that they never saw any exemption or resale certificates in records provided them by appellant. They did see invoices upon which someone else had indicated whether the sale was exempt. These invoices were used to prepare the tax returns. The tax returns, along with canceled checks (which evidenced payment of taxes reported by appellant), were introduced into evidence.

We hold that as a matter of law appellant has failed to present evidence which would overcome the delinquency certificate's presumed correctness. To allow appellant's evidence to overcome the presumption, especially in light of appellant's intentional destruction of his business records, would render meaningless the regulatory scheme requiring a taxpayer to keep and produce records to substantiate exclusion. *See Paine v. State Bd. of Equalization, supra; Urban Liquors, Inc. v. State Tax Com'n,* 90 A.D.2d 576, 456 N.YS.2d 138 (1982). Appellant's third and fourth points of error are overruled.

The trial court's judgment is affirmed.

INA Aviation Corp. and Ina Marx, as the Executrix of the Estate of Eric Marx v. UNITED STATES of America

468 F. Supp. 695

United States District Court, E. D. New York
April 1, 1979

* * * * *

Plaintiff Eric Marx was the Chairman of the Board, President and owner of plaintiff INA Aviation Corporation (INA), the registered owner of a twin engine Piper PA–31 Navajo aircraft bearing registration number N510BB. He was also the holder of an instrument pilot certificate issued pursuant to Instrument Flight rules (IFR) which permitted him to fly a properly equipped aircraft in weather conditions not suitable for flight under Visual Flight Rules (VFR) and N510BB was equipped with the necessary instrumentation. On September 20, 1974, Marx was the pilot and sole occupant of the aircraft N510BB and in attempting to land his plane crashed approximately seven miles from Joplin, Missouri airport. Since the crash occurred in inclement weather and plaintiffs charge defendant with negligence in failing to promptly notify Marx of changes in the weather conditions, a chronological account of the events preceding the crash is necessary.

* * * * *

At 4:11 A.M. (11011 GMT), Marx repeated

that he had an hour and 15 minutes of fuel remaining. Hultgren told Marx that there were no thunderstorms between his position and St. Louis and that he estimated that Marx could be in St. Louis in an hour and a half. Marx said it was "too close;" he could not take a chance on flying to St. Louis. Hultgren then asked Marx where he wanted to go. Marx said he wanted something on route that is, not too far out of his way.

* * * * *

Plaintiffs claim, however, that an inference that the weather deteriorated to below landing minimums before 4:15 A.M. must be drawn from the government's destruction of certain records, known as "traces," produced at Joplin FSS by two weather instruments, the ceilometer and Runway Visual Value (RVV). One may infer from the intentional destruction of evidence that its production would have been unfavorable to an intentional spoliator. *Dow Chemical Co. (U.K.) v. S. S. Giovanella D'Amico,* 297 F.Supp. 699, 701 (SDNY 1969). An inference that relevant evidence would be unfavorable is also justifiable where it is within the control of a party in whose interest it would naturally be to produce it and he fails to do so, without satisfactory explanation, and instead produces weaker evidence or no evidence. *Mid–Continent Petroleum Corp. v. Keen,* 157 F.2d 310, 315 (8th Cir. 1946). But one cannot justify the drawing of such an inference where the destruction of the evidence is unintentional or where failure to produce evidence is satisfactorily explained.

Steinkemp testified in particular with respect to the ceilometer trace that the normal procedure was to take place the rolled–up paper on which several day's or week's record appears into a storage bin for perhaps 15 or 30 days. After that time, the trace is discarded. He did not know what became of the traces from September 20, 1974. Counsel for the government confirmed that an FAA manual requires the orderly destruction of records, some within 20 or 60 days. Defendant contends that all papers potentially relevant to an accident cannot be saved, that FAA employees who are not lawyers cannot be expected to anticipate plaintiffs' requests for records were ambiguous at best and failed to

put FAA personnel on notice at the time that the traces should be retained, and finally, that, where weather reports were recorded in a log included among the documents preserved for plaintiff's case, destruction of the traces is satisfactorily explained. As a matter of law, we are inclined to agree with defendant that plaintiff's request for the retention of pertinent documents did not provide notice that the traces should be retained. We conclude that there is no showing that the government's destruction of the traces were intentional.

* * * * *

INDEADENT PETROCHEMICAL CORPORATION, et al. v. AETNA CASUALTY AND SURETY COMPANY, et al

654 F.Supp. 1334

United States District Court, District of Columbia
February 4, 1986

Plaintiff Independent Petrochemical Corporation ("IPC") is primarily in the business of terminaling and marketing various petrochemical products in Missouri. IPC is a wholly–owned subsidiary of plaintiff Chart Oil Company ("Charter"), which in turn is owned by plaintiff The Charter Company ("TCC"). Plaintiffs have filed for Chapter 11 bankruptcy in Florida.

Defendants are 23 insurance companies that sold 67 primary and excess liability insurance policies to plaintiffs from 1971 to 1983, for which plaintiffs paid in excess of $10 million and which provide coverage of approximately $1.115 million for each "occurrence" of certain "bodily injury" and "property damage."

In 1971, IPC agreed to help one of its customers, Northeastern Pharmaceutical and Chemical Company ("NEPACCO"), to remove waste products from a holding tank at NEPACCO's facility in Verona, Missouri. IPC did this by contacting an independent contractor, Russell Martin Bliss, who removed twenty thousand gallons of waste products. It is now alleged that this waste material contained a concentration of dioxin, a toxic element that can cause physical injury. Bliss allegedly mixed these waste products with waste oils he collected from other sources and sprayed the mixture as a dust suppressant at a number of sites in Missouri.

Fifty–seven civil actions involving more than 1,600 claimants have been filed in other courts against plaintiffs, as well as class actions and suits by the State of Missouri and the United States. Most of the claims allege bodily injury and property damage from exposure to the contaminated spray material. One aspect of the claims is that they allege "delayed–manifestation" injury, meaning continuous and progressive damage from the exposure. The individual claimants seek in aggregate $4 billion in bodily injuries and property damage, as well as $4 billion in punitive damages.

Some of the claims have been settled. Four of plaintiffs' six primary insurance companies have agreed to pay all of plaintiffs' defense costs for the time being in the remaining actions pursuant to a Standstill Interim Defense Agreement. Although the parties have attempted to negotiate a final settlement of defendants' obligation to defend and indemnify plaintiffs in the dioxin–related claims, no such settlement has been reached..

* * * * *

A. Destruction of documents

Hartford contends that the discovery that has taken place to date has been marked by a consistent pattern of obstructive and dilatory practices by plaintiffs. Central to this has been the destruction of various documents which may be relevant to Hartford's discovery efforts.

Through the deposition of Thomas Terbrueggen on July 17, 1985, Hartford learned that plaintiff Charter had no document retention policy and that numerous documents held by

Charter have been destroyed by Charter employees since this action was initiated. For instance, Terbrueggen himself had directed the disposal of 37 notebooks of insurance–related documents two weeks before his first deposition took place. The empty notebook binders were presented to Hartford at the second Terbrueggen deposition. Terbrueggen asserted that he only destroyed documents that he believed were duplicated in other files, but he was unable to describe in any depth the contents of the documents, nor whether they contained handwritten notations not found on their duplicates. Terrbrueggen stated that the notebooks contained "a lot of proposals that different people had made to us over the years on insurance programs that we may or may not have purchased." Deposition of Thomas Terbrueggen, July 19, 1985, at 133. Hartford believes that such documents are of critical importance since they may provide insight into Charter's intent and understanding of insurance policy terms that Charter agreed to over the past 15 years.

Hartford believes that Charter's obligation to preserve potentially relevant documents, *see Struthers Patent Corp. v. Nestle Co., Inc.*, 558 F.Supp. 747 (D.N.J. 1981), arose when the dioxin claims against plaintiffs were filed over a decade ago. As Hartford sees it, continuous destruction of documents in the Risk Management Department since that time was clearly a violation of Charter's obligation. Since reconstruction of the documents is not possible, Hartford's ability to receive a fair trial is lost, and dismissal of the case is appropriate.

Plaintiffs respond that the notebooks in questions contained old and useless documents which Terbrueggen, after review, determined were irrelevant to this litigation. Approximately 20 notebooks were retained as being possibly relevant. Those that were disposed of were extra copies, not originals. Deposition of Thomas Terbrueggen, July 19, 1985, at 133–139, 154. These notebooks dealt with subjects such as personnel practices, OSHA regulations, operating plans, seminar materials, and old proposals for insurance, including property insurance. *Id.*, at 290, 296, 299, and 303–04. Hartford has not shown willful misconduct, nor that its defense has in fact been prejudiced.

Plaintiffs contend that dismissal of this case under FRCP Rule 37 is appropriate only when a party fails to obey a court order to provide discovery. Since plaintiffs have not done this, dismissal is inappropriate absent repeated violations of a court order or proven record of bad faith. Hartford responds that this court has inherent equitable power beyond the confines of Rule 37 to dismiss this case. *See United States v. Moss–American, Inc.*, 78 F.R.D. 214 (E.D.Wis.1978).

While this court may have such power, this court declines to exercise it in this case. There is no question that when relevant documents are willfully destroyed by a party then that party is culpable and should be held responsible for the prejudice it has caused. *Wm. T. Thompson Co. v. General Nutrition Corp.*, 593 F.Supp. 1443 (C.D.Cal.1984). Hartford, however, has engaged in an insufficient showing that any relevant documents were in fact destroyed and that duplicates do not exist. Further, non–retention of such relevant documents must be a willful act, meaning deliberate obstructionist behavior. *See Societe Internationale v. Rogers*, 357 U.S. 197, 212, 78 S.Ct. 1087, 1096, 2 L.Ed.2d 1255 (1958). Terbrueggen's depositions make it clear that he sought to retain all potentially relevant documents and to destroy only documents duplicated elsewhere. Certainly there has been no violation of a court order and no clear intent to hinder Hartford's interests. Though it may be difficult for Hartford to make a stronger showing given that these are documents in Charter's control, this court is reluctant to engage in the extreme sanction of dismissal based on pure speculation by Hartford. This court, however, advises Charter that all additional documents that relate in any way to this case, duplicative or not, should be stored not destroyed, pending the outcome of this litigation.

INTERNATIONAL MINING v. ALLEN & CO., INC.

567 F.Supp. 777

Defendant Allen & Co., Inc. ("Allen") has moved pursuant to Fed.R.Civ.P. 56 for summary judgment dismissing the complaint of plaintiff International Mining Co., Inc. ("IMCO"). Allen has also moved pursuant to Fed.R.Civ.P. 37 to dismiss the complaint for IMCO's failure to comply with certain discovery orders issued by this court. For the reasons stated below, the motions will be granted.

Prior Proceedings

IMCO commenced this diversity action in July, 1980 seeking damages for tortious interference with contract. IMCO is a Pennsylvania corporation with its principal place of business in Pittsburgh, Pennsylvania. One of IMCO's business activities is the brokerage of coal. Allen, a New York corporation with its principal place of business in New York City, is engaged in the investment banking business.

The amended complaint asserts that a contract between IMCO and a third party, Kittanning Coal Co., Inc. ("Kittanning"), was repudiated pursuant to the "directions" of Allen and that this was done without any business justification and was undertaken out of spite. IMCO seeks damages of $500,000 in lost commissions under the brokerage agreement and $1,000,000 in lost sales of coal. Punitive damages "in excess of $1,000,000" are also sought.

* * * * *

In sum, IMCO did not produce answers and documents in response to Allen's initial discovery requests. When Allen moved to compel discovery, IMCO's counsel represented in open court that production was forthcoming. It was not. Allen was forced to file another motion to compel. In the meantime, IMCO filed answers to Allen's interrogatories that were woefully deficient. This court then awarded Allen its expenses on these motions and ordered production of answers by April 20, 1983. IMCO has yet to respond to Allen's document requests and its supplemental interrogatory answers, the second set of which were filed late and are still unsigned and not sworn to, fail to cure the inadequacies.

These events should be viewed in the context of the schedule for discovery and pretrial proceedings established by this court. As recounted above, following Allen's initial motion to dismiss, which was denied in December, 1981, the parties were given one year in which to conduct discovery. This was done primarily in the hope that the related Pennsylvania State court action could be resolved in the meantime. It subsequently became clear that trial was not imminent in Pennsylvania. Thus, the discovery deadline for this action was set for March 5, 1983, and the parties were directed to file all pretrial motions by the same date.

In the face of this proscription, IMCO's first response to Allen's interrogatories, which were prepounded in January, 1983, came on April 4, 1983, some two weeks after oral argument on Allen's motion for summary judgment and one month after the close of discovery. IMCO's dilatory conduct is unexplained.

Allen urges that the proper sanction for IMCO's dereliction is dismissal of the complaint pursuant to Fed.R.Civ.P. 37(b)(2)(C). The use of this harshest of sanctions is limited to cases involving "willfulness, bad faith, or any fault" on the part of the disobedient party. *Societe Internationale v. Rogers*, 357 U.S. 197, 212, 78 S.Ct. 1087, 1095, 2 L.Ed.2d 1255 (1958). Our Court of Appeals has held that gross negligence qualifies as "fault" under this doctrine. *Cine Forty–Second St. Theatre Corp. v. Allied Artists Pictures Corp.*, 602 F.2d 1062, 1065–66 (2d Cir.1979).

The sanctions available under Rule 37 should be employed with a view toward the three purposes they serve. First, they ensure that a party will not be able to profit from its own failure to comply with the requirements of discovery. *Id.* at 1066. Thus, a relevant consideration in choosing the appropriate sanction is the extent to which the other party's preparation for trial has been prejudiced. *Black Panther Party v. Smith*, 661 F.2d 1243, 1255 (D.C.Cir.1981), *vacated and remanded on other grounds*, _____ U.S. _____, 102 S.Ct. 3505, 73 L.Ed.2d 1381 (1982). Second, the sanctions act as specific deterrents in that they seek to secure compliance with the particular order at hand. *Cine Forth–Second St. Theatre Corp. v. Allied Artists Pictures Corp., supra,* 602 F.2d at 1066. Third, the general deterrent effect in enforcing the strict adherence to the responsibilities litigants owe to the court and their opponents is served. *Id.* at 1066–67. *See Roadway Express, Ind. v. Piper*, 447 U.S. 752, 764, 100 S.Ct. 2455, 2463, 65 L.Ed.2d 488 (1980); *National Hockey League v. Metropolitan Hockey Club, Inc.*, 427 U.S. 639, 643, S.Ct. 2778, 49 L.Ed.2d 747 (1976); *Black Panther Party v. Smith, supra,* 661 F.2d at 1256. *See generally* Note *The Emerging Deterrence Orientation in the Imposition of Discovery Sanctions*, 91 Harv.L.Rev. 1033 (1978). As the Court of Appeals for the District of Columbia Circuit has noted, the general deterrence purpose:

has special significance in the case of interrogatories which are supposed to be severed [sic] and answered without the need for judicial prompting. Indeed, Rule 37(d) plainly requires a party receiving interrogatories to make one of two responses: an answer or a motion for a protective order. If parties are allowed to flout their obligations, choosing to wait to make a response until a trial court has lost patience with them, the effect will be to embroil judges in day–to–day supervision of discovery, a result directly contrary to the overall scheme of the federal discovery rules.

Dellums v. Powell, 566 F.2d 231, 235 (D.C. Cir.1977) (citations omitted). The choice of the appropriate sanction lies within the discretion of the court after consideration of the full record in the case. *National Hockey League v. Metropolitan Hockey Club, Inc., supra,* 427 U.S. at 642, 96 S.Ct. at 2780; *Diapulse Corp. of America v. Curtis Pub. Co.*, 374 F.2d 442, 447 (2d Cir.1967).

This court has considered the above–enumerated factors and has determined that dismissal of the complaint is the appropriate sanction under the circumstances presented here. IMCO's complete failure to produce documents after the representation of its counsel in open court that production was forthcoming, can only be described as willful and shows its disrespect not only for its discovery obligations, but also for this court. Its intransigence in supplying adequate answers to Allen's interrogatories rises at least to the level of gross negligence. Indeed, the answers are sufficiently inadequate that an inference of willfulness is not unreasonable. IMCO has offered no excuse to explain its initial failure to answer. It could have sought a protective order if it considered Allen's requests too burdensome or otherwise objectionable, but it has not done so. Its second supplemental answers are not signed or sworn to and, as such, are not answers at all.

IMCO's defense on this motion is that it has proceeded in good faith and has laid out its case in its opposition to Allen's motion for summary judgment. It is required, however, to lay out adequate answers to interrogatories in a form to allow their use at trial as Rule 33 contemplates. It is not relieved of this duty simply because it has provided its theory of the case to the other side in attorneys' affidavits in response to a motion.

Furthermore, Allen has been prejudiced by IMCO's conduct. It was forced to file its motion for summary judgment without the benefit of discovery that it is entitled to. It still has not received documents or adequate answers to interrogatories. As noted, some of the interrogatories are so unresponsive as to be useless. A particularly egregious example is IMCO's response to Allen's interrogatory regarding the claim for $1,000,000 in damages for lost sales. No basis is given for this claim or for how this figure was arrived at.

* * * * *

INTERSTATE ELECTRIC CO. v. INTERSTATE ELECTRIC CO. OF SHREVEPORT, Inc.

33 So.2d 779

Court of Appeal of Louisiana, Second Circuit
February 2, 1948

* * * * *

As a background for an understanding of the original of the claims sued upon, it is desirable to set forth a brief history of the parties plaintiff and defendant which bear identical names, with the exception of the designation of the domicile of the Shreveport Company. There has never been any corporation relationship between the parties. Upon organization of the Interstate Electric Company of Shreveport the majority of the stock therein was subscribed by Percival Stern and members of his family. Stern became President of the Shreveport corporation and conducted its affairs for a period of years, being, during the same period, the President of the New Orleans Company. In or about the years 1930–31 the financial condition of the Shreveport Company deteriorated, because of general economic conditions, to such a point that the first National Bank of Shreveport, which carried substantial loans of the corporation felt required to select and install, in active management of the affairs of the company, one of its representatives as an alternative to foreclosing its loans, which would have been disastrous insofar as the continuance of business of the corporation was concerned. * * *

A short time after the change in the stock ownership of the Shreveport Company had taken place, the statement of the accounts between the New Orleans and the Shreveport Companies was prepared and forwarded by the Shreveport Company in accordance with the showing on its books, which statement disclosed a balance of $221.21 in favor of the New Orleans Company. After receipt of the statement the New Orleans Company protested the correctness thereof and countered with a statement of its own showing a balance in its favor in excess of $2,000. The disagreement as to the accounts existing between the two companies led to the institution of this action.

* * * * *

The character of the evidence which was tendered by plaintiff in support of this demand was made up of the testimony of its President, Stern, and its head bookkeeper, Breaud. The predicate for the introduction of secondary evidence on this point was attempted to be laid by the showing that plaintiff, in the regular course of business, periodically destroyed its vouchers, canceled checks and other records. But the significant fact was developed that the records bearing upon these particular items apparently were destroyed after the filing of this suit, and certainly after the dispute with reference to the repayment of these amounts became an issue between the parties.

The doubt cast upon plaintiff's explanation, and the acceptance thereof as a foundation for the introduction of secondary evidence, is further emphasized by the fact that other checks and vouchers bearing upon matters involved in this litigation, older in point of time, were produced and introduced in evidence. This circumstance clearly indicates that plaintiffs failed in their attempt to show such an enduring custom of periodic destruction of records as would justify the acceptance of secondary evidence.

* * * * *

Barbara JACKSON v. HARVARD UNIVERSITY and John H. McArthur

721 F.Supp. 1397

United States District Court, D. Massachusetts
August 14, 1989

Overview

This case concerns a faculty tenure decision upon which reasonable people could and did disagree. The plaintiff Jackson, although a talented academic, failed on two occasions to convince a critical mass of the tenured fac-

ulty at the Business School that she should herself be admitted to tenured status. Lacking that critical mass of support, Ms. Jackson's candidacy did not receive the necessary support of the defendant Dean McArthur.

* * * * *

The tenure process for Ms. Jackson followed the traditional pathway in 1981. A subcommittee, formed to review her work, generated a detailed report and made its own recommendation. By a 3–1 vote the Subcommittee found Ms. Jackson met the standards for tenure. The one dissenter took the position that while she did not meet the standards, she should nevertheless be granted tenure as an exceptional case.

The tenure question was then taken up by the tenured faculty as a whole. Following customary practice, a preliminary vote was taken after a preliminary discussion of Ms. Jackson's qualifications, and she received a substantial majority in support of tenure. However, when the final vote was taken less than one month later, Ms. Jackson's substantial majority had evaporated and only a slight majority continued to support her tenure candidacy. Although obviously relevant, this rapid evaporation of support was not the topic of any evidence adduced by the parties at trial.

Faced with only this slight majority of support for Ms. Jackson after the 1981 tenure votes, Dean McArthur chose a somewhat unusual approach. Rather than employing the customary one–year termination appointment ordinarily extended tenure candidates who fail to obtain substantial faculty support, the Dean organized a series of meeting designed to fashion a strategy to meet the perceived deficiency in the record Ms. Jackson presented: her lack of sufficient creativity. During the spring of 1982 interested members of the faculty met with her to define a project which would satisfy those who had opposed her tenure candidacy.

Such a project was developed that spring. And despite reservations about the definition given it, Ms. Jackson — who was relieved of any classroom responsibilities to allow her to devote full time to the project — began her work. Dean McArthur made clear that the project did not need to be completed before the end of February 1984. He further indicated that the final deadline could be extended to the later summer or fall of 1984. Nevertheless, Ms. Jackson decided to complete the project as quickly as possible. She submitted a draft to certain tenured professors in her area over the summer of 1983. In memoranda delivered in early August, two of the reviewers criticized this draft severely because of its superficiality. Heedless of these harbingers that her performance on the project was not meeting with support from interested representatives of the group whose substantial support she would need to achieve tenure, Ms. Jackson submitted her final version at the end of August 1983, within a month after receiving the severely negative comments and well before any deadline for submission.

Predictably, Ms. Jackson's rush to judgment in the face of adverse comments did not improve her tenure chances. The 1983 Subcommittee recommended unanimously against tenure for Ms. Jackson and the full tenured faculty voted in favor of tenure for her by only a modest majority, well short of the substantial majority Dean McArthur considered necessary before he would recommend tenure. At this point, Dean McArthur offered the termination appointment; Ms. Jackson left the Business School and this litigation ensued.

On their face, nothing in these proceedings fairly suggests Ms. Jackson was discriminated against on the basis of her sex in the Business School's tenure decision. I have found nothing in the direct evidence concerning that process to support such a claim. Ms. Jackson, however, has also raised a collection of circumstantial matters which she maintains support her contention. Broadly stated, these circumstantial matters relate to the environment at the Business School, purported irregularities in its procedures as applied to Ms. Jackson's candidacy, and alleged disparate treatment of male tenure candidates. I have analyzed these matters in great detail and find nothing beneath the surface which supports Ms. Jackson's position. The

circumstantial matters reduce to a collection of attenuated, dated, and immaterial incidents and stray remarks, *de minimus* procedural anomalies, and inapposite comparisons with other tenure candidates.

Viewing the appropriate judgment as extraordinarily clear, I was prepared to decide this case from the bench adversely to the plaintiff with an *ore tenus* decision dictated into the record. During the course of trial it also became clear, however, that the defendants, in addition to a very strong case, were benefiting improperly from their own discovery misconduct and the operation of certain misconceived pre–trial discovery rulings. Prior to trial the defendants destroyed documents they were under a court order to produce. They also availed themselves of a spurious privilege not to disclose the particulars of tenure discussions and evaluations. When it developed that the defendants had in addition not responded fully to pre–trial document demands, I offered the plaintiff *sua sponte* the opportunity to conduct further discovery to counteract these evidentiary limitations. She rejected this opportunity to adduce additional relevant evidence and pressed only for sanctions which would relieve her of the burden of proving her case by the introduction of evidence. The imposition of such sanctions, however, was unacceptable to me as a means of resolving factual disputes.

In deciding this case I found an absence of evidence which the parties should have adduced but for various reasons neither proposed to offer nor ultimately even sought to discover. Concerned that the defendants not benefit unfairly by their own misconduct and what I came to conclude were erroneous pre–trial privilege determinations, I found it necessary to read and reread the documentary submissions and trial testimony to assure myself that I had accounted for all the links — even those missing from the evidence offered by the parties — in the chains which bind this case together. After undertaking this extensive review, I am satisfied that my initial tentative judgment was correct.

In summary, there is in this case no basis on which to find gender discrimination against the plaintiff in her tenure review. It is simply a case presenting the supportable conclusion of a university and its responsible Dean that a member of a protected class — Ms. Jackson, a qualified female tenure candidate — did not satisfy the necessarily subjective standards which guide tenure determinations. There is here insufficient — indeed virtually no — evidence that illicit discriminatory motives were at work. Thus, I am not free to interpose whatever independent views I might harbor regarding the merits of Ms. Jackson's tenure candidacy but must enter judgment for the defendants.

Missing Evidence

Given the great subtlety and sensitivity required in assessing the evidence in this action, I am compelled to begin the detailed findings and conclusions by evaluating in depth the lack of certain evidence which might have been relevant and material to a determination in this case. Full development of the record has been hampered by what I shall call the problem of missing evidence, caused jointly and severally by the application of what I have now concluded was an erroneous extension of evidentiary privilege to the defendants, by the negligence of the defendants in preserving documents, by the inattentiveness of the defendants to their discovery responsibilities, and, ultimately, by the strategic judgment of the plaintiff herself not to pursue further discovery when it was offered her by the court.

The plaintiff sought to short circuit the judgment process and obtain the benefit of certain adverse inferences and preclusionary orders as a result of the missing evidence. She was, however, unwilling to accept an offer to conduct further discovery in order to remedy the advantage that she contended defendants had previously obtained improperly from the privilege, the documentary destruction, and the discovery defaults. For my part, I have been unwilling to decide this case on the basis of evidentiary constructs such as adverse inferences and preclusionary orders.

* * * * *

The Destruction of Documents

When the plaintiff commenced this action,

she served defendants with her First Request for Production of Documents. This included a request for the tenure files of every male who had ever been granted tenure at the Business School. On March 5, 1986, a Magistrate ordered that plaintiff be allowed discovery of the files of successful male candidates for tenure during only the 1981–1984 period. Plaintiff appealed the narrow scope of the Magistrate's ruling, and on August 12, 1986, Judge Garrity "modifie[d] the magistrate's order to permit discovery of the tenure files of men who were granted tenure between 1974 and 1984." *Jackson*, 111 F.R.D. at 476.

After Judge Garrity's August 1986 ruling, plaintiff and the court learned that defendants would not be able to comply fully with the Judge's discovery order, because the majority of the requested tenure files had been destroyed in April or May of 1986, shortly after issuance of the Magistrate's order.

The destruction of documents can merit the inference that the contents of the destroyed documents were unfavorable to the party that destroyed them. The First Circuit has observed that:

> The general principles concerning the inferences to be drawn from the loss or destruction of documents are well established. When the contents of a document are relevant to an issue in a case, the trier of fact generally may receive the fact of the document's nonproduction or destruction as evidence that the party which has prevented production did so out of the well–founded fear that the contents would harm him. Wigmore has asserted that nonproduction is not merely some evidence, but is sufficient by itself to support an adverse inference even if no other evidence for the inference exists:

> The failure or refusal to produce a relevant document, or the destruction of it, is evidence *from which alone* its contents may be inferred to be unfavorable to the possessor, provided the opponent, when the identity of the document is disputed, first introduces some evidence tending to

show that the document actually destroyed or withheld is the one as to whose contents it is desired to draw an inference.

Wigmore on Evidence § 291, at 288 (Chadbourne rev.1979) (emphasis added). The inference depends, of course, on a showing that the party had notice that the documents were relevant at the time he failed to produce them or destroyed them.

Nation–Wide Check Corp. v. Forest Hills Distribs., Inc., 692 F.2d 214, 217–18 (1st Cir.1982); *see also Petition of United States,* 255 F.Supp. 737, 740 n. (D.Mass. 1966), *aff'd in pertinent part and rev'd in part sub nom. United States v. Sandra & Dennis Fishing Corp.,* 372 F.2d 189, 196 (1st Cir.), *cert. denied,* 389 U.S. 836, 88 S.Ct. 48, 19 L.Ed.2d 98 (1967). Consequently, it is necessary for me to evaluate in detail the circumstances of Harvard's destruction of documents in order to evaluate what inferences, if any, should be drawn.

At the time this litigation commenced, the subject tenure files were stored in the office of Marrilyn Reid, the Administrator for Faculty Appointments and Procedures and Secretary of the Faculty of the Harvard Business School. The files remained in Ms. Reid's office until September 1985, at which time they were sent to the Inactive Records Center of Harvard University. Ms. Reid was "well aware" at the time the files were sent that they were needed for this litigation; she had been advised that the tenure files were to be preserved. However, she desperately needed to create file space in her office, and she believed the tenure files would be safe at the Inactive Records Center.

In selecting the particular files to be sent, Ms. Reid consulted with Amy Sugerman, who had become the Business School's Records Analyst in August 1985. The two women worked with one another in the selection process, but they did not communicate with respect to the various special considerations involved in the transfer. When the transfer was made, I find, Ms. Sugerman did not know about the pendency of this litigation or plaintiff's discovery request; she thought the tenure files were being transferred to be destroyed. Consequently, she filled out a "Records Disposition Application and Certificate" for the destruction of the files and sent it to the appropriate administrator at the Business School.

Ms. Sugerman also told Joan Glasser, the staff assistant to Richard Haas, the Records Management Officer of Harvard University's archives, that the files were to be destroyed. In fact, during September–October 1985, Ms. Sugerman and Ms. Glasser spoke between ten and twenty times. These conversations left Ms. Glasser with "no doubt" whatsoever that the records received from the Business School in September were to be destroyed.

When the tenure records arrived at the Inactive Records Center in September, they were placed in the area reserved for materials that are to be incinerated. Normally, records are not received and placed in that area unless they arrive with a completed Disposition Application. According to Mr. Haas, these records were received as an exception to the general rule because he was doing a favor for Ms. Sugerman and because he fully believed that the completed Application would be forthcoming.

On December 9, 1985, Ms. Sugerman received a memorandum from Dean Currie, the Business School's Assistant Dean for Administration and Policy Planning. This memorandum informed Ms. Sugerman, apparently for the first time, that the Business School was "in the early stages of litigation with someone who failed to be promoted to tenure. [And that] [f]or the time being, and especially now when we are in the 'discovery' process, our attorneys say that we shouldn't throw anything away." Ms. Sugerman sent a copy of Dean Currie's memorandum to Rich Haas and Marrilyn Reid two days after she received it.

On December 16, 1985, Rick Haas sent a memorandum to Ms. Sugarman in which he acknowledged his agreement with the directive expressed in Dean Currie's memorandum. Two days later, Ms. Sugerman called Mr. Haas to make sure that the tenure records which had been sent to the Inactive Records Center in September would not be accidentally destroyed. She memorialized her telephone conversation with a handwritten note to herself at the bottom of Mr. Haas's December 16th memorandum. The note states:

> Called Rick 18 Dec asking him if the records for Marrilyn now stored in the "hold" area for incineration would be safe there and wouldn't be destroyed accidentally with the Admissions files which were moved to the hold area at the same time. He said "absolutely not" — that he personally lets the movers in and supervises them as to which boxes to take.

Mr. Haas claims that following his conversation with Ms. Sugerman, he informed Ms. Glasser of the necessity of preserving the Business School's tenure records. He did not, however, write any sort of note or memorandum to this effect, and Ms. Glasser vehemently denies that she was ever told that the subject tenure records had to be preserved. Moreover, no one associated with the Inactive Records Center ever followed the Center's routine procedure of recording the subject tenure records on the "shelf list" of records to be preserved.

In late April or early May of 1986, a moving company employed by Harvard University to transport documents for purposes of destruction moved the boxes containing the subject tenure records from the Inactive Records Center. Ms. Glasser supervised the removal of the boxes, having been directed by Mr. Haas to let the movers take every box in the area of the Center where the tenure records had been stored since September.

The records were removed and destroyed without a Disposition Application ever having been presented to the Inactive Records Center. They appear to have been the first Business School records ever removed from the Inactive Records Center. They were apparently the only records of any sort to have been destroyed without a completed Disposition Application since the advent of the 1939 University–wide policy regarding records retention.

Remedies for the Limitations

Immediately after the plaintiff became aware of the defendants' discovery violations (and before she had obtained a copy of the tally sheet), she moved, pursuant to Fed.R.Civ.P. 26(g), 37(b), and 37(d), for sanctions. She requested that the defendants be precluded from offering any evidence concerning the votes of the tenured faculty in 1981 and 1983. This request was the culmination of plaintiff's efforts to obtain the benefit of affirmative evidentiary sanctions such as adverse inference and preclusion orders to overcome the effect of the evidentiary suppression caused by the erroneous privilege, documentary destruction, and discovery delay. My legal analysis of adverse inference sanctions and preclusionary remedies is set forth below in Section III.B.1 and III.B.2, respectively.

Instead of employing adverse inferences or preclusionary orders, I offered to remedy Harvard's negligent suppression of evidence by reopening discovery and allowing plaintiff to make further inquiry unconstrained by the limitations of an academic privilege. This offer provided plaintiff with the opportunity to develop for herself a remedial program closely tailored to meet the problems created by, for example, defendants' failure to disclose the tally sheet and other relevant information until the conclusion of trial in a four–year–old case. My offer, if accepted, could have made available to plaintiff — and the court — relevant evidence necessary to the determination of the ultimate issue in this case: whether defendants discriminated against plaintiff in denying her tenure. The plaintiff, however, rejected the offer and chose, as set forth more fully below in Section III.B.3, not to pursue further discovery.

There is no doubt that a major problem in this litigation has been the unavailability of relevant evidence, caused by the assertion of an unwarranted privilege, the destruction of relevant tenure records, and the belated and begrudging disclosure of critical ballot documents such as the tally sheet. As a policy matter, however, I rejected the adverse inference and preclusion remedies proposed by plaintiff because they would have exacerbated

the underlying problem further. Such remedies would have continued to circumscribe
unnecessarily the evidence available for my
fact finding.

1. The Adverse Inference Remedy for Document Destruction

Defendants offered two reasons why I should
not draw an adverse inference from the destruction of documents:

(1) The files destroyed presumably included
the tenure records of unsuccessful as well as
successful male candidates. Defendants
maintained that if the records of the unsuccessful males had been available, they would
have shown that men were denied tenure on
the same or similar grounds as plaintiff, and
that the Business School's promotion standards were applied in consistent, gender–blind
manner. They contended that the destruction
of the records therefore hurt their case as
much as, if not more than, plaintiff's.

(2) The records were inadvertently destroyed after the Business School sent them
out for safekeeping. Defendants averred
there was no intent to destroy evidence, and
in fact every intent to preserve it. They maintained that the loss of the evidence was due
to errors made at the Inactive Records Center, whose manager, Mr. Haas, was not directly affiliated with the Business School,
and who had assured the Business School
that he would personally see to the security
of the relevant documents; and whose negligence accordingly should not be imputed to
defendants. Defendants contended that they
should not suffer the extraordinary consequences of having a significant evidentiary
inference drawn against them because someone over whom they had little or no control
made a mistake.

I found defendants' first argument meritless.
Speculation that destroyed documents may
have proven helpful to defendants is hardly
a reason not to draw a negative inference
from what was at best negligent behavior on
defendants' part. While the records of unsuccessful male candidates could have aided
defendants' case, they also could have dam-

aged defendants' case, for instance, by showing that those men were denied tenure only
because their records were substantially
poorer than plaintiff's. The point is that we
do not know what those documents would
have shown. We are left with speculation,
attributable to defendants' failure to do what
they should have done.

However, defendants' failure was not intentional. And for that reason, I found compelling
defendants' second ground for opposing the
negative inference. Although there was initial
confusion as to whether the subject tenure
records were sent to the Inactive Records Center for preservation or for destruction, long
before the actual destruction of the records that
confusion had been cleared up.

Dean Currie specifically notified Amy
Sugerman in December 1985 that the subject
records were to be preserved. Amy Sugerman in turn passed this information on to
Richard Haas, who gave her absolute assurance that the records would not be destroyed.
Thus, five to six months before the records
were actually destroyed, defendants had
taken some precautions to make sure the
records would be protected. Of course, in
retrospect it is obvious that the precautions
were inadequate and that the Business
School should have done more to protect the
records. Ms. Sugerman should, for instance,
have requested that Mr. Haas immediately
transfer the records to the General Counsel's
Office of the University. However, I refused
to penalize defendants for having failed to
take the most prudent course. Defendants
were negligent, but they did not act in bad
faith: they did not intentionally have the
documents destroyed.

First Circuit case law suggests that my authority to draw a negative inference against defendants is not wholly dependent upon a finding
of bad faith. Under the principle adopted by the
First Circuit in *Nation–Wide Check*, I "*may
receive the fact of the document[s] . . . destruction as evidence that [defendants] fear[ed] that
the contents would harm [them]*," 692 F.2d at
217 (emphasis supplied), apparently regardless
of whether defendants acted in good or bad
faith. However, I am not obliged to draw that

inference, and here I chose to exercise my discretion by now drawing it.

I would, no doubt, have reached a different conclusion if plaintiff had produced any evidence showing that defendants destroyed the subject records to avoid disclosure in this litigation. However, the drawing of a negative inference under the circumstances of this case, an act which would be all but a declaration of victory for plaintiff, is unwarranted. Here, the evidence shows merely that a person — Richard Haas — who was not under the direct supervision or control of the Business School, made a mistake. To impute his error to Business School decision makers and declare that, as a result of it, defendants must set aside by default a tenure decision that was reached over painstaking hours by the tenured Business School faculty, would be an unduly harsh remedy. It is one I have chosen not to impose. *See Allen Pen Co., v. Springfield Photo Mount Co.*, 653 F.2d 17, 23–24 (1st Cir.1981) (Plaintiff "has not shown that the document destruction was in bad faith or flowed from the consciousness of a weak case. There is no evidence that [defendant] believed the [destroyed pieces of evidence] would have damaged it in a lawsuit. Without some such evidence, ordinarily no adverse inference is drawn from [defendant's] failure to preserve them."); *Eaton Corp. v. Appliance Valves Corp.*, 790 F.2d 874, 878 (Fed.Cir.1986) ("If a court finds that both conditions precedent, evidence destruction and bad faith, are met, it may then infer that the evidence would be unfavorable to the destroying party if introduced in court."); *Coates v. Johnson & Johnson*, 756 F.2d 524, 551 (7th Cir.1985) ("The prevailing rule is that bad faith destruction of a document relevant to proof of an issue at trial gives rise to a strong inference that production of the document would have been unfavorable to the party responsible for the destruction . . . [The facts of this case] suggest that the documents were destroyed under routine procedures, not in bad faith, and thus cannot sustain the inference that defendants' agents were conscious of a weak case.") (citations omitted); *S.C. Johnson & Son, Inc. v. Louisville & Nashville R.R. Co.*, 695 F.2d 253, 258–59 (7th Cir.1982) (Before

a court may draw a negative inference from a party's destruction of evidence, it must be convinced "that the party did so in bad faith.") (citing *Commercial Ins. Co. v. Gonzalez*, 512 F.2d 1307, 1314 (1st Cir.), *cert. denied*, 423 U.S. 838, 96 S.Ct. 65, 46 L.Ed.2d (1975)).

When Harley Holden, the Curator of the Harvard University Archives, learned of the destruction of the subject tenure records, he told Mr. Haas, "It's a terrible mistake and it should not have happened." Mr. Holden was correct. However, I find that although "terrible," the destruction of the tenure records was in fact a mistake. It was not a purposeful or intentional act on the part of the defendants designed to suppress evidence. I find that it is more likely than not that the records were destroyed because of miscommunication between Mr. Haas and Ms. Glasser, and because the records were stored at the Inactive Records Center directly adjacent to boxes containing material for which Disposition Applications had been properly completed. For this the sanction of adverse inference would be disproportionate.

JOBA CONSTRUCTION COMPANY, INC., a Michigan corporation v. BURNS & ROE INCORPORATED, a foreign corporation

329 N.W.2d 760

Court of Appeals of Michigan
December 6, 1982

On November 3, 1980, following an eight-week trial of plaintiff's action for tortious interference with prospective advantageous economic relations, the jury returned a verdict in favor of plaintiff in the amount of $272,368. Defendant appeals as of right raising a plethora of issues for our consideration, many of which have not been preserved for appeal, and the remainder of which do not require reversal.

Plaintiff is a Michigan corporation specializing in underground and heavy–duty construction.

Defendant is a New York based firm of consulting engineers which had been retained by the City of Detroit Public Lighting Commission (hereinafter PLC) in 1971 in connection with the expansion of the PLC's Mistersky Generating Station. Defendant's main responsibilities under its contract with PLC were to prepare construction specifications, evaluate bids made by contractors and make recommendations to the PLC as to which contractor should be awarded contracts.

In 1974, bids were solicited from contractors for performance of a contract designated as contract #306. Although plaintiff submitted the lowest bid, defendant recommended to the PLC that the contract be awarded to another contractor as it felt plaintiff was unqualified to perform the contract. Accordingly, the contract was awarded to another contractor. In 1976, bids were solicited for another project as Mistersky Station and a contract designated as contract 323 was awarded to a local construction company which had designated plaintiff as its proposed excavation and piling subcontractor. However, defendant informed that company that plaintiff was unacceptable as the subcontractor and plaintiff was thereafter removed as the subcontractor. Plaintiff then commenced this action alleging that defendant wrongfully persuaded the PLC not to award plaintiff the general contract on #306 and a subcontract on #323.

We consider defendant's allegations of error in the sequence in which they arose in trial court.

* * * * *

Similarly, we are unpersuaded by defendant's claim that the trial court erred in admitting a copy of the minutes in lieu of the original. Under MRE 1004, an original is not required and other evidence of the contents of a writing is admissible if the original is lost or destroyed, unless the proponent acted in bad faith. Here, there was testimony that the original of the minutes had been destroyed and there was no showing of bad faith on the part of the plaintiff and, therefore, the copy was properly introduced.

In addition, under MRE 1003, a duplicate such

as a photostatic copy is admissible to the same extent as the original, unless a genuine question is raised as to the authenticity of the original, or if it would be unfair to admit the duplicate in lieu of the original. Here, defendant never claimed the existence of a genuine issue regarding the authenticity of the original.

* * * * *

KANSAS–NEBRASKA NATURAL GAS COMPANY, INC. v. MARATHON OIL COMPANY and Double M Oil Company

109 F.R.D. 12

United States District Court D. Nebraska
April 28, 1983

The plaintiff has filed a motion for the imposition of sanctions, pursuant to the provisions of Rule 37(d), Fed.R.Civ. P., stemming from the defendant Marathon's destruction of certain documents claimed to be relevant to the issues pending before the court, at a time after such documents were requested to be produced pursuant to Rule 34, Fed.R.Civ. P.

* * * * *

The evidence, though voluminous, is not strong. In support of the motion, for example, there is no evidence giving a firm description of the documents destroyed; no evidence of which the destroyed documents, if any, have no duplicates available for counsel to use; no evidence tending to show that any of the destroyed documents were in any way tampered with or different from those copies which have been made available to counsel from other sources. Most importantly, there is no evidence tending to show that the destruction of these documents was in any way willful, or intended to thwart the plaintiff's discovery efforts and preparation for trial in this case.

* * * * *

While the above quoted language may not preclude an order imposing sanctions on Marathon at this point, it represents a formidable barrier which, at least to this point, the plaintiff has not overcome. The affidavit of Patrick G. Petit, an attorney for Marathon in its Casper Division, indicates that although the documents destroyed in Findlay, Ohio are not available to the plaintiff, duplicates of those documents were believed to exist in Marathon's Casper, Wyoming office, and that all of that office's records have been made available for inspection by plaintiff's attorneys. Although Petit was not so employed at the time these records were created, his affidavit does establish some familiarity with the records involved in this proceeding. Against this statement, it is possible to speculate that the "duplicates" sent to the Findlay, Ohio office of Marathon were either not true duplicates, or included marginal notes or other writings which would signify differences, or that the Findlay, office's records, particularly of the budget meetings involved, may be significantly different or more inclusive than those found at the Division office; this is, however, only speculation. There is no showing to that effect in support of the motion. In view of the fact that these records have now been destroyed, they cannot be inspected to determine any differences, and I cannot assume any. To the extent that their existence may have been used to show knowledge on the part of Marathon's management, of the claims of communication now being asserted by K N Energy, it is important to note that Marathon has not denied these records' existence. *Cf. Berkey Photo, Inc. v Eastman Kodak Co.*, 603 F.2d 263 (2nd Cir.1979), cert. denied 444 U.S. 1093, 100 S.Ct. 1061, 62 L.Ed.2d 783 (1980), and has made duplicates available. These factors lead me to conclude that, at least in the absence of a showing to the contrary, I must find that Marathon has met the standard of "substantial compliance" described in *Fox, supra*, so as to preclude the imposition of sanctions.

The evidence submitted tends to establish that these documents were destroyed by Marathon in the regular course of its business, although also, as the result of probable negligence on the part of Marathon's management, Marathon's house counsel, and/or Marathon's trial counsel in failing to prevent their destruction. While I in no way wish to convey acceptance of that low standard of care which seemingly allowed the destruction to occur*, under the circumstances shown by the evidence, I am unable to find the facts necessary to impose sanctions.

That is not to say, however, that K N Energy's motion could not be construed as a motion to compel the production (i.e. reconstruction) of these documents, pursuant to the provisions of Rule 37(a), Fed.R.Civ. P. Marathon states in its brief in opposition to the motion for sanctions that it believes these records can be reconstructed. If that be the case, they should be, if necessary. I will not comment further at this time on the matter of reconstructing these records, leaving it for the moment to counsel to seek agreement pursuant to the provisions of Local Rule 20I, after which, if necessary, the matter may be brought back before me.

United States v. Park, 421 U.S. 658 at 672, 95 S.Ct. 1903, 1911, 44 L.Ed.2d 489 (1975) (emphasis added), as quoted in Wessel, "Institutional Responsibility: Professionalism and Ethics," 60 Neb.L.R. 504, at 514 (1981). If the public, and incidentally the courts, have a right to expect such standards on the part of corporate management, it would seem that at least those standards might reasonably be expected from corporate counsel and trial counsel.

---

*As noted by Chief Justice Warren Burger, the "lack of knowledge" is no defense against a public policy which demands disclosure:

[A corporate manager has] not only a positive duty to seek out and remedy violations when they occur but also, and primarily *a duty to implement measures that will insure that violations will not occur*. The requirements of foresight and vigilance imposed on responsible corporate agents are beyond question demanding, and perhaps, onerous, but they are not more stringent than the public has a right to expect of those who voluntarily assume positions of authority in business enterprises whose services and products affect the health and well–being of the public that support them.

Brian KOSLOWSKI, PPA and Cynthia Karaffa, Plaintiffs, v. SEARS, ROEBUCK AND COMPANY and Russell Mills, Inc., Defendants. SEARS ROEBUCK AND COMPANY, Third-Party Plaintiff, v. RUSSELL MILLS, INC., Third-Party Defendant.

73 F.R.D. 73

United States District Court, D. Massachusetts
December 8, 1976

Court's Ruling on Defendant's Motion to Remove Default Judgment

JULIAN, Senior District Judge.

A brief statement of the prior events in this case suffices to explain the present posture of the defendant's motion to remove the default judgment.

Plaintiff, a minor, was severely burned on November 11, 1970, in Royal Oak, Michigan when a pair of pajamas allegedly manufactured and marketed by defendant was "cause to ignite" (Plaintiff's Complaint, Count #6). Plaintiff commenced this product liability action on April 9, 1975, asserting claims sounding in negligence, breach of warranty, and strict liability in tort.

On July 17, 1975, the plaintiff filed a "Request to Produce" pursuant to Rule 34, Federal Rules of Civil Procedure, seeking, among other items,[1] a record of all complaints and communications concerning personal injuries and death allegedly caused by the burning of children's nightwear which had been manufactured or marketed by the defendant, Sears, Roebuck & Co. On August 8, 1975, the defendant filed a motion to quash. The plaintiff opposed the defendant's motion to quash and filed a motion to compel discovery pursuant to Rule 37, Federal Rules of Civil Procedure. On January 22, 1976, United States Magistrate Princi filed a "Memorandum and Order," after a hearing on the motions, overruling the defendant's objections and ordering production within thirty days of all thirty-one items.[2] Because

the material was not forthcoming, the plaintiff filed, on August 16, 1976, a motion for entry of judgment by default against the defendant, pursuant to Rule 37, Federal Rules of Civil Procedure. On July 14, 1976, this Court, finding that the defendant's failure to comply with a previous discovery order was "willful and deliberate," entered a judgment by default against the defendant on the issue of liability, but conditioned its removal upon the defendant's "full compliance" with the Court's discovery order on or before September 15, 1976. The defendant filed the instant motion to remove the judgment by default. The Court held a hearing on the motion on October 20, 1976, and took it under advisement. On the basis of that hearing, the Court finds that the defendant has failed substantially to comply fully with the Court's July 14 Order, and thus has not fulfilled the condition for removal of the default judgment.

The Court now denies defendant's motion for reasons hereinafter stated.

* * * * *

In the instant case, information concerning accidents similar to the one alleged in the complaint is clearly relevant to the issues of whether the pajamas allegedly marked by the defendant were an unreasonably dangerous product and whether the defendant knew, or in the exercise of due care should have known, of that danger. Furthermore, even though the records of similar suits might be inadmissible in evidence (*Narring v. Sears, Roebuck & Co.*, 59 Mich.App. 717, 229 N.W.2d 901 (1975) (circumstances of prior accident were too dissimilar to accident alleged in complaint)), the records might contain facts which would lead to the discovery of admissible evidence. See Rule 26(b)(1), Fed.R.Civ.P., *Melori Shoe Corp. v. Pierce & Stevens, Inc.*, 14 F.R.D. (D.C.Mass.1953). Accordingly, most courts have held that the existence and nature of other complaints in product liability cases is a proper subject for pretrial discovery. See 20 A.L.R.3d 1430, Frumer and Friedman, *Products Liability*, § 47.01, but see *Proctor & Gamble Distributing Co. v. Vasseur*, 275 S.W.2d 941 (Ky. 1955).

Nevertheless, information of similar complaints has not been produced by the defendant.

The defendant has contended throughout this litigation and reiterated at the October 20 hearing that because of its longstanding practice of indexing claims alphabetically by name of claimant, rather than by type of product, there is no practical way for anyone to determine whether there have been any complaints similar to those alleged in the complaint at bar, "other than [by] going through all of the . . . claims . . . in the Sears Index . . . which is the equivalent of an impossible task." (Defendant's Supplementary Memorandum in Support of its Motion to Remove the Default.) No evidence has been produced tending to establish the truth of this presentation.

Under Rule 34, Fed.R.Civ.P., the party from whom discovery is sought has the burden of showing some sufficient reason why discovery should not be allowed, once it has been determined that the items sought are properly within the scope of Rule 26(b), Fed.R.Civ.P. See 8 Wright & Miller, *Federal Practice & Procedure*: Civil § 2214, p. 644 (1970). Merely because compliance with a "Request for Production" would be costly or time-consuming is not ordinarily sufficient reason to grant a protective order where the requested material is relevant and necessary to the discovery of evidence. *Luey v. Sterling Drug, Inc.*, 240 F.Supp. 632, 634-5 (W.D.Mich.1965).

In the instant case, the requested documents are clearly within the scope of Rule 26(b), Fed.R.Civ.P., the plaintiff has a demonstrable need for the documents, the defendant undisputedly has possession of them, and the plaintiff has not other access to them. Thus, the defendant has a duty pursuant to Rule 34, Fed.R.Civ.P., to produce its records of similar suits. The defendant seeks to absolve itself of this responsibility by alleging the herculean effort which would be necessary to locate the document. The defendant may not excuse itself from compliance with Rule 34, Fed.R.Civ.P., by utilizing a system of record-keeping which conceals rather than discloses relevant records, or makes it unduly difficult to identify or locate them, thus rendering the production of the documents an excessively burdensome and costly expedition. To allow a defendant whose business generates massive records to frustrate discovery by creating an inadequate filing system, and then claiming undue burden, would defeat the purposes of the discovery rules. See *Hickman v. Taylor*, 329 U.S 495, 500, 67 S.Ct. 385, 91 L.Ed. 451 (1947); Holtzoff, *Instruments of Discovery Under Federal Rules of Civil Procedure*, 41 Mich.L.Rev. 205, 224 (1942).

Apart from the defendant's failure to locate records of similar complaints in its own files, it appears that the defendant has never inquired of Russell Mills, Inc. (the manufacturer of children's nightwear) whether the corporation has any accessible information regarding the requested documents. It is undisputed that the defendant, Sears, Roebuck & Co., does have an indemnification agreement with its manufacturer, Russell Mills, Inc. Sears, Roebuck & Co. is a defendant in another, unrelated product liability case pending in this District, Wales, *Administratrix, et al. v. Sears, Roebuck & Co., et. al.*, Civil Action No. 73-564-S., District of Massachusetts. In that case, the defendant was in fact able to procure records of similar claims from its manufacturer/indemnitor.

It is well established that a private corporation cannot avoid producing documents by an allegation of "impossibility" if it can obtain the requested information from the sources under its control. (*In re Ruppert*, 309 F.2d 97 (6 Cir. 1962) (attorney); *Bingle v. Liggett Drug Co.*, 11 F.R.D. 593, 594 (D.C.Mass.1951) (insurer); *George Hantscho Co. v. Miehle-Goss-Dexter, Inc.*, 33 F.R.D. 332 (S.D.N.Y.1963) (corporate subsidiary).) The defendant's apparent failure in this case to impose any inquiry to Russell Mills, Inc., when a similar query proved fruitful in another case, undermines the defendant's assertion that it has produced all documents available to it.

Finally, the defendant makes a confusing offer to finance the transportation to Chicago, Illinois (where the records are kept), by the plaintiff's attorney so that he may either attempt to locate the desired documents among the defendant's massive files, or else verify for himself the impossibility of such a task. The defendant has in essence told the plaintiff that, if he wishes, he may hunt through all its documents and find the information for himself. "This amounts to nothing more than a gigantic 'do it yourself' kit." See *Harlem River Consumers Cooperative, Inc. v. Associated Grocers of Harlem, Inc.*, 64 F.R.D. 459 (S.D.N.Y.1974), quoting *Life Music Inc. v. Broadcast Music, Inc.*, 41 F.R.D. 16 (S.D.N.Y.1966). This Court will not shift the financial burden of discovery onto the discovering party, in this case an indigent plaintiff, where the costliness of the discovery procedure involved is entirely a product of the defendant's self-serving indexing scheme over which the plaintiff has no control.

While a judgment by default is the "most severe in the spectrum of sanctions," *National Hockey League v. Metropolitan Hockey Club, Inc.* (per curiam), 427 U.S. 639, 96 S.Ct. 2778, 49 L.Ed.2d 747 (1976), provided in Rule 37, Fed.R.Civ.P., it is appropriate where "one party has acted in willful and deliberate disregard of reasonable and necessary court orders and the efficient administration of justice." *Trans World Airlines v. Hughes*, 332 F.2d 602, 614 (2 Cir. 1964). The defendant's failure to produce records of similar complaints is due basically to an indexing system of its own devising, so maintained as to obstruct full discovery. Compare this situations with that prevailing in *Societe Internationale v. Rogers*, 357 U.S. 197, 78 S.Ct. 1087, 2 L.Ed.2d 1255 (1958) (reversing the dismissal of a complaint under Rule 37(b), Fed.R.Civ.P.), where the record clearly demonstrated that the petitioner had made "extensive efforts at compliance" with a court order for the production of certain records which were in the possession of Swiss banks and which could not have been produced without subjecting the petitioner to criminal penalties in Switzerland. *Id.*, at 211, 78 S.Ct. 1087.

This Court's finding, contained in its July 15 Order, that the defendant willfully failed to comply with the discovery rules, still stands. The record of this case to date discloses "either a total lack of diligence on the part of defense counsel, or extended indifference to its case on the part of defendant." *Sivelle v.*

Maloof, 373 F.2d 520, 521 (1 Cir. 1967). The Court finds and rules that the defendant has failed to show "full compliance" with the July 14 Order, and its motion to vacate the default judgment is therefore denied.

---

[1] The plaintiff's "Request for Production" sets forth six items (sample pajama fabrics) requested for testing and twenty-five items requested for inspection and copying. Following this Court's entry of judgment by default against the defendant, on July 14, 1976, Sear, Roebuck & Co. furnished certain documents for inspection in four separate installments: July 27, 1976, August 18, 1976, August 23, 1976, and September 14, 1976. The defendant maintains that it has produced all requested documents "which have been available since the commencement of this case"; the plaintiff contends that the items produced were only a part of the documents available to the defendant. It is clear, for example, that the defendant has not produced the requested records of similar complaints.
[2] The Magistrate's order modified the plaintiff's request to produce as to twenty-five of the items by imposing a time limit on the materials requested of five years prior and three years subsequent to November 11, 1970.

H.P. LAING v. LIBERTY LOAN COMPANY OF SMITHFIELD AND ALBEMARLE

264 S.E.2d 381

Court of Appeals of North Carolina
April 1, 1980

Plaintiff, a North Carolina attorney, instituted this action on 8 April 1978 against defendant, a former client, for breach of a contract to pay legal fees. Plaintiff alleged a contract to file suits and collect judgments on thirty–seven loans made by defendant totaling $30,326.43. Plaintiff maintains he obtained these judgments and that his fee would be a one–third contingent fee on all sums collected against the judgments. Plaintiff further alleged requests for accountings on the sums collected on the judgments which defendant continued to refuse to provide him. Defendant answered the complaint on 28 June 1978 wherein the allegations of plaintiff were "admitted in part." The answer failed to state which allegations were admitted and which were denied.

On 5 July 1978, plaintiff served interrogatories on defendant wherein he requested the "amounts and dates of all sums paid to the defendant" on the loans on which plaintiff alleged he had obtained judgments. Defendant filed an answer to interrogatories more than a month later which contained the following introductory statement:

> In answer to the interrogatories, the following is the best information available. The local office of Liberty Loan, Inc. was closed during the month of August, 1976 and most of the files at that time were removed. The work done by the Plaintiff was issued from that office.

Thereafter, defendant stated "[n]o monies were paid," as to twenty–five of the accounts on which information was sought. For the other eleven interrogatories, defendant provided an amount paid and whether it was refinanced, settled or charged off as a bad debt. Defendant admitted more than $4,000.00 had been collected.

On 18 July 1978, plaintiff served a request for production of documents upon defendant pursuant to Rule 34 in which plaintiff sought to examine the "original note, security agreement, and ledger card or cards of the note or notes" on each loan in question in this suit. In response to this request for production of documents, defendant, on 9 August 1978, filed a response in which it stated,

> The attached is the best information available in answer to the Mandatory Request for Production of Documents by the Plaintiff. The Wilmington office of the Defendant was closed in August 1976 and the records on the inactive accounts have been unavailable since then.

* * * * * No other information is avail-able on these accounts; however, prior to the Wilmington office closing, files of each of the accounts were always available to the Plaintiff.

Defendant produced information on some of the accounts, but for twenty–five, it merely stated "[i]nformation not available." These were the same twenty–five accounts on which defendant had earlier maintained in answers to interrogatories that "[n]o monies were paid." Plaintiff filed a motion for an order pursuant to Rule 37 to compel defendant to produce the documents he had earlier requested on the accounts for which defendant had made only the statement that information was not available and for several others where the information provided was incomplete. Defendant filed no response to plaintiff's Rule 37 motion. The motion was heard on 11 September 1978, and an order was entered requiring defendant to produce twenty–nine sets of documents sought by plaintiff. A specific time and place for production was provided in the order as well as a warning of sanctions pursuant to Rule 37 if the order was not heeded. Defendant did not produce the documents as ordered by the court or make any other response to the court's order.

Plaintiff also filed a request for admission on 26 August 1978. Plaintiff requested, among other things, admissions concerning the material allegations of the complaint on the contract for services and defendant's refusal to comply with its terms. No response whatsoever was ever filed by defendant to these requests for admissions.

On 1 February 1979, plaintiff made a motion for sanctions by the court pursuant to Rule 37(b)(2)c for defendant's refusal to produce. At the hearing on the motion for sanctions, defendant's attorney made the statement that the documents could not be produced because they had been destroyed but offered no testimony or other evidence that he had made repeated requests since 1975 to defendant to provide the information now sought through this unheeded court order to produce documents. For this failure to comply with a discovery order, the trial court sanctioned defendant by striking its answer and entering default judgment for plaintiff in the amount prayed for in the complaint. From this judgment, defendant appeals.

The issue raised by this case is whether the trial court acted properly in striking defendant's answer and entering judgment by default. We hold the trial court properly applied the discretionary powers of sanction for discovery abuse provided in Rule 37 of the North Carolina Rules of Civil Procedure.

Plaintiff has alleged performance of a contract to provide legal services, and defendant has never really denied this contract and its performance. To prove his damages, plaintiff would have to show money was collected on the thirty–seven judgments he obtained. Business records and documents consisting of notes, security agreements and payments cards held by defendant could provide this information. He sought this information through discovery procedures. To his interrogatories seeking the amounts and dates of payments on the loans, for all but eleven of the loans, defendant answered "[n]o monies were paid." Then, when the documentary evidence for those loans on which "[n]o monies were paid" was sought through voluntary production, the information sought became unavailable. Plaintiff sought and obtained a court order to produce these documents to which defendant made no response. At the sanctions hearing, defendant's attorney made the unverified statement on oral argument that the business documents sought which were no more than four years old were no longer in existence. Upon these circumstances, the trial court invoked one of the most severe sanctions pursuant to Rule 37 which provides in pertinent part the following:

If a party or an officer, director, or managing agent of a party or a person designated under Rule 30(b)(6) or 31(a) to testify on behalf of a party fails to obey an order to provide or permit discovery, including an order made under section (a) of this rule or Rule 35, a judge of the court in which the action is pending may make such orders in regard to the failure as are just, and among others the following:

* * * * *

c. An order striking our pleadings or parts thereof, or staying further proceedings until the order is obeyed, or dismissing the action or proceeding or any part thereof, or rendering a judgment by default against the disobedient party.

G.S. 1A–1, Rule 37(b)(2)c. The trial court had issued an order pursuant to section (a) of Rule 37 which was ignored. The trial court sanctioned defendant for this. The rule provides that the court "may make such orders in regard to the failure as are just . . ." G.S. 1A–1, Rule 37(b)(2). The issue is whether the trial court abused its discretion and entered an unjust order striking defendant's answers and entering default judgment for plaintiff.

The rule is very flexible and gives a broad discretion to the trial judge. *Telegraph Co. v. Griffin*, 39 N.C.App. 721, 251 S.E.2d 885, *cert. den.*, 297 N.C. 304, 254 S.E.2d 921 (1979). If a party's failure to produce is shown to be due to inability fostered neither by its own conduct nor by circumstances within its control, it is exempt from the sections of the rule. The rules do not require the impossible. It does require a good faith effort at compliance with the court order. *Societe Internationale v. Rogers*, 357 U.S. 197, 78 S.Ct. 1087, 2 L.Ed.2d 1255 (1958). In the case at hand, defendant made no good faith effort to comply with the order. No protective order was sought pursuant to G.S. 1A–1, Rule 26(c) against discovery of the material. No response was made by defendant to the motion seeking an order to produce. All these procedures are provided to benefit defendant. It took advantage of none of them. Defendant s own inactions and not the actions of the court in enforcing its own valid processes resulted in a failure to have the case heard on the merit of any deprivation or loss of property. There is no showing that defendants were punished for failure to do something it could not do. Defendant's counsel's unverified, sworn statement at oral argument is insufficient response to an order to produce. The general replies originally made to interrogatories and requests for production also present insufficient excuses for not heeding the order. Amplification and explanation is needed as to why no information on all but eleven of the thirty–seven accounts is the best information available. *See Norman v. Young*, 422 F.2d 470 (10th Cir. 1970); Shuford, N.C. Practice § 37–10 (1975).

* * * * *

Hobert R. LeMASTER v. CHICAGO ROCK ISLAND & PACIFIC RAILROAD COMPANY, a corporation

343 N.E.2d 65

Appellate Court of Illinois, First District, Third Division
February 10, 1976

Plaintiff, Hobert LeMaster, brought an action under the provisions of the Federal Employers' Liability Act (45 U.S.C., sec. 51, *et seq.*) against his employer, the Chicago Rock Island & Pacific Railroad Company, for personal injuries he sustained in the course of his employment. After hearing the evidence in the case, a jury returned a verdict of $1,000,000 for plaintiff, and the circuit court entered judgment thereon. The trial court denied the defendant's post–trial motion, and this appeal follows.

* * * * *

In his complaint filed pursuant to the provisions of the FELA, plaintiff alleged that the Railroad negligently failed to provide him with a reasonably safe place to work. At trial the plaintiff introduced evidence to prove that the train yard he had worked in the night of the accident was slippery as a result of a combination of spilled grain, water from a recent rainfall and an oil base weed killer sprayed on the tracks earlier in the day which formed a slippery "jello–like" mush that was struck to the plaintiff's shoes and gloves. Other evidence showed that the jolt plaintiff described in his testimony may have been caused by a minor derailment of the lead boxcar. Plaintiff's theory was that the derailment jolt combined with the slippery mush on his books and gloves caused him to lose

his hold on the train's ladder and fall to the tracks.

The Railroad's theory was that the plaintiff's fall was caused entirely by his own negligence, including the violation of certain railroad safety rules which specify the proper way to supervise a movement of boxcars.

At trial, the plaintiff proved actual damages amounting to over $180,000. After hearing all the evidence, the jury returned a verdict for plaintiff in the amount of $1,000,000.

* * * * *

On January 13, 1971, the third day of trial, defendant made certain oral amendments to its answers to plaintiff's interrogatories. On January 19, 1971, plaintiff's counsel stated to the court that although defendant had presented to him certain weed spray records on December 24, 1970, plaintiff now found that these records were incomplete. These records represented the log of the Railroad's weed spray program of June, 1969 in the West Davenport rail yards, where the injury occurred. Because of the plaintiff's allegation at trial that the oil based weed spray had contributed to cause his fall under the moving train, plaintiff's counsel brought the matter to the attention of the trial court when he discovered that the records he had been given omitted the log of weed spray operations for June 11 and June 12, 1969, the day before the day of the accident. Upon his representation the trial judge suggested that defendant's counsel make a search for the missing records. Defendant's counsel contended he had given plaintiff all of the weed spray records. Nevertheless, on the next day, January 20, 1971, defendant's counsel disclosed that he had found the weed spray records of June 11 and 12, 1969, and presented them to plaintiff.

On January 20, 1971, Charles Hill, a claim agent employed by the defendant who signed all of the defendant's written answers to the interrogatories, was called as an adverse witness by the plaintiff. The defendant immediately objected to Hill's testimony on the grounds of relevancy. Plaintiff's counsel argued that due to defendant's seeming reluctance to produce documents during the course of the discovery proceedings, he believed that there was further discoverable information which had not been disclosed by the Railroad. The trial judge overruled the objections and allowed Hill to be cross–examined as an adverse witness under section 60 of the Civil Practice Act (Ill.Rev. Stat.1971, ch. 110, par. 60).

Plaintiff's counsel questioned Hill about the answers to the interrogatories he had signed on behalf of the Railroad. During this questioning plaintiff's counsel read, in the presence of the jury, plaintiff's interrogatories No. 4 and No. 21, and the Railroad's original and amended answers to these interrogatories. Plaintiff's counsel also asked Hill whether the weed spray records were under his control; he responded that they were not. Counsel inquired whether Hill knew that certain of the week's spray records were not given to plaintiff until the 20th; Hill responded that he did not. Plaintiff further inquired whether Hill knew when the existence of Monahan was disclosed and certain diagrams prepared under his supervision were given to plaintiff; Hill said he did not.

After Hill's testimony defendant objected to the entire examination as being irrelevant and moved that the testimony be stricken and a mistrial declared. During argument on the motion plaintiff viewed the above mentioned sequence of discovery and stated that he believed that there were further week spray records which had not been produced by defendant. (The plaintiff contended that his examination of witness Cruse, another employee of defendant, disclosed that there may have been records showing the composition of the sprayed weed killer was mixed with water or oil, i.e., the actual "tank car consist.") Plaintiff concluded that all of these facts cast great doubt upon the defendant's contention that it had produced all the documents it had been ordered to produce, and that this failure to produce was a relevant fact for consideration by the jury. * * *

* * * * *

During his closing argument plaintiff's attorney again raised the issue when he argued that defendant had not disclosed the existence of Monahan in accordance with the ordered discovery. The defendant's objection was overruled and plaintiff continued, arguing that the reason the defendant never listed Monahan was "because Monahan had some goods that they didn't want revealed to the public eye."

On appeal defendant argues that it was error to allow the plaintiff's examination of Hill and the comments during closing argument, because through this evidence, innuendo and improper argument, plaintiff's counsel inflamed the jurors' emotions against the Railroad so that the Railroad was denied a fair trial. Defendant specifically complains that there was no basis for allowing plaintiff to read the interrogatories and answers during the examination of Hill, as answers to interrogatories may be used only for impeachment or as an admission of a party. We disagree and find that plaintiff's counsel's questioning of Hill and the subsequent argument to the jury were not improper when considered in this totality of events which occurred during the trial of this case.

To begin an analysis of this issue, it is clear that the authorities recognize that a party's failure to produce documents is conduct that can be evidence.

> "In the second class of cases it is to be included that sort of conduct which is received only when it emanates from a *party to the cause or a witness*, and can therefore be equally justified as involving an *admission* or a *discrediting circumstance*. Such conduct, for example, as the fabrication or suppression of evidence, the failure to produce important witnesses or documents, indicates a consciousness that one's cause is a bad one or a weak one, and from the consciousness or belief may be inferred the fact that it is bad or weak, *i.e.,* that facts essential for its support are lacking * * * ." (2 Wigmore, Evidence (3rd ed. 1940), sec. 267 at 95.)

Wigmore further states that this evidence, when confined to the conduct of parties in the cause, is receivable against them as an implied admission, and is receivable equally against civil parties and criminal defendants,

2 Wigmore, Evidence (3d ed. 1940), sec. 277.

"No useful purpose would here be served in undertaking to make further classification of the innumerable instances of conduct, both verbal and non–verbal, of a party indicating a consciousness of guilt. The common experience of mankind in dealing with the ordinary affairs of life should offer, it would seem, an indispensable test in making the determination as to whether or not the particular conduct encountered is calculated to raise the inference of a consciousness of guilt. And in this connection, common experience dictates that often times while an affirmative or negative act of a party may not in and of itself justify such an inference, considered in the light of the attendant facts and circumstances, an entirely different result is warranted." (2 Wigmore, Evidence (3d ed. 1940), sec. 178, 1975 Supp. at 53.)

This is also the law enunciated in Illinois. Gard, *Illinois Evidence Manual* (1963) Rules 22, 23; *Tepper v. Campo* (1947) 398 Ill. 496, 505, 76 N.E.2d 490.

Defendant contends that it has not suppressed or concealed any evidence inasmuch as all the evidence plaintiff alleges was withheld was eventually given to plaintiff either immediately before or during the trial. A similar argument was considered and rejected by this court in *Carlson v. General Motors Corp.* (1972) 9 Ill.App.3d 606, 289 N.E.2d 439, wherein the defendant refused to disclose certain discoverable material to the plaintiff prior to trial and, as this material was favorable to the defense case, disclosed the material for the first time through the testimony of witnesses during the trial of the case. The court reviewed the purpose of the discovery rules:

"In *Terry v. Fisher*, 12 Ill.2d 231, 239, 240, 145 N.E.2d 588, the court noted that the purpose of discovery rules was to enable attorneys to better prepare and evaluate their cases. In *Monier v. Chamberlain*, 35 Ill.2d 351, 361, 221 N.E.2d 410, the court stated that 'ascertainment of truth

and ultimate disposition of the lawsuit' is better served when parties are well educated as to their respective claims in advance of trial. In *Drehle v. Fleming*, 129 Ill.App.2d 166, 171, 263 N.E.2d 348, aff'd 49 Ill.2d 293, 274 N.E.2d 53, it was stated:

'[T]he principle is now well established that the purposes of litigation are best served when each party knows as much about the controversy as is reasonably practicable. It is the purpose of pretrial discovery procedures to enhance the truth seeking process, and good faith compliance with such procedures is both desirable and necessary.'

"These cases are cited not for purposes of factual analogy but rather the general principles they set forth, ones which we feel apply well to this case." (9 Ill.App.3d at 619, 289 N.E.2d at 449.)

The court concluded that although the defendant, General Motors, had technically complied with the rules of discovery, this type of compliance did not comply with the requirement of "full disclosure" contained in the discovery rules.

A review of the facts in the instant case indicates that the defendant Railroad technically complied with the discovery rules, but did not meets its responsibility of full disclosure. In *Carlson*, such an inadequate disclosure warranted the levying of judicial sanctions against the nondisclosing party. Herein, judicial sanctions were not sought; rather, plaintiff showed to the jury the extent of defendant's inadequate disclosure in the face of plaintiff's diligence in attempting to discover information known to the Railroad. Although an inadequate disclosure may not be as serious as a complete nondisclosure by a concealing party, there may be instances wherein a trial court may properly allow evidence of an inadequate disclosure to be presented to the jury. The admission of such evidence is within the discretion of the trial court. In the case at bar, considering the nature of the information concealed from discovery until the eve and the midst of trial, we do not feel that the trial court abused its discretion by permitting plaintiff to introduce evidence of the defendant's inadequate disclosure to the jury or to argue to the jury based upon this evidence.

* * * * *

Evelyn and Jack LEWY v. REMINGTON ARMS CO., INC.

836 F.2d 1104

United States Court of Appeals, Eighth Circuit
January 7, 1988

On November 14, 1982, Mike Lewy went deer hunting on the family land where he and his parents, Evelyn and Jack Lewy, lived. He returned home around noon and entered his basement living quarters, placing his loaded Remington Model 700 bolt–action center fire 30.06 rifle (M700) on a couch. Prior to going to bed at around 10:30 that evening, Mike remembered the loaded rifle and decided to unload it. Mike pointed the rifle toward the ceiling and proceeded to unload it. The design of the rifle required the safety to be moved to the fire position in order to lift the bolt handle to eject a chambered cartridge. When Mike placed the safety on the fire position the rifle discharged and the bullet penetrated the ceiling striking his mother in the upper left leg while she was seated in a living room chair. Mrs. Lewy required hospitalization for slightly more than a month, but she now has apparently recovered from the accident.

Mrs. Lewy and her husband filed suit against Remington Arms and the K–Mart Corporation for damages, alleging three separate theories of liability: strict liability — design defect, strict liability — failure to warn, and negligent failure to warn. The Lewys alleged two design defects: 1) the bolt lock feature which required the rifle to be in the fire position when unloading and 2) the fire control mechanism which is susceptible to firing on release of the safety (FSR). Evelyn Lewy claimed damages for personal injuries and Jack Lewy claimed damages for

loss of consortium. The jury returned a verdict in favor of the Lewys on all three theories of liability. Evelyn Lewy was awarded $20,000 in compensatory damages and $400,000 in punitive damages while Jack Lewy was not awarded monetary damages.

* * * * *

Evidentiary Rulings, Attorney Misconduct, Bias of the District Judge and Improper Jury Instructions

The final argument Remington raises is that the district court should have granted their motion for a new trial because the cumulative effect of erroneous evidentiary rulings, attorney misconduct, judicial bias, and an improper jury instruction deprived them of a fair trial.

* * * * *

The final error asserted by Remington refers to the propriety of a general instruction given to the jury. The instruction, taken from Devitt and Blackmar's *Federal Jury Practice and Instructions,* reads as follows:

> If a party fails to produce evidence which is under his control and reasonably available to him and not reasonably available to the adverse party, then you may infer that the evidence is unfavorable to the party who could have produced it and did not.

E. Devitt, C. Blackmar & M. Wolff, 3 *Federal Jury Practice and Instructions* § 72.16 (4th ed. 1987).

This instruction was requested by the Lewys because Remington was unable to produce several documents that were destroyed pursuant to Remington's "record retention policy." Remington argues that destroying records pursuant to routine procedures does not provide an inference adverse to the party that destroyed the documents. *Smith v. Uniroyal, Inc.,* 420 F.2d 438, 442–43 (7th Cir. 1970).

The record reflects that Remington had its record retention policy in place as early as 1970. In addition, the records that have been destroyed pursuant to the policy complaints and gun examination reports — were kept for a period of three years and if no action regarding a particular record was taken in that period it was destroyed. *Vick v. Texas Employment Commission,* 514 F.2d 734, 737 (5th Cir.1975) (records destroyed pursuant to regulations governing inactive records).

We are unable to decide, based on the record we have before us, whether it was error for the trial court to give this instruction. On remand, if the trial court is called upon to again instruct the jury regarding failure to produce evidence, the court should consider the following factors before deciding whether to give the instruction to the jury. First, the court should determine whether Remington's record retention policy is reasonable considering the facts and circumstances surrounding the relevant documents. For example, the court should determine whether a three year retention policy is reasonable given the particular document. A three year retention policy may be sufficient for documents such as appointment books or telephone messages, but inadequate for documents such as customer complaints. Second, in making this determination, the court may also consider whether lawsuits concerning the complaint or related complaints have been filed, the frequency of such complaints, and the magnitude of the complaints.

Finally, the court should determine whether the document retention policy was instituted in bad faith. *Gumbs v. International Harvester, Inc.,* 718 F.2d 88, 96 (3rd Cir.1983) ("no unfavorable inference arises when the circumstances indicate that the document or article in question has been lost or accidentally destroyed, or where the failure to produce it is otherwise properly accounted for."); *Boyd v. Ozark Air Lines, Inc., 568 F.2d 50, 53 (8th Cir.1977) ("We recognize, however, that the destruction of business records may be sufficient to raise an unfavorable inference.").* In cases where a document retention policy is instituted in order to limit damaging evidence available to potential plaintiffs, it may be proper to give an instruction similar to the one requested by the Lewys. Similarly, even if the court finds the policy to be reasonable given the nature of the documents subject to the policy, the court may find that under the particular circumstances

certain documents should have been retained notwithstanding the policy. For example, if the corporation knew or should have known that the documents would become material at some point in the future then such documents should have been preserved. Thus, a corporation cannot blindly destroy documents and expect to be shielded by a seemingly innocuous document retention policy. *Gumbs,* 718 F.2d at 96 ("Such a presumption or inference arises, however, only when the spoliation arises, however, only when the spoliation or destruction [of evidence] was intentional, and indicates fraud and a desire to suppress the truth, and it does not arise where the destruction was a matter of routine with no fraudulent intent.") (quoting 29 AM.Jur.2d *Evidence* § 177 (1967).

* * * * *

Dr. Charles E. MAY v. John A. MOORE, Jr., as Father and Personal Representative of the Infant Child Robert T. Moore, Deceased

424 So.2d 596

Supreme Court of Alabama
December 30, 1982

Fannie Moore, mother of the deceased infant, was admitted to Jackson Hospital in Jackson, Alabama, on 17 October 1977 by Dr. Charles May with a diagnosis of pregnancy, last trimester, premature rupture of the fetal membrane, slight cervical bleeding and false labor. She was treated and released but again returned to the hospital on 25 October 1977 at which time she was readmitted with a diagnosis of premature rupture of the fetal membrane and loss of amniotic fluids. Delivery of her infant did not take place for over 48 hours. Immediately prior to delivery Dr. May checked the mother and informed her the baby would be delivered within the hour or the next hour. However, shortly after he left the room, the mother delivered precipitously in her hospital bed without the assistance of any physician and in less than sterile conditions. After delivery, the child stopped

breathing and was resuscitated by the anesthetist on duty. Shortly afterwards a nurse
came on duty and received a report from the
anesthetist that the child had poor muscle
tone, was cyanotic around the mouth and
nose, was coughing up frothy white mucus
which required frequent suction and the infant was making grunting noises on exhalation. The nurse continued to follow the child
and noted a continuing bluish tinge around
the mouth, a fast rate of respiration, loud
grunting noises on exhalation together with
substernal retractions. She notified Dr. May
of the infant's condition and continued to
observe him. The infant showed signs of
respiratory distress from birth and on 30 October cardiac pulmonary resuscitation had to
be rendered when the infant ceased breathing
and its heart quit beating. At that time the
attending nurse on duty asked a licensed
practical nurse to reach Dr. May by phone
which could not be accomplished. Failing
that, the police were called to notify him to
come to the nursery. He called around 3:20
a.m. and spoke with the nurse on duty at
which time she requested that he come to the
hospital. At about 4:00 a.m. he was again
notified by telephone of the critical condition
of the infant and was again requested to come
to the hospital. Sometime shortly thereafter
Dr. May arrived at the hospital; however, the
attending nurse testified that she did not see
him do anything at all for the baby at that
time. During the early morning hours of 30
October, at approximately 8:15 a.m., Dr.
May ordered the child transferred to the University of South Alabama. The infant's condition continued to deteriorate with seizures,
severe respiratory distress, anemia and body
rigidity. On arrival of the transfer team from
the neonatal center at the University of South
Alabama, the infant was in an incubator and
its extremities appeared stiff. The transfer
team did a general assessment of the infant's
condition and attempted to stabilize it for the
return trip to the medical center.

At approximately 2:00 p.m. on 30 October, the
child was transferred to the neonatal care center
where, according to Dr. Hollis Wiseman, the
pediatrician in charge of that center, the baby
was critical if not terminal when it arrived. The
diagnosis of Dr. Wiseman was sepsis, a generalized bacterial infection in a newborn infant,
and probably meningitis, a part of the bacterial infection disease process. He also was of
the opinion that the child had central nervous
system injury, secondary either to the infection or to the deprivation of oxygen. The
infant died at the University of South Alabama Medical Center the next day at some
five days of age. In explaining the child's
death, Dr. Wiseman testified that it had developed congenital pneumonia as a result of
the long period following rupture of the
mother's fetal membranes before delivery.
The pediatric pathologist who performed the
postmortem on this infant agreed with this
conclusion and testified that when the fetal
membranes rupture there is a escalating incident rate of infection which, after 48 hours,
results in an 80 to 90% probability of infection.

In addition to the very high probability of
infection resulting from premature rupture of
the fetal membrane, the infant exhibited and
developed signs of respiratory infection. In
his testimony, Dr. May admitted that symptoms of grunting on exhalation, substernal
retraction, increased respiratory rate and cya-
nosis are indications, or manifestations, of
respiratory distress in newborn infants. Dr.
Wiseman also testified that these symptoms
are cardinal manifestations of respiratory
distress in newborn infants. In response to
these symptoms Dr. May failed to perform
any laboratory tests, other than a blood count.
Additionally, despite the fact the child
showed indications of infection to the central
nervous system, no antibiotics were prescribed, but rather than that being done, Dr.
May prescribed caffeine sodium benzoate
and decadron, as well as a procedure known
as hypodermoclysis.

A Birmingham pediatrician and clinical instructor at the University of Alabama Medical School testified that the treatment
rendered the infant by Dr. May was totally
inappropriate. He also noted that where 48
hours had lapsed from the rupture of the fetal
membrane, birth had occurred under less
than sterile conditions, respiratory distress
had existed for more than two hours, blood
cultures, skin cultures, spinal cultures and

other tests should have been obtained and antibiotics started immediately. This doctor also testified that the administration of caffeine sodium benzoate is totally inappropriate care for the stimulation of respiration in the primary care setting, as the Jackson Hospital was, and that hypodermocyclis is an antiquated and dangerous practice and should not have been used.

Not only was Dr. May's failure to do any laboratory testing or to prescribe proper medication improper treatment, another physician in the community of Jackson pointed out the availability of the neonatal center at the University of South Alabama only seventy miles from Jackson, Alabama. He explained the availability of consultation services from which the latest information could be obtained immediately. In the opinion of that doctor, Dr. May violated the standard of care in Clarke County when he failed to transfer the child to the neonatal center, or, in the alternative, to do the proper testing and render the appropriate treatment there at the Jackson Hospital.

Both the Birmingham pediatrician and clinical instructor as well as Dr. Wiseman of the University of South Alabama neonatal care center, testified that the administration of appropriate treatment would have resulted in a better than 50% chance that the infant would live.

* * * * *

Proof may be made concerning a party purposefully and wrongfully destroying a document which he knew was supportive of the interest of his opponent, whether or not an action involving such interest was pending at the time of the destruction. See Gamble, *Elroy's Alabama Evidence*, § 190.05 (3d.Ed.1977). Additionally, the spoliation, or attempt to suppress material evidence by a party to a suite, favorable to the adversary, is sufficient foundation for an inference of his guilt or negligence. *Home Southern Insurance Co. of the Carolinas v. Boatwright*, 231 Ala. 198, 164 So. 102 (1935); see also, Gamble, *McElroy's Alabama Evidence*, § 190.02 (3d.Ed.1977)

There was testimony to the effect that failure of Dr. May to properly treat the infant was almost concealed on the occasion of the loss of the child's original chart. One Louise Boykin, the hospital administrator, had made a copy of the chart before it disappeared. She testified she made the copy of the chart because of the disappearance of another child's chart before this, which child had also been a patient of Dr. May. Dr. May's own counsel in questioning Mrs. Boykin brought out the fact that hospital charts of a number of Dr. May's patients had disappeared prior to the treatment of this infant. She further testified that during the time she served as hospital administrator only the charts of Dr. May's patients were missing, not those of other doctors.

At an oral deposition of Dr. May before trial, he produced two copies of the infant's chart, both of which allegedly came from the original copy of Mrs. Boykin. He testified that one copy was received directly from her and the other one from Foster, who had obtained his copy from Mrs. Boykin. She denied ever giving Dr. May a copy of the record and compared her original copy to the two copies produced by Dr. May. She pointed out the discrepancies from her original copy of those copies produced by Dr. May and thus demonstrated that copies produced by him could not possibly have come from her original copy.

Admittedly, evidence adduced by plaintiff was circumstantial in nature; however, a fact may be established by either direct or circumstantial evidence, and the proof is sufficient if, from the facts and circumstances adduced, it can be reasonably inferred. *State v. Ludlam*, 384 So.2d 1089 (Ala.Div.App.1980). Furthermore, questions as to the relevancy of testimony are ordinarily within the discretion of the trial court and, unless much discretion has been grossly abused, it will not be considered on appeal. The trial court found the testimony of Mrs. Boykin relevant to the issue of whether Dr. May might have tampered with the original medical charge of the infant Moore in attempting to conceal his guilt or negligence and we see no error in its decision.

MONARCH FEDERAL SAVINGS AND LOAN ASSOCIATION, a Federal Association duly chartered by the Federal Home Loan Bank Board v. Lena GENSER, widow and Sidney Genser

383 A.2d 475

Superior Court of New Jersey
December 19, 1977

During the trial of the issues in this mortgage foreclosure action, plaintiff Monarch Federal Savings and Loan Association (Monarch) requested that certain computer records be admitted into evidence under the business records exception to the hearsay rule, *Evid.R.* 63(13). Defendants Lena Genser and Sidney Genser (Gensers) objected to their admission on the ground that plaintiff failed to lay the necessary foundation. Plaintiff produced three foundation witnesses and their testimony may be summarized as follows.

The first witness, Richard D. Russo, assistant vice–president of the Wood–Ridge National Bank (Wood–Ridge), testified that Monarch maintains a lock–box deposit account with Wood–Ridge for processing of their mortgage accounts. The mortgagors forward their payment together with an IBM card to the bank. After the monies are received, processed and checked, the computer cards are forwarded to Financial Services, Inc. (Financial Services) and the checks are forwarded to Monarch. Any problems or questions with the account are handled by Monarch. This witness also indicated that the account was maintained in the regular course of the bank's business and that Wood–Ridge provides similar services for other banks.

The next witness, Otto Kieffer, is the office manager of the mortgage department of Financial Services, a computer corporation located in Glen Rock, New Jersey. He testified that Financial Services, pursuant to an agreement with Monarch, has computerized the mortgage accounts of Monarch. When an account is initially opened, Monarch forwards all the relevant information to Financial Services which is transferred into the computer. Thereafter, all transactions between Monarch and the mortgagor are processed through the individual account. Monarch receives a daily read–out for each transaction and a monthly read–out for each individual account. Every mortgagor receives monthly and yearly statements.

The records of the Gensers' account were marked for identification and identified by Kieffer. He testified that this account, as well as the other accounts, are processed and maintained in the regular course of Financial Services' business.

The last witness, Victor Urbanovich, has been an employee of Monarch for the past 2 1/2 years and presently is an assistant vice–president. He testified that he is familiar with the operation of Monarch's mortgage department. This witness identified and reviewed the monthly and yearly computer printouts produced by Financial Services and supplied to and maintained by Monarch for the Genser account. He further testified that this account was maintained in the regular course of business since March 1968. Every transaction on the Genser account from March 1968 to the present was recorded with and reflected in the records processed by Financial Services and maintained by Monarch. He also testified that after reviewing the records the Gensers failed to make the payment for April 1976 and that this account remains in default as of that date.

Based on this evidence, defendants maintained that a proper foundation had not been established for the admission of these records.

The issue before this court is one of first impression in this State: What is the proper foundation to support the authenticity of a computer printout? The leading case in New Jersey on the admissibility of computer printouts is *Sears, Roebuck & Co. v. Merla*, 142 *N.J.Super.* 205, 361 A.2d 68 (App.Div.1976). In that case the Appellate Division reviewed the trial judge's refusal to admit a computer printout as evidence of the defendant's indebtedness to Sears. *Id.* at 206–207, 361 *MA.*2d 68. In reversing that trial judge's decision the court held "that as long as a proper foundation is laid, a computer printout is admissible on the same basis as any other business record." *Id*. at 207, 361 A.2d at 69. The *Merla* court, however did not specify what type of foundation would be required to establish admissibility.

In New Jersey the admissibility of business records is governed by *Evid.R.* 63(13), which provides as follows:

A writing offered as a memorandum or record of acts, conditions or events is admissible to prove the facts stated therein if the writing or the record upon which it is based was made in the regular course of business, at or about the time of the act, condition or event recorded, and if the sources of information from which it was made and the method and circumstances of its preparation were such as to justify its admission.

This rule, fashioned after the *Uniform Rules of Evidence* 63(13), see *Phillips v. Erie Lackawanna R. Co.*, 107 *N.J.Super.* 590, 595, 259 A.2d 719 (App.Div.1969); *State v. Hudes*, 128 *N.J.Super.* 589, 599–600, 321 A.2d 275 (Cty.Ct.1974), was promulgated by order of the Supreme Court of New Jersey, June 6, 1967, to be effective September 11, 1967, and superseded by New Jersey's Uniform Business Records as Evidence Act, *N.J.S.A.* 2A:82–34 *et seq*. See *Phillips v. Erie Lackawanna R. Co., supra* at *N.J.Super.* at 593, 594, 599, 259 A.2d 719; *Brown v. Mortimer*, 100 *N.J.Super.* 395, 403, 242 A.2d 36 (App.Div.1968). Although *Evid.R.* 63(13) differs from the Uniform Business Records as Evidence Act (UBREA) in that "the custodian need not be called as a witness to attest to its authenticity," *Samuel Sheitelman, Inc. v. Hoffman*, 106 *N.J.Super.* 353, 356–357, 255 A.2d 807, 809 (App.Div.1969); compare *Evid.R.* 63(13) with *N.J.S.A.* 2A:82–35, the purpose of the new rule is substantially the same as its former counterpart. *Sas v. Strelecki*, 110 *N.J.Super.* 14, 20, 264 A.2d 247 (App.Div.1970); *Brown v. Mortimer, supra* 100 *N.J.Super.* at 403, 242 A.2d 36. The court in *Mahoney v. Minsky*, 39 *N.J.* 208, 188 A.2d (1963) noted the rationale underlying the uniform evidence laws:

The basic theory of the uniform law is that records which are properly shown to have been kept as required normally possess a circumstantial probability of trustworthiness, and therefore ought to be received in evidence unless the trial court, after examining them and hearing the manner of their preparation explained, entertains serious doubt as to whether they are dependable or worthy of confidence. [at 218, 188 A.2d at 166.]

Accord, *Brown v. Mortimer, supra* 100 *N.J.Super.* at 403, 242 A.2d 36: *Falcone v. N.J. Bell Tel. Co.*, 98 *N.J.Super.* 138, 147, 236 A.2d 394 (App.Div.1967); *Carroll v. Houtz*, 93 *N.J.Super.* 215, 219–220, 225 A.2d 584 (App.Div.1966); see *Samuel Sheitelman, Inc. v. Hoffman, supra* 106 *N.J.Super.* at 356, 255 A.2d 807; *Webber v. McCormick* 63 *N.J.Super.* 409, 416, 164 A.2d 81 (App.Div.1960); *State v. Hudes, supra* 128 *N.J.Super.* at 599, 321 A.2d 275.

Both the UBREA and *Uniform Rule of Evidence* 63(13) liberalized and modernized the common law prerequisites for admission of business records. See *Smith v. First Nat'l Stores, Inc.*, 94 *N.J.Super.* 462, 467, 228 A.2d 874 (App.Div.1967); *State v. Scelfo, N.J.Super.* 472, 481, 156 A.2d 714 (App.Div.1959); *State v. Hudes, supra* 128 *N.J.Super.* at 599–600, 321 A.2d 275; *McCormick, Evidence* (2d ed. 1972) § 307 at 720; 5 *Wigmore, op. cit.*, § 1561b at 499. Under the common law four elements were needed to be proven:

(1) the entries have been original entries made in the routine of business, (2) must have been made upon personal knowledge of the recorder or of someone reporting to him, (3) must have been made at or near the time of the transaction recorded, and (4) the recorder and his informant had to be shown to be unavailable. [*State v. Hudes, supra* at 600, 321 A.2d at 281.]

Accord *McCormick, op. cit.*, § 306 at 720. The modern New Jersey approach has eliminated the common law requirement of unavailability of the recorder, *State v. Hudes, supra* at 600, 321 A.2d 275, and the requirement of personal knowledge of the recorder,

State v. Martorelli, 136 *N.J.Super.* 449, 453, 346 *A.*2d 618 (App.Div.1975). In *Martorelli* the Appellate Division set forth the three requirements for admissibility under *Evid.R.* 63(13):

> First, the record must be made in the regular course of business. Second, it must be prepared within a short time of the act, condition or event being described. Third, the source of information and the method of preparation must justify allowing it into evidence. [136 *N.J.Super.* at 453, 346 *A.*2d 618.]

Accord, *State v. Hudes, supra* 128 *N.J.Super.* at 600, 321 *A.*2d 275; see *Adams v. N.J. State Fair*, 71 *N.J.Super.* 528, 531, 177 *A.*2d 486, 488 (App.Div.1962) (UBREA decision finding "1955 balance" entry not to have been made 'at or near the time of the act * * * or event'"). In addition to the three elements of foundation set forth in *Martorelli*, the courts of New Jersey have mandated that the informant be "under a 'business duty' to supply honest information to the entrant." *Sas v. Strelecki, supra* 110 *N.J.Super.* at 20, 22, 264 *A.*2d at 250 (statements by third parties in police officer's report held inadmissible); see *State v. Taylor*, 46 *N.J.* 316, 330–331, 217 *A.*2d 1, *cert.* den. 385 *U.S.* 885, 87 *S.Ct.* 103, 17 *L.Ed*2s 83 (1966) (third–party statements in doctor's record held inadmissible).

Although the "business entry exception to the hearsay rule * * * is generally limited to *business* records," our courts have applied this exception to "[r]ecords other than commercial payment records." *State v. Connors*, 125 *N.J.Super.* 500, 506, 311 *A.*2d 764, 768 (Cty.Ct.1973) aff'd in part, rev'd in part, 129 *N.J.Super.* 476, 324 *A.*2d 85 (App.Div. 1974) (emphasis supplied); see e.g., *State v. Reddick*, 53 *N.J.* 66, 68, 248 *A.*2d 425 (1968) (autopsy report admitted after excising opinions as to cause of death); *State v. Gardner*, 51 *N.J.* 444, 462, *A.*2d 1 (1968) (hospital reports with medical facts admitted so long as opinions as to cause of injury excluded); *State v. Provoid*, 110 *N.J.Super.* 547, 556–557, 266 *A.*2d 307 (App.Div.1970) (police record of telephone calls reporting citizens' complaints admitted under *Evid.R.* 63(13));

Schneiderman v. Strelecki, 107 *N.J.Super.* 113, 118, 257 *A.*2d 130 (App.Div.1969) (police report of automobile accident admissible under *Evid.R.* 63(13)); *Falcone v. N.J. Bell Tel. Co., supra* 98 *N.J.Super.* at 146 and n.1 at 147, 236 *A.*2d 394 (treating physician's medical record admissible under UBREA); *Carroll v. Houtz, supra* 93 *N.J.Super.* at 221–223, 225 *A.*2d 584 (autopsy record containing reports of tissue and blood tests admissible under UBREA); *Hackensack Hosp. v. Tiajoloff*, 85 *N.J.Super.* 417, 419–420, 204 *A.*2d 902 (App.Div.1964) (hospital books of account admissible under UBREA to prove services rendered but not their value); *State v. Laster*, 69 *N.J.Super.* 504, 514, 174 *A.*2d 486 (App.Div.1961) (jail doctor's report book admissible under UBREA); *State v. Bassano*, 67 *N.J.Super.* 526, 534, 171 *A.*2d 108 (App.Div.1961) (insurance adjuster's memorandum of telephone report of auto theft admissible under UBREA); *Schwartau v. Miesmer*, 50 *N.J.Super.* 399, 405, 413, 142 *A.*2d 675 (App.Div.1958) (police blotter upon which time and date of an investigation was noted admissible under UBREA) (dictum); *Tsibikas v. Morrof*, 12 *N.J.Super.* 102, 111, 79 *A.*2d 64 (App.Div.1951) (attorney's notebooks admissible under UBREA) (dictum); *State v. Hudes, supra* 128 *N.J.Super.* at 601, 603, 321 *A.*2d 275 (certificate of operability of a breathalyzer machine admissible under *Evid.R.* 63(13)). But see, *Farber v. Shell Oil Co.*, 47 *N.J.Super.* 47, 54–55, 135 *A.*2d 243 (App.Div.1957) (lessor's internal proposal memorandum excluded under UBREA); *State v. Connors, supra* 125 *N.J.Super.* at 503, 507 311 *A.*2d 764 (certificate of operability of a breathalyzer machine excluded under *Evid.R.* 63(13)). The newest development in this State is the admissibility of computer printouts. See *Sears, Roebuck & Co. v. Merla, supra.*

Only recently have courts throughout this country faced the problem of admitting a new form of record — the computer printout. See *McCormick, op. cit.*, 314 at 733. Computer–kept records differ in some crucial respects from traditional business records. see generally Note, "Admissibility of Computer–Kept Business Records," 55 *Cornell*

L.Rev. 1033, 1034–36 (1970). Despite these differences, courts have acknowledged that "[c]omputerized bookkeeping has become commonplace," *Sears, Roebuck & Co. v. Merla, supra* 142 *N.J.Super.* at 207, 361 *A.*2d 68; see *e.g., United States v. Russo* 480 F A.2d 1228, 1239, (6 Cir.1973), *cert.* den. 414 *U.S.* 1157, 94 *S.Ct.* 915, 39 *L.Ed A.*2d 109 (1974), and that "the business records exception is intended to bring the realities of the business world into the courtroom." *Sears, Roebuck & Co., v. Merla, supra,* 142 *N.J.Super.* at 207, 361 *A.*2d at 69; accord, *Union Elec. Co. v. Mansion House Center No. Redev. Co.,* 494 *S.W.*2d 309, 315 (Mo.Sup.Ct.1973); *Transport Indem. Co. v. Seib* 178 *Neb.* 253, 259, 132 *N.W.*2d 871, 875 (Sup.Ct.1965).

In furtherance of the rationale behind this exception, state and federal courts have found computer printouts admissible as a business record according to their applicable evidence rules: (1) under the *Uniform Rules of Evidence.,* see *Sears, Roebuck & Co. v. Merla, supra,* 142 *N.J.Super.* at 207, 361 *A.*2d 68; (2) under the UBREA, see *Merrick v. United States Rubber Co.,* 7 *Ariz.App.* 433, 435–436, 440 *P A.*2d 314, 316–317 (App.Ct,1968); *State v. Veres,* 7 *Ariz.App.* 117, 125–26, 436 *P A.*2d 629, 637–638 (App.Ct.1968) (bank records prepared by automatic encoding machine), *cert.* den. 393 *U.S.* 1014, 89 *S.Ct.* 613, 21 *L.Ed A.*2d 559 (1969); *Union Elec. Co. v. Mansion House Center No. Redev. Co., supra* at 314–315; *Bobbie Brooks, Inc. v. Hyatt,* 195 *Neb.* 596, 598–600, 239 *N.W.*2d 782, 784–785 (Sup.Ct.1976); *State v. Watson,* 192 *Neb.* 44, 45–49, 218 *N.W.*2d 904, 905–907 (Sup.Ct.1974); *Transport Indem. Co. v. Seib, supra* 178 *Neb.* at 255–260, 132 *N.W.*2d at 873–876; *Endicott Johnson Corp. v. Golde,* 190 *N.W.*2d 752, 754–757 (N.D.Sup.Ct.1971) (computer–prepared invoices); *In re Matthews,* 47 *Pa.D. & C A.*2d 529, 531, 539 (Orph.D.Ct.1969); *Seattle v. Heath,* 10 *Wash.App.* 949, 956, 520 *P A.*2d 1392, 1396 (App.Ct.1974); but see *State v. Walker,* 16 *Wash.App.* 637, 639, 557 *P A.*2d 1330, 1332 (App.Ct.1976); (3) under the Commonwealth Fund Act, see *United States v. Fendley,* 522 *F.*2d 181, 187 (5 Cir.1975);

United States v. Liebert, 519 *F.*2d 542, 547 (3 Cir. 1975), *cert.* den. 423 *U.S.* 985, 96 *S.Ct.* 392, 46 *L.Ed.*2d 301 (1975); *United States v. Greenlee,* 517 *F.*2d 899, 902, 906 (3 Cir. 1975), *cert.* den. 423 *U.S.* 985, 96 *S.Ct.* 391, 46 *L.Ed.*2d 301 (1975); *United States v. Russo, supra* at 1239–1240; *United States v. Edick,* 432 *F.*2d 350, 354 (4 Cir.1970); *United States v. De Georgia,* 420 *F.*2d 889, 891, 893 and n.11, 894 (9 Cir.1969); *Olympic Ins. Co. v. H.D. Harrison, Inc.,* 418 *F.*2d 669, 670 (5 Cir. 1969); *D & H Auto Parts, Inc. v. Ford Marketing Corp.,* 57 *F.R.D.* 548, 551–552 (E.D.N.Y.1973); *Rogers v. Frank Lyon Co.,* 253 *Ark.* 856, 857–860, 489 *S.W.*2d 506, 507–509, (Sup.Ct.1973); *Smith v. Bank of the South,* 141 *Ga.App.* 114, 115, 232 *S.E.*2d 629, 630 (App.Ct.1977); *Cotton v. John W. Eshelman & Sons, Inc.,* 123 *Ga.App.* 360, 365, 223 *S.E.*2d 757, 761 (App.Ct.1976); *Sierra Life Ins. Co. v. First Nat'l Life Ins. Co.,* 85 *N.M.* 409, 412–413, 512 *P.*2d 1245, 1248 (Sup.Ct.1973); *Ed Guth Realty, Inc. v. Gingold,* 34 *N.Y.*2d 440, 451–452, 358 *N.Y.S.*2d 367, 374, 315 *N.E.*2d 441, 446 (Ct.App.1974); (4) under the new *Federal Rules of Evidence,* see *United States v. Scholle,* 553 *F.*2d 1109, 1124–1125 (8 Cir. 1977); (5) under the common law rule, see *Brown v. Commonwealth,* 440 *S.W.*2d 520, 524 (Ky.Ct.App.1969); *State v. Hodgeson,* 305 *So.*2d 421, 428 (La.Sup.Ct.1974); *King v. State ex rel. Murdock Acceptance Corp.,* 222 *So.*2d 393, 398 (Miss.Sup.Ct.1969); and (6) under distinct state statutes, see *People v. Cohen,* 59 *Cal.App.*3d 241, 249, 130 *Cal.Rptr* 656, 661 (D.Ct.App.1976) (ruling under *Cal.Evid. Code* § 1271 (West 1966)), *cert.* den. 429 *U.S.* 1045, 97 *S.Ct.* 748, 50 *L.Ed.*2d 758 (1977); *Dept. of Mental Health v. Beil,* 44 *Ill.App.*3d 402, 409, 2 *Ill.Dec.* 655, 660, 357 *N.E.*2d 875, 880 (App.Ct.1976) (ruling under *Ill.Rev.Stat.* c. 38, § 115–5 (1971)) (admissible but foundation in this case found inadequate); *People v. Gauer,* 7 *Ill.App.*3d 512, 514–515, 288 *N.E.*2d 24, 25 (App.Ct.1972) (same); *State v. Springer,* 283 *N.C.* 627, 636 197 *S.E.*2d 530, 536 (Sup.Ct.1973) (ruling under *N.C.Gen.Stat.* § § 55–37.1, 55A–27.1 (1965), a statute dealing specially with the admissibility of corporate computer records) (admissible but insufficient foundation in this case); *Texas*

Warehouse Co. of Dallas, Inc. v. Springs Mills, Inc. 511 *S.W.2d* 735, 743 (Tex.Civ.App.1974) (ruling under *Tex.Rev.Civ.Stat.Ann.* art. 3737e, § § 1–4 (1972)); *Railroad Comm'n v Southern Pac. R. Co.,* 468 *S.W.2d* 125, 128–29 (Tex.Civ.App.1971) (same); *Arnold D.Kamen & Co. v. Young,* 466 *S.W.2d* 381. 387 (Tex.Civ.App.1971) (same) (not admitted); *Gassett v. State,* 532 *S.W.2d* 328, 330–331 (Tex.Cr.App.1976) (same).

Although many courts have ruled upon the admissibility of computer printouts, only some of them have addressed the question of what foundation is required. See *United States v. Scholle, supra* at 1124–1125; *United States v. Fendley, supra* at 185–187; *United States v. Russo, supra* at 1239–40; *D & H Auto Parts, Inc. v. Ford Marketing Corp., supra* at 551–552; *Merrick v. United States Rubber Co., supra* 7 *Ariz.App.* at 435–436, 440 *P2d* at 316–317; *Rogers v. Frank Lyon Co., supra* 253 *Ark.* at 857–860, 489 *S.W.2d* at 507–509; *Smith v. Bank of the South, supra* 141 *Ga.App.* at 114–115, 232 *S.E2d* at 630; *Cotton v. John W. Eshelman & Sons, Inc., supra* 137 *Ga.App.* at 363–365, 223 *S.E.2d* at 760–761; *Dept. of Mental Health v. Beil, supra,* 44 *Ill.App.*3d at 409, 2 *Ill.Dec.* at 660, 357 *N.E.2d* at 880; *People v. Gauer, supra* 7 *Ill.App.*3d at 514–515, 288 *N.E.2d* at 24–25; *State v. Hodgeson, supra* at 427–428; *King v. State ex. rel. Murdock Acceptance Corp., supra* at 396–398; *Bobbie Brooks, Inc. v. Hyatt, supra* 195 *Neb.* at 599–600, 239 *N.W.2d* at 785–785; *State v. Watson, supra* 182 *Neb.* at 45–49, 218 *N.W.2d* at 905–907; *Transport Indem. Co. v. Seib, supra* 178 *Neb.* at 255–260, 132 *N.W.2d* 873–875; *State v. Springer, supra* 283 *N.C.* at 634–636, 197 *S.E.2d* 535–536; *Endicott Johnson Corp. v. Golde, supra* at 755–757; *In re Matthews Estate, supra* at 531–539; *Texas Warehouse Co. of Dallas, Inc. v. Springs Mills, Inc., supra* at 739–743; *Railroad Comm'n v. Southern Pac. R. Co., supra* at 128–129; *Arnold D. Kamen & Co. v. Young, supra* at 387; *Seattle v. Health, supra* 10 *Wash.App.* at 953–956, 520 *P.2d* at 1395–1397.

The foundation requirements as set forth in these cases can be broken down into six

elements. The first consideration is whether the foundation witness must have personal knowledge of the act or event recorded or, more specifically, the need to produce the witness who originally supplied the information recorded on the computer tape. The majority of courts that have discussed this issue have determined that such personal knowledge is not necessary. See *United States v. Fendley, supra* at 185 (no need for foundation to attest to accuracy of information contained in computer document), *Rogers v. Frank Lyon Co., supra* 253 *Ark.* at 860, 489 *S.W.2d* at 508–509 (lack of personal knowledge did not affect admissibility of computer records); *Smith v. Bank of the South, supra* 141 *Ga.App.* at 114, 232 *S.E.2d* at 630 (same); *Cotton v. John W. Eshelman & Sons, Inc., supra* 137 *Ga.App.* at 364, 223 *S.E.2d* at 760 (while employees who furnished entries had personal knowledge, foundation witness need not); *State v. Watson, supra* 192 *Neb,* at 46–48, 218 *N.W.2d* at 906 (personal knowledge not required) (by implication); *State v. Springer, supra,* 283 *N.C.* at 633–634, 636, 197 *S.E.2d* at 535–536 (same); *Endicott Johnson Corp. v. Golde, supra* at 756 (same) (by implication); *Seattle v. Heath, supra* 10 *Wash.App.* at 953–954, 520 *P.2d* at 1395–1397 (recorder of information need not have personal knowledge); *cf. Transport Indem. Co. v. Seib, supra* 178 *Neb.* at 256–258, 132 *N.W.2d* at 873–875 (court inferred that computations were within witness' knowledge but determined that production of persons who originally supplied information was unnecessary). But see *Railroad Comm'n v. Southern Pac. R. Co., supra* at 129 (court required proof that computer records "were based upon information within the personal knowledge of a person whose duties include collection of such information"); *Arnold D. Kamen & Co. v. Young, supra* at 387 (under statutory interpretation court required personal knowledge of act or event recorded), criticized in 24 *Baylor L.Rev.* 161 (1972) (Texas statute does not by its terms require such a showing).

The majority rulings on this point of the personal knowledge requirement are consistent with New Jersey's ruling which eliminated the common law requirement of personal knowledge.

See *State v. Martorelli, supra* 136 *N.J.Super.* at 453, 346 *A*2d 618. Thus, this court will not require proof of personal knowledge on the part of the entrant of the information recorded where computer printouts are being admitted as a business record.

The qualification of the foundation witness is the second consideration. Numerous cases in other jurisdictions have examined the issue of whether the witness in question is the custodian of the computer records or otherwise qualified to be the foundation witness. *Transport Indem. Co. v. Seib, supra*, the first case in this area, demanded the highest qualifications for the foundation. The witness was not only a director of the computer–processing company and the custodian of record, but he also had prepared and supervised the preparation of the computer records. *Id.* 178 *Neb.* at 255–256, 132 *N.W.*2d at 873. More recent decisions, however, have declared that there is no need for the preparer of the computer records to testify. See *United States v. Fendley, supra* at 185; *D & H Auto Parts, Inc. v. Ford Marketing Corp., supra* at 551; *King v. State ex rel. Murdock Acceptance Corp., supra* at 396; *cf. Bobbie Brooks, Inc. v. Hyatt, supra* 195 *Neb.* at 599–600, 239 *N.W.*2d at 784–785 (present custodian rather than custodian at the time of preparation of records allowed to testify). In some cases the courts have required that the supervisor of the computer–processing department testify, see *People v. Gauer, supra* 7 *Ill.App.*3d at 514, 288 *N.E.*2d at 25 (keeper of records who had direct supervision and control of records) (by implication); *King v. State ex rel. Murdock Acceptance Corp., supra* at 396 (assistant treasurer and accounting manager of data–processing department); *Railroad Comm'n v. Southern Pac. R. Co., supra* at 128 (person in charge of data–processing department who supervised computerized accounting records); whereas other courts have permitted different persons to be the foundation witness, see *United States v. Scholle, supra* at 1123 (section chief of department who developed computer system); *Merrick v. United States Rubber Co., supra* 7 *Ariz.App.* at 435, 440 *P.*2d at 316 (an employee of the credit office who was familiar with account); *State v. Hodgeson, supra* at 427 (comptroller–manager of company who supervised compilation of data which was later submitted

to a computer service); *Bobbie Brooks, Inc. v. Hyatt, supra* 195 *Neb.* at 599–600, 239 *N.W.*2d at 784–785 (present custodian rather than custodian who supervised making record in question). Witnesses have been found qualified to testify by reason of their expertise in computers, see *Id.* at 598, 239 *N.W.*2d at 784 (an expert in computer programming); *Texas Warehouse Co. of Dallas, Inc. v. Springs Mills, Inc., supra* at 742 (court–qualified expert in court programming), or by reason of their "training, experience and position to testify about the [computer] system." *United States v. Scholle, supra* at 1123, 1125 (witness also developed the computer retrieval system); accord, *United States v. Russo, supra* at 1241 (witness also "showed a familiarity with the use of the particular computers in question"). Other jurisdictions have gone so far as to eliminate any need for the witness's personal knowledge of the physical operations of the computer equipment and require only that the witness be generally familiar with the accounting and recording process. See *Merrick v. United States Rubber Co., supra* 7 *Ariz.App.* at 435, 440 *P.*2d at 316; *Cotton v. John W. Eshelman & Sons, Inc., supra* 137 *Ga.App.* at 363, 223 *S.E.*2d at 760–761 (but witness was direct supervisor who would certify a records' accuracy); *Endicott Johnson Corp. v. Golde*, 190 *N.W.*2d at 756–757; *cf. Smith v. Bank of the South, supra* 141 *Ga.App.* at 114, 232 *S.E.*2d at 630 (limited knowledge). See also *Bobbie Brooks, Inc. v. Hyatt, supra* 195 *Neb.* at 600, 239 *N.W.*2d at 785 (witness' personal knowledge of mode of preparation not required). Furthermore, in one case, the witness was permitted to testify from the company records rather than from his own general knowledge. *Rogers v. Frank Lyon Co., supra* 253 *Ark.* at 489 *S.W.*2d at 507.

All of the cases which have dealt with the qualifications of the foundation witness involve statutes or case law which delineate the type of witness required. New Jersey eliminated its prior requirement of having a custodian or other qualified witness testify when it adopted *Evid.R.* 63(13). See *Samuel Sheitelman, Inc. v. Hoffman, supra* 106 *N.J.Super.* at 356–357, 255 *A.*2d 807. No specific person must be called to supply the foundation testimony for the admission of business records. However, whoever testifies must be in a position to supply the foundation specified in *Evid.R.* 63(13), *i.e.,* the regular course of business, the time of the making of the record and the event recorded, the sources of information recorded, and finally, the methods and circumstances of the computer record's preparation. This court agrees with the following statement in *State v. Springer, supr* 283 *N.C.* at 636, 197 *S.E.*2d at 536:

> * * * a proper foundation for [computer] evidence is laid by testimony of a witness who is familiar with the computerized records and the methods under which they were made so as to satisfy the court that the methods, the sources of information, and the time of preparation render such evidence trustworthy.

Thus, in providing information as to the methods of preparation, the foundation witness should also be able "to testify as to the type of computer employed, the permanent nature of the record storage, and how daily processing of information to be fed into the computer was conducted, resulting in permanent records." *Railroad Comm'n v. Southern Pac. R. Co., supra* at 128.

The third element of foundation testimony is proof that the computer records were made in the ordinary course of business. See *United States v. Scholle, supra* at 1125; *United States v. Russo, supra* at 1241; *D & H Auto Parts, Inc. v. Ford Marketing Corp., supra* at 552; *Dept. of Mental Health v. Beil. supra, 44 Ill.App.*3d at 409, 2 *Ill.Dec.* at 660 357 *N.E.*2d at 880; *State v. Hodgeson, supra* at 428; *King v. State ex rel. Murdock Acceptance Corp., supra* at 398; *Bobbie Brooks, Inc. v. Hyatt, supra* 195 *Neb.* at 600, 239 *N.W.*2d at 785; *Transport Indem. Co. v. Seib, supra* 178 *Neb.* at 257–258, 260, 132 *N.W.*2d at 874; *State v. Springer, supra* 283 *N.C.* at 636, 197 *S.E.*2d at 536; *Railroad Comm'n v. Southern Pac. R. Co., supra* at 129; *Seattle v. Heath, supra* 10 *Wash.App.* at 956, 520 *P.*2d at 1397. This proof would include testimony that the computer printouts were routinely prepared, see *United States v. Scholle, supra* at 1125; *H & D Auto Parts, Inc. v. Ford Marketing Corp., supra* at 552; *King v. State ex rel. Murdock Acceptance Corp., supra* at

398, rather than specifically prepared for trial, see *D & H Auto Parts, Inc. v. Ford Marketing Corp., supra* at 552; but see *Transport Indem. Co. v. Seib, supra* 178 *Neb.* at 260, 132 *N.W.*2d at 875; *McCormick, op. cit.* § 314 at 734; that "they were relied upon by [the company involved] as sufficiently accurate for business purposes," *D & H Auto Parts, Inc. v. Ford Marketing Corp., supra* at 552; see *United States v. Russo, supra* at 1240, and where the computer processing is done by a third party, that the information was processed through the computer as agreed upon, see *Transport Indem. Co. v. Seib, supra* 178 *Neb.* at 258, 132 *N.W.*2d at 874. Requiring the above proof that the computer printout was made in the ordinary course of business is obviously mandated by *Evid.R.* 63(13) prior to the admission of such evidence. See *e.g., State v. Martorelli, supra* 136 *N.J.Super.* at 453, 346 *A.*2d 618.

In providing an adequate foundation, the fourth consideration is the time of preparation of the computer printout. The requirement that the entry be made "at or about the time of the act * * * recorded," *Evid.R.* 63(13), is satisfied so long as the input is placed into the computer "within a reasonable time after each act or transaction to which it relates." *United States v. Russo, supra* at 1240; see *Dept. of Mental Health v. Beil, supra, 44 Ill.App.*3d at 409, 2 *Ill.Dec.* at 660, 357 *N.E.*2d at 880; *State v. Hodgeson, supra* at 428; *King v. State ex. rel Murdock Acceptance Corp., supra* at 398; *Bobbie Brooks, Inc. v. Hyatt, supra* 195 *Neb.* at 600, 239 *N.E.*2d at 785 (transactions "recorded within one week of their occurrence within the regular course of business"); *Transport Indem. Co. v. Seib, supra* 178 *Neb.* at 259, 132 *N.W.*2d at 875 (information fed into computer in a systematic way on a day–to–day basis); *State v. Springer, supra* 238 *N.C.* at 636, 197 *S.E.*2d at 536. It is not required that the printout itself be made at that time. *United States v. Russo, supra* at 1240 (computer printout made 11 months after last transaction recorded). Although the printout can be made at some later date, it cannot be made specifically in preparation for trial or else it will not have been made in the regular course of business. See *D & H Auto Parts,*

Inc. v. Ford Marketing Corp., supra at 552. Requiring the above proof is also consistent with the mandates of *Evid.R.* 63(13).

The fifth element of a proper foundation is the source of information from which the computer printout was made. Consonant with the requisites of *Evid.R.* 63(13), the cases in other jurisdictions demand that the sources of information be specified. See *United States v. Scholle, supra* at 1125; *United States v. Russo, supra* at 1240; *D & H Auto Parts, Inc. v. Ford Marketing Corp., supra* at 552; *Dept. of Mental Health v. Beil, supra* 44 *Ill.App.*3d at 409, 2 *Ill.Dec.* at 660, 357 *N.E.*2d at 880; *State v. Hodgeson, supra* at 428; *King v. State ex rel. Murdock Acceptance Corp., supra* at 398; *Bobbie Brooks, Inc. v. Hyatt, supra* 195 *Neb.* at 600, 239 *N.W.*2d at 785; *Seattle v. Heath, supra* 10 *Wash,App.* at 956, 520 *P*2d at 1397 (gives complete list of sources). The original source of the computer program must be delineated, *United States v. Scholle, supra* at 1125, and the reliability and trustworthiness of the information fed into the computer must be established. *United States v. Russo, supra* at 1240; *King v. State ex rel. Murdock Acceptance Corp., supra* at 398, followed in *Dept. of Mental Health v. Beil, supra* 44 *Ill.App.*3d at 409, 2 *Ill.Dec.* at 660, 357 *N.E.*2d at 880, and *State v. Hodgeson, supra* at 428, and *Seattle v. Heath, supra* 10 *Wash.App.* at 956, 520 *P.*2d at 1397. The foundation witness should "describe[d] in detail the sources of information upon which the printout was based," *United States v. Scholle, supra* at 1125, explain, where necessary, the sources and meaning of any calculations, formulas or abbreviations appearing in the computer printout, see *Transport Indem. Co. v. Seib, supra* 178 *Neb.* at 258, 132 *N.W.*2d at 874, and show that the printouts were not only prepared by information supplied by a certain source but were capable of being verified by that source. *D & H Auto Parts, Inc. v. Ford Marketing Corp., supra* at 552.

The sixth, and perhaps the most important, element of foundation proof is the method and circumstances of the preparation of the computer printout. Most courts have required a complete and comprehensive de-scription of the method of preparation. See, e.g., *People v. Gauer, supra* 7 *Ill.App.*3d at 514, 288 *N.E.*2d at 25; *King v. State ex rel. Murdock Acceptance Corp., supra* at 398; *Transport Indem. Co. v. Seib, supra* 178 *Neb.* at 257, 132 *N.W.*2d at 874 (141 pages of record dealt with method of preparation — the most provided in any case). This description must include testimony as to (1) the competency of the computer operators, *King v. State ex. rel Murdock Acceptance Corp., supra* at 398; see *United States v. Russo, supra* at 1241 (persons who feed information to computer perform accurately); *Railroad Comm'n v. Southern Pac. R. Co., supra* at 129, (preparation of records done "by persons who understood operation of the equipment and whose regular duty was to operate it"); (2) the type of computer used and its acceptance in the field as standard and efficient equipment, *King v. State ex rel. Murdock Acceptance Corp., supra* at 397–398, followed in *Dept. of Mental Health v. Beil, supra* 44 *Ill.App.*3d at 409, 2 *Ill.Dec.* at 660, 357 *N.E.*2d at 880, and *State v. Hodgeson, supra* at 428; *Railroad Comm'n v. Southern Pac. R. Co., supra* at 129; *Seattle v. Heath, supra* 10 *Wash.App.* at 956, 520 *P.*2d at 1125 (assumption that equipment is functioning properly); accord, *United States v. Russo, supra* at 1239–40; (3) the procedure for the input and output of information, including controls, tests and checks for accuracy and reliability, see *United States v. Scholle, supra* at 1125; *United States v. Russo, supra* at 1239; *King v. State ex rel. Murdock Acceptance Corp., supra at 397–98; Bobbie Brooks, Inc. v. Hyatt, supra* 195 *Neb.* at 598–600, 239 *N.W.*2d at 785; *Texas Warehouse Co. of Dallas, Inc. v. Springs Mills, Inc., supra* at 742; see also, *People v. Gauer, supra* 7 *Ill.App.*3d at 514, 288 *N.E.*2d at 25 (mere conclusion on part of foundation witness that records were made in the ordinary course of business and were reliable, held to be an insufficient foundation for computer print-outs); but see *D & H Auto Parts, Inc. v. Ford Marketing Corp., supra* at 552 (no requirement for "'oral testimony concerning the reliability of the machine operations'") (quoting from Freed, "A Lawyer's Guide Through the Computer Maze," 6 *Prac.Law.* 15, 28 (1960)); (4) the mechanical operations of the machine, see *United States v. Scholle, supra* at 1125; *United States v. Russo, supra* at 1239; *King v. State ex rel. Murdock Acceptance Corp., supra* at 397 (provided but not specifically required); *Texas Warehouse Co. of Dallas, Inc. v. Springs Mills, Inc., supra* at 742; but see *State v. Watson, supra* 192 *Neb.* at 48–49, 218 *N.W.*2d at 906–907 (failure to explain the workings of the machine as was done in *Transport Indem. Co. v. Seib, supra,* did not affect admissibility of bank records distinguishes *Seib* decision on basis that bank was not party to this action as in *Seib*), and (5) the meaning and identity of the records themselves, see *People v. Gauer, supra* 7 *Ill.App.*3d at 514, 288 *N.E.*2d at 25; *Transport Indem. Co. v. Seib, supra* 178 *Neb.* at 258; 132 *N.W.*2d at 874. The five factors listed regarding the methods of preparation are not intended to be exhaustive. A trial court may require further proof as is necessary to justify the admission of a computer record.

In conclusion, under *Evid.R.* 63(13) a proper foundation for the admissibility of a computer printout as a business record should be provided by a person who may lack personal knowledge of the events recorded but is sufficiently familiar with the computerized record and the methods under which they were prepared so as to testify that (1) the computer record, as opposed to the printout, was made within a reasonable time after the happening of event or transaction recorded; (2) the computer record and printouts were made in the regular course of business; and (3) the methods and circumstances, as heretofore explained in this opinion, demonstrated that the computer and the printout were reliable and trustworthy so as to justify their admission.

Using the above principles to evaluate the foundation presented here, the court initially notes that in this case the actual route of the information from its source to the computer record is somewhat different from that of the previously cited cases. The mortgage payment, accompanied by a prepunched computer card, is sent by the mortgagee to the post office box of Wood–Ridge where the cards and the payments are matched and checked for the amounts. The checks are then forwarded to Monarch and the computer cards are sent to Financial Services. Financial Services processes these cards through its computer and obtains a daily readout of the total daily payments, which readout is then checked against the total amount on the checks received by Monarch. Financial Services then forwards the daily computer printout to Monarch, which receives it on the next day and cross–checks the totals. Three witnesses were called to explain the procedure involved in processing these checks and computer cards.

Defendants, however, have raised several objections to the admission of these computer printouts, including the qualifications of the foundation witnesses and the reliability and operations of the computer itself. Throughout the testimony of these witnesses defendants objected that they did not have personal knowledge of the mortgage transactions recorded on the computer printout. As I have previously noted, a foundation witness does not need to have personal knowledge of the transaction recorded. Therefore, as to all three witnesses this objection is without merit.

However, there is a question as to whether any of the three foundation witnesses was "familiar with the computerized records and the methods under which they were made so as to satisfy the court that the methods, the sources of information and the time of preparation render[s] [this] evidence trustworthy." *State v. Springer, supra* 283 *N.C.* at 636, 197 *S.E.*2d at 536. The first witness was in a position to testify as to the general practice of processing the mortgage checks and computer cards at Wood–Ridge since he had been the assistant vice–president of Wood–Ridge for 13 years and was familiar with the business transactions and work of Wood–Ridge. He did not necessarily have to be the direct supervisor of the bank's processing of defendant's checks and computer cards.

Urbanovich, the third witness called, has been the assistant vice–president of Monarch for the past ten years and was generally familiar with the workings of the mortgage department of the bank by reason of being in charge of the accounting at the bank. He was also familiar with the arrangements for processing mortgage payments that Monarch has with Wood–Ridge and Financial Services. This court finds that Urbanovich was sufficiently familiar with the methods and circumstances of processing mortgage payments from Monarch to Financial Services so as to be a proper foundation witness. Any objections made by defendant as to his qualifications are overruled.

The key foundation witness in this case was Kieper, the office manager of Financial Services, who is responsible for handling mortgage installment loans and has been in Financial Services employ for 17 years. He neither is a computer expert nor did he set up the computer mechanics of this particular service. However, expertise in computers or setting up the particular computer program is not required under the reasoning and holding of this decision. The objection as to Kieper's lack of personal knowledge as to the relationship between Monarch and Financial Services is not meritorious since he has demonstrated a general familiarity with the relationship and that is all that will be required by this court.

There is a question, though, as to whether Kieper is sufficiently familiar with the methods and circumstances of the computer printout's preparation. A review of the testimony before this court reveals that adequate proof has been presented to show that the computer record was made within a reasonable time of the receipt of the mortgage payments and that the computer records and the printouts were made in the ordinary course of business for Monarch and Financial Services. The problem arises when the testimony as to the actual preparation of the printout is examined. Kieper testified as to what information was received by Financial Services to initiate a new mortgage loan account but he did not explain what Financial Services does with this information or how the computer program on a new account originates. Further testimony revealed the method by which daily payment information is received from Wood–Ridge, the procedures for supplying daily, monthly and yearly readouts, the method of checking totals and the fact that the information received from Wood–Ridge

(or Monarch in irregular payment situations) is processed through the computer. He did not provide information on the type of computer used and its acceptance in the field as standard, efficient and accurate equipment. This witness did not testify as to the competency of those who program the computer and process the daily input, nor did he fully explain the input controls or the mechanics of the machines. In particular, Kieper had no knowledge of the procedure for handling "irregular payments" which came from Monarch.

On the evidence presented to this court plaintiff has failed to lay the proper foundation. But in light of the fact that no judgment has yet been entered here and the conclusions reached in this opinion are novel in this State, plaintiff will be permitted on a date to be fixed by the court to reopen its case in order to have an opportunity to submit additional evidence to lay the proper foundation in accordance with the rulings herein.

Charles W. MOORE, Jr. v. GENERAL MOTORS CORPORATION, a corporation

558 S.W.2d 720

Missouri Court of Appeals, St. Louis District, Division Three
August 16, 1977

In this case of first impression in Missouri the defendant, General Motors Corporation, appeals from a judgment of the Circuit Court of the City of St. Louis wherein the plaintiff, Charles W. Moore, Jr., was awarded $8,500.00 as damages by a jury for what the plaintiff contends was the failure of the defendant to pay him an amount of money to which he was entitled pursuant to the defendant's Employee Suggestion Plan.

At all relevant times the defendant has a Suggestion Plan (hereinafter referred to as the "Plan") which it promulgated to its employees and whereby it encouraged its employees to submit suggestions on forms identified as

"Suggestion Forms" made available to them by the defendant. A "Suggestion," according to the Plan, was a "proposal to submit something in a specified manner." When a suggestion was submitted on the form provided for that purpose, the Plan stated that it was to be "systematically investigated for merit" so that a sound decision would be made whether it should be adopted and was to be reviewed by the Suggestion Committee (hereinafter "Committee") made up of representatives of major departments of the defendant's plant. If a suggestion was not adopted the suggester was told the reason. Awards were to be paid after the suggestion was adopted and in effect.

According to the Plan, the function of the Committee was to decide (1) whether suggestions submitted to it were eligible for awards and (2) the amount of each award.

The Plan provided a formula for the making of awards which were adopted by the defendant. According to this formula, where the benefits resulting from a suggestion were *measurable* the award amount was to be one–sixth of the total gross savings to the division in which the employee worked during the twelve month period following adoption of the suggestion, up to a maximum award of $10,000.00. If a suggestion resulted in savings to the suggester's division but a loss in the same amount to another division, the suggestion would be considered to have resulted in no savings and the amount of the award would be based upon *other benefits*. When a suggestion resulted in a saving of capital expenditure, the amount would equal one–twelfth of the total savings, but again subject to the maximum award of $10,000.00. Where there were *no measurable savings* resulting from an adopted suggestion, the award would be determined by the Committee "in light of all available information concerning its other benefits." All decisions by the Committee were final; however, if at any time an employee wished to reopen a suggestion or present new or additional information, the Committee, at its discretion might review its decision.

* * * * *

Plaintiff's petition, as amended, alleged, among other things, that relying on defendant's suggestion plan and the monetary reward promised therein, he developed and manufactured a metal device or tool which, when used in hanging tail–gates on all station wagons produced by the defendant, with the exception of Cadillacs, eliminated any difficulty or delay in such hanging operation and the production of station wagons with defective tail–gates.

Plaintiff further alleged that he suggested that floor pans for such station wagons be cut to a standard length prior to assembly, and that pursuant to the suggestion plan he wrote up and described the metal device or tool he developed and manufactured, together with his suggestion as to floor pan lengths, submitted it to the defendant in the manner prescribed by the defendant; that these suggestions were used by the defendant in the manufacture of its station wagons; that he had repeatedly made demand for the monetary reward promised by the defendant in its suggestion plan, but that the defendant has failed and refused to pay plaintiff the monetary reward; that in making his suggestions he relied on defendant's promise of a $10,000.00 monetary award, but that defendant has refused to pay him the award. Plaintiff prayed judgment in the amount of $10,000.00.

Defendant's Answer, after admitting its corporate status, the nature of its business, plaintiff's employment, and the existence of the Suggestion Plan, denied each and every allegation of plaintiff's petition.

* * * * *

Missouri, since *Pomeroy v. Benton*, 77 Mo. 64 (1882), has followed the spoliation rule that the destruction of written evidence without a satisfactory explanation gives rise to an inference unfavorable to the spoliator, and he who destroys such evidence is thereby held to admit the truth of the allegations of the opposing party. As recently as *Brissette v. Milner Chevrolet*, 479 S.W.2d 176, 182–3[9–10] (Mo.App.1972), the rule has been discussed. The application of the rule is however limited to those cases where there is evidence of an intentional destruction of the evidence indicating fraud and a desire to suppress the truth. *Berthold–Jennings Lumber Co. v. St. Louis, I.M. & S. RY. Co.*, 80 F.2d 32 (8th Cir. 1936) 102 A.L.R. 688, certiorari denied, 297 U.S. 715, 56 S.Ct. 591, 80 L.Ed. 1001.

Records referred to during the course of trial included overtime equalization records, inspection records (also referred to as inspection tickets), payroll records, time cards, salvage records, and time studies. None of these were produced at trial by either party although testimony relevant to their content came into the record, and oftentimes said testimony was in conflict, dependent upon whether plaintiff or defendant adduced the evidence. The plaintiff contends that at least some of these records would have entries of the time spent as well as the number of tail–gates which had to be repaired by reason of the lack of clearance between the weatherstrip retainer and the interior of the tail–gate which resulted in the tearing off of the weatherstripping. Defendant, on the other hand, offered evidence that none of these records would contain that information. The issue to be decided is whether, on the basis of the evidence, plaintiff is entitled to the benefit of the spoliation doctrine.

Overtime equalization records were records required to be kept, pursuant to the collective bargaining contract with the Union so that the overtime worked by any employee would be posted to assure that overtime was equitably distributed among the employees of the various departments. The only witness who testified that this record would reflect the overtime money spent "on repair of tail–gates on station wagons in 1971," was Edward A. Gregory. Defendant's evidence was that these records were systematically destroyed at the end of the model year and for that reason were not available at trial time. Mr. Tisoto also testified, during defendant's case, that during the course of his investigation to ascertain the amount of award to be made to plaintiff after his suggestions were being reconsidered he was told that the overtime equalization records had been "pitched out."

While "payroll records" were referred to and it was established that they would show the amount of overtime worked, there was no evidence that they would show how much of that overtime was spent repairing station wagons with the problem plaintiff's suggestions were used to correct.

Inspection Tickets (or inspection records) are tickets which are made by an inspector when he "knocks–down" a vehicle for some repair. Although no one testified in detail what these records contain and no samples of such records were produced by either party, Mr. Gregory testified that an inspection ticket would show what was wrong with a car, e.g. "gate fit," and served the purpose of a quality control device, so that when an item showed up on the tickets frequently "they" would come back to the foreman of the department involved to find out why. According to this witness these records are required by the "Federal Motor Safety Standards Act" to be kept for every vehicle in the sequence as it is manufactured for a period of five years and they are kept on microfilm. According to Robert McGuire, these tickets would show what repair work was to be done but not how much overtime or work time was consumed in making the required repairs. He testified " . . . when we got a repair job we look at the repair ticket, we repair the items noted as defective by the inspector, and I know we were all involved in the tailgates."

During defendant's case Mr. Lance testified that there is an inspection ticket for every body produced. Mr. Hare, who was General Foreman of Inspection, testified that inspection tickets were retained for the current model year plus two years, but that the tickets for the period covered in this case had been disposed of. He was not asked nor did he testify when this occurred. They would indicate what defects were written up, that they had been repaired, and that the inspector "bought it off," i.e. passed the car for inspection. He denied that the ticket would show the length of time consumed in repairing the defects entered on the ticket. He confirmed the fact that the period those tickets were required to be maintained was regulated by the federal government.

Mr. Gregory testified that time studies were

made by assembly experts to see if an employee could do more work or if the number of men performing a particular function could be reduced and the same work performed by a fewer number. From these studies, he testified, the cost of hanging a tail–gate would be determined. These studies were performed by the Industrial Engineering Department according to Mr. Tisoto for the purpose of determining the time it takes an employee to do a certain function in the production of a car. According to Mr. Carl E. Barth, the department in which he is employed as a methods analyst conducts these "time studies whenever the circumstances dictate that they be done." Among the circumstances which might give rise to time studies are: 1) the beginning of each model year where there would be an operation which was different from the preceding year and a time study is made of the operation to bring files up to date, and 2) to ascertain the amount of time required to perform any function of work and thereby assist in setting up regroup operations to take into account time values. He testified that in October, 1971, a time study had been made on the tail–gate hanging operation but did not encompass adjusting, refitting and repairing of tail–gates.

Production records are those records which show the number of station wagons produced in an hour. When asked, Mr. Tisoto testified that somewhere, someone should have a copy of what defendant's production was during 1971.

Plaintiff relies on *State ex rel. St. Louis County Transit Company v. Walsh*, 327 S.W.2d 713 (Mo.App.1959) where the court, in a prohibition proceeding where the question was whether certain photographs taken by the operator of a relator's motor bus at the scene of an accident was subject to discovery, and whether they were, depended upon why they were taken. The spoliation question came into the case because at the taking of the bus operator's deposition when he was asked why the photographs were taken, whether relator had instructed him to take them, or whether it was part of his duty to take them, the relator's counsel instructed

him not to answer the questions. The court, 327 S.W.2d l. c. 717 said:

"The question as to why the photographs were taken was a question of fact, to be determined by the respondent. In his return respondent pleads that because the relator suppressed the evidence as to the reason the pictures were taken, he indulged the presumption that the evidence, if not suppressed, would have been favorable to the plaintiff and would have revealed that the photographs were in fact not privileged. We are of the opinion that under the circumstances of this case the respondent was entitled to indulge such a presumption, and to reach the conclusion that the photographs were taken for a reason which would not make them privileged. It has long been the rule in this state that the *spoliation or* suppression of evidence gives rise to an unfavorable inference. *Thus the destruction of written evidence without a satisfactory explanation gives rise to an unfavorable inference . . .* Similarly, where one party has obtained possession of physical evidence which he fails to produce or account for at the trial, an inference is warranted against that party . . . And where one conceals or suppresses evidence such action warrants an unfavorable inference . . . , and evidence of such suppression is . . . admissible as showing an admission that defendant was conscious of being in the wrong and that its cause was unjust." (emphasis supplied).

Defendant's overtime equalization records, according to all of the evidence in this case, were destroyed in accord with defendant's policy to destroy them at the end of the model year, July 27, 1971; exactly when they had been was not put into evidence other than Mr. Tisoto's testimony that he had been told they had been "pitched out" while he was investigating plaintiff's suggestion prior to the Committee meeting of September 21, 1971. There is no evidence that at the time defendant had any knowledge that it was facing litigation so that it was put on notice that it should not pursue its customary practice of destroying these records. Anyone knowledgeable of business practices and the cost of storing records in these times would find it reasonable and not smacking of fraud for the defendant, with no knowledge of pending litigation, to follow its customary practice. We hold that under these circumstances the spoliation doctrine is inapplicable to the overtime equalization records even if they did contain information on the time spent in repairing station wagon tail–gates with the rubber weatherstripping raked off by the clam style tail–gate on the 1971 Chevrolet station wagon.

* * * * *

MOORE v. JACKSON TUBE CO., INC.

286 N.Y.Supp.2d 488

Supreme Court, Special Term, New York
County, Part L
Jan. 20, 1949

Plaintiff moves, pursuant to Civil Practice Act, § 325, for an order punishing defendant for contempt, striking out the answer, and granting judgment for the relief demanded in the complaint.

The action is brought to recover $50,000 damages for breach of an oral contract employing plaintiff as a salesman. The contract is alleged to have been made in Chicago. The answer pleads general denials and the affirmative defenses of the Statute of Frauds of New York and Illinois. In order to establish the amount of sales made to certain of the defendant's customers, on which plaintiff claims commissions, plaintiff obtained an order of this court, date September 15, 1948, directing defendant to give plaintiff a discovery and inspection of all sales made by defendant to such customers during the period while the alleged contract of employment was in force (October 1, 1942 to September 30, 1943). The books and records containing this information were not produced.

Before defendant may be punished for contempt for violation of the discovery order, a finding must be made that the default is willful, i.e., that the party has refused to produce books and papers which were in existence. *Feingold v. Walworth Bros., Inc.,* 238 N.Y. 446, 455, 456, 144 N.E. 675, 678. The evidence here is sufficient to sustain such a finding. Defendant has offered affidavits by its president and former secretary. The former deposes that he made a thorough search in defendant's office in Piqua, Ohio, for the record of sales during the foregoing period and did not find any. The latter made a similar deposition regarding defendant's New York office. No explanation is advanced as to why records of sales made during 1942 and 1943 by a corporation apparently doing a large volume of business would have vanished without a trace. More important, the search by these two officers is alleged to have been made in June, 1948, yet the affidavits submitted by defendant in August, 1948, in opposition to the motion for discovery, made no claim that the books and records were unavailable, but opposed the motion on other grounds.

That makes it hardly credible that defendant had conducted a thorough search for the books in June but was unable to find them. The motion for contempt is therefore granted.

"The provisions of § 325, Civil Practice Act, are elastic enough to enable the court to fit the punishment to the offense, and to restrict the maximum punishment to 'a proper case.' The court is not limited to the alternatives of denying the motion or striking out the answer as a whole. It 'may make an order striking out one or more * * * defenses, counterclaims, * * * or that he (defendant) be debarred from maintaining a particular claim or defense in relation to which the discovery or inspection was sought.' * * * When a defendant refuses to produce books and papers relating to the merits of the action, he may be deprived of the right to assert that, so far as they relate to the merits of the action, he has a good defense. The presumption arises that a failure to produce such evidence is an admission that it exists. The punishment is for withholding proof, and is properly limited to excluding what the proof presumptively establishes. But to punish generally for a refusal to produce by striking out an entire answer, which not only puts in issue all the material allegations of the complaint, but includes affirmative defenses, comes perilously near the denial of due process of law." Pound, J., in Feingold v. Walworth Bros., Inc., supra, 238 N.Y. at pages 454, 455, 144 N.E. at page 678.

The cited case was in action for fraudulent representations by which plaintiff was included to sell stock to defendant for $20,000 whereas the value of the stock was $200,000. The answer contained a general denial and affirmative defenses. The order for discovery and inspection was obtained for the purpose of establishing the value of the stock. Special Term struck out the answer and granted judgment to plaintiff for the relief demanded in the complaint. The Court of Appeals modified by providing that defendant should be debarred solely from maintaining the particular claim that the value of the stock was less than $200,000.

The same result follows here. The books and records sought have no bearing on whether the contract was made or whether the Statute of Frauds is a valid defense. They would only go to prove plaintiffs damages if he establishes his cause of action. The defendant is therefore debarred from denying that the sales to the customers named in the discovery order during the period specified therein were less than the amount claimed in the complaint. Settle order.

NATION–WIDE CHECK CORPORATION, INC. v. FOREST HILLS DISTRIBUTORS, INC.

692 F.2d 214

United States Court of Appeals, First Circuit
November 15, 1982

In October 1973 Nation–Wide agreed with Forest Hills that Forest Hills would sell Nation–Wide's money orders to the public in return for a commission. The agreement specifically provided that Forest Hills would hold the sale proceeds apart from all its other assets and revenues, depositing those proceeds in a separate account with The First National Bank of Boston. This procedure, however, was not followed. Instead, the proceeds were deposited in various Forest Hills accounts in local banks near Forest Hills' stores, then transferred to various other Forest Hills accounts in Boston banks. From there, Forest Hills periodically remitted amounts due to Nation–Wide. Moreover, the proceeds were commingled with general Forest Hills revenues when they reached the Boston banks.

In late 1974 Forest Hills encountered financial difficulties and stopped sending money order proceeds to Nation–Wide. On December 18, Forest Hills executed an assignment of all its assets for the benefit of its creditors. At the time of assignment, Forest Hills owed Nation–Wide $71,417.69 for money orders issued between early November (when Forest Hills stopped paying Nation–Wide) and December 18 (when the assignment took place and money order sales were halted).

The assignees quickly liquidated most of Forest Hills' assets. By the end of December 1974 they apparently accumulated a fund of more than $600,000. Nation–Wide with equal promptness told the assignees about its claim against Forest Hills. Nation–Wide said that its claim took precedence of the claims of Forest Hills' general unsecured creditors because of the "separate–fund" provisions in its 1973 money order agreement. Nation–Wide's lawyers spoke to assignee Gordon around December 19 and wrote to Gordon about their claim a few days later. The assignees rejected Nation–Wide's priority claim and Nation–Wide filed suit against the assignees and Forest Hills on April 1, 1975, seeking payment of its $71,000 out of the $600,000 the assignees had accumulated.

On April 11, Gordon, an associate in a Boston law firm, wrote a letter to a senior partner in the same office about Forest Hills' business records. He noted that the records were being stored at some expense and asked if they could be discarded. In accordance with advice he received from the firm's partner, he then abandoned many of the documents — including all 1974 checks — to the landlord of the storage premises. Gordon's act of abandonment lies at the center of the controversy on this appeal.

In August 1979, when denying cross motions for summary judgment, the district court made clear just what Nation–Wide would have to prove to establish a preferred position vis–a–vis the general creditors and thereby to prevail. First, Nation–Wide would have to prove that Forest Hills breached a specific agreement to keep the money order sale proceeds separate. At that point Nation–Wide's claim would be like that of a secured creditor or a beneficiary of a trust, whose property the debtor or trustee has commingled with other property of his own. *See In re Dexter Buick–GMC Trust Co.*, 2 B.R. 247, 250 (Bkrtcy.D.R.I.1980). Second, Nation–Wide would then have to trace the funds from the sales themselves into the final $600,000 accumulated by the assignees.

* * * * *

At trial, Nation–Wide was able to present only limited evidence of the money order proceeds' "path" through Forest Hills' various accounts — in part because it had no recourse to the documents that Gordon discarded, in part because most of the banks involved had scanty records or no records at all. Nation–Wide produced records of the dates, locations, and amounts of money order sales for the relevant period, along with testimony that the proceeds were systematically deposited within a relatively short time by each local Forest Hills' store in a local bank. Nation–Wide also produced a list of the local bank accounts in both Massachusetts and New Hampshire and a compilation of the statements of those accounts in Massachusetts indicating that the aggregate balance for the period was always roughly equal to or substantially above the level of proceeds from all stores. Finally, it showed that the assignees deposited over $450,000 of Forest Hills' money in a new account within twelve days of the assignment, although it was unable (with one exception) to prove where the money came from.

While this evidence was consistent with the final accumulated fund containing proceeds of the original sales, in only one case did Nation–Wide produce conclusive documentary evidence of the route of the proceeds — a transfer of $1,204.85 from the Seabrook, New Hampshire, store and the New England Merchants' Bank, into the assignees' First National Bank of Boston account. The court found that the movement of funds from the Seabrook store was "typical" of the movement of funds from other stores, but Nation–Wide was unable to introduce parallel documentation to trace the balance of the proceeds from other accounts.

The district court filled this evidentiary gap by drawing an inference from the destruction of Forest Hills' business records by Gordon. The court found that Gordon had known as early as December 1974, from his communications with Nation–Wide's attorney, that the business records might be needed to trace the money order funds into the hands of the assignee. The court concluded that while Gordon had not acted in actual bad faith, he had "intentionally discarded" the documents "in knowing disregard of the plaintiff's claims," and that it was therefore proper to infer that the documents would have allowed Nation–Wide to trace the balance of the money order proceeds into the hands of the assignee.

The most recent authority in this circuit on the inferences to be drawn from the destruction of documents is *Allen Pen vs. Springfield Photo Mount Co.*, 653 F.2d 17 (1st Cir.1981). *Allen Pen* held that without some evidence that documents have been destroyed "in bad faith" or "from the consciousness of a weak case," it is "ordinarily" improper to draw an adverse inference about the contents of the documents. 653 F.2d at 23–24. The district court expressly found that Gordon did not act in bad faith, not because it believed that Gordon's behavior was in any sense proper, but because it felt that Gordon, as an assignee for the benefit of creditors, had no direct stake in the disposition of Forest Hills' assets among the claimants. However, the court did not interpret *Allen Pen* as establishing a *per se* requirement that bad faith be found before an adverse inference is drawn. It concluded that the inference was proper in this case because Gordon's conduct was not merely negligent but "purposeful" and "in knowing disregard" of Nation–Wide's claim. Unless an adverse inference were drawn, the court feared that other assignees might act like Gordon; they would be encouraged to destroy relevant documents and claimants in Nation–Wide's position would be denied their rightful property.

The general principles concerning the inferences to be drawn from the loss or destruction of documents are well established. When the contents of a document are relevant to an issue in a case, the trier of fact generally may receive the fact of the document's nonproduction or destruction as evidence that the party which has prevented production did so out of the well–founded fear that the contents would harm him. Wigmore has asserted that nonproduction is not merely "some" evidence, but is sufficient by itself to support an adverse inference even if no other evidence for the inference exists:

> The failure or refusal to produce a relevant document, or the destruction of it, is evidence *from which alone* its contents may be inferred to be unfavorable to the possessor, provided the opponent, when the identity of the document is disputed, first introduces some evidence tending to show that the document actually destroyed or withheld is the one as to whose contents it is desired to draw an inference.

Wigmore on Evidence § 291, at 228 (Chadbourn rev. 1979) (emphasis added). The inference depends, of course, on a showing that the party had notice that the documents were relevant at the time he failed to produce them or destroyed them.

The adverse inference is based on two rationales, one evidentiary and one not. The evidentiary rationale is nothing more than the common sense observation that a party who has notice that a document is relevant to litigation and who proceeds to destroy the document is more likely to have been threatened by the document than is a party in the same position who does not destroy the document. The fact of destruction satisfies the minimum requirement of relevance: it has some tendency, however small, to make the existence of a fact at issue more probable than it would otherwise be. *See* Fed.R.Evid. 401. Precisely how the document might have

aided the party's adversary, and what evidentiary shortfalls its destruction may be taken to redeem, will depend on the particular facts of each case, but the general evidentiary rationale for the inference is clear.

The other rationale for the inference has to do with its prophylactic and punitive effects. Allowing the trier of fact to draw the inference presumably deters parties from destroying relevant evidence before it can be introduced at trial. The inference also serves as a penalty, placing the risk of an erroneous judgment on the party that wrongfully created the risk. In McCormick's words, "the real underpinning of the rule of admissibility [may be] a desire to impose swift punishment, with a certain poetic justice, rather than concern over niceties of proof." *McCormick on Evidence* § 273, at 661 (1972).

That this policy rationale goes beyond a mere determination of relevance has been clear from the beginning. In the famous case of *Armory v. Delamirie*, 1 Stra. 505, 93 Eng.Rep. 664 (K.B.1722), the chimney sweep who sued the jeweler for return of the jewel he had found and left with the jeweler, was allowed to infer from the fact that the jeweler did not return the jewel that it was a stone "of the finest water." Were relevance all that was at issue, the inference would not necessarily be that the jewel was "of the finest water"; the fact that the jeweler kept the jewel proved that the jewel had value, but did not prove the value of the jewel. Nonetheless, the judge instructed the jury to "presume the strongest against him, and make the value of the *best* jewels the measure of their damages" — a clear sign that the inference was designed to serve a prophylactic and punitive purpose and not simply to reflect relevance.

In this case, both the evidentiary and the policy rationales, support the inference drawn by the district court. It is important as an initial matter to recall how much Nation–Wide had shown, directly or indirectly, without resort to the inference. It had established the precise dates and amounts of the money orders and the probable initial route of the proceeds into the local accounts. It had shown that at least some of the Massachusetts accounts had been sufficient balances at all relevant times to cover the proceeds. Although it was unable to introduce canceled checks or other records to trace most inter–account transfers, it was able to do so with regard to the Seabrook proceeds, and the court found that the flow of money from the Seabrook store's local account to the central accounts was "typical" of the flows from the other stores. Finally, it showed that some $88,000 came into the assignees' hands from a specific Forest Hills central account, and while it could not prove where the rest of the money collected by the assignees came from, it was not unreasonable to assume that some portion of it came from other Forest Hills accounts. In short, even without the inference from the destruction of the records, the court had significant circumstantial evidence that the proceeds were not dissipated before they could reach the assignees. The issue before the court was not whether the destruction was sufficient, standing alone, to warrant an adverse inference about the documents' contents; it was simply whether the destruction was at all relevant to the tracing issue, and if so, whether it was sufficiently probative in conjunction with the other evidence to support the tracing conclusion.

That the destruction was relevant is clear. As the district court found, Gordon had notice that the documents might be necessary to Nation–Wide's claim at the time he destroyed them. The assignees argue to the contrary on appeal, but there is sufficient evidence in the record to support the court's findings that Gordon was put on notice as early as late December, 1974, four months before he destroyed the documents, by his communications with Nation–Wide's attorney. More importantly, the court found that Gordon's conduct transcended mere negligence and amounted to "knowing disregard" of Nation–Wide's claim. The court's reluctance to label Gordon's conduct as "bad faith" is not dispositive: "bad faith" is not a talisman, as *Allen Pen* itself made clear when it stated that the adverse inference "ordinarily" depended on a showing of bad faith. Indeed, the "bad faith" label is more useful to summarize the conclusion that an adverse inference is permissible than it is actually to reach the conclusion. Here, although the

court found that Gordon might not have been "completely aware" of the significance of the records, he proceeded to destroy them without further inquiry even though they theoretically could have disproven as well as proven Nation–Wide's tracing claim. This conscious abandonment of potentially useful evidence is, at a minimum, an indication that Gordon believed the records would not *help* his side of the case — by proving, through the checks written, for example, that the accumulated funds could not contain the sale proceeds. In turn, such a belief by an assignee who was presumably familiar with records that included all 1974 checks, who knew of the assignee's denial of Nation–Wide's claim, and who knew of Nation–Wide's suit against him, is some (though perhaps weak) evidence that the records would have helped Nation–Wide.

Once this minimum link of relevance is established, however, we believe that the district court has some discretion in determining how much weight to give the document destruction, and prophylactic and punitive considerations may appropriately be taken into account. The court did consider the innocuous reason that Gordon claimed had led to his discarding the records — avoiding storage costs. The court also took account of the fact that an assignee ordinarily is supposed to be "neutral" as among claimants and thus would not wish to destroy evidence that would support a meritorious claim. It is also true that Gordon did not "destroy" the documents in an orthodox sense; he simply left them for the landlord to destroy.

While these considerations arguably reduce the probative value of Gordon's acts, they do not destroy the relevance of the acts altogether. Gordon's letter to his partners could be seen as self–serving. His neutrality also can be called into question, both because he had been made an assignee by the general creditors rather than by Nation–Wide, and because he was a defendant in Nation–Wide's suit. Moreover, while the mitigating circumstances surrounding Gordon's conduct might provide a basis for tempering a prophylactic or punitive use of the inference, the court was entitled to consider counter-

vailing factors. Among these were the improper of Gordon's conduct, the desirability
of deterring other assignees from engaging
in similarly reckless behavior, and the extent
to which fairness dictates making the assignees, rather than Nation–Wide, bear the financial risks arising from document loss. The
court could also take into account the other
evidence tending to show that the money
flows satisfied the "tracing" requirements
and reasonably conclude that the evidentiary
gap was not a large one. Taking these matters
into account, the district court decided to
give the act of document destruction sufficient weight to satisfy, in context, the tracing
burden the law imposed upon Nation–Wide.
Given that the act of destruction was logi-
cally connected to the ultimate fact proved
that the policy considerations militated in
favor of according that act significant
weight, we believe the district court's decision was reasonable and within its discretion.

We note that Nation–Wide has cross–appealed on the ground that the district court
erred in denying it attorney's fees and awarding it pre–judgment interest under the statutory provisions for tort actions. The district
court's reasoning in rejecting Nation–Wide's
requests below is entirely unobjectionable,
and Nation–Wide has not bothered to present
the case for its position either in its brief or
at oral argument other than by making the
contention (which we have rejected) that
Gordon should be found to have acted in bad
faith. We see no reason to upset the district
court's judgment in this respect.

The decision of the district court is *affirmed.*

NATIONAL ASSOCIATION OF RADIATION SURVIVORS, et al. v. Thomas K. TURNAGE

115 F.D.R. 543

United States District Court N.C. California
April 29, 1987

Plaintiff class is comprised of veterans exposed
to ionizing radiation during their service with

the United States armed forces, who now
allege that the Veterans Administration's
claims adjudication procedure violates due
process. The matter is currently before the
court on plaintiffs' motion for an award of
sanctions following the V.A.'s alleged destruction and nonproduction of documentary
evidence responsive to various discovery requests.

After a series of hearings on plaintiffs' earlier
motions for restraining orders and sanctions,
the court determined that an evidentiary
hearing was required to establish whether
defendant's conduct was sanctionable. On
December 3, 4, and 5, 1986, the court heard
testimony from a number of the defendant's
employees involved in discovery compliance and document destruction. On the basis
of the testimonial and documentary evidence
presented at that hearing, the court issued a
bench order on January 8, 1987, granting
plaintiffs' motion for sanctions. This written
order memorializes the court's ruling from
the bench.

I. Background

As set forth in the court's order dated November 26, 1986, plaintiffs' counsel received
an anonymous letter on July 11, 1986, indicating that the Compensation and Pension
Service ("CPS") of the Veterans Administration was in the process of destroying a significant number of documents relative to this
action. Plaintiffs subsequently sought a temporary restraining order enjoining further
document destruction, and an order to show
cause why the restraining order should not be
made permanent. On July 18, 1986, the court
granted plaintiffs' application.

After hearing on the order to show cause, the
court entered a permanent protective order on
September 26, 1986. The order issued upon
plaintiffs' undisputed showing that during June
and July 1986, the CPS destroyed numerous
discoverable documents relating to the processing of veterans' benefit claims, and had
planned to destroy additional documents specifically relating to the claims of ionizing radiation victims. Only the entry of the temporary
protective order saved these clearly relevant

materials from destruction. Counsel for the defendant explicitly conceded that the document purge reached relevant and discoverable material; he stated before the court on September 26, 1986, that "all sorts of documents, some of which could have been considered relevant and discoverable, have been and are being destroyed." R.T. at 5.

It remained to be determined whether the defendant's document destruction was willful, reckless, or merely the inadequate result of office housecleaning. At the hearing on the permanent protective order, the parties submitted conflicting deposition testimony regarding the motivation for the document destruction. Defendant claimed that the document destruction was part of an innocent filekeeping process, completed prior to the receipt of plaintiffs' Eighth Request to Produce Documents (which sought a number of the purged documents). Plaintiff countered with evidence suggesting that the document purge took place after the receipt of the discovery request, and was either an attempt to evade discovery or a reckless abrogation of the defendant's pretrial responsibilities.

The court determined that the extent and motivation of defendant's document purge could not be established without an evidentiary hearing. Accordingly, the court ordered that the employees of the CPS who participated in the document destruction appear at a hearing to testify before the court. Pursuant to that evidentiary hearing, the court now enters findings of fact, conclusions of law, and sanctions.

II. Findings of Fact

There are three primary allegations made by the plaintiff class: (1) that discoverable documents were destroyed or never produced; (2) that the destruction of documents postdated defendant's receipt of the eight document request; and (3) that defendant's overall failure to comply with discovery requests was intentional or reckless, and was concealed in part by threats of retaliation. The court enters findings of fact with respect to each.

A. Discoverability of the Destroyed or Unproduced Documents

Destroyed Documents in the Field Operations General Files

1. The first category of documents destroyed during the summer of 1986 were the general files of the Compensation and Pension Service's Field Operations staff. Vivian Drake, secretary to the CPS's Assistant Director for Field Operations, Michael Dunlap, maintained these files and conducted the purge of their contents. She stated that she "glanced through" the files and cleaned them out on the basis of age, using a V.A. publication providing guidelines for document retention. R.T. at 18, 19. While Drake could not identify the specific time frame utilized, she suggested that they had destroyed documents over two years old. R.T. at 21. Drake stated that everything she threw out had first been approved by Dunlap. R.T. at 20.

2. Ms. Drake testified that the general files contained interstaff correspondence within the V.A., internal memoranda generated by the Compensation and Pension Services, and staff analyses of field stations. R.T. at 18–19. The originals of the staff analyses are kept in the Field Operations general files, while additional copies are maintained in the Field Operations operating files and the regional offices. R.T. at 28. Dunlap stated that the staff analyses in the general files date back to the late 1970s and early 1980s. R.T. at 175. Drake testified that she destroyed none of these. R.T. at 28. Dunlap concurred. R.T. at 157. Dunlap testified that the general files also contain various blank forms and a "history" file. *Id.* The specific content of the forms and the history files was not established.

3. Drake averred that she recalls absolutely nothing about the specific documents which were destroyed, and would state only that no staff analyses were thrown out. Dunlap, who reviewed each document prior to its destruction, evinced a similar absence of memory. Drake's virtually complete lack of any specific recollection regarding the nature of the documents she destroyed only a few months earlier, and her highly nervous and recalcitrant demeanor on the

stand, cast serious doubt upon the credibility of her testimony. Unfortunately, Drake and Dunlap are the only individuals competent to testify to the specific documents destroyed, and their refusal or incapacity to do so precludes a determination of the specific relevance of the documents destroyed in the Field Operations general files.

Destroyed Documents in the Field Operations Operating Files

4. The Field Operations operating files were purged by consultants Stephen Tomasek, Doug Bissell, and Allen Zinn. Bissell estimated that he purged approximately half the contents of the files for which he was responsible — enough to fill approximately three to four government–issue garbage cans. R.T. at 311, 316–17. Zinn and Tomasek both testified that they used a 1980 cutoff date for purging documents, although both also testified that pre–1980 documents were saved if the consultants considered them particularly significant. R.T. at 219, 482. The documents destroyed were up to twenty years old; and permanent files apparently had not been purged in at least a decade. R.T. at 217, 310.

5. The operating files are maintained on a station–by–station basis for each of the 58 regional offices of the Veterans Administration. R.T. at 49. For each station, the operating file contains a permanent and temporary file. Of the three consultants purging these files, only Bissell purged the temporary files; the other two consultants focused exclusively on the permanent files. R.T. at 293, 309, 473.

6. The temporary files contain the raw data for the summary documents contained in the permanent files. This raw data includes a variety of documents. Exception sheets, generated by the CPS's Quality Review staff through random interviews of claim files in regional offices, R.T. at 137–38, contain analyses of processing errors found in individual cases. R.T. at 137. Each contains a claim number, the claimant's name, and "end product" indicating the agency action, the error made, and a notation of what should have been done. *Id.* By the terminal digit of the "end product" code, exception sheets can be linked to radiation claims. R.T. at 193. Three copies of these sheets exist: one in Quality Review, one in the Field Operations temporary operating file, and one in the regional office claim file. R.T. at 97–98. While two of the consultants did not purge the temporary files, the files are nonetheless maintained by CPS staff for only one year. Since Quality Review also retains its copies of exception sheets for no more than a year, R.T. at 189, the only available copies, if any, of exception sheets older than one year are contained in the various regional offices. It is doubtful that these copies are practically obtainable.

7. The temporary files also contain local "Systematic Quality Control" information and reports of corrective actions taken by regional offices in response to inquiries from the CPS central office. R.T. at 310. This data is also destroyed on a yearly basis, and is not otherwise practically obtainable.

8. The permanent files contain a variety of documents which are assembled from the raw data contained in the temporary files. These include staff analyses and site surveys of regional offices. R.T. at 46–47, 136. The permanent files also contain general correspondence between regional offices and the Field Operations central office staff. R.T. at 26. Staff analyses are prepared twice a year at the central office on the basis of information submitted from the regional offices. An analysis includes a "review of end product timeliness, average delay time to establish target claims, quality review . . . and assessment of the station's productivity statistics." R.T. at 136. Of the consultants, Tomasek purged the permanent files of all staff analyses more than one year old, while Zinn threw out none. R.T. at 221, 482. The original copies of the analyses are kept in the Field Operations general files. Dunlap testified that these originals were not purged, so the information remains available.

9. Site surveys differ from staff analyses insofar as they represent the findings of an actual visit to a regional office. R.T. at 46. Site surveys review a regional office's adherence to V.A. regulations governing the adjudication of benefit claims, and comment on due process violations. R.T. at 46–47. Copies

of the site surveys are kept only in the permanent operating files. R.T. at 295. Zinn and Bissell testified that they preserved all site surveys. R.T. at 313.482. Tomasek threw out all but the last two site surveys, which are prepared from once a year to once every eight years. R.T. at 295–96. The site surveys purged by Tomasek, some possibly only two years old, are thus irretrievably lost.

10. Other information in the permanent files includes inspector general reports and correspondence between the central and regional offices regarding corrective actions. Additional copies of this correspondence are found only in the files of the particular regional office which generally received it. R.T. at 168. Tomasek testified that he generally did not throw out any corrective action correspondence, though he "might" have. R.T. at 219–20. Tomasek admitted destroying an anonymous letter in a permanent file critical of Mr. Thomas Verrill, an adjudication officer in Philadelphia and later in San Francisco. R.T. at 224. Tomasek threw out inspector general reports, claiming that they are now maintained elsewhere in the Compensation and Pension Service; Bissell stated that he threw none away. R.T. at 246, 313. While Zinn and Bissell both stated that they threw out only mundane and outdated correspondence and forms, R.T. at 325, 483, and while Tomasek asserted to others within the CPS and he purged nothing of importance, R.T. at 102, Bissell admitted that there "may have been some quality control issues regarding due process that may have been destroyed." R.T. at 338. It is thus highly probable that relevant documentary evidence, including agency correspondence, was destroyed by the consultants. Copies, if any, exist only in the files of the various regional offices, and in all likelihood are not practically obtainable.

Nearly–Destroyed Ionizing Claim Documents

11. Twelve boxes of ionizing claim documents located in the Advisory Review offices of the Compensation and Pension Service were spared from destruction in July 1986 by this court's temporary restraining order. R.T. at 166. The boxes allegedly were to be destroyed to create more office space. R.T. at 185. The boxes

contained requests made to the Defense Nuclear Agency, the Department of the Navy, and the Department of the Army regarding the radiation exposure of particular veterans. R.T. at 162. The documents contained the names of the veterans, their service numbers, the V.A. claim file numbers, and the responses from the various agencies regarding the claimants' radiation exposure. *Id.* Some of the documents contained dose estimates. R.T. at 184. 12. These documents are located together only in the offices of the Advisory Review staff; the only other copies are contained in individual veterans' claim files maintained by the various regional offices of the V.A. R.T. at 164. Thus had the destruction taken place, the remaining copies would have been practically unobtainable.

Unproduced Documents: SIRS and PIF

13. The Special Issue Rating System ("SIRS") and the Pending Issue File ("PIF") are two V.A. computer systems capable of segregating and identifying the claims of ionizing radiation victims. The existence and capabilities of neither was revealed to plaintiffs until late 1986, though both have existed for a number of years.

14. Gary Hickman, a CPS Assistant Director, testified that SIRS had been used for several years. R.T. at 608. Dunlap knew of SIRS when he worked in the Washington, D.C. regional office of the V.A. in 1985, and testified that PIF has been in effect "a long time. Several years." R.T. at 200–01. Plaintiffs produced a recently–acquired document entitled "DVB Circular 20–82–39," which indicates that the PIF system has been capable of segregating ionizing radiation claims since 1982. R.T. at 553–59.

15. The SIRS field includes the claimant's file number and name, the date of the claim, and the agency disposition. R.T. at 199. Included among SIRS claims are those involving ionizing radiation. R.T at 200. SIRS is presently capable of segregating ionizing radiation claimants by specific disease. R.T. at 567. Hickman acknowledged that SIRS can readily identify all radiation claimants in whose case a ratings decision has been entered. R.T. at 570.

16. The PIF field includes a file number, end product code, the claimant's "stub" name, the date of filing of the claim, and information regarding the claim's disposition. PIF segregates ionizing radiation claims by the terminal digit of the end product code, and thus can identify all such pending claims. R.T. at 200.

17. Defendant has indicated throughout this litigation that it was incapable of identifying ionizing radiation claimants. *See, e.g.,*, Declaration of Jack Nagan, dated May 16, 1983, at 2–3; Defendant's Answers to Plaintiffs' First Set of Interrogatories, dated June 17, 1983, at 1, 11, 13; Defendant's Authorities in Opposition to Plaintiffs' Motion for Class Certification, dated April 1, 1986, at 10 ("no one knows the size of the proposed class [of ionizing radiation claimants] — not plaintiffs, not the Court, and certainly not this Agency.")

* * * * *

B. Timing of the Document Destruction Vis–a–Vis Receipt of the Eighth Document Request

20. Plaintiffs served defendant with their eighth document request on June 25, 1986. Plaintiffs allege that this request specifically sought a number of the documents destroyed. *See, e.g.,* Plaintiffs' Eighth Request to Produce Documents, Request Nos. 3, 6.

21. Vivian Drake testified that soon after being hired, she discussed with Dunlap the possibility of cleaning out and organizing the Field Operations general files. This conversation took place somewhere between October 1985 and April 1986; Drake could offer no greater specificity. R.T. at 27. Dunlap stated that he hold her to work on cleaning out the files on a "time available basis" when he hired her. R.T. at 181. Though Drake had nearly no recollection regarding the date of the second conversation with Dunlap that specifically led to the document destruction, Drake's affidavit dated August 4, 1986, places the conversation in June 1986.

22. Drake demonstrated a similar failure of recollection with respect to the time period during which she actually conducted the purge

of the general files. R.T. at 22. She left for another job on July 11, 1986, and stated that she could not remember whether she continued to work on the files until her departure. R.T. at 21. In her earlier deposition, she indicated that she worked on the file purge until she left. Drake Dep. at 55. Dunlap recalls that Drake worked on the purge up until the time she transferred, and recalls that she worked on it while he was gone in early July. R.T at 156, 195. Drake's purge of the general files can thus be reasonable placed after defendant's receipt of the eighth document request.

23. The date of the consultant's purge of the operating files is the subject of contradictory testimony. The consultants testified that the purge of the operating files was initiated by Vivian Drake, who had received authorization from Dunlap. They testified that Drake wanted to have the operating files thinned out because of their increasingly unwieldy bulk. R.T at 242–43. Drake passed Dunlap's authorization along to Tomasek, who testified that the conversation took place in mid–June. R.T. at 238.

24. Tomasek, Zinn, Bissell, and Dunlap all related nearly identical stories placing the subsequent document destruction during a short period in the middle of June, well before the receipt of the eighth document request. All testified that the document destruction began during the absence of Dunlap and Fay Norred, a supervisor in Field Operations, who was on vacation from June 10 through June 25. This apparently was her only absence. R.T. at 509. Dunlap was in Los Angeles from June 11 through June 13. R.T. at 160. They claimed that the operating file purge was conducted during a fairly short period of time, and was finished well before June 25. R.T. at 175, 236.

25. The evidence suggesting a later starting date, possibly after receipt of the eighth request, stems largely from the testimony of Barry Boskovich, a consultant working on the Adjudication Procedures staff of the CPS. Boskovich testified that he had two conversations with Tomasek about the purge — one in late June and another on July 7. R.T. at 49–

50. The second conversation, which took place with Bissell present, occurred after Boskovich had seen portions of the eighth document request. He teased Tomasek, who had worked in Baltimore, about the inclusion of the Baltimore office in the discovery request, and got the "impression" over the course of the conversation that the purge was continuing. R.T. at 52. In earlier deposition testimony, Boskovich was far more direct in his description of Tomasek's admission that documents had been destroyed after receipt of the request. *See* Boskovich Dep. at 14, 58, 65. Boskovich subsequently corrected these deposition statements and rendered them far more guardedly. He explained the changes as clarifications of those statements which he "didn't know for a fact," and which resulted from the confusion of the two conversations with Tomasek. R.T. at 108–09. The court observes that significant evidence exists of employee intimidation and harassment. *See infra* paragraphs 43 through 45. Boskovich's shifting testimony must be considered in light of this testimony.

26. In the second conversation, Boskovich raised the question of the propriety of the purge in light of the request, and Tomasek reportedly indicated that he had not seen the request, that he had done nothing wrong, and that the documents that he had thrown out were unimportant. R.T. at 69–70. Larry Nicholson, a supervisor within the CPS who had been present for some of the conversation, confirmed in his testimony that Tomasek stated he had done nothing wrong. R.T. at 347. There is agreement that Tomasek never denied that the purge of documents continued after receipt of the eighth document request. R.T. at 56–57, 346–47. Nicholson concluded, as did Boskovich, that on the basis of Tomasek's comments during various discussions, destruction of documents proceeded after receipt of the eighth request. R.T. at 370–71.

27. Two other considerations case doubt on Tomasek's rendition of the events. In his deposition on August 25, Tomasek stated that the purge began two to three weeks prior to the date when he gave his initial affidavit, which was conducted on August 1, 1986.

R.T. at 238. This deposition testimony placed the purge during the first few weeks of July. Tomasek subsequently testified that this was an "anomaly" in light of his testimony placing the purge in mid–June. *Id.* Second, the initial affidavits given by the three consultants were drawn up only after they had consulted among themselves regarding the date of the document purge. R.T. at 229, 319–20. The resulting affidavits are essentially identical, and wholly exculpatory.

28. While the date of the document purge cannot be identified with a high degree of specificity, and while there is substantial contradictory testimony regarding its occurrence, there is significant circumstantial evidence that the document purge continued after defendant's receipt of the Eighth Request for Documents.

29. Dunlap approved the shredding of the twelve boxes of ionizing claim documents in mid–July, well after receipt of the eighth request and following extensive discussion of this litigation within the Compensation and Pension Service. R.T. at 165. Only Dunlap's conversation with a number of CPS officials on July 21 or 22, in which he was instructed to save the documents pursuant to this court's temporary restraining order halted the plans for destruction from proceeding. R.T. at 166. These events occurred indisputably after Dunlap and others in the CPS had significant knowledge of this lawsuit.

C. Evidence of Culpable Intent in the Destruction and Nonproduction of Documents

30. Plaintiffs have offered significant evidence of the defendant's culpable intent in its pattern of noncompliance with discovery requests. This intent is reflected in two areas: evidence of CPS officials' failure to establish any systematic process to comply with plaintiffs' discovery requests, and evidence of the officials' affirmative attempts to stifle full compliance with discovery requests and disclosure to the court of past inadequacies.

* * * * *

Encouragement and Concealment of
Noncompliance and Destruction

43. Even more troubling than evidence of
the defendant's disregard of its obligations to
fully comply with discovery requests is evidence of its affirmative attempts to stifle such
compliance and its employees' cooperation
with this court's inquiry into discovery violations. A number of individuals testified to
efforts made by various CPS officials to restrain full disclosure of information — efforts which included threats of retaliation.

44. When Thomas Kenny went to Ted Spindle with his concerns that documents were
being destroyed which were responsive to
discovery requests, he was told to "keep his
nose out of it." R.T. at 379. In Boskovich's
first deposition, he stated that Spindle had
similarly told him to "stay out of it" after
Boskovich went to him with his concerns.
Boskovich Dep. at 49. Boskovich later de-
leted this statement — but left in its repeti-
tion only a few lines later. Boskovich later
repeated in testimony that Spindle had told
him to "stay out of it," not to put anything in
writing, to come to him if he discovered
additional information, and not to talk with
anyone else. R.T. at 112. In a transparent
threat of retaliation, Spindle indicated that
Boskovich should focus his attention and
concerns not on the agency, but on himself
and his family. *Id.*

45. Similarly, Ronald Abrams was told by
Deputy Director Herbert Mars, Hickman, and
Spindle not to put anything in writing after he
expressed concerns about discovery noncompliance. R.T. at 411–12. Abrams presently fears
retaliation from Dunlap for his role in exposing
due process violations within the V.A. R.T. at
395. Dunlap tore apart and discarded one of
Abrams' previous memoranda on due process
violations, contending that it was inappropri-
ately critical of regional offices; he was known
to Abrams as having little concern for "documentation of due process and providing full
notice." R.T. at 402, 404.

* * * * *

B. Sanctions for the Destruction of
Relevant and Discoverable Documents
Under the Court's Inherent Powers

The court has the inherent authority to sanction a litigant for the destruction of relevant
and potentially discoverable documents. As
the court in *Wm. T. Thompson Co. v. General
Nutrition Corp.*, 593 F.Supp. 1443
(C.D.Cal.1984), observed,

> [s]anctions may be imposed against a liti-
> gant who is on notice that documents and
> information in its possession are relevant
> to litigation, or potential litigation, or are
> reasonably calculated to lead to the dis-
> covery of admissible evidence, and de-
> stroys such documents and information.
> While a litigant is under no duty to keep
> or retain every document in its possession
> once a complaint is filed, it is under a duty
> to preserve what it knows, or reasonably
> should know, is relevant in the action, is
> reasonably calculated to lead to the dis-
> covery of admissible evidence, is reason-
> ably likely to be requested during discov-
> ery, and/or is the subject of a pending
> discovery request.

Id. at 1455; *See Graham v. Teledyne–Continental Motors*, 805 F.2d 1386, 1390 n. 9 (9th
Cir.1986) ("sanctions available to punish
those who alter or destroy evidence");
Struthers Patent Corp. v. Nestle Co., 558
F.Supp, 747, 765–66 (D.N.J.1981) (the destruction of documents which the party knew
or should have known would be relevant to
a lawsuit soon to be filed is sanctionable);
*Bowmar Instrument Corp. v. Texas Instru-
ments, Inc.*, 25 Fed.R.Serv.2d (Callaghan)
423, 426–27 (N.D.Ind.1977) (same).

There is no question that relevant documents
were destroyed and are now permanently lost;
defendant's counsel conceded this in open
court. Among the destroyed documents were
exception sheets, statistical quality control
data, and other information contained in the
CPS temporary files; the CPS site surveys
thrown out by Tomasek; and certain pieces of
agency correspondence, including a letter critical of Thomas Verrill. By the very fact of their
destruction, through, the vast majority of the

purged documents cannot now be identified. A striking absence of recollection regarding the content and nature of the destroyed documents characterized the testimony of Drake, Dunlap, and the consultants who conduced the purge, and makes the specific identification of the discarded materials even more difficult than it would be otherwise.

Needless to say, plaintiffs should not suffer because of this. Where one party wrongfully denies another the evidence necessary to establish a fact in dispute, the court must draw the strongest allowable inferences in favor of the aggrieved party. *Cecil Corley Motor Co. v. General Motors Corp.*, 380 F.Supp 819, 859 (M.D.Tenn.1974). As the court in *Alexander v. National Farmers Org.*, 687 F.2d 1173 (8th Cir.1982), *Cert. denied*, 461 U.S. 937, 938, 103 S.Ct. 2108, 2110, 77 L.Ed.2d 313, 314, (1938), observed,

> [o]bviously, the relevance of and resulting prejudice from destruction of documents cannot be clearly ascertained because the documents no longer exist. Under the circumstances, [the culpable party] can hardly assert any presumption of irrelevance as to the destroyed documents. On this record, the district court properly could have imposed the most severe sanctions upon [the culpable party] — dismissal of its claims and default judgment ... Nonetheless, we cannot say it was an abuse of discretion not to do so. It was error, however, not to draw factual inferences adverse to [the culpable party] on matters undertaken in or through offices and individuals involved in the destruction of documents.

Id, at 1205–06 (citations and footnote omitted). The court therefore infers and concludes that a significant portion of those materials purged from the CPS general and operating files which now cannot be identified were either "relevant in the action, ... reasonably calculated to lead to the discovery of admissible evidence, ... reasonably likely to be requested during discovery, and/or ... the subject of a pending discovery request." *Wm. T. Thompson,* 593 F.Supp. at 1455.

The court further concludes that the defendant knew or should have known that these destroyed materials were relevant and discoverable. After more than three years of litigation, the V.A. can hardly assert that it was not on notice of the issues involved in this lawsuit. It is no defense to suggest, as the defendant attempts, that particular employees were not on notice. To hold otherwise would permit an agency, corporate officer, or legal department to shield itself from discovery obligations by keeping its employees ignorant. The obligation to retain discoverable materials is an affirmative one; it requires that the agency or corporate officers having notice of discovery obligations communicate those obligations to employees in possession of discoverable materials. Certainly at this late stage in these proceedings, the responsibility lies with the Veterans Administration to inform its employees and agents of the substance of the litigation and to assure that relevant and discoverable materials are not destroyed. Far from achieving this objective, the procedures described by Mr. Hickman to manage discovery bordered on the anarchic. The V.A.'s reckless and irresponsible abrogation of its responsibility to assure full compliance with discovery requests cannot be tolerated and excused, and is most assuredly sanctionable where it results in the wholesale destruction of potentially relevant material.

C. Fees and Costs Under Rules 37(a)(4)

Finally, a prevailing party may recover its fees and costs in bringing motions to compel discovery under Fed.R.Civ.P. 37(a)(4). Plaintiffs' motions for temporary and permanent protective orders to spare discoverable and responsive documents from destruction were brought to compel discovery, and all costs and fees incurred to do so are thus recoverable.

IV. Sanctions

By its bench order dated January 9, 1987, this court imposed a variety of measures to sanction the defendant's multiple transgressions and to protect the court's jurisdiction and the integrity of these proceedings. These measures included the reimbursement of plaintiffs and the court of various expenses incurred as a result of defendant's sanctionable actions, the imposition of a number of requirements for the conduct of further discovery, and the appointment of a special master at defendant's expense to supervise all further discovery. Under the circumstances, the court determined that it was appropriate to direct the sanctions to both the defendant and its counsel, since responsibility for the conduct of the litigation was shared and since culpability could not be accurately apportioned between the two.

The court here details the sanctions ordered from the bench. These measures are without prejudice to subsequent requests by plaintiffs for the imposition of additional sanctions in the form of the exclusion of evidence or the admission of facts.

A. Monetary Sanctions

1. Defendant shall reimburse plaintiffs for all fees and costs incurred in depositions, discovery, preparation, the hearing, and other matters related to the bringing on of this motion for sanctions and of the plaintiffs' earlier motions for temporary and permanent protective orders. Defendant shall reimburse plaintiffs for all fees and costs incurred in ascertaining the documents destroyed during the defendant's purge and in reconstructing them, if possible. Defendant shall reimburse plaintiffs for all fees and costs incurred as a result of the defendant's failure to produce documents and information responsive to various discovery requests, as outlined in paragraphs 13 through 19 of the Findings of Fact, *supra*. This includes but is not limited to the fees and costs incurred as a result of supplemental discovery requests and as a result of the defendant's opposition to the motion for class certification based upon the plaintiffs' alleged failure to establish numerosity and impracticability of joinder.

2. On February 23, 1987, the parties stipulated that the fees and costs imposed by the January 9, 1987 bench order shall be satisfied by defendant's payment to the plaintiffs of the sum of $105,000.00. Further inquiry into the actual amount of the monetary sanctions therefore is unnecessary. The matter need not be referred to a magistrate and plaintiffs need not submit any further accounting of fees and expenses.

3. The defendant shall pay an additional sum of $15,000.00 to the clerk of this court for the unnecessary consumption of the court's time and resources *Olga's Kitchen of Hayward, Inc. v. Itel Containers Int'l Corp. v. Puerto Rico Marine Management, Inc.*, 108 F.R.D. 96, 106 (D.N.J.1985). In its bench ruling, the court ordered the defendant to pay the money into an extern fund to be used to compensate unpaid law students who assist in the work of the courts of this district. Defendant moved for reconsideration of that aspect of the ruling, arguing that the provisions of 28 U.S.C. § 751(e) (1982) require all funds received by the clerks of the court to be paid into the Treasury of the United States. After review of the applicable statutory authority, the court concludes that its prior bench ruling was inconsistent with the requirements of the law and thus modifies the ruling to require payment be made to the clerk of the court for disposition as required by law.

* * * * *

Benjamin R. NEIER v. UNITED STATES of America,

127 Bankr 669

United States District Court, D. Kansas
April 29, 1991

* * * * *

To prove the contents of the Certificates of Assessment and Payments regarding the alleged unemployment tax liabilities, the original documents are required. *See* Fed.R.Evid. 1002. The originals are not required, and other evidence of the contents of those documents is admissible to prove the contents of those documents if the originals are lost or have been destroyed, unless the government lost or destroyed them in bad faith. *See* Fed.R.Evid. 1004(1). Government Exhibit 4, which the parties refer to as a microfilm data printout, would be admissible at trial to prove the contents of the Certificates of Assessment upon a showing that the original Certificates of Assessment have been lost or destroyed without bad faith on the part of the government. If the government can make this showing of lack of bad faith, the exhibit would be admissible. In the absence of authority to the contrary, the court will allow the use of Government Exhibit 4, upon the proper showing by the government.

* * * * *

NEW HAMPSHIRE INSURANCE COMPANY, INC. v. ROYAL INSURANCE COMPANY

559 So.2d 102

District Court of Appeal of Florida, Fourth District
March 28, 1990

We reverse an order which entered final judgment in favor of an appellee after the trial court struck the appellant's pleadings for "intentional failure to comply with court's order and prejudice shown by [appellee]." The order which appellant failed to comply with directed the appellant to "comply with discovery" within ten days. The discovery requested consisted of a request to produce appellant's underwriting file together with interrogatories requesting information from that file. The discovery had been requested three months before, and one other ex parte order requiring answers had been entered.

Appellant's compliance with the order consisted of filing a response to the request stating that the underwriting file had been destroyed. Appellant's counsel signed interrogatories stating that the information requested could not be furnished because the files were destroyed. Appellee then filed a motion to strike the pleadings for failure to comply with the court order.

We confess that we have great sympathy for the trial court in dealing with the frustrations of requiring compliance with discovery orders. An undue amount of trial court time is spent policing what the Rules of Civil Procedure contemplated would be an orderly and expeditious discovery process in civil cases.

Unfortunately, in all too many cases, nothing could be farther from the truth. Nevertheless, using the ultimate sanction of dismissal should always be viewed as a remedy of last resort and only in cases where the conduct of the party evidences deliberate and willful failure to submit to discovery. *Mercer v. Raine*, 443 So.2d 944 (Fla.1983).

It seems to us that in this case appellant *did* comply, albeit with a response that appellee does not like. However, since there was compliance, the court cannot strike the pleadings and enter final judgment for "failure to comply." If appellant has destroyed relevant and material information by destroying the file, and that information is so essential to the appellee's defense that it cannot proceed without it, then the striking of appellant's pleadings may be warranted. *See Depuy, Inc. v. Eckes*, 427 So.2d 306 (Fla. 3d DCA 1983). Alternatively, where a party fails to produce evidence within his control, an adverse inference may be drawn that the withheld evidence would be unfavorable to the party failing to produce it. *Valcin v. Public Health Trust of Dade County*, 473 So.2d 1297 (Fla. 3d DCA 1984), *modified, Public Health Trust of Dade County v. Valcin*, 507 So.2d 596 (Fla.1987). Thus, the court could indulge such an inference of the facts of this case. However, for all we know, any evidence which might have been contained within those files might be legally irrelevant to the issues framed in the pleadings. Without a showing of prejudice to appellee on this record, we hold that the trial court reversibly erred when it entered final judgment in favor of appellee.

Reversed and remanded for further proceedings consistent with this opinion.

**P STONE, INC., Plaintiff v. KOPPERS
COMPANY, INC., and Lycoming Silica
Sand Company, Defendants**

94 F.R.D. 662

United States District Court, M.D. Pennsylvania
July 2, 1982

Memorandum

RAMBO, District Judge.

Defendants have moved, pursuant to Rule 37
of the Federal Rules of Civil Procedure, for
the sanction of dismissal of P Stone, Inc.'s
complaint.[1] They claim *inter alia* that plaintiff has deliberately concealed or destroyed
relevant evidence during the discovery process. The motion will be granted.

Plaintiff, a manufacturer of crushed limestone
for use in construction, filed its complaint on
July 26, 1978. It alleged that the defendants,
also manufacturers of crushed limestone, have
violated the Sherman Act, 15 U.S.C.§ § 1 and
2, and the Clayton Act, 15 U.S.C. § § 13a, 15
and 26. On March 16, 1979, defendant Lycoming filed its first request for production of documents seeking P Stone's business records for
the period covered by the complaint. The request at issue here was for:

> All worksheets, backup materials or other
> documents prepared or used by any per-
> son in connection with the preparation of
> any federal, state or local tax returns, fi-
> nancial statements, balance sheets,
> records and/or reports of P Stone, Inc.

Plaintiff's response was that the information
had already been supplied in connection with
three depositions. Plaintiff further replied
that: "[I]f any other information is needed, a
specific request should be filed." It is undisputed that at this time *no* inventory books had
been made available to the defendants. Plaintiff's business records became the subject of
a motion to compel. On July 19, 1979, Judge
Muir of this court ordered the plaintiff to
make available to the defendants production
records and some other items not relevant

here. Following that order plaintiff's counsel
sent the defendant copies of two inventory
books. One book covered production from
April 20, 1977 to October 18, 1978. The
second begins with November 6, 1978 and
ends on July 19, 1979. The cover letter accompanying these document stated: "Please
find enclosed documents responsive to Judge
Muir's July 19, 1979, order." That letter is
dated September 6, 1979.[2]

After receipt of the documents in September
of 1979, the defendants informed plaintiff's
counsel that they believed, on the basis of
deposition testimony, that there was a second
set of inventory records which had not been
produced. Counsel for the plaintiff replied:

> You state that only one set of inventory
> records was produced and that there has
> been extensive deposition testimony re-
> garding a second set of inventory records.
> I think you are incorrect and I think the
> testimony is clear that the records were
> kept at one office and later moved to an-
> other. Once again, if you would like to
> refer me to anything specific, I would be
> happy to see it and I will thereupon under-
> take diligent inquiry.[3]

Defendant answered this assertion specific
page references to three deposition transcripts all of which suggested that two inventory records were maintained. They received
no response from plaintiff.

Thereafter counsel met, on November 23,
1979, to resolve outstanding discovery disputes. At that meeting the matter of the dual
inventory records was raised again by the defendants. The following exchange occurred:

> MR. BODNER: The last item on this or-
> der that I will raise is, as you may recall,
> Mr. Rieders, this order requires the pro-
> duction of the inventory records of P
> Stone, and in the course of the deposi-
> tions, at least two, and possibly three sets
> of inventory records were referred to. We
> only have one set of inventory records.
> We would request any other sets of inven-
> tory records so we would have all inventory
> records that were either in the possession

of P Stone at the plant location or at the office location at the Newberry Garage or the other place.

MR. RIEDERS: I think I responded to that before, but let me tell you again what I know about it. It is my understanding that the production records that were kept at the quarry were at some point transferred physically to the office at Newberry Garage. Therefore, there was only one set of books. There may have been some sort of informal record kept on slips of paper, which one of the witnesses testified to, they are doing down at quarry and then sending up to the Newberry Garage office for transposition onto the records. I am certain those slips of papers have been destroyed, which came from the quarry.

Once again, all I can do is ask my client. I have asked for everything responsive to these orders, and I believe I have been given everything responsive, but I have no objection to checking back.

MR. BODNER: I would appreciate if you would make one final check on that and tell us in writing in a week whether there are any other inventory records in the possession or control of P Stone which have not previously been produced, and if there are, they would be so produced. Document number 448, pp. 7, 8.[4]

Plaintiff did not produce additional inventory records.

Defendants moved for the appointment of a special master to investigate the inventory keeping practices of the plaintiff. In the course of the briefing on this motion, plaintiff used three inventory records as exhibits. Two were the ones previously produced. The third was a new record duplicating one of the previous records in dates (November 10, 1978 to November 1980), but containing different inventory figures. The sudden appearance of these records more than two years after Judge Muir's order and nearly two years after counsel's promise to search for them was not explained.

* * * * *

James McKeag, P Stone's president, was asked at the hearing on this motion to dismiss, about Hoffman's work and whether he would have had access to records at the quarry office. He unequivocally said Hoffman only went to the quarry office once, accompanied by McKeag, Pressed as to how he was certain of this he stated, "Nobody would have got to the records without my approval." Mr. McKeag's extremely selective memory, his attitude and evasiveness on the witness stand, and the statement quoted above, lead ineluctably to the conclusion that he knew there were inventory records at the quarry office, that those records revealed a far more dismal financial position than McKeag was willing to disclose and that he decided to destroy or suppress that information.

This conclusion does not mean that plaintiff's counsel participated in an attempt to defraud the court. However there is certainly evidence of a lack of diligence on counsel's part, particularly in light of defendants' documentation of the references to dual inventory records. It may be that plaintiff's counsel had not knowledge of the existence of the second set of records. Yet he offered no explanation for the sudden appearance in August of 1981 of a partial second set of inventory records. He stated no testimony to demonstrate that a thorough search for the records was made. Frustrated by the lack of information being presented by plaintiff at the hearing on this motion, the court finally asked a paralegal assistant from plaintiff's counsel's office to testify. She testified after the objection of plaintiff's counsel was overruled. The assistant indicated that the late-produced partial set were handed to her, after a simple inquiry, out of a secretary's desk drawer at the plaintiff's quarry office. The visit to P Stone which revealed the whereabouts of the partial second set of inventory records was only the second she had made to the premises to look for the records. Apparently counsel's desperation at the thought that there might be an investigation of his compliance with this court's discovery order led him to make the inquiries of plaintiff that had been promised two years before.

The conclusion which has been reached compels dismissal of this action. Plaintiff has failed to comply with the order of July 19, 1979 requiring that production records be made available to the defendants. The sanction of dismissal is appropriate where there has been no good faith effort to obey the order. *National Hockey League v. Metropolitan Hockey Club, Inc.*, 427 U.S. 639, 96 S.Ct. 2778, 49 L.Ed.2d 747 (1976); *Societe Internationale v. Rogers*, 357 U.S. 197, 78 S.Ct. 1087, 2 L.Ed.2d 1255 (1958). Here there is not only untimely production of the partial second set of inventory records, and production of fraudulent reports but also no production of critical records that were in existence after the lawsuit began Plaintiff's costs of production would be a key factor in this antitrust case. Without accurate production figures defendants cannot determine what the costs were. To permit the action to continue when the production figures supplied the defendants are inaccurate, and plaintiff knew they were inaccurate, would be a mockery of justice.

Order

IT IS HEREBY ORDERED:

1. This case is dismissed with prejudice.

2. Costs of the action shall be paid by plaintiff.

3. The costs and expenses of the Special Master's investigation are assessed as follows:

　　Plaintiff shall pay 90% of the total;

　　Plaintiff's counsel shall pay 10% of the total.

----

[1] The relief requested in the motion included the additional sanction of a default in a related lawsuit, the taxation of costs and fees against plaintiff's counsel, the assessment of the costs and expenses of the Special Master's investigation against P Stone and its counsel referral of this matter to the United States Attorney for investigation into whether obstruction of justice has been committed, the referral of the case to a disciplinary committee of the bar to evaluate the conduct of plaintiff's counsel

in relation to the standards of professional responsibility.

Because there is no evidence showing that plaintiff's counsel had knowledge of the records which were either destroyed or suppressed, the court declines to sanction him directly except for a portion of the costs related to the special master's investigation. By the time of the briefing on the motion for the appointment of a special master there was sufficient evidence in the record of the existence of a complete second set of production records, that counsel had a duty to investigate the situation and offer an explanation to the court. The fact that no explanation was forthcoming, particularly of the sudden appearance of a partial second set of inventory and production records, necessitated the appointment. Thus counsel should bear part of the costs and expenses.

The court will not refer the matter for disciplinary action. Defendants have that option as private complainants.

The related lawsuit, Civil Action No. 78-1033, was filed by Lycoming Silica Sand Company against W. A. Emrick Trucking, Inc., James P. McKeag, P Stone, Inc. and Paul F. Moats. It also alleges violations of the antitrust laws, but the claims relate to boycotts, tying agreements and other common law causes of action.

P Stone's costs of production are not critical to the allegations of the complaint. Because of the difference in the issues and parties, the court will not grant a default in Civil Action No. 78-1033.

[2] Plaintiff's counsel seems to suggest in his brief in opposition to defendants' motion to dismiss and for sanctions (Doc. 627, p. 3) that inventory records were not subject to Judge Muir's July 19 order. However it is abundantly clear from the correspondence and the conferences between counsel that inventory records were very much at issue.

[3] The testimony is hardly clear that the records were moved from one office to another. Indeed plaintiff's counsel has himself espoused two different versions of the supposed scenario. In document number 482, filed on February 28, 1980, responding to defendant's motion for a special master,

he relates in his statement of facts:

Prior to <u>September 28, 1978</u>, or there-abouts P Stone maintained one inventory account at the P Stone quarry. When <u>William R. Hoffman</u> was retained at [sic] P Stone's accountant, he recommended that closer inventory records be kept, and pursuant to his recommendation, the inventory records were transferred from the P Stone quarry to the office of James McKeag in Linden.

Yet, in document number 570, filed on November 23, 1981, titled "Submission to the Master," counsel stated:

Beginning in April, 1977 (when the quarry began production) and continuing until February, 1978, one inventory book was maintained at the quarry. As of <u>February 27, 1978</u> upon the recommendation of <u>Don Herman</u>, P Stone's accountant at the time, the inventory book was physically transferred to the office in Linden where Melissa Young took over recording the daily production slips.

As the court added underlining demonstrates neither the date of the supposed transfer nor the individual recommending it are the same in those two versions supplied by plaintiff. Despite representations to the contrary, apparently the deposition testimony is not clear even to plaintiff's counsel.

[4] At the time counsel for plaintiff was making these assertions, there was on file with the bankruptcy court of this district the ensuing sworn statement, dated March 9, 1979 and signed by P Stone's president, James McKeag: "Daily estimated inventory records are located at P. O. Box 252, Jersey Shore, PA 17740 [the mailing address for the P Stone quarry], and R. D. #2 Box 131, Linden, PA 17744 [the mailing address for P Stone's business office]."

Rychen PADDACK, Arthur J. Darling, Henry Hannan, Donald D. Staudenmier, Marvin Hall, Carl M. Halvorson, et al. v. DAVE CHRISTENSEN, INC., dba Christensen Group, Inc., and David H. Christensen, an individual

745 F.2d 1254

United States Court of Appeals, Ninth Circuit
October 24, 1984

I. Facts and Proceedings Below

This case has its roots in two joint labor–management trust funds for carpentry industry employees created in compliance with § 302(c)(5) of the Labor–Management Relations Act, 29 U.S.C. § 186(c)(5) (1982), and two collective bargaining agreements entered into by the Employer and the Carpenters' Union between 1970 and 1978. One of the agreements was a field agreement covering employees who worked on location, and the other was a shop agreement covering employees who worked in the Employer's shop. Under the agreements, the Employer made payments to the Trust Funds for both field and shop employees and submitted monthly reports.

Apparently, the Trustees of the Trust Funds suspected that the Employer's reports were incorrect. As a consequence the Trust Funds employed Touche Ross & Company ("Touche Ross") to perform an audit of the Employer's contributions for shop employees between January 1, 1978 and December 31, 1978 and for field employees between January 1, 1973 and January 30, 1979. The accountants were not requested to undertake a traditional financial statement audit. Instead, they were requested to determine the extent of the Employer's compliance with the collective bargaining agreements. The compliance audit reports asserted that the Employer had wrongfully failed to contribute to the Trust Funds in the Amount of $12,108.75 for shop employees and $14,093.11 for field employees.

Five months after Touche Ross completed the audit, the Trustees filed suit in an Oregon state court against the Employer for breach of the collective bargaining agreements. The Trustees sought to recover $31,009 for the unpaid contributions, liquidated damages, interest, the accountants' fees, and attorneys' fees. The Employer removed the action to federal court pursuant to 28 U.S.C. § 1441 (1982).

During the bench trial, the Employer objected to the admission of the audit reports into evidence. The district court reserved ruling on the issue of admissibility and proceeded with the trial. After the trial, the district court found that the audits were based on hearsay and inadmissible under Federal Rules of Evidence 803(6), 1006, and 703. Because it found that the Trustees had introduced no other evidence to support their allegations of contribution deficiencies, the district court entered judgment for the Employer.

In order to preclude the need for a new trial in the event the evidentiary ruling was in error, the district court entered alternative conclusions of law and findings of fact. It found that if the audits had been admitted, it would have found the Employer liable for the alleged deficiencies with respect to the field employees' contributions, but not with respect to the shop employees' contribution deficiencies because the shop employee agreement did not satisfy § 302(c)(5) of the Labor–Management Relations Act. *See* 29 U.S.C. § 186(c)(5)(1982). The district court subsequently awarded $29,971.33 in attorney's fees to the Employer pursuant to 29 U.S.C. § 1132(g)(1982).

II. Admissibility of the Compliance Audit Reports to Prove the Contributions Deficiencies

In its compliance audit Touche Ross first used an audit program with statistical sampling techniques to identify "problem" employees. Once a problem employee was identified, the accountants examined both Employer and nonemployer sources to determine whether a contribution deficiency existed.

The audit resulted in the production of three separate documents: (1) the accountants' workpapers and exhibits showing the results of the

investigation of the Employers' contributions for every employee examined; (2) ,the audit reports which listed only those employees for whom, in the opinion of Touche Ross based on its investigation (as outlined in the workpapers and exhibits), insufficient contributions had been made by the Employer, and (3) certain one–page "summaries" of each of the audit reports. The Trust Funds sought to have both the audit reports and their summaries admitted as evidence of the amount of the deficiencies. They argued that the reports were admissible under: (1) the business records exception to the hearsay rule, *see* Fed.R.Evid. 803(6); (2) as summaries of voluminous writings, *see* Fed.R.Evid. 1006; and (3) as a basis of the expert's testimony, *see* Fed.R.Evid. 703. The district court concluded that the audit reports were inadmissible to prove the existence of the contribution deficiencies under each of these rules. We agree.

A. The Audit Reports Are Not Admissible Under Fed.R.Evid. 803(6)

Under Rule 803(6), for a memorandum or record to be admissible as a business record, it must be "(1) made by a regularly conducted business activity, (2) kept in the 'regular course' of that business, (3) 'the regular practice of that business to make the memorandum,' (4) and made by a person with knowledge or from information transmitted by a person with knowledge." *Clark v. City of Los Angeles*, 650 F.2d 1033, 1036–37 (9th Cir.1981), *cert. denied*, 456 U.S. 927, 102 S.Ct. 1974, 72 L.Ed.2d 443 (1982). Business records are admissible "unless the source of information or the method or circumstances of preparation indicate lack of trustworthiness." Fed.R.Evid. 803(6). In this case the district court found that the audit reports were not made or kept in the ordinary course of business and that they were prepared for purposes of litigation. We agree.

Clearly, the audit reports are not the business records of the Trust Funds or the Employer. The administrator of the Trust Funds testified that the Trustees had no regular compliance audit procedure. Once the Trustees suspected that a deficiency existed, they would employ an accountant to perform the compliance audit.

No evidence was submitted that such audits were conducted with any regularity. The irregular frequency and nature with which the audits were conducted also precludes their classification as business records of the Employer. Thus, the audit reports were not kept in the course of a regularly conducted business activity of the Trust Funds or the Employer.

We also believe that the compliance audit reports cannot be viewed as business records of Touch Ross. This was not a regularly conducted audit of the Employer; it was a special audit ordered in response to the Trustees' suspicion of irregularities. These reports, which are the direct product of the accountants, are not "business records" of the accounting firm within the meaning of Rule 803(6). A contrary interpretation would allow any firm to produce "business records" that would be automatically admissible. Such reports do not contain the same reliability that normally attends records kept in the course of a regularly conducted business activity.

Even if we were to say that the audit reports were Touche Ross' business records, the district courts finding that they were prepared in anticipation of litigation precludes their admission. In this case the Trustees employed Touche Ross only after they suspected that the Employer's contributions were deficient. "[A] document prepared for purposes of litigation is not a business record because it is lacking in trustworthiness." *Clark*, 650 F.2d at 1037 (citing *Palmer v. Hoffman*, 318 U.S. 109, 63 S.Ct. 477, 87 L.Ed. 645 (1943)). This is because "where the only function that the report serves is to assist in litigation or its preparation, many of the normal checks upon the accuracy of business records are not operative." *McCormick on Evidence* § 308, at 877 n. 26 (E. Cleary 3d ed. 1984). Thus, we affirm the district court's refusal to admit the audit reports under Rule 803(6).

B. The Audit Reports Are Not Admissible As A Summary Under Fed.R.Evid. 1006.

Under Rule 1006, "[t]he contents of voluminous writings, recordings, or photographs which cannot conveniently be examined in court may be presented in the form of a chart, summary, or calculation." The rationale behind the rule is to offer "the only practicable means of making their contents available to judge and jury." Fed.R.Evid. 1006 advisory committee note. The proponent of a summary must establish a foundation that (1) the underlying materials upon which the summary is based are admissible in evidence; and (2) the underlying documents were made available to the opposing party for inspection. *See United States v. Johnson*, 594 F.2d 1253, 1254–57 (9th Cir.), *cert. denied*, 444 U.S. 964, 100 S.Ct. 451, 62 L.Ed.2s 376 (1979). The Trust Funds have failed to establish both of these conditions.

1. Admissibility of the Underlying Documents

The Touche Ross accountant who supervised the audits testified that his employees relied on three sources of information to prepare the audit reports. These were: (1) the Employer's remittance reports of contributions submitted to the Trust Funds; (2) the rates of pay as evidenced by the payroll records, personnel files, and notations on the earnings records; and (3) "information from union sources that indicate [an] employee [had] worked for the employer but was not reported [on the Employer's records]". Transcript at 54–55. Because each of these sources is considered hearsay when introduced to support the existence of a contribution deficiency, the Trust Funds must establish an exception to the hearsay rule for each source in order for the audits to be admissible. *See* Fed.R.Evid. 802.

This presents no problem with respect to the first two sources relied upon by Touche Ross. Each are entries from the Employer's business records and admissible as such. *See* Fed.R.Evid 803(6). Therefore, summaries of such entries are also admissible under Rule 1006. The third source of evidence, however, is not admissible under any exception to the hearsay rule. Union sources, who were not subject to cross–examination, fall within no exception to the hearsay rule. The use of the union sources to establish the existence of deficiencies, the truth of that which was asserted, implicates the traditional "hearsay dangers." *See* Wellborn, *The Definition of hearsay in the Federal Rules of Evidence*, 61 Texas L.Rev. 49, 52–53 (1983).

It follows that the audit reports are based in part on inadmissible hearsay. And it is clear that a summary of both inadmissible and admissible hearsay should not be admitted under Rule 1006. *See Soden v. Freightliner Corp.,* 714 F.2d 498, 506 (5th Cir.1983) (summary charts based on statistics that were based on letters and conversations found inadmissible); 5 D. Louisell & C. Mueller, *Federal Evidence* § 599, at 36 (1983) Supp.) ("Where summary proof is offered, ordinarily it amounts to 'evidence,' particularly where the underlying material was not itself admitted or was not as a practical matter examinable by the jury. In such cases, it is especially important to insure that the summary *rests entirely* upon admissible evidence." The proponent of the summary of both admissible and inadmissible hearsay is entitled to admission of only those portions that he can demonstrate are entirely admissible. *See United States v. Johnson,* 594 F.2d at 1255. *Cf. Wilkes v. United States,* 80 F.2d 285, 291 (9th Cir.1935) (applying common law predecessor of Rule 1006 to exclude accountants' summaries because proponent could not segregate admissible from inadmissible); *McCormick on Evidence* § 51, at 125 (E. Cleary 3d ed. 1984) ("If part of the evidence offered . . . is admissible and a part is not, it is incumbent on the offeror, not the judge, to select the admissible part. If counsel offers both good and bad together and the judge rejects the entire offer, the offeror may not complain on appeal." (footnote omitted)).

The Touche Ross accountant, Thomas J. Godish, was unable to separate the admissible from the inadmissible and was largely unfamiliar with the actual procedures followed by his staff. During cross–examination, he could not indicate what sources were relied upon to determine the deficiencies for each individual employee listed in the audit report. He could do no more than recount the general procedures outlined in an audit program for compliance audits. Thus, neither the district court nor we know precisely what portions of the audit reports rest in part on the inadmissible hearsay. All is, therefore, inadmissible under Rule 1006.

2. Availability of the Underlying Documents

Moreover, all the underlying documents are not available. Availability of the employers' records alone is not enough. The purpose of the availability requirement is to give the opposing party an opportunity to verify the reliability and accuracy of the summary prior to trial. It is true that the Employer had access to his own records, but no access to the union sources was provided. To the extent that the audit reports relied upon this information, the Employer was powerless to verify their accuracy.

C. The Audit Reports Are Not Admissible Under Fed.R.Evid 703

Admissibility under Rule 703 presents a more difficult matter. Under it, "[t]he facts or data in the particular case upon which an expert bases an opinion or inference . . . need not be admissible in evidence." The Trustees attempt to employ this provision by arguing that, inasmuch as Godish relied on the audits as a basis for his opinion testimony, the audit reports are admissible to prove the existence of the contribution deficiencies. We disagree.

Rule 703 merely permits such hearsay, or other inadmissible evidence, upon which an expert properly relies, to be admitted to explain the basis of the expert's opinion. *See Fox v. Taylor Diving & Salvage Co.,* 694 F.2d 1349, 1356 (5th Cir.1983) ("An expert is permitted to disclose hearsay for the limited purpose of explaining the basis for his expert opinion, Fed.R.Evid 703, but not as general proof of the truth of the underlying matter, Fed.R.Evid. 802.") *See generally* S. Saltzburg & K. Redden, *Federal Rules of Evidence Manual* 467 (3d ed. 1982). It does not allow the admission of the reports to establish the truth of what they assert. Our opinion in *United States v. Sims,* 514 F.2d 147 (9th Cir.). *cert. denied,* 423 U.S. 845, 96 S.Ct. 83, 46 L.Ed.2d 66 (1975), was based on this interpretation of Rule 703:

Upon admission of such evidence, it then, of course, becomes necessary for the court to instruct the jury that the hearsay evidence is to be considered solely as a basis for the expert opinion and not as substantive evidence.

Id. at 149–50. The district court properly interpreted Rule 703 to find the audit reports inadmissible to prove the contribution deficiencies.

III. Examining The District Court's Judgment

It does not follow, however, that the district court was correct when it held that "judgment must be entered for the defendants because the plaintiffs introduced no other evidence that any employee performed work covered by the collective bargaining contracts for which the defendants failed to make contributions to the trust funds." *Paddock v. Dave Christensen, Inc.,* No. 80–257FR, at 9 (Aug. 12, 1982). This strongly suggests that the district court wholly disregarded both the audit reports and the opinion of Godish because of the inadmissibility of the audit reports to prove the truth of that which appears therein.

This was incorrect. The audit reports are admissible to show that basis of Godish's opinion. That opinion was evidence of the deficiencies. *See Bieghler v. Kleppe,* 633 F.2d 531, 533–34 (9th Cir.1980). It follows, therefore, that the district court had a duty to rule on the issue of the Employer's liability. In making this determination the audit reports were inadmissible *only* for the limited purpose of explaining the basis of Godish's testimony. *See* Fed.R.Evid. 793. We therefore reverse and remand this case for a redetermination of the existence and scope of the Employer's liability in light of a proper understanding of the applicable Federal Rule of Evidence.

* * * * *

Ceonia PAYTES, Plaintiff, v. Gerald A. KOST, Defendant, NATIONAL SURETY CORPORATION, Third–Party Plaintiff–Respondent, v. NATIONWIDE MUTUAL INSURANCE COMPANY, Third–Party Defendant–Appellant. Jeanette McMILLIAN, Jake McMillian and Travelers Plan Administrators, Plaintiffs, v. AMERICAN FAMILY MUTUAL INSURANCE COMPANY, Ceonia Paytes, Gerald A. Kost and Bulk Commodities Transport, Inc., Defendants, NATIONAL SURETY CORPORATION, Defendant–Respondent, NATIONWIDE MUTUAL INSURANCE COMPANY, Defendant–Appellant

482 N.W.2d 130

Court of Appeals of Wisconsin
February 10, 1992

Nationwide Mutual Insurance Company appeals a discovery sanction assigning Nationwide primary coverage for all lawsuits arising from an auto accident. Because the statute permitting discovery sanctions limits such sanctions to the case at hand, we conclude that a discovery sanction cannot extend to liability for damages in a case subsequently consolidated with the case in which the sanction was ordered.

Ceonia Paytes and Jeanette McMillian brought separate lawsuits to recover damages they sustained when a truck driven by Gerald Kost struck the car driven by Paytes. Paytes's lawsuit was commenced prior to McMillian's. Kost's insurer was National Surety Corporation, which filed a third–party complaint in Paytes's case against Nationwide Mutual Insurance Company. Nationwide insured Bulk Commodities Transport, Inc., which leased the truck driven by Kost. National Surety sought a declaratory judgment as to which company provided primary insurance coverage.

Prior to consolidation of Paytes with McMillian, Judge Stephen A. Simanek issued a discovery sanction against Nationwide in Paytes. The sanction assigned Nationwide primary coverage for any damages arising from the accident because of Nationwide's repeated failure to comply with the statutory and court–ordered deadlines for discovery requested by National Surety. Nationwide failed to produce the complete insurance policy covering its client, Bulk Commodities.

The trial court characterized the documents Nationwide did produce after several discovery requests as a "real hodgepodge."

After judge Emmanuel Vuvunas consolidated Paytes and McMillian, he adopted Judge Simanek's order as applicable to the consolidated case. However, Judge Vavunas indicated that he was simply reiterating the earlier order and was not issuing a new order in the consolidated case.

The consolidated case was tried before Judge Dennis Barry with Nationwide defending Kost. The jury awarded damages of $ 6750 to Paytes, $ 238,536.99 to McMillian, and $ 6,867.62 to McMillian's husband. Nationwide appeals two issues: first, whether the sanction order was appropriate in Paytes; second, whether the sanction order could extend to other cases not before Judge Simanek but which involved the same auto accident.

A circuit court's decision to impose a discovery sanction is discretionary and will not be disturbed unless the party claiming to be aggrieved by the decision establishes that the trial court has abused its discretion. See *Johnson v. Allis Chalmers Corp., 162 Wis. 2d 261, 273, 470 N.W.2d 859, 863 (1991).* A discretionary decision will be sustained if the circuit court has examined the relevant facts, applied a proper standard of law, and, using a demonstrated rational process, reached a conclusion that a reasonable judge could reach. Id.

Nationwide contends that the trial court abused its discretion in Paytes because there is no demonstration of a rational process since the court did not state on the record a finding of bad faith or egregious conduct on the part of Nationwide. Regarding McMillian, Nationwide argues that the court abused

its discretion by wrongly applying the law in extending a discovery sanction to a case not before the court.

Regarding the Paytes case, Nationwide argues that for such a drastic action, which prohibited them from asserting a defense, the law requires a court to make a finding of bad faith or egregious conduct. See *Englewood Apartments Partnership v. Alexander Grant & Co., 119 Wis. 2d 34, 39–40, 349 N.W.2d 716, 718–19 (Ct. App. 1984).* Nationwide contends that the court stated only that Nationwide was negligent, but negligence is not equivalent to bad faith or egregious conduct.

The law does not require a trial court to make an explicit finding of bad faith or egregious conduct before imposing a sanction. *Id. at 39n. 3, 349 N.W.2d at 719; Monson v. Madison Family Inst., 162 Wis. 2d 212, 215 & n. 3, 470 N.W.2d 853, 854 (1991).* It is sufficient if the record contains a reasonable basis for a determination that the sanctioned conduct was egregious and that there was no clear and justifiable excuse. *Id. at 215, 470 N.W.2d at 854.* We conclude that the record in Paytes contains a reasonable basis for such a determination and also for the circuit court's imposition of a sanction in that case.

National Surety served Nationwide with its first request for production of documents in the Paytes case on January 9, 1989. The request sought the production of the following: (1) a copy of the applicable Nationwide policies; (2) a copy of all regulatory filings made by Nationwide with respect to the policy. Nationwide failed to respond to the request within thirty days and did not respond to a follow–up letter sent by National Surety on February 22. National Surety pursued Nationwide's compliance with a verbal request on March 9, and Nationwide promised to produce the documents by April 1. When no response had been served by April 14, National Surety filed a motion to compel discovery. On May 1, Nationwide filed what it characterized as "portions" of the policy and "some" of the Interstate Commerce Commission regulatory filings.

The court held a hearing on National Surety's motion to compel discovery on May 3, and on May 15 ordered Nationwide to produce the requested documents by June 5. On May 31, Nationwide wrote to National Surety stating that the documents it had previously characterized as "partial" comprised "the entire policy documents" and stated it had "no more to furnish."

On August 10, National Surety filed a motion for a sanction which would order Nationwide to assume primary coverage for all actions arising from the accident. At the motion hearing on September 1, Nationwide filed an affidavit stating that the entire policy and all filings had been produced. This affidavit purported to be based on conversations with Nationwide employees, but no affidavits were produced from employees. The court found that the entire insurance policy had not been produced. It characterized what had been produced as a "real hodgepodge." It also stated, "I don't know how I can determine who's primary if I don't have the policy." The court imposed the sanction requested by National Surety. Two months later, at the reconsideration hearing, Nationwide produced more documents, which it claimed was the full policy.

We conclude that this record provides a basis for the determination that Nationwide exhibited bad faith and egregious conduct in its handling of the discovery request. At the very least, it provides no basis for finding either good faith or a lack of willfulness. See *Furrenes v. Ford Motor Co., 79 Wis. 2d 260, 268, 255 N.W.2d 511, 515–16 (1977).*

The most basic document governing the relations between an insurance company and its client is the insurance policy. It strains credibility to believe that a company with the experience of Nationwide cannot produce such a document on immediate demand or that partial policy documents comprised the entire contractual relationship between itself and its insured. While the trial court did not make an explicit finding of bad faith, it called the documents Nationwide produced a "real hodgepodge." The court also expressed incredulity at Nationwide's protestations of justified delay when Nationwide claimed that its far–flung offices in Ohio, Oregon,

and Chicago slowed down communications. The court pointed out that Nationwide had a FAX number on its letterhead. We conclude that it indicates bad faith when an insurance company ignores a discovery request for an insurance policy, then produces only portions of a policy, later claims the portion is the entire policy and, finally, after sanctions are imposed, produces still more documents that it claims is the complete policy.

Not only does the record show bad faith, it also shows egregious conduct. The basic issue in the third–party lawsuit between National Surety and Nationwide was a determination of which company provided primary coverage for the accident. There was no way for the court to determine this question on the merits without the insurance policy. The court itself explicitly stated this problem. Yet, in spite of the centrality of the insurance policy to this lawsuit, Nationwide ignored the statutory time limits for discovery, failed to keep a verbal promise to produce the documents — thereby making it necessary for the court to allocate scarce court time to a hearing on the discovery motion — and then ignored a court order to produce the entire policy. We conclude that this is evidence of egregious conduct.

The court's statement about Nationwide's negligence does not negate a determination that Nationwide's conduct was egregious and exhibits bad faith. The negligence statement was made at the hearing for reconsideration. There, the court concluded that "negligence cannot be a basis for relief from a Court order." This was not a finding about the reason for Nationwide's failure to comply with the discovery request. Moreover, the court explicitly contrasted the negligence of a professional business client like Nationwide, which knows the rules of litigation, from the negligence of a poorly–informed client.

Therefore, we conclude that the trial court's sanction of Nationwide in Paytes was not an abuse of discretion. Because of the sanction order, Nationwide is liable for the damages awarded to Paytes in the consolidated trial.

* * * * *

PEOPLE of the State of Illinois v. Arthur BOVIO

455 N.E.2d 829

Appellate Court of Illinois, Second District
October 18, 1983

Following a jury trial, defendant Arthur Bovio was found guilty of theft by deception (Ill.Rev. Stat.1981, ch. 38, par. 16–1(b)) and deceptive practices (Ill.Rev.Stat.1981, ch. 38, par. 17–1B(d)). Defendant was sentenced to two years imprisonment on the theft by deception offense, and the judgment on the verdict for deceptive practices was vacated by the trial court as constituting a lesser–included offense which arose from the same act as the theft by deception.

* * * * *

The State's next witness, Marilyn Long, assistant cashier at the Bank of Sugar Grove, testified that bank customers receive a monthly statement, and if there are any errors on it, the customer is to notify the bank within 10 days. She described the route a check takes once a customer drafts it on an account at the Bank of Sugar Grove and gives it to someone: the payee takes the check to his or her own bank; that bank forwards it to the Federal Reserve; the Federal Reserve Bank processes it and sends it to a data center used by the Bank of Sugar Grove. The data center makes all the computations of transactions for the account. The data center makes and keeps an original microfiche, makes a duplicate microfiche for the bank, and prints out a paper statement for the bank to send to its customer. Ms. Long testified that most banks use the same or a similar system. However, she did not describe the equipment that is used at the data center, or the method that is used there for entering deposits or withdrawals, or the type of program that is used. The microfiche is kept and relied on by the bank in its normal course of business. Ms. Long identified a copy of Bovio Automotive's checking account statement for April 1981, People's Exhibit No. 5, and said she verified its accuracy by checking it against the bank's microfiche that morning.

Counsel for the defendant objected to the foundation that had been laid for People's Exhibit No. 5. The judge overruled the objection and allowed the exhibit into evidence. The defendant's additional objection that the statement contained information of other checks which were not paid was also overruled and the court stated that any problems in that regard could be cured by instructions.

Ms. Long explained the meaning of the various columns on the monthly statement. She testified that the highest balance for the month was $3,591.26 and that the account was overdrawn on April 16 and 17. She identified the check that had been delivered in payment for the fuel and testified that the bank did not have anything called a "registered check." She said the check had not been paid because the signature did not match the one on the bank's signature card.

* * * * *

Defendant contends that a proper foundation had not been laid for the admission of People's Exhibit No. 5, a computer–generated bank statement of Bovio Automotive for April 1981. In Illinois, computer–generated business records are admissible under the business records exception to the hearsay rule if a proper foundation has been laid. To establish a foundation, it must be shown that the computer equipment is standard, that the entries are made in the regular course of business at or reasonably near the time of the happening of the event recorded, and that the sources of information and the method and time of preparation are such as to indicate trustworthiness and justify admission. *Grand Liquor Co. v. Department of Revenue*, (1977), 67 Ill.2d 195, 202, 10 Ill.Dec. 472, 367 N.E.2d 1238; see also *People v. Gauer* (1972), 7 Ill.App.3d 512, 514, 288 N.E.2d 24.

The State relies on the testimony of Marilyn Long, the assistant cashier of the Bank of Sugar Grove, to establish a proper foundation for the bank statement that was admitted into evidence and given to the jury to take back to the jury room. Her testimony also established that the bank statement was kept by the bank in the regular course of business after being received on microfiche from the data center. She also testified generally to the route a check takes once a customer of the bank drafts it and it is cashed at a different bank.

Nothing in the testimony, however, demonstrated that the computer equipment at the data center was standard and that the method of preparation at the data center indicates trustworthiness. Although Ms. Long testified that other banks used similar systems and computers, such general testimony is insufficient to prove that the particular equipment at the data center used by the Bank of Sugar Grove is standard and accurate. While Ms. Long compared the bank statement to the bank's microfiche and found the information on both to be identical, there is nothing in her testimony which described how transaction information was entered into and processed through the computer system at the data center which would verify the accuracy of the output on the microfiche. For example, the use of a keyboard in conjunction with a visual display screen is more error–free than a system that utilizes keypunched cards because of reduced human involvement. (*People v. Mormon* (1981), 97 Ill.App.3d 556, 567, 51 Ill.Dec. 856, 422 N.E.2d 1065, citing Roberts, *A Practitioner's Primer on Computer–Generated Evidence*, 41 U.Chi.L.Rev.254, 266 (1974).) Systems, like the one apparently in question, which perform calculations must be scrutinized more thoroughly than those systems which merely retrieve information. (97 Ill.App.3d 556, 567, 52 Ill. Dec. 856, 422 N.E.2d 1065.) No testimony established that the computer program at the data center was standard, unmodified, and operated according to its instructions. On the basis of these gaps in the foundation requirements, we hold that the trial court erred in admitting the bank statement in evidence. See generally, North, *Computer Evidence in Illinois*, 71 Ill.B.J. 590, 592 (1983).

* * * * *

PEOPLE of the State of Illinois v. Cornell BOYD and Raymond Williams

384 N.E.2d 414

Appellate Court of Illinois, First District, Fifth Division
November 9, 1978

* * * * *

Defendants finally contend that it was error for the trial court to admit into evidence certain computer print–outs, People's Exhibits 5–8, to rebut Boyd's testimony that he was employed at American Feather Products until December 1973. Although it is true that computer records may be admissible under Supreme Court Rule 236 (Ill.Rev.Stat.1975, ch. 110A, par. 236), a proper foundation must first be laid. (See *Grand Liquor Co., Inc. v. Department of Revenue* (1977) 67 Ill.2d 195, 10 Ill.Dec. 472, 367 N.E.2d 1238.) In *Department of Mental Health v. Beil* (1976), 44 Ill.App.3d 402, 409, 2 Ill.Dec. 655, 660, 357 N.E.2d 875, 880, the court stated that before computer records may be admitted into evidence:

"[I]t must be shown that the electronic computing equipment is recognized as standard, that the entries are made in the regular course of business at or reasonably near the time of the happening of the event recorded, and that the testimony satisfies the court that the sources of information, method and time of preparation were such as to indicate its trustworthiness and justify its admission."

In the present case the State failed to demonstrate that the computer from which the print–outs were obtained was properly operated, standard equipment. Moreover, witness Conwell, the bookkeeper for American Feather Products through whom the computer print–outs were introduced into evidence, did not testify that she had verified the accuracy of the print–outs. Accordingly, we agree that under the facts here a proper foundation was not established to justify the admission of the computer print–outs into evidence.

* * * * *

Harold PESKIN, Milton Peskin and Norman Peskin v. LIBERTY MUTUAL INSURANCE COMPANY

219 N.J. Super. 479; 530 A.2d 822

Superior Court of New Jersey, Appellate Division
August 3, 1987

* * * * *

Liberty had issued excess liability insurance policies to the three plaintiffs. These policies expired in May 1972 and were not renewed. In February 1972 fire destroyed an apartment building owned by the Peskins' real estate partnership. The fire killed one person, injured six others, including two children, and left 30 persons homeless. Plaintiffs gave timely notice to their primary liability insurance carrier, Progressive Casualty Insurance Company (Progressive), and to their fire insurance carrier. Plaintiffs did not notify Liberty at that time.

In July 1981, nine and one half years after the fire, an infant, Robert Wilcher, filed a complaint against the Peskins alleging that he sustained injuries in the 1972 fire.

On April 23, 1983, almost two years after the Wilcher complaint was filed, the Peskins, for the first time, notified Liberty of the fire and the pending suit. In July 1983 the Wilcher claim was settled for $250,000. Progressive paid its $100,000 policy limit and the Peskins paid the balance.

Peskins commenced this action to compel Liberty to contribute to the settlement. See *Fireman's Fund Ins. Co. v. Security Ins. Co. of Hartford*, 72 N.J. 63 (1976). Liberty contended that it was not obligated to provide coverage because the Peskins had violated their obligation to notify Liberty of the occurrence of the fire "as soon as practical" and because the policies which Liberty had issued to the Peskins did not cover business property.

On Liberty's motion for summary judgment, Judge Villanueva found that the Peskins had violated their obligation to give timely notice

to Liberty. The material facts as to the nature, circumstances and seriousness of the fire were not in dispute. The 11 year delay in giving notice of the Wilcher suite, was conceded. Accordingly, we affirm Judge Villanueva's finding that Peskins' notice to Liberty was untimely.

However, before late notice of an occurrence will void coverage, the insurer must prove that it was prejudiced. *Cooper v. Government Employees Ins. Co.*, 51 N.J. 86 (1968). Liberty's position with regard to prejudice in this case is novel. Liberty does not claim prejudice resulting from any impaired ability to adequately investigate the stale facts of the Wilcher claim. See *Cooper v. Government Employees Ins. Co.*, supra.; *Nat'l Newark & Essex Bank v. American Ins. Co.*, 76 N.J. 64, 82 (1978). Rather, Liberty contends that it has been prejudiced in its ability to establish whether its coverage extended to the business risk represented by the Peskin partnership's apartment house. According to Liberty, its prejudice results from the fact that it no longer possesses all the records necessary to establish the parameters of its coverage. Those records were destroyed by Liberty before it received notice of the fire. Judge Villanueva found that the absence of adequate coverage records constituted the prejudice to Liberty.

* * * * *

Our research has failed to produce any reported decisions which have applied this novel approach to the existence of prejudice. However, we express no opinion at this time as to the validity of this approach because of an unresolved threshold issue which requires disposition prior to evaluation of Liberty's claim of prejudice. The unresolved issue implicates Liberty's records retention practices. The prejudice, as found by the trial court, resulted in part from Liberty's records destruction schedule in effect between 1972 and 1983. Liberty's prejudice in this case is to some extent self–inflicted. Thus, the present case is distinguishable from the typical lack of notice case in which prejudice results from the insurer's inability to investigate an occurrence that is unknown to it. Consequently, the reasonableness of Liberty's destruction of the records must be considered before the prejudice found to exist in this case can be properly evaluated.

The record is silent as to industry standards or practices governing records retention. Therefore, this matter must be remanded to determine whether Liberty's records retention policy comported with industry standards or practices and was otherwise reasonable. The trial court's conclusions as to prejudice must be reconsidered in light of the determination to be made on remand regarding the reasonableness of Liberty's records retention policy.

Affirmed in part and remanded for further proceedings consistent with this opinion. We do not retain jurisdiction.

PETROLEUM INSURANCE AGENCY, INC., et al., v. HARTFORD ACCIDENT AND INDEMNITY COMPANY, et al., v. John H. SULLIVAN

106 F.R.D. 59

United States District Court, D. Massachusetts
May 14, 1985

Introduction

The Complaint in this case was filed in the Superior Court of the Commonwealth of Massachusetts on November 14, 1980 and was removed to this Court on December 12, 1980. In Count III of the Complaint, the plaintiffs claim that as to certain insurance policies, the defendants, on many occasions, gave an oral quotation as to the amount which the premium would be for a particular policy or renewal and then later billed the plaintiffs for a premium which was larger than the premium orally quoted. In sum, plaintiffs claim that they were overcharged.

Count III was referred to the undersigned for a Master's Hearing pursuant to 28 U.S.C. § 636(b)(2). On December 5, 1984, a Master's Hearing on Count III of the plaintiffs' Complaint commenced before the undersigned. The plaintiffs' first witness was John H. Sullivan, President of the plaintiff–agencies. During the course of plaintiffs' counsel's direct examination, counsel for the defendants objected when counsel sought to have the witness authenticate a document which was requested during discovery pursuant to Rule 34, F.R.Civ. P. and which allegedly was not produced by the plaintiffs.

The document was obviously relevant to the issue which I, as Master, must decide, i.e. whether or not the plaintiffs were overcharged on premiums for the policies which the plaintiffs have listed.

Although the defendants' objection at the Master's Hearing on December 5th was to a single document, further inquiry has revealed that the alleged non–disclosure pertained to several so–called "quote files" relative to the insurance policies as to which overcharges are claimed. The defendants claim that the plaintiffs failed in their discovery obligations in two ways. First, they claim that the documents were not produced pursuant to a request for production made in December, 1980. Second, they claim that the documents were not identified in response to interrogatories which were filed in January, 1982 seeking a specification of documents upon which the plaintiffs would rely in attempting to prove each of the overcharge claims.

The Document Request — December, 1980

As stated, the first method by which documents were sought was through a request pursuant to Rule 34, F.R.Civ. P. On December 19, 1980, the defendants filed Defendants' First Request for Production of Documents (#06). Paragraph 1 of this request sought all documents relative to any communications (oral and written) between the parties which pertain to the allegations of the Complaint. The plaintiffs did not file a response until September 14, 1981 when Plaintiffs' Response to Defendants' First Request for Production (#20) was filed. The response was to the effect that, with certain exceptions not here relevant, ". . . [a]ll documents in plaintiffs [sic] possession described in paragraph 1 have been turned over . . .".

Nine months after the request for documents had been made, at the deposition of John H. Sullivan on September 22, 1981, the existence of "quote files" was revealed. These quote files had never been produced in response to Defendants' First Request for Production of Documents. Defendants filed Defendants' Second Request for Production of Documents (#22) seeking production of the quote files specifically. This request sought "Plaintiffs' complete quote files, as described in his deposition testimony on September 22, 1981, for the period from May 1, 1976 through November 14, 1981 for each customer of plaintiffs who had any policy with any defendant." In addition, the defendants filed Defendants' Motion To Compel Production of Documents (#23) on October 8, 1981 which sought to compel the production of the documents as being within Defendants' First Request for Production of Documents.

This motion to compel was never acted upon because plaintiffs' counsel agreed to produce the documents. Counsel for the defendants made arrangement whereby the original files would be picked up at plaintiffs' counsel's office by Xerox Corporation, copied by Xerox, and returned to plaintiffs' counsel's office. This was done, and the copies were delivered by Xerox to defendants' counsel's office. The cost to the defendants in having this copying done was $8,143.67.

On December 30, 1981, defendants' counsel prepared a list of the quote files which had been produced. Defendants' counsel claims that the quote files for the Draper, Reynolds, Semple and Servitor policies and the 1979–80 quote file for the Litchfield policies were not produced by the plaintiffs and, thus, not picked up by Xerox and copied.

A request for the files was made by letter on the day before the Master's Hearing; plaintiffs' counsel did not respond.

The Interrogatories — January, 1982

The second manner in which the defendants

sought to procure documents relative to the overcharge claims was through interrogatories. On January 11, 1982, after receiving the copies of the quote files which had been made by Xerox, defendants' counsel filed a set of interrogatories numbered 12 through 37 (#30). Timely answers were not filed, so defendants' counsel filed a motion to compel on April 9, 1982 (#33). The Court denied the motion on May 19, 1982 because by the time of the hearing on that date, the plaintiffs had answered the interrogatories. In fact, Plaintiffs' Answers to Interrogatories ##12–37 By Defendants (#40) were filed on May 4, 1982.

Interrogatories ##14–16 and plaintiffs' answers thereto read as follows:

Interrogatory #14 — For each policy identified in your answer to interrogatory No. 12, [the list of policies on which the plaintiffs claim they were overcharged] please state the author and date of each document in your business records that you claim is evidence of the amount or date of the oral quote or the person giving or receiving it.

Answer — The attached documents which follow each of the thirteen–page summary are the business records which support plaintiffs' claims.

Interrogatory #15 — For each such document that was among the business records you have already produced for the defendants' inspection and copying, please describe the individual file in which the document was located and the document itself with sufficient particularity to permit defendants to find the document among those produced.

Answer — For the convenience of the defendants the documents are produced herewith.

Interrogatory #15 — Please describe each such document that has not yet been produced with sufficient particularity to allow you to produce it in response to a request from defendants.

Answer — For the convenience of the defendants the documents are produced herewith.

A number of documents were attached to the answers. The answers were never supplemented.

The Master's Hearing — December 5 & 6, 1984

When, at the first day of the Master's Hearing on December 5, 1984, defendants' counsel objected to the introduction of the document which had not been produced, the Court attempted to ascertain the extent of any failure to produce. At that time, the Court learned, as stated *supra*, that on December 4th, defendants' counsel had written a letter to plaintiffs' counsel, the last two paragraphs of which listed five quote files which had not been produced and which defendants' counsel stated he " . . . would like to inspect and have copied immediately." The last line of the letter read: "Please let me know when these files will be available." Since plaintiffs' counsel had not responded to the letter, the Court took a recess in order to allow counsel for the plaintiffs the opportunity to determine whether any of the five quote files existed, and if so, to produce them in Court.

On the next day, December 6, 1984, counsel for the plaintiffs produced the quote files for Draper, Litchfield, Reynolds, and Servitor. The plaintiffs indicated that there were no quote files for Semple.

In response, the defendants orally moved for an order precluding the plaintiffs from introducing into evidence any of the documents not previously produced and from introducing any documents in support of any overcharge claim that were not identified in the answers to interrogatories. (Transcript of 12/6/84 hearing, [#217] at pp. 2—15–17.

After hearing arguments on the motion, the Court ordered the plaintiffs' counsel to prepare a list of each document which he intended to introduce in support of the overcharge claim or which would be used to refresh a witness' recollection with respect to an overcharge

claim. The matter of sanctions was deferred. (Transcript, [#217] at pp.2—45–46).

Plaintiffs' counsel filed a list of documents (#216) on December 17, 1985. It appears that of the five hundred odd documents on the list, only twenty–nine documents appear both on the list and as attachments to the interrogatory answers.

Defendants' Present Motion for Sanctions

Defendants' Motion for Sanctions For Failure to Make Discovery (#225) was filed on March 22, 1985 and, in essence, reduces to writing the oral motion on December 6, 1984. Defendants seek orders (1) precluding the plaintiffs from introducing any of the "quote files" which were not produced until December 6, 1984 into evidence or using the files to refresh any witness' recollection and (2) precluding the defendants from introducing into evidence or refreshing any witness' recollection with any document not identified in the interrogatory answers.

Imposition of Sanctions

After hearing and considering the respective memoranda filed by counsel, I am of the opinion that imposition of sanctions upon plaintiffs and their counsel is fully warranted and, in fact, required on the facts of this case.

First, based on the evidence before me, I find that plaintiffs and their counsel were clearly negligent in failing to produce the quote files for the Draper, Reynolds, Semple and Servitor policies and the 1979–80 quote file for the Litchfield policies.

So far as appears, counsel for the plaintiffs requested that Mr. Sullivan deliver the quote files to counsel's office, which he did, and then counsel for the plaintiffs gave the files to the representatives of Xerox for copying as per the defendants' direction. Mr. Sullivan did not inventory the quote files he produced to his attorneys, nor did he make any list of what files were produced. Plaintiffs' attorney did nothing to verify that all the quote files had been produced, nor did plaintiffs' counsel make any list of what quote files were delivered to his office. This is inexcusable. The identity of the policies on which over-charges were claimed was known to the plaintiff and their counsel. Despite this, it appears that neither Mr. Sullivan nor plaintiffs' counsel did anything to verify that the quote files relevant to the claimed over-charges had been produced. In my view, this method of responding to discovery requests represents a careless disregard of a party's obligations. Not only was there no effective review to determine that production was complete but no record was made of what was produced. Since no record was made, plaintiffs' counsel argues that it cannot be proved that these five quote files were not produced. The failure to keep a record of what was produced is just another aspect of the carelessness of plaintiffs and their counsel. Plaintiffs' counsel's argument seeks to bar sanctions based on this further aspect of carelessness.

The evidence that the documents were not produced is strong. Defendants' counsel listed each file which was received from Xerox, and these five were not among them. The argument that Xerox made a mistake and did not copy these five files is, in my view, not credible on this record.

In short, I find that the five files were not produced, and the cause for their non–production was the negligence and carelessness of plaintiffs and their counsel in responding to discovery requests.

Plaintiffs' argument that the defendants have waived any objection to the non–production because of defendants' counsel's failure to in-quire about the missing files is without merit. When one party serves a document request on another party, it is very often the case that the requesting party does not know whether any documents exist responsive to the request. This is such a case. Defendants' counsel was entitled to rely on the representation that all quote files were being produced, especially in view of the fact that Mr. Sullivan, at his deposition, was unable to state that there existed a quote file for every insured. In addition, defendants' counsel did write a letter on the day before the hearing seeking production if the files existed; plain-

tiffs' counsel never bothered to respond. I find that there has been no waiver by the defendants.

Second, I find that the plaintiffs and their counsel were equally careless in answering interrogatories ##14, 15 & 16. Interrogatory #14 asked the plaintiffs to identify from their own business records each document which ". . . you claim is evidence of the amount or date of the oral quote or the person giving or receiving it . . . " as to each policy on plain-tiffs' overcharge list. Interrogatory #15 asked the plaintiffs to identify the file in which any document identified in answer to the preced-ing interrogatory which had already been produced could be found. Interrogatory #16 asked the plaintiffs to identify with sufficient particularity any document identified in an-swer to interrogatory #14 which had not been produced so that the defendants could file specific requests to produce such documents. The purpose of the interrogatories is plain. The defendant sought to have the plaintiffs specify the documents in their business records which were evidence of the claimed overcharges so that they could discover what documentary evidence existed which, ac-cording to the plaintiffs, supported each of the claimed overcharges. This is a perfectly legitimate and proper purpose of discovery, i.e. to narrow and clarify the issues. *Shelak v. White Motor Co.* 581 F.2d 1155, 1159 (5 Cir., 1978). This purpose is fully sanctioned by the Federal Rules of Civil Procedure. Rule 33(b), F.R.Civ. P., provides that "[i]nterroga-tories may relate to any matter which can be inquired into under Rule 26(b), [F.R.Civ. P.] . . .". Rule 26(b), F.R.Civ. P., provides, in pertinent part that:

Parties may obtain discovery regarding any matter, not privileged, which is rele-vant to the subject matter involved in the pending action, . . . *including the exist-ence*, nature, custody, condition and loca-tion *of any books, documents*, or other tangible things . . .[Emphasis supplied]

For the plaintiffs to have attached only 29 of the over 500–odd documents which the plain-tiffs plan to introduce to prove the overcharge claims makes a mockery of the discovery process and, when considering the purpose for which the defendants propounded the interrogatories, renders the answers worthless to the defendants.

Plaintiffs' argument that they should be excused because they produced a great volume of documentation during discovery is totally without merit. It is precisely because there was so much documentation in the case the defendants sought to have the plaintiffs specify, in answer to interrogatories ##14, 15 & 16, what particular documents were going to be introduced in support of the overcharge claims.

In sum, I am of the opinion that sanctions must be imposed in connection with the plaintiffs' failure to provide requested discovery in the form of producing the five quote files and answering fully interrogatories ##14, 15 & 16. As the Second Circuit Court of Appeals has written:

> Where justified, . . . the imposition of sanctions for discovery abuse is essential to the sound administration of justice.

Penthouse International, Ltd. v. Playboy Enterprises, 663 F.2d 371, 372, 392 (2 Cir., 1981).

The Appropriate Sanction in This Case

As stated *supra*, the defendants seek sanctions in the form of an order precluding the plaintiffs from introducing into evidence or using at trial any document which was not produced pursuant to the document request and any document which was not identified in answers to interrogatories ## 14, 15 & 16. While, in my opinion, the record in this case would fully support such sanctions, I decline to issue any orders precluding the use of this evidence. The reasons are two-fold.

First, an order of preclusion would prolong rather than advance this litigation. Quite simply, if such an order were issued, I can foresee endless litigation at the resumed Master's Hearings over the extent to which Mr. Sullivan has "used" a document which has been precluded to refresh his recollection before testifying. Mr. Sullivan is President of the plaintiff–agencies and the documents are ones kept in the usual course of business of those agencies; Mr. Sullivan has seen the documents, and in many cases, is presumably the author of all or part of some of the documents. The extent to which Mr. Sullivan "used" the documents in preparing for his testimony or the extent to which his memory is based on his prior reference to the documents would be extremely difficult to sort out and would, in my opinion, unnecessarily prolong this litigation.

Second, I am of the view that there is a two–part sanction which will avoid the problems inherent in an order of preclusion and not only will sanction the plaintiffs and their counsel for their conduct but also minimize the prejudice to the defendants. This sanction involves first the granting of a continuance so that the defendants' counsel can review the documents which are contained on the list (#216) prepared by plaintiffs' counsel and filed on December 17th and fully prepare his case with those documents disclosed. The second part of the sanction is an order requiring the plaintiffs and their counsel to pay the reasonable expenses, including attorney's fees, which will be incurred by the defendant in having their counsel re–prepare their case during the period of the continuance. This, in my opinion, is essential. Merely granting a continuance would not be in the interests of justice. There is no question but that the defendants will be put to added expense during the period of the continuance due to the failure of the plaintiffs and their counsel to abide by their discovery obligations; it is patently unfair to require that the defendants bear those expenses which were plainly caused by plaintiffs and their counsel.

The Power to Impose the Two–Part Sanction

There is no question but that the Court has the power to grant the continuance. However, on the facts of this case, there is an issue of whether the Court has the power to impose the second part of the sanction, i.e. the award of reasonable expenses, including attorney's fees, to the defendants.

A. Rule 37(b) F.R.Civ. P.

The first point to be made is that sanctions cannot be imposed in this case pursuant to Rule 37(b), F.R.Civ. P. by reason of the plaintiffs having failed to obey an order compelling discovery. The reason is simple. No order pursuant to Rule 37(a)(2), F.R.Civ. P., was ever entered. The reason for this is not that motions to compel were not filed; as noted *supra*, the defendants filed motions to compel production of the quote files and motions to compel answers to interrogatories. Rather, the reason that no orders pursuant to Rule 37(A)(2), F.R.Civ. P., were entered is that plaintiffs produced documents and filed answers to the interrogatories before the time at which the Court was to act on the motions and the Court, on the basis that documents had been produced and interrogatories had been answered, issued no orders compelling discovery.

This would seem to eliminate Rule 37(b)(2), F.R.Civ. P., as a basis for imposing the sanction of requiring payment of reasonable expenses, including attorney's fees, since, by its terms, Rule 37(b)(2), F.R.Civ. P., permits imposition of sanctions for failure to obey an order pursuant to subsection (a) of Rule 37. *Israel Aircraft Industries, Ltd. v. Standard Precision*, 559 F.2d 203, 208 (2 Cir., 1977); *Britt v. Corporacion Peruana De Vapores*, 506 F.2d 927, 932 (5 Cir., 1975). The Second Circuit Court of Appeals has written that it is "doubtful whether sanctions for non–production of documents could be imposed without [a party] first obtaining a Rule 37(a) order for their production, except perhaps in the unusual situation where the exercise of the inherent power to impose sanctions is appropriate, see *Roadway Express, Inc. v. Piper, supra* [447 U.S. 752, 764–67, 100 S.Ct. 2455, 2463–65, 65 L.Ed.2d 488 (1980)] . . .". *Penthouse International, Ltd. v. Playboy Enterprises, supra*, 663 F.2d at 389.

B. Rule 37(d), F.R.Civ. P

Nor do I believe that the sanction can be supported by Rule 37(d), F.R.Civ. P. That rule provides, in pertinent part:

If a party . . . fails (1) to appear before the officer who is to take his deposition after being served with proper notice, or (2) to serve answers or objections to interrogatories submitted under Rule 33, after proper service of the interrogatories, or (3) to serve a written response to a request for inspection submitted under Rule 34, after proper service of the request, the court in which the action is pending on motion may make such orders in regard to the failure as are just, and among others, it may take any action authorized under paragraphs (A), (B), and (C) or subdivision (b)(2) of this rule. In lieu of any order or an addition thereto, the court shall require the party failing to act or the attorney advising him or both to pay the reasonable expenses, including attorney's fees, caused by the failure, unless the court finds that other circumstances make an award of expenses unjust.

In the instant case, the plaintiffs *did* "serve a written response to a request for inspection." I am of the opinion that the power to impose sanctions for failure to produce all the documents requested or to respond fully to the interrogatories cannot be found in Rule 37(d), F.R.Civ. P., if answers or objections have been filed to the interrogatories if a written response has been filed to a request for production of documents.

There is authority which holds that even if a response to a Rule 34 request is made, ". . . a culpable failure to produce documents in response to a request to produce can be the basis for sanctions under Rule 37(d)." *Fautek v. Montgomery Ward & Co., Inc.*, 96 F.R.D. 141, 145 (N.D.Ill., 1982). In a footnote, the Court in that case explained its reasoning:

Rule 37(d) speaks to the case where a party "fails . . . to serve a written response to a request . . . " Here, defendant did serve a written response. The problem is that the response contained serious misrepresentations and failed to provide the material requested. Despite this, defendant appears to concede that Rule 37(d) is applicable, since a response containing misrepresentations denying the existence of requested materials is as good as no response at all. Indeed, "dilatory and partial compliance" with a request to produce does not remove a case from the ambit of Rule 37(d). *Charter House Insurance Brokers, Ltd. v. New Hampshire Insurance Co.*, 667 F.2d 600, 607 (7th Cir., 1981) Moreover, apart from rule 37, sanctions can be imposed under the inherent powers of this court. *See Roadway Express, Inc. v. Piper*, 447 U.S. 752, 764–67, 100 S.Ct. 2455, 2463–65, 65 L.Ed.2d 488 (1980).

Id. at 145, footnote 5.

With all due respect, I think equating "failing to respond" with filing a response containing "serious misrepresentations" and a "failure to provide the material requested" with "failing to file a response" does some violence to the plain terms of Rule 37(d), F.R.Civ. P. This becomes clearer when the type of response which is required by Rule 34(b), F.R.Civ. P., is considered. That Rule provides:

> The response shall state, with respect to each item or category, that inspection and related activities will be permitted as requested, unless the request is objected to, in which event the reasons for the objection shall be stated.

Commentators have written that, in filing a response pursuant to Rule 34(b), F.R.Civ. P.:

> . . . it should be enough for the party to respond by saying that a particular document is not in existence or that it is not in his possession, custody, or control.

Wright & Miller, *Federal Practice And Procedure: Civil*, § 2213, p. 641.

> . . . the party making [the response] must indicate as to each item or category described in the request that he will comply, or state the reasons for objection.

4A *Moore's Federal Practice*, ¶ 34.05[3], p. 34–31. In addition, courts have held that if a party is suspicious as to the accuracy of a response to the effect that certain documents

" . . . were not available and therefore could not be produced", the requesting party accepts the response unless the requesting party files a motion to compel discovery. *Clinchfield Railroad Co. v. Lynch*, 700 F.2d 126, 132 (4 Cir., 1983). It is hard to reconcile that exposition of the law with the notion that a false response or a failure to produce all documents requested is the equivalent of a "failure to respond" as that term is used in Rule 37(D), F.R.Civ. P.

In addition, I am of the opinion that the Court in *Fautek* read too much into the holding of *Charter House Insurance Brokers, Ltd. v. New Hampshire Insurance Co.*, 667 F.2d 600 (7th Cir., 1981). In the *Charter House* case, there was plainly a failure to respond by Charter House and a motion filed by New Hampshire Insurance pursuant to Rule 37(d). *Id.* at 602. However, before the Court acted on the motion, the attorney for Charter House promised to produce the documents. When some were produced but not all, the Court allowed the Rule 37(d) motion. On appeal, the Charter House argued that its "late and incomplete tender should have ended the applicability of Rule 37(d)". *Id.* at 604. It was in this connections that the Court wrote that:

> Charter House's position . . . overestimates the curative effect of dilatory and partial compliance.

Id.

I agree completely that dilatory and partial compliance *after a failure to file a response* does not prevent the applicability of sanctions pursuant to Rule 37(d) for failure to file a response. But I disagree that "dilatory and partial compliance" after a response has been filed permits the imposition of sanctions pursuant to Rule 37(d), F.R.Civ. P. if all documents are not produced or if the response is found to have been untrue. Rule 37(d), F.R.Civ. P., is applicable only when there has been a "complete failure to comply with discovery". *Israel Aircraft Industries, Ltd. v. Standard Precision, supra*, 559 F.2d at 208.

Accordingly, I do not find in Rule 37(d), F.R.Civ. P., the power to impose the sanction of requiring payment of reasonable expenses, including attorney's fees which I find to be the most just sanction in the circumstances.

C. Rule 26(e), F.R.Civ. P.

Defendants argue that sanctions can be imposed on the basis that the plaintiffs failed to supplement their answers to interrogatories ## 14, 15 & 16 by either identifying the additional documents which had not been identified in the original answers to the interrogatories but which the plaintiffs later determined were evidence of the overcharges.

Rule 26(e), F.R.Civ. P., provides, in pertinent part:

A party who has responded to a request for discovery with a response that was complete when made is under no duty to supplement his response to include information thereafter acquired, except as follows:

(1) A party is under a duty reasonably to supplement his response with respect to any question directly addressed to (A) the identity and location of persons having knowledge of discoverable matters, and (B) the identify of each person expected to be called as an expert witness at trial, the subject matter on which it is expected to testify, and the substance of his testimony.

(2) A party is under a duty reasonably to amend a prior response if he obtains information upon the basis of which (A) he knows that the response was incorrect when made, or (B) if he knows that the response though correct when made is no longer true and the circumstances are such that a failure to amend is in substance a knowing concealment.

It is clear that subsection (1) of Rule 26(e), F.R.Civ. P., is not applicable to the facts of this case, for the matter called for in interrogatories ## 14, 15 & 16 did not fall within the categories of identify of persons having knowledge or identity of experts.

The question then is whether subsection (2) of Rule 26(e), F.R.Civ. P., applies in the instant case. " . . . [B]efore any duty [under Rule 26(e)(2) arises, it must also be shown that the failure to disclose the new facts would amount to a knowing concealment." *Havenfield Corporation v. H & R Block, Inc..*, 509 F.2d 1263, 1272 (8 Cir., 1975), *cert. den.* 421 U.S. 999, 95 S.Ct. 2395, 44 L.Ed.2d 665 (1975). As is stated in one treatise:

The critical word here is "knows". This requires both actual knowledge of the new information and actual knowledge that it is inconsistent with a response previously made. Though the rule refers to the "party" as the one who "knows," it is apparent that knowledge of his lawyer must be regarded as knowledge of the party for this purpose, as it is for purposes of discovery generally.

Wright & Miller, Federal Practice and Procedure: Civil § 2049, p. 323. (footnotes other than 91 omitted).

Footnote 91 reads:

The Advisory Committee Note to Rule 26(e) says in part: "Another exception is made for the situation in which a party or more frequently his lawyer, obtains actual knowledge that a prior response is incorrect. This exception does not impose a duty to check the accuracy of prior responses, but it prevents knowing concealment by a party or attorney." 48 F.R.D. 508.

Id.

On the facts of this case, I cannot find a "knowing" in the sense of "intentional" concealment. I do not view the evidence as supporting a finding that Mr. Sullivan or counsel for the plaintiffs answered interrogatories ## 14, 15 & 16 with the purpose of intentionally concealing documents upon which they would rely in proving their overcharge claims. Rather, it is again a case of negligence and carelessness. I am of the view that Mr. Sullivan and counsel for the plaintiffs attached the documents to the answers to interrogatories ## 14, 15 & 16 without much thought as to the purpose of the interrogatories themselves and without much thought as to whether they were attaching all the documents upon which they would rely in proving their overcharge claims. After that, I doubt if they ever looked at the answers again until the first day of the Master's Hearing, and I am confident that when they were preparing for the Master's Hearing, it did not occur to them that their answers were woefully deficient. In short, I cannot find that either Mr. Sullivan or plaintiffs' counsel acted knowingly or intentionally in failing to supplement their answers to the three interrogatories. Thus, I do not see a basis for imposing sanctions upon Mr. Sullivan or plaintiffs' counsel on the basis of Rule 26(e)(2), F.R.Civ. P.

D. 28 U.S.C. § 1927

Consideration must be given to whether authority to impose the second part of the two–part sanction can be found in 28 U.S.C. § 1927, which reads as follows:

> Any attorney or other person admitted to conduct cases in any court of the United States or any Territory thereof who so multiplies the proceedings in any case as to increase the costs unreasonably and vexatiously may be required by the court to satisfy personally such excess costs, expenses, and attorney's fees reasonably incurred because of such conduct.

While I have no difficulty in finding that the plaintiffs and their counsel have multiplied the proceedings in this case " . . . as to increase costs unreasonably . . . ", I cannot find that they have acted vexatiously. The stature requires " . . . a clear showing of bad faith . . . ", *State of West Virginia v. Charles Pfizer & Co.*, 440 F.2d 1079, 1092 (2 Cir., 1971), *cert. den.* 404 U.S. 871, 92 S.Ct. 81, 30 L.Ed.2d 115 (1971) or a showing of action "lacking justification and *intended* to harass." *United States v. Ross*, 535 F.2d 346, 349 (6 Cir., 1976) quoting definition of "vexatious" found in Webster's Third International Dictionary (1971) (emphasis supplied by Court). After quoting the definition, the Court in *Ross* went on to write:

> Personal responsibility should, in this in-

stance, flow only from an *intentional* departure from proper conduct, or at a minimum, from a reckless disregard of the duty owed by counsel to the court.

Ross, ante, 535 F.2d at 349 (emphasis supplied).

For the reasons stated *supra*, I do not think the actions of plaintiffs, through Mr. Sullivan, and plaintiffs' counsel were either in bad faith or intended to harass or intentionally committed. Rather, I find that both were irresponsibly careless and negligent, even grossly so.

E. Inherent Power of the Court

There is no question but that the Court possesses inherent powers with respect to the conduct of litigation before it which are not delineated in rules and statutes. The inherent powers are those which " . . . are necessary to the exercise of all others." *Roadway Express, Inc. v. Piper, supra*, 447 U.S. at 764, 100 S.Ct. at 2463 quoting *United States v. Hudson*, 7 Cranch. 32, 34, 3 L.Ed. 259 (1812). In certain circumstances, this may include the power to assess attorney's fees against counsel. *Roadway Express, supra*, 447 U.S. at 765, 100 S.Ct. at 2463. The Supreme Court noted that in *Link v. Wabash R. Co.*, 370 U.S. 626;.632, 82 S.Ct. 1386, 1389, 8 L.Ed.2d 734 (1962), it upheld the *dismissal* of action for failure to prosecute as an 'inherent power' which is " . . . 'governed not by rule or statute but by the control necessarily vested in courts to manage their own affairs . . .'." *Roadway, supra*, 447 U.S. at 765, 100 S.Ct. at 2463, quoting from *Link, supra*, 370 U.S. at 630, 82 S.Ct. at 1389. The Court then wrote:

> Since assessment of counsel fees is a less severe sanction than outright dismissal, *Link* strongly supports Roadway's contention here.

Roadway, supra, 447 U.S. at 765, 100 S.Ct. at 2464.

However, in *Roadway*, the Court went on to note that they were limited on this inherent power to depart from the general rule that a litigant cannot recover his counsel fees. Certainly, the Court has the power to depart from the general rule when the conduct of the litigation is in bad faith. *Roadway, supra*, at 766 100 S.Ct. at 2464. Whether the power extends to sanctions for "mere negligence" was not addressed by the Court. *Roadway, supra* at 767, 100 S.Ct. at 2464, footnote 13.

On the facts of the instant case, I believe that I have the inherent power to impose the second part of the two–part sanction discussed *supra*, i.e. an order requiring the plaintiffs and their counsel to pay the reasonable expenses, including attorney's fees, which will be incurred by the defendant in having their counsel re–prepare their case during the period of the continuance. I base this opinion on several factors.

First, there appears to be no questions but that I have the discretion under the Court's inherent powers to exclude the evidence. *Campbell Industries v. M/V Gemini*, 619 F.2d at 27; *Davis v. Marathon Oil Co.*, 528 F.2d at 395; *Coalition of Black Leadership v. Doorley*, 349 F.Supp. 127, 129 (D.R.I., 1972). However, the discretion may not be abused. *Halverson v. Campbell Soup Co.*, 374 F.2d 810, 812 (7 Cir., 1967).

Second, I am of the opinion that the Court has inherent power to impose a sanction which is lesser than the sanction of exclusion. In the instant case, I view the two–part sanction which is proposed to be a lesser sanction than the sanction of exclusion. That the inherent power to exclude includes within it the lesser sanction is supported by the Supreme Court's statement in *Roadway Express, Inc. v. Piper, supra*, 477 U.S. at 765, 100 S.Ct. at 2464, that the "assessment of counsel fees is a less severe sanction than outright dismissal" and that if the Court had the power to dismiss, it had the power to impose the lesser sanction. The use of the power to impose a lesser sanction is also recommended by the Second Circuit in *Schwartz v. United States*, 384 F.2d 822 (2 Cir., 1967) in which the Court wrote:

Under the circumstances, we cannot say that the remedy of dismissal of this five

year old action was an abuse of discretion. We would, however, suggest that the court keep in mind the possibility, in future cases of inexcusable neglect by counsel, of imposing substantial costs and attorney's fees payable by offending counsel personally to the opposing party as an alternative to the drastic remedy of dismissal.

Id. at 836.

The *Schwartz* decision is cited by the Supreme Court in the *Roadway Express* case, 447 U.S. at 767, 100 S.Ct. at 2464, footnote 13, as a case in which the suggestion that costs and attorney's fees be assessed in cases of "inexcusable neglect" by counsel when the neglect does not rise to intentional or vexatious conduct or an inference of bad faith.

The Court has inherent powers to impose sanctions, even though "no technical violation of any particular rule" was made. *Guidry v. Continental Oil Co.*, 640 F.2d 523, 534 (5 Cir., 1981). This power may be exercised to sanction non–production of documents even when no order compelling production pursuant to Rule 37(a)(2), F.R.Civ. P., was obtained. *Penthouse International, Ltd. v. Playboy Enterprises, supra*, 663 F.2d 389–90. I also find support for the inherent power to impose lesser sanctions in the cases of *Flaksa v. Little River Marine Construction Co.*, 389 F.2d 885, 887–88 (5 Cir., 1968) cited with approval in *Ramos Colon v. U.S. Attorney for the District of Puerto Rico*, 576 F.2d 1, 3 (1 Cir., 1978); *Richman v. General Motors Corporation*, 437 F.2d 196, 199–200 (1 Cir., 1971), and *Schneider v. American Export Lines, Inc.*, 293 F.Supp. 117, 119 (S.D.N.Y., 1968).

Thus, I shall impose the two–part sanction pursuant to the inherent power of the Court. Perhaps the bottom line is that the inexcusable neglect and carelessness of plaintiffs' counsel and Mr. Sullivan have forced the Court to suspend the Master's Hearing for a period of over seven months. The power to impose a sanction is inherent in the Court's power to set a schedule for the litigation of cases and hold to that schedule.

Order

For the foregoing reasons, it is ORDERED that the Master's Hearing be, and the same hereby is, CONTINUED to *Monday, July 15, 1985 at 9:00 A.M.*

Further, it is ORDERED that counsel for the plaintiffs personally and the plaintiff–agencies reimburse the defendants for the costs, including reasonable attorney's fees, which will be incurred by defendants' counsel in re–preparing his case for the Master's Hearing. The total sum will be determined after counsel for the defendants has reviewed the documents which were produced on December 6, 1984 and the documents contained in Plaintiff's List of Documents (#216) filed December 17, 1984 and after the Court holds a hearing on the total sum to be reimbursed. However, the sum of attorney's fees to be reimbursed shall not exceed reimbursement for more than fifty (50) hours at defendants' counsel's customary rate. In this connection, counsel for the defendants shall FORTH-WITH file and serve an affidavit setting forth the hourly rate he is billing his clients at the present time.

It is FURTHER ORDERED that plaintiffs' counsel shall pay one–half the total; the plaintiff–agencies shall pay the other half of the total.

PHILLIPS PETROLEUM COMPANY v. LUJAN, Secretary of the Interior

Unpublished Opinion

United States Court of Appeals, Tenth Circuit
December 1, 1991

Defendants–appellants, the Secretary of the Interior and his department, the Mineral Management Service which is a division within the Department of the Interior, and two other administrative officials of the Mineral Management Service, appeal the district court's order granting summary judgment to plaintiff–appellee, Phillips Petroleum Company, in a declaratory action. We have jurisdiction under 28 U.S.C. § 1291. Our review of orders granting motions for summary judgment is de novo. *United States v. Gammache,* 713 F.2d 588, 594 (10th Cir. 1983). We reverse and remand to the district court with instructions to enter judgment for defendants.

Defendants are responsible for issuing and administering oil and gas leases for federal lands, *see* 30 U.S.C. § § 181, 223–237, and for approving issuance of and administering such leases for lands allotted to Indians and tribal lands. *See* 25 U.S.C. § § 396–396g. Congress has directed defendants to "establish a comprehensive inspection, collection and fiscal and production accounting and auditing system to provide the capability to accurately determine oil and gas royalties, interest, fines, penalties, fees, deposits, and other payments owed, and to collect and account for such amounts in a timely manner." 30 U.S.C. § 17173(a). Further, defendants are required to "audit and reconcile, to the extent practicable, all current and past lease accounts for leases of oil or gas and take appropriate actions to make additional collections or refunds as warranted, . . . and may also audit accounts and records of selected leases and operators." *Id.* § 1711(c)(1).

Plaintiff holds oil and gas leases for both federal and Indian lands. These leases contain an inspection clause which requires, in relevant part, that the lessee "keep open . . . for the inspection of any duly authorized officer of the Department . . . all books, accounts, maps and records relative to operations and surveys or investigations on the leased lands or under the lease." As a lessee of oil and gas rights, plaintiff is required to "establish and maintain any records, make any reports, and provide any information that the Secretary may, by rule, reasonably require for the purpose of implementing this chapter or determining compliance with rules or orders under this chapter." 30 U.S.C. § 1713(a). Further, "[u]pon the request of any officer or employee duly designated by the Secretary . . . the appropriate records, reports, or information which may be required by this section shall be made available for inspection and duplication . . . " *Id.* Plaintiff is also required to maintain records of its oil and gas leases for six years after the records are generated "unless the Secretary notifies [plaintiff] that he has initiated an audit or investigation involving such records and that such records must be maintained for a longer period"[1] *Id.* § 1713(b).

On September 30, 1988, defendants ordered plaintiff to provide records relating to thirty–two leases for the period October 1, 1980, through September 30, 1983. The order stated that plaintiff previously had been notified of an impending audit for the period October 1, 1980 through September 30, 1986, and that this particular order pertained only to the first segment of the audit. The stated purpose of the audit was to ascertain "the propriety of the royalty payments made by [plaintiff]."

On October 28, 1988, plaintiff filed the present action seeking declaratory and injunctive relief. The complaint contended that, pursuant to the general federal statute of limitations, 28 U.S.C. § 2415, defendants must audit and file claims for under payment or mispayment of royalties within six years after royalty payments are made or due. Plaintiff sought a judgment that the order which requested records that were more than six years old was unenforceable, arbitrary, capricious, an abuse of discretion, and otherwise not in accordance with law.[2] *See* 5 U.S.C. § 706 (scope of judicial review of agency actions). Plaintiff argued that a cause of action on royalty payments accrues at the time of payment; therefore, any cause of action on payments made more than six years earlier was barred by the statute of limitations. As plaintiff's argument goes, the six–year limitation of maintaining records deprived defendants of their authority to audit records that were more than six years old.

On cross–motions for summary judgment, the district court denied defendants' motion[3] and granted plaintiff's motion. The district court declared that there was no authority for defendants' action unless they could show that the statute of limitations was tolled. The district court determined that the statute was not tolled and granted the declaratory relief requested by plaintiff because defendants' request for records was untimely.[4]

Congress has vested federal courts with the power to review agency actions. 5 U.S.C. § 704. However, the scope of review is a "narrow one." *Edwards v. Califano*, 619 F.2d 865, 868 (10th Cir. 1980). The fact that plaintiff has brought this action not on appeal from an administrative ruling but rather as a preemptive declaratory action makes no difference as to the substantial deference we afford to the actions of administrative agencies in compliance with their statutory enforcement obligations. Indeed, unless the agency's order can be considered "arbitrary, capricious, an abuse of discretion, or otherwise is not in accordance with law," 5 U.S.C. § 706(2)(A), we cannot set it aside.

The district court viewed the six–year limitation on the recordkeeping requirement and the six–year statute of limitations on actions to collect royalty payments as dispositive on whether defendants could compel disclosure of the records. The district court framed the issue as "whether [defendants] must audit and file claims for underpayment or mispayment of royalties within 6 years after the royalty payments are made or due." We cannot agree with that characterization.

Defendants were not asserting a claim for underpayment of royalties. Had they been, plaintiff might have very well been able to assert a statute of limitations defense. *See* 28 U.S.C. § 2415 (six–year statute of limitations on "action for money damages brought by the United States . . . which is founded upon any contract.) Rather, defendants were merely ordering plaintiff to provide records. Such an order is well within defendants' authority under the lease agreements and under the pertinent statutes and regulations governing the management of royalty payments.

The lease agreements require plaintiff to permit defendants to inspect "all books, accounts, maps and records . . . " The inspection clause of the agreement is not limited to records generated within the past six years. Indeed, the only limitation on the disclosure of records that plaintiff and defendants have formally agreed upon is that the records must be "relative to operations and surveys or investigations on the leased lands or under the lease." We will not read a limitation into a lease provision which was not part of the agreement between the parties. *See Yankee Atomic Elec. Co. v. New Mexico & Ariz. Land Co.*, 632 F.2d 855, 858 (10th Cir. 1980) ("courts cannot change or alter contract language for the benefit of one party and to the detriment of another party"). *See also Williams Petroleum Co. v. Midland Cooperatives, Inc.*, 539 F.2d 694, 696 (10th Cir. 1976).

In addition to the lease terms requiring disclosure, the statutes and regulations governing the payment of royalties on oil and gas leases also require disclosure of the records. Upon the request of defendants, plaintiff is required to make available for inspection and duplication "the appropriate records, reports, or information." 30 U.S.C. § 1713(a). *See also* 30 C.F.R. § 212.51(c) (1991). While plaintiff is required to maintain the records for six years, unless otherwise notified, 30 U.S.C. § 1713(b); 30 C.F.R. § 212.51(b) (1991), plaintiff's duty to disclose records is not limited to records which plaintiff could have lawfully destroyed but, instead, has retained.[5]

Administrative agencies vested with investigatory power have broad discretion to require the disclosure of information concerning matters within their jurisdiction.[6] *See, e.g., United States v. Morton Salt Co.*, 338 U.S. 632, 642–43 (1950) (agency could compel the production of information even if action was a "fishing expedition"); *Endicott Johnson v. Perkins*, 317 U.S. 501, 509 (1943) (district court must enforce administrative subpoena unless the evidence sought was "plainly incompetent or irrelevant to any legal purpose" of the agency). Further, the Supreme Court has held that a summons issued by an enforcement agency, specifically the Internal Revenue Service, need not make any showing of an act which would toll the statute of limitations, such as fraud, in order to enforce a summons for documents which relate to a period outside the statute of limitations, *United States v. Powell*, 379 U.S.

48, 57–58 (1964). Ironically, defendants could obtain the records under normal civil discovery procedures. Indeed, the records are relevant to the present declaratory action because plaintiff's contention is premised on the absence of some event, such as fraud, which would toll the statute of limitations. Plaintiff cannot avoid disclosure of the records simply by asserting that any action defendants might bring to which the documents relate is barred by the statute of limitations.[7]

We REVERSE the district court's order granting summary judgment for plaintiff and REMAND to the district court with instructions to enter judgment for defendants.

---

[1] Once an audit or investigation is underway, the lessee is required to maintain the records until the Secretary releases it from such obligation. 30 U.S.C. § 1713(b).

[2] Plaintiff agreed to produce the records for the period October 1, 1982 through September 30, 1983, which were requested within the six–year period.

[3] Defendants initially moved to dismiss the amended complaint contending that plaintiff should be required to exhaust its administrative remedies prior to seeking judicial review, and that the order was not a final agency action. *See* 5 U.S.C. § 704. Defendants have not appealed the denial of their motion to dismiss, and, accordingly, we express no opinion on these issues.

[4] Finding that the declaratory relief granted fully disposed of the issues, the district court denied plaintiff's request for injunctive relief. The district court denied defendants' subsequent motion to alter or amend the judgment.

[5] Plaintiff contends that the order violates the six–year statutory and regulatory limitation on record maintenance, *see* 30 U.S.C. § 1713(b), 30 C.F.R. § 212.51(b) (1991), because the order requires it to maintain the records indefinitely. However, by giving the Secretary the authority to unilaterally extend the period for maintaining records, 30 U.S.C. § 1713(b), Congress has recognized that the six–year limitation is not

absolute. The fact that defendants did not examine this authority within six years does not negate plaintiff's duty to disclose records which it was legally required to compile and voluntarily chose to retain beyond six years.

[6] Plaintiff's attempt to distinguish orders by defendants premised the investigatory power and orders by defendants premised on their power to audit is without merit. Defendants' investigatory power *is* their power to audit records maintained by lessees such as plaintiff. *See* 30 U.S.C. § 1711(c).

[7] Because we believe that the statute of limitations, 28 U.S.C. § 2415, is irrelevant to defendants' authority to obtain the records, we need not address the questions of when a cause of action on royalty payments accrues or whether the statute was tolled under the facts before us. Further, we have considered plaintiff's additional arguments concerning laches and defendants' failure to follow required procedures, and find them to be without merit.

Jo Ann PIECHALAK, a minor, by Patricia Piechalak, her mother and next friend v. LIBERTY TRUCKING COMPANY, an Illinois Corporation, and Marvin C. Lembke

208 N.E.2d 379

Appellate Court of Illinois, First District, Fourth Division
April 28, 1965

Action for personal injuries brought against truck driver by child injured when struck by truck running across street. The Circuit Court, Cook County, Charles R. Barrett, J., entered judgment on verdict for driver and child appealed. The Appellate Court, Drucker, J., held that verdict was not contrary to weight of evidence and that there was no prejudicial error in conduct of trial.

* * * * *

Plaintiff claims error in the court's refusal to give her Instruction No. 1 (I.P.I. 20.01) relat-

ing to a party's failure to produce evidence. The evidence related to the maintenance of defendant's truck prior to the time of the accident. These records were subpoenaed by plaintiff during the trial. A witness called by plaintiff testified that the 1959 records had been destroyed in 1962. The accident happened in 1960. There was no basis in this evidence for plaintiff's tendered instruction. *Turner v. Seyfer*, 44 Ill.App.2d 281, 290, 194 N.E.2d 529. Nevertheless, the court allowed plaintiff to comment on the unavailability of the 1959 records.

Ike W. PITTMAN v. DIXIE ORNAMENTAL IRON COMPANY

177 S.E.2d 167

Court of Appeals of Georgia, Division No. 2
September 8, 1970

Dixie Ornamental Iron Company brought an action against Ike W. Pittman seeking recovery for $1,265.82 as an alleged balance due on an account. The account showed five charges, one of which was sales tax, making a total of $3,210.82 and showing two credits, one of $1,500, and one of $445, leaving a balance due of $1,265.82. The sales tax item was $93.33. The other four items were as follows: "200 ft. square picket rail with castings $1,495, 1 pair gates 21 ft. with castings, 450, adding double pickets to fence, 847.50, adding double pickets to gate and castings, 325." On the trial of the case, a Mr. Hayes, who was president of the plaintiff company testified that he kept all the books and records of the plaintiff, that he was familiar with the account and that the copy of the statement of accounts attached to the pleadings (described above) was the only record made or kept, that the job was completed and the balance owed was $1,265.42 in one place in this testimony and $1,265 in another place and in another place $1,279 and in another place $1,265.82; that a statement of the account had been mailed to the defendant. Certain checks written by the defendant and payable to the plaintiff were exhibited to the witness, and he testified that all of these checks were endorsed and payment received thereon. These checks totaled the amount of credits shown on the statement attached to the petition. He was unable to say whether the check for $445 exhibited to him was any different from the original. Two of the workmen who put up the fence testified that during the construction and before the fence was completed, the smaller of the two dogs of the defendant got through the fence and that they added extra pickets to those sections already installed and to those subsequently installed. The defendant testified that through Mr. Hayes he had an oral contract with the plaintiff to put up an ornamental iron fence which would keep his two dogs in and that Mr. Hayes stated that he could erect such a fence for the price of $1,945.00. He also testified about the dogs getting through that portion of the fence already constructed and that this was reported to the workmen who saw the smaller dog go through, and extra pickets were added to the fence. The defendant further testified that he had torn up and put in the wastebasket the original checks showing payments, but testified that the photostatic copies which he got from the bank were the exact copies of the original checks, and sought to introduce those photostatic copies, as well as a photostatic copy of bank records showing his accounts, deposits and charges. The last of these checks had written across the face thereof "iron fence in full." The trial judge refused to admit them in evidence. Upon the trial of the case before the trial judge without the intervention of a jury, judgment was rendered against the defendant for the principal sum of $1,265.62. He appealed, enumerating as error (a) the entry of judgment in favor of the plaintiff without sufficient evidence, (b) the exclusion from evidence of the photostatic copies of the checks and the bank statements, and (c) the overruling of defendant's counter claim seeking expenses of litigation.

* * * * *

(a) The trial court erred in refusing to admit in evidence the photostatic copies of the checks as evidence in uncontradicted that the originals thereof had been torn up and thrown in the wastebasket and disposed of as trash. A copy thereof is admissible. Code § 38–702. That these copies were made from a

negative film at a bank does not make the film the best evidence. The film is only a copy and it makes no difference how many copies of the original are made, any copy of the original identified as a correct copy, is admissible in evidence in lieu of the original. These certified copies were therefore admissible irrespective of whether a proper foundation had been laid for their admission under the Business Records Statute. As to these requirements, see *Smith v. Smith*, 224 Ga. 442(1), 162 S.E.2d 379; Ga.L.1950, pp. 73, 74 (Code Ann. § 38–710).

(b) The photostatic copies of the bank statements were not shown to be correct copies nor was the proper foundation laid for their admission as business records of the bank. The trial court, therefore, did not err in refusing to admit them in evidence.

* * * * *

Vincent N. POLEO and Ann N. Poleo, his wife v. GRANDVIEW EQUITIES, LTD., an Arizona Corporation, and William Parker and Sharon Parker, his wife

692 P.2d 309

Court of Appeals of Arizona, Division 1,
Department B
November 8, 1984

Grandview Equities appeals from a default judgment entered against it as a sanction for failure to comply with an order for production of documents.

The Poleos purchased a business from Grandview known as The Aquarium. The purchase price was $95,000, with a $23,000 down payment. Grandview provided the Poleos with a profit and loss statement and warranted it as a fair and accurate summary of the financial status of the business.

In late 1980, the Poleos brought a suit alleging that Grandview had induced the purchase by making fraudulent representations about payment be declared the purchase price of the business and that the $72,000 promissory note be canceled.

In February of 1981, the Poleos made two separate discovery requests which were disregarded. First, they requested that certain documents be produced at the office of Grandview's counsel in late March of 1981. The Poleos also served nonuniform interrogatories which were likewise due to be answered by the end of March. There was no response to either request and the Poleos, in early April, moved for an order compelling discovery. Grandview responded with a motion for a protective order, citing privacy and irrelevancy as justifications for the failure to produce. In late May, the trial court ordered that some, but not all, of the requested documents be produced by June 19, 1981.

Two weeks before the deadline for production, Grandview asked for and received an extension of time until July 8, 1981 to produce the documents. On July 9, one day after the trial court's deadline for production, Grandview responded to the order to produce which the court had entered in May. While Grandview did submit some of the requested documents, the company inexplicably "refuse(d) to submit" a variety of account books.

In late July, the Poleos requested that Grandview's answer be stricken and that default be entered for Grandview's refusal to comply with various discovery requests. Following a hearing, the trial court ordered that the defendant's answer be stricken and that default on the issue of liability be entered against Grandview. In late September, without notice or hearing, judgment was entered on Poleos' motion pursuant to Rule 55(b)(1), Arizona Rules of Civil Procedure. The trial court reformed the underlying sales agreement, specifying that the $23,000 already paid for the Aquarium was commensurate with the value of the business. The balance due under the promissory note was canceled. Subsequently, the trial court denied Grandview's motion for a new trial.

* * * * *

The Default Judgment

Grandview next claims that the imposition of default was an abuse of the trial court's discretion. Rule 37(b)(2)(C) authorizes "[a]n order striking out pleadings or parts thereof, or staying further proceedings until the order is obeyed, or dismissing the action or proceeding or any part thereof, or rendering a judgment by default against the disobedient party . . . " The trial court has discretion in imposing sanctions pursuant to Rule 37(b). *Fleitz v. Van Westrienen*, 114 Ariz. 246, 560 P.2d 430 (App.1977). This discretion is more limited, however, where the ultimate sanctions of dismissal or entry of default judgment are involved. *Golleher v. Horton*, 110 Ariz. 604, 583 P.2d 260 (App.1978). The trial court is to make "such orders in regard to the failure as are just" under Rule 37(b). Interpreting this language, the Supreme Court has held:

> [W]e think that Rule 37 should not be construed to authorize dismissal . . . when it has been established that failure to comply has been due to inability, and not to willfulness, bad faith, or any fault of [the party].

Societe Internationale v. Rogers, 357 U.S. 197, 212, 78 S.Ct. 1087, 1096, 2 L.Ed.2d 1255, 1267 (1958); *Sears, supra*. It is our function to review the records and determine whether there is a reasonable basis for the trial court's ruling. *Sears, supra*.

In this case there was ample indicia of appellant's willful and bad faith failure to produce. Initially, separate requests were made for the production of documents and for answers to interrogatories. At no time before the respective deadlines for discovery did Grandview object to production. Two weeks before the production ordered by the court was due, Grandview asked for and received and extension. Grandview then failed to meet the extended deadline, and later filed a "response" in which it flatly "refuse(d) to submit" to the court's order. Even when Grandview produced some of the ordered documents, it did not comply completely. For example, it produced only the first page of various tax returns. It was not until it filed its motion for a new trial, months after the first request for production, that Grandview first asserted that the documents were unavailable. The tenor of Grandview's lack of cooperation is readily apparent.

* * * * *

Melva PRESSEY, individually and as next Friend for William H. Pressey v. Kendall R. PATTERSON, W.L. Brasher, etc. and City of Houston

898 F.2d 1018

United States Court of Appeals, Fifth Circuit
April 23, 1990

In this section 1983 action, the City of Houston appeals a default judgment in excess of $8 million entered against it after the district court struck its answer for discovery abuse. We reverse the default judgment and remand for a trial on liability and to allow the district court to consider a more appropriate sanction.

On October 14, 1983, a truck driven by William Pressey, the plaintiff, approached the scene of a traffic accident that was under investigation and supervision of Houston police officers Kendall Patterson and W.L. Brasher. Pressey failed to move through the accident scene promptly despite Officer Patterson's signals and Patterson approached Pressey's truck. As the truck began to move, Patterson ran alongside it and shot Pressey in the head. Patterson and Brasher later fabricated a story to justify the shooting.

Pressey sued Patterson, Brasher, and the City of Houston under both 42 U.S.C. § 1983 and state law. One theory of Pressey's case was that the City of Houston had violated section 1983 by failing to investigate officers with violent propensities, thereby allowing dangerous officers such as Patterson to remain on duty.

The discovery phase of the lawsuit was punctuated by a number of discovery disputes and refusals by the City to produce evidence. The most serious discovery incidents concerned the destruction of two cassette tapes. The tapes contained an interview of Sergeant Steve Reiser, a supervisor and spokesperson for the Houston Police Department's internal affairs division, by a Houston Post reporter. Based in part on this interview, the Houston Post published a series of articles exposing inefficiency and incompetence in the internal affairs division. Reiser, who made the tapes, retained them until after the articles appeared. But in late December 1986 or early January 1987, around the time Reiser was transferred from internal affairs to another post, Reiser burned the interview tapes.

Before Pressey's attorney learned of the tapes' existence, he had made a number of broad discovery requests concerning the internal affairs division; the City did not produce the tapes of Reiser's interview. When Pressey's attorney did learn that the interview had been taped (well after the tapes had been destroyed) he specifically requested production of the tapes. The City did not respond for several months, but finally informed the court the tapes had been erased through routine reuse.

In November 1987, Pressey asked the court to strike the City's answer for discovery abuses. During a deposition ordered as part of the litigation over the sanctions motion, Pressey's attorney learned the tapes of Reiser's interview had not in fact been destroyed through routine reuse but instead had been burned by Reiser. Pressey added this to the reasons why the court should strike the City's answer.

The trial judge held a hearing on the sanctions motion and, without issuing specific findings of fact, ordered the City's answer struck "[b]ecause of abuse in the discovery process . . . " The judge then granted a default judgment against the City on liability.

Following a trial on damages, the jury returned a verdict of over $6.7 million. The trial court added prejudgment and postjudgment interest and an award for over $900,000 in attorneys' fees. The City appeals the judgment on liability, the damages award, and the attorneys' fees award. One of the City's code-fendants, W.L. Brasher, also appeals the judgment entered against him. Pressey cross–appeals the trial court's calculation of prejudgment interest.

* * * * *

B. Discovery Misconduct

The trial court did not make specific findings when imposing the sanctions. In its oral reasons for judgment, however, the judge alluded to the destruction of the tapes, the City's misrepresentations concerning those tapes, and the City's recalcitrance during the entire discovery process.

Destruction of the Reiser Interview Tapes

The plaintiff primarily seeks to justify the sanction because the City of Houston, through Sergeant Steve Reiser, deliberately destroyed the tapes. The trial court indicated in its oral reasons for judgment that it was primarily concerned with destruction of the tapes.

It is disputed that Sergeant Reiser intended to destroy the tapes. It is less clear why he did it. As Pressey points out, the record contains some evidence that Reiser knew that the information contained on these tapes might have been relevant to the Pressey case. The City has been served with a number of very broad discovery requests that arguably covered the tapes, and Reiser was one of the City employees involved in satisfying these production requests. Shortly before he destroyed the tapes, Reiser was subpoenaed to testify in another civil rights case involving allegations similar to those Pressey had made. At about the same time, Pressey filed a request that the City admit that Reiser had made the statements attributed to him in the Post articles. From all this, the plaintiff asks us to infer, or more specifically, to uphold the trial court's apparent conclusion that Reiser destroyed the tapes to prevent Pressey from using them as evidence against the City.

But other undisputed circumstances sur-rounding this case make us unable to accept this conclusion. The interview recorded on the tapes was used as the basis for an article exposing poor practices in the internal affairs division. No reason is suggested why the Houston Post, after conducting a long and tedious investigation of the internal affairs department, would have declined to print any detrimental information it discovered about the department. In other words, anything contained on the tapes that was helpful to Pressey and similarly situated plaintiffs would have almost certainly been printed in the news articles. Hence, destroying the tapes would have been of very little use to the City or to Sergeant Reiser, because presumably all damaging information was already public.

Likewise, the record reflects that the Houston Post reporter, Ira Perry, made his own tapes of the interview. Reiser obviously was aware that Perry had these tapes. Hence, even if the tapes contained some damaging information not printed in the articles, as far as Reiser knew, the Houston Post held an identical recording of the interview. We therefore fail to see what Reiser could have hoped to gain by destroying his tapes.

It is true that this second copy of the tapes was ultimately unavailable to Pressey's counsel because the trial judge refused to compel Perry to produce it based on the journalist's first amendment privilege to protect confidential sources. However, we cannot conceive that at the time Reiser burned the tapes, he could have anticipated the eventual exclusion of the tapes based on the trial court's interpretation of this privilege. In short, a decision to destroy the tapes in hopes of preventing the information contained on them from being used as evidence would have been an entirely irrational act.

Finally, the City had a plausible explanation for Reiser's conduct. Reiser was leaving his post at the internal affairs division at the time he destroyed the tapes and explained that destroying the tapes was simply part of cleaning out his office. When questioned why he did not retain the tapes, Reiser testified that he had made and kept the tapes only as protection against misquotation by the

Post, and that because the articles had already appeared, he felt no need to retain the tapes any longer.

We are bound by the trial court's findings of fact unless they are "clearly erroneous." Fed.R.Civ.P. 52(a). Insofar as the trial judge found that Reiser destroyed the tapes to prevent their use as evidence, we have "the definite and firm conviction that a mistake has been committed." *United States Gypsum Co.*, 333 U.S. 364, 395, 69 S.Ct. 525, 542, 92 L.Ed. 746, 766 (1948). Because no other evidence supports a conclusion that the City was in bad faith or willfully destroyed the tapes to deprive the court of probative evidence, that destruction alone cannot support the sanction imposed by the trial judge.

PROFESSIONAL SEMINAR CONSULTANTS, INC., a corporation v. SINO AMERICAN TECHNOLOGY EXCHANGE COUNCIL, INC., and G.Y. Lin

727 F.2d 1470

United States Court of Appeals, Ninth Circuit
March 13, 1984

PSC conducts professional seminars abroad. In 1980, PSC paid SATEC to make tour arrangements for a doctor's group traveling to Hong Kong and China. G.Y. Lin, the owner of SATEC, agreed to handle all land arrangements, including visas, for PSC.

PSC sent checks to Lin, one for $11,450.70 payable to SATEC, the other for $102,042.63 payable to the Peking Medical College for tour accommodations. PSC alleges that Lin deposited funds in his own name and withdrew all the money.

SATEC failed to make arrangement for visas, which complicated the tourists' plans for accommodations and meetings. As a result, angry patrons sued PSC, Lin, and SATEC in California state court.

Before this incident, PSC had conducted two

to three study trips a year for each of the groups of medical specialists involved in this case. They were pathologists and plastic surgeons. Both have since discontinued business with PSC.

PSC brought a district court action for conversion of the $102,042.63 check, libel, and other damages. SATEC counterclaimed. The parties agreed to trial before a federal magistrate.

During discovery, PSC requested an inspection of documents, including, "all books, records, canceled checks, receipts or other documentation showing what you did with the proceeds of the $102,042.63 check." SATEC agreed to produce these documents as soon as they were sent from Hong Kong.

Pursuant to a discovery order, SATEC produced documents, including photocopies of checks purportedly paid to Peking Medical College, but PSC argued at a pretrial conference that the documents were falsified. PSC brought a motion for sanctions under Fed.R.Civ.P. 37(b). The motion was granted; the defendants' answer and counterclaim were stricken and a default judgment was entered.

SATEC raises six issues on appeal.

1. *Sufficiency of the Evidence of Falsity.* We review findings of fact related to a motion for sanctions under the clearly erroneous standard. *Wyle v. R.J. Reynolds*, 709 F.2d 585, 589 n. 2 (9th Cir.1983).

Contrary to SATEC's assertion that there is no evidence that the documents were false, PSC filed two affidavits and a letter in support of its motion for sanctions. Although one affidavit was based on hearsay, the magistrate could reasonably have found the evidence to be reliable, probative, and admissible. *See* J. Weinstein & M. Berger, 4 *Weinstein's Evidence* ¶ 800[03] (Supp.1982).

SATEC did not challenge the evidence or offer other evidence that the documents were not false. We do not review an issue not raised or objected to below except to prevent a manifest injustice. *Komatsu, Ltd. v. States*

Steamship Co., 674 F.2d 806, 812 (9th Cir.1982). There is no showing of manifest injustice here.

SATEC's failure to object to the hearsay allowed the magistrate to consider it for its probative value. *United States v. Jamerson*, 549 F.2d 1263, 1266–67 (9th Cir.1977). It also bars SATEC from raising the issue on appeal unless plain error exists. Fed.R.Evid. 103(d). The admission of the hearsay was not plain error because the evidence was relevant and probative.

The magistrate's finding that the documents were false was not clearly erroneous.

SATEC contends that the trial court's failure to conduct an evidentiary hearing about the documents' falsity violated due process.

Due process is a flexible concept which requires "such procedural protections as the particular situation demands." *Dash, Inc. v. Alcoholic Beverage Control Appeals Board*, 683 F.2d 1229, 1233 (9th Cir.1982) (citing *Matthews v. Eldridge* 424 U.S. 319, 334, 96 S.Ct. 893, 902, 47 L.Ed.2d 18 (1976)).

What the situation demands is determined by balancing the competing governmental and private interests affected. *Matthews*, 424 U.S. at 334, 96 S.Ct. at 902.

A balance of the competing interests weighs in favor of the court's interest in efficiency, compliance with its orders, and deterrence. SATEC had two weeks to respond to the claim of falsified documents. It did not assert that the documents were genuine. Since no evidentiary issue was raised prior to the hearing, it was reasonable for the magistrate to find that an evidentiary hearing was unnecessary. *See Charter House Insurance Brokers v. New Hampshire Insurance*, 667 F.2d 600, 605 (7th Cir.1981).

There was no abuse of discretion in ordering sanctions without an evidentiary hearing. *Charter House*, 676 F.2d at 605.

* * * * *

Charles RICE v. UNITED STATES of America

411 F.2d 485

United States Court of Appeals
June 11, 1969

The defendant, Charles Rice, was convicted of violating § 659, Title 18, United States Code, for stealing two suitcases from the Greyhound Lines, Incorporated, on January 9, 1968, while the suitcases were moving in interstate commerce. He was sentenced to one year in prison.

* * * * *

Owens testified that the luggage of each Greyhound passenger is checked before he boards a bus. A separate baggage tag is prepared for each bag. One portion of a numbered tag is attached to the bag and another portion of the tag — a claim check — with a matching number is given to the passenger. The claim check includes a statement that "this check must be surrendered in order to obtain baggage." Owens testified that this requirement was uniformly followed in St. Louis. The baggage strap tag and the claim check show the point of origin and destination of the bag. The tag indicated that the suitcase, to which the strap had been attached, had been checked at Los Angeles and was destined for Evansville. On cross–examination, Owens testified that he solicited the return of Exhibit 2–a, the claim check, from the terminal manager at Evansville. No other record of the transaction is made by Greyhound.

The exhibits constituted hearsay as they were offered to prove the truth of their contents, but a proper foundation was laid for their admission under the business record exception to the hearsay rule. See, *Palmer v. Hoffman*, 318 U.S. 109, 112, 63 S.Ct. 477, 87 L.Ed. 645 (1943); *Standard Oil Company of California v. Moore*, 251 F.2d 188 (9th Cir.), cert. denied, 356 U.S. 975, 78 S.Ct. 1139, 2 L.Ed.2d 1148 (1958). This is an exception sanctioned by statute.

Section 1732(a), Title 28, United States Code, provides in part:

"(a) In any court of the United States, * * * any writing or record, whether in the form of an entry in a book or otherwise, made as a memorandum or record of any * * *, transaction, * * * shall be admissible as evidence of such * * * transaction, * * *, if made in the regular course of any business, and if it was the regular course of such business to make such memorandum or record at the time of such * * * transaction * * * within a reasonable time thereafter.

"All other circumstances of the making of such writing or record, including lack of personal knowledge by the entrant or maker, may be shown to affect its weight, but such circumstances shall not affect its admissibility."

The baggage strap tag and the claim check were writings, they were made as a memorandum of a transaction in the regular course of business, and it was in the regular course of Greyhound's business to make them. See, *Doss v. United States*, 355 F.2d (8th Cir. 1966).

The defendant's contention that Exhibits 2 and 2–A should not have been admitted into evidence because Owens, who identified them, neither prepared them nor had them prepared under his supervision is without merit. Owens, as manager of the St. Louis Terminal, was thoroughly familiar with Greyhound's baggage procedure, and was responsible for baggage in the terminal. His testimony amply demonstrated that the strap tag and claim check were prepared pursuant to the established procedures of a form specifically devised for the purpose and used routinely by the company. Under such circumstances, it is unnecessary to require a Greyhound employee at the point of origin to testify with respect to the baggage documents. *United States v. Olivo*, 278 F.2d 415 (3rd Cir. 1960).

In *Olivo*, the defendant was convicted of possession of an air compressor stolen from the Spector Freight System, Inc., while it was moving in interstate commerce from Peoria, Illinois to South River, New Jersey. The government sought to prove the interstate nature of the shipment by introducing a waybill,

prepared by Spector employees at Peoria, through the manager of the Spector terminal at Newark, New Jersey. The Court held the waybill was properly admitted and stated:

"Specifically, appellant's objection is grounded upon the fact that the witness who testified concerning the waybill and its preparation did not actually prepare it himself nor did he directly supervise its preparation. Rather, Mr. Dillman, Spector's Newark terminal manager, testified to the company procedures concerning preparation of waybills in general and indicated that they were prepared at the point of origin within the Spector transportation system. Where Newark was the point of origin they were prepared under his supervision, but since this shipment had originated with another carrier it was waybilled by Spector when delivered to it at Peoria, Illinois. Extensive testimony was taken from Dillman concerning the preparation, use and billing procedures connected with Spector waybills. We are asked to hold that this waybill is inadmissible under the Business Records Act since no official or employee of the Spector system at Peoria testified regarding these matters. We are not prepared to place such stringent restrictions on this Act, for it was intended to eliminate the technical requirements of proving the authenticity of records and memoranda by the testimony of the maker. The Supreme Court has said that the Federal Business Records Act 'should of course be liberally interpreted so as to do away with the anachronistic rules which gave rise to its need and at which it was aimed.' *Palmer v. Hoffman*, 1943, 318 U.S. 109, 115, 63 S.Ct. 477, 481, 87 L.Ed. 645. The witness testified to a well–established business procedure not only in the trade, but specifically in the very company which had prepared the document. All the hallmarks of authenticity surround this document, since it was made pursuant to established company procedures for the systematic, routine, timely making and preserving of company records. As the Court of Appeals so aptly stated in *Korte v. New York, N.H. & Hartford R.R. Co.*, 2

Cir., 191 F.2d 86, 91, certiorari denied 1951, 342 U.S. 868, 72 S.Ct. 108, 96 L.Ed. 652, the statute was intended 'to bring the realities of business and professional practice into the courtroom in usable form,' and the statute should not be interpreted in a 'dryly technical' way which would 'reduce sharply its obvious usefulness.'"

RICHMARK CORP., a California Corporation, Plaintiff, v. TIMBER FALLING CONSULTANTS, an Oregon Corporation, Defendant. TIMBER FALLING CONSULANTS, an Oregon Corporation, Counterclaim Plaintiff–Appellee, v. RICHMARK CORP., A California Corporation, Peacock Mfg. Co., a Texas Corporation, Zhu Yuanchang, Eugene Wang, James Yang, and Francis Tong, Counterclaim Defendants, and Beijing Ever Bright Industrial Co., a foreign Corporation, Counterclaim Defendant–Appellant.

959 F.2d 1468

United States Court of Appeals, Ninth Circuit
March 30, 1992

This case presents a number of difficult questions regarding a sensitive area of law and foreign relations. Timber Falling Consultants, Inc. (TFC) won a default judgment for fraud and breach of contract against Beijing Ever Bright Industrial Co. (Beijing), a corporation organized under the laws of the People's Republic of China (PRC) and an arm of the PRC government. As part of an effort to execute that judgment, TFC sought discovery of Beijing's assets worldwide. Beijing resisted those discovery efforts, and refused to comply when ordered to do so by the district court. The district court imposed discovery sanctions, held Beijing in contempt, and ordered contempt fines of $10,000 a day. Beijing contends that PRC secrecy laws prevent it from complying with the discovery order and that it would be subject to prosecution in the PRC were it to comply. It appeals the discovery order, the discovery sanction, the contempt order, and the district courts' refusal to vacate the contempt order.

While we acknowledge the importance of the interests the State Secrecy statute is designed to protect, we conclude in the circumstances of this case that the PRC's laws limiting disclosure cannot excuse Beijing's failure to comply with the district court's orders. For this reason, we affirm the discovery and contempt orders. We modify the contempt order, however, to make it payable to the court, rather than to TFC.

Factual and Procedural Background

Beijing contracted to purchase lumber from Richmark Corp. Richmark in turn retained TFC to procure the timber. After the contract fell through, Richmark sued TFC. TFC counterclaimed against Richmark and cross–claimed against all other parties involved, including Beijing, alleging fraud and breach of contract. Beijing failed to appear, apparently because of the interruption in United States–PRC relations which followed the Tienanmen Square incident. All other claims on both sides were dismissed by the district court, but TFC was awarded a $2.2 million default judgment against Beijing. This judgment was entered on June 5, 1990.

Beijing appealed this judgment to the Ninth Circuit. Beijing did not post a supersedeas bond or letter of credit, however, so TFC was free to begin efforts to collect this judgment while the appeal was pending. In an attempt to do so, TFC served Beijing with a number of discovery requests and interrogatories which sought to identify Beijing's assets worldwide. Beijing did not respond to those requests, and instead moved for a stay of discovery pending resolution of its Rule 60(b) motion for relief from the judgment. TFC in turn filed a motion to compel discovery.

On October 15, 1990, the district court denied Beijing's Rule 60(b) motion, mooting Beijing's request for a stay, and granted TFC's motion to compel discovery. *Richmark Corp. v. Timber Falling Consultants*, 747 F.Supp. 1409 (D.Or.1990). Beijing then appealed the denial of its Rule 60(b) motion, and on November 27, 1990, petitioned the district court for a stay of discovery pending appeal. The district court denied this motion on January 11, 1991. Beijing promptly petitioned the Ninth Circuit for a stay of discovery. Its petition was denied on February 19, 1991.

On January 28, 1991, Beijing for the first time requested advice from its government on how to respond to TFC's discovery requests. Specifically, Beijing sought guidance as to whether PRC "State Secrecy Laws" prohibited it from disclosing the requested information concerning its assets. This request was passed by the State Secrecy Bureau to another arm of the State Council, the Ever Bright Group, which was in charge of overseeing Beijing's operations. On April 16, 1991, the Ever Bright Group sent written notification to Beijing that almost all of its financial information was classified a state secret and could not be disclosed.

Meanwhile, following the denial of the stay petition by the Ninth Circuit, TFC moved for contempt and discovery sanctions against Beijing. In its answer, Beijing for the first time raised the issue of the State Secrecy Laws. The district court denied the request for sanctions on March 4, but it rejected Beijing's contention that PRC law prevented it from complying as "untimely and without merit," and again ordered Beijing to respond to TFC's discovery requests. On March 5, Beijing moved the district court for a protective order against discovery, on the same grounds. The district court denied this motion on March 14.

Beijing still refused to comply with the discovery orders. On April 4, 1991, the district court held Beijing in contempt of its October 15 and March 4 orders. It awarded TFC its attorney's fees and costs incurred in seeking discovery as a discovery sanction, and imposed contempt fines of $10,000 a day, payable to TFC, until Beijing complied with the discovery orders. However, the district court indicated that it would vacate the contempt order if Beijing complied with the discovery orders within 60 days.

On Mary 15, 1991, Beijing provided the limited amount of information the Ever Bright Group allowed it to disclose, and moved the district court to vacate the contempt sanctions. On July 24, 1991, the district court denied the motion to vacate.

Richmark Corp. v. Timber Falling Consultants, 138 F.R.D. 132 (D.Or.1991).

Beijing appeals on a variety of grounds from the March 4 discovery order, the April 4 contempt order, and the July 24 denial of its motion to vacate.

* * * * *

Deference to PRC Law

Beijing contends that the state secrecy laws prohibit it from disclosing the information the district court ordered it to provide, that it would be subject to criminal prosecution if it did disclose such information, and that this prohibition necessitates the reversal of the discovery order and the contempt sanctions against it. The district court explicitly accepted Beijing's contention that the PRC's State Secrets Act barred disclosure of the information in question. We do so as well.

That does not end the inquiry, however. The PRC's admitted interest in secrecy must be balanced against the interests of the United States and the plaintiffs in obtaining the information. In *Societe Internationale Pour Participations Industrialles et Commerciales v. Rogers*, 357 U.S. 197, 78 S.Ct. 1087, 2 L.Ed.2d 1255 (1958) (*Societe Internationale*), The Supreme Court confronted a similar issue. In that case, the petitioner, a Swiss Company, objected to discovery requests on the grounds that producing Swiss bank records would violate Swiss law. The Swiss Federal Attorney had issued an order prohibiting their disclosure. The district court expressly concluded that the Swiss company acted in good faith in seeking to comply, and the company did disclose over 190,000 documents during discovery. The Supreme Court held that the company had failed to comply with the order, *id.*, at 208, 78 S.Ct. at 1094, but concluded that the sanction of dismissal of its complaint was inappropriate. It reached this conclusion because "petitioner's failure to satisfy fully the requirements of this production order was due to inability fostered neither by its own conduct nor by circumstances within its control. It is hardly debatable that fear of criminal prosecution constitutes a weighty excuse for nonproduction. . . ." *Id.* at 211, 78 S.Ct. at 1095.

Cases since *Societe Internationale*, however have emphasized that a foreign–law prohibition will not always excuse compliance with a discovery order. In *Societe Nationale Industrielle Aerospatiale v. United States District Court*, 482 U.S. 522, 544 n. 29, 107 S.Ct. 2542, 2556 n. 29, 96 L.Ed.2d 461 (1987) (*Aerospatiale*), the Supreme Court states that "[i]t is well settled that such [foreign 'blocking'] statutes do not deprive an American court of the power to order a party subject to its jurisdiction to produce evidence even though the act of production may violate that statute." *Accord United States v. Vetco, Inc.*, 691 F.2d 1281, 1287 (9th Cir.) ("*Societe Internationale* did not erect an absolute bar to summons enforcement and contempt sanctions whenever compliance is prohibited by foreign law."), *cert. denied*, 454 U.S. 1098, 102 S.Ct. 671, 70 L.Ed.2d 639 (1981).

Instead, *Aerospatiale* endorsed the balancing test contained in the Restatement (Third) of Foreign Relations Law § 442(1)(c). Under that test, factors that are relevant in deciding whether or not foreign statutes excuse noncompliance with discovery orders include:

> the importance to the investigation or litigation of the documents or other information requested; the degree of specificity of the request; whether the information originated in the United States; the availability of alternative means of securing the information; and the extent to which noncompliance with the request would undermine important interests of the United States, or compliance with the request would undermine important interests of the state where the information is located.

Id; *Aerospatiale*, 482 U.S. at 544 n. 28, 107 S.Ct. at 2556 n. 28. As the Court noted, this list of factors is not exhaustive. Other factors that we have considered relevant are "'the extent and the nature of the hardship that inconsistent enforcement would impose upon the person, . . . [and] the extent to which enforcement by action of either state can

reasonably be expected to achieve compliance with the rule prescribed by that state,'" *Vetco*, 691 F.2d at 1288 (quoting the Restatement (Second) of Foreign Relations Law § 40. We consider each factor in turn.

Importance of the Documents. Where the outcome of litigation "does not stand or fall on the present discovery order," or where the evidence sought is cumulative of existing evidence, courts have generally been unwilling to override foreign secrecy laws. *See In re Westinghouse Elec. Corp. Uranium Contracts Litigation*, 563 F.2d 992, 999 (10th Cir.1977). Where the evidence is directly relevant, however, we have found this factor to weigh in favor of disclosure. *Vetco*, 691 F.2d at 1290. In this case, the information sought is not only relevant to the execution of the judgment, it is crucial. Without information as to Beijing's assets, TFC cannot hope to enforce the judgment. The execution proceedings, and in some sense the underlying judgment itself, will be rendered meaningless. The importance of the documents to the litigation weighs in favor of compelling disclosure.

Specificity of the Request. A second consideration in evaluating a discovery request is how burdensome it will be to respond to that request. Generalized searches for information, the disclosure of which is prohibited under foreign law, are discouraged. In this case, Beijing has not objected to the burdensome nature of the discovery request, apart from the fact of its illegality. While TFC sought a great deal of information, all of it was directed at identifying Beijing's current assets in order to execute the judgment. Further, TFC's request was reasonably limited in time; it sought only recent financial documents. Beijing has not made this factor an issue, and it does not favor nondisclosure here.

Location of Information and Parties. The fact that all the information to be disclosed (and the people who will be deposed or who will produce the documents) are located in a foreign country weighs against disclosure, since those people and documents are subject to the law of that country in the ordinary course of business. *Reinsurance Co. of America v. Administratia Asigurarilar de*

Stat, 902 F.2d 1275, 1281 (7th Cir.1990); *Westinghouse,* 563 F.2d at 998. In this case, Beijing has no United States office. All of its employees, and all of the documents TFC has requested, are located in the PRC. This factor weighs against requiring disclosure.

Alternative means of Obtaining Information. If the information sought can easily be obtained elsewhere, there is little or no reason to require a party to violate foreign law. *Cf. In re Sealed Case,* 825 F.2d 494, 499 (D.C.Cir.) (reversing contempt sanction, noting that it is "relevant to our conclusion that the grand jury is not left empty–handed by today's decision"), *cert. denied,* 484 U.S. 963, 108 S.Ct. 451, 98 L.Ed.2d 391 (1987). In this circuit, the alternative means must be "substantially equivalent" to the requested discovery. *Vetco,* 691 F.2d at 1290; *see SEC v. Minas de Artemisa,* 150 F.2d 215, 219 (9th Cir.1945). Beijing has not suggested any such alternatives, as did the appellants in *Vetco.*

One possible alternative would be to seek information from Beijing's nominal parent corporation, China Ever Bright Holdings Co., which is incorporated in Hong Kong. However, as Beijing itself takes pains to note, China Ever Bright is a separate entity from Beijing, and financial information about China Ever Bright is not relevant to Beijing's financial position. A second alternative would be to subpoena information from sources in the United States who have dealt with Beijing and might have financial information. TFC in fact has attempted to do this, issuing subpoenas to the Bank of China, Mesta Engineering Corp., Shougang Mechanical Equipment of Pennsylvania, and Solid Beam Industrial Co. TFC was not successful in obtaining information from these sources. Indeed, it failed in part because Beijing and its affiliates actively opposed those subpoenas. Further, Beijing concedes that any information received from these sources should not include the core financial information requested by TFC. Finally, TFC has requested depositions of various Beijing officials, which obviously cannot be provided by anyone other than Beijing.

TFC appears to have done everything in its

power to collect information which will enable it to enforce the judgment. To date, it has been unsuccessful. The absence of other sources for the information TFC seeks is a factor which weighs strongly in favor of compelling disclosure.

Balance of National Interests. This is the most important factor. We must assess the interests of each nation in requiring or prohibiting disclosure, and determine whether disclosure would "affect important substantive policies or interests" of either the United States or the PRC. *Restatement (Third) of Foreign Relations Law* § 442 comment c. In assessing the strength of the PRC's interests, we will considerer "expressions of interest by the foreign state," "the significance of disclosure in the regulation . . . of the activity in question," and "indications of the foreign state's concern for confidentiality *prior to the controversy." Id.* (emphasis added).

In this case, the PRC's State Secrecy Bureau has directly expressed an interest in the outcome of this case. In its response to Beijing's request for guidance, the Bureau wrote: "[T]his Bureau hereby orders your Company not to disclose or provide the information and documents requested by the United States District Court for the District of Oregon except Items 1, 2, 3(f), 9 and 10. Your Company shall bear any or all legal consequences should you not comply with this order."

However, the State Secrecy Bureau did not express interest in the confidentiality of this information prior to the litigation in question. Indeed, Beijing routinely disclosed information regarding its assets, inventory, bank accounts, and corporate structure to the general public, for example through a trade brochure, and to companies with whom it did business, *see Richmark* 937 F.2d at 1447; *Timber Falling,* No. 90 Civ. 6838 (KTD) (S.D.N.Y. July 19, 1991). The State Secrecy Bureau did not object to the *voluntary* disclosure of any of this information. It is only now, when disclosure will have adverse consequences for Beijing, that the PRC has asserted its interest in confidentiality.

Further, neither Beijing nor the PRC has

identified any way in which the disclosure of the information requested here will significantly affect the PRC's interests in confidentiality. Those interests, as set forth by the State Secrecy Laws themselves, are in matters involving national security and interest." Collection of the Laws of the People's Republic of China 1363 Art. 2 (1989). This is defined to include information which "concern[s] the national economy and social development" or disclosure of which may "diminish the country's economic, technological and scientific strength." *Id.* at Art. 8. Art. 4(7). There is no indication that Beijing, much less the economy of the PRC as a whole, will be adversely affected at all by disclosure of this information. The only likely "adverse" affect on the PRC economy will be that TFC may be able to collect its judgment, something the PRC has no legitimate state interest in preventing.

The PRC, then, has asserted an interest (albeit one whose strength is unknown) in the confidentiality of the information in question. This interest must be weighed against the United States' interests in vindicating the rights of American plaintiffs and in enforcing the judgments of its courts. The former interest has been described as "substantial" *see In re Insurance Antitrust Litigation*, 938 F.2d 919, 933 (9th Cir.1991), *petitions for cert. filed* Jan. 9 and 13, 1992, and the latter as "vital," *Reinsurance*, 902 F.2d at 1280. To be sure, these interests are not so strong that they would compel disclosure in all cases. *See id.* at 1281 (Romanian interest in secrecy outweighs United States' interest in enforcing private judgments). In this case, however, because Beijing and the PRC have been unable to identify any way in which the PRC's interests will be hurt by disclosure, the interests of the United States must prevail. The balancing of national interests is therefore a factor which weighs in favor of disclosure.

Hardship to Beijing. The effect that a discovery order is likely to have on the foreign company is another factor to be considered. If Beijing is likely to face criminal prosecution in the PRC for complying with the United States court order, that fact constitutes a "weighty excuse" for nonproduction.

Societe Internationale, 357 U.S. at 211, 78 S.Ct. at 1095. In this case, Beijing has in fact been ordered by the Chinese government to withhold the information, and has been told that it will bear the "legal consequences" of disclosing the information. Beijing therefore seems to be placed in a difficult position, between the Scylla of contempt sanctions and the Charybdis of possible criminal prosecution.

However, if the hardship is self–imposed, or if Beijing could have avoided it, the fact that it finds itself in an undesirable position will not work against disclosure of the requested information. *See Vetco*, 691 F.2d at 1289–90 (hardship not a factor because it was "avoidable"). In this case, the discovery dispute arose only because Beijing refused to post a supersedeas bond or letter of credit to stay execution of the judgment pending appeal, as required by Fed.R.Civ.P. 62(d). *See United States v. $2,490.00 in United States Currency*, 825 F.2d 1419, 1421 (9th Cir.1987). Beijing even now could post a supersedeas bond pending the outcome of its petition for certiorari, or it could pay the judgment. Either of these courses of action would keep it from having to violate either the district court's orders or the PRC's laws.

Beijing objects that requiring either course of action would violate its "immunity" from execution under the Foreign Sovereign Immunities Act, 28 U.S.C.§ 1610(b). Beijing misreads that provision. Section 1610 provides for the execution of judgments against foreign sovereigns. It is true that section 1610 does not empower United States courts to levy on assets located outside the United States. That provision merely limits the power of United States courts, however; it does not vest in Beijing a "right" not to pay a valid judgment against it. *See Frolova v. Union of Soviet Specialist Republics*, 558 F.Supp. 358, 361 (N.D.Ill.1983) (purpose of section 1610 is to provide a remedy against foreign states who fail to pay judgments against them) *aff'd.* 761 F.2d 370 (7th Cir.1985). TFC can seek to execute the judgment in whatever foreign courts have jurisdiction over Beijing's assets, *see Nippon Emo–Trans Co. v. Emo–Trans, Inc.*, 744

F.Supp. 1215, 1218 (E.D.N.Y.1990), but TFC needs discovery in order to determine which courts those are. Beijing may be *able* as a practical matter to conceal its assets from the district court and therefore avoid execution of TFC's judgment, but it has no *right* to do so, and it certainly has no right to avail itself of the United States judicial system for purposes of appeal while at the same time seeking to evade the judgments of that judicial system.

Because Beijing could — and still can — avoid the hardship disclosure would place on it, that hardship is not a factor weighing against disclosure.

Likelihood of Compliance. If a discovery order is likely to be unenforceable, and therefor to have no practical effect, that factor counsels against requiring compliance with the order. In this case, it may be impossible to force Beijing to comply. The imposition of sanctions in the amount of $10,000 a day, sanctions which have already grown larger than the underlying judgment, has failed to move Beijing. It is perhaps unrealistic to expect that a PRC court will enforce an order requiring Beijing to violate PRC law. Compliance therefore seems unlikely, a factor counseling against compelling discovery.

Nonetheless, the discovery and contempt orders may be of some significance. While Beijing apparently has no assets in the United States, it has in the past done substantial business in this country. Should it wish to do business here in the future, it would have to pay the judgment or risk having its assets seized and its business interrupted. In addition, a clear statement that foreign corporations which avail themselves of business opportunities in the United States must abide by United States laws might have a substantial effect on the way Beijing and other corporations do business in the United States in the future. Our recent decision in *Insurance Antitrust* is instructive. In that case, the court concluded that an injunction against Lloyd's of London would not be enforced by the British courts. It nonetheless upheld the injunction because it could be enforced within the United States, and because it would send a message to companies who wished to do business in the United States in the future. 938 F.2d at 933.

In short, full compliance by Beijing with the order of the district court is unlikely. The order may nonetheless produce partial compliance, and might be effective in other ways as well. While the likelihood of noncompliance does weigh against compelling disclosure, we think the weight of this factor is lessened by these mitigating circumstances.

Conclusion. Taking all of the aforementioned factors into consideration, the balance tips significantly (although not overwhelmingly) in TFC's favor. The United States has a strong interest in enforcing its judgments which outweighs the PRC's interest in confidentiality in this case. The information sought is vital to the litigation and cannot be obtained elsewhere. Finally, Beijing can avoid any hardship it may face by following normal litigation procedure and posting a supersedeas bond. If it does so, both the district court and TFC have indicated a willingness to forego contempt sanctions. The only factors weighing against compelling disclosure are that Beijing has the information in the PRC and may choose not to disclose it in spite of the court's order. Were these factors alone sufficient, a foreign corporation could avoid its discovery obligations in almost every instance. We therefore conclude that the order compelling discovery should be upheld in spite of the PRC secrecy statute.

In reaching this conclusion, we are not unmindful of the difficulties foreign corporations face in doing business in the United States, nor of the rather delicate nature of relations between sovereign states. We sincerely hope that today's decision will not adversely affect the cordial business relationship between the United States and the PRC. However, international business requires the accommodation of different legal climates. Just as United States companies doing business in the PRC must expect to abide by PRC law, when Beijing availed itself of business opportunities in this country, it undertook an obligation to comply with the lawful orders of the United States courts. We do not minimize the difficult situation in which Beijing has been placed. Here, however, where the PRC has not demonstrated a strong interest in keeping the requested information confidential, and where Beijing has options open to it which violate neither United States nor PRC law, Beijing cannot escape compliance with the district court's discovery orders.

C. Good Faith Compliance

Beijing next contends that, even if the discovery order was valid, the contempt sanction should be vacated because Beijing has attempted in good faith to comply with the court's orders. It is true that contempt is inappropriate where a party has taken "all the reasonable steps" it can take to comply. *Balla v. Idaho State Bd. of Corrections*, 869 F.2d 461, 466 (9th Cir. 1989). The Restatement (Third) of Foreign Relations Law § 442(2)(b) provides that "a court or agency should not ordinarily impose sanctions of contempt . . . on a party that has failed to comply with the order for production, except in cases of deliberate concealment, or removal of information, or of failure to make a good faith effort to secure permission from the foreign government to disclose the information."

In *Vetco*, we required a foreign corporation asserting a blocking statute as a defense to make an *affirmative showing* of its good faith in seeking permission to disclose the information. 691 F.2d at 1287 ("This case is not controlled by *Societe Internationale*. We have no finding that appellants have made good faith efforts to comply with the summonses.) *Compare Societe Internationale*, 357 U.S. at 201, 78 S.Ct. at 1090 (explicit finding by Special Master of good faith confirmed by district court)." *see also* Restatement (Third) of Foreign Relations Law § 442 comment h ("Parties to litigation . . . *may be required to show that they have made serious efforts* before appropriate authorities of states with blocking statutes to secure release or waiver from a prohibition against disclosure.") (emphasis added).

Beijing has made no such affirmative showing here. The district court did not find that Beijing acted in good faith in attempting to obtain a waiver. Nor is good faith evident from the record. Beijing fought for several

months before raising the foreign law problem, even after the district court issued an order on October 15, 1990 compelling disclosure. Beijing's effort to seek a waiver consisted of a letter to the Ministry of Justice on January 28, 1991, in which it noted the "broad scope" of the discovery order, pointed out to the Ministry the legal provision it felt barred disclosure, and asked whether it was permitted to disclose the information under the State Secrets Act. While Beijing did ask whether there was "a procedure through which Beijing Ever Bright May seek the permission of the government to disclose the information it is not presently permitted to disclose," it did not in fact seek such permission, but rather requested only "guidance" on a legal question. In spite of this, Beijing asserted that the State Secrets Act prevented it from complying in February 1991, two months *before* the Ministry even responded to this request. Beijing does not appear to have made a good faith effort to clarify PRC law or to seek a waiver of the secrecy statutes before refusing to comply with the district court order. For these reasons, the district court acted within its discretion in sanctioning Beijing for noncompliance.

* * * * *

RIVER DOCK and PILE, INC. v. O & G INDUSTRIES, INC., et al.

595 A.2d 839

Supreme Court of Connecticut
July 30, 1991

Action to recover damages for, *inter alia*, wrongful termination of a construction contract, brought to the Superior Court in the judicial district of New Haven, where the action was withdrawn as against the defendant Hartford Fire Insurance Company and where the named defendant filed a counterclaim; thereafter, the case was tried to the jury before Downey, J.; verdict and judgment for the plaintiff on the complaint and for the named defendant on the counterclaim, from which the named defendant appealed.

The principal issue in this appeal is whether certain documents offered into evidence by the plaintiff were admissible under the business records exception to the hearsay rule, as set forth in General Statutes § 52–180. The trial court concluded that the requirements of § 52–180 had been satisfied and admitted the documents. The named defendant seeks a new trial on the ground that the documents in question should not have been admitted.

* * * * *

The facts relevant to this appeal are largely disputed. The named defendant, O and G Industries, Inc., was the general contractor for the renovation of Union Station in New Haven, which is owned by the New Haven Parking Authority (NHPA). On August 25, 1983, the named defendant entered into a subcontract with the plaintiff, River Dock and Pile, Inc., in which the plaintiff agreed to provide all the labor, material and equipment necessary to design and install piling and a sheeting system required for the construction of platforms A and D and a passenger tunnel leading from the railroad station to the platforms. The contract provided that the plaintiff would receive $476,000 for performing this work. On April 15, 1985, the roof of one of the platforms and some of the catenary wires that provide electricity for the trains were damaged as a result of an accident involving the plaintiff's crane, which was being used for pile driving. The parties dispute whether, at this point, the named defendant wrongfully terminated the contract or whether the plaintiff simply refused to perform any more work under the contract. The named defendant subsequently hired another subcontractor to complete the work that the plaintiff originally had agreed to perform.

* * * * *

The series of documents that the defendant claims were improperly admitted as business records concerned negotiations between the defendant and the NHPA over the resolution of two separate "delay claims" arising from the renovation of Union Station. The delay claims represented amounts that the defendant sought to recover from the NHPA to compensate it for increased construction costs arising from delays in the timetable of

its work for which the defendant contends that it was not responsible.

The first delay claim involved the period from May 19, 1985, to November 30, 1986. It concerned work that was done on platform D and the main building. The plaintiff performed work on platform D during this period and, therefore, the defendant's first delay claim included amounts related to delay costs incurred by the plaintiff. Greiner Engineering Sciences (Greiner) served as construction manager on the Union Station renovation for the NHPA during the period involved in the first delay claim. Greiner's duties included inspecting the renovation work to verify that it conformed to the contract requirements and reviewing requisitions submitted by the named defendant. In addition, at the request of the NHPA, Greiner assisted the NHPA in evaluating the first delay claim submitted by the defendant.

The second delay claim involved delay costs related to the completion of work remaining on April 3, 1987. As of that date, the plaintiff had ceased to work on the site, and therefore the defendant's second delay claim did not involve work actually performed by the plaintiff. Hill International, Inc., served as construction manager for NHPA for the period relevant to the second delay claim and therefore assisted the NHPA in negotiating the settlement of that claim of the defendant.

* * * * *

Exhibit OO

Exhibit OO is a critical analysis of the defendant's first delay claim. This document was prepared by Greiner, NHPA's construction manager at the time, at the request of the NHPA in order to assist it in negotiating the settlement of the defendant's claim. The exhibit includes an evaluation of the claims submitted by the plaintiff as well as claims submitted by numerous other contractors who have no connection to this case. Michael Robinson, a construction inspector who began working for the NHPA in October of 1988, testified that the exhibit was a copy of the original, which was kept in the NHPA's files, and that the document was prepared in the ordinary course of business of the NHPA. Robinson did not testify as to whether it was in the regular course of the NHPA's business to make such a record or whether the record was made at or within a reasonable time of the act described in the exhibit.

The defendant objected to Robinson testifying that the document was made in the ordinary course of business on the ground that Robinson was not employed by the NHPA in February, 1987, when exhibit OO was prepared. After the trial judge sustained this objection, he ordered a recess to give the defendant an opportunity to review the document. After the recess, the trial judge implicitly reversed its prior ruling since it admitted the exhibit on the basis of Robinson's testimony that the exhibit was made in the ordinary course of business. We note that this result is consistent with the fact that the witness, whose testimony is used as the basis for admitting a business record, need not have been employed by the business at the time that the record was made. *State v. Damon*, 214 Conn. 146, 157, 570 A.2d 700, *cert. denied*, U.S., 111 S.Ct. 65, 112 L.Ed.2d 40 (1990).

Albert Landino, an employee of Greiner who was involved in the preparation of the analysis of the first delay claim, testified that the analysis was prepared pursuant to Greiner's duties as project manager. The trial court, however, relied solely on the testimony of Robinson in admitting the exhibit.

The plaintiff sought to introduce Greiner's report into evidence in order to show Greiner's analysis of its delay claim and for use during the testimony of the director of the NHPA and of Albert Landino, an employee of Greiner. The defendant objected to the admission of this exhibit on the grounds that: (1) there was insufficient testimony to support the conclusion that the three requirements of § 52–180 were satisfied; (2) the bulk of the information in the exhibit was irrelevant to this case; (3) the exhibit included several prejudicial references to the defendant; and (4) the exhibit contained opinion and analysis not subject to cross–examination and therefore it was not properly admissible under the business records exception.

The Greiner report states that the plaintiff's claim that it was delayed in starting "is justified," but it assigned a value of $7500 to the delay claim, which was significantly less than the $33,200 of delay damages claimed by the plaintiff.

With respect to the defendant's first ground for objection, we note that there was no testimony as to whether it was the regular course of business to make such a record or whether the record was made at or near the time of the act described in the report. A brief examination of the document indicates that the latter requirement was satisfied by notations in the document itself, but we find nothing in the testimony of Robinson to indicate that it was in the regular course of business of the NHPA to prepare such a record. Although § 52–180 is to be liberally construed, we cannot allow any of the three statutory requirements for the admission of business records to be ignored completely. *McCahill v. Town & Country Associates, Ltd.*, 185 Conn. 37, 40, 440 A.2d 801 (1981); *Weller v. Fish Transport Co.*, 123 Conn. 49, 60, 192 A. 317 (1937); cf. *Emhart Industries, Inc. v. Amalgamated Local Union 376, U.A.W., supra*, 388–89 (inability of witness to testify to the exact time a record was made did not render the record inadmissible because the witness stated that the report was completed at or near the time of the incident). We, therefore, conclude that the trial court improperly admitted exhibit OO as a business record. Because that report includes a statement that the plaintiff's delay claim "is justified," we cannot conclude that its admission constituted harmless error and therefore a new trial is necessary.

We note, however, that the record does not indicate that the trial court conducted an examination of the exhibit prior to admitting it. It is possible that on retrial the plaintiff may be able to provide sufficient testimony to demonstrate that exhibit OO satisfies the requirements set forth in § 52–180. We shall therefore address the other issues raised by the defendant concerning this exhibit because they are likely to arise again during the retrial.

* * * * *

Exhibit RR

Exhibit RR is a copy of a letter dated November 12, 1986, that was sent to the director of the NHPA by Greiner. The letter indicates that Greiner reviewed the delay claim submitted by the defendant dated June 17, 1976, and recommended an allowable compensation of $587,870 out of the total claim of $3,091,923. The letter states that the claim is "grossly exaggerated" and "flawed on several important counts." The only reference in the letter to the plaintiff states that the claim for the plaintiff contains $123,067 in charges that were not related to the delay claim. Robinson testified that the document was included in the NHPA's files and that it would have been received in the ordinary course of business. The defendant objected on the grounds that it was irrelevant and that it had not been qualified as a business record under § 52–180.

Exhibit RR relates to an earlier version of the first delay claim. The delay claim was submitted by the defendant on December 10, 1986, which was summarized and analyzed in exhibit OO, replaced the claim dated June 17, 1986.

Exhibit RR, like exhibit OO, notes that the delay claim for the plaintiff's work includes charges unrelated to the delay. The charges were for unpaid billings ($72,063), lost profits ($29,672) and damage to the catenary wires ($21,332).

On retrial, the trial court should reconsider whether exhibit RR satisfies the requirements of § 52–180. Robinson testified that the document would have been received in the ordinary course of business, not that it would have been made in the ordinary course of business. The presumption that a business record is reliable is based in large part on the entrant having a business duty to report. *D"Amato v. Johnson, supra,* 59–60; *C. Tait & J. LaPlanta, supra,* § 11.14.5; *see State v. Paulette,* 158 Conn. 22, 255 A.2d 855 (1969). The mere fact that the NHPA received this letter in the ordinary course of business and included the document in its files tells us nothing about the motivation of the maker of the record, and therefore would not ordinarily satisfy the requirements of § 52–180. *White Industries v. Cessna Air-*

craft Co., 611 F.Sup. 1049, 1059 (W.D.Mo. 1985); *Orzechowski v. Higgins,* 146 Conn. 463, 152 A.2d 510 (1959).

In light of Robinson's testimony concerning exhibit OO, it seems like that on retrial he would be able to testify that exhibit RR was prepared in the ordinary course of business pursuant to Greiner's duties as project manager for the NHPA. We emphasize, however, that the mere receipt of documents in the ordinary course of business, in the absence of any duty owed by the entrant to the business to prepare the record, would not ordinarily establish such documents as business records.

We also note that, in light of some of the statements made in exhibit RR concerning the defendant's delay claim, the trial court should consider whether the probative value of this document is outweighed by its prejudicial effect. *See State v. Higgins,* 201 Conn. 462, 469, 518 A.2d 631 (1986).

* * * * *

Kevin ROGERS v. CHICAGO PARK DISTRICT et al.

89 F.R.D. 716

United States District Court
April 22, 1981

The primary issue raised in plaintiff's motion for an order that certain facts be taken as established is what sanction should be imposed for the defendant's failure to produce documents pursuant to a discovery request and subsequent court order.

On December 19, 1979, shortly after his suit was filed, the plaintiff served upon the defendant a request to produce. On February 13, August 18 and September 18, 1980, the plaintiff's attorneys went to the defendant's offices to inspect and copy documents specified in the request. They were particularly interested in patronage or sponsorship letters recommending the hiring of certain employment applicants or recommending certain

employees for promotion and so forth. Although the attorneys were told that all such
letters were kept in the General Supervisor's
office, they were never given the opportunity
to inspect or copy the letters.

When the plaintiff had not received copies of
any patronage or sponsorship letters pursuant to his request by September, he moved
for an order compelling production of the
documents. The motion was granted on
September 4.

On September 18, the defendant's counsel informed the plaintiff that all patronage letters had
been destroyed. The plaintiff, to confirm this
information, took second depositions of Horace
Lindsey and Ann Herman, two of the defendant's employees. In her deposition, Ms. Herman stated that, since 1980, the park district had
refused to accept patronage letters. (Tr. 7) Prior
to 1980, Ms. Herman testified that she accepted
and kept such letters for five or six months, but
eventually destroyed them. (Tr. 8–9) She explained that she, personally, burned the letters in
the boiler in the park district office's basement.
(Tr. 12) When asked when she last destroyed
letters, Ms. Herman replied that it was "around
the first of the year." (Tr. 10) Although this was
well after this action was instituted and a request
to produce had been filed and served, she denied
that she knew the letters were important and
relevant to unfair employment practices suites,
or that she had been told by anyone to retain the
letters. (Tr. 10, 13)

Shortly thereafter, the plaintiff filed a motion
for default judgment or, in the alternative, for
an order that certain facts be taken as established. We granted this motion insofar as the
plaintiff sought to have certain facts deemed
established, and asked the parties to prepare
an order setting out the facts to be deemed
established.

Although the parties apparently tried to reach
an agreement on the order, they failed to do
so. The plaintiff now argues that the following facts should be ordered established:

1. Defendant Chicago Park District established and administered a patronage system

within the Park District during the course of
plaintiff's employment.

2. That patronage system played a dominant
or significant role in the Park District's employment decisions.

3. Upon his promotion by the defendant to
the position of natatorium instructor on or
about September 30, 1972, plaintiff tendered
a patronage or sponsorship letter from Neal
Hartigan, a ward committeeman.

4. Defendant is aware of the plaintiff's
aforesaid sponsorship by Neal Hartigan.

5. Thereafter, plaintiff moved from Mr. Hartigan's ward.

6. Defendant is aware of the aforesaid move
by the plaintiff out of Mr. Hartigan's ward.

7. Defendant treated plaintiff differently in
his employment once he no longer enjoyed
the benefits of Mr. Hartigan's political sponsorship.

The defendant apparently believes that the
sanctions which the plaintiff seeks are
harsher than warranted.

We agree with the defendant that the plaintiff's proposed order is in some respects a
harsher sanction than warranted in this case.
The proper sanction under Rule 37(b) for a
party's failure to obey a court order regarding
discovery should be no more severe than
necessary to prevent prejudice to the other
party. *Wilson v. Volkswagen of America, Inc.*,
561 F.2d 494, 504 (4th Cir. 1977). Thus, the
extent to which one party's failure to produce
documents impairs the other party's ability
to prosecute or defend should be the focus of
any attempt to frame sanctions under this
rule. *Id.* at 516.

It is clear that the plaintiff in this case has been
seriously prejudiced by the defendant's destruction of all patronage and sponsorship letters, since there is no other record of which or
how many employees had patronage letters. As
a result, the plaintiff will have difficulty proving that the park district made hiring, retention,

and promotion decisions based on such letters. Nevertheless, some of the facts that plaintiff asks us to deem established are facts which, even if he had the patronage letters, he might not be able to prove.

For example, the plaintiff asks us to deem established the fact that the park district "established and administered a patronage system during the course of Plaintiff's subject employment." Although it certainly will be harder for plaintiff to prove that the park district adhered to a patronage system without the patronage letters, it won't be impossible. He may be able to establish the existence of such a system via the testimony of park district employees and administrators. Moreover, even with the patronage letters, the plaintiff might not be able to prove the existence of such a system; that the park district had patronage letters in its files, at best, is only circumstantial evidence that the park district used the letters in making employment decisions. On the other hand, the fact that the defendant had patronage letters in its files and destroyed them after this action was instituted strongly suggests that they were significant evidence with respect to whether or not it adhered to a patronage system. It does not, however, justify deeming that fact to be established.

For similar reasons, we will deny the plaintiff's request that proposed facts 3 and 4 be deemed established. At the time we granted the plaintiff's motion for sanctions, we recommended that he depose his former sponsor, Mr. Hartigan. According to the docket sheet, the plaintiff took our advice. Through the information he obtained from Mr. Hartigan and through his own testimony, the plaintiff should be able to establish that he tendered a patronage letter from Mr. Hartigan to the park district shortly before his promotion, and that the park district was aware of Mr. Hartigan's sponsorship of the plaintiff. Consequently, since the plaintiff's ability to establish these two allegations is not seriously impaired by the defendant's destruction of patronage letters, there is insufficient reason to deem these facts established, although again the fact of destruction is relevant and defendant certainly is foreclosed from denying that a patronage letter from Mr. Hartigan was in plaintiff's file.

We also deny plaintiff's request that we deem proposed facts 5, 6 and 7 established. The patronage letters, even if the defendant had produced them, would be irrelevant to whether the plaintiff moved from Mr. Hartigan's ward after his promotion, whether the park district was aware of his move, and whether the plaintiff was treated differently after he lost Mr. Hartigan's sponsorship. These allegations could be established only through the plaintiff's own testimony and through that of park district employees and administrators. Thus, the destruction of the park district's patronage letters has not prejudiced the plaintiff insofar as proof of these allegations is concerned.

Proposed fact 2, in contrast, presents a closer question. The plaintiff requests that we deem established that the "patronage system played a dominant or significant role in the Park District's employment decisions." Using the sponsorship letters in the park district's files, the plaintiff could have compared the employment histories of park district employees, if any, who did not have sponsorship letters to establish that patronage letters significantly influenced the park district's employment decisions or whether the identities of the sponsors were significant. In the absence of sponsorship letters or a list of persons who sent or had such letters, however, it undoubtedly will be difficult for the plaintiff to establish this allegation.

Consequently, we will deem established (1) that the park district accepted sponsorship or patronage letters from prospective and current employees, (2) that these letters were retained as part of employees' files for an indefinite period of time, (3) that these letters were intentionally destroyed shortly after the present lawsuit was filed, and (4) that patronage played a significant role in the park district's employment decisions.

An order prohibiting the defendant from using at trial the absence of patronage letters in a park district employee's file — including the plaintiff's file — as evidence that such letters played no part in employment decisions will also be entered.

One other issue which was raised in the plaintiff's original motion for sanctions and which has not yet been addressed is whether we should order the defendant to reimburse the plaintiff for the additional costs he incurred as a result of its destruction of the sponsorship letters. We believe that we should assess costs against the park district, particularly those costs that the plaintiff incurred in searching for the letters after they had been destroyed. The plaintiff apparently was put to significant expense trying to locate these documents, seeking an order to compel production, deposing for a second time two park district employees in order to find out what happened to the letters, and bringing this motion for sanctions. These expenses would not have been incurred had the park district told the plaintiff a year ago that these documents had been destroyed. Since the defendant knew about the destruction a year ago, its waiting until September 20, 1980, to tell the plaintiff about it is inexcusable. There is considerable support, as the plaintiff contends, for awarding costs in a situation like the present one. *See, e.g., Bell v. Automobile Club of Michigan*, 80 F.R.D. 228, 235 (E.D.Mich.1978). In fact, F.R.Civ.P. 37(b) provides that a court "*shall* require the party failing to obey the order . . . to pay the reasonable expenses, including attorney's fees, caused by the failure, unless the court finds that the failure was substantially justified or that other circumstances make an award of expenses unjust" (emphasis added). The circumstances surrounding the destruction of the letters and the silence regarding the destruction indicate that the failure to obey the order in this case was not substantially justified.

If plaintiff will tender evidence as to the additional expenses and fees he incurred as a result of the defendant's actions, giving defendant an opportunity to review and object to the same, we will enter an appropriate order. Meanwhile, an order consistent with the foregoing as to facts deemed established and prohibiting defendant from using at trial the absence of a patronage letter in its file will enter.

Gladys E. ROGERS and Margaret A. Rogers, as Co–Executrices of the Estate of Dilworth T. Rogers v. EXXON RESEARCH AND ENGINEERING COMPANY, a Delaware Corporation

550 F.2d 834

United States Court of Appeals, Third Circuit
January 20, 1977

Although involuntary retirement after lengthy service may be a traumatic experience for an employee, statutory silence circumscribes the relief that can be obtained. We conclude that an Age Discrimination in Employment Act suit may be a proper subject for a jury trial but that there can be no monetary damages for "pain and suffering" in the nature of emotional distress. Accordingly, we vacate a district court's judgment which incorporates a substantial award for such damages.

Dr. Dilworth T. Rogers worked for the Exxon Corporation from 1938, except for a one year absence, until his involuntary retirement on September 1, 1969. He contended that his separation from the company was the result of age discrimination and brought suit under the Age Discrimination in Employment Act of 1967. (ADEA), 29 U.S.C. § § 621 *et seq*. Dr. Rogers died on March 29, 1973 and his executrices were substituted as plaintiffs. A jury awarded the plaintiffs $750,000 for pain and suffering as well as $30,000 in compensatory damages. The latter amount was doubled by the court because the defendant's conduct had been willful. After plaintiffs accepted a remittitur of $550,000 on the pain and suffering verdict, defendant's post–trial motions were denied, and judgment was entered in favor of plaintiffs.

Dr. Rogers was a research scientist who had done extensive post–graduate work in chemistry and had earned a doctorate in that field. Active in professional societies, he was credited with fifty–one patents and, during his service with Exxon, was designated as its first Senior Research Associate. In his early years with the company, promotions and salary increases came fairly frequently but, beginning in 1959, when Dr. Rogers became 50 years of age, his relations with the company began to deteriorate. The plaintiffs asserted that the reversal of his fortunes was the result of Exxon's policy of age discrimination which included a policy of harassment designed to make him leave the company. The defendant, however, contended that Dr. Rogers became frustrated and dissatisfied because he could not climb the administrative ladder of the company.

Dr. Rogers, unhappy with his job assignments, the technical facilities designated for his use, and the failure to receive periodic salary increases, found his relationships with superiors and co–workers becoming strained. The tensions of his employment were accompanied by emotional problems which in turn were reflected in his physical health.

On March 7, 1969, after a disagreement with a superior over his work, Dr. Rogers left his employment in an emotional turmoil, taking an extended sick leave. In the ensuing months, he suffered a number of physical ailments and a condition diagnosed in part as a situational neurosis. During this period, Dr. Rogers' attending physician and the company medical director exchanged information, the nature of which was disputed at the trial. On August 1, 1969, the company wrote to Dr. Rogers that he would be retired for medical reasons. Despite his protests, the retirement became effective September 1, 1969, and he received benefits thereafter in accordance with the company retirement plan. At trial, the defense contended that the sole reason for his retirement was medical disability.

Plaintiffs claimed damages for earnings lost because of the company's failure to grant salary increases before 1969, in addition to the differential between the pension payments and what would have been received had Dr. Rogers continued in active service. Further, claims were made for the emotional and physical problems caused by Dr. Rogers' involuntary retirement, as well as the onerous treatment he had received before that time. The trial court rules that the plaintiffs were entitled to a jury trial and the ADEA permitted a recovery of damages for pain and suffering.

After the jury in the bifurcated trial found liability against the defendant, the parties stipulated that compensatory damages were $30,000. Following the verdict on damages, the parties agreed to submit the question of willfulness to the judge rather than the jury. The district judge determined the actions of the defendant to have been willful and doubled the compensatory damages to $60,000 as permitted by the statute, 29 U.S.C. § 626(b). However, he held the doubling provision inapplicable to the pain and suffering award.

* * * * *

One matter of evidence does deserve discussion: the destruction of diaries which Dr. Rogers prepared. Defendant contended that Dr. Rogers' emotional problems centered on his inability to get along with fellow–employees, and a number of its witnesses testified to this point. The diaries for the period from 1955 to 1969 related personal difficulties with other Exxon employees as well as details of inventions. Dr. Rogers destroyed the diaries after commencing this litigation and after showing them to the attorney he had originally retained [not present counsel]. To justify adverse comment on the incident, the defense offered to read relevant portions of Dr. Rogers' discovery deposition describing the contents of the diaries and his reasons for destroying them. The trial judge refused to admit this evidence on the rationale that the destruction could have been due to many reasons unrelated to the lawsuit and, moreover, defendant had produced other testimony on Dr. Rogers' interpersonal relationships. We believe the proffered testimony should have been received in evidence. Under the circumstances, the destruction of the records could reasonably raise an unfavorable inference. *See Stoumen v. Commissioner of Internal Revenue* 208 F.2d 903, 907 (3rd Cir. 1953). The reasons for the action are more properly matters for argument to the jury rather than grounds for exclusion. If the jury accepted the inference, it would corroborate the defendant's witnesses on an important part of the case.

* * * * *

RUSSO et al., d.b.a. Par–Oak Confectionery v. DONAHUE, Tax Commr.

226 N.E.2d 747

Supreme Court of Ohio
May 24, 1967

This appeal by the Tax Commissioner from a portion of a decision of the Board of Tax Appeals, modifying and reducing the basic sales tax assessed against appellee by a final order of the Tax Commissioner, is before this court under the direct appeal provisions of Section 5717.04, Revised Code.

The vendors in this instance operate a combined confectionery and beer and wine carry–out store and did not maintain the records required to be kept by § 5739.11, Revised Code, i.e., they kept no records of the sales of taxable property and no records of the tax collected thereon.

The business was audited and the Tax Commissioner, on August 23, 1965, issued a final order of assessment in the amount of $1,005.38. This amount was subject to the 15% penalty prescribed by statute, but 5% of the penalty was conditionally remitted.

The record disclosed that the vendors' records consisted only of invoices of purchases and gross receipts.

The Tax Commissioner arrived at the assessment by making a detailed listing of the taxable merchandise shown by invoices for the months of May and June 1964. Selling prices of all listed items were furnished by the vendors and the percentage of markup was computed. The cost of all taxable merchandise purchased during the audit period was multiplied by this percentage figure to obtain the dollar amount of the gross taxable sales. Taxable sales were then computed to be 27.4% of gross sales.

* * * * *

"It appears to be the general rule, *and common sense would dictate,* that if a taxpayer fails to keep proper records, or for some other reason exact information is unavailable, some formula must be devised to determine the tax established by legislative authority. *Vale v. Du Pont,* 37 Del. 254, 182 A. 668, 103 A.L.R. 946; *W.T. Grant Co. v. Joseph,* 2 N.Y.2d 196, 159 N.E.S.2d 150, 140 N.E.2d; *Mason and Dixon Lines v. Commonwealth,* 185 Va. 877, 41 S.E.2d 16; *Gasper v. Commissioner of Internal Revenue,* 6 Cir., 225 F.2d 284."

* * * * *

§ 5739.13, Revised Code, imposes a duty upon the vendor both to collect and remit to the state the bracket tax imposed by § 5739.02, Revised Code, and makes him subject to assessment and personally liable in the event he fails in either respect. § 5739.11, Revised Code, imposes upon the vendor the duty to maintain records. The vendor has the burden of providing such records or of being assessed on the basis of test checks or of any other information in the possession of the Tax Commissioner. In the absence of a clear prohibition in any part of the statute against the use of such information as the Tax Commissioner may have in his possession as a result of test checks of representative periods of a particular vendor's business, we see no reason why such test–check information may not be used by the Tax Commissioner alone or together with other information as the basis of an assessment.

* * * * *

S.C. JOHNSON & SON, INC. v. LOUISVILLE & NASHVILLE RAILROAD COMPANY

695 F.2d 253

United States Court of Appeals, Seventh Circuit
November 29, 1982

In a period of our industrial history when one sometimes finds consumer goods failing to be of the quality expected, it is refreshing to find a manufacturer being insistent upon its products not going into the stream of commerce unless those products meet its own high quality standards. Such an insistence can, of course, be directly reflected in an increase in manufacturing costs. The present case demonstrates that a hidden cost may also occur as a result of taking steps to pull defective products from the flow of commerce even though the diminished quality has come about without fault on the part of the manufacturer.

Seeking damages in such a situation, S.C. Johnson & Son (Johnson) brought suit under the Carmack Amendment, 49 U.S.C. § 20(11) (recodified at 49 U.S.C. § 11707), against a rail carrier for damage incurred when the carrier delivered a shipment of Johnson products some of which appeared to be frozen. The district court tried the case without a jury and held that Johnson failed to prove the amount of damages with the requisite certainty. The court accordingly entered judgment for the defendant. Johnson now challenges this finding on two grounds: the court erred in discrediting the testimony of Johnson's main witness and in rejecting the sampling method employed by Johnson to determined the extent of the damage.

I. Facts.

Johnson manufactures a large number of household products in its plant in Racine, Wisconsin. In January 1977, Johnson shipped by the Chicago, Milwaukee, St. Paul & Pacific Railroad Company (Milwaukee Road) and the Louisville and Nashville Railroad Company (L&N) various products to a customer of Johnson, Houchen Industries, in Bowling Green, Kentucky. Johnson employees loaded the cases onto the floor of the insulated rail car. To preheat the car, the employees had previously placed the car in a heated warehouse. When loaded into the car the lading was three to four feet high. No heater was placed in the car, some of the products being of a volatile nature.

The Milwaukee Road pulled the sealed car from Johnson's warehouse on January 10, 1977. The L&N delivered the car to Houchen's rail dock on January 25. It is not clear why this 400 mile trip took 15 days to

complete. Earl Felts, receiving foreman for Houchens, broke the seals and inspected approximately 20 cases of various products from the sides, top, and each end of the car. Felts found the contents of these cases appeared to be frozen. He later could not remember which products he had examined.

Houchens notified Johnson that the shipment had arrived with frozen contents. Johnson directed Houchens to return the car to Racine. This request was in accordance with Johnson's policy of conducting all quality control tests through its own quality control department in Racine. Johnson believed that a customer such as Houchens, which operates a chain of grocery stores, was not qualified to determine if Johnson products had been damaged. Houchens complied and released the resealed car to the L&N on January 26. The Milwaukee Road returned the car to Racine on February 21. Johnson employees unloaded the car and stacked the cases on pallets in the warehouse.

Fred Manske, Technical Specialist in Johnson's quality control department, was responsible for determining the extent of the loss. Manske first segregated those products not susceptible to damage from freezing and returned them to stock. Over 2,000 cases remained to be tested. Manske did not know where the cases had been located in the car. He recognized, however, that products near the perimeter of the car would freeze faster than those in the center, so he chose cases from each pallet in an attempt to obtain a representative sample from every location in the car. He followed the sampling method set forth in Military Standard 105–D in choosing the number of cases to inspect.

The tests conducted by Manske were simple. He tested Glade Solid, a gel–based air freshener, by checking for any free water that would leak from the gel during freezing. Glo–Coat, a floor polish, was tested by inspection for lumps or grain in the liquid. Aerosol products were tested by measuring the free water produced when the contents of the cans was sprayed. He found that all of the Glade Solid, Glo–Coat, Klear, Step Saver, Pledge Liquid, Pledge Aerosol, Favor and

Jubilee had been damaged and ordered them scrapped. He also tested several products that were susceptible to freezing damage in theory, but which had never exhibited any actual damage in Manske's experience. None of these products were damaged. All of the testing was conducted in late March.

Manske took notes regarding the condition of each product as he performed the tests. Based upon these notes he prepared a memorandum for the salvage department, which was typed by his secretary. After reviewing the memorandum Manske disposed of the handwritten notes. He testified that he had not preserved the notes because they were illegible to anyone but himself and because all of the necessary information was contained in the memorandum.

* * * * *

IV. Proof of Damages.

A. Negative Inferences from Destruction of Manske's Notes

The success of Johnson's case rests upon its ability to prove the amount of damages at Bowling Green. The first issue in this respect is whether the trial court erred in inferring that the contents of Manske's notes would reveal that he had not sampled the products properly. The court based this inference upon the maximum *omnia praesumunteur contra spoliatorem*, application of which involves a two step process. First, the court must be of the opinion from the fact that a party has destroyed evidence that the party did so in bad faith. Only then may the court infer from this state of mind that the contents of the evidence would be unfavorable to that party if introduced in court. The crucial element is not that the evidence was destroyed but rather the reason for the destruction. This has been recognized by most courts that have addressed the issue. The First Circuit stated the general rule:

It is elementary that if a party has evidence . . . in its control and fails to produce it, an inference may be warranted that the document would have been unfa-

vorable. However . . . it must appear that the party has some reason to suppose that non–production would justify the inference . . . the totality of the circumstances must bring home to the non–producing party notice that the inference may be drawn.

Commercial Insurance Co. of Newark v. Gonzalez, 512 F.2d 1307, 1314 (1st Cir.1975), *cert. denied*, 423 U.S. 838, 96 S.Ct. 65, 46 L.Ed.57 (emphasis added). *See also Vick v. Texas Employment Commission*, 514 F.2d 734 (5th Cir.1975); *Smith v. Uniroyal*, 420 F.2d 438 (7th Cir.1970); *INA Aviation Corp. v. United States*, 468 F.Supp. 695 (E.D.N.Y. 1979), *aff'd mem.*, 610 F.2d 806 (2nd Cir.).

We do not think that the facts surrounding Manske's destruction of his notes support an inference of bad faith. Manske prepared the notes in the course of determining which products should be scrapped by the salvage department. The information in the notes was typed in the form of a memorandum. At that time Manske would have had no reason to alter or omit necessary information. It is not clear to us that the notes contained any information that did not also appear in the final memorandum. Manske testified that: "I made handwritten notes on my findings, the actual condition of the product, whether there was or was not damage." There is no indication that Manske went beyond this and made notes regarding the sample size or tests performed. The salvage department was only interested in knowing which products should be saved. Under these circumstances we find that there was no basis for rejecting Manske's explanation for the destruction of his notes. We reject any inference that Manske did not perform the tests or follow the sampling method set forth in Military Standard 105–D. Our reading of the record indicates that this was the sole reason for discrediting Manske's testimony. Of course, had the court found that Manske was an incredible witness for other reasons, such as his demeanor, we would respect that finding. This was not the case, however, so we will proceed on the assumption that Manske testified truthfully.

* * * * *

Tony SCHROEDL and Catherine Schroedl v. Leo V. McTAGUE and Frances McTague

129 N.W.2d 19

Supreme Court of Iowa
June 9, 1964

* * * * *

II. Next we come to the question of the letters, which the plaintiffs testified they had received through the years and which they had destroyed. They offered secondary evidence, some of which was received and some excluded upon objection. The tenor of the evidence received was that some twenty letters had been sent them by the defendant Leo V. McTague, in each of which he acknowledged the indebtedness. The contents of one letter in particular, which plaintiffs said was received in 1956, were testified to that the writer said "he absolutely could not pay anything on the note at that time and the interest at that time." Both plaintiffs testified to this. When asked as to the substance of other letters received, as to which they could not quote the contents verbatim, an objection that the question called for a conclusion was sustained; an obviously erroneous ruling. No offer of proof was made, and the defendants rely upon this to uphold the refusal. Whether this was a situation in which the answer was so obvious that no offer was necessary we do not decide, in view of a re–trial required because of other errors.

The substantial question at this point concerns the contention of the defendants that secondary evidence of the contents of the letters was not admissible because the plaintiffs had destroyed them and so took it out of the power of the defendants to show what the contents really were. Each plaintiff testified that the letters were received over a period of years, at least from 1956 to 1961. We have pointed out there was a close family relationship. The evidence of the plaintiffs is that the families visited often, went to conventions together, and generally were on excellent terms, until the friendship was terminated by the not uncommon method of one friend

loaning the other money. They said they did not ordinarily keep letters about their home, and although they had searched every possible place they could not find them. They had been destroyed.

The general rule is thus stated in 20 Am.Jur., Evidence, section 438, page 391: "A party to a trial is not precluded from introducing secondary evidence of the contents of a destroyed instrument although he himself destroyed the instrument deliberately and voluntarily, if, at the time he did so, he acted under an erroneous impression as to the effect of his act or under other circumstances which render his act free from all suspicion of intentional fraud." To the same effect is 32 C.J.S. Evidence § 824, page 752.

The rule has been applied in several cases from other jurisdictions. *In re Bakers' Estate*, 144 Neb. 797, 14 N.W.2d 585, 591, 155 A.L.R. 950, is this language: "* * * and even if their destruction is voluntary, secondary evidence of their contents may be given if the circumstances accompanying the act are free from suspicion of intent to defraud and consistent with an honest purpose." See also *Booher v. Brown*, 173 Or. 464, 146 P.2d 71, 75, where in an equity case the court, although stating the rule, weighed the evidence and found it against admission; *Crosby v. Little River Sand & Gravel Development*, 212 La. 1, 31 So.2d 226, 229; and *Reynolds v. Denver & Rio Grande Western Railroad Company*, C.C.A. 10th Cir., 174 F.2d 673, 676.

There seems no good reason for holding here, as a matter of law, that the destruction of the letters by the plaintiffs was so tainted with fraud that secondary evidence of the contents should be excluded. The parties were on intimate terms; no litigation was foreseen, so far as the record shows; in fact the interest was unpaid for five years before this suit was commenced; Tony Schroedl believed, in fact had been advised by a Nebraska attorney, that the payment of interest, which was through 1955, stopped the running of the statute; and both plaintiffs testified to the reason for destroying the letters, which was, according to them, nothing more than that they had no system for keeping correspondence and did not usually keep it. At all times in our consideration of this case we must keep in mind the settled rule that when a verdict has been directed against a plaintiff, his evidence must be given the most favorable construction it will reasonably bear. There was a jury question as to the contents of the letters and the good faith of the plaintiffs in destroying them. In fact, the learned trial court seemed to recognize this when, in directing the jury to return the verdict, it said: "I would be placing before this jury a terrific job to decide who was telling the truth." We suggest that such a burden is a normal part of a jury's function.

We come next to a determination whether secondary evidence may be received under any circumstances to show the contents of writings claimed to have admitted an indebtedness so as to bar the defense of the statute. It is said the admission of such evidence opens the door to fraud. The same claim may be made against any secondary evidence of the contents of lost or destroyed writings. Such evidence is usually material and important to the issues in the various cases in which it is employed. So secondary evidence of what was claimed to be written recognition of an illegitimate son was held admissible in *Watson v. Richardson*, 110 Iowa 673, 677, 80 N.W. 407, 409. *In re McCullum's Estate*, Fla., 88 So.2d 537, 539, holds: "* * * the fact of written acknowledgment of paternity may be established by secondary evidence under the general rules relating to the admissibility of secondary evidence or lost or destroyed writings."

It seems to follow that, if secondary evidence of a writing which would establish the important rights of an illegitimate son to a share in the property of the putative father is admissible, such evidence of lost or destroyed letters which admit an indebtedness so as to toll the statute or revive a cause of action should likewise be admitted. In fact, we have ourselves considered it to be so, without question. In *Craig v. Welch*, 231 Iowa 1009, 1014, 2 N.W.2d 745, 747, an action to foreclose a real estate mortgage, the statute was pleaded as a bar. An attempt was made to show that a written instrument admitting the debt was lost, and evidence was offered as to its contents. The action being in equity, we said: "It is the settled rule that the former existence, execution, delivery, loss and contents of a lost instrument must be shown by clear, satisfactory and convincing evidence in order to establish the same. * * * " In a law action, of course, the required proof would be by a preponderance of the evidence.

In *Barton v. Boland*, supra, there was again a claim of a lost instrument, the contents of which were in dispute. The action being in equity, we weighed the conflicting testimony and followed the findings of the trial court as to the facts. Loc. cit. 224 Iowa 1217, 1219, 279 N.W. 89. In neither of these cases was there any suggestion that secondary evidence of the contents of lost writings could not be received to show an admission of indebtedness within the purview of § 614.11. It was accepted, as we think it should be, that such evidence is admissible; it was considered, and weighed, and found wanting; not because it was inadmissible, but because it lacked sufficient probative value.

The infirmity of possible fraud exists in all cases where secondary evidence of lost writings is admitted. The writings themselves would be far preferable in ascertaining the true facts. But when they are lost or destroyed, the law does the best it can subject to the rules set out in our foregoing discussion. Most oral testimony is subject to the same objection, whether it concerns lost instruments, or other matters which admit of factual disputes. There is always the possibility that a case may be made by someone bearing false witness. But lost wills, and deeds, and other instruments of the greatest importance may be proven by parol testimony; if the proper foundation is laid. There is no reason for making an exception to secondary evidence of lost writings claimed to be admissions of the existence of a debt. The human infirmities of lack of knowledge, or understanding, or recollection, or, unfortunately at times, of character and integrity, will usually deprive oral testimony of that certainty desirable in all cases and generally found in written documents. The trier of facts must decide.

It should be noted that there is no evidence that the defendant Frances McTague signed any of the letters which plaintiffs claim to have received. So if the same situation exists on a retrial, the evidence of the lost writings should be limited to its applicability to Leo V. McTague; and the jury should be so instructed.

* * * * *

Mark SHATZKAMER and Gail Shatzkamer v. Sidney ESKIND, Claire Schwartz and the City of New York

528 N.Y.S. 968

Civil Court of the City of New York, Kings County, Special Term, Part I
April 29,1988

The issue in these two motions, relating to different cases, initially concerns whether the defendant City of New York conducted proper searches for prior notices of defect pursuant to this Court's orders of January 14, 1987. The adequacy of the search in each case turns in part on whether the defendant City is obligated to index notices of claim and/or notices of defect by location under the applicable statutes and cases.

The importance of this aspect of pre–trial discovery results from the crucial burden placed upon a plaintiff under the "Pot Hole Law". The "Pot Hole Law", as § 7–201 subd (c) of the Administrative Code of the City of New York is popularly known, requires prior notice of defect as a condition precedent to a successful action against the City of New York for damages sustained on its roadways or sidewalks.

In the first case, *Shatzkamer v. City of New York*, the plaintiffs' attorney served a Notice of Discovery and Inspection on the defendant City in May 1986, requesting inspection of any notices of defect, notices of claim, work permits, accident or inspection reports, repair reports and other items relating to the location of the accident. Thereafter plaintiffs moved to strike the answer of the defendant

City for failure to comply with such Notice. On January 14, 1987, this Court conditionally granted the motion to the extent that the sanction of preclusion was to be implemented, unless disclosure in compliance with the demand, as modified by the Court, was supplied.

Thereafter the defendant sent a letter to plaintiffs' attorney in April 1987, stating that it had searched but had failed to find any prior notices, reports, work permits or any other items demanded, relating to the location involved, during the relevant time period. Plaintiffs then re–applied to strike the answer of the defendant City, this time for failure to comply with the Court order directing discovery. Plaintiffs argued that the defendant City was frustrating discovery by its refusal to index notices of claim by location.

On November 9, 1987, this Court issued an interim order directing the defendant City to furnish the Court and the plaintiffs with two affidavits; one setting forth essentially the manner in which the City keeps all notices of defect per Section 50–g of the General Municipal Law and the number of pages in such book for the relevant time period; the other by the individual who conducted the search per the earlier Court order as to how, when and where the search was made and how long it took. Affidavits, which purported to comply with the order, were received at the beginning of January 1988. Oral argument was made and memoranda of law were then submitted.

The pattern in the companion case *Termine v. City of New York* is almost identical. A Notice for Discovery and Inspection regarding prior notices of defect was served, followed by a motion to strike the answer of the City. The Court issued an order conditionally precluding the City, identical to that in Shatzkamer and on the same date. The City reported after a search that it had found no notices of defect prior to the date of the accident on December 15, 1981.

The plaintiffs in *Termine*, who are represented by the same attorney as the plaintiffs in *Schatzkamer*, then similarly moved to strike the answer of the defendant City for noncompliance. The motions in both cases were returnable on the same date and since that time they have proceeded together in all respects.

* * * * *

At the outset, it should be noted that it is the defendant and not the plaintiff who is required to have the actual notice, but it is the plaintiff who is required to prove knowledge which is exclusively within the ken of the defendant City.

Thus, the obligations of the plaintiff can only be fulfilled by the diligent and good faith effort of the defendant City to search its internal records. The effort of the City of New York to comply with this Court's order in each case must be measured by both the extent and the quality of its search.

Unfortunately, the defendant, by active concealment, lackadaisical effort or a refusal to intelligently compile its records, may be rewarded by its own imperfections. Article 31 CPLR, however, indisputably provides the mechanism by which a recalcitrant defendant may be compelled to engage in meaningful disclosure.

The most critical documents submitted during the course of these motions were the affidavits from the defendant City per this Court's interim orders of November 9, 1987. The affidavit in each case as to how the City maintains its records to comply with Section 50–g of the General Municipal Law and the number of pages in the record book for the relevant time period is the same. Both affidavits are given yearly page numbers for the Borough of Brooklyn. This is actually an error on the part of the City, because the accident in the *Termine* case occurred in Queens and as a result, the data given in that affidavit should have been for Queens County.

But the information given, even if just for the Borough of Brooklyn, is inadequate. According to the affidavit from a supervisor in the Comptroller's Office, it was the procedure of that office, prior to the 1987 amendment of Section 50–g, that "Upon the receipt of a notice of claim, each claim was assigned a number, and that number, together with the

claimant's name, the date of the accident, the nature of the claim *and the location of the accident* as described in the notice of claim, *were entered into this office's computer"*. *(Emphasis added)*.

From time to time the City would print out all sidewalk and roadway "defect claims" received in that year in alphabetical order, by claimant's name, for each borough. (Apparently, the term "defect claims" describes notices of claim relating to defects in the roadways and sidewalks.) The printouts were then bound in books. For the calendar year of 1980 the index book for Brooklyn had 147 pages, 80 pages for 1981, 124 pages for 1982; 104 pages for 1983, 46 pages for January 1, 1984 through April 30, 1984; 151 pages for May 1, 1984 through June 30, 1985; and 83 pages for July 1, 1985 through February 2, 1986.

It had been this Court's distinct impression from the prior papers and arguments in these motions that the City objected to making a search of prior notices of claim and other data requested by the plaintiffs because it involved a review of thousands upon thousands of claims. The Court had also been led to believe that indexing notices of claim or notices of defect by location would involve a tremendous amount of work for the City.

At no time was it mentioned by the City's attorneys that the data in question was already computerized, including information relating to location, and that it was merely a matter of further printouts of relatively small size.

It would also appear that there are very few notices of claim relating to defects in the roadways or sidewalks in any given year. At one point in the argument of these motions on January 25, 1988, the plaintiffs' attorney stated that the most pages in any one year was 151, "which means 151 notices of claim, because each would be a page." This allegation was noticeably never denied by the City's attorney at that argument.

In the second affidavit submitted by the City in each case, the individual in the Comptroller's Office who made the search of the

City record for prior notices of defect, as ordered by this Court, stated that the search of the notices of claim in the *Shatzkamer* case took 1 1/2 hours, while the search in *Termine* took 1 hour. The notice of claim index for Brooklyn was reviewed in the *Shatzkamer* search and the index for Queens in the *Termine* search.

These affidavits refer only to searches of the notices of claim filed by claimants with the City. Yet the Notice for Discovery and Inspection served by plaintiffs' attorney in each case requested not only notices of claim at the accident location but also reports and notices of defect (which include but are not limited to notices of claim). This Court, in its orders of January 14, 1987, did not modify the items demanded, only the time period of the search. Moreover, this Court, in its orders of November 9, 1987, directed the City to supply it with affidavits relating to the manner in which the City complies with Section 50–g of the General Municipal Law, which relates to recording notices of defect, not notices of claim. This Court now holds first that the search made by the City in each case was inadequate because the City, according to its own affidavits, searched only the index of notices of claim. For this reason alone, the Court must find that the City failed in each case to comply with this Court's order of January 14, 1987.

While it is not the function of this Court to tell a defendant the manner in which it is required to keep its records, nevertheless, the recordkeeping which, unintentionally or otherwise, *results* in the frustration of discovery, mandates appropriate sanctions pursuant to Section 3126 of the CPLR.

While the defendant was not required to use any particular system of indexing under Section 50–g prior to September 2, 1987, it could not and cannot choose to index notices of defect filed prior to that date in so scattered and Byzantine a fashion as to deprive those with legitimate claims against the City of the right to maintain civil actions for damages because prior notices of defect that exist cannot be found, either by the City or by the plaintiff.

It would seem that any search would be questionable as long as this defendant does not keep all such notices of defect, including but not limited to notices of claim relating to a defect in the roadway or sidewalk, received on or after June 4, 1980 and before September 2, 1987, in a separate book indexed by location, which book would be available for inspection by the general public.

Under the pot hole law it is the City which must not only keep accurate records of all prior notices of defect, but also make same accessible to its adversaries. Absent this diligence then it should not be permitted to avail itself of the benefits of such a law.

* * * * *

SHINRONE, INC., and Francis G. Bridge v. TASCO, INC.

283 NW.2d 280

Supreme Court of Iowa
September 19, 1979

In this law action, tried to the court, $206,877.22 was awarded for consequential damages in the sale of two calf confinement buildings. On defendant's appeal we affirm the trial court.

Tasco, Inc. is an Iowa company which manufacturers, distributes, and assembles livestock confinement buildings. Shinrone, Inc., owns land in Nebraska and Iowa which it farms and on which it raises cattle. As a part of its business Shinrone operates cow–calf operations, in which it raises Simmental and Maine–Anjou breeding stock, described by the trial court as "purebred, exotic animals."

As a result of prior purchases of swine confinement buildings from Tasco, Shinrone purchased calf nurseries from Tasco in 1973, one for the operation in each state. These buildings were purchased to house sick calves, orphan calves, and otherwise normal calves which were not achieving full growth potential. This intended use was made known to Tasco prior to purchase. Shinrone first began using a Tasco building at its Nebraska location. The use of the Tasco building at the Iowa farm began several weeks later, approximately May 1, 1974. By this time Shinrone had already stopped using the building at the Nebraska farm. The use of the building at the Iowa farm continued for several weeks, until temporarily suspended due to an almost 100 percent loss of calves placed in the building due to pneumonia. Tasco then sent experts to advise Shinrone on how to cure the problem. After following the experts' recommendations the building was reopened but, after several weeks, was again closed because of continuing losses.

Taking the evidence in the light most consistent with the verdict, poor ventilation in the buildings caused dampness which in turn caused calves confined there to catch pneumonia. The pneumonia resulted in the deaths of 379 calves.

* * * * *

VI. Tasco also objected to the introduction of plaintiff's exhibit 10. This was a log kept by Dr. Craig Schwartz while he served as veterinarian at Shinrone's Iowa farm. A record was kept on each calf placed in the Tasco nursery. Before leaving Shinrone's employment, in October 1975, a secretary transcribed the handwritten log. Dr. Schwartz testified that he verified this copy when it was completed. Thereafter the handwritten log was lost and Dr. Schwartz testified he was unable to locate it.

When the typed transcription was introduced as plaintiff's exhibit 10, it was objected to as hearsay and not the best evidence. Tasco argued that the exhibit, being secondary evidence, should not have been admitted at trial, citing *Schroedl v. McTague*, 256 Iowa 772, 129 N.W.2d 19 (1964). In *Schroedl*, the plaintiffs offered secondary evidence of original documents which they testified had been destroyed. Despite arguments that the secondary evidence should not have been admitted because plaintiffs had destroyed the originals, we held the evidence was admissible. We pointed out that there was nothing appearing in that record which would justify holding as a matter of law that the destruction of the original was " . . .

so tainted with fraud that secondary evidence of the contents should be excluded . . . " 256 Iowa at 779–80, 129 N.W.2d at 23–24.

In order to hold exhibit 10 inadmissible by reason of loss of the original documents, we would have to find (1) that the original log was intentionally destroyed, and (2) that the destruction was under circumstances indicating intentional fraud. There was no evidence of either in this record. Tasco's contention to the contrary is without merit.

Tasco argues that the transcript was not admissible under section 622.28, The Code 1979, which provides for the admission of business records if the judge finds they were made in the regular course of business or at or about the time of the act or event recorded and if the records' sources indicate their trustworthiness. *See, e.g., State v. Fisher*, 178 N.W.2d 380, 382 (Iowa 1970). Even if we were to distrust Dr. Schwartz's powers of comparison, the statutory allowance that a record need be made only "about the time" of its subject deserves an especially liberal application given the rather minimal possibilities of error here. The trial court did not abuse its wide discretion in applying section 622.28. *Prestype, Inc. v. Carr*, 248 N.W.2d 111, 117 (Iowa 1976).

VII. Records of Shinrone's Nebraska operation were received in evidence over Tasco's objection that their custodian lacked personal knowledge of their preparation. Foundation for admitting the records was laid through the testimony of Delbert Johnson, the Nebraska operation general manager. Preparation of these records started prior to Johnson's employment and Tasco objected that he therefore did not possess sufficient personal information for a proper foundation.

This contention was answered by *Culligan Soft Water Service v. Berglund*, 259 Iowa 660, 664–65, 145 N.W.2d 604, 607 (1966). In that case we denied a similar contention. Foundation for Culligan's office records of sale was laid through the testimony of a company officer who joined the company after the sale in question.

* * * * *

Thomas SILKE, d/b/a Potters' Pantry Caterers v. UNITED STATES of America et al.

Unpublished Opinion

United States District Court of the District of Massachusetts
February 3, 1987

Plaintiff's catering business was crippled by a fire which swept through its Lynn, Massachusetts, outlet on November 28, 1981. President Reagan declared that part of Lynn a disaster area, making it eligible for federal aid under 42 U.S.C. § 4151 (1982). With the help of Lynn city officials, plaintiff prepared a loan application to the Small Business Administration ("SBA"), a federal agency authorized to make loans to businesses affected by the Lynn fire. Plaintiff eventually received a loan of $41,700, approximately half of what he requested. Failing to obtain satisfaction from either local or federal authorities, plaintiff filed a complaint in the Court, naming a panoply of defendants and seeking damages in excess of $5,000,000.00

* * * * *

Furthermore, plaintiff has produced no evidence that the SBA determination in his case was arbitrary, capricious or an abuse of discretion, as required by the APA, 5 U.S.C. 706(2)(A) (1982). Therefore, even if this Court had authority to review the SBA decision under 15 U.S.C. § 634(b) (1982), plaintiff's failure to show the existence of a genuine dispute of material fact regarding the allegedly irregular conduct necessitates summary judgment for the defendant. *Palmer v. Weaver*, 512 F.Supp. 281 (E.D. Pa. 1982).[1]

* * * * *

_____

[1] It is the routine practice of the SBA to destroy loan application records at the end of the two years of storage. As a result, there is almost no factual record to support either plaintiff's case or today's holding. I do not applaud this practice, as it empowers the SBA to insulate itself from any form of review of its decisions. Were the case against the plaintiff not so clear, SBA's

practice could well have worked to its own detriment in this case.

SKIBS AKTIESELSKAPET ORENOR, as owner of THE Steamship MOISIE BAY, and Tankore Corporation v. THE Steamship AUDREY, her engines, boilers, etc. and Constantine G. Gratsos, her owner

181 F.Supp. 697

United States District Court E.D. Virginia, Norfolk Division
February 10, 1960.
Supplemental Opinion, March 18, 1960

At approximately 2021 (Moisie Bay bridge time) on March 24, 1957, during darkness and clear weather, with visibility good, wind moderate, and tide ebb, the Moisie Bay and Audrey collided in the vicinity of the approach to the Maryland Pilot Station off Cape Henry, Virginia. In separate proceedings consolidated for trial we have for consideration the determination of liability for damages occasioned by the impact.

* * * * *

The credible evidence supports the contentions of the privileged vessel. The testimony likewise conclusively establishes that the engine log book of the Audrey was fabricated. Manifestly, the page of the original entries for March 24, 1957, in the Audrey's rough engine log book had been removed and presumably destroyed, and in its place appeared a new page of entries on both sides. The log book consists of a number of double-page sheets, printed on both sides to form four pages, and bound in the middle with three staples. When folded from the middle, the book is complete. It is obvious that pages may be removed and replaced with little or no difficulty.

At first blush the continuity of dates before and after the collision would not disclose any irregularity without the aid of a handwriting expert. But when we examine the corresponding pages of the double page sheet it is

clear that a deliberate fraud had been perpetrated. Entries between December 6, 1956,
and December 31, 1956, are missing. On
December 6, 1956, it is noted that entries
were made for sea steaming watches from
Portland to Japan, and, on the following page
dated December 31, 1956, from Japan to
Canada. The Audrey argues that engine log
entries are only made while entering and
leaving port, and that a record is not maintained while in port except while the vessel
is maneuvering. In answer, it is said that the
routine revolution counter readings normally
recorded at the end of the sea passage when
the pilot boards, and again recorded at the
commencement of the outbound voyage
when the pilot departs, are both missing.
These entries, if made, would have appeared
on December dates in the forward part of the
sheet which, when the same sheet is continued, would include the entries of March 24,
1957, in the latter part of the book.

The fraudulent acts are buttressed by the
testimony of a handwriting expert (Hilton)
who has pointed to certain embossed impressions on the page dated March 22, 1957, and
the absence of such impressions on the page
now dated March 23, 1957, which latter page
would normally reveal the results of any
heavy writing on the opposite side of the
pages dated March 22, 1957. Nor is the Court
impressed with the suggestion that engine
movement orders may have been written on
scraps of loose paper and thereafter copied
into the log book following the collision. The
evidence presented by the Audrey points to
the fact that all entries on March 24, 1957,
were made directly into the log. When we
consider the fact that the entries for March
23–24 were made in the same handwriting
(presumably that of the third engineer) and
that the third engineer did not go on watch
until 1955 (although the entries for the 1600–
2000 watch are in the same handwriting), the
perpetrated fraud is complete.

As was so aptly said by judge Learned Hand
in *Warner Barnes & Co. v. Kokosai Kisen
Kabushiki Kaisha*, 2 Cir., 102 F.2d 450,
quoted with approval by Judge Dobie in *The
Anaconda*, 4 Cir., 164 F.2d 224, 226:

When a party is once found to be fabricating, or suppressing, documents, the natural, indeed the inevitable, conclusion is
that he has something to conceal, and is
conscious of guilt."

The authorities are legion to the effect that
intentional falsification of material records
presumptively destroys the weight of the offender's evidence as to the entire case. *Allen
v. United States*, 164 U.S. 492, 499–500, 17
S.Ct. 154, 41 L.Ed. 528; *Gung You v. Nagle*,
9 Cir., 34 F.2d 848; *The Silver Palm*, 9 Cir.,
94 F.2d 754, 762; *Broomfield v. Texas General Indemnity Co.*, 5 Cir., 201 F.2d 746, 748;
Capehorn Steamship Corp. v. Texas Co.,
D.C., 152 F.Supp. 33, 36.

While there are many inconsistencies and
discrepancies in the Audrey's testimony,
these only point significantly to a continuation of efforts to conceal the true facts. To
detail the theory of the Audrey's case would
unduly emphasize the fraud, and perhaps
lend dignity to the fraudulent scheme.

* * * * *

SOCIETE INTERNATIONALE POUR PARTICIPATIONS INDUSTRIELLES ET COMMERCIALES, S.A., etc. v. William P. ROGERS, Attorney General of the United States, and Ivy Baker Priest, Treasurer of the United States

78 S.Ct. 1087

June 16, 1958

The question before us is whether, in the
circumstances of this case, the District Court
erred in dismissing, with prejudice, a complaint in a civil action as to a plaintiff that had
failed to comply fully with a pretrial production order.

This issue comes to us in the context of an
intricate litigation. Section 5(b) of the Trading
with the Enemy Act, 40 Stat. 415, as amended,
50 U.S.C.Appendix, § 5(b), 50 U.S.C.A.Ap-
pendix § 5(b), sets forth the conditions under

which the United States during a period of war or national emergency may seize " * * * any property or interest of any foreign country or national * * *." Acting under this section, the Alien Property Custodian during World War II assumed control of assets which were found by the Custodian to be "owned by or held for the benefit of" I.G. Farbenindustrie, a German firm, valued at more than $100,000,000, consisted of cash in American banks and approximately 90% of the capital stock of General Aniline & Film Corporation, a Delaware corporation. In 1948 petitioner, a Swiss holding company also known as I.G. Chemie or Interhandel, brought suit under § 9(a) of the Trading with the Enemy Act, 40 Stat. 419, as amended, 50 U.S.C.Appendix,§ 9(a), 50 U.S.C.A.Appendix, § 9(a), against the Attorney General, as successor to the Alien Property Custodian, and the Treasurer of the United States, to recover these assets. This section authorizes recovery of seized assets by "[a]ny person not an enemy or ally of enemy" to the extent of such person's interest in the assets. Petitioner claimed that it had owned the General Aniline stock and cash at the time of vesting and hence, as the national of a neutral power, was entitled under § 9(a) to recovery.

The Government both challenged petitioner's claim of ownership and asserted that in any event petitioner was an "enemy" within the meaning of the Act since it was intimately connected with I.G. Farben and hence was affected with "enemy taint" despite its "neutral" incorporation. See *Uebersee Finanz–Korp., A.G. v. McGrath*, 343 U.S. 205, 72 S.Ct. 618, 96 L.Ed 888. More particularly, the Government alleged that from the time of its incorporation in 1928, petitioner had conspired with I.G. Farben, H. Sturzene & Cie, a Swiss banking firm, and others "[t]o conceal, camouflage, and cloak the ownership, control and domination by I.G. Farben of properties and interests located in countries, including the United States, other than Germany, in order to avoid seizure and confiscation in the event of war between such countries and Germany."

At an early stage of the litigation the Government moved under Rule 34 of the Federal Rules of Civil Procedure, 28 U.S.C.A., for an order requiring petitioner to make available for inspection and copying a large number of the banking records of Sturzenegger & Cie. Rule 34, in conjunction with Rule 26(b), provides that upon a motion "showing good cause therefor," a court may order a party to produce for inspection nonprivileged documents relevant to the subject matter of pending litigation " * * * which are in his possession, custody, or control * * *." In support of its motion the Government alleged that the records sought were relevant to showing the true ownership of the General Analine stock and that they were within petitioner's control because petitioner and Sturzenegger were substantially identical. Petitioner did not dispute the general relevancy of the Sturzenegger documents but denied that it controlled them. The District Court granted the Government's motion, holding, among other things, that petitioner's "control" over the records had been *prima facie* established.

Thereafter followed a number of motions by petitioner to be relieved of production on the grounds that disclosure of the required bank records would violate Swiss penal laws and consequently might lead to imposition of criminal sanctions, including fine and imprisonment, on those responsible for disclosure. The Government in turn moved under Rule 37(b)(2) of the Federal Rules of Civil Procedure to dismiss the complaint because of petitioner's noncompliance with the production order. During this period the Swiss Federal Attorney, deeming that disclosure of these records in accordance with the production order would constitute a violation of Article 273 of the Swiss Penal Code, prohibiting economic espionage, and Article 47 of the Swiss Bank Law, relating to secrecy of banking records, "confiscated" the Sturzenegger records. This "confiscation" left possession of the records in Sturzenegger and amounted to an interdiction on Sturzenegger's transmission of records to third persons. The upshot of all this was that the District Court, before finally ruling on petitioner's motion for relief from the production order and on the complaint, referred the matter to a Special Master for findings as to the nature of the Swiss laws claimed by petitioner to block production and as to petitioner's good faith in seeking to achieve compliance with the court's order.

The Report of the Master bears importantly on our disposition of this case. It concluded that the Swiss Government had acted in accordance with its own established doctrines in exercising preventive police power by constructive seizure of the Sturzenegger records, and found that there was " * * * no proof, or any evidence at all of collusion between plaintiff and the Swiss Government in the seizure of the papers herein." Noting that the burden was on petitioner to show good faith in its efforts to comply with the production order, and taking as the test of good faith whether petitioner had attempted all which a reasonable man would have undertaken in the circumstances to comply with the order, the Master found that " * * * the plaintiff has sustained a burden of proof placed upon it and has shown good faith in its efforts [to comply with the production order] in accordance with the foregoing test."

These findings of the Master were confirmed by the District Court. Nevertheless the court, in February 1953, granted the Government's motion to dismiss the complaint and filed an opinion wherein it concluded that: (1) apart from considerations of Swiss law petitioner has control over the Sturzenegger records, (2) such records might prove to be crucial in the outcome of this litigation, (3) Swiss law did not furnish an adequate excuse for the petitioner's failure to comply with the production order, since petitioner could not invoke foreign law to justify disobedience to orders entered under the laws of the forum; and (that the court in these circumstances has power under Rule 37(b)(2), as well as inherent power, to dismiss the complaint in 111 F.Supp. 435. However, in view of statement by the Swiss Government following petitioner's intercession, that certain records not deemed to violate the Swiss laws would be released, and in view of efforts by petitioner to secure waivers from those persons banking with the Sturzenegger firm who were protected by the Swiss secrecy laws, and hence whose waivers might lead the Swiss

Government to permit production, the court suspended the effective date of its dismissal order for a limited period in order to permit petitioner to continue efforts to obtain waivers and Swiss consent for production.

By October 1953, some 63,000 documents had been released by this process and tendered the Government for inspection. None of the books of account of Sturzenegger were submitted, though petitioner was prepared to offer plans to the Swiss Government which here too might have permitted at least partial compliance. However, since full production appeared impossible, the District Court in November 1953 entered a final dismissal order. This order was affirmed by the Court of Appeals, which accepted the findings of the District Court as to the relevancy of the documents, control of them by petitioner, and petitioner's good–faith efforts to comply with the production order. The court found it unnecessary to decide whether Rule 37 authorized dismissal under these circumstances since it ruled that the District Court was empowered to dismiss both by Rule 41(b) of the Federal Rules of Civil Procedure, and under its own "inherent power." It did, however, modify the dismissal order to allow petitioner an additional six months in which to continue its efforts. 96 U.S.App.D.C. 232, 225 F.2d 532. We denied certiorari. 350 U.S. 907, 76 S.Ct. 302, 100 L.Ed. 818.

During this further period of grace additional documents, with the consent of the Swiss Government and through waivers, were released and tendered for inspection, so that by July of 1956, over 190,000 documents had been procured. Record books of Sturzenegger were offered for examination in Switzerland, subject to the expected approval of the Swiss Government, to the extent that material within them was covered by waivers. Finally, petitioner presented the District Court with a plan, already approved by the Swiss Government, which was designed to achieve maximum compliance with the production order: A "neutral" expert, who might be an American, would be appointed as investigator with the consent of the parties, District Court, and Swiss authorities. After inspection of the Sturzenegger files, this investigator would submit a report to the parties identifying documents, without violating secrecy regulations, which he deemed to be relevant to the litigation. Petitioner could then seek to obtain further waivers or secure such documents by letters rogatory or arbitration proceedings in Swiss courts.

The District Court, however, refused to entertain this plan or to inspect the documents tendered in order to determine whether there had been substantial compliance with the production order. It directed final dismissal of the action. The Court of Appeals affirmed, but at the same time observed: "That [petitioner] and its counsel patiently and diligently sought to achieve compliance * * * is not to be doubted." 100 U.S.App.D.C. 148, 149, 243 F.2d 254, 255. Because this decision raised important questions as to the proper application of the Federal Rules of Civil Procedure, we granted certiorari. 355 U.S. 812, 78 S.Ct. 61, 2 L.Ed.2d 30.

We consider first petitioner's contention that the District Court erred in issuing the production order because the requirement of Rule 34, that a party ordered to produce documents must be in "control" of them, was not here satisfied. Without intimating any view upon the merits of the litigation, we accept as amply supported by the evidence the findings of the two courts below that, apart from the effect of Swiss law, the Sturzenegger documents are within petitioner's control. The question then becomes: Do the interdictions of Swiss law bar a conclusion that petitioner had "control" of these documents within the meaning of Rule 34?

We approach this question in light of the findings below that the Swiss penal laws did in fact limit petitioner's ability to satisfy the production order because of the criminal sanctions to which those producing the records would have been exposed. Still we do not view this situation as fully analogous to one where documents required by a production order have ceased to exist or have been taken into actual possession of a third person not controlled by the party ordered to produce, and without that party's complicity. The "confiscation" of these records by the Swiss authorities adds nothing to the dimensions of the problem under consideration, for possession of the records stayed where it was and the possibility of criminal prosecution for disclosure was of course present before the confiscation order was issued.

In its broader scope, the problem before us requires consideration of the policies underlying the Trading with the Enemy Act. If petitioner can prove its record title to General Aniline stock, it certainly is open to the Government to show that petitioner itself is the captive of interests whose direct ownership would bar recovery. This possibility of enemy taint of nationals of neutral powers, particularly of holding companies with intricate financial structures, which asserted rights to American assets was of deep concern to the Congress when it broadened the Trading with the Enemy Act in 1941 " * * * to reach enemy interests which masqueraded under those innocent fronts." *Clark v. Uebersee Finanz–Korp.*, 332 U.S. 480, 485, 68 S.Ct. 174, 176, 92 L.Ed.88. See Administration of the Wartime Financial and Property Controls of the United States Government, Treasury Department (1942), pp. 29–30; H.R.Rep. No. 2398, 79th Cong., 2nd Sess. 3.

In view of these considerations, to hold broadly that petitioner's failure to produce the Sturzenegger records because of fear of punishment under the laws of its sovereign precludes a court from finding that petitioner had "control" over them, and thereby from ordering their production, would undermine congressional policies made explicit in the 1941 amendments, and invite efforts to place ownership of American assets in persons or firms whose sovereign assures secrecy of records. The District Court here concluded that the Sturzenegger records might have a vital influence upon this litigation insofar as they shed light upon petitioner's confused background. Petitioner is in a most advantageous position to plead with its own sovereign for relaxation of penal laws or for adoption of plans which will at the least achieve a significant measure of compliance with the production order, and indeed to that end it has already made significant progress. United States courts should be free to require claimants of seized assets who fact legal obstacles under the laws of their own countries to make all such efforts to the maximum of their ability where the requested records promise to bear out or dispel any doubt the Government may introduce as to true ownership of the assets.

We do not say that this ruling would apply to every situation where a party is restricted by law from producing documents over which it is otherwise shown to have control. Rule 34 is sufficiently flexible to be adapted to the exigencies of particular litigation. The propriety of the use to which it is put depends upon the circumstances of a given case, and we hold that only that accommodation of the Rule in this instance to the policies underlying the Trading with the Enemy Act justified the action of the District Court in issuing this production order.

* * * * *

We turn to the remaining question, whether the District Court properly exercised its powers under Rule 37(b) by dismissing this complaint despite the findings that petitioner had not been in collusion with the Swiss authorities to block inspection of the Sturzenegger records, and had in good faith made diligent effort to execute the production order.

We must discard at the outset the strongly urged contention of the Government that dismissal of this action was justified because petitioner conspired with I. G. Farben, Sturzenegger & Cie, and others to transfer ownership of General Aniline to it prior to 1941 so that seizure would be avoided and advantage taken of Swiss secrecy laws. In other words, the Government suggests that petitioner stands in the position of one who deliberately courted legal impediments to production of the Sturzenegger records, and who thus cannot now be heard to assert its good faith after this expectation was realized. Certainly these contentions, if supported by the facts, would have a vital bearing on justification for dismissal of the action, but they are not open to the Government here. The findings below reach no such conclusions; indeed, it is not even apparent from them whether this particular charge was ever passed upon below. Although we do not

mean to preclude the Government from seeking to establish such facts before the District Court upon remand, or any other facts relevant to justification for dismissal of the complaint, we must dispose of this case on the basis of the findings of good faith made by the Special Master, adopted by the District Court, and approved by the Court of Appeals.

The provisions of Rule 37 which are here involved must be read in light of the provisions of the Fifth Amendment that no person shall be deprived of property without due process of law, and more particularly against the opinions of this Court in *Hovey v. Elliott*, 167 U.S. 409, 17 S.Ct. 841, 42 L.Ed. 215, and *Hammond Packing Co. v. State of Arkansas*, 212 U.S. 322, 29 S.Ct. 370, 53 L.Ed. 530. These decisions establish that there are constitutional limitations upon the power of courts, even in aid of their own valid processes to dismiss an action without affording a party the opportunity for a hearing or the merits of his cause. The authors of Rule 37 were well aware of these constitutional considerations. See Notes of Advisory Committee on Rules, Rule 37 28 U.S.C. (1952 ed.) p. 4325, 28 U.S.C.A.

* * * * *

These two decisions leave open the question whether Fifth Amendment due process is violated by the striking of a complaint because of a plaintiff's inability, despite good–faith efforts, to comply with a pretrial production order. The presumption utilized by the Court in the Hammond case might well falter under such circumstances. *Cf. Tot v. United States*, 319 U.S. 463, 63 S.Ct. 1241, 87 L.Ed. 1519. Certainly substantial constitutional questions are provoked by such action. Their gravity is accented in the present case where petitioner, through case in the role of *plaintiff*, cannot be deemed to be in the customary role of a party invoking the aid of a court to vindicate rights asserted against another. Rather petitioner's position is more analogous to that of a *defendant*, for it belatedly challenges the Government's action by now protesting against a seizure and seeking the recovery of assets which were summarily possessed by the Alien Property Custodian without the opportunity for protest by any party claiming that seizure was unjustified under the Trading with the Enemy Act. Past decisions of this Court emphasize that this summary power to seize property which is believed to be enemy–owned is rescued from constitutional invalidity under the Due Process and Just Compensation Clauses of the Fifth Amendment only by those provisions of the Act which afford a non–enemy claimant a later judicial hearing as to the propriety of the seizure. See *Stoehr v. Wallace*, 255 U.S. 239, 245–246, 41 S.Ct. 293, 296, 65 L.Ed. 604; *Guessefeldt v. McGrath*, 342 U.S. 308, 318, 72 S.Ct. 338, 344, 96 L.Ed. 342; *cf. Russian Volunteer Fleet v. United States*, 282 U.S. 481, 489, 51 S.Ct. 229, 231, 75 L.Ed. 473.

The findings below, and what has been shown as to petitioner's extensive efforts at compliance, compel the conclusion on this record that petitioner's failure to satisfy fully the requirements of this production order was due to inability fostered neither by its own conduct nor by circumstances within its control. It is hardly debatable that fear of criminal prosecution constitutes a weighty excuse for nonproduction, and this excuse is not weakened because the laws preventing compliance are those of a foreign sovereign. Of course this situation should be distinguished from one where a party claims that compliance with a court's order will reveal facts which may provide the basis for criminal prosecution of that party under the penal laws of the foreign sovereign thereby shown to have been violated. *Cf. United States v. Murdock*, 284 U.S. 141, 149, 52 S.Ct. 63, 76 L.Ed. 210. Here the findings below establish that the very fact of compliance by disclosure of banking records will itself constitute the initial violation of Swiss laws. In our view, petitioner stands in the position of an American plaintiff subject to criminal sanctions in Switzerland because production of documents in Switzerland pursuant to the order of the United States court might violate Swiss laws. Petitioner has sought no privileges because of its foreign citizenship which are not accorded domestic litigants in United States courts. *Cf. Guaranty Trust Co. of New York v. United States*, 304 U.S. 126, 133 135, 58 S.Ct. 785, 82 L.Ed. 1224. It does not claim that Swiss laws protecting banking records should here be enforced. It explicitly recognizes that it is subject to procedural rules of United States courts in this litigation and has made full efforts to follow these rules. It asserts no immunity from them. It asserts only its *inability* to comply because of foreign law.

In view of the findings in this case, the position in which petitioner stands in this litigation, and the serious constitutional questions we have noted, we think that Rule 37 should not be construed to authorize dismissal of this complaint because of petitioner's noncompliance with a pretrial production order when it has been established that failure to comply has been due to inability, and not to willfulness, bad faith, or any fault of petitioner.

This is not to say that petitioner will profit through its inability to tender the records called for. In seeking recovery of the General Aniline stock and other assets, petitioner recognizes that it carries the ultimate burden of proof showing itself not to be an "enemy" within the meaning of the Trading with the Enemy Act. The Government already has disputed its right to recovery by relying on information obtained through seized records of I. G. Farben, documents obtained through petitioner, and depositions taken of persons affiliated with petitioner. It may be that in a trial on the merits, petitioner's inability to produce specific information will prove a serious handicap in dispelling doubt the Government might be able to inject into the case. It may be that in the absence of complete disclosure by petitioner, the District Court would be justified in drawing inferences unfavorable to petitioner as to particular events. So much indeed petitioner concedes. But these problems go to the adequacy of petitioner's proof and should not on this record preclude petitioner from being able to contest on the merits.

* * * * *

SOCIETE NATIONAL INDUSTRIELLE AEROSPATIALE and Societe de Construction d'Avions de Tourisme, Petitioners v. UNITED STATES DISTRICT COURT for the SOUTHERN DISTRICT OF IOWA, etc.

482 U.S. 522, 107 S.Ct. 2742, 96 L.Ed.2d 461

United States Supreme Court
June 15, 1987

Justice STEVENS delivered the opinion of the Court.

The United States, the Republic of France, and 15 other Nations have acceded to the Hague Convention on the Taking of Evidence Abroad in Civil or Commercial Matters, opened for signature, Mar. 18, 1970, 23 U.S.T. 2555, T.I.A.S. No. 7444.[1] This Convention — sometimes referred to as the "Hague Convention" or the "Evidence Convention" — prescribes certain procedures by which a judicial authority in one contracting state may request evidence located in another contracting state. The question presented in this case concerns the extent to which a federal district court must employ the procedures set forth in the Convention when litigants seek answers to interrogatories, the production of documents, and admissions from a French adversary over whom the court has personal jurisdiction.

The petitioners are corporations owned by the Republic of France.[2] They are engaged in the business of designing, manufacturing, and marketing aircraft. One of their planes, the "Rallye," was allegedly advertised in American aviation publications as "the World's safest and most economical STOL plant."[3] On August 19, 1980, a Rallye crashed in Iowa, injuring the pilot and a passenger. Dennis Jones, John George, and Rosa George brought separate suits based upon this accident in the United States District Court for the Southern District of Iowa, alleging that petitioners had manufactured and sold a defective plane and that they were guilty of negligence and breach of warranty.

Petitioners answered the complaints, apparently without questioning the jurisdiction of the District Court. With the parties' consent, the cases were consolidated and referred to a Magistrate. See 28 U.S.C. § 636(c)(1).

Initial discovery was conducted by both sides pursuant to the Federal Rules of Civil Procedure without objection.[4] When plaintiffs[5] served a second request for the production of documents pursuant to Rule 34, a set of interrogatories pursuant to Rule 33, and requests for admission pursuant to Rule 36, however, petitioners filed a motion for a protective order. App. 27-37. The motion alleged that because petitioners are "French corporations, and the discovery sought can only be found in a foreign state, namely France," the Hague Convention dictated the exclusive procedures that must be followed for pretrial discovery. App. 2. In addition, the motion stated that under French penal law, the petitioners could not respond to discovery requests that did not comply with the Convention. *Ibid.*[6]

The Magistrate denied the motion insofar as it related to answering interrogatories, producing documents, and making admissions.[7] * * *

* * * * *

In the District Court and the Court of Appeals, petitioners contended that the Hague Evidence Convention "provides the exclusive and mandatory procedures for obtaining documents and information located within the territory of a foreign signatory." 782 F.2d, at 124.[11] We are satisfied that the Court of Appeals correctly rejected this extreme position. We believe it is foreclosed by the plain language of the Convention. * * *

* * * * *

In arguing their entitlement to a protective order, petitioners correctly assert that both the discovery rules set forth in the Federal Rules of Civil Procedure and the Hague Convention are the law of the United States. Brief for Petitioners 31. This observation, however, does not dispose of the question before us; we must analyze the interaction between these two bodies of federal law. Initially, we note that at least four different interpretations of the relationship between the federal discovery rules and the Hague Convention are possible. Two of these interpretations assume that the Hague Convention by its terms dictates the extent to which it supplants normal discovery rules. First, the Hague Convention must be read as requiring its use to the exclusion of any other discovery procedures whenever evidence located abroad is sought for use in an American court. Second, the Hague Convention might be interpreted to require first, but not exclusive, use of its procedures. Two other interpretations assume that international comity, rather than the obligations created by the treaty, should guide judicial resort to the Hague Convention. Third, then, the Convention might be viewed as establishing a supplemental set of discovery procedures, strictly optional under treaty law, to which concerns of comity nevertheless require first resort by American courts in all cases. Fourth, the treaty may be viewed as an undertaking among sovereigns to facilitate discovery to which an American court should resort when it deems that course of action appropriate, after considering the situations of the parties before it as well as the interests of the concerned foreign state.

In interpreting an international treaty, we are mindful that it is "in the nature of a contract between nations," *Trans World Airlines, Inc. v. Franklin Mint Corp.*, 466 U.S. 243, 253, 104 S.Ct. 1776, 1783, 80 L.Ed.2d 273 (1984), to which "[g]eneral rules of construction apply." *Id.*, at 262, 104 S.Ct., at 1788. See *Ware v. Hylton*, 3 Dall. 199, 240-241, 1 L.Ed. 568 (1796) (opinion of Chase, J.). We therefore begin "with the text of the treaty and the context in which the written words are used." *Air France v. Saks*, 470 U.S. 392, 397, 105 S.Ct. 1338, 1341, 84 L.Ed.2d 289 (1985). The treaty's history, "'the negotiations, and the practical construction adopted by the parties'" may also be relevant. *Id.*, at 396, 105 S.Ct.., at 1341 (quoting *Choctaw Nation of Indians v. United States*, 318 U.S. 423, 431-432, 63 S.Ct. 672, 677-678, 87 L.Ed 877 (1943)).

We reject the first two of the possible interpretations as inconsistent with the language and negotiating history of the Hague Con-

vention. The preamble of the Convention specifies its purpose "to facilitate the transmission and execution of Letters of Request" and to "improve mutual judicial co-operation in civil or commercial matters." 23 U.S.T., at 2557, T.I.A.S. No. 7444. The preamble does not speak in mandatory terms which would purport to describe the procedures for all permissible transnational discovery and exclude all other existing practices.[15] The text of the Evidence Convention itself does not modify the law of any contracting state, require any contracting state to use the Convention procedures, either in requesting evidence or in responding to such requests, or compel any contracting state to change its own evidence gathering procedures.[16]

* * * * *

An interpretation of the Hague Convention as the exclusive means for obtaining evidence located abroad would effectively subject every American court hearing a case involving a national of a contracting state to the internal laws of that state. Interrogatories and document requests are staples of international commercial litigation, no less than of other suits, yet a rule of exclusivity would subordinate the court's supervision of even the most routine of these pretrial proceedings to the actions or, equally, to the inactions of foreign judicial authorities. As the Court of Appeals for the Fifth Circuit observed in *In re Anschuetz & Co., GmbH*, 754 F.2d 602, 612 (1985), cert. pending, No. 85-98:

> "It seems patently obvious that if the Convention were interpreted as preempting interrogatories and document requests, the Convention would really be much more than an agreement on taking evidence abroad. Instead, the Convention would amount to a major regulation of the overall conduct of litigation between nationals of different signatory states, raising a significant possibility of very serious interference with the jurisdiction of the United States courts.

* * * * *

> "While it is conceivable that the United States could enter into a treaty giving other signatories control over litigation

instituted and pursued in American courts, a treaty intended to bring about such a curtailment of the rights given to all litigants by the federal rules would surely state its intention clearly and precisely identify crucial terms."

The Hague Convention, however, contains no such plain statement of a pre-emptive intent. We conclude accordingly that the Hague Convention did not deprive the District Court of the jurisdiction it otherwise possessed to order a foreign national party before it to produce evidence physically located within a signatory nation.

While the Hague Convention does not divest the District Court of jurisdiction to order discovery under the Federal Rules of Civil Procedure, the optional character of the Convention procedures sheds light on one aspect of the Court of Appeals' opinion that we consider erroneous. That court concluded that the Convention simply "does not apply" to discovery sought from a foreign litigant that is subject to the jurisdiction of an American court. 782 F.2d, at 124. Plaintiffs argue that this conclusion is supported by two considerations. First, the Federal Rules of Civil Procedure provide ample means for obtaining discovery from parties who are subject to the court's jurisdiction, while before the Convention was ratified it was often extremely difficult, if not impossible, to obtain evidence from nonparty witnesses abroad. Plaintiffs contend that it is appropriate to construe the Convention as applying only in the area in which improvement was badly needed. Second, when a litigant is subject to the jurisdiction of the district court, arguably the evidence it is required to produce is not "abroad" within the meaning of the Convention, even though it is in fact located in a foreign country at the time of the discovery request and even though it will have to be gathered or otherwise prepared abroad. See *In re Anschuetz & Co., GmgH*, 754 F.2d, at 611; *In re Messerschmitt Bolkow Blohm GmgH*, 757 F.2d 729, 731 (CA5 1985), cert. vacated, 476 U.S. 1168, 106 S.Ct. 2887, 90 L.Ed. 975 (1986); *Daimler-Benz Aktiengesellschaft v. United States District Court*, 805 F.2d 340, 341-342 (CA10 1986).

Nevertheless, the text of the Convention draws no distinction between evidence obtained from third parties and that obtained from litigants themselves; nor does it purport to draw any sharp line between evidence that is "abroad" and evidence that is within the control of a party subject to the jurisdiction of the requesting court. Thus, it appears clear to us that the optional Convention procedures are available whenever they will facilitate the gathering of evidence by the means authorized in the Convention. Although these procedures are not mandatory, the Hague Convention does "apply" to the production of evidence in a litigant's possession in the sense that it is one method of seeking evidence that a court may elect to employ. See Briefs of *Amici Curiae* for the United States and the SEC 9-10, the Federal Republic of Germany 5-6, the Republic of France 8-12, and the Government of the United Kingdom and Northern Ireland 8.

Petitioners contend that even if the Hague Convention's procedures are not mandatory, this Court should adopt a rule requiring that American litigants first resort to those procedures before initiating any discovery pursuant to the normal methods of the Federal Rules of Civil Procedure. See *e.g., Laker Airways, Ltd. v. Pan American World Airways*, 103 F.R.D. 42 (DC 1984); *Philadelphia Gear Corp. v. American Pfauter Corp.*, 100 F.R.D. 58 (ED Pa.1983). The Court of Appeals rejected this argument because it was convinced that an American court's order ultimately requiring discovery that a foreign court had refused under Convention procedures would constitute "the greatest insult" to the sovereignty of that tribunal. 782 F.2d, at 125-126. We disagree with the Court of Appeals' view. It is well known that the scope of American discovery is often significantly broader than is permitted in other jurisdictions, and we are satisfied that foreign tribunals will recognize that the final decision on the evidence to be used in litigation conducted in American courts must be made by those courts. We therefore do not believe that an American court should refuse to make use of Convention procedures because of a concern that it may ultimately find it necessary to order the production of evidence that a foreign tribunal permitted a party to withhold.

Nevertheless, we cannot accept petitioners' invitation to announce a new rule of law that would require first resort to Convention procedures whenever discovery is sought from a foreign litigant. Assuming, without deciding, that we have the lawmaking power to do so, we are convinced that such a general rule would be unwise. In many situations the Letter of Request procedure authorized by the Convention would be unduly time consuming and expensive, as well as less certain to produce needed evidence than direct use of the Federal Rules.[26] A rule of first resort in all cases would therefore be inconsistent with the overriding interest in the "just, speedy, and inexpensive determination" of litigation in our courts. See Fed. Rule Civ.Proc. 1.

Petitioners argue that a rule of first resort is necessary to accord respect to the sovereignty of states in which evidence is located. It is true that the process of obtaining evidence in a civil-law jurisdiction is normally conducted by a judicial officer rather than by private attorneys. Petitioners contend that if performed on French soil, for example, by an unauthorized person, such evidence-gathering might violate the "judicial sovereignty" of the host nation. Because it is only through the Convention that civil-law nations have given their consent to evidence-gathering activities within their borders, petitioners argue, we have a duty to employ those procedures whenever they are available. Brief for Petitioners 27-28. We find that argument unpersuasive. If such a duty were to be inferred from the adoption of the Convention itself, we believe it would have been described in the text of that document. Moreover, the concept of international comity[27] requires this context a more particularized analysis of the respective interests of the foreign nation and the requesting nation than petitioners' proposed general rule would generate.[28] We therefore decline to hold as a blanket matter that comity requires resort to Hague Evidence Convention procedures without prior scrutiny in each case of the particular facts, sovereign interests, and likelihood that resort to those procedures will prove effective.[29]

Some discovery procedures are much more "intrusive" than others. In this case, for example, an interrogatory asking petitioners to identify the pilots who flew flight tests in the Rallye before it was certified for flight by the Federal Aviation Administration, or a request to admit that petitioners authorized certain advertising in a particular magazine, is certainly less intrusive than a request to produce all of the "design specifications, line drawings and engineering plans and all engineering change orders and plans and all drawings concerning the leading edge slats for the Rallye type aircraft manufactured by the Defendants." App. 29. Even if a court might be persuaded that a particular document request was too burdensome or too "intrusive" to be granted in full, with or without an appropriate protective order, it might well refuse to insist upon the use of Convention procedures before requiring responses to simple interrogatories or requests for admissions. The exact line between reasonableness and unreasonableness in each case must be drawn by the trial court, based on its knowledge of the case and of the claims and interests of the parties and the governments whose statutes and policies they invoke.

American courts, in supervising pretrial proceedings, should exercise special vigilance to protect foreign litigants from the danger that unnecessary, or unduly burdensome, discovery may place them in a disadvantageous position. Judicial supervision of discovery should always seek to minimize its costs and inconvenience and prevent improper uses of discovery requests. When it is necessary to seek evidence abroad, however, the district court must supervisor pretrial proceedings particularly closely to prevent discovery abuses. For example, the additional cost of transportation of documents or witnesses to or from foreign locations may increase the danger that discovery may be sought for the improper purpose of motivating settlement, rather than finding relevant and probative evidence. Objections to "abusive" discovery that foreign litigants advance should therefore receive the most careful consideration. In addition, we have long recognized the demands of comity in suits involving foreign states, either as parties or as sovereigns with a coordinate interest in the litigation. See *Hilton v. Guyot*, 159 U.S. 113, 16 S.Ct. 139, 40 L.Ed. 95 (1895). American courts should therefore take care to demonstrate due respect for any special problem confronted by the foreign litigant on account of its nationality or the location of its operations, and for any sovereign interest expressed by a foreign state. We do not articulate specific rules to guide this delicate task of adjudication.

In the case before us, the Magistrate and the Court of Appeals correctly refused to grant the broad protective order that petitioners requested. The Court of Appeals erred, however, in stating that the Evidence Convention does not apply to the pending discovery demands. This holding may be read as indicating that the Convention procedures are not even an option that is open to the District Court. It must be recalled, however, that the Convention's specification of duties in executing states creates corresponding rights in requesting states; holding that the Convention does not apply in this situation would deprive domestic litigants of access to evidence through treaty procedures to which the contracting states have assented. Moreover, such a rule would deny the foreign litigant a full and fair opportunity to demonstrate appropriate reasons for employing Convention procedures in the first instance, for some aspects of the discovery process.

Accordingly, the judgment of the Court of Appeals is vacated, and the case is remanded for further proceedings consistent with this opinion.

It is so ordered.

---

[1] The Hague Convention entered into force between the United States and France on October 6, 1974. The Convention is also in force in Barbados, Cyprus, Czechoslovakia, Denmark, Finland, the Federal Republic of Germany, Israel, Italy, Luxemburg, the Netherlands, Norway, Portugal, Singapore, Sweden, and the United Kingdom. Office of the Legal Adviser, United States Dept. of State, Treaties in Force 261-262 (1986).

[2] Petitioner Societe National Industrielle Aerospatiale is wholly owned by the Government of France. Petitioner Societe de Construction D'Avions de Tourisme is a wholly owned subsidiary of Societe Nationale Industrielle Aerospatiale.

[3] App. 22, 24. The term "STOL," an acronym for "short takeoff and landing," "refers to a fixed-wing aircraft that either takes off or lands with only a short horizontal run of the aircraft." *Douglas v. United States*, 206 Ct.Cl. 96, 99, 510 F.2d 364, 365, cert. denied, 423 U.S. 825, 96 S.Ct. 40, 46 L.Ed.2d 41 (1975).

[4] Plaintiffs made certain requests for the production of documents pursuant to Rule 34(b) and for admissions pursuant to Rule 36. App. 19-23. Apparently the petitioners responded to those requests without objection, at least insofar as they called for material or information that was located in the United States. App. to Pet. for Cert. 12a. In turn, petitioners deposed witnesses and parties pursuant to Rule 26, and served interrogatories pursuant to Rule 33 and a request for the production of documents pursuant to Rule 34. App. 13. Plaintiffs complied with those requests.

[5] Although the District Court is the nominal respondent in this mandamus proceeding, plaintiffs are the real respondent parties in interest.

[6] Article 1A of the French "blocking statute," French Penal Code Law No. 80-538, provides:

"Subject to treaties or international agreements and applicable laws and regulations, it is prohibited for any party to request, seek or disclose, in writing, orally or otherwise, economic, commercial, industrial, financial or technical documents or information leading to the constitution of evidence with a view to foreign judicial or administrative proceedings or in connection therewith."

"*Art.* ler bis. — [French version omitted]

Article 2 provides:

The parties mentioned in [Article 1A] shall forthwith inform the competent minister if they receive any request concerning such disclosures.

[French version omitted]

[7] *Id.*, at 25a. The Magistrate stated, however, that if oral depositions were to be taken in France, he would require compliance with the Hague Evidence Convention. *Ibid.*

[11] The Republic of France likewise takes the following position in this case:

"The Hague Convention is the exclusive means of discovery in transnational litigation among the convention's signatories unless the sovereign on whose territory discovery is to occur chooses otherwise." Brief for Republic of France as *Amicus Curiae 4.*

[15] The Hague Convention on Private International Law's omission of mandatory language in the preamble is particularly significant in light of the same body's use of mandatory language in the preamble to the Hague Service Convention, 20 U.S.T. 361, T.I.A.S. No. 6638. Article 1 of the Service Convention provides: "The present Convention shall apply in all cases, in civil or commercial matters, where there is occasion to transmit a judicial or extrajudicial document for service abroad." *Id.*, at 362 T.I.A.S. No. 6638. As noted, *supra*, at 7, the Service Convention was drafted before the Evidence Convention, and its language provided a model exclusivity provision that the drafters of the Evidence Convention could easily have followed had they been so inclined. Given this background, the drafters' election to use permissive language instead is strong evidence of their intent.

[16] At the time the Convention was drafted, Federal Rule of Civil Procedure 28(b) clearly authorized the taking of evidence on notice either in accordance with the laws of the foreign country or in pursuance of the law of the United States.

[26] We observe, however, that in other instances a litigant's first use of the Hague Convention procedures can be expected to yield more evidence abroad more promptly than use of the normal procedures governing pre-trial civil discovery. In those instances, the calculations of the litigant will naturally lead to a first-use strategy.

[27] Comity refers to the spirit of cooperation in which a domestic tribunal approaches the resolution of cases touching the laws and interest of other sovereign states. This Court referred to the doctrine of comity among nations in *Emory v. Grenough*, 3 Dall. 369, 370, n., 1 L.Ed. 640 (1797) (dismissing appeal from judgment for failure to plead diversity of citizenship, but setting forth an extract from a treatise by Ulrich Huber (1636-1694), a Dutch jurist):

"'By the courtesy of nation, whatever laws are carried into execution, within the limits of any government, are considered as having the same effect every where, so far as they do not occasion a prejudice to the rights of the other governments, or their citizens.

* * * * *

"'[N]othing would be more convenient in the promiscuous intercourse and practice of mankind, than that that what was valid by the laws of one place, should be rendered of no effect elsewhere, by a diversity of law . . . .'" *Ibid.* (quoting 2 U. Huber, Praelectiones Juris Romani et hodiemi, bk. 1, tit. 3, pp. 26-31 (C. Thomas, L. Menke, & G. Gebauer eds. 1725)). See also *Hilton v. Guyot*, 159 U.S. 113, 163-164, 16 S.Ct. 139, 143, 40 L.Ed. 95 (1895):

"'Comity,' in the legal sense, is neither a matter of absolute obligation, on the one hand, nor of mere courtesy and good will, upon the other. But it is the recognition which one nation allows within its territory to the legislative, executive or judicial acts of another nation, having due regard both to international duty and convenience, and to the rights of its own citizens or of other persons who are under the protection of its law."

[28] The nature of concerns that guide a comity analysis by the Restatement of Foreign Relations Law of the United States (Revised) § 437(1)(c) (Tent.Draft No. 7, 1986) (approved May 14, 1986) (Restatement). While we recognize that § 437 of the Restatement may not represent a consensus of international views on the scope of the district court's power to order foreign discovery in the face of objections by foreign states, these factors are relevant to any comity analysis:

"(1) the importance to the . . . litigation of the documents or other information requested;

"(2) the degree of specificity of the request;

"(3) whether the information originated in the United States;

"(4) the availability of alternative means of securing the information; and

"(5) the extent to which noncompliance with the request would determine important interests of the United States, or compliance with the request would determine important interests of the state where the information is located." *Ibid.*

[29] The French "blocking statute," n. 6, *supra*, does not alter our conclusion. It is well settled that such statutes do not deprive an American court of the power to order a party subject to its jurisdiction to produce evidence even through the act of production may violate that statute. See *Societe International Pour Participations Industrielles et Commerciales, S.A. v. Rogers*, 357 U.S. 197, 204-206, 78 S.Ct. 1087, 1091-1092, 2 L.Ed.2d 1255 (1958). Nor can the enactment of such a statute by a foreign nation require American courts to engraft a rule of first resort onto the Hague Convention, or otherwise to provide the nationals of such a country with a preferred status in our courts. It is clear that American courts are not required to adhere blindly to the directives of such a statute. Indeed, the language of the statute, if taken literally, would appear to represent an extraordinary exercise of legislative jurisdiction by the Republic of France over a United States district judge, forbidding him or her to order any discovery from a party of French nationality, even simple requests for admissions or interrogatories that the party could respond to on the basis of personal knowledge. It would be particularly incongruous to recognize such a preference for corporations that are wholly owned by the enacting nation. Extraterritorial assertions of jurisdiction are not one-sided. While the District Court's discovery orders arguably have some impact in France, the French blocking statute asserts similar authority over acts to take place in this country. The lesson of comity is that neither the discovery order nor the blocking statute can have the same omnipresent effect that it would have in a world of only one sovereign. The blocking statute thus is relevant

to the court's particularized comity analysis only to the extent that its terms and its enforcements identify the nature of the sovereign interests in nondisclosure of specific kinds of material.

The American Law Institute has summarized this interplay of blocking statutes and discovery orders: "[W]hen a state has jurisdiction to prescribe and its courts have jurisdiction to adjudicate, adjudication should (subject to generally applicable rules of evidence) take place on the basis of the best information available . . . . [Blocking] statutes that frustrate this goal need not be given the same deference by courts of the United States as substantive rules of law at variance with the law of the United States." See Restatement, § 437, Reporter's Note 5, pp. 41, 42. "On the other hand, the degree of friction created by discovery requests . . . and the differing perceptions of the acceptability of American-style discovery under national and international law, suggest some efforts to moderate the application abroad of U.S. procedural techniques, consistent with the overall principle of reasonableness in the exercise of jurisdiction." *Id.*, at 42.

Dennis L. SORIA v. OZINGA BROS., INC.,

704 F.2d 990

United States Court of Appeals, Seventh Circuit
April 7, 1983

This Title VII matter comes before us on appeal from the district court's finding after a bench trial that plaintiff Dennis Soria, a Catholic of Italian background, was not discharged from his employment as a cement truck driver with defendant Ozinga Bros., Inc., a company largely owned and managed by individuals who were of traceable Dutch ancestry or members of the Christian Reformed Church, or both, due to his differing religion or national origin. On appeal, plaintiff chiefly argues that the district court erred in its refusal to consider as decisive certain statistical evidence offered by him linking company disciplinary patterns and religion and national origin. Plaintiff also contends that the district court erred in refusing to consider a relevant statistical evidence concerning the ethnic composition of defendant's work force, and claims that the court erred in certain findings of fact. Because we find no significant error in the district court's consideration of the evidence and no error at all in its ultimate findings, we affirm.

Defendant Ozinga Bros., Inc. (the company) is a small family–owned and –operated business which prepares and delivers building materials such as ready–mix concrete. It was founded by a Dutch immigrant whose son and three grandsons occupy the crucial management positions. Of the other managers, one is of Italian origin and two others are affiliated with the Catholic church. Although roughly half the company's employees are of traceable Dutch ancestry or Christian Reformed Church members (CRC), there was no allegation that plaintiff was discriminated against in regard to hiring or promotion. Instead, the sole issue at trial was whether plaintiff would not have been fired but for his non–Dutch, non–CRC background, or whether, as the company claimed, he was fired solely for persistently uncooperative and hostile behavior toward management and carelessness and irresponsibility in performance of his duties throughout his five years of employment, culminating in two serious truck accidents in the several days prior to his final discharge.

The evidence adduced at trial established a lengthy history of job–related problems between plaintiff and the company. The company's chief truck dispatcher and supervisor testified that during the 1977 season, plaintiff was the only cement truck driver with whom he experienced a significant difficulty in the assignment of deliveries. Indeed, at least one contractor–customer has requested that the company not send plaintiff to its job site because of plaintiff's uncooperative attitude. There was also testimony that on several occasions, plaintiff displayed a careless attitude toward his delivery obligations. For example, the company's dispatcher testified that even during busy periods, plaintiff several times stated in mid–afternoon that he

would not accept any more deliveries for the remainder of the day; when queried as to the reason for his early departure, plaintiff was either silent or responded, at least on one occasion, "Well, I'll be sick after this [delivery]." In addition, the dispatcher testified that, as supervisor, his attempts to communicate with the plaintiff were unavailing, as plaintiff repeatedly ignored him or walked away. Further attempts to address the communications problem were rebuffed with the same behavior.

The supervisor's testimony was buttressed by that of a manager of Italian origin who noted what, while Soria may have had a "roughly average" record in regard to vehicle maintenance, the plaintiff manifested a "[v]ery unconcerned" and "lackadaisical" attitude toward specific problems noted to him. This picture was confirmed by one of plaintiff's witnesses, a fellow driver of Irish Catholic origin, who noted that plaintiff had a bad attitude at times and argued with the company's dispatcher and customers.

During plaintiff's final ten days of employment, he was involved in two serious accidents. Plaintiff's conduct in connection with these accidents apparently crystallized the company's long–standing dissatisfaction with plaintiff and served as a catalyst for his final discharge. In the first of these accidents, plaintiff, failing to watch his right hand mirror, drove his truck into a large ditch. Plaintiff and an assisting driver attempted to remove the truck from the ditch, but in so doing caused it to tip over, causing great damage. A member of company management arrived at the scene and concluded that the accident was due to plaintiff's carelessness. After consultation with other management members, plaintiff was laid off for the balance of that week. More important than the tip–over accident itself (other drivers employed by the same company had been involved in similar accidents), the company testified, was the fact that the plaintiff belligerently denied responsibility for the accident and offered what management considered to be inappropriate excuses (*e.g.*, that the accident was caused by the distraction of another car and the failure of the contractor to cooperate).

When a manager admonished plaintiff that he was responsible for control over his vehicle despite the claimed distractions, plaintiff "proceeded to tell [him] that he didn't like what [he] was saying and that if [he] didn't back off, that he was going to straighten [him] out." Plaintiff offered no testimony to rebut this recollection. Even though such hostility was unprecedented in the manager's experience, plaintiff was allowed to return to work the following week.

The second accident occurred ten days later, when plaintiff ran his truck into a viaduct, causing damage to the cement–mixing barrel. Plaintiff again denied responsibility for the accident, claiming that he did not know the height of his truck, and that a company dispatcher had concurred in the choice of the route taken. The first excuse compounded the company's belief in plaintiff's irresponsibility, since the height of the truck was a readily ascertainable fact which other company drivers had taken the trouble to learn. At trial, the company dispatcher also denied having concurred in plaintiff's delivery route, and noted that such consultation was infrequent. Moreover, plaintiff appeared to acknowledge the depth of his dereliction and its natural consequences when, in returning to the company yard, he told the dispatcher, "This will probably be my last load, I just hit a viaduct." When a company manager met with plaintiff after the accident and heard the plaintiff's excuses and plaintiff's statement that he refused to drive the type of truck involved in the accident again, the manager rebuked him for his lack of responsibility and carelessness. Plaintiff was indefinitely laid off, and after a consultation among management in which the plaintiff's history of non-cooperation and refusal to accept basic responsibility was discussed, it was decided to permanently discharge plaintiff.

One week after his discharge, plaintiff filed a grievance with the labor–management grievance committee empowered to reinstate him, in which, significantly, he did not allege any religious or ethnic discrimination. The committee rejected his demand to be reinstated. Several months thereafter, plaintiff filed a discrimination charge with the Equal Employment Opportunity Commission (EEOC), claiming discrimination on the basis of his Italian ancestry and Catholic affiliation; the EEOC rejected his claim. Finally, plaintiff instituted this action under Title VII of the Civil Rights Act of 1964, 42 U.S.C. § 20002–2(a)(1), changing his discrimination theory to allege that he was victimized as a non–Dutch, non–CRC affiliated employee rather than specifically an Italian Catholic.

At trial, plaintiff attempted to demonstrate unlawful discrimination against him through two doctrinal avenues — — "disparate impact" and "disparate treatment." First, he alleged that the company's informal, subjective system of discipline resulted in markedly more severe discipline being applied to non–Dutch and non–CRC drivers. Second, he alleged that his specific discharge resulted from discriminatory treatment based on his non–Dutch, non–CRC background. To establish his claim of disparate impact and to paint as pretextual the company's claim of legitimate, nondiscriminatory discharge, plaintiff relied chiefly upon comparative and statistical evidence purporting to demonstrate worse treatment of non–Dutch, non–CRC drivers. The district court, however, found the statistical data presented by both sides irreparably flawed and of "minimal assistance;" it also found the comparative evidence indeterminate. The district court concluded that plaintiff had proven neither disparate impact nor disparate treatment. Instead, the district court found that plaintiff had been discharged for "careless and unsafe attitudes, noncooperation with management, and lack of responsibility toward his job." From that determination, plaintiff appeals.

* * * * *

Even were the sample size adequate, however, the district court noted a still more decisive flaw in the sample: its radical incompleteness. The plaintiff's data base includes only *recorded* disciplinary actions. Since the company's disciplinary system is largely informal and unwritten, the few recorded disciplinary incidents could scarcely provide a balanced picture of the company's overall disciplinary pattern. Moreover, the plaintiff significantly chose to omit from its analysis thirteen additional incidences of *unwritten* discipline recalled by the company management in deposition. This court has previously recognized that such deposition evidence from company officials is especially crucial in Title VII actions involving small employers who do not keep extensive personnel records. *Kephart v. Institute of Gas Technology*, 630 F.2d 1217, 1220 (7th Cir.1980), *cert. denied*, 450 U.S. 959, 101 S.Ct. 1418, 67 L.Ed.2d 383 (1981).[7]

* * * * *

[7] Plaintiff suggests that the company should be required to bear the consequences of maintaining incomplete records, citing *Equal Employment Opportunity Commission v. American National Bank*, 652 F.2d 1176 (4th Cir.1981), *cert. denied*, — U.S. — 103 S.Ct. 235, 74 L.Ed.2d 186, 30 EPD 33,080 (1982). In that case, however, the company was simply made to bear the consequences of having voluntarily *destroyed* the relevant records. 652 F.2d at 1195. Where, as here, the incomplete recording of discipline is due to the admittedly informal nature of the company's policy rather than willful destruction of existing records, it would be unfair to create an evidentiary presumption against the company.

In re SOUTH FLORIDA TITLE, INC. In re German LUENGO. In re Caridad LUENGO. Steven FRIEDMAN v. German LUENGO and Caridad Luengo

102 Bankr. 266

United States Bankruptcy Court, S.D. Florida
June 8, 1989

Defendants' Answer invokes their Fifth Amendment and their common law interspousal immunity privileges to excuse their refusal to either admit or deny the trustee's allegations (CP 4). The Answer incorporates a motion for a grant of immunity under 11 U.S.C. § 344 (which only the Attorney General or U.S. Attorney may request; neither has done so) and a motion to dismiss. The

motions were heard May 12. The motion to dismiss was abandoned at the hearing. The motion for grant of immunity was orally denied at the hearing and by a subsequent Order. (CP 32).

* * * * *

The defendants were the initial and only directors of the bankrupt South Florida Title, Inc., a Florida Corporation, from its incorporation, on February 16, 1982, until its involuntary dissolution, on November 14, 1986. Throughout the life of this corporate debtor, the debtor wife was its vice-president, and both of the defendants were persons in control of the corporation. I find, therefore, that each defendant was an insider of South Florida Title, Inc., at all times relevant to this decision, that is to say, when their actions as more fully described below occurred.

The corporate bankruptcy began September 29, 1988, with the filing of an involuntary petition under chapter 7. The Order for Relief was entered October 16 (CP 46). All of the pertinent activity of the debtors, which is more fully described below, occurred within the year before that date.

The corporate debtor sold title insurance policies, as agent for title insurance underwriters, and also served as closing, escrow, and disbursing agent in connection with real estate closings where the title was insured by those policies. On Friday, August 19, 1988, the last day the corporation was open for business, the two Luengos were observed systematically removing files, documents and checkbooks from file drawers and filing cabinets in the business premises and stuffing them into plastic garbage bags. In mid-afternoon of that day, the Receiver appointed for the corporation by the State Court attempted to take possession of the corporate premises and its records, but found the premises locked and could not get in.

When he gained access the next day, he found the file drawers and cabinets open and the remaining records in disarray. He found that the books of 23 to 25 of the most recent closings, as reflected in the corporate transaction register, were missing, together with the corporate escrow account documents and other financial records. Despite extensive and repeated efforts, he has been unable since to discover the whereabouts or recover any of those records from the Luengos or otherwise. All of the missing records are known to have been maintained on the premises up to August 19.

I infer from these disputed circumstances that the missing records were removed from the business premises on Friday, August 19, 1988, by the Luengos and have since been concealed or destroyed by them. I also find that the Luengos were under a deputy to keep and preserve the missing records and have failed to do so.

The State court receiver and Commonwealth, one of the title insurance underwriters represented by the corporate debtor, has since been obliged to pay over $1 million in title insurance claims to vendees on account of undischarged liens which had been fully covered by escrowed funds entrusted to the Luengos on behalf of the corporate debtor.

An independent fraud examiner has inventoried and examined all of the corporate records which remain, and has verified that the essential transactional records had existed but had been systematically removed, together with the associated corporate financial books and records.

The Luengos, who alone were in complete control of the corporate records through August 19, 1988, have refused to explain the disappearance of any of these essential financial and business records, and have refused to produce them, invoking their privileges against self-incrimination.

I agree with the trustee that it is appropriate for this Court, in this civil matter, to draw a negative inference from the invocation by each of the Luengos of their Fifth Amendment privileges. *Baxter v. Palmigiano*, 425 U.S. 308, 96 S.Ct. 1551, 47 L.Ed.2d 810 (1976); *RAD Services, Inc. v Aetna Casualty and Surety Co.*, 808 F.2d 271 (3rd Cir.1986); *In re Stelweck*, 86 B.R. 833 (Bankr.E.D.Pa.1988).

With that inference, but also from the evidence before me without the benefit of that inference, I find that, during the year preceding the filing of the bankruptcy petition for South Florida Title, Inc., each of the defendants has deliberately concealed or destroyed and has failed to preserve recorded information, including books, documents, records and papers, from which the financial condition and business transactions of the bankruptcy debtor, South Florida Title, Inc. (of which they were then insiders) might be ascertained.

I conclude that each defendant has, therefore, committed an act specified in § 727(a)(3) and that the bankruptcy discharge of each defendant must, therefore, be denied under the provisions of § 727(a)(7).

* * * * *

In the Matter of STANDARD LAW ENFORCEMENT SUPPLY COMPANY OF WISCONSIN, d/b/a Standard Equipment Company, John Louis CASTELLANI, Trustee, v. FIRST WISCONSIN NATIONAL BANK OF MILWAUKEE and Clifton G. Owens, Trustee

89 B.R. 24

United States Bankruptcy Court, E.D. Wisconsin
July 22, 1988

Standard Law Enforcement Supply Co., also known as Standard Equipment Co. (SECO), filed its voluntary petition under Chapter 7 of the Bankruptcy Code in 19893, and John Castellani was appointed as its trustee. Thereafter, Castellani served also as bankruptcy trustee of Lentech International Corporation, a related corporation, until discovering that SECO was a creditor of Lentech. Castellani then resigned as Lentech's trustee and Clifton Owens was appointed his successor.

Subsequently, Castellani instituted this adversary proceeding to recover an alleged fraudulent transfer made by SECO to First

Wisconsin National Bank of Milwaukee through Lentech. While the suit was pending, Castellani filed a motion in the underlying bankruptcy case seeking authority to abandon voluminous, unidentified commingled documents regarding SECO, Lentech and other related businesses, he considered unnecessary for continued administration of the bankruptcy estate. Those documents had been stored in a suite next to Castellani's office for three years, at a cost of $180 a month, paid by First Republic Bank–Dallas, SECO's largest creditor.

After notice to all known parties in interest and a hearing, Castellani's motion was granted without objection on March 3, 1987. Thereafter, the documents were destroyed.

On November 21, 1987, First Wisconsin served Castellani with a subpoena and request to produce documents relating to transfers between SECO and Lentech during the period January 1, 1981, to December 31, 1983. When Castellani replied that he did not have the documents and that they may have been destroyed, First Wisconsin filed the pending motion asking for various sanctions, including dismissal of Castellani's complaint; dismissal of Owens' cross claim seeking recovery of the funds from First Wisconsin as a preference; a determination that SECO owed Lentech less that $356,800 when the alleged fraudulent transfer was made; striking Castellani's assertion that the alleged fraudulent transfer was for less than reasonably equivalent value; and ordering Castellani to produce all documents that in any way related to SECO and Lentech. First Wisconsin claimed that some, if not all, of the sanctions were warranted because failure to produce the documents impaired its primary defense that the transfer from SECO to Lentech was for reasonably equivalent value.

* * * * *

First Wisconsin argues that the court must infer that Castellani destroyed relevant documents, relying on *Turnage*. In *Turnage*, the defendant admitted to destroying relevant documents, and the court imposed monetary, discovery, and other sanctions against the defendant. The court stated that it "must draw the strongest allowable inferences in favor of the aggrieved party . . . Obviously, the relevance of and resulting prejudice from destruction of documents cannot be clearly ascertained because the documents no longer exist. Under the circumstances, the culpable party can hardly assert any presumption of irrelevance as to the destroyed documents." *Id.* at 557 (citations omitted).

Here, there is no admission to the destruction of relevant documents and Castellani has stated that he does not believe that he destroyed any documents relating to transfers between SECO and Lentech. But, even if relevant documents were among those purged, Castellani sought and received court approval for the abandonment of materials which he felt burdened the bankruptcy estate. Furthermore, First Wisconsin was aware of Castellani's motion to abandon and intention to destroy documents and yet, failed to object or seek to inspect the documents before they were destroyed. First Wisconsin cannot now complain that the destroyed documents were relevant when it chose not to inspect the documents. Under the circumstances, First Wisconsin's tardy complaints are to no avail. Castellani reasonably relied on First Wisconsin's silence following his motion to abandon and he properly obtained a court order approving his request.

For the foregoing reasons, First Wisconsin's motion for sanctions is denied.

STATE OF NEBRASKA, Appellee, v. Odell FORD, Appellant.

501 N.W.2d 318

Nebraska Court of Appeals
March 16, 1993

I. Introduction

This appeal arises from the conviction of the appellant, a hotel porter, on two counts of theft by unlawful taking. The appellant challenges the admission into evidence of computer–generated records which indicated that

during the time periods when the thefts occurred, the appellant had gained entry to the
hotel rooms from which the missing property
had been taken. The appellant also argues
that the trial court's jury instruction on reasonable doubt erroneously diminished the
State's burden of proof. We affirm.

II. FACTS

1. Reports of Stolen Property

The Appellent, Odell Ford, began working as
a porter at the Homewood Suites hotel complex the morning of June 6, 1991. His job was
to empty trash collected by the hotel's maids
and stock guestrooms with new linens. The
evening of June 6, two Homewood guests
reported that personal items were missing
from their rooms. Curtis VanDeen in room
318 was missing a key chain with two men's
rings attached, and Kristy Oehlert in room
233 was missing a pair of diamond earrings.

2. Homewood's Computer System

The doors to Homewood's guestrooms can
be opened with keys, but Homewood does
not issue keys to its guests. Instead, Homewood utilizes the Cellular Lock System, a
computerized lock system, to control access
to its guestrooms. All the doors to guestrooms are equipped with security devices
that are unlocked by cards rather than keys.
At check–in, the guest's credit card is run
through a machine, which sends a message
to the system's lock computer. The lock computer then signals the device on the guest's
door to allow access to the room whenever
the guest's credit card is inserted into the
device. If the guest does not want to use his
or her own credit card to open the door,
Homewood issues the guest a plastic card
that functions in the same manner as the
credit card. Homewood employees whose
duties require entry into guestrooms also receive access cards.

The computer system records the opening of
every guestroom door on the Homewood
property, whether by card or key. The computer records the date and time of access,
whether access was obtained by card or key,

and, if by card, the name of the person to
whom the card was issued. There is no human input into the recordkeeping process,
and no calculation of figures is involved.

3. Records Implicate Ford

The access cards for Homewood employees
are identified by the employees' names. A
card had not yet been prepared for Ford on
his first day of work, so he was issued the
card assigned to "Mary CC," who was not
working that day. Ford was the only employee authorized to use the "Mary CC" card
on June 6.

In response to the reports of stolen items by
guests VanDeen and Oehlert, Glenda Willmon, Homewood's general manager, consulted the hotel's computerized records to
determine who had entered rooms 318 and
233 through the course of the day.

VanDeen left room 318 the morning of June
6 between 8 and 8:30. Before leaving, he
removed from his pocket a key chain with
two men's rings attached and placed it on the
kitchen table. He returned at 5:14 p.m. The
"Mary CC" card had been used to gain entry
to VanDeen's room at 10:35 a.m. and again
at 3:51 and 3:54 p.m. The computer records
also showed that a regular key had been used
to open the door to VanDeen's room at 11:08
a.m. and 3:54 p.m.

Before taking an early afternoon nap in room
233, Oehlert had taken off her diamond earrings. Oehlert wore a different pair of earrings when she next left the room. She placed
the earrings on a glass shelf in the vanity area
of the room. Oehlert left the room at approximately 3:30 p.m. and returned at 10:44 p.m.
The "Mary CC" card had been used to gain
entry to Oehlert's room at 5:15 p.m. That was
the only entry into Oehlert's room during her
afternoon and evening absence.

When questioned on June 7, 1991, by Willmon, Ford initially denied ever entering
rooms 318 and 233. After Willmon explained
the computerized recordkeeping system and
produced printouts of the entries to rooms
318 and 233 on June 6, Ford admitted that he

had used both the "Mary CC" card and a regular key to enter the two rooms, but denied taking the missing items. Ford was charged with two counts of theft by unlawful taking.

4. Trial

At trial, Willmon testified to the manner in which the computerized access and recordkeeping system functioned, and the State offered into evidence exhibits 10 to 14, the computer printouts detailing Ford's multiple entries into rooms 318 and 233 while the occupants were gone. Arguing hearsay and lack of foundation, defense counsel continually objected to Willmon's testimony and the offers of exhibits related to the computerized recordkeeping system. The objections were overruled. Willmon was allowed to testify about the computerized recordkeeping system, and the computer printouts were admitted into evidence.

The jury found Ford guilty of both counts of theft by unlawful taking. On count I, theft of Oehlert's diamond earrings, Ford was sentenced to a prison term of 6 2/3 to 20 years. For theft of VanDeen's rings, count III of the amended information, Ford was sentenced to a prison term of 20 months to 5 years, to run concurrently with the sentence on count I.

III. Assignments of Error

Ford assigns as error the admission into evidence of Homewood's computer printouts and the overruling of his objection to the jury instruction on reasonable doubt.

* * * * *

V. Analysis

1. Admission of Computer Printouts

Ford's objection to the computer printouts were based on lack of foundation and on hearsay. Neb. Rev Stat. § 27–803(5) (Reissue 1989) establishes a hearsay exception for business records. The three foundational requirements for admission of business records under the hearsay exception are: (1) the activity recorded must be a type which

regularly occurs in the course of the business' day–to–day activity, (2) the record must have been made at or near the time of the event recorded, and (3) the record must be authenticated by a qualified witness. *State v. Wilson, 225 Neb. 466, 406 N.W.2d 123 (1987).*

In the case at bar, there is no question that the first two requirements of the business records exception were satisfied. First, the activity recorded was the unlocking and opening of the doors to rooms 318 and 233, an activity which regularly occurs and is regularly recorded in the course of Homewood's day–to–day business. Second, the records were made instantaneously; entry by card or key is recorded into the computer's memory at the moment the device on the door is unlocked.

Ford's argument focuses on the third requirement of the business records exception. He argues that Willmon was not qualified to testify about the computer system and authenticate the computer–generated records. In addition, Ford contends that "the State failed to lay a proper foundation as to whether the computer security system was standard within the industry and whether retrieval of information from the system occurs in the ordinary manner which indicates trustworthiness." Brief for appellate at 5.

(a) Qualification of Witness

At trial, as the State began using Willmon's testimony to explain the computerized lock system and authenticate the printouts, defense counsel objected and asked for permission to voir dire Willmon for foundation. The court granted defense counsel's request. Defense counsel established that Willmon did not have a degree in computers, did not invent the computer used at Homewood, and was unfamiliar with the computer's components. Willmon testified that the company that had installed the computer system at Homewood gave her 3 weeks of training in how to operate the computer system.

The facts before us are analogous to those in *State v. Estill, 13 Kan. App. 2d 111, 764 P.2d 455 (1988)* in which a records custodian testified about computer–generated "phone trap" records. In a phone–trap arrangement, a telephone company computer traces all calls made to a certain number and records and stores the numbers of the phones from which the calls originated. At trial, the records custodian explained the computerized phone trap and testified that the computerized records were made at the time a harassing call was reported and were kept in the ordinary course of business. However, she could not explain how the computer itself operated. The court noted that it previously had held that a police officer operating a radar unit did not have to be an expert in the science or theory underlying the instrument; the fact that the officer was trained to operate the device was sufficient foundation for admitting evidence produced by the radar unit. In *Estill*, the court held that admission of the computer–generated phone–trap evidence under the business records exception was proper.

In the case at bar, Willmon explained how the computer system worked and testified that the computer instantaneously recorded the opening of every guestroom door on the property. Her testimony indicated that she was proficient in retrieving and printing out information stored in the computer system. Willmon's situation is analogous to that of the records custodian in *Estill* or the officer, referred to in *Estill*, who uses a radar device. The record on appeal shows that Willmon was trained and competent in the use of the computer system. For purposes of foundation, it did not matter whether Willmon could discuss the components or engineering principles of the computer. Willmon was qualified to testify about the computer system and authenticate the system's printouts. The third requirement of the business records exception was satisfied.

(b) Proof of Industry Standard

Ford cites *People v. Bovio, 118 Ill. App. 3d 836, 455 N.E.2d 829 (1983)*, for the proposition that one of the foundational requirements for admission of computerized business records is proof that the computer equipment is standard within the industry. *Bovio* cites Illinois case law and recites the foundational requirement of proof of indus-

try standard, but offers no rationale for the requirement. One of the two cases cited in *Bovio* to support the requirement does not mention proof of industry standard as a foundational requirement for admission of computerized records. *See People v. Gauer, 7 Ill. App. 3d 512, 288 N.E.2d 24 (1972)* (the court must be satisfied from the foundation testimony that the sources of information, method, and time of preparation were such as to indicate [the computer's] trustworthiness.) *Bovio* does not cite any Illinois statutory authority for requiring proof of industry standard to admit computer–generated records or business records in general. *Bovio* is not persuasive authority for adopting the foundational requirement at issue.

Although some jurisdictions have sided with *Bovio* and required proof that computer equipment is standard within the industry, we side with jurisdictions that have rejected such a requirement. See McCormick on Evidence § 294 n.7 (John W. Strong 4th ed. 1992) (for citations to cases on both sides of the issue). "Testimony describing [computer] equipment should ordinarily be limited to the function that each unit performs in the process and that each is adequate for the purpose. Excursions into theory are not required or ordinarily appropriate." McCormick on Evidence, supra, § 294 at 284. McCormick points out that with time, a type of technology becomes so commonplace and reputable that detailed foundational evidence is no longer necessary:

As new technologies develop and win acceptance, courts move in the direction of taking judicial notice of the validity of the underlying scientific principle. Radar is a case in point . . . Similarly, the principles of electronic data processing are now a proper subject of judicial notice and should not require proof.

Id. at n.9. Of course, a specific computerized system must be shown to be reliable, but the imposition of the burden of proving industry standard is not justifiable. At this state in the evolution of computer technology, there is no need to require proof of industry standard. Concern over whether a computer system is reliable is addressed by § 27–803(5)'s requirement that the recordkeeping method be proven trustworthy.

We also are bound by the rule that admissibility of evidence is controlled by statute, not judicial discretion. See *State v. Timmerman, 240 Neb. 74, 480 N.W.2d 411 (1992)*. In *McAllen State Bank v. Linbeck Const. Corp., 695 S.W.2d 10, 17 (Tex. App. 1985)*, the court made the following observation:

"The [Texas] legislature did not see any necessity for additional requirements where the records sought to be introduced into evidence were electronically produced. Once the [foundational] requirements [set out in Texas' business records exception statute] are met the records are admissible and are to be given whatever weight they are entitled to."

Section 27–803(5) of the Nebraska rules of evidence does not require a party offering business records to prove that the recordkeeping system is standard within the industry. It is not within the province of an appellate court to amend § 27–803(5) by incorporating into the statute such a foundational requirement for computerized records.

For the reasons discussed above, we reject Ford's assertion that the State was required to prove that Homewood's computer system was standard within the industry.

(c) Trustworthiness of Recording System

Section 27–803(5) states that business records evidence may be excluded if "the source of information . . . indicates lack of trustworthiness."

On cross–examination of Willmon, defense counsel asked about an occasion on which Homewood's computer system had generated faulty information. In December 1991, defense counsel himself had gone to Homewood for a demonstration of how the system functioned. The computer's time–recording mechanism was out of order because the hotel's computer maintenance worker happened to be backing up the system's records during the time of the demonstration. Defense counsel questioned Willmon about the inaccuracy of the information produced by the computer system during the December demonstration:

[Defense]: So what was printed out there as a date and time was in fact not what the actual date and time [were]; is that correct?

[Willmon]: Right. The time was off. If you remember, [the computer maintenance worker] said that he could reset the time and show you again, as he was in the middle of backing up some records.

[Defense]: So it's possible to run something on the machine and not have it reflect the accurate date and time; is that right?

[Willmon]: If you're backing up some records, yes.

The assertion that the computerized recordkeeping system was not trustworthy on June 6, 1991, is without merit. The computer–recorded times of entry into rooms 318 and 233 on June 6 were corroborated by Ford, VanDeen, Oehlert, and other hotel personnel. For instance, VanDeen testified that he returned to room 318 sometime between 5 and 5:30 p.m. Oehlert testified that she returned to room 233 sometime after 10:30 p.m. The computer system shows that Oehlert returned at 10:44 p.m. The record on appeal indicates that the system was functioning properly on June 6. Defense counsel's emphasis on the inaccurate computer readings generated while the system was being backed up in December 1991 is irrelevant.

(d) Conclusion

The State satisfied the foundational requirements for the business records exception, and the record on appeal indicates the computer's recordkeeping system was trustworthy. Therefore, the trial court properly admitted the printouts into evidence.

* * * * *

STOUMEN v. COMMISSIONER OF INTERNAL REVENUE

208 F.2d 903

United States Court of Appeals, Third Circuit
December 8, 1953

STALEY, Circuit Judge.

This is a petition for review of a decision of the Tax Court which sustained the Commissioner's deficiency assessments in petitioner's income taxes for the years 1943, 1944, and 1945.

Petitioner, Bernard Stoumen, and his brother Abraham were equal partners in the firm Fairplay Knitting Mills, engaged in the manufacture and jobbing of knit goods. During the times which concern us here, petitioner's principal duties consisted of expediting shipments to the firm and working in the shipping end of the business. He did not handle the books and knew nothing of their details, Abraham being the managing partner and responsible for the firm's finances. Samuel Schwartz, petitioner's brother-in-law and an employee of the firm, did the buying for the business and supervised mill operations.

For the taxable years in question, Abraham had an accountant audit the firm's records and determine its income. Using the information obtained from that accountant, another accountant made up the firm's and petitioner's income tax returns. Petitioner's returns showed his full share of partnership income as reflected by the firm's books. It was learned in 1946, however, that Abraham and Schwartz had engaged in transactions which did not appear on the books.

* * * * *

On the night of May 6, after receiving two extensions of time within which to submit the partnership books for examination by the Internal Revenue agents, Abraham destroyed al the partnership records except the general ledger for 1945. The next morning, after

writing notes to petitioner, Schwartz, and the investigating agents, he committed suicide.

The Commissioner, in reliance upon Section 182 of the Internal Revenue Code, 26 U.S.C. § 182, determined that all the money in the New York accounts represented partnership income and charged petitioner with one-half of that amount and assessed a 50 per cent fraud penalty. The deficiencies total about $180,000, plus substantial interest. The Tax Court sustained the deficiency assessments but cancelled the fraud penalties, which holding the Commissioner does not question.

* * * * *

Petitioner's entire case is based upon his wholly unsupported assertion that Abraham was off on a criminal frolic and was not acting for the partnership. Abraham, of course, is dead and cannot further clear up the matter. But Schwartz, who participated in all of Abraham's alleged machinations, was alive, available, and, in fact, was still employed by petitioner at the time of trial. Certainly, Schwartz could throw some light on the validity of petitioner's theory of the case. Yet petitioner did not call Schwartz. Indeed, the trial was adjourned at petitioner's request in order to afford him an opportunity to put Schwartz's testimony in the record, but petitioner declined to do so. From this failure to call Schwartz, the Tax Court inferred, as was clearly within its province, that his testimony would have been unfavorable to petitioner. Under the circumstances of this case, petitioner's neglect to call Schwartz "* * * becomes evidence of the most convincing character." *Interstate Circuit v. United States*, 1939, 306 U.S. 208, 226, 59 S.Ct. 467, 474, 83 L.Ed. 610; *Wichita Terminal Elevator Co. v. Commissioner of Internal Revenue*, 1946, 6 T.C. 1158, 1165, affirmed, 10 Cir., 1947, 162 F.2d 513; 2 Wigmore, op.cit. supra, § 285. Petitioner would avoid that unfavorable result by pointing out that it was the Commissioner who subpoenaed Schwartz but did not call him. The Commissioner might well have expected Schwartz to be hostile, while petitioner, would have had every reason to expect Schwartz to be friendly and cooperative. Whatever may have motivated the Commissioner's decision not to call Schwartz need not concern us here, however, for the Commissioner made out his case without Schwartz. Petitioner was the one who needed Schwartz, not the Commissioner.

Petitioner did not testify that Schwartz had told him that all the money and bonds that he had withdrawn from the New York accounts had been turned over to Abraham. This, we are told, shows that Abraham and not the partnership benefited, and, thus, Abraham realized income, but the partnership did not. Even if Schwartz did turn the withdrawals over to Abraham, it does not follow that the latter converted or embezzled them. Petitioner showed no inordinate increase in Abraham's net worth. Indeed, his studied indifference as to what did become of the money from the New York accounts, considering the importance of the matter to him, was truly astounding. Furthermore, Schwartz was an employee and Abraham the managing partner. There is nothing sinister in an employee turning over to his employer money received from the sale of firm property. We may not assume that Abraham was an embezzler or a thief.

Petitioner overemphasizes the effect of his success in defeating the imposition of the fraud penalty. The fact that he was unaware of the New York funds, received none of them knowingly, and justifiably relied upon the information contained in the partnership books, was sufficient to show that, though false, his returns were not filed with intent to evade the tax. That, however, has nothing to do with the operation of Section 182(c). By virtue of that section, one-half of the partnership's ordinary net income automatically became his income even through he actually received none of it knowingly and was ignorant of its existence at the time.

The judgment of the Tax Court will be affirmed.

STRUTHERS PATENT CORPORATION v. The NESTLE COMPANY, INC., Defendant, v. STRUTHERS WELLS CORPORATION, et al

558 F.Supp. 747

United States District Court, D. New Jersey
October 13, 1981

Plaintiff, Struthers Patent Corporation, filed its complaint on April 13, 1972, alleging that defendant, The Nestle Company, Inc., was infringing ten Struthers patents by its manufacture and sale of soluble coffee. Nestle denied infringement and asserts that each of the patents is invalid and unenforceable. Nestle filed a counterclaim seeking, in one Count, a declaratory judgment of invalidity and unenforceability of each of the ten patents and asserting, in a second Count, a claim alleging unfair competition. Nestle joined as defendants on the counterclaim two corporations which are affiliated with plaintiff — Struthers Wells Corporation and Struthers Scientific and International Corporation. The three affiliated corporations will be referred to collectively as "Struthers".

The case has had a protracted pretrial history. Two matters are now ripe for disposition: (i) Struthers' motion to confirm the report and recommendation of a special master concerning sanctions to be imposed by reason of Struthers' destruction of relevant documents prior to institution of this action, and (ii) Nestle's motions for summary judgment of invalidity and/or unenforceability of the ten patents in suit.

For the reasons which are set forth in Parts I through V of this opinion, the findings of the special master will be adopted in part, modified in part, and rejected in part, but his recommendations that no sanctions will be imposed will be adopted; Nestle's motions for summary judgment of invalidity of the ten patents will be granted.

A. Background

Struthers is in the business of licensing and selling technical information and know-how. It owns the ten patents in suit, which deal generally with freeze concentration in the manufacture of instant or soluble coffee and certain other food products. Nestle is the world's largest seller of soluble coffee.

In simple terms, freeze concentration of coffee extract (derived by brewing coffee from coffee beans) involves removing water from the extract by chilling the extract sufficiently to form ice particles and then removing the ice particles, leaving a more concentrated solution. After the concentration stage the concentrated solution may be dried by various means to form the powder or granules constituting the soluble coffee. Nestle uses a freeze *drying* process but denies that it freeze *concentrates* coffee. For the most part the patents in suit contemplate that the freeze concentration processes described therein either will be or may be followed by freeze drying.

Events pertinent to the pending motion took place as early as the mid–1960's. At that time Struthers entered into a contractual relationship with General Foods Corporation to assist General Foods in developing equipment for the freeze concentration of coffee extract. During the course of that relationship Struthers disclosed and sold or offered to sell to General Foods various processes and items of equipment relating to freeze concentration. According to General Foods it did not find the processes or equipment useful in its business and terminated its relationship with Struthers.

Thereafter extensive litigation between General Foods and Struthers took place, most of which ultimately was consolidated in the United States District Court in Delaware. Struthers charged General Foods with infringement of six of the ten patents at issue in the present action. Each party charged the other with theft of trade secrets and know-how. After extensive discovery and other pretrial proceedings the parties settled, signing a settlement agreement on February 9, 1972.

After February 9 and prior to April 13, 1972, when the present action was filed, Struthers collected and destroyed a very substantial part of the documents and depositions which it had assembled in the course of the General Foods case. This document destruction is the subject of Nestle's motion for sanctions and the special master's report and recommendation recommending against sanctions.

* * * * *

The Special Master's Report

In December, 1975 Nestle filed a motion pursuant to *Fed.R.Civ.P.* 37 seeking sanctions against Struthers for alleged destruction by Struthers just prior to the institution of this action of a very substantial quantity of documents relevant to the issues in this action.

These documents were voluminous in nature and were assembled during the course of the litigation between Struthers and General Foods Corporation. In that action Struthers asserted against General Foods six of the ten patents which it now asserts against Nestle.

Judge Meanor, to whom the case was then assigned, reviewed the papers which Nestle submitted in support of its motion for sanctions on account of the document destruction, and he heard argument on the motion. As set forth in his opinion filed September 15, 1976, he concluded that he was "[u]nable to determine from the written record what documents were destroyed or how they related to the issues in this action." Further, on the record before him, he was unable to "determine the appropriateness of the many forms of sanctions sought by Nestle." He reserved decision until a hearing could be conducted.

In order that resolution of the document destruction issues would not delay prosecution of the other phases of this case I appointed The Honorable Harold R. Tyler, Jr., a former United States District Court Judge, Special Master to supervise discovery, conduct hearings, and file a report containing his findings of fact, conclusions of law, and recommendations with respect to the document destruction charge. Inquiry into the following factual and legal questions was to be made: (i) identification, with as much specificity as possible, of the documents which were destroyed; (ii) the relationship of those documents to the issues in the present action; (iii) the extent to which such documents can now be obtained from other sources; (iv) whether Struthers knew or should have known at the time it caused the destruction of the documents that litigation against Nestle on the patents at issue was a distinct possibility, and (v) whether, in the light of the circumstances disclosed by the factual inquiry, sanctions should be imposed upon Struthers and, if so, what the sanctions should be.

By pretrial order #2 Judge Tyler was appointed Special Master. Thereafter very extensive work was performed by the Special Master and the parties with respect to the document destruction phase of the case. Had it not been for the efforts of the Special Master, it would have been impossible for me to have proceeded with the discovery and summary judgment phases of the case.

On June 8, 1981 the Special Master filed his report and recommendations, which concluded that no sanctions should be imposed upon Struthers. Struthers filed a motion to confirm the Special Master's report and to deny Nestle's motion for sanctions. Nestle filed objections to the report and recommendation. A hearing on the motion and objections was held on September 10, 1981. Most of the grounds of Nestle's objections are addressed in this Part I. In view of my conclusions set forth below it is unnecessary to address the remaining grounds.

A. The Destroyed Documents

During the course of the General Foods litigation Mr. Drucker, patent counsel and an officer of Struthers, was in general charge of assembling and controlling documents. He arranged for all Struthers' documents pertaining to freeze concentration to be assembled and sent, ultimately, to the Texas law firm representing Struthers in that litigation, Fulbright and Jaworski. Mr. Drucker retained in his own custody the files relating to

the processing of the pertinent patent applications. Through the discovery process in the General Foods litigation depositions were acquired and thousands of documents produced. Struthers kept these documents in Houston and copies were kept by Mr. Drucker in New York City, by John G. Muller, a Vice President of one of the Struthers companies, in Washington, D.C., and by Struthers' Delaware counsel in Wilmington, Delaware. In addition, the Fulbright firm sent to Westheimer Transfer & Storage Co., Inc., for storage, certain documents which included those known as the Office of Saline Water ("OSW") documents. These were documents relating to work carried out by Struthers for the Office of Saline Water, United States Department of the Interior.

A protective order was entered in the Delaware federal district court in the General Foods litigation covering some, but by no means all, of the depositions and documents produced by General Foods. It provided, in part:

> 2. At the conclusion of this litigation, all information received by any party from an opposing party and designated as secret, or determined to be secret by Court order, *shall be deposited by the party then in possession of it in a secure place*, still subject to the terms of this order, protected from access by any person other than a person authorized to see it by the terms of this order, or the terms of some subsequent Court order. (Emphasis added.)

On February 9, 1972 Struthers and General Foods signed an agreement terminating their litigation.

At Mr. Drucker's instructions, some OSW documents had been destroyed at the Westheimer warehouse on January 12, 1972. Struthers can give no explanation of this destruction, which took place just prior to a court-ordered document inspection by General Foods of the OSW documents. The remaining documents stored at Westheimer were destroyed on March 7, 1972, pursuant to Mr. Drucker's instructions.

On February 14 or 15, 1972 (less than a week after the Struthers–General Foods settlement agreement was signed) Mr. Drucker ordered that all the General Foods litigation documents be shipped to Houston for destruction. The exact dates when the destruction of the documents in Houston took place (except for the documents destroyed on January 12 and March 7, 1972 in the Westheimer warehouse) are not known precisely. Many were probably destroyed in late February and early March, 1971. Some must have been destroyed in or after May, 1972, when Struthers' Delaware attorneys shipped documents to Houston in response to Mr. Drucker's instructions.

On March 6, 1972, Mr. Muller burned the documents under his control in Washington, D.C. Struthers' Delaware counsel destroyed certain of the documents in their control in February, 1972 and, as mentioned above, shipped others to Houston in May, 1972.

Mr. Drucker's files contained documents underlying or pertaining to the patents in suit in the present case or relating to freeze concentration. This included documents relating to the prosecution and the file history of abandoned, pending and issued applications. These were destroyed, according to Struthers, as a "routine housekeeping practice" and "began in the early 1960s and continued subsequent to April 13, 1972" (the date when Struthers filed its complaint against Nestle).

The Special Master found that this document destruction program resulted in the destruction of the following categories of documents:

1. Copies of transcripts of depositions of General Foods personnel.

2. Copies of exhibits marked during the depositions of General Foods personnel.

3. Copies of documents, which copies were produced to Struthers to General Foods in the course of discovery.

4. All copies of the OSW records except copies of government contracts and a North American Aviation contract.

5. Copies of Struthers' correspondence and related materials pertaining to customers or potential customers of Struthers for a period during the mid–1960s.

6. Materials in the files of Struthers designated as "privileged" in relation to the litigation with General Foods.

7. Copies of documents in the files of Struthers relating to the prosecution and file history of some or all of the freeze concentration patents here in suit.

This finding requires a modification to reflect two events which occurred during the proceedings before the Special Master.

Shortly before the March 21, 1981 hearing before the Special Master, Struthers reported that "portions" of its customer correspondence in the mid–1960s had been discovered. Thus at least part of the customer records previously reported to have been destroyed evidently were not destroyed and, very belatedly, have been produced. The day before the hearing before the Special Master Nestle was informed that the original index cards of documents from the Struthers–General Foods litigation were in existence and in the possession of Struthers' counsel. Early in this litigation Struthers denied the existence of such a list. With these modifications, the findings of the Special Master as to the documents which were destroyed are supported by the records and will be adopted.

B. Struthers' Knowledge of Impending Litigation

The Special Master found that "[t]he record does not indicate when Struthers decided to institute suit against Nestle, nor does it establish who, acting on behalf of Struthers, made that decision. The complaint herein was filed April 13, 1972." This is a correct finding.

In addition, however, I believe it necessary to determine whether Struthers knew or should have known at the time it caused the destruction of the documents that litigation against Nestle on the patents at issue was a distinct possibility. The Special Master did not make a specific finding on this point, but the record leaves no question as to what the answer to this question must be.

Struthers' proposed Contentions of Fact filed with the Special Master conceded that "After the settlement of the General Foods litigation, Struthers knew or should have known that litigation against Nestle on the patents at issue in its present action against Nestle was contemplated."

A recital of Struthers' position on this issue is pertinent, because it bears upon Struthers' motives when destroying the documents and it bears upon its good faith in the present proceedings.

In 1976, in opposition to Nestle's motion for sanctions, Struthers filed an affidavit of Mr. Drucker which stated in part:

> I also want to emphasize that at the time the documents were destroyed Struthers had not turned its attention to preparation for litigation with Nestle and indeed was not prepared for litigation with anyone. I was not at the time aware of any plan by Struthers to conduct further litigation nor have I subsequently become aware that such a plan was in existence at that time.
>
> * * * Struthers has not concealed from Nestle any information appropriate to the matters in dispute in the present litigation. From the beginning of the present litigation until this time there has been absolutely no document destruction on behalf of Struthers. *Indeed, no document destruction occurred from the moment that litigation between Struthers and Nestle was contemplated by Struthers.* [Emphasis in original.]

In its Interrogatory 81(a)(C)(xii) Nestle had requested Struthers to identify "memoranda of counsel, diary and timebook entries of counsel and employees of respondents, bills and statements of counsel," etc. In its answers (which list William Drucker, James Weiler and Dudley Dobie (of the Fulbright firm)) of counsel, Struthers responded:

Objection is made to identification of memoranda of counsel, diary and timebook entries of counsel and bills and statements of counsel on the basis of privilege. However, without waiving the foregoing objection, *there are no such documents* relating, pertaining, referring to or bearing upon the foregoing. In addition, there *are no other documents of the nature requested.* (Emphasis added.)

Nestle also served further document requests (Nos. 7–9) relating to destruction, to which Struthers replied: "There are no documents relating to the solicitation or giving of advice concerning document destruction."

Discovery of the Fulbright firm's time sheets in the proceedings before the Special Master disclosed that Mr. Drucker's statements and the answers to these interrogatories were not true.

It will be recalled that the Struthers–General Foods settlement agreement was signed on February 9, 1972 and that Mr. Drucker issued the document destruction orders on February 14 or 15, 1972. The Fulbright records show that on February 11, 1972, Mr. Drucker entered into discussions with the Fulbright firm regarding the disposition of documents *and* institution of new legal proceedings. The Fulbright and Jaworski time record of Dudley R. Dobie dated February 11, 1972, reads as follows:

> Conf. T. Clark re document retention; T/T W.A. Drucker re doc. disposition and new litigation; continue review of files for storage. (Chargeable Hours Card No. 000037; Tab 18.)

Mr. Dobie testified that the new litigation mentioned in his card referred to either Nestle or Coca–Cola (Dobie Tr., p. 192.)

During February, 1972 letters proposing non–exclusive licenses were sent over the signature of Struthers' litigation counsel, Mr. Weiler, to Nestle and several other companies in the soluble coffee industry. These letters were dated February 15, 1972, the very time when Mr. Drucker issued his instructions for the destruction of documents.

Again, on February 22, 1972, Mr. Dobie had another telephone conversation with Mr. Drucker regarding the Nestle matter. His Time Card of that date reads as follows:

T/T Drucker re Nestle matter and re storage of files. (Fulbright and Jaworski Chargeable Hours Card No. 000002, Tab. 19.)

On February 23, 1972 — the same date on which the order of dismissal was filed in the Delaware District Court terminating the Struthers/General Foods litigation — Mr. Drucker had further discussions with the Fulbright lawyers regarding the Nestle litigation. Mr. Dobie's Time Card for February 23, 1972 reads as follows:

T/T Richards re entry of Order of Dismissal; *T/T W.A. Drucker re Nestle litigation*; review Rule 60 requirements re Court's jurisdiction after judgment; *investigate jurisdiction re Nestle litigation.* (Fulbright and Jaworski Chargeable Hours Card No. 000001, Tab. 20; emphasis added)

On the same date Mr. Drucker also conferred with James F. Weiler, the partner in charge of the litigation. Weiler's Time Card for February 23, 1972 reads:

Confer Drucker re bringing suit against Nestle in Houston; drafting Complaint and venue questions; confer Dobie re same. Fulbright and Jaworski Chargeable Hours Card No. 000161, Tab. 21; emphasis added.)

Confronted with these records, Struthers had little choice but to concede that at the time it caused the destruction of the documents it knew or should have known that litigation against Nestle on the patents at issue was a distinct possibility. The Special Master's report will be modified to include a finding to the effect that Struthers had actual knowledge that such litigation was a distinct possibility at the time of its destruction of documents in and after February, 1972. Further, there will be included a finding that during the course of the present litigation Struthers sought to conceal the fact that it had

such knowledge until, during the proceedings before the Special Master, it was confronted with records from its former attorneys' files — which demonstrated that Struthers' original contentions in this regard were untrue.

C. Relationship of the Documents to the Issues

The Special Master did not make findings as to the relationship of the destroyed documents to the issue in the present action, perhaps because it is so obvious that each category of destroyed documents (with the possible exception of the OSW documents) was likely to contain relevant information or material which might lead to relevant information.

The General Foods litigation in which the destroyed documents were assembled included a number of separate actions, the claims in which were eventually dealt with in the district court action in Delaware. Struthers filed actions in Texas charging that General Foods was infringing certain of Struthers' patents. General Foods began a declaratory judgment action with respect to the patents in Delaware and thereafter the Texas actions were transferred there. As additional patents were issued to Struthers, additional infringement actions were filed by Struthers in Delaware. Ultimately, six patents (all in suit in the instant action) were in suit in Delaware. In addition, Struthers filed an action in the New York State courts alleging theft of trade secrets by General Foods. General Foods' amended complaint in Delaware also contained a count alleging unfair competition by reason of Struthers' wrongful misappropriation of General Foods' confidential information and Struthers' use of that information to obtain the Muller '007 patent (*see* Part II of this opinion) and the Reimus '302 dewaxing patent (*see* Part IV of this opinion). The relationship of the unfair competition and patent claims was discussed in *General Foods Corp. v. Struthers Scientific and International Corp.*, 297 F.Supp. 271 (D.Del.1969).

The six patents asserted against General Foods are among the ten patents which are the subject of this suit and of Nestle's summary judgment motion. They are dealt with in this opinion as follows:

Both patents in this group, viz., Muller 3,404,007 and Muller 3,495,522, were in suite in Delaware.

Part III — Ganiaris 3,531,295 and Ganiaris 3,620,034 were not in suit in Delaware. Their disclosure of washing the ice to recover coffee solids is, however, included in the claims of other of the patents which were in suit.

PART IV — Reimus 3,381,302, Reimus 3,449,129 and Reimus 3,474,723 were in suit in Delaware. The fourth Reimus patent (3,632,353) purports to derive from the same applications.

PART V — Of the two hollow agitator shaft patents, Howell 3,367,126 was in suit in Delaware; Ganiaris 3,636,722 was not.

In Documentary Requests Nos. 1–6 in the present action Nestle asked for all documents and other products of discovery in the General Foods–Struthers litigation. Concluding that this was a proper subject of discovery, Judge Lacey, who was then handling this case, entered an order on February 15, 1973 which provided, in part:

That Defendant's [Nestle's] motion to compel Respondents [all three Struthers companies] to produce for inspection and copying all documents which are the subject of Defendant's first documentary request (Nos. 1–6) is hereby GRANTED, except insofar as such documents have been produced or marked as Defendant's Deposition Exhibits in this litigation.

Having heard Nestle's summary judgment motions before addressing the document destruction issues, I am able to evaluate the relationship between the destroyed documents and major issues in the case. There can be no question that Judge Lacey correctly concluded that the documents generated in the earlier litigation are pertinent to the present case.

Given the fact that six of the ten patents involved in the present action were the subject of the earlier action, and that the present and former actions involve similar claims and defenses, transcripts of the depositions of General Foods personnel, copies of exhibits marked during those depositions, and copies of documents produced to Struthers by General Foods in the earlier litigation must be highly relevant in the present action. Among other things, they would bear upon the validity of Struthers' patents under paragraphs (a), (b), (f) and (g) of 35 U.S.C. — 102 and under 35 U.S.C. § 103.

There is a dispute between the parties as to the relevance of the OSW documents which involved a development program for freeze desalination of water which Struthers had undertaken for the United States government. Nestle contends that freeze concentration and desalination are essentially the same process and therefore Struthers' work on desalination would bear upon its freeze concentration efforts. Struthers, on the other hand, urges that the processes are essentially different and that the OSW documents produced in the General Foods action related to issues unrelated to patent validity. There is insufficient evidence in the record to make a finding on the relevance of these documents in the present litigation, but, of course, destruction of the documents compounds the difficulty of making such a determination.

The Special Master recited Struthers' rationale for destroying its correspondence and related materials pertaining to customers or potential customers for the period during the mid–1960s: "Struthers made the decision to destroy these documents because of their age and because of the view of Struthers' counsel, at the time of destruction, that such documents were wholly irrelevant to any litigation with Nestle and any other company."

The conclusion of Struthers' counsel in this regard (if, indeed, he did so conclude) was unjustified. As the summary judgment motions in this case amply demonstrate, an important basis for attacking the validity of Struthers' patents is that the subject matter claimed in the patents was offered for sale or

sold more than one year prior to the applications therefor, 35 U.S.C. § 102(b). Correspondence with customers during the
mid–1960s, a period one year or more prior
to the applications for the patents now in
litigation, had potential relevance to the on
sale defense. It is inconceivable that Struthers' counsel, an experienced patent attorney
who had only recently wrestled with this
issue in the General Foods litigation, would
not have appreciated the significance of this
kind of document.

Whether or not the materials in the files of
Struthers designated as "privileged" in the
General Foods litigation is discoverable in
the present action, they are in all likelihood
relevant to the issues now before the Court.
Given the substantial overlap of the patents
involved in the present and former case and
the similarity of the patent claims and defenses, much of the "privileged" materials,
like the General Foods case deposition transcripts, exhibits and documents, must bear
upon the issues in this case.

The documents in Struthers' files relating to
the prosecution and file history of some or all
of the freeze concentration patents now in
suit also had a potential relevance in the
present case. It became evident during the
review of the papers in support of Nestle's
motions for summary judgment (papers
which were not available to the Special Master) that there are major deficiencies and gaps
in the Patent Office files of the prosecution
of the pertinent patent applications. This will
be developed more fully in Parts II through
V of this opinion. Suffice it to say at this point
that it is quite likely that Struthers' files
would have filled these gaps and helped explain or amplify questions relating to the
prosecution of the patents. Thus, the destroyed files were also potentially relevant to
the issues in this case.

Inasmuch as the Special Master made no
findings as to the relevance of the destroyed
documents to the issues in the present case,
his report and recommendation will be modified to include the factual findings contained
in this section C.

D. Present Availability of the Destroyed Documents

The Special Master's findings with respect to
the present availability of the destroyed
documents appear at different places in his
report and recommendation, quite often in
connection with his discussion of other issues. I shall discuss them as they apply to
each category of documents destroyed.
There is one general observation in the report
which is incorrect.

At page 11 of the report it is stated: "That
deposition [of General Foods' Delaware
counsel] reveals that the Connolly firm has
copies of *all* or "virtually all" of the materials
destroyed by or at the direction of Struthers
in 1972." The following discussion of the
present availability of the documents will
show that that conclusion is too broad.

Turning now to the present availability of the
seven categories of documents:

The Special Master found (at pp. 8, 9) that
"Copies of the transcripts of depositions of
General Foods personnel, together with the
exhibits thereto, are still in existence and in
the possession of Messrs. Connolly, Bove &
Lodge of Wilmington, Delaware, attorneys
for General Foods. The same law firm also is
currently in possession of documents which
were produced by General Foods to Struthers
in the course of the General Foods litigation." This finding is amply supported by
the deposition testimony of Paul Crawford
taken during discovery undertaken in connection with the proceedings before the Special Master.

The Special Master also found that "the originals of [the documents which were produced
by General Foods to Struthers] appear to be still
in the possession of General Foods." This finding has some support in the record in the form
of deposition testimony of Michael J. Quillinan, General Foods' Manager of Patent Litigation, given in October, 1972. However,
according to that testimony, the original documents, contained in five five–drawer filing
cabinets, are not assembled in one place. The
documents probably had been returned to the

places from which they had come. In the words of Mr. Quillinan: "The simplest way would be to simply return to the corporate arms that provided these documents, the various haystacks thereof that existed. And I am not sure that even today [October, 1972] such haystacks exist. They may be in the form of hay. Where and what degree they are stacked, I really cannot say."

.Thus it is highly probable that the original documents were still in the possession of General Foods at the start of the Struthers litigation against Nestle. However, it also appears that they had been scattered throughout General Foods' corporate departments. It had required strenuous discovery efforts on Struthers' part to obtain production of those documents in the earlier litigation. That work, in all likelihood would have had to have been repeated by Nestle if it sought to obtain the documents from General Foods. Its task would have been complicated by the fact that General Foods is not a party to the present litigation.

However, it appears, as the Special Master found, that the first three categories of documents are available in that they are in the possession of General Foods' Delaware counsel and that, at least in October, 1972, General Foods had the original category 3 documents scattered throughout the corporation's offices.

As to the availability of the remaining four categories of documents, the Special Master made the additional finding that the items referred to in categories, 4, 5, 6, and 7 above "were in fact received from Struthers by General Foods." From this it might be inferred that the documents were therefore available in the files of General Foods' counsel. The finding on which this inference is based is clearly erroneous, at least as to categories 4, 6 and 7. The finding will not be adopted.

As to category 4, some of the OSW records were destroyed on January 2, 1972 before General Foods' inspection, and it is not known whether General Foods made copies of the balance of the OSW records which were inspected by General Foods and which

Struthers subsequently destroyed. At page 9 of his report and recommendation the Special Master wrote: "I note that there is some evidence that the originals of the OSW records may still be in the possession of the United States Government." This observation can only be applicable to OSW documents which were generated by or submitted to the United States government. It cannot be applicable to Struthers' internal documents relating to the OSW project. Further, according to evidence submitted by Nestle long after the Special Master had filed his report and recommendation, the government's copies of the OSW documents were disposed of even before Struthers destroyed its copies in 1972.

As to category 5, it may well be that General Foods did receive copies of Struthers' customer correspondence, although discovery in connection with the document destruction proceeding raises a question as to whether it received all such documents. It now seems likely that most of the customer records have finally been located through Nestle's discovery efforts during the proceeding before the Special Master.

As to category 6, pursuant to the order of the Delaware district court, General Foods received copies of a *portion* of the documents as to which Struthers claimed a privilege. It did not receive those which were not ordered to be produced. The Special Master recognized this fact and he may have intended to limit the overly broad language appearing on page 6 of his report by the observation appearing on page 9 to the effect that "[c]opies of *some*, at least, of the Struthers files designated 'privileged' in the litigation with General Foods are currently to be found in the offices of Messrs. Connolly, Bove and Lodge." (emphasis added)

As to category 7, General Foods did not receive Mr. Drucker's prosecution and file history. As found by the Special Master, it did receive a very substantial documentation relating to freeze concentration, including laboratory notebooks, data sheets, weekly reports, etc., as listed in the footnote commencing on page 6 of the Special Master's report. To the extent that General Foods' counsel did not receive the Struthers' "privileged" documents (category 6) and the documents in the Struthers prosecution files (category 7) these destroyed documents were and remain unavailable in the present litigation.

Therefore, the Special Master's findings as to the present availability of copies or originals of the destroyed documents will be adopted, modified and rejected to the extent indicated in this section D.

E. Sanctions to be Imposed

The Special Master recommended that no sanctions be imposed upon Struthers for the destruction of the documents. His recommendation was based upon his findings concerning the matters discussed in section A through D above, and it was based upon certain other factual findings.

The Special Master found that Struthers' motives for destroying the documents were proper, namely:

1. ". . . when the decision was made by Drucker on behalf of Struthers in February, 1972 to destroy documents, that decision was in large measure motivated by the existence of a protective order entered in the General Foods litigation on or about April 24, 1969 . . . " (p. 7).

2. "Counsel for Struthers knew that originals or copies of some or all of the documents were in the possession or control of General Foods; they also believed that it would be impossible to reach an agreement with General Foods regarding the disposition of all these documents." (p. 8).

3. "The proof indicates that Struthers and its counsel were motivated to destroy some of the OSW records because they perceived no need to continue storage, particularly since, in their view, copies or originals of all these documents were on file with the United States government." (p. 8).

4. "As to the files of correspondence and related materials pertaining to Struthers' potential customers in the mid–1960s, Struthers made the decision to destroy

these documents because of their age and because of the view of Struthers' counsel, at the time of the destruction, that such documents were wholly irrelevant to any litigation or any other company."

Nestle urges rather substantial reasons to reject these findings.

As to the finding that the destruction of the documents was occasioned by the existence of the protective order, Nestle notes: (i) Struthers' action constituted a violation of that order, which required that upon termination of the litigation the documents subject thereto be kept "in a secure place," (ii) Struthers' destruction of its *own* documents could not possibly have been occasioned by the existence of the protective order which was designated to protect General Foods' documents, and (iii) even as to the depositions of General Foods' personnel and even as to the General Foods' documents, only a portion were subject to the protective order.

As to the finding that counsel for Struthers knew that *some or all* of the documents were in the possession or control of General Foods, Nestle notes: (i) clearly not *all* the documents were in the possession or control of General Foods or its counsel (and I have so found in an earlier section of this opinion), and (ii) since Struthers had no discussions with General Foods concerning preservation of documents, Struthers had no basis for relying on General Foods to preserve indefinitely documents which might be relevant in a new litigation to which it was not a party.

As to the finding that Struthers destroyed the OSW documents to avoid the burdens of storage and because copies or originals were on file with the government, Nestle notes: (i) the so–called "burden" of storing the OSW documents was a $7.50 per month storage bill of Westheimer Transfer & Storage Co., Inc. and (ii) internal Struthers OSW documents would not have been on file with the government (and I have so found in an earlier section of this opinion).

As to the finding that Struthers destroyed its customer records because of their age and lack of relevance, Nestle notes the high degree of relevance of such documents in connection with the on–sale defense. (I have found, in Section C, that it is inconceivable that Struthers' counsel would not have appreciated the significance of this kind of document.)

Were I to make a finding on the evidence which was before the Special Master as to Struthers' motives in destroying the documents, my finding would differ from his. The reasons Struthers advances smack to me of after–the–fact rationalizations. I note the significance of Struthers' vigorous denials, early in this litigation, that suit against Nestle was contemplated when the documents were destroyed, and the reversal of this position only when confronted in the document destruction proceeding with records which demonstrated conclusively that Struthers and its attorneys were discussing document destruction and suit against Nestle at the very same time. This indicates to me that Struthers knew perfectly well that it should not have destroyed the documents when suit against Nestle was contemplated.

Nevertheless, in some measure this finding rests upon credibility evaluations, and the Special Master heard certain pertinent testimony on this issue. I conclude, therefore, that the finding as to Struthers' motivation is not clearly erroneous.

Another finding on which the Special Master based his recommendations was that "the instant motion was filed in December 1975 but not brought on by Nestle for argument and decision by this Court until 1980." This statement is clearly erroneous, but for understandable reasons. The Special Master could not be expected to have a familiarity with the involved procedural history of this case. Nestle brought on the sanctions motion in December, 1975, as the Special Master observed. It was heard and argued before Judge Meanor, who wrote an opinion disposing of that and other motions. He concluded that he could not decide the sanctions motion without an evidential hearing. Thereafter, the case was assigned to different judges and the delay in scheduling the evidential hearing and resolving the motion was attributable to

the inability of the Court to reach the matter, not Nestle's dilatoriness.

The Special Master further found that "not until the spring of 1981 did counsel for Nestle make any effort to obtain existing copies of the documents in question from General Foods or its attorneys."

In October, 1972, Nestle took the deposition of General Foods' Manager of Patent Litigation, Mr. Quillinan, and sought to ascertain the whereabouts of General Foods' copies of all the documentation generated in its case against Struthers. At that time Mr. Quillinan testified, as noted above, that the haystacks of documents had been redistributed throughout the corporations and "may be in the form of hay." Nestle's attorney then asked if General Foods' counsel had possession of the documents General Foods produced to Struthers. Mr. Quillinan said, "I really don't know." General Foods' patent counsel, who were present, did not disclose that they had in their possession a complete set of such documents. Nestle did not learn of this fact until such counsel were deposed in connection with the proceeding before the Special Master.

Again, I might have reached a different conclusion, but the Special Master's finding that if Nestle really wanted the documents it would have gone after General Foods and its counsel more aggressively, is not clearly erroneous and will be adopted.

The Special Master found that "the belated motion for sanctions was finally pressed in 1980 more to obtain some tactical advantage over Struthers than to achieve true discovery." I have noted above that the motion was pressed in 1975 and that the five–year delay is attributable to problems which confronted the Court and not to Nestle's inaction. It may well be that Nestle has been primarily interested in the tactical advantages which it could derive from the document destruction caper rather than in the wish to obtain additional discovery, and the Special Master's finding in this regard will be adopted.

On the basis of the findings of the Special Master as adopted, modified and rejected by me, I will adopt his sanctions recommendation, although for somewhat different reasons from those set forth in his report and recommendation.

I do not think there is any basis for imposing sanctions for violating Judge Lacey's order to produce. Long before he had entered that order Struthers had destroyed the documents. It was unable to comply and, therefore, cannot be held to have willingly violated the order.

The issue is whether Struthers should be penalized for destroying the documents in 1972 under the circumstances of this case.

I conclude that the destruction of the documents was clearly improper. It is immaterial, in arriving at this conclusion, that Struthers thought the destruction was a convenient way to handle the Delaware district court's protective order or that it sought relief from the burden of storing the documents or that it thought other parties or counsel or the government would have originals or copies of the documents. Similarly, it is immaterial, in arriving at this conclusion that Nestle, once having learned of the event, exploited it to the full as a matter of litigation tactics, perhaps thereby seeking to divert the Court from the substantive issues in the case. All that may affect the ultimate relief to be accorded. It does not in any way cure the essential wrongness of what Struthers did.

Struthers had in its possession a vast collection of documents which had been gathered through great effort in an earlier litigation. It was contemplating new litigation involving substantially the same subject matter and issues as were involved in the litigation in which the documents had been assembled. It knew that a substantial portion of the documents would be relevant in the litigation about to be instituted. Yet it nevertheless destroyed those documents. As a result, some became forever unavailable; many would have to be acquired once again through the long and difficult process of discovery; imposing on the Court and litigants unnecessary, heavy burdens, of which these sanction proceedings are but a part. Regardless of its avowed reasons for the destruction (which

the Special Master found to be genuine reasons), Struthers' actions in 1972 were highly improper.

The applicable rule is set forth in *Bowmar Instrument Corp. v. Texas Instruments, Inc.*, 25 Fed.R.Serv.2d 423, 427 (N.D. Ind.1977):

> The proper inquiry here is whether defendant, with knowledge that this lawsuit would be filed, willfully destroyed documents which it knew or should have known would constitute evidence relevant to this case.

Struthers' conduct clearly comes within these criteria. In February and March, 1972 Struthers had in its possession vast quantities of documents. It was actively planning to institute a complex patent action against Nestle. It knew that the documents included material relevant to the issues which would be involved in that action. Yet, on the eve of filing its complaint, Struthers embarked upon an extensive program to assemble and then destroy these documents, thus placing itself in a position where it could not comply with future discovery requests of the parties or orders of the Court with respect to those documents. It makes no difference what other reasons Struthers had for destroying those documents; its actions in the circumstances which prevailed in 1972 constitute *willful* destruction of documents in anticipation of litigation.

Had this conduct resulted in demonstrable injury to Nestle, there is no question in my mind that whatever sanctions as would be necessary to undo harm would be in order, *National Hockey v. Metropolitan Hockey Club, Inc.*, 427 U.S. 639, 96 S.Ct. 2778, 49 L.Ed.2d 747 (1976). I have concluded, however, in conformity with the recommendation of the Special Master, that Nestle has not been harmed in its defense on the substantive issues in this case.

In Parts II through V of this opinion I set forth my reasons for granting Nestle's motions for summary judgment of invalidity of the ten patents in suit. Even without the destroyed documents Nestle has been able to assemble a comprehensive record with respect to these patents sufficient to demonstrate that there is no genuine issue of material fact as to the invalidity. Access to the destroyed documents might have provided a few more nails to drive into the coffin, but even without those documents Nestle secured sufficient nails to inter decently the ten patents in suit.

So, in the last analysis, Nestle's ability to meet the substantive issues in the case has not been impaired significantly by the destruction of the documents. The necessity to pursue the matter has imposed a very heavy, unnecessary burden on the litigants and upon the Court. The appointment of the Special Master was required in order to ease the Court's burden and to make it possible for the Court to deal with discovery and substantive matters. Nestle urges that these burdens, which flowed from the document destruction, require that attorneys' fees and other costs incurred by Nestle as a result of the document destruction proceedings be assessed against Struthers. This would be a reasonable sanction in some circumstances. However, in the course of the present case Nestle's own conduct when discovery was sought from it has been far from exemplary. At every opportunity it sought to delay and obstruct necessary discovery. It evaded and even violated orders of the Court. It, too, has cast unnecessary burdens on the litigants and the Court. Under the circumstances each party should bear its own attorneys' fees and costs incurred in the document destruction proceedings.

An order will be entered which will recite simply that the report and recommendations of the Special Master are adopted, modified and rejected in the manner set forth in this opinion.

TELECTRON, INC. v. OVERHEAD DOOR CORPORATION

116 F.R.D. 107

United States District Court, S.D. Florida
June 4, 1987

The issue squarely presented by this case is what sanction should be imposed for the flagrant and willful destruction of records specifically called for in a production request served upon the Defendant in a complex antitrust case. We undertake this inquiry pursuant to a Renewed Motion for Default Judgment and Sanctions, filed by the Plaintiff on October 28, 1985.

The Defendant, Overhead Door Corporation (hereinafter "ODC") is engaged in the manufacture and nationwide distribution of garage doors, garage door operators, and related products. The Plaintiff, Telectron, Inc. (hereinafter "Telectron"), is a manufacturer of radio receivers and transmitters which, until the early 1970's, were commonly sold by OHD distributors as companion equipment for OHD door operators. On April 10, 1979, Telectron filed a Complaint, alleging that OHD, after its 1971 acquisition of Advance Industries, a company engaged in the manufacture of radio controls, undertook various measures to induce OHD distributors to purchase Advance radio controls rather than Telectron controls, in violation of this nation's antitrust laws.

* * * * *

From the array of evidence brought before this Court, it is disturbingly apparent that Mr. Richard B. Arnold, the Secretary and Corporate Legal Counsel to OHD, ordered the immediate destruction of documents directly pertaining to Plaintiff's Complaint and Request for Production, on the very day that these papers were served personally upon him. The evidence also establishes beyond any real doubt that Mr. Arnold ordered this destruction in a willful and intentional attempt to place documentation which he anticipated to be damaging to OHD's interests in this litigation forever beyond the reach of Telectron's counsel. Specifically, Mr. Arnold called for the immediate destruction of all sales correspondence, over two years old, generated by OHD's Advance radio control division. Given the repeated and prominent references to Advance in both the Complaint and the Request for Production, and given the centrality of that plant's product to Telectron's allegations of exclusive dealing, illegal tying, attempted monopolization, and tortious interference with an advantageous business relationship, we cannot escape the conclusion that Mr. Arnold's directive was specifically designed and intended to obscure OHD's history of anticompetitive endeavor, and to impede and obstruct Telectron's right to an honest and open discovery process. Sadly, we can only conclude on this ample record that the Defendant intentionally meant to prevent the full and fair adjudication on the merits of this serious case.

It is also abundantly clear that numerous documents were destroyed in direct and immediate response to Mr. Arnold's directive, the testimony of several employees at the Advance plant reveals in no uncertain terms that such destruction occurred. While it is now impossible to determine precisely what the destroyed documents contained or how severely the unavailability of these documents might have prejudiced Plaintiff's ability to prove the claims set forth in its Complaint, we find OHD's contention that no significant prejudice has resulted from this pattern of destruction to be wholly unconvincing. The inescapable fact is that documents falling within a category directly pertinent to Telectron's claims *were* destroyed, willfully and intentionally, under urgent orders of OHD's chief legal officer and secretary in the immediate aftermath of his receipt of Telectron's Complaint and Request for Production. Moreover, this same corporate officer lied in his testimony before this Court, in an obvious attempt to conceal his role in instigating this premeditated destruction.

In reviewing the range of potential sanctions available to this Court, we have concluded that no sanction less than the entry of default judgment as to Defendant's liability can fairly and adequately redress this willful obstruction of the discovery process. We are fully aware of the enormity of this sanction, but we find that all lesser sanctions such as the imposition of attorneys' fees and court costs, evidence preclusion, and other similar measures, standing alone or in the aggregate, would neither ensure this Plaintiff's basic right to a fair trial nor provide a truly meaningful deterrent to future acts of willful disregard for our rules of discovery. In short, we have determined that the entry of default as to OHD's liability is a sanction precisely proportionate to the Defendant's conduct. Accordingly, it is hereby

ORDERED AND ADJUDGED as follows:

* * * * *

I. Findings of Fact

* * * * *

D. The April 23 Order to Destroy Documents at Advance

* * * * *

In addition to meeting with Messrs. Hagman and O'Neil to discuss the Telectron Complaint, Mr. Arnold made a fateful phone call on the same date to Harold Stevens, General Manager of the Advance division. [Tr. 390.] This phone conversation revealed both the seriousness with which Mr. Arnold regarded Telectron's claims against OHD and the extraordinary extent of his willingness to defy the rules of discovery in seeking to place potentially damaging documentation beyond Telectron's reach. In a memorandum addressed to sales–related personnel at the Advance division the very same day (April 23, 1979), Mr. Stevens relayed the orders which he had received over the phone from Mr. Arnold. The memorandum, identifying "Sales Correspondence" as its subject, stated in full:

> We have been directed by our legal counsel, Richard Arnold, to destroy today, April 23, 1979, all of *our generated* sales correspondence which is over two years old. Also we are to get rid of all our old files today. If there is a question about what is to be kept, Richard will provide the answer.

> This just means if you have a letter or memo which deals with pricing in your files which we wrote to a prospect or customer and it's over two years old, get rid of it.

[Plaintiff's Ex. 4 (emphasis in original).]

Mr. Stevens unequivocally testified that the above–quoted memorandum emanated directly from his phone conversation with Mr. Arnold on April 23, 1979. [Tr. 390–94.]

When asked whether the memorandum accurately reflected the orders given to him by Mr. Arnold during the phone call, he responded: "I tried to make it that way." [Tr. 390.] Mr. Stevens reported that he had even taken notes during the course of the phone conversation, and had immediately thereafter drafted the memorandum relying upon those notes. [Tr. 391–92.] The conversation was reportedly brief — only a minute or two — but it dealt solely with the issues addressed in the memorandum. [Tr. 392]

In describing the specific contents of his memorandum, Mr. Stevens consistently cast himself as merely a messenger for OHD's corporate counsel. He made it clear that Mr. Arnold had specified that the document destruction was to be carried out that same day. [Tr. 393.] When asked whether the instruction to destroy documents which were over two years old was Mr. Arnold's idea, he responded: "It wasn't mine." [Tr. 397.] The focus upon sales correspondence, moreover, was clearly identified as Mr. Arnold's idea. [Tr. 393, 397.]

Not only did Mr. Stevens, in his hearing testimony, point clearly and unequivocally to Mr. Arnold as the source of the document destruction orders in the memorandum, he also made an obvious effort, within the body of the memorandum itself, to identify Mr. Arnold as the responsible party. As the above–quoted text reveals, Mr. Stevens' memorandum opened with the declaration that Mr. Arnold had ordered the document destruction, and, in the very next sentence, the memorandum's recipients were advised that, if they had any questions about what should be kept, "Richard [Arnold] will provide the answer." [Plaintiff's Ex. 4]. Acknowledging that Mr. Arnold had not instructed him to include Mr. Arnold's name in the memorandum as the person to whom questions about document retention should be addressed, Mr. Stevens explained: "I couldn't answer the questions, so that's the reason I put [Mr. Arnold's name] in there." [Tr. 394.]

Mr. Arnold, while claiming incredibly to have "no recollection" of a phone conversation with Mr. Stevens on April 23, 1979, has

nevertheless stated that he could not dispute "Mr. Stevens' version" of that exchange. [Arnold Dep. II, at 74, 76.] He has further commented that the subject matter of the memorandum was "certainly not" something about which Mr. Stevens would have had any reason to lie. [Tr. 75.] Moreover, he has admitted that the document destruction order communicated by the April 23 memorandum was of such significance that he would not likely have forgotten having issued it. [Arnold Dep. II, at 82.] The following exchange is revealing as to Mr. Arnold's professed befuddlement on this issue:

Q: As an attorney, did it occur to you . . . that this would be an extraordinary act for an attorney to call a corporate employee and to tell him to destroy documents the very day a request for production was served on him?

A: That's what makes it all the more mystifying to me, because if I had this call with Mr. Stevens, it probably should have registered as more significant with me. Clearly, my lack of recollection indicates to me that whatever communication I had with Mr. Stevens, I didn't consider it significant, and obviously, the memo here suggests that something significant occurred. So, that's a contradiction which I'm hard pressed to reconcile.

In considering the above–cited testimony of Messrs. Stevens and Arnold, we find Mr. Arnold's professed lack of recollection as to his role in ordering the document destruction at Advance to be wholly implausible. We find no reason to doubt the veracity of Mr. Stevens' account of his telephone conversation with Mr. Arnold on the date in question, which, as we have already noted, Mr. Arnold himself has refrained from challenging. Moreover, we agree with Mr. Arnold that such an exchange would not have been easily forgotten, given its obvious, momentous implications. The most benevolent interpretation which might therefore attach to Mr. Arnold's testimony is that he is an unusually forgetful individual. We unequivocally reject this possible interpretation, however, as Mr. Arnold has offered no testimony to advance such a theory, nor has Defendant come forward with any independent evidence showing Mr. Arnold — a young, practicing attorney with rather impressive academic credentials — to suffer from any such mental impairment. To the contrary, we believe and find explicitly that Mr. Arnold willfully and intentionally ordered this documentation destruction, that he did so fully aware of the decided impact upon the Telectron litigation, that he did so specifically in order to obscure OHD's history of anticompetitive endeavor, and that he sought to conceal this flagrant and contumacious conduct by testifying falsely before this Court as to his professed lack of recollection.

An additional reason for rejecting Mr. Arnold's testimony as to his asserted inability to recall the April 23 phone conversation arises from the deposition testimony of OHD's President, Robert Haugh. According to his testimony, Mr. Haugh first learned of the Stevens memorandum sometime in March 1981 in a phone conversation with Mr. Paul Trigg, chairman of OHD's executive committee and outside legal counsel to the corporation, while he was on an out-of-town trip. [Haugh Dep. at 20; Arnold Dep. II, at 9–10.] Upon his return to the office, Mr. Haugh has testified that he "severely reprimanded" Mr. Arnold:

> I faced up to Mr. Arnold and we had a serious discussion. He was severely reprimanded for this, if he had in fact done this . . . Mr. Arnold's answer to me was that he could not recall making such a phone call; *he could have, but he did not recall it.* It hung in the balance, and I subsequently advised Mr. Arnold he was in a very tenuous position because of this — if he, in effect, had done this — and that he was, in essence, on a probationary status as far as the company was concerned, and that I was going to continue to investigate it, and look into it, and if it ever came foolproof where I was convinced that he had done this, he'd be terminated.

[Haugh Dep. at 21–22.]

Further describing his interchange with Mr. Arnold, Mr. Haugh declared: I raised hell

with him totally. I don't think many people would have gone through what he went through." [*Id.* at 22.] Mr. Haugh further reported that OHD was conducting "a continuous investigation of Mr. Arnold's performance as it pertains to this and . . . other matters." [*Id.* at 23.] We note, in passing, that Mr. Arnold was removed from his position as corporate secretary a few months after being reprimanded by Mr. Haugh, and was terminated by OHD in April 1983, for reasons not revealed by the record. [Tr. 159, 290.]

Whether or not OHD's decision to fire Mr. Arnold emanated in whole or in part from a more conclusive determination that he had, in fact, ordered the destruction of records at Advance on the date in question, it is clear from Mr. Haugh's testimony that OHD's chief executive officer looked upon the document destruction order with utmost disapproval and regarded it as sufficiently violative of acceptable corporate practice to warrant placing its suspected instigator on probation. We applaud Mr. Haugh's candid reportage of his confrontation with Mr. Arnold, but unfortunately, no amount of such *ex post facto* disapproval can place within Plaintiff's reach the uncertain number of documents discarded by officials at the Advance division plant pursuant to the April 23, 1979 order.

E. Document Destruction at Advance

As the text of the Stevens memorandum indicates, four Advance personnel were designated by Mr. Stevens to receive a copy of the destruction order: Maynard Geske, Advance's Sales Manager; Paul Buntin, a sales engineer for Advance; Arcelia Crupi, the purchasing and office manager; and Hubert Nelson, the division's accountant. [Plaintiff's Ex. 4; Tr. 388.] From the deposition and hearing testimony of these individuals, it is clear that a considerable — though indeterminate — number of documents were discarded in immediate response to the memorandum, and that additional document destruction occurred in subsequent months.

Mr. Stevens, who testified that he personally had destroyed documents from his own files on April 23, was unable to say with certainty what or how many documents had been destroyed. [Stevens Dep. at 8–10.] He did recall looking through two files, one marked "Competitor Companies" and the other titled "Pricing." Out of the "Pricing" file, which he described as containing materials pertaining to "special pricing to certain kinds of customers," Mr. Stevens recalled having removed a competitive price table, which compared the prices set by "all" operator and radio control manufacturers. [*Id.* at 9, 11]. While he did not specifically remember discarding any other documents from this file, he stated that he could not be certain that nothing else had been removed. All that he could say for certain was that he "really didn't get rid of much." [*Id.* at 9–10.] In searching through the "Competitor Companies" file, he threw away an unspecified number of sales–related documents. In total, he reported having thrown away documents which, if stacked, would have produced a pile one–quarter–of–an–inch thick. [Tr. 409.]

Maynard Geske, immediately upon receiving the Stevens memorandum, searched through two file folders in his desk titled "correspondence" and "price quotes." From these he remembered extracting ten to twelve letters, which he then discarded. [Tr. 65.] He acknowledged having found the destruction order to be "somewhat unusual," and recalled having questioned Mr. Stevens about it. When Steven reassured him that the order reflected "company policy," Mr. Geske apparently inquired no further. [Tr. 69; Geske Dep. at 21.]

A dozen or two pieces of paper were reported to have been discarded upon receipt of the Stevens memorandum by Paul Buntin, Advance's sales engineer. [Tr. 101.] The discarded documents, he recalled, included old sales literature and other pricing–related documents. [Tr. 106–107.] Although he didn't recall destroying any correspondence with OHD distributors, he admitted that he did not specifically recall *not* destroying any sales correspondence. [Tr. 109.]

Neither Arcelia Crupi nor Hubert Nelson, the purchasing and officer manager and the accountant, respectively, recalled having discarded any documents on April 23, 1979, or immediately thereafter. [Tr. 302–03, 355.] Both, however, noted that they had received the Stevens' memorandum [Tr. 302, 345–46.], and that subsequent to receiving it, they periodically discarded various documents to make room in their files. [Tr. 304, 356.] Ms. Crupi reported that she periodically weeded out purchasing–related correspondence with vendors as well as vendor brochures and price quotations once they became, in her view, obsolete. [Tr. 306.] Mr. Nelson recalled having periodically discarded accounting materials when the "retention period" had expired and he needed more space in his files. [Tr. 355–56.]

Crupi and Nelson were not alone among Advance personnel in periodically purging their files of materials which they regarded as obsolete, long after the Telectron Complaint and Request for Production had been filed and without having been informed as to the nature of the suit or the scope of documents sought to be produced. Mr. Stevens himself has acknowledged that he — the top executive at the OHD division most directly implicated by the suit — did not even learn that the suit had been filed until "about a year" after he circulated the memorandum calling for document destruction. [Tr. 411.] The suit was, in his words, "a pretty closely guarded secret." [*Id.*] Stevens further admitted that he continued to discard documents in his personal files until September 18, 1990, some seventeen months after receiving the directive to destroy, when he at last received a memorandum from Richard Arnold establishing a new policy of indefinite document retention. [Tr. 430–35; Defendant's Ex. 1.]

When he received the September 18 memorandum, Mr. Stevens circulated it to only three Advance employees; Arcelia Crupi, Hubert Nelson, and an individual named Mark Galozzi. [Tr. 430–31.] As Maynard Geske had been terminated by Advance in May 1979, it is clear why he was not provided with a copy of this memo. [Tr. 74.] It is not apparent, however, why the fourth recipient of the earlier document destruction order, Paul Buntin, was not sent a copy of the memorandum. Mr. Buntin attested to the fact that he *never* received instructions to cease destroying documents, and that he continued to throw away files, including sales–related correspondence, on a periodic basis after April 23, 1979. [Tr. 149.]

An inevitable and, we must assume, a desired byproduct of OHD's internal secrecy about the suit was a pervasive state of ignorance, among employees at Advance as well as at other OHD facilities, about the sorts of documents which fell within the scope of Telectron's discovery requests. The predictable result of this ignorance was the loss forever of records whose value to Telectron can never be determined with any certainty.

F. Document Destruction at Other OHD Facilities

The absence of a coherent document retention policy during the pendency of this lawsuit has extended beyond the Advance division, with possibly damaging document destruction occurring in both routine and non–routine manners at other OHD plants as well as at OHD's corporate headquarters in Dallas. On May 7, 1979, only two weeks after being served with Telectron's Complaint and Request for Production, Mr. Arnold sent a memorandum to seven OHD personnel, asking them to assist in a continuing effort to reduce the quantity of materials being kept at the basement storage room at OHD headquarters. [Tr. 256–59; Plaintiff's Ex. 20.] Specifically, these individuals were asked to "pull any possible obsolete files from the shelves and review them" leaving "[a]ny material to be discarded in the middle of the floor." [Plaintiff's Ex. 20.] Mr. Arnold maintained that, before these materials were actually carted away, he periodically combed through them, "to make sure there was nothing responsive to the request for production or even further that there was nothing that appeared to be relevant to the lawsuit." [Tr. 258.]

In addition to his direct involvement in document destruction in the basement storage room, Mr. Arnold was aware that OHD employees at the Dallas facility continued to follow the pre–established procedure of reviewing the Dallas corporate files at year–

end, pulling out material which they believed would be discarded under OHD's Standard Operating Procedure. [Tr. 265.] In this regard, Mr. Arnold stated: "I am sure a substantial amount of material was discarded at year end. That was the procedure." He further admitted that no one who was familiar with Telectron's production request screened these documents prior to their disposal. [Tr. 269.] As a result, according to Mr. Arnold's own admission, it is now impossible to determine whether the discarded documents might have fallen within the ambit of Telectron's Request for Production. [*Id.*]

Mr. Arnold did address the Telectron litigation in two memoranda sent to OHD personnel in 1979 and 1980. [Tr. 283–85; Defendant's Ex. 1 & 1A.] The first such memorandum, dated December 27, 1979, was directed to all employees at OHD's Dallas headquarters. It stated in full:

As you are closing out your files and desks in preparation for the move to our new corporate office, you should be aware that we are involved in a substantial lawsuit with Telectron, Inc. If you encounter any papers which you suspect may have a bearing on this case, please check with me prior to their disposal.

[Defendant's Ex. 1.]

The failings of this communique are obvious and numerous. First, it was issued more than eight months after Telectron's Complaint and Request for Production had been served and after Mr. Arnold had specifically ordered the destruction of documents related to this litigation. Second, as discussed above, substantial destruction of documents possibly pertinent to this action had already occurred by that point both at OHD headquarters, at the Advance division plant, and at other OHD facilities. Third, rather than calling for the *retention* of all documents during the pendency of the suit, the memorandum merely suggested that documents appearing to have some relationship to the litigation be brought to Mr. Arnold's attention before being discarded. Given the memo's failure to describe, even in the briefest terms, the nature of Telectron's claims or the scope of its production requests, it is difficult to imagine how an OHD employee, after reading this memorandum, would have been able to conduct an intelligent screening of documents before disposing of them. Finally, even if the memorandum *had* included details sufficient to enable employees to screen documents effectively, the memo was addressed only to "corporate office employees" — i.e., those in OHD's Dallas headquarters. [Defendant's Ex. 1.] Mr. Arnold has acknowledged that the memo was not sent to employees at any other facilities. [Tr. 293.]

It was not until September 18, 1980, nearly seventeen months after the Complaint was served, that a memorandum finally went out, calling generally for the retention of documents during the pendency of the suit. [Defendant's Ex 1A.] This document, addressed to "All Managers of U.S. Door Plants — Advance, Shelbyville," was explicit in suspending the "normal records retention/destruction program" and in instructing that obsolete records be boxed and stored rather than destroyed. [*Id.*] Even this communication, however apparently did not reach all OHD personnel. Robert Hagman, OHD's Senior Vice–President in charge of manufacturing from 1976 until 1981, testified in July 1981 that he had *never* received instructions not to destroy documents in light of the Telectron suit. [Hagman Dep. at 7–9, 19.] Disturbingly, Mr. Hagman further revealed that he had destroyed documents contained in his desk file as recently as December 1980.

Not only did Mr. Hagman maintain that he had never been told to retain documents in his personal files during the pendency of the Telectron suit; he was also not even aware of whether OHD had a document retention policy at all. [*Id.* at 15.] Furthermore, even if he had been told not to discard documents which might be related to the Telectron litigation, he would have been ill–prepared to make such determinations as he had never read any of Telectron's requests for production. [*Id.* at 41–32.]

Deposition testimony of OHD's President, Robert Haugh, makes embarrassingly apparent the corporation's utter neglect in ensuring that documents relevant to this litigation would be retained. When asked whether he had instructed corporate employees and officers not to destroy documents since the initiation of the suit, Mr. Haugh responded that instructions of this nature had been issued orally at a staff meeting in the spring or summer of 1979. [Haugh Dep. at 26.] Even assuming, *arguendo*, that such instructions were actually given at a staff meeting in 1979, the ineffectuality of this communication was highlighted by further questioning of Mr. Haugh:

Q: Who would be at a staff meeting? What kind of people?

A: Senior vice–presidents, Richard Arnold; probably vice–president of marketing.

Q: Would Bob Hagman be there?

A: Yes, he would have been there.

Q: Then, why would he not know that this directive had been given?

A: He may not have been there. They weren't always at the meetings. He could have been out of town.

Q: Would there be minutes of such a meeting?

A: No. Most of those meetings were of a verbal nature.

Q: And you couldn't recall who was at that specific meeting and who was not?

A: No, I could not.

[*Id* at 26–27.]

The failure of OHD's top management to provide any leadership or effective oversight regarding document retention is further evidenced by Mr. Haugh's acknowledged ignorance as to the corporation's on–going document retention policy allegedly set forth in OHD's Standard Operating Procedure manual. He believed that such a policy had been established in 1966 or 1967, but he knew none of the policy's provisions and stated that he did not know if anybody was formally charged with implementing the policy. [*Id.* at 7–8.] He guessed that OHD's financial department, legal counsel, and senior vice–presidents would be involved, but he emphasized: "I don't think it's really formalized." [*Id.* at 8–9.]

Within this context of indifference and professed ignorance among OHD's top management, Mr. Arnold, the corporation's chief legal office, allowed and orchestrated the destruction of documents at OHD–Dallas and various of OHD's manufacturing plants over many months, free from the scrutiny of superior corporate officers. As we noted earlier, Mr. Haugh did reprimand Mr. Arnold for having apparently ordered the destruction of documents at Advance on April 23, 1979, but this reprimand can only be described at best as "too little, too late." By the spring of 1981, when this reprimand was issued, document destruction, both calculated and inadvertent, had been proceeding under Mr. Arnold's guidance for approximately two years. Moreover, Mr. Arnold retained his position as corporate legal counsel for more than two years *after* being reprimanded by Mr. Haugh.

II. Conclusions of Law

* * * * *

In the case at bar, there is disturbingly similar evidence of willful document destruction by a corporate defendant, carried out in an unabashed — and successful — attempt to render irretrievable records clearly pertinent to the claims brought against it. As our recitation of the facts reveals, OHD's chief legal counsel and corporate secretary, Richard Arnold, has acknowledged that he was served with Telectron's Complaint and First Request for Production on April 23, 1979. [Tr. 192–93; Arnold Dep. II, at 58.] His testimony establishes that he read through these documents on the day he received them. [Tr. 193–201; Arnold Dep. II, at 58–59.] Given the manner in which these two papers were drafted, even a brief reading would have alerted Mr. Arnold to the central role which

Advance Industries played in Telectron's claims against OHD. Indeed, the entire Complaint takes as its starting point the acquisition of Advance by OHD in November 1971. [Complaint, ¶ 18.] It is from this time forward that OHD is alleged to have induced its distributors to purchase only radio controls manufactured by Advance, in violation of the antitrust laws of the United States and in tortious interference with Telectron's established business relationship with these distributors. [Complaint, Counts I–IV.]

In addition to the numerous prominent references to Advance in the Complaint, Telectron's Request for Production unambiguously targeted documents related to and likely to be found at Advance. Moreover, essentially all of the documents requested from Advance fall quite clearly under the general rubric of "sales correspondence." [*See* Request for Production, ¶¶ 58, 65, 86, 87, 96–98, 101–103.] It was precisely this category of documentation at Advance which Mr. Arnold ordered immediately destroyed on the very date that the Complaint and Request for Production were served. In immediate response to this bold directive, at least three employees at Advance, including the plant's general manager, Harold Stevens, destroyed a substantial number of sales–related documents. In addition, periodic and unsupervised document destruction persisted both at the Advance plant and at other OHD facilities for many months following service of the Complaint and the Request for Production.

The contents of the correspondence and other records destroyed pursuant to Mr. Arnold's order can no longer be fairly determined, as secondary evidence of the contents of destroyed writings is prohibited where "the proponent lost or destroyed them in bad faith." Fed.R.Evid. 1004(1)

It is well settled, under the best evidence rule, that in proving the contents of a document, the document itself must be produced unless it is shown to be unavailable through no fault of the proponent, If it is satisfactorily shown to be unavailable, secondary evidence as to its contents may be received.

Bendix Corp. v. Untied States, 600 F.2d 1364, 1371–72, 220 Ct.Cl. 507 (1979) (citations omitted) (where blueprint of contractor's drawings was unavailable through no fault of proponent, secondary evidence was deemed admissible as to its content). In the present case, we are faced with a defendant which seeks to establish, through secondary evidence, that the numerous documents destroyed at the Advance division facility in the immediate aftermath of Mr. Arnold's order were not pertinent to Telectron's claims and therefore did not prejudice Telectron's ability to litigate the case. [OHD's Memorandum of Law in Opposition to Telectron's Motion for Default and Sanctions, at 9–30.] We emphatically reject this line of argument, for two reasons. First, Plaintiff's right to a full and fair adjudication of its claims on the merits would be poorly protected if OHD, having purposefully, willfully, and in bad faith destroyed an indeterminate number of documents, were subsequently allowed to introduce extraneous evidence for the purpose of showing that no real prejudice had resulted from its bald defiance of Telectron's production request. Second, we have no reason to doubt that the documents admittedly destroyed — sales and pricing–related correspondence, literature, and records held by Advance's general manager and sales personnel — would have been highly relevant to Telectron's grievances, given the Complaint's central focus upon Advance's allegedly unlawful intrusion upon Telectron's business relations with OHD distributors.

In light of OHD's willful destruction of documents and the prejudice to Telectron caused by this activity, we find that the entry of default judgment as to OHD's liability is a measure falling appropriately within this Court's inherent authority to sanction litigants who consciously seek to determine the very foundations of our discovery process.

* * * * *

From the descriptions of documents destroyed at Advance, offered by the very personnel who destroyed them, a strong inference can thus be drawn that some or all of the discarded materials were relevant to Telectron's Complaint and Request for Pro-

duction. Moreover, while it is now impossible to determine precisely what or how many documents were destroyed, the bad–faith destruction of a relevant document, by itself, "gives rise to a strong inference that production of the documents would have been unfavorable to the party responsible for its destruction." *Coates v. Johnson & Johnson.* 756 F.2d 524, 551 (7th Cir.1985) (citations omitted); *see also Nation–wide Check Corp. v. Forest Hills Distributors*, 692 F.2d 214, 217 (1st Cir.1982); *National Association of Radiation Survivors v. Turnage*, 115 F.R.D. 543 (N.D. Calif.1987); *Wm. T. Thompson Co. V. General Nutrition Corp.*, 593 F.Supp. 1443, 1455 (C.D.Calif.1984).

The "adverse inference rule" has also been applied by the former Fifth Circuit in *Vick v. Texas Employment Commission*, 514 F.2d 734, 737 (5th Cir.1975). The Court in *Vick* upheld a trial court's finding for the defendant employment commission in a sex discrimination case, despite the fact that records relevant to the plaintiff's employment had been destroyed prior to trial. In so ruling, the court explained that, in the absence of a finding that the employment commission had acted in bad faith, no adverse inference as to the probative value of the destroyed documents was called for:

[The Commission's] records on [the plaintiff] were destroyed before trial, apparently pursuant to Commission regulations governing disposal of inactive records . . . The adverse inference to be drawn from destruction of records is predicated on bad conduct of the defendant. "Moreover, the circumstances of the act must manifest bad faith. Mere negligence is not enough, for it does not sustain an inference of consciousness of a weak case." McCormick, Evidence § 273 at 660–61 (1972), 31A C.J.S. Evidence § 156(2) (1964). There was indication here that the records were destroyed under routine procedures without bad faith and well in advance of [plaintiff's] service of interrogatories. Certainly, there were sufficient grounds for the trial court to so conclude.

Id.

The facts in the present case differ strikingly from those which led the Fifth Circuit in *Vick* to uphold the trial court's decision not to draw an adverse inference from the defendant's destruction of records. Here the Defendant's actions were unequivocally motivated by the flagrant bad faith of OHD's in–house counsel and corporate secretary, who explicitly and urgently called for the destruction of records in a category directly related to the opposing party's claims, on the very date he became aware of those claims. This willful and premeditated scheme, thoroughly revealed through the testimony of several of the Defendant's employees, warrants the inference that the destroyed documents would have been harmful to OHD, had they been produced. The unavailability of these documents today must therefore be seen as prejudicial to Telectron's interest in pursuing the full and fair litigation of its claims.

* * * * *

III. OHD's "Unclean Hands" Defense

In defending against Telectron's Motion for Default and Sanctions, OHD has argued, among other things, that Telectron is guilty of "unclean hands," because certain of its officers and personnel discarded documents during the pendency of this litigation. While the record evidence does establish that some document disposal occurred since the filing of this suit, we find absolutely no evidence that *any* of Telectron's officers or staff destroyed *any* documents in a deliberate attempt to hinder discovery efforts by OHD.

A major focus on OHD's "unclean hands" claim pertains to certain actions taken by Mr. William Foster, Telectron's Vice President and Treasurer, during the summer of 1980. Mr. Foster has described himself as the person responsible for maintaining Telectron's business records, although the actual task of reviewing Telectron's files for discovery purposes in this litigation was left to OHD's attorneys, with the assistance of Telectron's counsel. [Foster Dep. (March 31, 1982), at 12.]

During the summer of 1980, Telectron moved its Fort Lauderdale facilities to a new location in the same city. [*Id.* at 22, 46, 66.]

In preparing for this move, Mr. Foster determined that some of the corporation's older records should be discarded due to limited storage space in the new building. [*Id.* at 46, 66.] While it is undisputed that Mr. Foster did actually dispose of certain documents at the time, there is strong evidence that he did so in the good faith belief that OHD had completed its review of these files and had photocopied all relevant materials. It is also clear from the evidence that Mr. Foster, in discarding certain records, adhered to Telectron's pre–existing document retention policy, which called for the preservation of corporate records for a minimum of seven years, in conformity with the presumed mandates of the Internal Revenue Service. [Foster Dep. at 15; Arthur Horvath Dep. at 49; John J. Lucca Dep. at 53; Tr. 483.]

Our belief that Mr. Foster acted in good faith is not at all tantamount to an endorsement of his sense of judgment; nor is it a denial of the fact that records potentially useful to OHD may have been destroyed by his actions. [*See* Defendant's proposed Order Denying Telectron's Motion for Sanctions, at 52.] We simply observe that nothing in Mr. Foster's actions rises to a level of calculated mischief sufficient to give credence to OHD's assertion of "unclean hands."

Similarly ill–suited to an "unclean hands" defense is OHD's contention that Arthur Horvath, a Telectron vice president in charge of the company's Cleveland operations, had improperly destroyed records at Telectron's plant in Cleveland, Ohio. Among the records discarded by Mr. Horvath were the correspondence files of a former Telectron vice president and sales manager, Frank Oates, who left the company in 1978. [Defendant's Proposed Order Denying Telectron's Motion for Sanctions, at 53; Horvath Dep. at 12.] Mr. Horvath's candor in acknowledging that he had disposed of these files contrasts dramatically with Mr. Arnold's disingenuous representation that he could not recall having ordered the destruction of documents at Advance. [Horvath Dep. at 12–13.] A further crucial distinction lies in the timing of Mr. Horvath's actions. Whereas Mr. Arnold ordered the destruction of key documents immediately after being served with Plaintiff's

Complaint and Request for Production, Mr. Oates' correspondence was disposed of in June 1979, five months *prior* to Telectron's receipt of OHD's first and only Request for Production, on November 8, 1979. [Horvath Dep. at 13; Defendant's Ex. 20 (OHD Request for Production.] In light of these circumstances, we are at a loss to find even the slightest hint of willful wrongdoing on Mr. Horvath's part.

OHD additionally maintains that Lester Norman and Harry Sundberg, two of Telectron's' regional sales representatives, discarded documents possibly relevant to OHD's Request for Production, subsequent to Telectron's receipt of the Request in November 1979. [Defendant's Proposed Order at 55–58.] None of the evidence shows that the two sales representatives, both of whom worked out of their homes, bore any responsibility for retaining corporate documents beyond the time of their immediate use. [Sundberg Dep. at 76–79; Norman Dep. at 21–24.] Moreover, there is no intimation that these individuals were acting under Telectron's instructions when they periodically cleaned out their files. [Sundberg Dep. at 9, 37; Norman Dep. at 22.]

* * * * *

In the evidence presented to this Court, we find absolutely no support for the proposition that the Plaintiff has sought equitable relief with unclean hands. Not even the slightest indication of willful misconduct or bad faith emerges from the testimony regarding Telectron's disposal of certain records.

In light of the absence of any support for the Defendant's argument, we cannot attach any legal significance to the "unclean hands" defense.

For the reasons set forth above, the sanctions outlined at the commencement of this Order are hereby imposed upon the Defendant, Overhead Door Corporation.

In Re Marvin THIRTYACRE, Debtor, Jody THORP, Plaintiff, v. Marvin THIRTYACRE, Defendant.

154 Bankr. 497

United States Bankruptcy Court for the Central District of Illinois
May 19, 1993

JODY THORP (Plaintiff) filed an adversary action to determine the dischargeability of a debt owed her by the Debtor, MARVIN THIRTYACRE (Defendant) arising out of an assault. At the time of the incident, the Defendant was the sheriff of Mercer County, Illinois. He was also suffering from depression. In part, his depression was caused by his suspicion his wife was having an affair with Jim Brokaw (Brokaw), the Chief of Police for the City of Aledo, Illinois. He received treatment for his depression at the Veterans Administration Hospital in Iowa City, Iowa (VA Hospital). As part of his treatment, the drug Pamelor was prescribed. He was instructed not to drink alcoholic beverages while taking this drug.

Subsequently, the Defendant and his wife were divorced and she married Brokaw.

Sometime prior to the incident, the Defendant had obtained a tape recording of a telephone conversation between Brokaw and his wife which confirmed in his mind that an affair was occurring. The day before the incident, the Defendant saw Brokaw and his wife driving in the same direction, but in separate cars, which added to his belief about an affair. The day of the incident the Defendant and his wife had an argument and that afternoon the Defendant started drinking. That evening he returned home and struck his wife.

During this period of time Brokaw was dating the Plaintiff. The defendant wanted to tell the Plaintiff what he thought was going on between Brokaw and his wife. The Defendant went to the Plaintiff's home. No one was present. In the process, the Defendant kicked in the back door.

The defendant then went to the police station in Aledo, Illinois. Brokaw and the Plaintiff returned to her home and found the damage. Brokaw called the Aledo police department and a telephone conversation between Brokaw and the Defendant occurred. In that telephone conversation the Defendant told Brokaw he was going to return to the Plaintiff's home and physically attack him.

The Defendant returned to the Plaintiff's home. The Plaintiff attempted to intercede, and an altercation ensued between the Plaintiff and the Defendant, with the Defendant striking the Plaintiff. The Aledo police then arrive and subdued the Defendant.

The Plaintiff sued the Defendant in state court and obtained a default judgment for $25,000.00. The Defendant filed a Chapter 7 case in bankruptcy, and the Plaintiff filed this adversary proceeding to have the judgment debt declared nondischargeable as a willful and malicious injury under § 523(a)(6) of the Bankruptcy Code, 11 U.S.C. § 523(a)(6). The Defendant contends because he was taking Pamelor and drinking alcoholic beverages, his mental capacity to form an intent to act in a willful and malicious manner was impaired. The parties stipulated that was the only issue and a trial was held. The matter was taken under advisement and the parties were given an opportunity to file written briefs, which they did.

* * * * *

The next evidentiary issue involves the admissibility of the VA Hospital records. Relying on *Pieters v. B–Right Trucking, Inc.*, 669 F.Supp. 1463 (N.D.Ind.1987), the Defendant contents they are admissible under the "business records" exception to the hearsay rule. However, the court's reasoning in *Pieters* clearly is contrary to the Defendant's contention. In that case the court stated:

The business records exception to the hearsay rule found in Federal Rule of Evidence 803(6) does not require a showing of chain of custody. In pertinent part, the Rule excludes from the hearsay rule:

[a] memorandum, report, record or data compilation, in any form, of acts, events,

conditions, opinions or diagnoses, made at or near the time by, or from information transmitted by, a person with knowledge, if kept in the course of a regularly conducted business activity, and if it was the regular practice of that business activity to make the memorandum, report, record, or data compilation, all as shown by the testimony of the custodian or other qualified witness, unless the source of information or the method or circumstances of preparation indicate lack of trustworthiness.

Fed.R.Evid. 803(6). In order for evidence to be admissible under Rule 803(6), it must be "transmitted by" a declarant "with knowledge" in the ordinary course "of a regularly conducted business activity . . . ." *Cook v. Hoppin*, 783 F.2d 684, 689 (7th Cir.1986) While the Rule requires that a custodian or qualified witness testify that the requirements of the business records exception have been met, there is no requirement that the "qualified witness" must have personally participated in or observed the creation of the document. *United States v. Moore*, 791 F.2d 566, 574 (7th Cir.1986). *See also United States v Keplinger*, 776 F.2d 678, 693 (7th Cir.1985). "The phrase 'qualified witness' is to be broadly interpreted as requiring only someone who understands the system." (Citations.) In the case of a hospital, evidence is admissible under the Rule if transmitted by a declarant (such as a doctor or a nurse) who reports to the recordkeeper as part of a regular business routine in which they are participants.

In *Belber v. Lipson*, 905 F.2d 549 (1st Cir.1990), the court reached the same conclusion, holding that medical records were not admissible because there was a lack of testimony by the custodian or other qualified witness, stating:

This testimony is essential. Without such a witness the writing must be excluded. "Obviously a writing is not admissible . . . merely because it may appear on its face to be a writing made by a physician in the regular course of his practice."

* * * * *

TORRIDGE CORPORATION, a New Mexico corporation, and El Camino Motel, Inc., a New Mexico corporation v. COMMISSIONER OF REVENUE, State of New Mexico,

506 P.2d 354

Court of Appeals of New Mexico
December 29, 1972

* * * * *

This is an appeal from the Commissioner's Decision and Order assessing emergency school tax, gross receipts, compensating tax, municipal tax, penalty and interest against Torridge Corporation, d/b/a/ El Camino restaurant and Lounge (Torridge) for the reporting period January 1, 1966 to March 31, 1971 and emergency school tax, gross receipts tax, municipal tax, penalty and interest against El Camino Motel, Inc. (El Camino) for the reporting period January 1, 1966 to March 31, 1971.

We affirm in part and reverse in part. Torridge is a New Mexico corporation which operates a package liquor store, a lounge and a restaurant. El Camino is a New Mexico corporations which operates a motel. Both corporations have the same accountant. All tax returns for the period in question were timely filed.

During October, 1970 a fire occurred on the Torridge premises which destroyed, among other things, its entire books and records (ledgers, journals, bank statements, deposit slips and checks). The same fire also destroyed the entire records of El Camino except for a journal and ledger for 1970 which were not on the premises at the time of the fire. The Commissioner does not challenge the accidental nature of the fire.

Subsequently, the Commissioner conducted an audit from January 1, 1968 to March 31, 1971. The auditor made a finding that the gross receipts had been understated by 25%. Pursuant to § 72–13–33(D), N.M.S. A.1953 (Repl.Vol. 1961, pt. 2, Supp.1971) the audit was extended to cover the years 1966 and 1967.

For the audit period, the auditor computed the gross receipts of both taxpayers based upon bank deposits, eliminating such bank deposits as could be determined from bank microfilm records to be either interdepartmental transactions or bank transfers. Subsequent to the original audit a second audit was made and a partial abatement was provided for in the Commissioner's Decision and Order.

Bank Deposit Method.

This is a matter of first impression. It is taxpayers' contention under this point that the Commissioner is not justified in using this method unless there is either a strong suspicion that taxpayer has received income from undisclosed sources or the taxpayer has failed to keep any records or that the records are inadequate. Taxpayers state that the mere fact that their records were destroyed by fire should not justify the Commissioner's resort to the bank deposit method with its inherent inaccuracies. We disagree.

Section 72–13–22(A), NMSA1953 (Repl.Vol.1961, pt. 2, Supp.1971) states: "72–13–22. *Investigative authority and powers.* A. For the purpose of establishing or determining the extent of the liability of any person for any tax, for the purpose of collecting any tax or for the purpose of enforcing any statute administered by the bureau, the commissioner or his delegate is authorized to examine equipment and to examine and require the production of any pertinent records, books, information or evidence, to require the presence of any person and to require him to testify under oath concerning the subject matter of the inquiry and to make a permanent record of the proceedings."

We deem this statute only as authority to examine pertinent books and records for the purpose of verification but also as authority to reconstruct records when they are destroyed. The fact of an accidental destruction is not material. The nonexistence of records, for whatever reasons, is the pertinent fact.

We are not impressed by taxpayers' argument that the cases cited for the proposition of using the bank deposit method only relate to fraud and criminal prosecution. See Standard Federal Tax Reporter CCH, Vol. 3, § 2767.051–2767.052 (1972) and cases cited therein. The issue is: when records do not exist, for whatever reason, what methods are available and reasonable in order to reconstruct the records?

Both taxpayers argue that since the two corporations had the same accountant this was evidence that the books of both corporations were kept in the same way and, thus, the 1970 records of El Camino which corresponded with the returns filed that year created a presumption that the records of both corporations for the prior years would correspond with the returns filed for those years. We cannot say, as a matter of law, that such a presumption exists under the record as presented. To the contrary, once the notice of assessment of taxes is delivered to the taxpayer, the statutory presumption, of the correctness of the assessment, applies. Section 72–13–32(C), NMSA1953 (Repl.Vol.1961, Pt. 2, Supp.1971). See *McConnell v. State ex rel. Bureau of Revenue*, 83 N.M. 386, 492 P.2d 1003 (Ct.App.1971).

We conclude that the bank deposit method is a reasonable method of reconstruction of records, regardless of what the reasons are for not having records. After the audit and the notice of assessment of taxes is delivered to taxpayer, taxpayer must carry the burden of proof in order to negate the presumption of correctness.

The Audit.

It is the taxpayers' contention that the audit was "fraught with so many errors as to result in an arbitrary and capricious result."

The Commissioner used the "test months" technique in performing the audit. After the first audit, a second and final audit was prepared and certain adjustments were made in favor of taxpayers. Taxpayers state: "[t]he question naturally arises in one's mind what a third audit would reveal." Our answer to this is the same as under the first point. The notice of assessment of taxes based on the audit is presumed to be correct. § 72–13–32

(C), supra. Absent a showing of incorrectness by taxpayers, the audit and notice of assessment of taxes must stand.

The "test months" method was used for the audit period, January 1, 1968 to March 31, 1971. The test months were used to determine gross receipts subject to tax. There is evidence that the test months method is acceptable practice. Although there is conflicting evidence, the Commissioner could draw the inference from the evidence of the auditor, that the gross receipts were the amount computed by use of the test months and bank deposit methods. See *Archuelta v. O'Chesky*, 84 N.M. 428, 504 P.2d 638 (Ct.App.), decided November 30, 1972. The Commissioner's decision, that the taxpayers failed to establish the inaccuracy of the gross receipts ascertained by the audit, is supported by evidence. Accordingly, the presumption of correctness of the assessments for January 1, 1968 to March 31, 1971, has not been overcome.

TP ORTHODONTICS, INC. v. PROFESSIONAL POSITIONERS, INC., a Wisconsin corporation, Professional Positioners, Inc., a Delaware corporation, Gerald W. Huge, Richard W. Allesee, Donald S. Riegelman and Albert Weiss, individuals

Unpublished Opinion

United States District Court for the Eastern District of Wisconsin
June 9, 1990

This is the damages phase of a patent infringement suit. This Court found U.S. Patent No. 3,178,820 not invalid and infringed by defendant Professional Positioners, Inc. in an August 11, 1988 Decision and Order. The parties to this suit include: plaintiff PT Orthodontics, Inc., defendant Professional Positioners, Inc. ("Pro"), defendant and third–party plaintiff Bristol–Myers Co. ("B–M"), and third–party defendants Albert Weiss, Gerald W. Huge, Donald S. Riegelman, and Richard W. Allesee ("the founders").

* * * * *

Plaintiff's Motion for Sanctions for Pro's Destruction of Invoices:

Plaintiff's second motion for sanctions is of a more serious nature. Plaintiff has moved the Court to sanction Pro for the destruction of Pro positioner sales invoices. Plaintiff bases this motion on exhibits and the testimony of Ms. Williams, who testified that pursuant to the Pro document retention policy, Pro destroyed positioner sales invoices in January of 1988. Ms. Williams testified that the 1984 and 1986 Pro Record Retention Policy was to retain invoices for a period of seven years, and prescription sheets for two years. She also testified that the 1988 Pro Record Retention Policy required keeping invoices for seven years and prescription sheets for five years. Exhibit A to plaintiff's motion. Plaintiff states that at the March 29, 1990 deposition of Pro maintenance man John Vander Hoef, plaintiff's deposition exhibit 551 was produced, which states which documents should be destroyed or thrown away before which dates. Exhibit C to plaintiff's motion. Plaintiff concludes that the testimony of Williams and Vander Hoef, in addition to that exhibit, demonstrate the destruction of the positioner sales invoices for the years before 1980.

Defendants aver that Ms. Williams in her testimony states that she may have authorized this destruction of documents in January 1988. Defendants state: "The destruction of invoices was performed pursuant to Pro's document retention policy, and was not influenced by this litigation." Defendants' Response to Plaintiff's Three Motions for Sanctions p. 5. Defendants also advance that the Vander Hoef testimony evidences he was instructed to discard various Pro documents, not limited to invoices or other sales documents, pursuant to the document retention schedule. Defendants again assert that plaintiff has failed to allege how the absence of these invoices has prejudiced its case, and that there has been no suggestion that the sales summaries, which exist and have enabled the parties to stipulate to Pro's sales during the infringement period, are not an accurate indicator of those sales.

But plaintiff has pointed out how it has been prejudiced by this destruction. Neither of the defendants can contend that they were not aware of this action during the time period when the destruction of documents occurred. Plaintiff has correctly advanced that defendants had a duty during the pendency of this litigation to take reasonable care to assure retention of relevant documents, including invoices. The invoices contain a level of particularity material to the damages calculation which the sales summaries do not contain. See Plaintiff's Reply Brief to its Motions for Sanctions pp. 3–4 (listing founders' testimony regarding the value of invoices over sales summaries in determining damages). In this way they are relevant documentation that defendants should have taken every reasonable step to see that they had been retained. Standard questioning regarding Pro's record retention policy and instructions to Pro not to destroy the documents could have ensured the existence of the invoices through discovery and trial. The Court determines that based on Pro's failure to retain relevant documents through the damages phase of this litigation, it must be sanctioned. The scope and nature of this sanction will have to be determined based on the parties' arguments and perhaps a separate presentation of evidence. Accordingly, this Court will grant the plaintiff's motion but hold in abeyance the nature of the sanction pursuant to Fed.R.Civ. P. 37.

* * * * *

TRACY v. BUCHANAN

151 S.W. 747

Court of Appeals. Missouri
December 9, 1912

JOHNSON, J. Plaintiff sued to recover damages for the breach by defendant of a contract for the sale and delivery of shares of stock in a telephone corporation. The answer is a general denial. A trial resulted in a verdict for defendant, but, on motion of plaintiff, the court set aside the verdict and granted a new trial, on the ground, stated in the order, of error in giving instructions B and C, asked by defendant. Dissatisfied with this action of the court, defendant brought the case here by appeal.

Defendant was the president and manager of the California Telephone Company, a corporation owning and operating a telephone exchange in the city of California. The capital stock of the company was $9,000, divided into 90 shares of the par value of $100 each. Defendant owned 20 shares, and the remaining stock was held by various persons residing in California. Plaintiff lived in Shelbina, and was engaged in the business of buying and selling telephone exchanges. In July, 1910, the parties began negotiations for the purchase by plaintiff of a controlling interest in the stock of the company. The negotiations were conducted chiefly by correspondence, and the letters written by plaintiff were not preserved by defendant, and, as no copies of them were kept by plaintiff, their contents were the subject of a sharp dispute at the trial. Plaintiff testified that the proposals he made in them were for the purchase of stock from defendant; while defendant testified that in the purchase of the stock it was understood he was acting as the agent of plaintiff as to all the shares except those owned by him, which were to be included in the sale.

It is conceded plaintiff did not offer to pay the full purchase price of the stock at the time of delivery. At first he offered to make a down payment of $2,000, and to give defendant his notes for the remainder, secured by a chattel mortgage on all of the stock to be purchased. Later he found it would be inconvenient for him to pay more than $1,500 on the purchase price, and he wrote defendant to that effect, and further objected to going into debt so deeply. Under date of July 16, 1910, defendant wrote plaintiff as follows: "Yours of the 15th inst. recd. Contents noted. You say you do not want to go in debt so much. Now if you want the exchange I will make you a proposition that you cannot afford to pass up for any trade. I will retain $2,000.00 instead of $1,000.00. You will have $9,000.00 only invested. As to terms you can pay $1,500 down and balance as you want to. Now if you want the chance of your life, come at once, as I am going to make a deal in a few days.

In regard to your farm you can trade it for real estate here I think without any trouble. Let me hear at once."

On August 11, 1910, plaintiff, according to his testimony, mailed an offer to defendant to purchase 70 shares for $8,500, to pay down $1,500, and to discharge the remainder of the purchase price in deferred payments. Defendant replied by letter, but his reply is not in the record, and we do not know its contents. Evidently it was favorable to the continuance from plaintiff to the effect that he would go to California to close the deal in person. The record relating to the correspondence preceding plaintiff's visit to California, which occurred August 22, 1910, is very unsatisfactory, but we are able to say with certainty that the letters do not evidence a binding contract between the parties. Plaintiff himself testified that there were some "variations" between the terms of sale agreed upon in the letters and those in the contract finally made by the parties at the end of their personal negotiations. One of the conceded changes was an increase of the purchase price of the 70 shares from $8,500 to $8,554. The contract that was finally entered into was made at California, and the terms of that contract are a matter of controversy.

We shall not go into the details of the evidence bearing on this subject. The evidence of plaintiff, to the effect that defendant undertook the sale and delivery on the first day of the following month of 70 shares of stock at the agreed price, is not only substantial, but, as we shall show, must be treated as conclusive. The day after the contract had been made, and after plaintiff had returned home, defendant telephoned him that the contract could not be carried out, and also wrote him a letter, in which defendant said: "Complications have arisen which cannot be adjusted. I am returning your papers as per agreement." The papers referred to were plaintiffs check of $1,500 for the down payment and notes he had executed for the deferred payments. These papers, together with a chattel mortgage executed by plaintiff to secure the deferred payments, and which covered the stock to be transferred, had been placed by the parties in the hands of a banker at California, with the understanding that the check, notes, and mortgage were to be delivered to defendant on delivery by him to the banker for plaintiff of the 70 shares of stock. These deliveries were to be made on the first day of the following month, and the papers were to remain in the banker's hands until that time. But, finding that he could not procure the stock necessary to consummate the sale, defendant obtained the papers from the banker, destroyed the chattel mortgage, and sent the other papers to plaintiff. Plaintiff states that a bill of sale executed by defendant, conveying to him the 70 shares of stock, was placed in the hands of the banker with the other papers; but this statement is denied by defendant. The excuses offered by defendant for procuring these papers from their custodian and destroying at least one of them are too flimsy to merit serious consideration. His conduct was high–handed and inexcusable; and, as it resulted in the destruction of important documentary evidence, we shall accept as proved the statement of plaintiff that there was a bill of sale among the papers deposited with the banker which, in form and substance, bound defendant, as vendor, to deliver the shares of stock to the banker for plaintiff's benefit. Every presumption is against the despoiler of documentary evidence. "His conduct is attributed to his supposed knowledge that the truth would have operated against him." 1 Greenleaf on Ev. § 37. It is said by our own Supreme Court, in *Pomeroy v. Benton*, 77 Mo. loc. cit. 87: "Numerous instances are given in the books of the like application of the rule, where it is held that spoliation of documentary evidence being proved against a defendant that thereby he is held to admit the truth of the plaintiff's allegations; and this upon the ground that the law, in consequence of the fraud practiced, in consequence of the spoliation, will presume that the evidence destroyed would establish the plaintiff's demand to be just."

To permit the despoiler to dispute his adversary's statement of the contents of the destroyed document would be to permit him to profit by his own wrong — to gain the very advantage his lawless act was designed to secure. Applying this rule, we must hold that, inasmuch as defendant admits the destruc-

tion of certain papers having an important bearing on the relation existing between him and plaintiff, we should assume, as a matter of law, that the papers deposited with the banker evidenced a contract of sale in which defendant was the vendor and plaintiff the vendee, and disproved the assertion of defendant that he was merely the agent of plaintiff.

* * * * *

TRANSPORT INDEMNITY COMPANY v. John SEIB, Impleaded with John Seib d/b/a Shipper's Motor Express et al.

132 N.W.2d 871

Supreme Court of Nebraska
February 5, 1965

This is an action for insurance premiums. From a jury verdict and judgment for the plaintiff in the sum of $6,639.46 John Seib, hereinafter referred to as defendant, appeals.

The defendant operated a fleet of trucks in various states. The plaintiff writes retrospective insurance. By the terms of the contract, exhibits 1 and 2, the defendant pays an advance premium based on a percentage of his gross monthly receipts. The insurance covers bodily injury, property and material damage, and cargo liability. As the losses are reported to the plaintiff, it processes and pays them. The defendant is given a quarterly report of his loss experience. The defendant pays all losses and expenses up to $1,000 and the plaintiff pays all over that sum. According to the formula agreed to by the parties, the earned premium is calculated retrospectively. The loss experience of other operators is not a factor. Each loss has added to it certain investigation, overhead, taxes, fees, and management costs, and the net sum is charged back against the defendant as earned premium. The sum, so computed on cash loss, cannot be more than $1,000. The plaintiff pays the balance of the loss. If the advance premiums exceed the losses, the defendant gets a refund; if they are less, he is obliged to pay the balance as an earned premium. The object of the insurance is to give an operator the opportunity to take advantage of a good safety record in his insurance costs. The contract and policy may be canceled at any time by either party. The insurance went into force in April 1960 and was canceled on May 16, 1961.

To establish the amount of premium due, the plaintiff, whose home office is in Los Angeles, California, offered in evidence exhibit 14 which was received over objection as to foundation. Its admission now is assigned as prejudicial error.

The evidence supports the following summary of the nature of exhibit 14 and the foundation for its admission. Exhibit 14 is prepared and printed by electronic equipment. It was prepared by, and under the direction of, Leland S. Thomas, a director of the company, who is director of accounting for plaintiff, and whose testimony is the foundation for the admission of exhibit 14. Records, such as exhibit 14, are under the custody and control of Thomas. A fair inference from the record is that the figures reported and the computations made are accurate calculations within his personal knowledge. On direct examination, this witness, Leland S. Thomas, testified: "Q. (BY MR. ACKLIE) Mr. Thomas, was Exhibit 14 computed, say, by an I.B.M. or other tabulating machine? A. Those calculations are prepared by machine, yes. They are all electric computers. We have our formulas set out, first, as to the type of policy this is. There are different plans of insurance which you can pursue, on all retrospective policies, so you have to have a formula in order to feed this particular information into the machine, and each time you have a case, we feed that formula into the machine, and the machine does the calculating work, whether multiplying or subtracting the premiums. It just does what used to be done by keeping books. We feed the formulas, and the machine will do that, and keep them on tape."

The information as to the losses is fed into the machine, the machine records them, makes the necessary formula calculations, and it is stored on tape. On four of the large pages of this exhibit is recorded each accident by date, name of driver, type of accident (coded), amount and type of loss, allocated expenses according to the policy contract, and other information from which the premium can be computed. The total of the paid losses chargeable as premiums for policy year is found on the first two pages of exhibit 14. There is recorded the amount of advance premiums paid. The individual loss records on the last four pages support the figures in the calculation of premiums owed and due on pages 1 and 2. On pages 1 and 2, the machine takes the composite totals of the losses allocated to premiums, subjects them to the formula of the contract (exhibits 1 and 2), computes the total premium owed for the year, deducts the payments made, and enters the total due. It is a bookkeeping record made in the usual course of business. It was sent quarterly to the insured, Seib, and it is a cumulative record. The information is stored on the tape and at any time the machine can retrieve a record such as exhibit 14 giving the losses paid to date and the premium paid and due according to the formula. Thomas testified that the calculations on exhibit 14 are made exactly in conformity with the defendant's premium formula in the contract. This witness, Thomas, made a detailed explanation of each item on exhibit 14. He took the entire list of claims shown on exhibit 14, computed the amounts charged and due according to the contract formula, and reconciled these figures with the machine–produced results on exhibit 14. This witness' testimony, mostly as to foundation for exhibit 14, stretches across 141 pages of this record. All of it cannot be summarized. It shows that this record and computation were made as the usual part of plaintiff's business operation, that the keeping of this record was an indispensable part of the business, and that the record was kept separate for the insurance contract of the defendant. This exhibit shows $39,828.50 paid claims for the policy year April 1, 1960, to April 1, 1961. After processing through the contract formula, it shows a total earned premium charge of $10,301.45, with payments of $3,046.18 by defendant as advance premiums and a payment balance of $2,069.03 on the deficit, leaving a balance due of $5,186.24. The same process applied to the year April 1, 1961, to April 1962, results in a net due the plaintiff of $1,453.22 or a total due of $6,439.46. This is the verdict the jury returned.

Section 25-12,109, R.R.S.1943, is as follows: "A record of an act, condition, or event, shall, insofar as relevant, be competent evidence if the custodian or other qualified witness testifies to its identity and the mode of its preparation, and if it was made in the regular course of business, at or near the time of the act, condition, or event, and if, in the opinion of the court, the sources of information, method, and time of preparation were such as to justify its admission."

In construing this statute, our court said in *Higgins v. Loup River Public Power Dist.*, 159 Neb. 549, 68 N.W.2d 170, as follows: "The purpose of the act is to permit admission of *systematically entered records* without the necessity of *identifying, locating, and producing as witnesses the individuals who made entries in the records in the regular course of the business* rather than to make a fundamental change in the established principles of the book–shop exception to the hearsay rule." (Emphasis supplied.)

It seems to us that the foundation testimony here follows the statute and indirectly the scope of the purpose of the statute as stated in the Higgins case, supra. It was not necessary to produce and identify the witnesses who originally supplied the information as to losses that is recorded on the tape.

The defendant has failed to point out to us wherein the foundational requirements of this statute have not been met. Identification and the mode of its preparation, and that it was made in the regular course of business, were fully testified to. A complete and comprehensive explanation of its meaning and "identity" was given. As we see it, defendant's objections go only to the weight and credibility of exhibit 14 and not its admissibility. Exhibit 14 constitutes the accounts receivable record of the plaintiff as to defendant. It responds to the reports as to gross

receipts and claims furnished by the defendant himself. It was fed into the electronic equipment, processed as to the formula agreed upon, all as a part of the usual and necessary business operations and record of the plaintiff company. The calculations were authenticated by the testimony of the witness, Thomas, which reconciled the figures of the original losses with the calculation of the final amount due. This procedure fit squarely that approved in *United States v. Olivo*, 3 Cir., 278 F.2d 415, wherein it was said: "The witness testified to a well–established business procedure not only in the trade, but specifically in the very company which had prepared the document. All the hallmarks of authenticity surround this document, since it was made pursuant to established company procedures for the systematic, routine, timely making and preserving of company records."

No particular mode or form of record is required. The statute was intended to bring the realities of business and professional practice into the courtroom and the statute should not be interpreted narrowly to destroy its obvious usefulness. *United States v. Olivo*, supra.

The machine here performs the bookkeeping task in the usual course of business. Instead of on paper, the information and calculations are stored on tape and may be retrieved and printed at any time. The taped record furnished a cumulative record based on information flowing into the office of the plaintiff company day by day and fed into the machine in response to a systematic procedure for processing each insured's account.

In the terms of the statute, we are of the opinion that the "sources of information, method, and time of preparation" were such as to justify its (exhibit 14) admission. To hold otherwise would require the production of the original claims files and reports, which in turn would probably be inadmissible under a strict application of the hearsay rule.

Defendant was sent a quarterly report in the same form as exhibit 14, and prepared from the same tape, showing his loss experience and expense, and the calculation of his premium due. During the period of his business with plaintiff he did not question the accuracy of this record. Exhibit 14 is merely cumulative of these quarterly reports. The original sources came from the defendant himself. The amounts and character of the payments on the losses are not questioned. This situation bears on the authenticity and probative source of the document and aids the conclusion that, "the sources of information, method, and time of preparation were such as to justify its admission." Section 25–12,109, R.R.S.1943.

Defendant argues exhibit 14 is inadmissible because it was prepared for use in this litigation and trial, citing *Higgins v. Loup River Power Dist.*, supra.

This argument exalts the form over the substance. The retrieval from the taped record (exhibit 14) was made for the purposes of the trial. But, the taped record and the information and calculations thereon were made in the usual course of business and for the purpose of the business alone. There is no merit to this contention.

* * * * *

Leonard TRUPIANO, d/b/a Trupiano Plumbing & Heating Co. v. George H. CULLY, d/b/a Spartan Engineering & Construction Company

284 N.W.2d 747

Supreme Court of Michigan
September 4, 1957

A building contractor and a plumber had a dispute about whether or not the former owed the latter for fixtures and plumbing work performed under an oral contract on a certain house. The plumber sued. In two jury trials he prevailed. (A new trial was granted in the first.) The record of the second jury trial is before us.

The only legal issue presented on appeal pertains to the effect of plaintiff's action in having a set of books made up for him and thereafter discarding the original notes and memoranda. Defendant claims that this action represented spoliation and cites the rule thereon from American Jurisprudence.

"It is a general rule that the intentional spoliation or destruction of evidence raises the presumption against the spoliator where the evidence was relevant to the case or where it was his duty to preserve it, since his conduct may properly be attributed to his supposed knowledge that the truth would operate against him." 20 Am.Jur., Evidence, § 185, p. 191.

The full section continues, however:

"Such a presumption can be applied only where there was intentional conduct indicating fraud and a desire to destroy and thereby suppress the truth. Moreover, while the spoliation of evidence raises a presumption against the person guilty of such act, yet such presumption does not relieve the other party from introducing evidence tending affirmatively to prove his case, in so far as he has the burden of proof. The spoliation or suppression of evidence is a circumstance open to explanation."

See, also, *Davis v. Teachout's Estate*, 126 Mich. 135, 85 N.W. 475, 86 Am.St.Rep. 531; *Pitcher v. Rogers' Estate*, 199 Mich. 114, 165 N.W. 813.

We cannot hold as a matter of law from the evidence contained in the record that there was "intentional conduct indicating fraud and a desire to destroy and thereby suppress the truth." At best, in the event the jury found destruction of records with an intent to suppress the truth, defendant was entitled to an inference that the original records, if available, would not prove favorable to plaintiff. The facts were certainly before the jury. Presumably they were argued.

* * * * *

Nathan TURNER, Plaintiff, – against – HUDSON TRANSIT LINES, INC. and SHORT LINE TERMINAL AGENCY, INC., Defendants. HUDSON TRANSIT LINES, INC. and SHORT LINE TERMINAL AGENCY, INC., Third–Party Plaintiffs, – against – Joseph ZOZICHOWSKI and Denise ZOZICHOWSKI, Third–Party Defendants.

142 F.R.D. 68

United States District Court for the Southern District of New York
September 27, 1991

This is a personal injury action arising out of a motor vehicle collision on the New Jersey Turnpike. Nathan Turner, who was a passenger in a bus involved in the accident, has sued the owner and operator of the bus, alleging that he sustained injuries because the bus was improperly equipped or negligently driven. Jurisdiction is based on diversity of citizenship.

The parties have now submitted cross–motions for sanctions based on purported discovery abuses, including the destruction of evidence. Each motion will be analyzed in turn, together with the relevant factual and procedural background.

I. Destruction of Maintenance Records

The plaintiff's first motion arises out of the destruction of the bus maintenance records by defendants Hudson Transit Line, Inc. and Short Line Terminal Agency, Inc. (collectively referred to as "Hudson Transit"). The plaintiff contends that the defendants' conduct has deprived him of potentially valuable evidence. Consequently, the plaintiff argues, he is entitled to an "adverse inference" charge: an instruction that the jury may infer from the destruction of these maintenance records that they would have been detrimental to Hudson Transit's case.

A detailed chronology is important to an understanding of this issue. The accident in which the plaintiff was injured took place on

October 8, 1986. On September 23, 1987, the defendants sold the bus that had been involved in the accident to Hausman Bus Sales, a company in Illinois. Affidavit of Andrew T. Houghton dated February 28, 1991, Exh. J. The plaintiff served a state court complaint in this action on October 24, 1988. Petition for Removal at P 1. He then served an Amended Complaint on June 12, 1989, Petition for Removal at P 3, and defendants thereafter removed the action to this Court on the basis of diversity jurisdiction. The Amended Complaint alleged, among other things, that the defendants had failed to provide the bus with good and sufficient brakes. Amended Complaint at P 8.

The plaintiff's efforts to obtain the maintenance records began on December 29, 1989, the date of the plaintiff's Request for Production of Documents. Houghton Aff., Exh. B. Defendants' counsel responded to the request on January 18, 1990, by noting that no such records were in the possession, custody, or control of the defendants. Houghton Aff., Exh. C. Thereafter, in a letter to the Court dated April 27, 1990, defendants' counsel stated that the bus had been sold and that copies of the maintenance records were not retained. Houghton Aff., Exh. D. Yet in a deposition taken on April 19, 1990, the bus driver seemed to indicate that there were two sets of maintenance records, one that accompanied the bus and another that was retained by the defendants. Affidavit of Andrew T. Houghton dated May 9, 1990, Exh. K. On the basis of this testimony the plaintiff moved to compel production of the records. Defendants' counsel responded that he then made further inquiry and was advised by his clients that all maintenance records had been transferred with the bus when it was sold. Affidavit of Haydn J. Brill dated May 17, 1990 at P 10. This was reiterated in the defendants' Response to Plaintiff's Second Request for Production of Documents. Houghton Aff., 2/28/91, Exh. G. On the basis of these representations, I denied plaintiff's application for an order compelling production of the maintenance records. I did, however permit the plaintiff to pursue discovery regarding the disposition of the records. See Order dated May 22, 1990 at P 4.

After seeking unsuccessfully to obtain the maintenance records from the company to which the bus had been sold, the plaintiff took the deposition of Hudson Transit's Director of Maintenance, William Huddleston, on August 28, 1990. He testified that in March or April, 1990, he had been asked by Catherine Jones, a claims administrator for Hudson Transit, whether he had any records for the bus. Houghton Aff., 2/28/91, Exh. O at 14–15. Mr. Huddleston further stated that in response to Mr. Jones' inquiry, he searched the files but found no records. Houghton Aff., 2/28/91, Exh. O at 15–16.

Mr. Huddleston also testified about Hudson Transit's document retention policies. He stated that records are maintained for one year pursuant to Federal Highway Administration regulations. Houghton Aff., 2/28/91, Exh. O at 12. When a bus is sold, Hudson Transit generally transfers the maintenance records to the new owner but keeps copies for six months. Houghton Aff., 2/28/91, Exh. O at 19–20.

Then, on October 29, 1990, in response to the plaintiff's supplemental interrogatories, the defendants issued answers prepared by Mr. Huddleston. Houghton Aff., 2/29/91, Exh. R. This time he stated that he personally transferred the original maintenance records to the new bus owner at the time of the sale. Further, he acknowledged that Hudson Transit had retained a copy of the records. Now, however, Mr. Huddleston admitted that he had personally destroyed these copies in December, 1989.

At the close of discovery, the plaintiff moved for sanctions in connection with the destruction of the maintenance records, and a hearing was held on June 19, 1991. Remarkably, the defendants did not offer Mr. Huddleston as a witness. Instead, they produced Catherine Jones, the claims administrator who had asked Mr. Huddleston about the records. She testified that she had contacted him in early January of 1990, not in March or April as he had stated. Tr. 11–12. According to Ms. Jones, Mr. Huddleston told her that the maintenance documents had been transferred with the bus but never stated that he had destroyed copies. Tr. 13–14. With respect to Hudson Transit's document retention policy, Ms. Jones stated that records are retained as long as federal regulations require; after that they may be discarded even if someone has asserted a claim or initiated Litigation because of an accident. Tr. 18–19. Ms. Jones never advised Mr. Huddleston that the claim at issue here was in litigation. Tr. 19–20.

A. Authority for Imposing Sanctions

Where a party has destroyed evidence, the court's authority to impose sanctions derives from two sources. First, Rule 37(b) of the Federal Rules of Civil Procedure provides that a party that fails to comply with a discovery order is subject to sanctions. Thus, when noncompliance results from the spoliation of evidence, Rule 37(b) comes into play. See *Marking Specialists, Inc. v. Bruni, 129 F.R.D. 35, 53 (W.D.N.Y. 1989)*. Even though a party may have destroyed evidence prior to issuance of the discovery order and thus be unable to obey, sanctions are still appropriate under Rule 37(b) because this inability was self–inflicted. See *In re Air Crash Disaster near Chicago, Illinois on May 15, 1979, 90 F.R.D. 613, 620–21 (N.D. Ill. 1981)*.

Occasionally, courts are hesitant to rely on Rule 37, believing that it does not deal specifically with the issue of spoliation. For example, in *Capellupo v. FMC Corp., 126 F.R.D. 545 (D. Minn. 1989)*, the court found this rule applicable only to "'normal' disputes, delays, or difficulties occurring in civil litigation," and refused to apply it to the destruction of documents prior to the initiation of litigation. *Id. at 550–51 & n. 14*. Yet in such cases courts may still impose sanctions, relying on their "inherent power to regulate litigation, preserve and protect the integrity of proceedings before [them], and sanction parties for abusive practices." *Id. at 551* (citation omitted); see also *National Ass'n of Radiation Survivors v. Turnage, 115 F.R.D. 543, 556 (N.D. Cal. 1987)*.

Courts thus have the power to sanction the destruction of evidence, whether that authority is derived from Rule 37 or their inherent powers.[1]

B. Obligation to Preserve Evidence

In determining whether a court should exercise its authority to impose sanctions for spoliation, a threshold question is whether a party had any obligation to preserve the evidence. One court has articulated the general rule as follows:

Sanctions may be imposed on a litigant who is on notice that documents and information in its possession are relevant to litigation, or potential litigation, or are reasonably calculated to lead to the discovery of admissible evidence, and destroys such documents and information. While a litigant is under no duty to keep or retain every document in its possession once a complaint is filed, it is under a duty to preserve what it knows, or reasonably should know, is relevant to the action, is reasonably calculated to lead to the discovery of admissible evidence, is reasonably likely to be requested during discovery and/or is the subject of a pending discovery request.

Wm. T. Thompson Co. v. General Nutrition Corp., 593 F.Supp. 1443, 1455 (C.D. Cal. 1984) (citations omitted).

Thus, no duty to preserve arises unless the party possessing the evidence has notice of its relevance. *See Danna v. New York Telephone Co., 752 F.Supp. 594, 616 n.9 (S.D.N.Y. 1990)* Of course, a party is on notice once it has received a discovery request. Beyond that, the complaint itself may alert a party that certain information is relevant and likely to be sought in discovery. *See Computer Associates International, Inc. v. America Fundware, Inc., 133 F.R.D. 166, 169 (D. Colo. 1990); Telectron, Inc. v. Overhead Door Corp., 116 F.R.D. 107, 127 (S.D. Fla. 1987).* Finally, the obligation to preserve evidence even arises prior to the filing of a complaint where a party is on notice that litigation is likely to be commenced. *See Capellupo v. FMC Corp., 126 F.R.D. at 550–51 & n. 14; Alliance to End Repression v. Rochford, 75 F.R.D. 438, 440 (N.D. Ill. 1976).*

Here, Hudson Transit's contention that it had no notice of the relevance of the maintenance records is unavailing. The defendant argues that the central issue in this case is whether the bus was negligently operated, not whether it was properly maintained. Yet the complaint in this action explicitly charges that the bus lacked "good and sufficient brakes." Thus, at least by the time the complaint was served, Hudson Transit was on notice that maintenance records should be preserved.

This obligation ran first to counsel, who had a duty to advise his client of the type of information potentially relevant to the lawsuit and of the necessity of preventing its destruction. *See Kansas–Nebraska Natural Gas Co. v. Marathon Oil Co., 109 F.R.D. 12, 18 & n. Similarly, the defendants' corporate managers were responsible for conveying this information to the relevant employees. Id.*

It is no defense to suggest, as the defendant attempts, that particular employees were not on notice. To hold otherwise would permit an agency, corporate officer, or legal department to shield itself from discovery obligations by keeping its employees ignorant. The obligation to retain discoverable materials is an affirmative one; it requires that the agency or corporate officers having notice of discovery obligations communicate those obligations to employees in possession of discoverable materials.

National Ass'n of Radiation Survivors, 115 F.R.D. at 557–58 (footnote omitted).

Hudson Transit and its counsel failed to meet these obligations, and the excuses offered are without merit. For example, Hudson Transit relies on *INA Aviation Corp. v. United States, 468 F.Supp. 695 (E.D.N.Y. 1979),* for the proposition that it is immune from sanctions because it followed governmental regulations in preserving the maintenance records for the required period of time. But in INA, the regulations required the destruction of documents after a given period. *Id. at 700.* Here, the Federal Highway Administration regulations permitted the maintenance records to be destroyed after a particular period but did not conflict with discovery obligations requiring that they be preserved longer. Moreover, the decision in INA has been properly criticized:

The court overlooked a real problem. The FAA manual could have provided explicit guidance on exceptions to its destruction procedures for accidents. The manual's inadequate guidance protects federal employees who wish to destroy relevant documents with an intent to keep them out of court and later argue that the act was routine.

Dale A. Oesterle, A Private Litigant's Remedies for an Opponent's Inappropriate Destruction of Relevant Documents, 61 Tex. L. Rev. 1185, 1216 (1983). Thus, the government regulations on which Hudson Transit relies do not excuse its destruction of records.

Similarly, it is immaterial that Hudson Transit may have believed that the original records would be available from the new bus owner. In fact, this assumption proved unwarranted, since efforts to obtain the records from the new owner have failed. Nor was it a reasonable assumption: according to the government regulations that Hudson Transit itself cites, the new owner would only have been required to preserve the records for a year after the sale in 1987. In any event, a party's discovery obligations are not satisfied by relying on non–parties to preserve documents. *See Struthers Patent Corp. v. Nestle Co., 558 F.Supp. 747, 765 (D.N.J. 1981).*

Hudson Transit, then had an obligation to preserve the maintenance records, and it failed to do so. It is therefore necessary to consider the appropriate relief.

C. Adverse Inference

The plaintiff requests an instruction that the jury may infer from Hudson Transit's destruction of the maintenance records that these documents would have demonstrated that the brakes were not in good order. The concept of an adverse inference as a sanction for spoliation is based on two rationales. The first is remedial: where evidence is destroyed, the court should restore the prejudiced party to the same position with respect to its ability to prove its case that it would have held if there had been no spoliation.

The second rationale is punitive. "Allowing

the trier of fact to draw the inference presumably deters parties from destroying relevant evidence before it can be introduced at trial." *Nation–Wide Check Corp. v. Forest Hill Distributors, Inc., 692 F.2d 214, 218 (1st Cir. 1982).* Of course, it also serves as retribution against the immediate wrongdoer. "The law, in hatred of the spoiler, baffles the destroyer, and thwarts his iniquitous purpose, by indulging a presumption which supplies the lost proof, and thus defeats the wrongdoer by the very means he had so confidentially employed to perpetrate the wrong." *Pomeroy v. Benton, 77 Mo. 64, 86 (1882)* quoted in McCormick on Evidence § 273, at 809 n. 14 (Edward W. Cleary ed.. 3d ed. 1984).

Particular courts relying exclusively on one or the other of these rationales, may lose sight of the need to consider both principles in determining the appropriate remedy in any specific case. Cf. John M. Maguire & Robert C. Vincent, Admissions Implied from Spoliation or Related Conduct, *45 Yale L. J. 226, 230–31 (1935)* (inconsistency of cases attributed to "intertwining of punitive and remedial ideas"). In particular, a court should keep both principles in mind when considering the two objective factors that weigh most heavily in determining the appropriateness of an adverse inference: the intent of the party responsible for the destruction and the content of the evidence destroyed.

1. Intent

The state of mind of a party that destroys evidence is a major factor in determining whether an adverse inference is the appropriate sanction. Where the destruction is intentional — that is, where the destroyer intended to prevent use of the evidence in litigation — courts clearly have the power to invoke such an inference. *See Capellupo, 126 F.R.D. at 552; INA Aviation Corp., 468 F.Supp at 700.* Indeed, under some circumstances it may be an abuse of discretion not to draw an adverse inference when the party destroying evidence has been shown to have acted willfully. *See Alexander v. National Farmers Organization, 687 F.2d 1173, 1205–06 & n. 40 (8th Cir. 1982).* Moreover, the even harsher sanction of judgment by default may be imposed as a sanction for the intentional destruction of evidence if the party seeking the evidence has been severely prejudiced and no lesser sanction would be adequate. *See Computer Associates Int'l, Inc., 133 F.R.D. at 169–70; Capellupo, 126 F.R.D. at 552; Carlucci v. Piper Aircraft Corp., 102 F.R.D. 472, 486 (S.D. Fla. 1984).*

While a finding of bad faith, then, is sufficient to trigger an adverse inference, the courts are divided on whether it is necessary. Some say that the adverse inference may be drawn only when it has been shown that the destruction of evidence was intentional. See *Allen Pen Co. v. Springfield Photo Mount Co., 653 F.2d 17, 23–24 (1st Cir. 1981); Britt v. Block, 636 F.Supp. 596, 606–07 (D. Vt. 1986); INA Aviation Corp., 468 F.Supp. at 700.* Others hold that the negligent or reckless destruction of evidence may warrant such a sanction. See *Pressey v. Patterson, 898 F.2d 1018, 1024 (5th Cir. 1990)*, the Court quoted *INA Aviation Corp., 468 F.Supp. at 700*, for the proposition that "'one cannot justify the drawing of . . . an [adverse] inference where the destruction of evidence is unintentional.'" However, by prefacing this statement with the phase "on the facts of this case," *Berkovich, 922 F.2d at 1024*, the Court implied that in other circumstances it might indeed be appropriate to draw an adverse inference even though the destruction was merely negligent.

That appears to be the conclusion that has been reached in the First Circuit. In *Allen Pen, 653 F.2d at 23–24*, the court seemed to erect bad faith as a prerequisite for drawing an adverse inference. However, in *Nationwide Check Corp. v. Forest Hills Distributors, Inc.*, the court stated:

> The [district] court's reluctance to label [the spoliator's] conduct as "bad faith" is not dispositive: "bad faith" is not a talisman, as Allen Pen itself made clear when it stated that the adverse inference "ordinarily" depended on a showing of bad faith. Indeed, the "bad faith" label is more useful to summarize the conclusion that an adverse inference is permissible than it is actually to reach the conclusion.

692 F.2d at 219.

Courts that require a showing of bad faith do so on the theory that, without it, the adverse inference lacks logic:

> The litigant's conduct indicates a belief relevant and detrimental to some feature of his case; therefore he holds that belief; therefore his case is in this feature defective. But if the litigant's conduct results only from happy–go–lucky carelessness, and not from specific motive or intention to achieve a specific end, the whole backbone of the formula breaks. The necessary showing of belief is lacking.

Maguire & Vincent, supra, at 235 (footnote omitted); see also *Allen Pen Co., 653 F.2d at 23–24; McCormick on Evidence, supra*, § 273, at 809 ("Mere negligence is not enough, but it does not sustain the inference of consciousness of a weak case."). In other words, if a party destroys evidence carelessly, rather than because he believes that the evidence is damaging to him, there is no logical reason for the trier of fact to conclude that the evidence would have been damaging to him.

The flaw in this analysis is that it assumes that the only basis for the adverse inference is this evidentiary syllogism. But this sanction should be available even for the negligent destruction of documents if that is necessary to further the remedial purpose of the inference. It makes little difference to the party victimized by the destruction of evidence whether that act was done willfully or negligently. The adverse inference provides the necessary mechanism for restoring the evidentiary balance. The inference is adverse to the destroyer not because of any finding of moral culpability, but because the risk that the evidence would have been detrimental rather than favorable should fall on the party responsible for its loss.[2]

In other contexts, courts commonly preclude a party from introducing certain evidence without any finding that the sanctionable conduct was intentional. For example, a party that fails to identify an expert witness when required to do so by a scheduling order may be precluded from offering the witness's testimony at trial.

See *Hull v. Eaton Corp., 825 F.2d 488, 451–52 (D.C. Cir. 1987).* More broadly, a party that fails to seek or comply with a scheduling order may even be subject to judgment by default without inquiry into the party's motives. See C.E. *Bickford & Co., v M.V. "Elly", 116 F.R.D. 195, 195–96 (S.D.N.Y. 1986).* Although there may be no suggestion that these parties failed to comply with scheduling or discovery orders because of any weakness in their own cases, they are nevertheless subject to orders of preclusion because their conduct has unfairly prejudiced their adversaries.

The same rationale is applicable here. An adverse inference is the mirror image of a preclusion order: it supplies evidence which was once in the power of one party to produce, but which, because of the conduct of that party, can not now be offered at trial. The evidentiary imbalance caused by the spoliation does not depend on that party's intent; therefore, bad faith, while a significant consideration, should not be an absolute prerequisite to drawing an adverse inference.

In this case, there is insufficient evidence to demonstrate that Hudson Transit deliberately destroyed copies of the maintenance records to prevent their discovery. First, the company does have some document retention policy, though it is geared to federal regulation and is not sensitive to obligations arising from litigation. Second, the documents were destroyed here long after the litigation had commenced, but before Hudson Transit received the document demand. Had the destruction been deliberate, it would more likely have been accomplished either immediately after suit was filed or after the plaintiff sought the documents. Finally, if Hudson Transit believed that the original maintenance records were in fact transferred when the bus was sold, then it would also have known that destruction of the copies would be futile.

Hudson Transit's conduct is nonetheless disturbing. As discussed above, it clearly violated its obligation to maintain these records once the litigation had been filed. In addition, the discovery responses provided by Hudson Transit were misleading at best. Counsel repeatedly represented to the Court that the records had been transferred with the bus and that copies had not been retained. In deposition, Mr. Huddleston testified that he searched for copies of the records in response to the discovery request but found none. Later, however, he admitted in interrogatory answers that he had destroyed the documents before they had been requested. This admission renders his deposition testimony wholly incredible, since it is inconceivable that he would have searched for documents that he himself had recently destroyed. Likewise, his answers to questions suggested that he had destroyed copies. The only explanation offered by counsel is that Mr. Huddleston was carefully coached for his deposition and answered each question in the narrowest possible terms. (Tr. 32–38). Such an excuse is hardly adequate, and it does little to breed confidence in the conduct of counsel.

Thus, although Hudson Transit did not intentionally destroy evidence, its reckless conduct did result in loss of the records, and its subsequent discovery responses misled the Court and opposing counsel. In order to determine whether an adverse inference is warranted under these circumstances, we must turn to the second critical factor: the content of the lost evidence.

2. Content of the Evidence Destroyed

Before an adverse inference may be drawn, there must be some showing that there is in fact a nexus between the proposed inference and the information contained in the lost evidence. Wigmore articulates this requirement as follows:

> The failure or refusal to produce a relevant document, or the destruction of it, is evidence from which alone its contents may be inferred to be unfavorable to the possessor, provided the opponent, when the identity of the document is disputed, first introduces some evidence tending to show that the document actually destroyed or withheld is the one as to whose contents it is desired to draw an inference. In applying this rule, care should be taken not to require anything like specific details of contents, but merely such evidence as goes to general marks of identity.

Wigmore on Evidence § 291, at 228 (Chadbourn rev. 1979) (emphasis omitted). According to this formulation, the plaintiff here need only show that the documents destroyed were in fact the maintenance records and not some other papers. Hudson Transit has, of course, admitted the identity of the documents.

But in fact courts have generally required some greater showing of the content of the destroyed evidence before drawing an inference. In *Stanojev v. Ebasco Services, Inc., 643 F.2d 914 (2d Cir. 1981)*, for example, the Second Circuit refused to infer from the defendant's destruction of personnel records that it had engaged in discrimination, because "it is unlikely that documents containing evaluations relevant to an earlier time and prior positions would support a charge that [the plaintiff's] dismissal in 1978 was the result of age discrimination." *Id. at 923–24).* Similarly, in *Nation–Wide Check Corp.*, the court drew an adverse inference only after observing that substantial circumstantial evidence supports the facts to be inferred. *692 F.2d at 218–19).*

A showing of bad faith by itself is the basis for some inference that the evidence destroyed was detrimental to the destroyer:

> a party who has notice that a document is relevant to litigation and who proceeds to destroy the document is more likely to have been threatened by the document than is a party in the same position who does not destroy the document.

Nation–Wide Check Corp., 692 F.2d at 218. Nevertheless, some extrinsic evidence of the content of the evidence is necessary for the trier of fact to be able to determine in what respect and to what extent it would have been detrimental.

This corroboration requirement is even more necessary where the destruction was merely negligent, since in those cases it cannot be inferred from the conduct of the spoliator that the evidence would even have been harmful to him. See *Stanojev, 643 F.2d at 924 n. 7* (proper inference to be drawn from failure to call witness is to give strongest weight to evidence

already in case favorable to other side: "The jury should not be encouraged to base its verdict on what it speculates the absent witnesses would have testified to, in the absence of some direct evidence."), quoting *Felice v. Long Island Railroad, 426 F.2d 192, 195 n2 (2d Cir.)*, cert. denied, *400 U.S. 820 (1970); Maguire & Vincent, supra, at 240–42.*

Here, there is no evidence that the destroyed records would have shown whether the brakes were in good working order. Notations of work on the brakes prior to the accident would not likely have revealed whether any problems were successfully corrected by the time of the accident. Notations after the accident would probably not show how long any problem had persisted. At best, then, the records would have contained ambiguous information. Moreover, the plaintiff has offered no extrinsic evidence to corroborate the suggestion that the brakes were faulty. No affidavit has been offered attributing the accident to the bus's inability to stop. Nor has the plaintiff ascertained that the new bus owner found the brakes to be defective or to have been recently repaired. Thus, the maintenance records themselves would not have shown the brakes to be defective, and therefore no inference to that affect is appropriate. See *Allen Pen, 653 F.2d at 24.*

In order to remedy the evidentiary imbalance created by the destruction of evidence, an adverse inference may be appropriate even in the absence of a showing that the spoliator acted in bad faith. However, where the destruction was negligent rather than willful, special caution must be exercised to ensure that the inference is commensurate with information that was reasonably likely to have been contained in the destroyed evidence. Where, as here, there is no extrinsic evidence whatever tending to show that the destroyed evidence would have been unfavorable to the spoliator, no adverse inference is appropriate.

D. Costs

Denial of the requested relief does not, however, leave the plaintiff without a remedy. Even when rejecting an adverse inference, courts impose monetary sanctions for the destruction of evidence. See *Harkins Amusement Enterprises, Inc. v. General Cinema Corp., 132 F.R.D. 523, 524 (D. Ariz. 1990); Capellupo, 126 F.R.D. at 553* (double costs and attorneys' fees). Like an adverse inference, an award of costs serves both punitive and remedial purposes: it deters spoliation and compensates the opposing party for the additional costs incurred. Such compensable costs may arise either from the discovery necessary to identify alternative sources of information, see *Allen Pen, 653 F.2d at 23; Capellupo, 126 F.R.D. at 552; In re Air Crash Disaster, 90 F.R.D. at 621,* or from the investigation and litigation of the document destruction itself. See *Capellupo, 126 F.R.D. at 552; National Ass'n of Radiation Survivors, 115 F.R.D. at 558.*

Here, an award of costs, including attorneys' fees, is entirely warranted. Hudson Transit unjustifiably destroyed documents after litigation had been commenced, causing the plaintiff to expend time and effort in attempting to track down the relevant information. It then caused the expenditure of additional resources by misleading the plaintiff and the Court regarding the actual disposition of the records.

* * * * *

---

[1] In addition, where a discovery response fails to acknowledge spoliation because of the failure to make reasonable inquiry, sanctions may be imposed under Rule 26(g) of the Federal Rules of Civil Procedure. See *National Ass'n of Radiation Survivors v. Turnage, 115 F.R.D. at 554–55.*

[2] The adverse inference thus acts as a deterrent against even the negligent destruction of evidence. This is perfectly appropriate: deterrence is not a function limited to punitive sanctions where intent has been demonstrated. In the law of torts for example, damages for negligence serve to deter such conduct in the future.

UNITED NUCLEAR CORPORATION v. GENERAL ATOMIC COMPANY and Indiana & Michigan Electric Co.

629 P.2d 231

Supreme Court of New Mexico
August 29, 1980

This is an appeal from a default judgment entered against General Atomic Company (GAC) in Santa Fe District Court for its alleged willful and bad faith failure to comply with the court's discovery orders.

This case is by far the single largest litigation in the history of New Mexico, both in terms of the dollar value of the judgment, which approaches one billion dollars, and the sheer volume of the record, which contains more than 28,000 pages in the record proper, 13,000 pages of transcripts, thousands of documents, and over 100 depositions containing approximately 16,000 pages of testimony and 2,700 exhibits. The facts are largely disputed and are extremely complex. Although we begin with a general factual background and summary of the proceedings below, additional factual details are contained in the separate discussions of the issues raised on appeals.

This action was instituted by United Nuclear Corporation (United) against GAC, a partnership made up of Gulf Oil Corporation (Gulf) and Scallop Nuclear Corporation (Scallop). Scallop is a wholly–owned subsidiary of Dutch Shell Oil Company. As amended, United's complaint sought a declaratory judgment that two contracts under which United was to apply approximately twenty–seven million pounds of uranium to GAC were void and unenforceable. The complaint alleged that GAC and Gulf committed fraud and economic coercion, breached their fiduciary duties to United, and violated the New Mexico Antitrust Act. United also contended that its performance under the contracts had been rendered commercially impractical. GAC counterclaimed for actual and punitive damages for United's alleged violations of the New Mexico Antitrust Act, and for specific performance of the two contracts, or alternatively, for damages of almost eight hundred million dollars.

GAC impleaded Indiana and Michigan Electric Company (I&M), a public utility company which provides electrical service to customers in the states of Indiana and Michigan. GAC contended that if United's obligations to supply uranium to GAC were excused, GAC's obligations to supply uranium to I&M from the supplies United was to deliver should also be excused. I&M counterclaimed against GAC for specific performance and for other relief.

The trial of this case began on October 31, 1977. It was terminated on March 2, 1978, when the trial judge entered a sanctions order and default judgment against GAC. The court found that GAC had exercised "the utmost bad faith in all stages of the discovery process." The court entered forty–eight recitals relating to GAC's discovery failures, twelve findings of fact as to sanctions pursuant to N.M.R. Civ. P. 37(b)(2)(i), N.M.S.A. 1978, and a default judgment under N.M.R. Civ. P. 37(b)(2)(iii), N.M.S.A. 1978. The judgment invalidated United's uranium supply contracts with GAC, declared that United had no other obligations to deliver uranium to GAC, and struck GAC's defenses, counterclaims and crossclaims.

A hearing on damages followed, after which the court entered a final judgment, amended final judgment, and second amended final judgment. In addition to invalidating the United–GAC contracts, the court awarded damages to United of $8,264,723 (reduced by an offset for prepayments that had been made) and to I&M of $15,950,752. The court also granted specific performance of I&M's contract for the supply of five million pounds of uranium from GAC.

GAC appeals from the default judgment, arguing ten main grounds for reversal. We have consolidated these points in this opinion into the following five sections: (1) The propriety of the court's discovery orders; (2) GAC's non–compliahce with those orders and the propriety of the sanctions entered for non-compliance; (3) the court's failure to disqualify United's counsel; (4) the trial judge's

refusal to disqualify himself; and (5) the propriety of the remedies.

* * * * *

C. The International Uranium Cartel

Several months after this case was filed, United raised a new allegation — that Gulf's and GAC's monopolistic efforts were part of a worldwide conspiracy of certain international uranium producers to fix the prices, allocate the markets, and control the production of uranium. United's efforts to secure discovery of records relating to this international uranium cartel became the major focus of this litigation, and GAC's failure to supply cartel–related information was the principal basis for the sanctions order and default judgment entered by the trial court.

The precise facts regarding the development and operation of the cartel are not completely clear, largely because full cartel–related discovery was not made in this case. However, several matters are well–established.

First, as GAC concedes, there was a uranium cartel made up of various international uranium producers, which operated from at least 1972 to 1975. Foreign governments, including those of Canada, South Africa, France and Australia, played some role in the formation and operation of the cartel. The nature of the roles played by those governments, particularly by the Canadian Government, is a disputed question in this case, the resolution of which is critical to the disposition of one of the major issues raised by GAC on appeal. We will examine this question in Section II C, *infra*, of this opinion.

* * * * *

D. History of the Proceedings in the Trial Court

In Section III A, *Infra*, of this opinion we will discuss in detail the chronology of the proceedings in the court below in the context of analyzing GAC's efforts to comply with the court's discovery orders. At this point, however, it is necessary to provide a brief outline of those proceedings in order to facilitate an understanding of the overall posture of the case and the various issues on appeal.

On December 31, 1975, United filed this action in Santa Fe District Court. On the same day, United served lengthy interrogatories on GAC. This set of interrogatories will be referred to as the First Set of Interrogatories. The interrogatories called for detailed information concerning the uranium and fuel fabrication businesses of Gulf, Scallop and GAC. Many of the interrogatories specifically asked for information from "the partnership and the partners." Neither the complaint nor the interrogatories specifically mentioned the international uranium cartel.

On April 6, 1976, GAC filed the first of two sets of answers to the First Set of Interrogatories. The answers provided no information on the cartel and virtually no information on the separate uranium business activities of Gulf and Scallop. The trial court eventually found answers to have been "wholly inadequate and evasive."

During the summer of 1976, extensive discovery efforts were conducted by United. GAC produced its business records, but it did not produce documents which were in the separate possession of Gulf or Scallop. On September 23, 1976, the Canadian Government promulgated the Canadian Uranium Information Security Regulations, which prohibited the release of cartel information from Canada. One week later, United pointed out for the first time that GAC had failed to produce documents from Gulf and Scallop. GAC then contended that it was not obligated to produce records which were in the separate possession of the partners. *See* Section II A, *infra*. The trial court rejected this argument on November, 30, 1976. The court held that both the partnership and the partners were subject to its discovery orders, and it warned that sanctions would be imposed if either the partnership or the partners failed to comply with those orders.

United then moved to compel production of partner documents and supplemental answers to the First Set of Interrogatories. GAC continued to assert that partner documents were not discoverable, and the court again rejected this argument at three different hearing in January 1977. It ordered GAC to provide supplemental answers and to provide supplemental answers and to produce partner documents by April 15, 1977.

In February 1977, United moved to compel production of cartel–related documents Gulf had produced in other litigation. GAC resisted production of these documents, once again rearguing the question of partner discovery. GAC also suggested for the first time that United's counsel, who had represented Gulf until November 1976 on its operations at Mt. Taylor, might have to be disqualified in this case. *See* Section IV, *infra*. On March 1, 1977, for the first time GAC specifically asserted that the Uranium Information Security Regulations were a bar to the discovery of cartel information. At a hearing on March 7, the court reiterated its previous rulings on Gulf were subject to its discovery orders, granted United's motion to produce the cartel records, and again warned that sanctions, including a default judgment, would be imposed if good faith discovery efforts were not made. GAC then formally moved to disqualify United's counsel. The court denied this motion. In March 1977, I&M, which had been joined as a party in January 1977, filed claims against GAC, specifically asserting Gulf's cartel activities as a basis for the relief it sought. GAC's supplemental answers were filed on April 15. They made no mention of the cartel.

In August 1977, United filed its Second Set of Interrogatories. This set was specifically addressed to the activities of the cartel. GAC filed objections to these interrogatories. The objections made no mention of the Uranium Information Security Regulations or any other Canadian secrecy laws. The court overruled most of the objections. GAC then filed answers to these interrogatories, which included the assertion that Canadian laws barred production of cartel documents.

United moved to compel further answers to the interrogatories and the production of cartel documents, and to have sanctions imposed. The trial court granted the request for further answers. The court found that GAC had not acted in good faith regarding the production of cartel documents up to that time. It ordered GAC to produce cartel records to the extent lawful, and to the extent that it was unlawful, to seek a waiver of Canadian nondisclosure laws. The court again warned that sanctions would be imposed if its order was not complied with. GAC unsuccessfully sought permission from the Canadian Government to produce cartel documents located in Canada. GAC then submitted its second set of answers, which did not identify any cartel documents located in Canada or contain information from such documents.

Five days after the trial began, United again moved to compel the production of cartel documents and for sanctions for GAC's alleged discovery failures. At a hearing on November 8, 1977, the trial judge accused GAC of "stonewalling" information. The following day, GAC moved to disqualify the judge. The motion was denied. *See* Section V, *infra.* The trial court, after a hearing, found that GAC had deliberately housed cartel documents in Canada in an attempt "to court legal impediments" to their production. It also found that GAC had violated its prior order to identify cartel documents, and it again ordered such identification.

In December 1977, United and I&M filed objections to GAC's second set of answers to the Second Set of Interrogatories and moved to compel further answers. The trial court granted this request. On February 1, 1978, GAC filed its third set of answers. Thereafter, United filed its fourth motion for a default judgment, in which I&M joined. The trial court granted the motion, and entered the sanctions order and default judgment which is the subject of this appeal. The trial court found all issues of liability against GAC and in favor of I&M and United. The court found that GAC had acted in bad faith throughout the discovery process, and had "willfully, intentionally and in bad faith covered up"[1] "highly relevant" information concerning the cartel and Gulf's role therein. The court said that GAC's answers to the First Set of Interrogatories were "wholly inadequate

and evasive," and that its series of answers to the Second Set of Interrogatories amount to a willful, intentional, deliberate and bad faith failure and refusal to answer. *See* Section III, *infra.*

A lengthy trial on the question of damages was conducted following entry of the sanctions order and default judgment. *See* Section VI, *infra.* On May 16, 1978, the court entered a final judgment against GAC.

II. Propriety Of Discovery Orders

The first area we examine is whether the trial court's discovery orders, which the court found GAC had willfully failed to comply with, were within the court's authority to enter. If, as GAC contends, the court's orders were invalid from the outset, then GAC could not have been sanctioned for its failure to comply with them.

The orders involve the production of documents or the furnishing of information regarding the international uranium cartel. GAC contends that they were invalid for four reasons: (1) information and documents in the possession of the partners cannot be the subject of discovery orders in a case in which only the partnership, and not the individual partners, is a party; (2) the cartel documents and information are not relevant to any issue in this case; (3) adjudication of any issues regarding the cartel and, therefore discovery orders directed at cartel–related information and documents, are barred by the act of state doctrine and the exclusive federal power over the conduct of foreign relations; and (4) the New Mexico Antitrust Act cannot be applied to the 1973 and 1974 uranium supply agreements and, therefore, the court was without jurisdiction to enter discovery orders based on the appellee's allegations of violations of that Act. Each of these contentions will be separately discussed in the sections that follow:

* * * * *

Although the Uranium Information Security Regulations were not in effect during the period the cartel was apparently in existence, the Ontario Business Records Protection Act was in effect. Although that Act is not a significant impediment to discovery, it was relied on by GAC in the court below as a total bar to the discovery of cartel records. If documents were housed in Canada with the expectation that the Ontario Act would be applicable, it is largely immaterial that the expectation was later realized in the form of a different secrecy law. When a party places documents outside this country with the expectation that production of those documents will be frustrated in litigation here, the strong policy in favor of a broad discovery dictates that that party bear the consequences of the dilemma created by the realization of its expectations.

It is not required that the actual litigation in which the documents are ordered produced must either be pending or contemplated at the time the housing policy is initiated and followed. In *Societe*, the Court suggested that an attempt to take advantage of foreign secrecy laws *before* the United States entered World War II would have "a vital bearing" on litigation which commenced many years later under the Trading with the Enemy Act. The evidence demonstrates that Gulf was very concerned about possible liability under American antitrust laws resulting from its participation in the cartel. *See* n. 127, *supra*, and Section II C(1), *supra*.

We hold that GAC was not deprived of its right to notice of, and a hearing on, the housing allegations against it and Gulf. We also hold that there is substantial evidence to support the court's finding that Gulf followed a deliberate policy of storing cartel documents in Canada, and that this policy amounted to courting legal impediments to their production. Under *Societe*, these findings alone may be the basis for imposition of such a discovery sanction as a default judgment.

The Snyder and Grand Jury Documents

The last two recitals of bad faith we examine concern documents which, for the most part, GAC did not produce until after the commencement of the trial. These documents consisted of two categories — the so-called Snyder and Grand Jury documents.

The term Snyder documents refers to a group of documents Gulf produced in another case involving the cartel. In that case, Westinghouse subpoenaed certain documents concerning the cartel from Gulf. Gulf claimed that the documents were subject to the attorney–client privilege. In mid–August 1977, United States District Judge Daniel J. Snyder, Jr. held that many of the documents were not privileged, and ordered that they be turned over to Westinghouse. However, Judge Snyder maintained a confidentiality order prohibiting their disclosure to outsiders. *In Re Westinghouse Elec. Corp., Etc.*, 76 F.R.D. 47 (W.D.Pa.1977)

The trial court in this case found that (1) GAC wrongfully failed to inform it and the opposing parties of Judge Snyder's rulings of August 1977; (2) GAC never accurately disclosed to the court or to United the existence of all the Snyder documents; (3) these documents were called for by the First Set of Interrogatories, but the existence of most of them was not disclosed in this case until over a year after the interrogatories were filed; (4) the existence of some of the documents was not disclosed until after Judge Snyder held them to be public and not subject to claims of privilege; and (5) some of the documents were not identified or produced until after United brought the matter to the attention of the trial court in October 1977. The trial court concluded that GAC's failure to reveal the existence of, and to identify, the Snyder document in a timely manner was a deliberate attempt to conceal relevant evidence.

As we have previously discussed, documents such as these were called for by the First Set of Interrogatories. Further, on January 11, 1977, the court had specifically ordered the production of such documents, and had set a deadline of April 15, 1977, for complete production or the submission of those documents as to which GAC was claiming a privilege to the court for an *in camera* review.

By April 1977, GAC had produced only a few of the Snyder documents. It had claimed a privilege on many others, but had not submitted any of the documents for an *in camera* review by the April 15 deadline. It was not until late August 1977, that GAC listed twelve of the documents on a privilege list. GAC did not submit the documents as to which its claim of privilege had been challenged for an *in camera* review until September 16, 1977 — five months after the deadline for their submission, over two weeks after the deadline for the completion of all discovery, and six weeks before the scheduled commencement of the trial.

On October 5, 1977, the court upheld GAC's claim of privilege in many of the instances in which it had been challenged. The remaining documents were turned over a week later. On October 7, 1977, United raised the question of the Snyder documents, stating that it had received only a few, despite Judge Snyder's rulings in August that many of the documents were not privileged. On October 11, the court held that documents de–privileged by another court were not subject to a claim of privilege in this case. On October 20, GAC produced the documents Judge Snyder had held were non–privileged, including documents which the court in this case had held to be privileged. On October 28, Judge Snyder ordered Gulf to produce the remaining documents he had not previously ruled on. On November 7 — eight days after the trail commenced — GAC produced all of the remaining Snyder documents.

We cannot agree in all respects with the court's recital on the production of the Snyder documents. The court was incorrect in ruling that Judge Snyder made the documents public; although produced to Westinghouse, the documents were still subject to a confidentiality order. The court also erred in faulting GAC for its failure to bring Judge Snyder's August order to its attention, since the court had stated prior to October 11 that it would not be bound by other judges' rulings on claims of privilege. Despite those errors, however, the court's conclusion that GAC did not fulfill its obligations to make full and complete discovery of the Snyder documents in a timely fashion is not manifestly erroneous.

GAC did not identify all of the documents in a timely manner. It did not submit the documents as to which it claimed privilege for an *in camera* review until long after the date set for their submission. By failing to submit them until after the completion of the period set for discovery, appellees were effectively precluded from using the documents during depositions of key individuals taken during the summer of 1977. GAC's excuse for these delays is that discovery was an on going process which took a great deal of time. However, the court had made it clear throughout 1977 that adherence to the deadlines it set was a matter of considerable importance. After GAC failed to produce Gulf's records in response to United's original discovery requests, the court had ordered production of them to commence on January 24 and to continue diligently thereafter. Instead of producing the documents, GAC continued to reargue the production of partner records, despite several previous rulings on that subject. It waited until March 1977 to bring production of Gulf's records. The consequences which flowed from GAC's inability to comply with the court's orders in a timely fashion were self–inflicted wounds.

The second group of documents consisted of records Gulf produced to the federal grand jury. The trial court found that GAC had in bad faith failed to reveal the existence of these documents to the court or the other parties until after United learned of their existence from a third party and had made a demand on GAC for them. The facts concerning these documents are largely uncontested; the only issue is the correctness of the trial court's conclusion that GAC had acted in bad faith with respect to their production.

When these documents were produced to the grand jury in January 1978, copies were apparently sent to GAC's counsel in Santa Fe, but they were not turned over to the court or the opposing parties. United filed a demand for them on February 15, 1978, after learning of their existence from Westinghouse.

GAC contends that it did not act in bad faith because it was still reviewing the documents at the time United filed its demand, and that it turned them over before completing its review. It contends that in view of the constraints involved in reviewing the documents while the trial was continuing, it acted as expeditiously as possible.

The trial court's finding on this subject was not erroneous. On October 7, 1977, GAC's counsel represented to the trial court that "every document that is available in the United States that are responsive to [the Second Set of Interrogatories] has been produced." That representation could not be made in good faith at a time when a file search was continuing. *Compare Armour & Co. v. Enenco, Inc., supra*, 17 F.R.Serv.2d at 515 and 519. When the documents were sent to Santa Fe, GAC could have informed the trial court and opposing counsel that it was reviewing additional material; however, it did not. These documents were called for by United's first discovery requests. Their production had specifically been ordered as early as January 1977, over a year before they were eventually produced. "Such a dilatory response . . . hardly bespeaks of the good faith compliance which [defendant] repeatedly assets." *State of Ohio v. Crofters, Inc., supra*, 75 F.R.D. at 19. *See also Perry v. Golub, supra, 74 F.R.D. at 365; Von Brimer v. Whirlpool Corporation*, 362 F.Supp. 1182, 1186 (N.D.Cal.1973), *aff'd*, 536 F.2d 838 (9th Cir. 1976); *Armour & Co. v. Enenco, Inc., supra*, 17 F.R.Serv.2d at 515–16. Under these circumstances, it was reasonable for the trial court to conclude that GAC's actions as to the production of these documents were improper. *See generally Link v. Wabash Railroad Co.*, 370 U.S. 626, 634–35, n. 11, 82 S.Ct. 1836, 1391 n. 11, 8 L.Ed.2d 734 (1962).

If GAC's conduct with regard to the production of the Snyder and Grand Jury documents were the only matters at issue, we might take a different view. But they are just two instances to be considered in the pattern of intransigence which characterized GAC's actions during discovery. *DiGregoria v. First Rediscount Corporation*, 506 F.2d 781, 787 (3rd Cir. 1974). *See also Link v. Wabash Railroad Co., supra*, 370 U.S. at 634, 82 S.Ct. at 1390; *Diapulse Corporation of America v. Curtis Publishing Co., supra*, 374 F.2d at 446; *Riverside Memorial, Etc. v. Sonnenblick Goldman*, 80 F.R.D. 433, 436 (E.D.Pa. 1978), *aff'd mem., Riverside Mausoleum, Inc. v. Umet Trust*, 605 F.2d 1196 (3rd Cir. 1979), *cert. denied*,

444 U.S. 1075, 100 S.Ct. 1022, 62 L.Ed.2d 757 (1980). In light of the full record, the trial court did not err in reaching the conclusions it did regarding the production of these two categories of documents.

* * * * *

The other aspect of GAC's attack upon the procedures by which the judgment was entered — the lack of an evidentiary hearing — is also without merit. There is no requirement under Rule 37(b) that an evidentiary hearing be held before sanctions are imposed. *See Norman v. Young*, 422 F.2d 470, 474 (10th Cir. 1970). Under our rules, a court may decide motions on the basis of affidavits, oral testimony or depositions. N.M.R.Civ.P. 43(e), N.M.S.A.1978 (current version at N.M.R.Civ.P. 43(c), N.M.S.A.1978 (1980 Repl.Pamp.)). Evidentiary hearings in cases involving the imposition of discovery sanctions have been required under some, but not all circumstances. *Compare Flaks v. Koegel*, 504 F.2d 702, 712 (2nd Cir. 1974) *and McFarland v. Gregory*, 425 F.2d 443, 450 (2nd Cir. 1970) *with Margoles v. Johns*, 587 F.2d 885, 888–89 (7th Cir. 1978) *and Norman v. Young, supra*.

In a previous opinion in this case, we considered the question of the circumstances under which a trial court is required to hold an evidentiary hearing. In *United Nuclear Corp. v. General Atomic Co., supra*, 93 N.M. at 123–24, 597 P.2d at 308–09, we rejected GAC's argument that the trial court erred in failing to hold an evidentiary hearing on GAC's motion to stay the proceedings pending arbitration. We noted that the critical question is "what type of hearing is 'appropriate to the nature of the case.'" *Id.* at 123, 597 P.2d at 308 (citation omitted). The following general principles, set forth in our earlier decision, are equally applicable here:

> The requirements of due process are not technical, and no particular form of procedure is necessary for protecting substantial rights. The circumstances of the case dictate the requirements. The integrity of the fact–finding process and the basic fairness of the decision are the principle considerations.

Id. (citations omitted).

GAC's failure to make good faith discovery are "mirrored in the record." *In Re Liquid Carbonic Truck Drivers Chemical, Etc., Supra,* 580 F.2d at 822; *DiGregorio v. First Rediscount Corporation, supra,* 422 F.2d at 474. The initial, self–serving misconstruction of the scope of the First Set of Interrogatories, the unjustified failure to include cartel information in the supplemental answers to those interrogatories, the contradictory representations GAC made to the trial court at various stages of the proceedings, the series of inadequate answers to the Second Set of Interrogatories, and the unfulfilled commitments to produce cartel documents, are all apparent from the face of the record. No amount of oral testimony could alter those aspects of the history of this litigation.

Further, the affidavits GAC filed on February 13 and March 13, 1978, in connection with its request for an evidentiary hearing did not demonstrate any need for such a hearing. Rather, portions of those affidavits are themselves evidence of the lack of good faith on GAC's part. For example, the Ross affidavit of February 13, which stated that GAC understood its obligation under the First Set of Interrogatories to include the furnishing of at least some records in the custody of the partners, contradicted the March 13 affidavits of five GAC attorneys stating that they understood that only documents in the possession of GAC were required. One of the March 13 affidavits contained the assertion that United's allegation that documents in Gulf's possession were required was "patently false," which was rather startling in light of the Ross affidavit and the fact that *some* information from Gulf was provided in GAC's original answers to the First Set of Interrogatories. The trial court afforded these contradictory sets of affidavits the weight to which they were entitled.

Even if GAC's representations of February and March 1978 concerning its understanding of the scope of its obligations had been consistent, they would not have established that it had acted in good faith nor would they have demonstrated the presence of factual issues to be resolved at an evidentiary hearing. The undisputed fact is that without objecting to the interrogatories, without disclosing its understanding of its obligations to opposing counsel, and without seeking guidance from the court, GAC made a unilateral, self–serving construction of the scope of the interrogatories. "The wording of the interrogatories and answers themselves would not lead to any other reasonable conclusion." *Hunter v. International Systems & Controls Corp., supra,* 56 F.R.D. at 625 (footnote omitted). It is no defense to say that GAC simply made an innocent mistake of law in determining that information and documents in the possession of the partners were not subject to discovery under Rules 33 and 34. *Compare Unger v. Los Angeles Transit Lines,* 180 Cal.App.2d 174, 4 Cal.Rptr. 370, 378 (1960). As we have previously noted, the rules call for such a question to be presented in advance to the court for its determination.

The affidavits GAC submitted concerning its failure to provide information on the cartel in its supplemental answers to the First Set of Interrogatories similarly failed to present any factual issue as to the good faith of this failure. In one affidavit, a GAC attorney stated that they did not consider the cartel to be an issue when the supplemental answers were filed in April 1977, and only appreciated that it had become "a significant issue" when United filed its Second Set of Interrogatories on August 16, 1977. However, on March 25, 1977, almost three weeks before the supplemental answers were filed, this same attorney had objected in the presence of the trial court to United's "continual reference to the so–called international uranium cartel." In a second affidavit the GAC attorney who prepared the supplemental answers to questions 30–34 of the First Set of Interrogatories stated that no information on the cartel was provided in those answers because the cartel was not mentioned in United's complaint or in the interrogatories, and therefore, had not yet been raised as an issue. We have previously reviewed the evidence which contradicts these assertions or demonstrates the unreasonableness of them.

Finally, these affidavits did not create an issue as to the trial court's finding that GAC had, in bad faith, concealed the existence of the cartel and Gulf's participation in it. It was permissible for the trial court to conclude that GAC's excuses for not producing cartel information early in the litigation were inadequate. And it could reasonably be inferred from GAC's conduct in various aspects of the proceedings throughout the course of this litigation, as well as from the nature of the cartel evidence that was eventually made available, that GAC had deliberately concealed cartel information. *Compare Link v. Wabash Railroad Co., supra,* 370 U.S. at 633, 82 S.Ct. at 1390.

Even if GAC's failure to provide information on the cartel in response to the First Set of Interrogatories was not the product of a calculating, illicit attempt to conceal damaging information, the record compels the conclusion that, at best, it could be characterized as "gross disregard for the requirements for the discovery process." *Amour & Co., v. Enenco, Inc., supra,* 17 F.R.Serv.2d at 519. However, whether GAC's original failures to make cartel discovery were the result of a willful, intentional and bad faith attempt to conceal evidence, as the trial court found, or were due to a gross indifference to its discovery obligations, is immaterial. The willfulness required to sustain the severe sanctions of Rule 37(b)(2)(iii) may be predicated upon either type of behavior. *See Rio Grande Gas Company v. Gilbert, supra,* 83 N.M. at 278, 491 P.2d at 166; *Cine Forty–Second St. Theatre v. Allied Artists,* 602 F.2d 1062, 1066–68 (2nd Cir. 1979); *Kozlowski v. Sears, Roebuck & Co., supra,* 73 F.R.D. at 77; *Armour & Co. v. Enenco, Inc. supra.* The two types of misconduct differ only in degree as to culpability, and they differ not at all in terms of the adverse affects that GAC's discovery failures have had on the due process rights of appellees and the integrity of the truth–seeking function of the trial court.

* * * * *

The Breadth of the Sanctions for Non–Compliance

GAC contends that even if sanctions should have been entered under Rule 37 for its discovery failures, a default judgment on all issues was unconstitutionally overbroad. GAC makes two points in this regard. First, GAC contends that the trial court could have imposed lesser sanctions to resolve the problem of the nonproduction of cartel documents. Second, GAC argues that its discovery failures, particularly those relating to the cartel, did not relate to all dispositive issues, and that a default judgment depriving it of a trial on the merits on other issues amounted to "mere punishment." We are not persuaded by this argument either.

It is well–settled that the choice of sanctions under Rule 37 lies within the sound discretion of the trial court. Only an abuse of that discretion will warrant reversal. Although the severest of the sanctions should be imposed only in extreme circumstances, "in this day of burgeoning, costly and protracted litigation courts should not shrink from imposing harsh sanctions where, as in this case, they are clearly warranted." As one court stated:

> [W]hen a defendant demonstrates flagrant bad faith and callous disregard of its responsibilities, the district court's choice of the extreme sanction is not an abuse of discretion. It is not our responsibility as a reviewing court to say whether we would have chosen a more moderate sanction.

* * * * *

UNITED STATES of America v. ABC SALES & SERVICE, INC., et al.

95 F.R.D. 316

United States District Court, D. Arizona
February 18, 1982

The court has had under advisement the Government's Motion for Partial Summary Judgment. In its motion the Government requests that the facts set forth in 148 consumer complaints be established as a sanction pursuant to Rule 37(b) of the Federal Rules of Civil Procedure because of the defendant's failure to produce their files relating to those complaints, and that the facts established by the consumer complaints constitute violations of the Fair Debt Collection Practices Act [the Act], 15 U.S.C. § 1692 et seq., and of the Federal Trade Commission Order Number C–2608 (December 4, 1974) [the Order] against the defendants. However, the defendants have now produced the file of Helen Lumerman (34). It also appears that the defendants carried the accounts of Lee Halsey (28) under the name "Lee Holsey", and of Carolyn Venditti (100) under the name of "Wheeler", which could account for the failure of the defendants to locate those two accounts. The facts will be deemed established only with respect to the 145 other complaints. The motion for partial summary judgment will be granted in part.

On February 25, 1981, pursuant to the Government's Motion to Compel Production, the Court entered an order requiring the defendants to produce by March 27, 1981 debtor files and other documents reflecting the defendants' debt collection activities regarding each of 582 named debtors. By March 27, 187 files had been produced. On April 29, 1981 the Government filed a motion for sanctions because of the failure of the defendants to produce the other 395 files. The defendants claimed that they had been making diligent efforts to locate the files but that they were "buried among several million files" they maintain. On May 26, 1981 the Court entered an order extending the time for production for 60 days and providing that if production was not made by then the facts set forth in the various debtors' complaints would be deemed to be established. On November 5, 1981 the Government filed the pending motion for partial summary judgment. In response thereto, for the first time, the defendants claimed that their failure to make production may have been because the files had been discarded since they are kept only as "space allows," which is usually not more than two years. The reasons given for non–production are entitled to little weight.

In the first place, a business which generates millions of files cannot frustrate discovery by creating an inadequate filing system so that individual files cannot readily be located. *See Kozlowski v. Sears, Roebuck & Co.*, 73 F.R.D. 73 (D.Mass.1976).

In the second place, any destruction of files of named complaining debtors appears to have been motivated more from an attempt to suppress evidence than from the need of additional filing space for new files. Three of defendants' offices are in California and defendants admit in their answers to interrogatories that debt collectors in that state are required to maintain collection files for a period of at least four years. The defendants were given notice that many of the named debtors were complaining to the Federal Trade Commission or had complained to lawyers regarding the conduct of defendants' employees. Given that notice, one would reasonably think that the defendants would have taken steps to preserve the files relating to those complaining debtors if there were any information in the files which would tend to refute the complaints. Accordingly, the Court will order as a sanction for failure to produce, pursuant to Rule 37(b)(2)(A) of the Federal Rules of Civil Procedure, that the facts set forth in 145 of the 148 debtor complaints attached to the motion for summary judgment shall be deemed established.

* * * * *

UNITED STATES of America, Plaintiff–Appellee, v. Craig Lee CHILDS, Defendant–Appellant.

5 F.3d 1328

United States Court of Appeals for the Ninth Circuit
July 12, 1993

Defendant Craig Lee Childs appeals his conviction on four counts of possession of a stolen vehicle in violation of 18 U.S.C. § 2313 and his sentence of one year incarceration and five years probation. * * *

Background

Five vehicles were reported stolen in Arizona between May and July of 1987. During this same period of time, Craig Lee Childs registered these cars in Calgary, Alberta, Canada, using the name Craig Lee Connors. Childs, along with another man, was identified as having test–driven one of the cars in Arizona shortly before it was stolen.

On April 19, 1989, Childs was indicted in Arizona on five counts of Possession of a Stolen Vehicle Transported in Interstate Commerce in violation of 18 U.S.C. § 2313. Childs was arrested on March 8, 1991 in Oklahoma. He was released on bond and ordered to appear before a Magistrate Judge in Phoenix. Childs made a motion to dismiss the case, arguing that venue was improper. This motion was denied after a hearing. A jury trial was held in Phoenix and Childs was found guilty of four counts of the indictment.

* * * * *

B. Admission of Documents as Business Records

Childs argues that the district court erroneously admitted a number of documents as business records without proper foundation. District court decisions to admit evidence under the business records exception to the hearsay rule are reviewed for abuse of discretion. *See United States v. Bland*, 961 F.2d 123, 126 (9th Cir.), *cert. denied*, 121 L.Ed.2d 117, 113 S.Ct 170 (1992).

Fed.R.Evid. 803(6) provides:

A memorandum, report, record, or data compilation, in any form, of acts, events, conditions, opinions, or diagnoses, made at or near the time by, or from information transmitted by, a person with knowledge, if kept in the course of a regularly conducted business activity, and if it was the regular practice of that business activity to make the memorandum, report, record, or data compilation, all as shown by the testimony of the custodian or other qualified witness, unless the source of information or the method

or circumstances of preparation indicate lack of trustworthiness. The term "business" as used in this paragraph includes business, institution, association, profession, occupation, and calling of every kind, whether or not conducted for profit.

Childs challenges the admission of the government's exhibit 34, an application for Alberta, Canada license plates in the name of Craig Lee Connors. Exhibit 34 was admitted as a business record of the Alberta Division of Motor Vehicles ("Alberta DMV"). Childs argues that the admission of exhibit 34 was improper because the exhibit was not made by the Alberta DMV, but by a private auto club that was contracted by the Alberta DMV to issue licenses.

Testimony indicated that the private auto club was hooked directly into the DMV's computer system and could perform transactions on–line. The private auto club was following the DMV's procedures for issuing licenses and was performing the transactions directly on the DMV's computer system. For the purposes of issuing license plates, the private auto club and the DMV were essentially acting as one business entity. Accordingly, we find that the district court did not abuse its discretion in admitting exhibit 34 as a business record of the Alberta DMV.

When the DMV had an overload of work, it contracted the work out to small issuing offices which were given computers by the DMV and were hooked directly into the DMV's computer system.

Childs objects to the admission of the government's exhibits 4, 5, 6, 7, 8, and 13, arguing that the circumstances surrounding their preparation indicate a lack of trustworthiness. The government alleged at trial that Childs manipulated the Canadian system. Childs argues that he may have had the help of an accomplice within the Canadian system, and if so, "the documents would lack trustworthiness and would not have been made in the regular course of business." Childs does not point to any evidence in the record suggesting the presence of such an accomplice within the Canadian system. There is no support for this frivolous argument.

Childs next argues that the government's exhibits 19, 20, 23, 31 and 32 were erroneously admitted. These exhibits include several types of documentation kept by auto dealers in connection with the stolen cars, such as certificates of title, purchase orders and odometer statements. They were introduced to show that the stolen automobiles were the same cars that Childs possessed in Canada. These documents were admitted as business records of the automobile dealers. Childs argues that the documents were improperly admitted because, although the documents were kept by the automobile dealers in the regular course of business, the dealers did not make the documents.

Several circuits have held that exhibits can be admitted as business records of an entity, even when that entity was not the maker of those records so long as the other requirements of Rule 803(6) are met and the circumstances indicate the records are trustworthy. *See, e.g., United States v. Doe*, 960 F.2d 221, 223 (1st Cir.1992) (upholding admission of pistol invoice as a business record of the sports shop which received the invoice where witness testified that he received the invoice and that he relied on "'documents such as those,' in his business to show 'acquisition' of the pistol."); *United States v. Parker*, 749 F.2d 628, 633 (11th Cir.1984) (upholding admission of customs certificate for liquor as a business record of a distilling company) ("That the witness and his company had neither prepared the certificate nor had first–hand knowledge of the preparation does not contravene Rule 803(6)."); *Mississippi River Grain Elevator, Inc. v. Bartlett & Co., Grain*, 659 F.2d 1314, 1318–19 (5th Cir.1981) (upholding admission of grain weight certificates prepared by government entities as business records of private grain company).

In *United States v. Ullrich*, 580 F.2d 765 (5th Cir.1978), the Fifth Circuit considered and rejected the same argument as Childs is now making before this court. The prosecutor in *Ullrich* introduced documents to prove the identity of a stolen automobile through the testimony of an employee of an automobile dealership. *Id.* at 771. The documents were prepared by a credit company and an automo-

bile manufacturer, and sent to the dealership. The defendant argued that the documents were improperly admitted as business records because they were not prepared by the dealership. The Fifth Circuit found it "obvious" that the documents were admissible as business records. *Id.* at 772. "Although these documents were furnished originally from other sources, [the dealership employee] testified that they were kept in the regular course of the dealership's business. In effect, they were integrated into the records of the dealership and were used by it." *Id.* at 771.

In this case, as in Ullrich, the witnesses from the auto dealerships testified that the documents in question were kept in the regular course of business at the dealerships. Additionally, the auto dealerships relied on the documents' identification of individual cars in keeping track of their cars. The district court did not err by admitting these documents as business records.

The reasoning in *NLRB v. First Termite Control Co.*, 646 F.2d 424 (9th Cir.1981) does not apply to this case. In *First Termite*, the NLRB sought to introduce a freight bill which came from the files of a lumber company through the testimony of the lumber company's bookkeeper. The freight bill was prepared by a railroad company, not by the lumber company, *Id.* at 425–26.

We reversed the district court's decision to admit the freight bill as a business record. In reaching this decision, we emphasized the fact that the lumber company did not rely on the portion of the record at issue and "had no interest in the accuracy of that portion of the [record]." *Id.* at 429.

In contrast, the auto dealers in this case did rely on the records at issue and had substantial interest in their accuracy. The circumstances of this case support the conclusion that the records are trustworthy.

Lastly, Childs argues that the government's exhibits 19, 20, 23, 24, 25, 26, 27, 31, and 32 were erroneously admitted because the foundational evidence offered was not presented by the custodians of these documents or by other qualified witnesses. The witnesses who testified concerning these exhibits were former employees of the auto dealerships whose cars were stolen. Although these witnesses were not employees of the auto dealerships at the time they testified at trial, they were employees of the dealerships when the cars were stolen.

A witness does not have to be the custodian of documents offered into evidence to establish Rule 803(6)'s foundational requirements. *United States v. Ray*, 930 F.2d 1368, 1370 (9th Cir.1991); *See also Bergen v. F/V St. Patrick*, 816 F.2d 1345, 1353 (9th Cir.1987), modified on other grounds, 866 F.2d 318 (9th Cir.), *cert. denied*, 493 U.S. 871 (1989). "The phrase 'other qualified witness' is broadly interpreted to require only that the witness understand the recordkeeping system." *Ray*, 930 F.2d at 1370. A review of the record indicates that the former employees were familiar with the contents and preparation of the exhibits in question. It was not an abuse of discretion to allow the former employees to lay the foundation for these exhibits.

* * * * *

UNITED STATES of America v. Leonard A. PELULLO, Appellant.

964 F.2d 193 (3rd Cir. 1992)

May 18, 1992

Leonard A. Pelullo appeals from a judgment conviction entered in the United States District Court for the Eastern District of Pennsylvania following a three–week jury trial. The jury convicted Pelullo of 49 counts of wire fraud in violation of 18 U.S.C. § 1343, and one count of racketeering under the Racketeer Influenced and Corrupt Organizations Act (RICO), 18 U.S.C. §§ 1962(c) and 1963. He was, however, acquitted of five additional counts of wire fraud. On August 30, 1991, Pelullo was sentenced to a term of 24 year's imprisonment, assessed $4,400,000 in fines and ordered to pay restitution of $2,071,000 and $114,000.

* * * * *

We set forth the evidence at length as this is required for an understanding of this case, our description being from a view of the evidence in a light favorable to the Government as the verdict winner. The indictment charged Pelullo with engaging in a pattern of illegal racketeering activity by abusing his position as chief executive officer of The Royale Group, Limited ("Royale"), a publicly held corporation. In the fall of 1983, Royale, through wholly owned subsidiaries, acquired six "art deco" hotels in Miami Beach, Florida: the Cardozo, the Victor, the Senator, the Leslie, the Carlyle and the Cavalier. In June 1984 the hotels obtained a $13.5 million loan from FCA Mortgage Corporation ("FCA Mortgage"), a wholly owned subsidiary of American Savings and Loan Association ("American"). Approximately $10 million of the loan was earmarked for acquisition costs, while the remaining $3.5 million was to be used for renovation. The loan was increased twice, by $2.2 million in January 1985 and $1.4 million in September 1985. By September 1985, $6.2 million of the loan proceeds was to be used for renovation. Under the agreement, American retained this portion of the loan and would disburse funds as the renovation costs were incurred. To obtain a disbursement, Royale was required to submit draw requests setting forth a certified itemization of these costs.

The indictment charged Pelullo with three fraudulent schemes. First, the Government alleged that Pelullo defrauded American, Royale and Royale's shareholders of approximately $1.6 million by submitting false documentation in connection with certain draw requests on the project. This scheme is reflected in wire fraud counts 1 through 53 and racketeering acts 1 through 59 of count 55, the RICO count, which referred to the same transfers as those in the wire fraud counts, as well as several additional transfers. The second scheme, reflected in wire fraud count 54 and RICO racketeering act 60, involved Pelullo's defrauding Royale of $114,000 in February 1986 by diverting cash from one of its subsidiaries to repay a debt Pelullo owed to a loanshark connected with the Philadelphia mafia. The third scheme which is reflected only in racketeering acts

61–72, and not in individual wire fraud counts, charged Pelullo with defrauding Royale of approximately $500,000 by diverting money for uses other than the purposes of the loans that American had loaned to Royale.

Under the terms of the loan Royale was permitted to draw loan money to pay for so–called "hard costs" associated with the renovation work, such as labor, materials and supplies. Pelullo, who certified most of the draw requests, overstated the renovation costs and submitted false documentation upon which American relied to support these costs.

Pelullo directed the bank to transfer the disbursements by wire transfers to Delta Development and Construction Corporation ("Delta"), a company owned and controlled by Pelullo or his family, which acted as general contractor for the renovation project. He thereupon diverted the proceeds for his personal use through various corporations he owned and controlled. Some of the proceeds were used to purchase or run two farms in Chester County, Pennsylvania; to purchase a sheep ranch in Montana; for operating corporations set up to run restaurants in the Philadelphia area; and to repay a loan on behalf of his father. In addition, $100,000 of the loan was converted to cash and delivered to Pelullo at a casino in Puerto Rico.

* * * * *

Admission of Bank Documents and Summaries

To the extent the district court's admission of evidence was based on an interpretation of the Federal Rules of Evidence, our standard of review is plenary. But we review the court's decision to admit the evidence if premised on a permissible view of the law for an abuse of discretion. *United States v. Furst*, 886 F.2d 558, 571 (3rd Cir.1989), *cert. denied*, 493 U.S. 1062, 110 S.Ct. 878, 107 L.Ed.2d 961 (1990).

The Bank Documents

At trial, Wolverton, who is a certified public accountant, described how he traced funds diverted by Pelullo, by examining subpoenaed wire transfer documents, statements and checks. Wolverton testified that wire transfer documents are bank–generated documents that record the date, amount and source and destination account numbers of each wire transfer. The court admitted these documents over Pelullo's objections that the evidence was hearsay.

The documents were hearsay. Each was an out–of–court statement offered to prove the truth of the facts described in the document, such as the identity of the sender and recipient, and the amount of the transaction. *Cf. United States v. Hathaway*, 798 F.2d 902, 905–08 (6th Cir.1986) (in mail and wire fraud prosecution arising out of fraudulent investment schemes, transaction statements, trade tickets, advertising materials, cancelled checks, client files, correspondence and client account agreements were only admissible because these documents were not offered for truth of the matters asserted therein but were offered to prove defendant's possession of the documents).

The Government makes a litany of arguments in support of the admissibility of the documents. Initially, it contends that the documents were not hearsay since, as records of corporations controlled by Pelullo, they constituted admissions. However, while the documents purport to record transactions of Pelullo–controlled companies, the testimony shows that these were bank records and not records made by Pelullo or corporations controlled by him. Additionally, there is nothing in the record to indicate that Pelullo directed or authorized the creation of any of the documents. Thus, the documents cannot be admissions since they are not attributable to Pelullo or to corporations controlled by him.

At oral argument before us the Government argued that the documents were adoptive admissions since they were sent to Pelullo and he failed to deny their accuracy. *See* Fed.R.Evid. 801(d)(2)(B). Again, however, there is nothing in the record that establishes this significant fact. In fact, the record shows the contrary. Following Pelullo's hearsay objections, Mr. Cole (the Assistant United States Attorney) elicited the following from Agent Wolverton on direct examination:

Q: Just for the record, [these are] government exhibits 15 through 84, government exhibit 87 and government exhibit 161. Would you tell the jury what these documents are and how they tie into your schedules?

A: These relate to each of the wire transfers that are on my schedules and they will show records concerning the receipt of the money and what happened to the money when it was traced out of the accounts . . . .

Q: Are they all bank documents?

A: Yes.

Q: And were they all — how were they obtained?

A: Through the use of grand jury subpoenas.

Q: *To banks?*

A: *Yes.*

6/26/91, 10:01:56–10:02:42 (emphasis added)

Additionally, the government argues that, even if the documents were hearsay, they were admissible under the business records exception to the hearsay rule. Fed.R.Evid. 803(6). The business records exception permits admission of documents containing hearsay provided foundation testimony is made by "the custodian or other qualified witness" that: (1) the declarant in the records had personal knowledge to make accurate statements; (2) the declarant recorded the statements contemporaneously with the actions that were the subject of the reports; (3) the declarant made the record in the regular course of the business activity; and (4) such records were regularly kept by the business. *Furst*, 886 F.2d at 571; Fed.R.Evid. 803(6). With the exception of certain documents relat-

ing to counts 7, 11, 14, 49 and 54 (racketeering acts, 10, 14, 17, 55 and 60), however, no such foundation was ever laid for their admission.

The Government, citing *Furst*, 886 F.2d at 572, and *Hathaway*, 798 F.2d at 905–07, contends that the documents could have been admitted even without the testimony of a custodian since surrounding circumstances provided the necessary foundation for trustworthiness. Here, the Government maintains that there are sufficient circumstantial guarantees of trustworthiness since: (1) the records were obtained in response to grand jury subpoenas directed to the corporations and their banks; (2) testimony of witnesses involved in the transactions corroborated the information in the bank records; and (3) Pelullo has not stated any reason why the records are not reliable. However, these reasons are not sufficient to overcome the express requirements of Rule 803(6).

It is, of course, true that Rule 803(6) does not require foundation testimony from the custodian of records for the rule states that such testimony may be provided by either the custodian or "other qualified witness." Furthermore, "[t]he phrase 'other qualified witness' should be given the broadest interpretation; he need not be an employee of the entity so long as he understands the system." Jack B. Weinstein & Margaret A. Berger, *Weinstein's Evidence* ¶803(6)[02], at 803–178 (footnote omitted) (hereinafter "Weinstein & Berger"). Thus, courts have held that a government agent may provide a foundation where the agent is familiar with the record–keeping system. *See, e.g., United States v. Franco*, 874 F.2d 1136, 1139–40 (7th Cir.1989); *See also Hathaway*, 798 F.2d at 906 ("there is no reason why a proper foundation for application of Rule 803(6) cannot be laid, in part or in whole, by the testimony of a government agent"). In *In re Japanese Elec. Prod. Antitrust Litig.*, 723 F.2d 238, 288 (3rd Cir.1983), *rev'd on other ground sub. nom. Matsushita Elec. Indus. Co. v. Zenith Radio Corp.*, 475 U.S. 574, 106 S.Ct. 1348 89 L.Ed.2d 538 (1986), we approved of the district court's holding that:

the testimony of the custodian or other qualified witness is not a sine qua non of admissibility in the occasional case *where the requirements for qualification as a business record can be met* by documentary evidence, affidavits, or admissions of the parties, *i.e., by circumstantial evidence, or by a combination of direct and circumstantial evidence.*

Id. (quoting *Zenith Radio Corp. v. Matsushita Elec. Indus. Co.*, 505 F.Supp. 1190, 1236 (E.D.Pa.1980)) (emphasis added).

However, none of these authorities holds that the court may admit into evidence under the business exception to the hearsay rule documents containing hearsay simply because there are some indicia of the trustworthiness of the statements. While a noncustodial witness such as a government agent, or even documentary evidence, may be used to lay the foundation required by Rule 803(6), that witness or those documents must still demonstrate that the records were made contemporaneously with the act the documents purport to record by someone with knowledge of the subject matter, that they were made in the regular course of business, and that such records were regularly kept by the business. *Cf. Franco*, 874 F.2d at 1140 (agent gave thorough description of the manner in which records were prepared and maintained based on agent's conversations with owner and employee of business as well as agent's own observations); *Hathaway*, 798 F.2d at 906 (FBI agent permitted to lay foundation where agent had familiarity with the record–keeping system). *But see United States v. Hines*, 564 F.2d 925, 928 (10th Cir.1977) (automobile manufacturers' invoices admissible without foundation since such documents possess a high degree of trustworthiness and necessity of admitting them outweighs inconvenience in having custodian testify), *cert. denied*, 434 U.S. 1022, 98 S.Ct. 748, 54 L.Ed.2d 770 (1978). Here, agent Wolverton did not purport to have familiarity with the record–keeping system of the banks, nor did he attest to any of the other requirements of Rule 803(6). Therefore, as proponent of the evidence, the Government failed to lay a proper foundation as required by the business records exception.

Alternatively, the Government argues that the documents were admissible under Rule 803(24), the residual hearsay exception. That provision creates a general exception to the inadmissibility of hearsay where there are adequate "circumstantial guarantees of trustworthiness . . . ." Fed.R.Evid. 803(24). But Rule 803(24) is subject to the following proviso: "However, a statement may not be admitted under this exception unless the proponent of it makes known to the adverse party sufficiently in advance of trial or hearing to provide the adverse party with a fair opportunity to prepare to meet it, the proponent's intention to offer the statement and the particulars of it, including name and address of declarant." *Id.* If notice is given, the statement(s) may be admitted where there are:

equivalent circumstantial guarantees of trustworthiness [to the other hearsay exceptions], if the court determines that (A) the statement is offered as evidence of a material fact; (B) the statement is more probative on the point for which it is offered than any other evidence which the proponent can procure through reasonable efforts; and (C) the general purposes of these rules and the interests of justice will best be served by admission of the statement into evidence.

Fed.R.Evid. 803(24).

Bank documents like other business records provide circumstantial guarantees of trustworthiness because the banks and their customers rely on their accuracy in the course of their business. In fact, in the context of discussing the foundation requirements of the business records exception, one leading authority has noted that "[a] foundation for admissibility may at times be predicated on judicial notice of the nature of the business and the nature of the records as observed by the court, *particularly in the case of bank and similar statements.* Weinstein & Berger ¶803(6)[02], at 803–178 (emphasis added) (footnote omitted); *see also Karme v. Commissioner*, 673 F.2d 1062, 1064–65 (9th Cir.1982) (bank records provided pursuant to treaty admissible under Rule 803(24) given circumstantial guarantees of trustworthiness even though inadmissible as business records because there was not foundation testimony). Nevertheless, the residual hearsay exception may not be used as a substitute for the business records exception when counsel has not complied with the requirements of 803(6) unless the requirements of Rule 803(24) have been met. *Cf. In re Japanese Elec. Prod. Antitrust Litig.*, 723 F.2d at 302 (courts may consider admissibility of documents under Rule 803(24) despite having failed the requirements of another exception; rejecting "near miss" theory).

The Government, in an attempt to satisfy the notice requirement, argues that the documents were made available to Pelullo months before trial. Although Rule 803(24) may be read as requiring only that the proponent give notice of the hearsay "statement" (and its particulars, including the name and address of the declarant), in *Furst* we construed the notice provision to require the proponent to give notice of its intention specifically to rely on the rule as grounds for admissibility. *See Furst*, 886 F.2d at 574. *See also United States v. Tafollo–Cardenas*, 897 F.2d 976, 980 (9th Cir.1990) (prosecutor must give notice of Rule 803(24) as basis for admissibility); *but see United States v. Benavente Gomez*, 921 F.2d 378, 384 (1st Cir.1990) (requiring that notice be given of the existence of the evidence). At oral argument, the Government conceded that it did not notify Pelullo that it intended to rely on the residual exception to the hearsay rule for admission of the documents. Therefore, under *Furst*, it may not rely on Rule 803(24) as a basis or admissibility.

In addition, because the Government first made the "residual exception" argument on appeal, the district court did not make any findings regarding the statements' or documents' admissibility under Rule 803(24), and perhaps we should not consider their admissibility for this reason alone. *See, e.g., Tafollo–Cardenas*, 897 F.2d at 980 (prosecutor must either state the exception as grounds for the admissibility or district court must find that the statement met requirements of the rule in order for appellate court to consider admissibility of statement under 803(24)); *but cf. United States v. Nivica*, 887 F.2d 1110,

1127 (1st Cir.1989) ("If the trier incorrectly admits evidence under a hearsay exception, we will not reverse so long as the material was properly admissible for the same purpose under a different rule of evidence"), *cert. denied*, 494 U.S. 1005, 110 S.Ct. 1300, 108 L.Ed.2d 477 (1990). While the reasoning of *Nivica* may be preferable where it is clear that the district court's error in admitting evidence was harmless, we are unwilling to dispense in this case with the requirement of notice expressly provided for in Rule 803(24). Additionally, Rule 803(24) requires that the court make factual findings and the district court is in a better position to make these findings in the first instance, such as that the statement is more probative on the point for which it is offered than any other evidence that the proponent can procure through reasonable efforts. *See* Weinstein & Berger ¶803(24)[01], at 803–373–79. Furthermore, although the court of appeals in *Nivica* relied on Rule 803(24) where the district court erroneously relied on Rule 803(6) to admit certain bank records, the district court in that case made express findings that the documents were authentic, reliable and trustworthy and that, given the provenance and character of the materials, their admission was justified. *See* 887 F.2d at 1127. The district court did not make such findings here. Accordingly, Rule 803(24) does not support the Government's position.

Much has been made by the Government of the inherent trustworthiness of the documents at issue in this case. It has repeatedly stressed that these documents are nothing more than ordinary bank statements and the like, obtained by subpoena. We recognize that the Government relied on not a few but many such documents in presenting its case, and we are not unmindful of the purposes of the Federal Rules of Evidence, as stated in Rule 102:

These rules shall be construed to secure fairness in administration, elimination of unjustified expense and delay and promotion of growth and development of the law of evidence to the end that the truth may be ascertained and proceedings justly determined.

Moreover, we recognize that, given Pelullo's theory of defense, the policies underlying the hearsay rule may have been only marginally implicated by the admission of these documents. The hearsay rule provides that an out–of–court statement cannot be admitted for the truth of the matter asserted since the statement is inherently untrustworthy: the declarant may not have been under oath at the time of the statement, his or her credibility cannot be evaluated at trial, and he or she cannot be cross–examined. The documents at issue here were admitted to prove that transfers of funds were made to individuals and entities in specific amounts. As indicated above, they are out–of–court statements by a declarant that the transactions took place in the manner described by the documents, which is what they were offered to prove. At trial, however, Pelullo's defense was not predicated on a denial that the transactions had occurred in the manner described, through he preserved his objection to the admissibility of the evidence, but rather that the transfers were not fraudulent at all. Thus, considering the trustworthiness of the documents and Pelullo's theory of his case, we are tempted to question whether Pelullo has been prejudiced by the admission of these documents.

In the final analysis, however, an accused is under no duty to rebut bare allegations by the prosecutor that documents are what they purport to be and establish the truth of what they represent. *Cf.* Fed.R.Evid. 901 (dealing with requirements for authentication or identification). Business records are not self–proving documents as public records may be. *See* Fed.R.Evid. 803(8). In our view, the goals underlying the Federal Rules of Evidence would not be furthered by upholding the admissibility of these documents as the record now stands, since to do so we would necessarily eviscerate the requirements of Rules 803(6) and 803(24). Although the Federal Rules of Evidence are to be liberally construed in favor of admissibility, this does not mean that we may ignore requirements of specific provisions merely because we view the proffered evidence as trustworthy. We thus conclude that the documents constitute hearsay, that they were not admissible under the business records exception since a proper foundation for them was not laid, that the residual hearsay exception was inappli-

cable since the Government did not give Pelullo notice of its intention to rely on Rule 803(24) and the district court did not make the findings as required by that rule, and that the documents were not admissible under any other exception or exclusion to Rule 801's prohibition of hearsay.

In view of the critical importance of this evidence we cannot conclude that the error was harmless, except with respect to counts 7, 11, 14, 49 and 54, which Pelullo concedes were verified through admissible testimony. *See* n. 6, *supra.* Indeed, the Government itself concedes that "the bank records were material . . . [and that] [t]he government had no other evidence to complete the tracing process showing the movement of funds from American to PBH to appellant." Government's Brief at 41. Accordingly, except for the five foregoing counts, it was reversible error to admit the documents.

* * * * *

UNITED STATES et al. v. Max POWELL et al

379 U.S. 48, 85 S.Ct. 248

November 23, 1964

* * * * *

In March 1963, the Internal Revenue Service, pursuant to powers afforded the Commissioner by § 7602(2) of the Internal Revenue Code of 1954, summoned respondent Powell to appear before special Agent Tiberino to give testimony and produce records relating to the 1958 and 1959 returns of the William Penn Laundry (the taxpayer), of which Powell was president. Powell appeared before the agent but refused to produce the records. Because the taxpayer's returns had been once previously examined, and because the three–year statute of limitations barred assessment of additional deficiencies for those years[1] except in cases of fraud (the asserted basis for this summons),[2] Powell contended that before he could be forced to produce the records the Service had to indicate some grounds for its belief that a fraud had been committed. The agent declined to give any such indication and the meeting terminated.

Thereafter the Service petitioned the District Court for the Eastern District of Pennsylvania for enforcement of the administrative summons. With this petition the agent filed an affidavit stating that he had been investigating the taxpayer's returns for 1958 and 1959; that based on this investigation the Regional Commissioner of the Service had determined an additional examination of the taxpayer's records for those years to be necessary and had sent Powell a letter to that effect; and that the agent had reason to suspect that the taxpayer had fraudulently falsified its 1958 and 1959 returns by overstating expenses. At the court hearing Powell again stated his objections to producing the records and asked the Service to show some basis for its suspicion of fraud. The Service chose to stand on the petition and the agent's affidavit, and, after argument, the District Court ruled that the agent be given one hour in which to re–examine the records.[3]

* * * * *

We reverse, and hold that the Government need make no showing of probable cause to suspect fraud unless the taxpayer raises a substantial question that judicial enforcement of the administrative summons would be an abusive use of the court's process, predicated on more than the fact of re–examination and the running of the statute of limitations on ordinary tax liability.

* * * * *

Respondent primarily relies on § 7605 (b) to show that the Government must establish probable cause for suspecting fraud, and that the existence of probable cause is subject to challenge by the taxpayer at the hearing. That section provides: "No taxpayer shall be subjected to unnecessary examination or investigations, and only one inspection of a taxpayer's books of account shall be made for each taxable year unless the taxpayer requests otherwise or unless the Secretary or his delegate, after investigation, notifies the taxpayer in writing that an additional inspection is necessary."

We do not equate necessity as contemplated by this provision with probable cause or any other like notion. If a taxpayer has filed fraudulent returns, a tax liability exists without regard to any period of limitations. Section 7602 authorizes the Commissioner to investigate any such liability. If, in order to determine the existence or nonexistence of fraud in the taxpayer's returns, information in the taxpayer's records is needed which is not already in the Commissioner's possession, we think the examination is not "unnecessary" within the meaning of § 7605(b). Although a more stringent interpretation is possible, one which would require some showing of cause for suspecting fraud, we reject such interpretation because it might seriously hamper the Commissioner in carrying out investigations he thinks warranted, forcing him to litigate and prosecute appeals on the very subject which he desires to investigate, and because the legislative history of § 7605(b) indicates that no severe restriction was intended.

* * * * *

Congress recognized a need for a curb on the investigating powers of low echelon revenue agents, and considered that it met this simply and fully by requiring such agents to clear any repetitive examination with a superior. For us to import a probable cause standard to be enforced by the courts would substantially overshoot the goal which the legislators sought to attain. There is no intimation in the legislative history that Congress intended the courts to oversee the Commissioner's determination to investigate. No mention was made of the statute of limitations[4] and the exception for fraud.

We are asked to read § 7605(b) together with the limitations sections in such a way as to impose a probable cause standard upon the Commissioner from the expiration date of the ordinary limitations period forward. Without some solid indication in the legislative history that such a gloss was intended, we find it unacceptable.[5] Our reading of the statute is said to render the first clause of § 7605(b) surplusage to a large extent, for, as interpreted, the clause adds little beyond the relevance and materiality requirements of § 7602. That clause does appear to require that the information sought is not already within the Commissioner's possession, but we think its primary purpose was no more than to emphasize the responsibility of agents to exercise prudent judgment in wielding the extensive powers granted to them by the Internal Revenue Code.[6]

* * * * *

Reading the statutes as we do, the Commissioner need not meet any standard of probable cause to obtain enforcement of his summons, either before or after the three-year statute of limitations when ordinary tax liabilities has expired. He must show that the investigation will be conducted pursuant to a legitimate purpose, that the inquiry may be relevant to the purpose, that the information sought is not already within the Commissioner's possession, and that the administrative steps required by the Code have been followed — in particular, that the "Secretary or his delegate," after investigation, has determined the further examination to be necessary and has notified the taxpayer in writing to that effect. This does not make meaningless the adversary hearing to which the taxpayer is entitled before enforcement is ordered.[7] At the hearing he "may challenge the summons on any appropriate ground." *Reisman v. Chaplin*, 375 U.S. 440, at 449, 84 S.Ct. at 513. Nor does our reading of the statutes mean that under no circumstances may the court inquire into the underlying reasons for the examination. It is the court's process which is invoked to enforce the administrative summons and a court may not permit its process to be abused. Such an abuse would take place if the summons had been issued for an improper purpose, such as to harass the taxpayer or to put pressure on him to settle a collateral dispute, or for any other purpose reflecting on the good faith of the particular investigation. The burden of showing an abuse of the court's process is on the taxpayer, and it is not met by a mere showing, as was made in this case, that the statute of limitations for ordinary deficiencies has run òr that the records in question have already been once examined.

The judgment of the Court of Appeals is reversed, and the case is remanded for further proceedings consistent with this opinion.

It is ordered.

Reverse and remanded.

_____

[1] I.R.C., § 6501(a).

[2] I.R.C., § 5501(c) (1), which in relevant part provides: "In the case of a false or fraudulent return with the intent to evade tax, the tax may be assessed, or a proceeding in court for collection of such tax may be begun without assessment, at any time."

[3] The parties subsequently agreed that if the Government was upheld in its claim of the right to examine without showing probable cause, the one–hour time limitation would be removed.

[4] Revenue Act of 1921, § 250(d), 42 Stat. 265, provided a four–year period of limitation on ordinary tax liability.

[5] The contrary view derives no support from the characterization of the limitations provision as a "statute of repose." The present three–year limitation on assessment of ordinary deficiencies relieves the taxpayer of concern for further assessments of that type, but it by no means follows that it limits the right of the Government to investigate with respect to deficiencies for which no statute of limitations is imposed.

[6] The Court of Appeals appears to have been led astray by the fact that the Government argued its case on the premise that § 7604(b) was the governing statute.

[7] Because § 7604(a) contains no provision specifying the procedure to be followed in invoking the court's jurisdiction, the Federal Rules of Civil Procedure apply, *Martin v. Chandis Securities Co.*, 9 Cir., 128 F.2d 731. The proceedings are instituted by filing a complaint, followed by answer and hearing. If the taxpayer has contumaciously refused to comply with the administrative summons and the Service fears he may flee the jurisdiction, application for the sanctions available under § 7604(b) might be made simultaneously with the filing of the complaint.

**UNITED STATES of America,
Plaintiff–Appellee v. Sidney
ROSENSTEIN, Irving BRAVERMAN,
FOREMOST BRANDS, INC. and
McINERNEY SALES INC.,
Defendants–Appellants**

474 F.2d 705

United States Court of Appeals for the Second
Circuit
January 26, 1973

These are appeals by Sidney Rosenstein, Irving Braverman, Foremost Brands, Inc. and McInerney Sales, Inc. from judgments of conviction entered in the United States District Court for the Southern District of New York on January 11, 1972 after trial before Hon. Thomas F. Croake, United States District Judge, and a jury. Judgments affirmed.

* * * * *

I. The Facts

The investigation of this complicated case was commenced by Internal Revenue Service in 1964 and did not terminate until late in 1967. It involved interviewing a great number of witnesses in the United States as well as foreign nationals in Switzerland and Liechtenstein. In a trial which lasted six weeks, the Government presented some 75 witnesses and over 1000 documents as exhibits. The defendants did not testify.

The Government's proof established without any doubt that from May, 1960 until 1967 Braverman and Rosenstein and their wholly owned corporations, Foremost and McInerney, brazenly and fraudulently evaded United States income taxes by creating a dummy Liechtenstein corporation, called Continental Trade Establishment (CTE), to which they diverted payments of $1.6 million in commissions from October 1, 1961 to January 31, 1965 and which, in turn, were deposited in a secret account at the Bank Leu, Zurich, Switzerland.

Braverman and Rosenstein and their corporate alter egos, Foremost and McInerney, acted as sales representatives for American manufacturers in the sale of their products to United States Military Post Exchanges throughout the world. In return for their services, they received commissions of about 6% on gross sales. In May, 1960, Braverman and Rosenstein created CTE in Liechtenstein and opened an account at the Bank Leu in Zurich. Their American clients were then asked to make all commission checks on sales to overseas PX's payable to CTE and to forward them to Dr. Herbert Batliner, Haupstrasse 22, Vaduz, Liechtenstein, instead of to Foremost or McInerney, the previous payees. Sometime in 1966 the instructions were changed and the checks were forwarded to Dr. Alfred Buehler at the same Liechtenstein address. Batliner and Beuhler were both Liechtenstein attorneys and Haupstrasse 22 was a two–story building which housed Batliner's law office and a shoe store. Representatives of 42 American manufacturers testified at trial as to the payment arrangements and the Government produced checks, payable to CTE and deposited in the Swiss Bank, totaling $1,604,409.59 for foreign PX commissions from October 1, 1961 through January 31, 1965. It is not disputed that no United States income tax have ever been paid by the appellants on these commissions.

* * * * *

The principal argument raised on appeal is that the admission into evidence of the records of CTE, Government Exhibits 1020–23 and 1025–29, constituted reversible error.

II. The Liechtenstein Documents

(a) The Business Records Exception

The exhibits in question were produced toward the close of its case, but a Government witness, Dr. Peter Monauni, one of three Liechtenstein attorneys resident at Hauptstrasse 22, Liechtenstein. Dr. Batliner had refused to come to the United States at the time of the trial to testify. Instead he sent Dr. Monauni who had been associated with him for ten years. Dr. Monauni's direct testimony bolstered the other evidence in the case as to CTE's true character. He knew it simply as a client of his firm; to his knowledge it conducted no business of any description at the law office headquarters except for the forwarding of mail and checks.

Monauni produced a CTE file containing Exhibits 1020–23 and 1025–29. The Government offered the documents under the business records exception to the hearsay rule, 28 U.S.C. § 1732. Essentially the statute provides that any writing or record, made as a memorandum of any act, transaction, occurrence or event, if made in the ordinary course of one's business and if it was the regular course of such business to make such records at the time or reasonably thereafter, is admissible as evidence of the act, transaction, occurrence, or event. We agree with the appellants that the documents were not properly admissible under the statutory business record exception. The fact that Dr. Monauni did not personally keep the books and records would not render them inadmissible (*United States v. New York Foreign Trade Zone Operators,Inc.*, 304 F.2d 792, 796 (2nd Cir.1962)), but someone who is sufficiently familiar with the business practice must testify that these records were made as part of that practice. *United States v. Delgado*, 459 F.2d 471, 472 (2nd Cir.1972); *Cullen v. United States*, 408 F.2d 1178 (8th Cir.1969); *United States v. Dawson*, 400 F.2d 194, 198–99 (2nd Cir.1968), *cert. denied*, 393 U.S. 1023, 21 L.Ed.2d 567, 89 S.Ct. 632 (1969). Dr. Monauni's testimony did not rise to this level of requisite knowledge. He not only did not keep the records, he did not even know from his own personal knowledge that they were kept in Batliner's office. He did not testify to the business practice of CTE or that it was the practice to keep the documents which were introduced.

* * * * *

Some of the Liechtenstein documents were letters from third parties who clearly were not working for CTE. They "were not made in the regular course of the business of the company in whose files they were found . . . ." *Phillips v. United States*, 356 F.2d 297, 307 (9th Cir.1965), *cert. denied*, 384 U.S. 952, 16 L.Ed.2d 548, 86 S.Ct. 1573 (1966). The requirements of the Business Records

Rule are not fulfilled by a showing that the addressee routinely kept a file of such correspondence. It must appear that the letter was written in the regular course of its author's business. *See Johnson v. Lutz*, 253 N.Y. 124, 170 N.E. 517 (1930).

While the records were not admissible as business records, we cannot agree with the appellant's contention that we cannot sustain their admission on the basis of some other exception to the hearsay rule. * * *

* * * * *

UNITED STATES of America v. Joseph RUSSO

480 F.2d 1228

United States Court of Appeals, Sixth Circuit
July 6, 1973

Appellant, Joseph Russo, is an osteopathic physician licensed to practice in Michigan. He and an associate were charged in a single indictment containing 51 counts of violating the mail fraud statute, 18 U.S.C. § 1341. Count one of the indictment was divided into paragraphs I and II. Paragraph I charged that the two physicians "devised and intended to devise a scheme and artifice to defraud Blue Shield of Michigan, . . . by filing claims for services not performed on patients on dates specified and for obtaining money from such organization by false and fraudulent pretenses and representations well knowing at the time that the pretenses and representations would be and were false when made." Subparagraphs A through G set forth in detail the manner in which the alleged scheme and artifice to defraud was carried out. Paragraph II of Count one then recited that on July 14, 1966 at Detroit in the Eastern District of Michigan the defendant, Joseph Russo, did knowingly and willfully cause Blue Shield of Michigan to mail a check, identified by number, to him in violation of the mail fraud statute. Each of the subsequent 50 counts realleged and adopted the allegations of paragraph I of Count one and in its paragraph

II charged one or the other of the named defendants with willfully causing a check to be placed in the mail by Blue Shield of Michigan for delivery to that defendant. No conspiracy was charged in the indictment.

The evidence reveals that during the period covered by the indictment which was part of the year 1966, all of 1967 and part of 1968 Dr. Russo leased a group of offices in the basement of a building in a "blue–collar" neighborhood in Detroit. These offices, referred to in the testimony as Dr. Russo's clinic, consisted of four examination rooms, an office and a long hallway where patients waited. Although Dr. Russo was associated with several other doctors in a partnership known as The Midwest Clinical Group, only one of the other members of that partnership practiced in the same building with Dr. Russo and there was no sharing of facilities or personnel by them. The Midwest Clinical Group was a loose sort of arrangement in which each of the partners contributed income for the purpose of maintaining one or more osteopathic hospitals in Detroit. It appears from the testimony that the doctors who belonged to the Midwest Clinical Group had problems obtaining hospital beds for their patients and that it was necessary for them to operate, through the partnership, hospitals known as Palmer East and Palmer West for the treatment of their patients. Although the testimony indicates that the Midwest Clinical Group received a portion of its funds from Dr. Russo, presumably including payments from Blue Shield of Michigan which the indictment charges were procured by fraud, there is no evidence that any other member of the Midwest Clinical group was involved in, or had any knowledge of, the scheme charged in the indictment. The co–defendant, Dr. Lieberwitz, was not a member of the Midwest Clinical Group, but was an employee of Dr. Russo.

The Russo office or clinic was kept open throughout the day until late at night and hundreds of patients were seen in a single day. Most of the time Dr. Russo had at least two other doctors working for him at the clinic and each worked on certain days during the week. The other doctors who worked for Dr. Russo gave him a portion of their gross receipts and paid none of the overhead expenses of the offices. The co–defendant who was indicted and tried with Dr. Russo was a younger osteopathic physician who testified to treating an average of 150 patients per day while working at Dr. Russo's office and who stated that he often stayed until 1:00 or 2:00 o'clock in the morning since the office was never closed as long as there were any patients waiting to be seen. Several of the doctors who had worked at the clinic testified that it was Dr. Russo's office and that when they came to work, all of the patients were Dr. Russo's patients, although after they had been there a while some of the patients became theirs. Several witnesses attributed the large number of daily patients at the Russo clinic to the fact that it was located in a densely populated section of Detroit where few doctors' offices were situated.

It was testified that Blue Shield of Michigan furnishes to the doctors who practice in that state printed forms known as "Doctor Service Reports" (hereinafter DSR). In order to be paid by Blue Shield it is necessary for a doctor to complete a DSR for each treatment and submit it for payment. Each doctor is assigned a provider's code number and this and his name are both imprinted on the DSR's furnished to him by Blue Shield. The DSR is completed by filling in the name of the patient, the name of the subscriber, which might be different from that of the patient, and the address, identification number and certain other statistical data of the subscriber. Often the subscriber is the employer of the patient. In addition, the treating physician must indicate the date of the service and a description of the service rendered together with a diagnosis. Each physician is supplied with a manual containing approximately 8,000 different procedures with a four–digit code number for each such procedure. There is an established fee which Blue Shield agrees to pay for each particular type of medical service under its various contracts, and the amount of its liability is determined by the procedure code number and description of services performed as indicated on the DSR. Not all medical services are covered by Blue Shield and the coverage can vary between contracts of various subscribers.

The prosecution did not contend that the appellant submitted DSR's to Blue Shield for patients that he had not seen on the dates indicated. What was contended was that in many cases the treatment received by the patients was of such a nature that it was not covered by Blue Shield and was not compensable under the particular subscriber contract involved and that if the services actually performed had been disclosed on the DSR, no payment would have been due from Blue Shield. Instead of making a charge to the patient for the actual services which were not compensable under the patient's Blue Shield coverage, it was the contention of the prosecution that the defendants caused a DSR to be prepared showing that some procedure had been followed with the patient which would have been compensable.

* * * * *

II. The Computerized Statistical Evidence

Appellant has mounted a broad attack on the admission by the court of the 1967 annual statistical run of Blue Shield of Michigan. In the first place it is claimed that this evidence does not qualify as a business record under 28 U.S.C. § 1732(a), the Federal Business Records Act. That statute establishes the admissibility in federal courts of any writing or record, made as a memorandum or record of an act or transaction, as evidence of such act or transaction if made in the ordinary course of business. This is an exception to the hearsay rule. The uncontradicted testimony of two witnesses established that the 1967 statistical run was a regularly maintained business record of Blue Shield and was made in the ordinary course of business. It was also shown that this record was relied upon by the company in conducting its business, particularly with reference to its auditing and actuarial procedures. The appellant maintains that the annual statistical run is not the record of any act or transaction and that only the original DSR's should have been admitted to prove the "act" of payment for medical procedures.

Computer printouts are not mentioned in the Federal Business Records Act. However, no court could fail to notice the extent to which businesses today depend on computers for a myriad of functions. Perhaps the greatest utility of a computer in the business world is its ability to store large quantities of information which may be quickly retrieved on a selective basis. Assuming that properly functioning computer equipment is used, once the reliability and trustworthiness of the information put into the computer has been established, the computer printouts should be received as evidence of the transactions covered by the input. No evidence was introduced which put in question the mechanical or electronic capabilities of the equipment and the reliability of its output was verified. The procedures for testing the accuracy and reliability of the information fed into the computer were detailed at great length by the witnesses. The district court correctly held that the trustworthiness of the information contained in the computer printout had been established.

The appellant also maintains that the computer printout should not have been received in evidence because it was not prepared at the time the acts which it purports to describe were performed or within a reasonable time thereafter as required by 28 U.S.C. § 173(a). However, the evidence clearly shows that a record of payment was made at the time each DSR was paid by Michigan Blue Shield and that this record was referred to as the paid claims file. This file consisted of reels of magnetic tape which reflected every payment to a doctor in the year 1967. Since the computer printout is just a presentation in structured and comprehensible form of a mass of individual items, it is immaterial that the printout itself was not prepared until 11 months after the close of the year 1967. It would restrict the admissibility of computerized records too severely to hold that the computer product, as well as the input upon which it is based, must be produced at or within a reasonable time after each act or transaction to which it relates.

The Federal Business Records Act was adopted for the purpose of facilitating the admission of records into evidence where experience has shown them to be trustworthy. It should be liberally construed to avoid the difficulties of an archaic practice which formerly required every written document to be authenticated by the person who prepared it. *Gilbert v. Gulf Oil Corporation*, 175 F.2d 705 (4th Cir.1949); *Gradsky v. United States*, 342 F.2d 147 (5th Cir. 1965), vacated and remanded on other grounds, 383 U.S. 265, 86 S.Ct. 925, 15 L.Ed.2d 737 (1966). The Act should never be interpreted so strictly as to deprive the courts of the realities of business and professional practices. *Harris v. Smith*, 372 F.2d 806 (8th Cir.1967). Appellant insists that the 1967 statistical record was a "summary" which is not admissible, citing *Melinder v. United States*, 281 F.Supp. 451 (W.D.Okl.1968). That case involved an exhibit prepared by an Internal Revenue agent for use at the trial of an income tax case. It was not a record produced in the ordinary course of business and was merely a recapitulation of certain information which had not been introduced to verify it in the case. The annual statistical run of Blue Shield of Michigan is not a summary, since it contains a record of every claim paid by the organization during a given year. The information contained in it is arranged in a predetermined manner and classified according to medical procedures. However, all paid claims are included and all compensable procedures are covered. It is important to distinguish the entire printout of the 1967 annual statistical run from a separate item of evidence consisting of a summary of portions of the printout. The witness Smith did summarize portions of the annual statistical report and did relate these summaries to the individual doctor's profiles of the defendants. Nevertheless, the entire statistical run was produced by the prosecution as a business record prepared in the ordinary course of business long before the time of the trial. Although summaries may or may not be admissible in evidence according to the circumstances of a particular case, we hold that the computer printout offered in evidence in this case was an original record and not a mere summary.

The appellant maintains that no proper foundation was laid for the admission of the 1967 annual statistical record. We disagree. The witnesses Smith and Mrachina were qualified as experts by education, training and experience and they showed a familiarity with the use of the particular computers in question. The mechanics of input control to assure accuracy were detailed at great length as was the description of the nature of the information which went into the machine and upon which its printout was based. In *United States v. De Georgia*, 420 F.2d 889 (9th Cir. 1969), the computerized records of Hertz Corporation were admitted for the purpose of showing that a particular automobile was not involved in any rental or lease activity during a certain period of time. An employee of Hertz was permitted to testify, based on the computer information, that an automobile found in the custody of the defendant at the time of his arrest was stolen from the Hertz lot since it had not been rented or leased. As the opinion points out, the foundation for admission of such evidence consists of showing the input procedures used, the tests for accuracy and reliability and the fact that an established business relies on the computerized records in the ordinary course of carrying on its activities. The defendant then has the opportunity to cross–examine concerning company practices with respect to the input and as to the accuracy of the computer as a memory bank and retriever of information. The concurring opinion in *De Georgia* emphasizes the necessity that the court "be satisfied with all reasonable certainty that both the machine and those who supply its information have performed their functions with utmost accuracy." 420 F.2d at 895. This opinion goes on to say that the trustworthiness of the particular records should be ascertained before they are admitted and that the burden of presenting an adequate foundation for receiving the evidence should be on the parties seeking to introduce it rather than upon the party opposing its introduction. We believe that in this case the prosecution proved the essential elements upon which the district court could, and did, conclude that the annual statistical run of Blue Shield of Michigan was a trustworthy record which was entitled to be received in evidence under the Federal Business Records Act. Two well–reasoned state court opinions support this conclusion. *See Transport Indemnity Company v. Seib*, 178 Neb. 253, 132 N.W.2d 871 (1965); *King v. State ex rel. Murdock Acceptance Corporation*, 222 So.2d 393 (Miss.1969).

Appellant also complains that he was not given an opportunity to prepare his defense to the computerized material used by the prosecution. In *United States v. Stifel*, 433 F.2d 431 (6th Cir.1970), cert. denied, 401 U.S. 994, 91 S.Ct. 1232, 28 L.Ed.2d 531 (1971), this Court held that if the Government uses highly sophisticated scientific evidence (in that case, neutron activation analysis) involving time consuming and expensive laboratory tests, it must allow time for a defendant to make similar tests. The Manual for Complex and Multidistrict Litigation deals at some length with the use of computer evidence. Its admissibility is strongly defended where the records have been kept in the regular course of business and its reliability has been demonstrated. The Manual further states,

It is essential that the underlying data used in the analysis, programs and programming method and all relevant computer inputs and outputs be made available to the opposing party far in advance of trial. This procedure is required in the interest of fairness and should facilitate at the introduction of admissible computer evidence. Such procedure provides the adverse party and the court with an opportunity to test and examine the inputs, the program and all outputs prior to trial. (p. 88).

On March 22, 1971 appellant filed a request for particulars in which he sought information about the evidence which would be used in support of the charges against him. On April 27, 1971 the government filed its response and forwarded to the attorneys for appellant a number of documents relating to the request for particulars. At the same time the Assistant U.S. Attorney forwarded to the attorneys for the appellant certain documents, including — "[A] statistical summary for 1967 compiled from the records of Blue Shield of Michigan. It compares the number of claims filed for certain services by the defendants as against the total number filed by all doctors in the State of Michigan." So far as the record shows, no discovery steps

were taken by the appellant between the time of the disclosure by the prosecution of the nature of this particular evidence and the beginning of the trial on September 14, 1971 despite the fact that Rule 16(b) Fed.R.Crim.P. provides for discovery and inspection by a defendant in a criminal case. At the trial Charles Smith's testimony compared the number of claims made by Drs. Russo and Lieberwitz for five particular medical procedures with those made by all of the doctors in Michigan. This summary was prepared by the witness from two sources. The number of claims paid to Drs. Russo and Lieberwitz was determined from the individual doctor's profiles prepared for each one of the defendants concerning which there is no contention on appeal. The information as to the total number of claims paid all doctors in Michigan in the five categories of medical procedures was based on the annual statistical run which was offered and accepted in evidence. In view of the enclosure of the identical summary in the letter of April 27, there was no surprise or sudden, unexpected production of this evidence. Mr. Smith was cross–examined vigorously as to the manner in which the annual statistical run was produced.

Furthermore, on the third day of the trial, September 16, 1971, there was a discussion between the court and counsel concerning exhibits. The prosecuting attorney referred to the fact that he had furnished statistics to counsel for the defendant pursuant to the court's pretrial order and stated that statistics showing the volume of claims in certain categories by the defendants would be compared with the total volume of such claims paid to all doctors throughout Michigan. On September 24, 1971 the witness Smith was recalled for the purpose of testifying about individual doctor's profiles and the annual statistical run of his employer. The court recalled to the attorneys that there had been a previous discussion of this offer of proof and that he had requested attorneys to be prepared to offer authority for their positions. When counsel for appellant complained that the information included in the annual statistical run was exclusively in the control of Blue Shield the court reminded him that he had a right to get an order which would have permitted him to go into the plant and study the whole process, and had not done so. The court ruled that the summary evidence offered by the witness Smith could be introduced because the primary evidence upon which the summary was based was in the courtroom and available for inspection and use in cross–examination by appellant. The prosecuting attorney pointed out again that the original of the computer run for the 1967 annual statistical report was available to counsel for the defendants, that the doctors' profiles and the vouchers from which they were constructed were also available for examination by counsel.

In cross–examining the witness Smith on September 28, 1971 the defense for the first time asked about other information that Blue Shield might furnish from its computer for comparison with the statistics included in his testimony. At no time prior to the trial or after the September 14th conference with the court did the defense make any effort to require the prosecution or Blue Shield to make its computers available to the defendants or to an expert employed by them or even to provide other information from the computers which was not then available. The computerized annual statistical run was not introduced into evidence and presented to the jury until September 30, 1971. Defense counsel were given an opportunity to examine the exhibit and to cross–examine both Mr. Smith and Mr. Mrachine extensively concerning it. The prosecuting attorney stated that the reason for introducing the annual statistical run as an exhibit was to provide a foundation for the testimony of Mr. Smith. The court pointed out that the annual statistical run itself was not a summary but a primary and original record constantly used by the company and was admissible in support of the testimony relating to portions of the exhibit by the person under whose supervision it was prepared.

* * * * *

UNITED STATES of America, owner of the U.S.S. DARBY (DE 218) v. S.S. SOYA ATLANTIC, her engines, boilers, tackle, etc., in rem and against Rederi A/B Walltank, owner of the S.S. Soya Atlantic, in personam

213 F.Supp. 7

United States District Court D. Maryland
January 2, 1963

These actions arise out of a collision between the U.S.S. DARBY (DE 218), a destroyer escort of the United States Navy, and the S.S. SOYA ATLANTIC, a Swedish vessel owned by Rederi A/B Walltank. The United States has filed a libel against the SOYA ATLANTIC and her owners, who, in turn, have filed a cross–libel against the United States. Also, two seamen aboard the DARBY were killed as a result of the collision; their legal representatives have brought two separate wrongful death actions against the SOYA ATLANTIC and her owners, who there have impleaded the United States. The cases have been consolidated and presently are before the court on the question of liability only.

* * * * *

Finally, the government claims that alterations and erasures in the log of the SOYA ATLANTIC cast suspicion upon her entire case. A government expert testified that three entries in the Swedish vessel's rough deck log, posted immediately after the collision, appeared over obliterations made by a simple pencil erasure; what the original entry was, in each instance, the expert was not prepared to state. The government's argument correctly presents the rule with respect to log alterations, but the rule is not applicable where, as here, the alterations are satisfactorily explained. The first erasure, made by Chief Officer Leman, was of the same information that was written over it, and the erasure was made solely because of insufficient space within which to write. The second erasure pertained to the time of collision, and also was made by the Chief Officer. He admitted he did not remember the change, but, as the logged collision time was only an estimate and not an observed time, the alteration is of little consequence. The Chief Officer was so candid in his testimony with respect to erasures that he acknowledged an additional alteration not even identified by the government expert. Immediately opposite the logged collision time appears the word "kolliderat" ("hit and damaged") which was substituted for the word "Stottepo" [?] ("hit, but not necessarily damaged"). The third alteration was made by Captain Bakke, and he testified that the material erased had no relation to the navigation of the ship, but was an irrelevant marginal note. The word under which the erasure appears is "strax" which simply means "soon after." All of these changes appear to be innocent and, probably, are most adequately explained by the turmoil and haste immediately following the collision.

* * * * *

UNITED STATES of America, v. Daniel UNGAR and Peter Giambalvo

648 F.Supp. 1329

United States District Court, Eastern District
New York
November 25, 1986

The defendant Peter Giambalvo, convicted on a conspiracy charge at his jury trial of August, 1986, moves for a judgment of acquittal on the ground that the evidence was insufficient to establish his guilt beyond a reasonable doubt. He also moves to dismiss the indictment on the ground the preindictment delay prejudiced his own defense, and for dismissal of the indictment or for a new trial on the ground that the government destroyed discoverable and potentially exculpatory material. His co–defendant Daniel Ungar joins these motions. For the reasons set forth below, the motions are denied.

Background

Giambalvo was previously a Supervisory Consumer Safety Inspector for the New York Import District of the United States Food and Drug Administration (FDA). As a supervi-

sory inspector, he had responsibility for determining what goods imported into New York would be inspected. Daniel Ungar is a retired Chief of the FDA Import Section of the New York Import District. In January 1986, Giambalvo, Ungar and other persons were indicted on a charge of conspiring, between June 1981 and July 1984, to defraud the United States government of the right to have the faithful and honest service of Giambalvo as an FDA employee and to have the laws and regulations of the FDA administered honestly and impartially. Giambalvo was also charged with bribery in connection with the inspection and release of foods entering the United States; Ungar was charged with aiding and abetting that bribery. Following a jury trial, Giambalvo and Ungar were convicted on the conspiracy charge and acquitted of the bribery charge.

The members of the alleged conspiracy included Giambalvo, Ungar, Demetrius Christophides, a customs broker who became a government informant during the course of the conspiracy, and Mr. Kefaleas, an importer of figs. Pursuant to the conspiratorial agreement, Christophides received money from agents of Kefaleas in exchange for Christophides' agreement that figs imported by Kefaleas would not be inspected by the FDA. Such an assurance on non–inspection enabled Kefaleas to save money by removing the necessity of obtaining insurance against the possibility of FDA rejection of the figs, and by hastening the appearance of the figs on the market. Christophides represented that he had connections at the FDA who would ensure that the figs would be released without inspection. One of those connections was Giambalvo. The agreement was that Christophides would pay the money received from Kefaleas to Ungar, who in turn would pass the money to FDA inspectors, including Giambalvo.

The FDA form used during the period in question to authorize the entry and release of imported goods, with or without inspection, consisted of four attached, identical forms separated by carbon paper inserts. The top form was numbered FDA form 701 (701 form). The second form was numbered FDA form 702 (702 form). After completion, the

701 form was kept by the FDA; the 702 form was kept by whatever customs broker was involved in the importation. On each of the identical forms was a box which included the words "This Importation May Proceed Without FDA Examination" (release box). The signature of an FDA inspector in the release box indicated that the goods referred to in the form had been admitted into the United States without inspection. A large majority of the goods entering the New York ports were not inspected, for legitimate reasons.

Evidence at trial established that despite the fact that the 701 and 702 forms are identical forms of a single carbon set they may, after use, contain different information. When an FDA inspector decided that certain imported goods should be inspected, he would make a notation as to the nature of the inspection on the 701 form in a felt–tip pen that would not leave a mark on the lower copies of the forms. For example, an inspector might use the pen to write "insan" on the 701 form, indicating that the goods in question should be inspected for insanitation; the 702 copy would not show that notation.

Even where in inspector had written in felt pen on a 701 form to request inspection, the goods in question would sometimes be released without inspection due to shortage of manpower or to other legitimate factors. An inspector would then ultimately sign the release box, using a regular pen that would show through onto the second, 702, copy. In consequence, a top, 701, form, might indicate that inspection of goods had initially been required, but the 702 copy of the form would show only that release had been authorized without inspection, with no indication that inspection had been originally requested.

Key evidence in the government's case was a large number of 702 forms that the government obtained from customs broker Christophides. Those forms concerned importations of figs by Kefaleas between September and November 1983, and each form showed a signature in the release box by an FDA inspector, some of them by Giambalvo. The government did not introduce into evidence the top, 701, copies of the forms. The defense had requested the corresponding 701 forms

but had been informed by the government that the forms had been destroyed by the FDA in the regular course of business. Trial testimony of Mr. Joseph Faline, District Director of the FDA, established that it is FDA practice to retain 701 forms for only six months. On this motion the government represents to the court that in November 1984 it subpoenaed all original release forms from the FDA and that the FDA indicated that the forms for 1983 had already been destroyed. The FDA did produce the 701 forms for 1984, which were turned over to the prosecutor and, subsequently, to the defense.

Giambalvo at trial introduced into evidence the 701 forms for 1984 that had been obtained from the FDA. Those forms had felt pen markings showing that Giambalvo had requested inspection of 1984 shipments of figs by Kefaleas, although certain of the forms also had signatures in the release boxes indicating that the requested inspections had not in fact occurred. Defense counsel argued in summation that those requests for inspection made in 1984 indicated that Giambalvo had been requiring inspections of Kefaleas's figs, and that Giambalvo was therefore not party to the conspiracy to let the figs enter without inspection.

* * * * *

Giambalvo contends that, regardless of whether the destruction of the 701 forms were causally related to preindictment delay, his right to due process was violated because the forms were discoverable and exculpatory and the government destroyed them. He therefore asks for either dismissal of the indictment or for a new trial; Ungar joins this motion.

Under *California v. Trombetta*, 467 U.S. 479, 104 S.Ct. 2528, 81 L.Ed.2d 413 (1984), government destruction of exculpatory evidence violates due process only if the exculpatory value of the material was apparent before the material was destroyed, and if the nature of the material was such that the defendant would not be able to obtain comparable evidence by other reasonably available means. *Id.* at 488–89, 104 S.Ct. at 2534; according *United States v. Fletcher*, 801 F.2d 1222 (10th Cir.1986).

Under this stringent test, Giambalvo has failed to establish a due process violation. Assuming arguendo, that the destroyed 701 forms did contain exculpatory notations, there is nothing to suggest that their exculpatory value "was apparent before the evidence was destroyed." *Trombett*, 467 U.S. at 489, 104 S.Ct. at 2534. For there is no indication that FDA officials responsible for the destruction were aware of the ongoing investigation or able to assess the value to an unknown prospective defendant of particular FDA files kept in the regular course of business. Nor is there any indication that the investigatory agents who were involved in this case had reason to know prior to the forms' destruction that there was an FDA practice of putting felt–tip pen notations on the 701 forms or that the forms might be exculpatory. It is true, as Giambalvo points out, that the agents did have reason to know this after receiving the 701 forms for 1984 in response to the November 1984 subpoena. By that time, however, the 1983 forms had been destroyed. Giambalvo has therefore failed to establish that the exculpatory value of the 701 forms was apparent before their destruction. Consequently, his due process claim must fail, as must Ungar's.

Giambalvo argues further that, under the law of this Circuit, this court should impose sanctions for the FDA's destruction of the 701 forms. In this circuit, in cases of government destruction of evidence, a balancing test is used for determining when sanctions are appropriate. *See United States v. Grammatikos*, 633 F.2d 1013, 1019–20 (2d Cir.1980) (balancing test should be employed in cases of destruction of evidence); cf. *United States v. Mayersohn*, 452 F.2d 521, 525 n. 11 (2d Cir.1971) (the law that has evolved from the federal court suppression of cases appears to be rooted in the appellate courts' supervisory powers); *United States v. Consolidated Laundries Corp.*, 291 F.2d 563, 571 (2d Cir.1961) (court did not need to decide if negligent suppression of evidence violated due process where to deny new trial would be inconsistent with correct administration of justice). Under the test employed by the Second Circuit:

the appropriateness and extent of sanctions . . . depends upon a case–by–case assessment of the government's culpability for the loss, together with a realistic appraisal of its significance when viewed in light of its nature, its bearing upon critical issues in the case and the strength of the government's untainted proof.

United States v. Grammatikos, 633 F.2d at 1019–20; see *United States v. Quintana*, 673 F.2d 296, 299 (10th Cir.1982) (in cases of lost evidence, courts apply pragmatic balancing test) (citing cases), cert. denied, 457 U.S. 1135, 102 S.Ct. 2963, 73 L.Ed.2d 1353 (1982). Additionally, the Circuit had indicated that it will look with an exceedingly jaundiced eye upon . . . efforts to justify non–production of a Rule 16 or Jencks Act 'statement' by reference to a 'department policy' or 'established practice' or the like and that "[w]here . . . destruction is deliberate, sanctions will normally follow." *United States v. Bufalino*, 576 F.2d 446, 449 (2d Cir.), cert. denied, 439 U.S. 928, 99 S.Ct. 314, 58 L.Ed.2d 321 (1978); accord *United States v. Sanchez*, 635 F.2d 47, 65–66 (2d Cir.1980).

Applying the Second Circuit test, sanctions in this case are not appropriate. As to the first prong of the test, government culpability, Giambalvo does not dispute that the 701 forms were destroyed in the regular course of FDA business, nor does he allege bad faith. The forms were not in the possession of an investigatory agency nor kept primarily for prosecution purposes, and there is no indication that the investigatory agents had reason to know the forms would be destroyed by the FDA, or that the forms might contain exculpatory information. In light of these factors, the government was at most negligent regarding destruction of the forms. Specifically, it may have been negligent in waiting until November 1984, four months after the end of the charged conspiracy, to serve a subpoena on the FDA, or in failing to earlier determine which, if any, FDA documents were normally destroyed in the regular course of business.

Bufalino, 576 F.2d at 449, and *Grammatikos*, 633 F.2d at 1019–20, do warn that government destruction of documents as a matter of "department policy" will not protect the government from a claim of violation of its duty to preserve evidence, and that sanctions will "normally follow" when destruction is "deliberate." However, it is not clear that these strong warnings are directed at the routine destruction of documents by non–investigatory agencies not requested to maintain the documents. Rather, the cases pertain to destruction of documents by investigatory agencies, or by non–investigatory agencies requested to maintain the documents. Thus, in *Grammatikos*, tape recordings made by the DEA were destroyed by the DEA; in *Bufalino*, a tape made by the FBI was destroyed by the FBI. See also *United States v. Henriquez*, 731 F.2d 131, 137–38 (2d Cir.1984) (Coast Guard acted improperly in destroying tape in regular course of business; Second Circuit requires prosecutors to instruct various agencies that tapes are not to be destroyed); *United States v. Sanchez*, 635 F.2d at 64–66 (reports of informant destroyed by DEA); *United States v. Arra*, 630 F.2d 836, 849 (1st Cir.1980) (destruction of tapes was good faith administrative error where tapes not primarily for prosecutorial purposes were erased in accordance with routine procedures having no relation to case); *United States v. Carrasco*, 537 F.2d 372 (9th Cir.1976) (reversal of conviction where DEA destroyed informant's diary). It does not appear that sanctions should "normally follow" good faith, routine destruction of records that are kept by a non–investigatory agency which is not asked to preserve the records, so long as there is no bad faith by the investigatory agency or indication that it should have known the documents would be destroyed, or of their possible exculpatory value. Rather, the appropriateness of sanctions in such a case must depend upon a pragmatic case–by–case analysis in which all factors are taken into account. Grammtikos, 633 F.2d at 1019–20.

Giambalvo, correctly points out, however, that where destruction of documents was deliberate, cases indicate that a heavy burden is on the government to show that no prejudice resulted to the defendant. See *United States v. Sanchez*, 635 F.2d at 65 (when destruction

is deliberate, government has heavy burden of showing no prejudice); *United States v. Bufalino*, 576 F.2d at 449 (same); *United States v. Miranda*, 526 F.2d 1319, 1326 (2d Cir.1975) (government has burden of showing loss of evidence was not intentional, deliberate, or in bad faith), cert. denied. 429 U.S. 821, 97 S.Ct. 69, 50 L.Ed.2d 82 (1976). If literally denied, 429 U.S. 821, 97 S.Ct. 69, 50 L.Ed.2d (1976). If literally interpreted, these cases would require that sanctions be imposed, as there is no question but that the FDA deliberately destroyed the 701 forms and that the government has not affirmatively proved that there were no notations by Giambalvo on those forms. But, again, it is not clear that the Circuit's concept of "deliberate" destruction encompasses all routine destructions of documents by non–investigatory agencies. Moreover, *Grammatikos*, 633 F.2d 1013 — which requires use of a balancing test" suggests that the appropriateness of sanctions does not stand or fall upon a government showing as to any single factor. *See id.* at 1019–20 (although government has long been on notice of duty to preserve evidence, appropriateness of sanctions depends on case–by–case analysis).

The balancing test requires an appraisal, not only of government culpability, but also of the significance of the destroyed material and its bearing upon critical issues. *Id.* As is discussed above, the defendants' claim that the destroyed 701 forms in fact contained requests by Giambalvo for inspection is speculative. Furthermore, even if the forms contained such notations and even had the forms been available to the defense at trial, such evidence, although helpful to the defense, would not have belied the fact that Kefaleas's figs were not inspected in 1983. It is also relevant that the 1984 forms containing Giambalvo's requests for inspection were placed in evidence by the defense and that counsel argued in summation that the 1983 forms might also have contained such requests. Cf. *United States v. Miranda*, 526 F.2d at 1328 (factor in court's decision not to impose sanctions for destruction of evidence was that loss of evidence was brought out in summation).

A further requirement under the balancing test is an assessment of the strength of the government's untainted proof. On these facts, "tainted" proof would presumably encompass the 702 forms corresponding to the destroyed 701 forms, and any other evidence that Kefaleas's shipments had entered the United States without inspection. Such proof, although probative, was not essential to the government's case. Proof of participation in a conspiracy does not require evidence that the objectives of the conspiracy were accomplished, and here the government had other evidence of Giambalvo's membership in the conspiracy. Specifically, there was the evidence that Ungar told Christophides that Giambalvo was his FDA contact; that Ungar regularly called the homes of Giambalvo and another supervisor at times corresponding with entries of Kefaleas's figs (with or without inspection), that those calls ceased when notice was given of the subpoenaing of phone records; that Giambalvo made a false exculpatory statement regarding those calls; that Christophides made a recorded call to Giambalvo in which Giambalvo commented that he could not talk in the office; and that Christophides called asking Giambalvo about the Zim Kelung and that Ungar had characterized Giambalvo's statement to Christophides during that call as a threat. While this "untainted" evidence is not overwhelming, it is not unsubstantial. The untainted evidence against Ungar is overwhelming, given the videotapes of Ungar and Christophides.

In sum: 1) it is highly speculative whether there were requests for inspection on the destroyed forms; 2) the government was most negligent insofar as destruction of the 701 forms is concerned; 3) the destroyed forms, although significant to the defense if they did contain notations, were not necessarily exculpating; and 4) the untainted evidence against both Giambalvo and Ungar was not insubstantial. Weighing these factors, the court denies the defendant's motions for sanctions.

SO ORDERED.

UNITED STATES of America v. Ricardo "Ricky" VELA

673 F.2d 86

United States Court of Appeals, Fifth Circuit
April 2, 1982

I. Background

On November 12, 1980, a grand jury sitting in the Southern District of Texas' Laredo Division handed down a five–count indictment charging Ricky Vela with: conspiring to possess with intent to distribute cocaine in violation of 21 U.S.C. § § 846 & 841(a)(1), possession of a small sample of cocaine with intent to distribute it in violation of 21 U.S.C. § 841(a)(1), distribution of that small sample of cocaine in violation of 21 U.S.C. 841(a)(1), possession of 639.1 grams of cocaine with intent to distribute it in violation of 21 U.S.C. § 841(a)(1), and distribution of 639.1 grams of cocaine in violation of 21 U.S.C. § 841(a)(1). Vela was tried before a jury which acquitted him of the four counts alleging substantive offenses, but convicted him of the conspiracy count. He was sentenced to serve a six–year prison term and fined $10,000.

* * * * *

III. Admission of Telephone Records

Vela argues that the district court erred in admitting copies of the telephone bills of Vela, Caballero, and Gutierrez under the business records exception to the hearsay rule because a proper foundation was not laid to support the reliability of Southwestern Bell Company's computer–billing process. We hold that the foundation was adequate to support admissibility under Rule 803(6).

At trial, an employee of Southwestern Bell described as custodian of records sponsored copies of the telephone bills. He testified that the copies were made from microfiche records prepared by the comptroller's department of the company, that the records were prepared in the usual course of the company's regularly–conducted business activity, and that it was part of that activity to prepare such records. When questioned by Vela's counsel outside of the jury's presence, the employee explained the process by which automatic call identification equipment registers the dialing of long–distance telephone calls on electronic tapes. The tapes are then transmitted to the comptroller's office where the information is transferred into billing tapes. Computers are used at two stages: first, in the recording of the initial dialing, and second, in the computation and preparation of bills in the comptroller's office. The testifying employee vouched only for the general reliability of the process. He was unable to identify the brand, type, and model of each computer, and to vouch for the working condition of the specific equipment during the billing periods covered.

The district court admitted the bills under Rule 803(6) declaring that they "would be even more reliable than . . . average business record[s] because they are not even touched by the hand of man." The defense had previously examined the custodian outside of the jury's presence. Before the jury returned, the court advised the defense that it might want to attack the credibility of the bills on cross–examination. However, the defense never cross–examined the telephone company employee in the presence of the jury. Moreover, the defense did not attack the accuracy of the bills during its closing argument. Indeed, the only reference made to the bills during the defense's closing argument is a suggestion that the jury consult the bills for information tending to exonerate Vela.

Vela's central attack of admissibility of the bills under Rule 803(6) is that the prosecution did not lay a satisfactory foundation. Vela does not dispute that insofar as the custodian of the records testified that the records were kept in the regular course of business the dictates of Rule 803(6) were satisfied. What Vela does argue is that by failing to establish that the computers involved in the billing process were in proper working order a satisfactory foundation was not made and Vela was denied confrontation rights.

Our review of a trial court's decision to admit business records is a limited one. We test it only for abuse of discretion. *See Rosenberg v. Collins*, 624 F.2d 659, 665 (5th Cir. 1980). While the suggestion has been made that there are unique foundation requirements for the admission of computerized business records under Rule 803(6), *see generally United States v Scholle*, 553 F.2d 1109, 1125 (8th Cir.), *cert. denied*, 434 U.S. 940, 98 S.Ct. 432, 54 L.Ed.2d 300 (1977); *McCormick's Handbook of the Law of Evidence* 733–34 (2d ed. 1972), this court has previously held that "computer data compilations . . . should be treated as any other record of regularly conducted activity." *Rosenberg v. Collins*, 624 F.2d at 665. Like the computer records in the *Rosenberg* case, the telephone company's long distance billing records are "sufficiently trustworthy in the eyes of this disinterested company to be relied on by the company in conducting its day to day business affairs." *Id.*

The prosecution laid a proper predicate for the admission of the bills. A telephone company employee explained the precise manner in which the billing data are compiled. The failure to certify the brand or proper operating condition of the machinery involved does not betray a circumstance of preparation indicating any lack of trustworthiness. Fed.R.Evid. 803(6). This court has previously stated that computer evidence is not intrinsically unreliable. *United States v. Fendley*, 522 F.2d 181, 187 (5th Cir.1975); *Olympic Insurance Co. v. H.D. Harrison, Inc.*, 418 F.2d 669, 670 (5th Cir. 1969). Vela's arguments for a level of authentication greater than that regularly practiced by the company in its own business activities go beyond the rule and its reasonable purpose to admit truthful evidence. The court did not abuse its discretion in admitting the bills or deny Vela his confrontation rights. At best, the arguments made go to the weight that should be accorded the evidence, not its admissibility. *See United States v. Scholle*, 553 F.2d at 1125.

UNIVERSAL FILM EXCHANGES, INC., et al. v. BENBAR CINEMA CORP., et al.

370 N.Y.S.2d 311

Supreme Court, Special Term, New York County
October 11, 1975

A motion was filed to confirm the report of a referee directed to hear and report as to credibility of defendants' claim of inability to locate records required to be produced by plaintiffs' notice and by order of the court. The Supreme Court, Irving H. Saypol, J., held that where defendants wholly failed to explain or justify in any credible manner their failure to produce records required by licensing agreement, and a notice to produce and a court order, defendants' answers would be stricken and an inquest directed to determine damages to be assessed.

Order in accordance with opinion.

Motion to confirm the report of a referee is consolidated for decision with motion numbered 99 of November 13, 1974, to reject the report.

The court directed the referee to hear and report as to the credibility of the defendant's claim of inability to locate the records required to be produced by the plaintiffs' notice and by order of this court.

This action was commenced to recover license fees in excess of those reported and paid by the defendants due from the defendants for the leasing by them of the plaintiffs' film for exhibition to the public. The documents which were not produced are the documents which prove actual attendance and box office receipts needed definitively to determine the fees due the plaintiffs.

The license agreements on which this action is based all provide that the plaintiffs shall have the right to examine these records and to audit the defendants' admission and box office receipts. In 1972, prior to the commencement of this action, the plaintiffs requested such examination and audit. It was after the defendants' refusal that this action was brought. The defendants' chief executive officer has admitted that he saw the records requested in January of 1973, after the pre–action audit demand, and that they were stored in a room on the defendant's premises.

For this reason and based on the testimony adduced before the referee, the court is constrained to agree with the referee who heard the testimony. The defendants have wholly failed to explain or justify in any credible manner their failure to produce the records required by the agreement, the notice to produce and the order of this court. In these circumstances to permit the defendants so to frustrate the plaintiffs' rights would frustrate too any opportunity for the plaintiffs ever to ensure that they get an "honest count" from the licensees.

The plaintiffs' motion to confirm the referee's report is granted and the cross motion to reject denied.

For failure to produce the records required the answers will be stricken and an inquest directed to determine the damages to be assessed. Settle order.

Gregoria VALCIN and Gerard Valcin, her husband v. PUBLIC HEALTH TRUST OF DADE COUNTY, d/b/a Jackson Memorial Hospital

473 So.2d 1297

District Court of Appeal of Florida, Third District
June 5, 1984

In May 1978, after Gregoria Valcin had given birth to her fifth child at Jackson Memorial Hospital, she asked to be sterilized. Accordingly, Dr. Shroder, a member of the hospital staff, performed a Pomeroy tubal ligation on Valcin six days after the birth. About a year and a half later, Valcin suffered a ruptured ectopic (tubal) pregnancy which almost caused her death. According to Valcin, this near fatality caused her permanent physical and emotional problems.

In 1981, Valcin, joined by her husband brought suit against the defendant, Public Health Trust of Dade County, d/b/a Jackson Memorial Hospital, alleging that the hospital, through its agents, (1) breached its warranty that the sterilization procedure performed on Mrs. Valcin would be one hundred per cent effective, (2) failed to fully inform her of the risks of a sterilization procedure in obtaining her consent, and (3) negligently performed the procedure. From a summary judgment entered in the hospital's favor on all three counts, the Valcins appeal.

* * * * *

There is little question that Valcin's ability to prove her negligence claim against the hospital has been substantially prejudiced by the absence of critical hospital records. Whether the ultimate sanction of entering a judgment as to liability against the hospital should be imposed depends, in our view, on what the proof ultimately shows as to the reason the records cannot be produced. Since the evidence concerning the reason the records cannot be produced is peculiarly within the knowledge of the hospital, we deem it fair to preliminarily impose upon the hospital the burden of proving by the greater weight of the evidence that the records are not missing due to the intentional or deliberate act or omission on the part of the hospital or its employees. If the fact–finder, under appropriate instructions, determines that the hospital has sustained its burden of showing that Dr. Shroder did not deliberately omit making an operative report or, if one was made, that the hospital did not deliberately remove or destroy the report, then the fact that the record is missing will merely raise a presumption that the surgical procedure was negligently performed, which presumption may be rebutted by the hospital by the greater weight of the evidence. However, if the fact–finder is not satisfied that the records are missing due to inadvertence or negligence, then a conclusive, irrebuttable presumption that the surgical procedure was negligently

performed will arise, and judgment as to liability shall be entered in favor of Valcin.

Thus, we hold that where a health care provider, statutorily and morally charged with the responsibility of making and maintaining records as a part of its obligation to promote the safe and adequate treatment of patients, negligently fails to do so, such health care provider shall have the burden of proving that the treatment which such missing records would reflect was performed non–negligently; and that where such health care provider intentionally fails to make or maintain such records, the treatment which such missing records would reflect shall be deemed negligent and the provider adjudged liable.

In so holding, we plow no new ground. The burden–shifting principle is not new or novel. There are no hard–and–fast standards governing the allocation of the burden of proof in every situation. The issue, rather, "is merely a question of policy and fairness based on experience in different situations." 9 Wigmore, *Evidence ¶ 2486 (Chadbourn rev.1981)*. Likewise, the remedy of imposing liability for an intentional interference with an opposing party's right to seek redress in the courts is well precedented. *See Mercer v. Raine*, 443 So.2d 944; *Agencias Maritimas Nicaraguenses v. Usatorres*, 435 So.2d 247.

Our holding takes into account that the maintenance of thousands of hospital records is a burdensome undertaking in which errors may be expected to occur, but it is nonetheless the hospital's duty to maintain such records for, *inter alia*, the benefit of the patient. Because, as a matter of policy and fairness, we believe it would be unduly harsh to impose liability on the hospital where it has negligently failed in this duty, but unduly lenient to simply condone such errors at a patient's expense, we have concluded that the burden should shift to the hospital to prove that it was not guilty of medical malpractice. Where, however, the patient has been deprived of access to essential records through the deliberate acts or omissions of the hospital, we deem it appropriate that the hospital be foreclosed from any opportunity to rebut the presumption of medical malpractice and that liability be imposed on it, the patient being left with the burden of proving damages only. We trust this will encourage the implementation of appropriate safeguards to avoid negligence in the maintenance of hospital records and, at the same time, deter intentional and deliberate misconduct.

* * * * *

Mary P. VALENTINO, individually and on behalf of all other persons similarly situated, Appellant v. UNITED STATES POSTAL SERVICE

674 F.2d 56

United States District Court, District of Columbia
March 26, 1982

GINSBURG, Circuit Judge: This action, brought under Title VII of the Civil Rights Act of 1964, as amended, 42 U.S.C. § 2000e et. seq. centers on the promotion system for upper echelon positions instituted in January 1976 at United States Postal Service (USPS) Headquarters. Plaintiff-appellant Mary P. Valentino charges that the system, in operation, accords women disadvantageous treatment based upon their sex. Valentino pursues on appeal an individual charge that, under the promotion system in question, she was discriminatorily denied advancement to the position of Director of the Office of Employee Services, an office within the Employee and Labor Relations (E&LR) Group at USPS Headquarters. She also pursues, on behalf of a class, a charge that women holding upper echelon posts at USPS Headquarters since June 16, 1976, have been denied promotions on the basis of their sex.

* * * * *

I. The Individual Claim

A. Facts

Mary P. Valentino has had a long career in the personnel field in government service. Her USPS employment, however, has been relatively short-term. She was initially engaged by the Post Office Department in October 1970 to work as an Employment Specialist (Women). Prior to that assignment, she held the post of Director of Personnel at the Equal Employment Opportunity Commission. The Post Office position increased her annual salary by approximately $2,000. She remained in this position only seven months. The functions of the Post Office Department were being transferred to USPS during this period and Valentino was among a group of employees eligible to retire early with a six-month pay bonus. She opted for early retirement and accepted a bonus of approximately $13,600.

Nine months later, in February 1972, Valentino reentered federal service first at the Food and Drug Administration and, in December 1972, at the Consumer Product Safety Commission (CPSC), where she became Director of Personnel. In late 1973 and early 1974, USPS officials sought out Valentino and she accepted work at USPS Headquarters commencing February 1974 as Director, Office of Career Planning, in the E&LR Group. At CPSC, her annual salary was $32,932. Her starting salary at USPC was $33,500; unlike most early retirees who returned to postal employment, she was not required to repay the six-month bonus paid to her in May 1971. Valentino's new office at USPS had a total staff of three; it was responsible for supervision of Women's Program and career planning for postal employees.

In sum, until 1976, it appears that Valentino's own Post Office and USPS employment experience entailed no gender-based unfavorable treatment, and we do not understand Valentino to contend otherwise. Rather, her individual claim stems from a 1987 efficiency-oriented realignment of the E&LR Group, which eliminated the Office of Career Planning, and her unsuccessful bids for promotion to two newly-created posts.

* * * * *

The great debates concerning the nature and use of statistical proof in employment discrimination cases should not obscure the fact that nonstatistical proof also plays an important role in the determination of the prima facie case in many class actions, particularly where . . . the statistical sample is small or the disparity not egregious.

B. Schlei & P. Grossman, *supra,* 1976 main text at 1193. When the capability of statistics to show discrimination is limited, see, *e.g., id.* at 1190, 1979 Supp. at 329-30, plaintiffs can press into better service nonstatistical proof of disparate treatment. See *supra,* pp. 19-20; F. Morris, Current Trends in the Use (and Misuse) of Statistics in Employment Discrimination Litigation 49 (1977).

In this case, the combination of unrefined statistics and thin proof of individual instances of discrimination leaves the adjudicator without any basis for concluding that gender impeded Valentino and the class she would represent from moving into the highly skilled, diverse positions in the upper ranks at USPS Headquarters. If race or sex bias in fact infects selection across-the-board for jobs at the top, however, it should not be impossible to assemble the evidence from which a pattern of discrimination can be inferred. "[P]ractitioners should not lose sight of the fact that employment discrimination cases require the same ingenuity regarding methods of proof as any other court litigation." B. Schlei & P. Grossman, *supra,* 1976 main text at 1193 (footnote omitted).

From January 1976 to October 1979, 831 vacancy announcements resulted in promotions to jobs at level 17 or higher. 579 of the files in question were complete, 86 were incomplete, and 166 had been destroyed pursuant to routine USPS record destruction procedures. Valentino contends the "spoliation" doctrine should have been invoked against USPS for its destruction of relevant EVS files. See *Boyd v. Ozark Air Lines, Inc.,* 568 F.2d 50, 53 (8th Cir. 1977); *Vick v. Texas Employment Comm'n.* 514 F.2d 734, 737 (5th Cir. 1975); *United States v. Roelof Const. Co.,* 418 F.2d 1328, 1331 (9th Cir. 1969). However, the circumstances of the destruction here provide no basis for attributing bad faith to USPS. See *Vick,* 514 F.2d

at 737. Until the June 13, 1978, certification of a class the district court considered appropriate and manageable, USPS had not clear indication of its obligation regarding record preservation. (Valentino's initial delineation of the class to encompass all past, present, and future female USPS employees and applicants for employment addressed a work force of over 650,000.) Upon certification of the class, USPS immediately acted to preserve records relating to the class claim. We find no reason to disagree with the district court's disposition of this issue. See 511 F.Supp. at 938-39, 953-54. *EEOC v. American Nat'l. Bank,* 652 F.2d at 1195-96, cited by Valentino, holds that an employer who destroys records cannot use the lack of records to lessen its burden on rebuttal; it does not address the relationship between an employer's routine destruction of records no longer in use and the plaintiff's burden.

* * * * *

Nancy W. VEEDER v. TRUSTEES OF BOSTON COLLEGE

85 F.R.D. 13

United States District Court, D. Massachusetts
October 12, 1979

Plaintiff, a college professor, brought action against her employer alleging discrimination on account of her sex in pay as well as promotion and tenure. Upon defendant's motions for sanctions for failure to produce a requested document in response to discovery efforts, the District Court, Zobel, J., held that although plaintiff violated both letter and spirit of discovery by attempting to destroy all copies of documents which defendant had sought to recover, trial court could not impose sanctions of dismissal for reason that defendant was able to obtain copy of the document but court would assess attorney fees.

Order in accordance with opinion.

Defendant has moved for sanctions including dismissal of this action and an order awarding reasonable attorney's fees and expenses because plaintiff not only failed to produce a requested document in response to defendants' discovery efforts, but, in fact, destroyed all copies of the document known to her. Plaintiff, a professor at Boston College, brought this action under Title VII of the Civil Rights Act of 1964, 42 U.S.C. § § 2000e *et seq.*, and under the Equal Pay Act, 29 U.S.C. § 206(d). She alleges that defendant discriminated against her on account of her sex in pay as well as promotion and tenure. The document in issue is a "final reference" which was part of her file and part of her record as a graduate student at the Smith College School of Social Work.

The facts underlying defendants' motion are not in dispute. Defendants requested the production of documents and a waiver of privacy as to certain of these documents at Smith college which were protected by the so–called Buckley Amendment, 20 U.S.C. § 1232g. Counsel for the parties disagreed as to the right of defendants to production of these papers, plaintiff refused to produce them or authorize their disclosure, and defendants undertook to obtain them by means of a subpoena duces tecum directed to Smith College. After receiving notice of defendants' intention to serve that subpoena, but before the taking of the deposition of Smith College, plaintiff traveled to Smith, requested to see her records, and after reviewing them, destroyed all copies of the "final reference" in her file. Defendants thereafter did take the deposition of the Dean of the Smith College School of Social Work and thus learned of the plaintiff's actions, but also obtained a copy of the destroyed document which had been found in yet another file in the basement of the School.

Rule 37(d), Fed.R.Civ.P., 28 U.S.C., authorized the imposition of various sanctions for failure to respond to certain discovery requests including an order of dismissal and an order for the payment of the reasonable expenses caused by the failure.

There is no question that plaintiff violated both the letter and the spirit of the discovery rules. Whatever legitimate grounds she may have had for contesting defendants' right to inspect the "final reference," she was bound to assert them in court in accordance with the rules which are designed to afford both sides a fair and impartial hearing. This system of deciding disputes cannot tolerate self–help such as plaintiff's in the instant case, and survive.

The matter of an appropriate sanction is more difficult. In the final analysis defendants were not harmed in the preparation of their case as plaintiff did not succeed in destroying all copies of the document. Dismissal is not, therefore, an appropriate sanction. Defendants were, however, put to the expense of searching out the document by means of a deposition and subpoena duces tecum. That expense shall be borne by plaintiff. Defendants seek an additional order prohibiting plaintiff from destroying any other documents and requiring her to file a statement attesting to the accuracy of all answers she has heretofore given in response to various requests for discovery. That request is denied.

The motion for sanctions is allowed and plaintiff is ordered to pay defendants the expenses of taking the deposition of Smith College School of Social Work in the total amount of $1,323 including attorney's fees in the amount of $1,225 and disbursements of $98. Said payment shall be made by plaintiff within 20 days.

Mary VICK v. TEXAS EMPLOYMENT COMMISSION

514 F.2d 734

United States Court of Appeals, Fifth Circuit
June 12, 1975

Mary Vick, a mathematical analyst laid off by TRW Systems, Inc. applied to the Texas Employment Commission for job referrals and unemployment compensation. Despite her initial eligibility, the Texas Employment Commission (TEC) deemed Vick unavailable for work and thus ineligible to receive further unemployment compensation benefits during the last trimester of her pregnancy.

This was in accordance with general and settled Commission policy and despite medical evidence submitted by Vick of her individual continuing ability to work. Ineligibility for benefits, under further general Commission policy, continued until six weeks after childbirth, at which time Vick could produce proof, inter alia, of her ability to return to work. Vick alleges, as well, that TEC refused to refer her to jobs during her last trimester. Claiming to be a victim of sex discrimination, Vick filed a suit in federal district court, alleging unlawful employment practices under Title VII of the 1964 Civil Rights Act, 42 U.S.C. § 2000e et seq. and violation of Fourteenth Amendment rights, and seeking declaratory relief and damages. After consideration, the lower court concluded and so declared that TEC had employed an impermissible sex stereotype in arriving at an across–the–board, three–month cutoff date, that Vick could have performed the job requirements of her job up to a period six weeks prior to the scheduled birth of her child and would have again been able to work — subject to submission of proof in compliance with TEC guidelines — 30 days after giving birth. Thus, she was available for work as required under the Texas Unemployment Compensation statute. However, the court found Vick had failed to show TEC negligent or in malfeasance in referring her to jobs. Acting under 42 U.S.C. § 2000e–5(g), the court deemed the "appropriate affirmative action" to be award of back unemployment benefits, excluding the postnatal period since Vick had never complied with the TEC proof requirements. Attorneys' fees were awarded as well. Both parties appealed.

* * * * *

* * * As a final point, Vick contends that the court should have used the adverse inference rule to find TEC in violation of Title VII. Specifically, TEC records on Vick were destroyed before trial, apparently pursuant to Commission regulations governing disposal of inactive records. Vick's argument is unpersuasive. The adverse inference to be drawn from destruction of records is predicated on bad conduct of the defendant. "Moreover, the circumstances of the act must manifest bad faith. Mere negligence is not enough, for it does not sustain an inference

of consciousness of a weak case." McCormick, Evidence § 273 at 660–61 (1972), 31A C.J.S. Evidence § 156(2) (1964). There was indication here that the records were destroyed under routine procedures without bad faith and well in advance of Vick's service of interrogatories. Certainly, there were sufficient grounds for the trial court to so conclude.

* * * * *

VILLANEUVA COMPANIA NAVIERA, S.A., owner of the Liberian S.S. Devon v. S.S. MATILDE CORRADO, her furniture, engines, tackle, apparel, etc., in rem, and "Corrado" Societa Di Navigazione, a foreign corporation, as owner and/or operator of said vessel in personam

211 F.Supp. 930

United States District Court, E.D. Virginia, Norfolk Division
December 31, 1962

Actions *in rem* and *in personam* are pending by and between the owners of the bulk carrier DEVON and the owners of the Canadian liberty–type vessel MATILDE CORRADO. Each vessel claims that the other dragged anchor and drifted. A collision occurred on the night of January 24, 1958. For all practical purposes the only factual issue for determination is an inquiry as to which vessel dragged anchor. For reasons hereinafter stated the Court concludes that the MATILDE CORRADO was the offending vessel and appropriate decrees should be entered in these consolidated actions in admiralty.

* * * * *

The Court has previously expressed its views with respect to changes and erasures in log books. *Skibs Aktieselskapet Orenor v. The Audrey*, D.C., 181 F.Supp. 697, affirmed sub nom., *Gratsos v. The Moisie Bay*, 4 Cir., 287 F.2d 706. It is sufficient to state that an intentional falsification of material records presumptively destroys the weight of the offender's evidence as to the entire case. The master of the MATILDE CORRADO, who made the entries for the night of January 24, 1958, insists that there were no erasures but it does not require the services of an expert to conclude that erasures were made at the pertinent times noted. This is not to say that every erasure on a log book is fatal. Proctors for the MATILDE CORRADO point to erasures in the DEVON's log. Two minor changes do appear at the time of the collision entry but the gist of what happened appears to be a continuous entry made immediately after the collision. However, while the log erasures are persuasive, the case need not be determined solely on the fact that they were made. The Court does feel that such erasures, coupled with the master's denial that any were made, tend to destroy the credibility of the testimony given by the master of the MATILDE CORRADO.

* * * * *

Charles G. VOGLER and Elizabeth Vogler v. COMMISSIONER

T.C. Memo. 1975–357

December 18, 1975

Respondent determined deficiencies in petitioners' Federal income tax for the tax years 1970 and 1971 in the amounts of $2,778.36 and $3,072.71, respectively. The only issue for decision is whether petitioners have substantiated business expenses and charitable contributions in the amounts deducted for the years in issue.

Findings of Fact

Some of the facts have been stipulated and are found accordingly. The petitioners, husband and wife, filed joint individual income tax returns for 1970 and 1971 with the Central Service Center in Covington, Kentucky. Their residence at the time the petition was filed was in Dearborn, Michigan.

Petitioner, Charles G. Vogler, earned

$18,764.13 and $19,005.92 in 1970 and 1971, respectively, as a stockbroker with Reynolds and Company. Petitioners on their returns for 1970 and 1971 deducted $11,191.38 and $11,914.58, respectively, as employee business expenses related to the income from Reynolds and Company. Respondent allowed the deduction for both years only to the extent of $5700, approximately 30 percent of Charles Vogler's income as a stockbroker. Respondent also reduced the charitable contributions deduction claimed by petitioners and allowed a deduction of $850 for each year as contrasted to $3201 and $3234 claimed by petitioners for 1970 and 1971, respectively.

The records of business expenses and charitable contributions were maintained by petitioner, Charles G. Vogler, and consisted of slips of paper prepared by him from bills, canceled checks and receipts. No expense books or diaries were maintained by petitioners for 1970 or 1971.

On or about May 2, 1972 when the petitioners were in Tennessee, their residence was burglarized. A neighbor reported the burglary and on May 16, 1972 petitioners made a supplementary report to the police, but at the time did report any missing business records. On June 24, 1972, after an audit was commenced, petitioners in an inventory of items missing after the burglary, reported that documents pertaining to business expenses and charitable contributions had been stolen.

Opinion

The sole issue is whether petitioners are entitled to deductions for business expenses and charitable contributions in the amounts claimed on the returns for the years in issue. Respondent contends that petitioners have failed to substantiate the disputed deductions and the deductions in excess of amounts allowed by the respondent must, therefore, be denied. We are compelled to agree.

Petitioners claimed travel expenses were inconsistent with the total mileage on the odometers of their cars. Additionally, the amount of the charitable contributions involved were very large to have been made in cash, and many of the organizations involved would presumably have records available to substantiate some of the contributions made. Yet petitioners have failed to produce any secondary evidence, other than their oral testimony, which would verify the amount and nature of the disputed deductions. See sections 1.162–17(d) and 1.170–1(a), Income Tax Regs. Petitioners' vague testimony regarding both the business expense and charitable contributions deductions is clearly insufficient to carry their burden of proof. *Robert Neaderland* [Dec. 29,255], 52 T.C. 532 (1969), affd. on other grounds [70–1 USTC ¶ 9340] 424 F.2d 639 (2d Cir. 1970); Rule 142, Tax Court Rules of Practice. Moreover, we cannot agree that respondent's determination was, as petitioners contend, arbitrary and unreasonable. On the contrary, respondent's determination was, under the circumstances, generous. Consequently,

Decision will be entered for the respondent.

W.T. GRANT COMPANY v. Lazarus JOSEPH, as Comptroller of the City of New York

159 N.Y.S.2d 150

Court of Appeals of New York
Jan. 10, 1957

* * * * *

The system used by Grant for collection of the sales tax was, in general, as follows. A metal box, with a coin slit in it, was attached to the side of each cash register; a copy of the comptroller's bracket schedule was affixed to the register; and the sales clerk would consult the schedule to determine the amount of the tax to be collected and would then deposit that amount in the metal box. The proceeds of the sale, exclusive of the tax, were separately rung up on the cash register and deposited in the register drawer. No written record, however, was kept of the individual tax items collected, either in the form of sales slips, cash register tapes or otherwise, nor apparently was there any permanent record of the individual sales transactions. At the end of the work day, the

manager or assistant manager of the store would unlock the metal tax box, the tax receipts would be counted and inserted in a special "tax bag" and the total entered on a special form. The tax receipts would subsequently be recounted by the cashier, and the aggregate figure recorded on a daily cash statement. Upon the basis of such weekly cash statements, Grant filed quarter–annual sales tax returns with the city.

* * * * *

Upon the auditing of its returns by the comptroller, Grant failed to produce or make available any records of the individual sales, of the amount collected as tax on each such transaction or of the number of sales falling into each particular sales tax bracket. Taking the position that Grant had failed to comply with the recordkeeping requirements of the law, Administrative Code, § N41–2.0, subd. e; § N41–4.0, and that the returns were insufficient, § N41–7.0, the comptroller's auditors proceeded to have a test check made, and the deficiency here under attack was assessed on the basis of that check.

* * * * *

Since, as we have indicated, the vendor occupies the role of taxpayer, as well as collector, and is liable to the city for the taxes which should have been paid by his purchasers (or the amount of taxes actually collected, if that be greater), we would expect the local law to require the vendor to maintain such records, including a record of individual sales, as bear on determining his liability. And, sure enough, so the local law plainly provides. Thus, the statute mandates "Every person * * * [to] keep records of receipts and of the tax payable thereon," Administrative Code. § N41–4.0, and further declares that "Upon each taxable sale * * * the tax to be collected shall be stated and charged separately from the sale price * * * and shown separately on any record thereof, § N41–2.0, subd. e. Moreover, by article 24 of the regulations promulgated by the comptroller in 1938, and effective during the entire period here involved, a vendor is called upon to maintain "such other records as may be necessary or required to determine his tax liability or the extent thereof."

Obviously, these requirements cannot be satisfied by keeping records only of *total* sales receipts and of *total* collections, without any record of taxes payable on *individual* sales where, as here, the extent of the vendor's tax liability turns on the individual sales receipts and the tax payable thereon in each instance. If no records were kept of individual sales, if the appellant's system were sanctioned, there would be no way of ascertaining whether the vendor's sales clerks were collecting, or whether the vendor was remitting, the full amount of taxes required to be collected from the purchasers. The sales clerks themselves would, for all practical purposes, be the ones administering the sales tax law. Certainly, the collection of the sales tax was never intended to be solely dependent on, and measured by, the honesty, efficiency and accuracy of the vendor's sales personnel.

Since Grant kept no records whatsoever, not even cash register tapes, adequately reflecting the factors essential to the computation and determination of the sales taxes which should have been collected for the years gone by, it became necessary for the comptroller, pursuant to the authority vested in him, to estimate them "on the basis of external indices * * other factors," Administrative Code, § N41–7.0; Sales Tax Regulations, art. 24. * * *

* * * * *

WASCO, INC. v. ECONOMIC DEVELOPMENT UNIT, INC.

461 So.2d 1055

Court of Appeal of Louisiana Fourth Circuit
October 22, 1984

* * * * *

On March 3, 1978, plaintiff–appellee, WASCO, INC., a corporation wholly owned by Spencer Washington and his wife, and defendant–appellant, ECONOMIC DEVELOPMENT UNIT, INC., a non profit community services corporation ("E.D.U.") entered into a written contract whereby WASCO, Inc. agreed to provide manage-

ment and janitorial services for certain commercial real estate owned by E.D.U. The term of the contract was from March, 1978 through December, 1982. On November 8, 1978, the contract was amended to delete management services; WASCO, INC. was to provide janitorial services only at a monthly rate of $3500.00. Provision was made for termination or suspension by E.D.U. upon written notice of twenty–one days.

On the night of May 11, 1979, A fire occurred in the offices of Total Community Action, Inc. (hereinafter T.C.A.) which were located in the building which formed the basis of contract. Mr. Spencer Washington (the President of WASCO, Inc.) and two WASCO employees were subsequently arrested on suspicion of aggravated arson in connection with that fire.

By letter dated August 3, 1979, E.D.U. informed WASCO that it "ha[d] no alternative, but to indefinitely suspend your maintenance contract with E.D.U. A determination will be made to resume services based on the outcome of the alleged charges filed against you by the District Attorney's Office. This suspension has an effective date as of Friday, August 31, 1979."

Plaintiff performed no further services nor did it make any formal protest of the contract termination until September 23, 1981. On October 19, 1981, WASCO filed suit seeking $640,000.00 as damages for breach of contract by E.D.U., through its trial attorney, filed an answer in which it denied that it breached the contract with WASCO. On May 3, 1982, a set of Interrogatories to E.D.U. was filed by WASCO. On May 24, 1982, WASCO filed a Motion to Compel Answers to Interrogatories. That matter was heard on October 22, 1982. E.D.U.'s attorney made no appearance on behalf of his client. The Court ordered E.D.U. to answer the interrogatories prior to November 8, 1982, in default of which, "defendant shall not be allowed to utilize any information not produced, at trial."

The interrogatories remained unanswered. The matter proceeded to trial on April 28, 1983. After plaintiff presented its case, the trial judge refused to allow defendant's witnesses to testify because E.D.U.'s trial attorney had failed to answer WASCO's interrogatories. The trial was conducted essentially as a default except that defendant's counsel was allowed to proceed with cross–examination of plaintiff's witnesses.

Because we reverse this judgment on other grounds, we do not address the correctness of the action of the trail judge in prohibiting the introduction of any evidence by defendant.

Assuming, arguendo, that E.D.U. unilaterally breached the contract without legal cause and, therefore, is liable for any damages resulting therefrom, including loss of profits, did WASCO sustain the burden of proof required for such an award? We find it did not.

In *Al Smiths's Plumbing & Heating Service, Inc. v. River Crest, Inc.,* 365 S.2d 1122 (La.App. 4th Cir.1978), this court held as follows: "Lost profits are recoverable in an action for breach of contract where the amount can be proved with reasonable certainty. *George W. Garig Transfer v. Harris,* 226 La. 117, 75 S.2d 28 (1954). Loss of profit awards may not rest on speculation or conjecture (citations omitted) unless direct evidence is not available to establish this element of damage."

In the recent case of *F & F Transfer, Inc. v. Tardo,* 425 S.2d 874 (La.App 4th Cir., 1983) we stated:

The allowance of loss of profits as an element of damages is more liberal in actions purely in tort, as opposed to actions for breach of contract. See: C.C. Art. 2315. *Shreveport Laundries v. Red Iron Drilling Co.,* 192 S. 985 (La.App., 2nd Cir., 1939). In such cases, the loss of profits is recoverable as an element of damages, if they are proven with reasonable certainty. *Mire v. Timmons,* 155 S.2nd 265 (La.App., 2d Cir., 1959). That is, the plaintiff must show that the loss of profits is more probable than not. *Jordon v. Travelers,* 257 La. 995, 245 S.2d 151 (1971). A claim for loss of profits will not be supported by estimates of loss. *Shreveport Laundries v. Red Iron Drilling Co., supra.* This is especially true in those cases in which corroborative evidence is shown to be available and is not produced. *Peoples Moss Gin Co., Inc. v.*

Jenkins, 270 S.2d 285 (La.App., 3rd Cir., 1972). Although the absence of independent corroborative evidence is not always fatal, the lack of even a minimal degree of detail and specificity in the plaintiff's testimony, regarding the issue of lost profits, would preclude recovery of this item of damages. *Casadaban v. Bel Chemical & Supply Co., Inc.,* 322 S.2d 854 (La.App., 1st Cir., 1975).

* * * * *

There is no presumption that a corporation will make a profit solely because of the existence of a contract. Loss of profits as an element of damages, must be proved in accordance with the principles earlier enunciated.

In support of WASCO's claim for damages for breach of contract, WASCO offered the testimony of Spencer Washington, its President, and copies of two acts of sale of immovable property. The properties were alleged to have been lost by foreclosure because of E.D.U.'s breach of contract causing WASCO to have insufficient revenues to pay the mortgage notes.

No business records of WASCO were introduced in support of its claim for damages. When questioned by the Court, Mr. Washington stated that "all the records were seized by the Federal Government" and that WASCO's income tax returns for 1978, 1979 and 1980 "were still pending," and that returns for 1981 and 1982 were filed. The 1981 and 1982 tax returns were not offered into evidence nor did plaintiff offer any corroborating documentary evidence.

No evidence of any attempt to recover the allegedly missing records was introduced. WASCO offered no evidence of correspondence requesting the return of the records. No one was deposed or subpoenaed to testify as to the whereabouts of the records or to substantiate WASCO's claim of their unavailability. WASCO failed to seek the issuance of a subpoena duces tecum addressed to the U.S. Attorney or any other U.S. government employee ordering the production of the missing records before or at trial. Under these circumstances we find that WASCO failed to show that corroborative evidence of claimed loss of profits was unavailable.

In lieu of the business records of WASCO, plaintiff relied upon the testimony of Mr. Washington. He testified that WASCO had approximately five or six employees in 1978 and that the weekly payroll was approximately $300.00 to $500.00. He declined to estimate the exact cost of janitorial supplies; stating that some of the supplies were purchased once every six months. He concluded by estimating a profit margin on the contract of sixty percent (60%).

Although Spencer Washington testified that WASCO retained the services of a prominent C.P.A., the accountant was not called as a witness to testify on behalf of WASCO or to furnish information from his records in lieu of the missing records.

WASCO did not offer any expert testimony to establish the anticipated profits that would be customary in the janitorial service industry as a measure of damages in lieu of the proof that would normally be supplied by its missing business records.

Our examination of the record discloses that the award of damages was based solely upon the uncorroborated testimony of Spencer Washington. His testimony dealt in generalities, estimates and speculation, including his estimate of a corporate profit margin on this contract of sixty percent (60%). Since the unexpired term of the contract was forty months with the monthly fee of $3,500.00, the claimed sixty (60%) percent margin of profit would have amounted to $84,000.00. WASCO offered no evidence of its margin of profit on any other contract that it performed during the period 1979–1982, or to the date of trial.

The trial judge rejected Mr. Washington's sixty (60%) percent profit estimate and then substituted his own conjecture the "$25,000.00 is a reasonable amount of damages to be awarded to plaintiff." This would have been a margin of profit of 17.86%. The trial judge, in his reasons for judgment, offered no explanation, formula, or evidentiary basis for his selection of this profit margin in assessing his award of damages, nor did the trial court cite any authority for the award of the attorney's fees in the sum of $5000.00 in the absence of any provision for attorney's fees in the contract.

Our review of the record discloses that the trial judge was clearly wrong in awarding a judgment for loss of profits in this case, as such award is purely speculative and unsupported by any competent evidence. WASCO may not substitute for the records it failed to produce, an uncorroborated estimate as to its loss of profits as proof of such loss. We further find that the lack of competent evidence of damages is such as to preclude any award, even under the holding in *Jordan v. Travelers Insurance Co., supra,* relative to the degree of certainty required to support an award of monetary damages.

Accordingly, the judgment of the trial court is reversed; plaintiff to pay all costs of these proceedings.

WM. T. THOMPSON CO., a Missouri corporation v. GENERAL NUTRITION CORPORATION, INC., a Pennsylvania corporation, dba GNC and General Nutrition Center, Inc., a subsidiary of General Nutrition Corporation, a Pennsylvania corporation. GENERAL NUTRITION CORPORATION, INC., et al v. WM. T. THOMPSON CO., a Missouri corporation

593 F.Supp. 1443

United States District Court, D.C. California
September 7, 1984

Findings of Fact

1. GNC operates the nation's largest chain of health food and health products stores. For many years preceding this litigation, GNC stores sold vitamins manufactured by Thompson, along with competing "national brand" vitamins and GNC's private label vitamins. In May of 1978, GNC commenced a "national brands" sales campaign, featuring extensive newspaper advertisement stating that its national brand vitamins, including Thompson's, were on sale at 20 percent off.

Thompson subsequently concluded that GNC's advertisements were false and misleading on a variety of grounds, chief among them the charge that many GNC stores maintained inadequate stocks of Thompson products to meet expected customer demand. By letter dated July 28, 1978, counsel for Thompson notified GNC that Thompson was terminating sales of its products, on the ground that GNC's stores "either do not have the products in stock, have wholly inadequate inventory and/or outdated or reduced potency merchandise available for sale . . . " Thompson further charged that GNC was engaging in "bait and switch" advertising, using Thompson's products as the "bait," and invited GNC to immediately conduct a shelf inventory to determine for itself the accuracy of Thompson's allegations.

On August 17, 1978, Thompson filed its complaint in case No. CV 78–3206, asserting that GNC's advertising practices violated federal antitrust and state law.

3. On August 18, 1978, GNC filed suit against Thompson in the United States District Court for the Western District of Pennsylvania alleging essentially that Thompson had participated in an unlawful conspiracy to restrain trade in violation of the federal antitrust laws by suspending sales of its products to GNC. ("*General Nutrition Corporation, etc. v. Wm. T. Thompson Co.*, Civil Action No. 78–911").

4. The litigation referred to in paragraph 3 above was transferred to this Court on October 2, 1978, and assigned No. CV 78–3891 for identification purposes.

5. In each action, Thompson served discovery upon GNC in August and September, 1978 within a few weeks after the filing of each action. In No. CV 78–3206, Thompson served its initial Request for the Production of Documents on August 21, 1978, its First Interrogatories on August 23, 1978, and Notices of Depositions accompanied by subpoenas duces tecum to GNC directors and officers on August 25, 1978. In *General Nutrition Corporation, etc. v. Wm. T. Thompson Co.*, Civil Action no. 78–911, Thompson

filed its Notices of Depositions and Requests for Production of Documents to GNC directors and officers on September 13, 1978.

6. Thereafter, Thompson brought on a Motion for Preliminary Injunction pursuant to Rule 65, Federal Rules of Civil Procedures, which was served upon GNC along with accompanying points and authorities and other supporting affidavits and papers, on September 15, 1978. By this motion, Thompson sought to enjoin GNC from advertising Thompson products for which it did not have adequate inventories or supplies. Thompson's supporting and supplemental papers contained, among other things, a study and sworn findings by its retained consultant, Dr. Donald W. Vinson, in which that consultant had compared statistical samples of inventories of products in GNC stores with GNC's advertising claims and concluded that such claims were erroneous, false and deceptive. GNC opposed Thompson's preliminary injunction motion by alleging, *inter alia*, that its records reflected inventories of Thompson and other nationally–branded products in sufficient quantities to avoid the allegations of illegality made by Thompson, thus itself placing in further dispute the facts pertaining to inventory of products in GNC stores and the demand for such products.

7. From a time no later than August 25, 1978, and continuing at least until December 30, 1980, GNC created and maintained the following types of purchase, sale and inventory record, among others, which records are no longer available:

(a) Store Order Books, containing such information as a listing of each product which may be ordered by a given store, the maximum inventory level which that particular store was permitted to order of particular products (maximum inventory levels varied from product to product and from store to store), the prices at which individual products were to be sold in individual stores, and the location (by reference to shelf) of individual products in individual stores. Two copies of each Store Order Book were maintained by GNC, one in the Merchandising Department at GNC's headquarters in Pittsburgh and the other in the individual GNC stores, which were used by stores on a biweekly basis (each order book covering a 6 to 8 week order cycle) for taking inventory counts of what was in the store and for ordering additional products;

(b) Store Order Strips (for the time period between no later than August 25, 1978 and ending no earlier than the last week of September, 1979) which are strips of paper taken from each store's Order Book every other week and shipped to Pittsburgh for computer and other processing, and which contained such information as biweekly inventory counts and the amount of each item being ordered by the store;

(c) Store Invoices (otherwise sometimes called Stores–In–Detail Reports by GNC). These invoices, created each time an order was shipped from GNC's warehouse to a store in response to the store's previous biweekly order, contained the following information, *inter alia*: the date of the shipment, the number of units of each product ordered or demanded by the store, the number of units of each product shipped on that particular date to the store, the number of units in the store's inventory of particular products (as reported by the store on its biweekly order forms), and the price at which the shipped units of products were to be sold in individual stores;

(d) Fiscal year–end inventory count sheets, showing product–by–product unit counts (1) for 40% of the GNC stores taken in connection with the fiscal year–end inventory completed on or about January 29, 1979, and (2) for 100% of the GNC stores in connection with the fiscal year–end inventory completed by GNC on or about February 26, 1980;

(e) Quarterly inventory count sheets, showing product–by–product unit counts for each GNC store for inventories completed on or about November 4, 1979, May 2, 1980, August 3, 1980, and October 29, 1980;

(f) Daily Inventory Status Reports con-

taining, *inter alia*, product–by–product inventory data for the GNC warehouses;

(g) Daily and Weekly Ship/Non–Ship Reports containing product–by–product data concerning the failure or success of GNC warehouses in meeting the demand on the warehouses created by GNC store orders;

(g) Lost Sales Reports, which were produced at least weekly and which set forth the amounts of "non–shipments" (the difference between the amount ordered and amount shipped of a particular product) on a product–by–product basis from GNC's central warehouse facility at Preble Avenue, Pittsburgh, Pennsylvania; and

(i) Retail Level Summary Reports, which were produced by GNC every 4 to 8 weeks, and which showed average maximum inventory levels for each product in the GNC order book, as well as product–by–product price, cost and gross ˙profit percentage date.

8. GNC also maintained at its headquarters in Pittsburgh, between at least June 15, 1978 and December 31, 1980, computer files (electronically readable tapes, discs and/or cards) on which the following types of data appearing on the records set forth in paragraph 7 above were retained for a period of between 2 and 12 weeks, depending on the particular type of data: fiscal year–end inventory data, quarterly inventory data, biweekly inventory data, biweekly store order demand data, and biweekly maximum allowable inventory level data on a product–by–product basis.

9. On August 25, 1978, GNC had in its possession at least the following records:

(a) Store Order Books for each GNC store (with biweekly inventory data, biweekly maximum inventory level data, and biweekly store order demand data) containing information for the period from 10 to 16 weeks prior to August 25, 1978;

(b) Store Order Strips for each GNC

store containing biweekly inventory data and store order demand data for approximately 2 to 3 months prior to August 25, 1978;

(c) Store Invoices for at least 2 to 4 weeks prior to August 25, 1978; and

(d) Electronically–recorded computer historical records of biweekly store inventories, biweekly maximum store inventory levels, and biweekly store order demand data for approximately 4 months prior to August 25, 1978.

GNC's Violation of Its Duties to Preserve

10. All of the records set forth in Findings 7 and 9 above have been destroyed by GNC (here and hereafter "destroyed" includes the physical destruction, discarding, failure to retain in its possession, and — in the case of electronically–readable records — the erasure of records). None of these records is now available or recreatable.

11. GNC was on notice from the inception of the litigation that the records identified in Findings 7 and 9 above were relevant to the litigation or at least were reasonably calculated to lead to the discovery of admissible evidence. Notice was provided by the pre–litigation correspondence between counsel for the parties; the Complaint filed by Thompson on August 17, 1978; Thompson's request for discovery served in August and September 1978 and the depositions conducted in September 1978; and Thompson's Motion for Preliminary Injunction filed on September 15, 1978. GNC's senior management knew, or should have known at the inception of this litigation that the records identified in Findings 7 and 9 above were relevant to the matters in issue, reasonably calculated to lead to the discovery of admissible evidence, and reasonably likely to be requested by Thompson during discovery in the litigation.

12. GNC destroyed the records identified in Finding 9 above and continued to destroy the documents identified in Findings 7 above after August 25, 1978. GNC also destroyed, at some time after the filing of the complaint and its receipt of Thompson' initial discovery

requests, the electronically–maintained computer files containing the data described in Finding 8 above (except for maximum inventory level information which was retained beginning in February 1980).

13. GNC could have preserved and retained on computer tape or disc all of the purchase, sale and inventory information and data which was on the now–destroyed records described in Findings 7 and 9 above without undue burden. GNC admits that it already possesses a computer tape and disc library of over 2000 tapes. The information contained on those remaining library tapes, however, cannot replicate the documents destroyed by GNC.

14. GNC did not instruct its employees to preserve the records set forth in Finding 7 and 9 above, or make any other efforts reasonably calculated to ensure that those records would be preserved, following the inception of this litigation. As a result of GNC's omission to take steps necessary to ensure the preservation of such records, they were destroyed by GNC employees.

15. On October 2, 1978, the Honorable Albert Lee Stephens, Jr., District Judge, United States District Court for the Central District of California, entered an order staying all proceedings in this litigation. At that time Thompson's initial discovery requests were still pending and had not been complied with by GNC or resolved by any order of the Court. GNC destroyed the records described in Findings 7, 8 and 9 above without regard to the stay order and without regard to Thompson's pending discovery requests. Neither GNC nor its counsel informed Thompson or the Court of this destruction, nor did GNC or its counsel seek leave of the Court or obtain permission to destroy any of these records.

16. On March 9, 1979, Thompson moved to vacate the stay of discovery; GNC opposed Thompson's motion on March 16, 1979. On April 13, 1979, the Court entered an order setting a date for the filing of answers and appointing the Honorable Parks Stillwell as Special Master (the "Special Master"). In the Stipulation and Order of Reference dated

July 2, 1979, the District Court ordered, and the parties agreed to, the granting of pretrial powers and duties for the purpose of having the Special Master supervise and govern all discovery and pretrial proceedings The order of Reference authorized the Special Master, in addition, to issue protective orders, determine whether discovery orders had been complied with, and submit to the District Court a final pretrial order. Under paragraph A.4 of the Order of Reference, all unreviewed orders of the Special Master became the orders of the District Court. Neither GNC nor its counsel took steps to prevent or defer the destruction of the documents or information identified in Findings 7, 8 or 9 above, pending the assumption by the Special Master of his formal duties.

17. Prior to the entry of the Special Master's July 1979 preservation order, counsel for Thompson attempted to negotiate an agreement with counsel at GNC whereby GNC would voluntarily preserve certain documents, including documents described in Findings 7 and 9 above and which GNC destroyed before, during and after the period in which negotiations were conducted. GNC did not agree to voluntarily preserve documents as requested by Thompson.

GNC's Violations of the July 1979 Order

18. On July 17, 1979, at the first proceedings of the parties before the Special Master, the Special Master ordered GNC to preserve all purchase, sale and inventory records maintained by GNC in the ordinary course of business at its headquarters in Pittsburgh, Pennsylvania. Such order was based, in part, upon representations made by GNC's counsel that GNC routinely maintained copies of all purchase, sale and inventory records, or their originals, as well as other documents, at its headquarters in Pittsburgh, Pennsylvania. This July 1979 Preservation Order (the "July 1979 Order") was embodied in a written order which was executed by the Special Master and, thereafter, the District Court in September 1979.

19. GNC's employees were not instructed by GNC or its counsel to preserve purchase,

sale and inventory records as required by the July 1979 Order. GNC's president, Mr. Gary Daum, issued a memorandum dated July 27, 1979, to all GNC personnel advising them that the Orders "should not require us to change our standard document retention or destruction policies or practices." This instruction on its face appears to instruct GNC employees to conduct their destruction procedures as they had done in the past and it was so interpreted by GNC employees. This memorandum did not result in the retention of records as required in the July 1979 Order and operated to authorize or condone GNC practices which resulted in the destruction of critical evidence.

20. GNC's general counsel, Mr. George Basco, GNC's counsel of record herein, attended the July 17, 1979, hearing before the Special Master. Neither Mr. Basco, who drafted Mr. Daum's memorandum, nor counsel of record herein, instructed GNC employees to preserve purchase, sale and inventory records as ordered.

21. Neither GNC nor its counsel made any credible attempt to insure or monitor GNC's compliance with the July 1979 Order. Mr. Daum's memorandum was itself insufficient means to insure or monitor compliance with the Order.

22. GNC contends that it has never had a formal or written document retention or preservation policy. Furthermore, GNC contends that the practices of retention and destruction of all records described in Findings 7, 8 and 9 above, were left up to individual GNC departments, and sometimes individual employees, for their decision. The individual GNC departments and employees maintaining those documents were not, however, contacted by GNC or its counsel in order to insure that any of GNC's duties to preserve documents or to comply with the July 1979 Order were being met.

23. The July 1979 Order, and any reasonable construction thereof, required GNC beginning on July 17, 1979, and continuing to the present, to preserve all purchase, sale and inventory records which were in its possession on the date

of the Order, as well as such records created on or after July 17, 1979. No reasonable construction of the July 1979 Order, or its written memorialization of September 5, 1979, could limit GNC's continuing obligation to preserve such documents.

24. The record indicates that the only documents which GNC preserved at any time as a result of the July 1979 Order were bulk cash register tapes and, belatedly, Store Order Strips (beginning in late September 1979 at the earliest). No one could have attended the hearing before the Special Master on July 17, 1979, and have reasonably concluded that the Order was intended to have such negligible effects.

25. At a minimum, all of the records identified in Finding 7 above which were created on or after July 17, 1979, as well as all of the following purchase, sale and inventory records predating July 17, 1979 (which, among others, were in GNC's possession on July 17, 1979), were required by the July 1979 Order to be preserved by GNC:

(a) Store Order Books for each GNC store (containing historical store order demand, biweekly inventory, maximum store inventory level, and related data) for 10 to 16 weeks prior to July 17, 1979;

(b) Biweekly Order Strips for each GNC store dating back approximately 2 to 3 months prior to July 17, 1979;

c. Store invoices for at least 2 to 4 weeks prior to July 17, 1979, and

d. Full store order information (including such data as biweekly inventory counts, store order demand, and maximum inventory levels) which was retained on computer tape for the period covering approximately 4 months prior to July 17, 1979.

26. After July 17, 1979, GNC destroyed at a minimum both (a) the records in its possession as identified in Finding 25 above, as well as (b) those records identified in Finding 7 above which were created by GNC on or after July 17, 1979. This destruction was in violation of the July 1979 Order, as well as GNC's other legal duties.

27. GNC also destroyed the computer files from which the data identified in Finding 8 above might have been alternatively obtained for the time period covered by the destroyed documents (with the exception of maximum store inventory level limitations which began to be preserved by GNC for the first time, and then solely in electronically readable form, in approximately February of 1980).

28. Records containing warehouse shipment data (information concerning amounts shipped from GNC warehouses to retail stores) were covered by the July 1979 Order, and the Order was so understood by GNC. The July 1979 Order was interpreted by GNC to cover documents which contain warehouse shipment data, including such documents as Inventory Status Reports and Store Inventories. GNC, however, destroyed such documents after the entry of the July 1979 Order.

29. At no time did GNC or its counsel inform the Special Master or Thompson of its ongoing destruction of documents, seek leave of the Special Master or the Court to destroy such documents, or intercede to prevent the destruction of any of the record set forth in Findings 7, 8, 9, and 25 above.

30. GNC alleges that it may have retained certain warehouse shipment data for certain four–week periods. Such data, if it still exists, is not duplicative of the inventory, demand and maximum inventory level data which GNC destroyed. The inventory, demand, and maximum inventory level data which was lost in connection with GNC's destruction of the records identified in Findings 7, 8, and 9 above, is not recreatable from the information which GNC now alleges it may have retained.

31. The documents and other evidence destroyed by GNC are not capable of reconstruction or replication.

GNC's Violations of the January 1980 Order

32. On August 10, 1979, Thompson submitted to GNC its "First Request for the Production of Documents and Things Propounded by Plaintiff to Defendant General Nutrition Center, Inc." and its "First Request for the Production of Documents and Things Propounded by Plaintiff to Defendant General Nutrition Corporation" (hereinafter collectively referred to as "the First Requests"). These discovery requests were the first in a schedule of discovery expressly adopted by the Special Master and ordered to be implemented on July 17, 1979, at the first hearing before him.

33. On August 10, 1979, the date of Thompson's submission of the First Requests, GNC had in its possession at least the following records which GNC destroyed after August 10, 1979:

(a) Store Order Books for each GNC store (with biweekly inventory data, maximum inventory level data, and biweekly store order demand data) containing information for the period from 10 to 16 weeks prior to August 10, 1979;

(b) Store Order Strips for each GNC store containing biweekly inventory data and store order demand data for a period of approximately 2 to 3 months prior to August 10, 1979;

(c) Store Invoices for a period of at least 2 to 4 weeks prior to August 10, 1979; and

(d) Electronically–recorded records of biweekly store inventories, maximum store inventory levels, and biweekly store order demand data for a period of approximately 4 months prior to August 10, 1979.

34. GNC objected to Thompson's First Requests and Thompson moved for an order compelling production.

35. At a hearing before him on January 21, 1980, the Special Master entered an order (the "January 1980 Order") compelling GNC

to produce documents in response to certain of the requests contained in Thompson's First Requests. At that hearing, counsel for GNC represented to the Special Master that GNC's headquarters in Pittsburgh and its six regional offices received and maintained the documents responsive to Thompson's discovery requests. Accordingly, the Special Master confined GNC's search to its headquarters and six regional offices. The January 1980 Order further required GNC to preserve all documents at its headquarters and six regional offices responsive to Thompson's First Requests until all such documents were either produced to Thompson, or the matter further resolved by the Special Master. The Special Master further ordered GNC not to alter its document retention practices at its other business locations until further notice. On March 7, 1980, the January 1980 Order was embodied in a written stipulation and order.

36. After being served with Thompson's First Requests, GNC destroyed, at a minimum, the documents and data set forth in Finding 33 above. Each of these documents which contained information for the period between July 1, 1977 to August 1, 1979, was responsive to Thompson's First Requests.

37. The January 1980 Order did not, nor could it have been reasonably construed or interpreted to have, modify or supersede the July 1979 Order or GNC's continuing duty to comply with the July 1979 Order. GNC did not interpret the January 1980 Order to modify or supersede the July 1979 Order at the time the January 1980 Order was entered. For example, GNC requested leave of the Special Master as late as July 1980 to be relieved of its obligations under the July 1979 Order as it applied to the preservation of certain store cash register tapes.

38. Each of the documents identified in Finding 33 above which contained information from the period from July 1, 1977 to August 1, 1979, was ordered by the Special Master to be produced by GNC in the January 1980 Order. These documents were not produced to Thompson in response to the January 1980 Order, to Thompson's First Requests, or otherwise.

39. The documents identified in Finding 33 above were destroyed after August 10, 1979. The destruction of each of these documents which contained information from the period from July 1, 1977 to August 1, 1979, were violations of the January 1980 Order. The destruction was also in violation of GNC's continuing duties to preserve records. The destruction of all of the records identified in Findings 7, 8, 9, 25 and 33 above in existence on or created after July 17, 1979, also violated the July 1979 Order.

Prejudice to Thompson

40. GNC's violations of orders and of its duties here has caused prejudice to Thompson. The records destroyed by GNC were relevant, at a minimum, to Thompson's allegations and contentions that: (a) GNC's advertisements were false and deceptive due to the inadequate inventories of Thompson and other products in GNC's stores, by showing, *inter alia*, the actual inventories which GNC's own records showed it had on hand; (b) such false advertisements formed part of marketing devices used to sell GNC's own products as opposed to those products advertised by GNC, by showing, *inter alia*, the numbers and types of GNC's own products which GNC's own records showed it had on hand; (c) said marketing devices were deliberately and intentionally implemented by GNC and that GNC purposefully set maximum inventory levels for Thompson and other products at low levels in order to sell GNC's own products to customers, by showing, *inter alia*, the levels actually set by GNC and any written instructions regarding those levels; (d) GNC imposed these levels at artificially low amounts regardless of demand, by showing, *inter alia*, the actual level and demand information; (e) GNC targeted local and regional competitors and utilized unlawful predatory pricing and advertising practices to cause harm to local and regional competition as part of its attempted monopolization, by showing, *inter alia*, local or regional differences in inventory, levels, sales, pricing and demand; and (f) these marketing and advertising practices were a part of a deliberate pattern of predatory conduct engaged in by GNC in an attempt to monopolize, by showing, *inter alia*, a persistent false adver-

tising scheme and a persistent targeting of competitors.

41. The records destroyed by GNC were relevant, at a minimum, to Thompson's allegations and contentions that GNC's practices caused damage to Thompson by *inter alia*, diverting trade from Thompson products to GNC's own products. GNC's records would have reflected any shifts or diversion in sales over time, among other data trends, and would have tended to show any damages Thompson suffered from GNC's activities.

42. The records destroyed by GNC also were relevant, at a minimum, to Thompson's defenses and counterclaims in *General Nutrition Corporation, etc. v. Wm.T. Thompson Co.*, No. CV 78–3891.

43. The records destroyed by GNC also were relevant, at a minimum, to Thompson's defenses to GNC's allegations of damages. GNC has alleged that its damages for a period from prior to the filing of its complaint to the present would consist largely of lost sales of Thompson products, of other national brands, and of GNC's own products due to the unavailability of Thompson products in GNC's stores.

44. The records destroyed by GNC have impaired Thompson's ability to effectively obtain consulting and expert advice on the liability and damage issues referred to above and to utilize such advice for discovery and trial purposes.

45. The records found herein to have been destroyed by GNC are not available from any other source and are not recreatable.

46. Delay in these proceedings caused by GNC's order violations and violations of its duties has caused additional prejudice to Thompson. Witnesses may be difficult to locate, memories may have faded or been distorted, and other documentary evidence may now be destroyed.

47. GNC's destruction of relevant records appears to have deprived Thompson of the best objective evidence on many central is-

sues for presentation to an independent trier of fact and has impaired Thompson's ability to obtain a full and fair trial by jury on all issues raised by Thompson. This is particularly so where issues of intent and conduct have been raised on both sides and where conflicting oral testimony may be offered by both parties.

The Supplier Documents

48. On August 10, 1979, Thompson served GNC with its First Request for the Production of Documents and Things ("First Request"). The First Request sought from GNC, among other things, documents pertaining to the alleged "suppliers" of Thompson products to GNC (other than Thompson itself). When GNC did not produce the documents requested in Thompson's First Request, Thompson filed a motion seeking a Rule 37(a) order compelling production. On January 21, 1980, the Special Master heard oral argument on Thompson's Rule 37(a) motion, granted it, and ordered GNC to produce the requested records on a date certain. This January 21 Order was reduced to writing on March 7, 1980.

49. GNC did not produce a single identifiable supplier document in response to the Special Master's January 21, 1980 Order as required. GNC was, accordingly, in violation of said Order.

50. On February 9, 1981 (and again on April 8, 1981) Thompson served Notices of Deposition on a number of GNC executives and employees. Each Notice contained a request for the production of documents under Rule 30(b), including documents with respect to GNC's alleged suppliers of Thompson products.

51. On February 18, 1981, a telephonic hearing was held concerning Thompson's request to compel production of the documents. The Special Master again ordered GNC to produce all requested documents with respect to the alleged suppliers of Thompson products with the proviso that, subject to a future motion by Thompson, GNC could delete portions revealing the identity of a supplier directly or by implication.

Other than a single document produced at the deposition of Mr. Joseph Bresse, not a single supplier document was produced by GNC to Thompson at any deposition as a result of the Special Master's February 18, 1981 order.

52. On May 15, 1981, Thompson filed a motion for the imposition of Rule 37(b) sanctions upon GNC and for a further order directing GNC to produce all supplier–related documents as previously ordered and without further delay. After hearings on May 30, 1981 and July 9, 1981, the Special Master found that GNC had, in fact, violated the previous Orders referred to above and announced his intention to sanction GNC for its refusal to comply with the aforesaid January 21, 1980 and February 18, 1981 Orders on the subject.

53. By a written Order dated August 12, 1981, the Special Master imposed upon GNC sanctions in the amount of $14,068.

The August 12, 1981 Order also directed GNC to again produce all supplier documents specified in the Order itself (this time without deletion of any information) and required that this be accomplished "within twenty (20) days" (i.e. by September 2, 1981). The Order specifically set forth the precise document and discovery requests of Thompson with which GNC was to comply.

54. Despite the express requirement that GNC produce all supplier documents "with twenty (20) days," GNC did not produce all documents as ordered by September 2, 1981. GNC did produce some supplier documents on that date but said that others could only be identified and produced if GNC made a "special computer run" and GNC demanded that Thompson pay for such a program. As of September 2, 1981, GNC was in violation of the August 12, 1982 Order — the second written order on this one subject by failing to produce all documents in its possession as ordered.

55. GNC was again ordered (on October 13, 1981) to produce all requested documents as ordered August 12, 1981 on or before October 21, 1981. This Order also imposed sanctions on GNC for its refusal to comply fully with the August, 1981 Order and GNC paid

$1,376.00 to Thompson for the fees and other expenses incurred by Thompson.

56. GNC did not produce all documents on October 21, 1981 as ordered. Initially, counsel for GNC represented to Thompson's counsel that a full and proper search had occurred. However, and only after persistent inquiry by Thompson's counsel, GNC produced over 150 pages of additional documents on December 8 and December 11, 1981 — over 6 weeks later than required by the explicit terms of the October 13, 1981 Order. Furthermore, GNC did not even conduct a formal inquiry of its regional offices and stores until March, 1982 and that inquiry itself did not constitute an adequate search for documents ordered to be produced. Thereafter, GNC produced additional documents on May 18, 1982 — almost 7 months after the date set for full and final compliance and only after Thompson had filed a motion seeking sanctions for GNC's failure to comply and seeking a further order compelling complete production.

57. GNC's failure to produce, in a timely fashion, the subject documents violated the October 13, 1981 Order and its mandate that all documents be produced on or before October 21, 1981.

58. By failing to again adequately search for and produce all documents as expressly ordered, GNC's conduct was tantamount to contempt of the Special Master's orders.

59. Even after the belated productions in December, 1981, and May, 1982, GNC still has not searched for and produced all documents as ordered. Despite the express terms of the August 12, 1981 and October 13, 1981 Orders specifically identifying the deposition notices of Messrs. Dobies, Eby, Withrow, Bresse, Bentley, Sulik, Rawlik, Rusnak and Lied, some of these employees were never instructed to search files under their control for documents responsive to their deposition Notices. GNC has yet to produce documents that others of these employees had testified existed. Moreover, GNC's middle–level managers and store managers were not contacted and expressly instructed to conduct a thorough search for all the requested documents (despite the fact that Thompson's requests to produce as well as the court's Orders called for a company–wide search for responsive documents). Although the evidence establishes that Thompson products were purchased by non–headquarter's personnel, Thompson has received no documents from the store or regional levels of GNC's operations that were identifiable as such. Nor did GNC circulate anything in writing or give any oral instructions on a corporate–wide basis requesting or instructing its employees to conduct an actual and thorough search for, or to identify, any documents relating to those persons identified by GNC as "potential", rather than "actual" sources of Thompson products. Thus far, GNC has yet to produce any documents covering "potential suppliers" of Thompson products despite the fact that Thompson's requests and the Special Master's Orders cover such documents. GNC thus remains in violation of the October 13, 1981 Order and its predecessor Orders to this day and a further corporate–wide search will be required to insure that all documents ordered to be produced will, in fact, be produced to the extent they have not been lost or destroyed.

60. There is a strong and compelling inference that GNC destroyed or failed to retain supplier–related documents despite the requirements of the Special Master's July, 1979 and January, 1980 document preservation Orders and that GNC has violated said preservation Orders. By destroying said documents, GNC disabled itself from complying fully with the Special Master's subsequent document production Orders referred to above.

* * * * *

Bad Faith 63.

GNC's destruction of documents, violations of court orders, and violations of its duties reflect bad faith. This bad faith is demonstrated, at a minimum, in GNC's failure to preserve critical documents after commencement of these actions; its failure to implement procedures to monitor or control document destruction after the commencement of these actions; its erroneous or negligent representations to the court and counsel; its failure to preserve any records other than relatively useless bulk cash register tapes and store order strips in response to a clear preservation order of the court; its erasure of computer tapes and discs which could have been utilized to store some of the destroyed information relatively simply; its failure to implement any procedures to monitor or control document destruction after entry of the Special Master's orders; its providing employees with instructions that amounted to approval for document destruction; its belated attempt to exonerate itself from its order violations by proffering a series of contradictory and factually unsupportable excuses; its attempts to obstruct or delay the court's inquiry into the scope and import of GNC's destruction as alleged by Thompson; and its indifference to the authority of the court and its violations of other discovery orders of the court.

64. GNC's destruction of relevant records has caused Thompson to divert substantial sums of money in attempting to discover and obtain the records GNC wrongfully destroyed and in bringing on motions and requests to the court for relief from GNC's wrongful conduct.

65. GNC's and its counsel's conduct of discovery in this litigation was intended and has unfairly expanded the proceedings so as to unreasonably burden and vex Thompson and divert Thompson's resources unnecessarily.

66. GNC has sought to and has succeeded in frustrating and obstructing discovery and the advancement of these litigations. GNC's conduct during discovery in the litigation has been either in derogation of or in disregard for the authority of the court.

67. GNC has engaged in a pattern of order violations and discovery abuse, including defiance and indifference to the orders of the court, to their obligations and duties as litigants, and to the discovery process under the Federal Rules of Civil Procedure.

68. Any Conclusion of Law deemed a Finding of Fact is incorporated herein.

* * * * *

Propriety of Sanctions

6. This Court possesses an inherent power to sanction litigants for abusive litigation practices that are taken in bad faith. *Roadway Express, Inc. v. Piper*, 447 U.S. 752, 100 S.Ct. 2455, 65 L.Ed.2d 488 (1980); *Link v. Wabash Railroad Co.*, 370 U.S. 626, 82 S.Ct. 1386, 8 L.Ed.2d 734 (1962); *Chism v. National Heritage Life Insurance Co.*, 637 F.2d 1328 (9th Cir.1981). Sanctions may be imposed against a litigant who is on notice that documents and information in its possession are relevant to litigation, or potential litigation, or are reasonably calculated to lead to the discovery of admissible evidence, and destroys such documents and information. While a litigant is under no duty to keep or retain every document in its possession once a complaint is filed, it is under a duty to preserve what it knows, or reasonably should know, is relevant to the action, is reasonably calculated to lead to the discovery of admissible evidence, is reasonably likely to be requested during discovery, and/or is the subject of a pending discovery request. *Bowmar Instruction Corp. v. Texas Instruments, Inc.*, 25 Fed.R.Serv. 2d 423 (N.D.Ind.1977); *In re Agent Orange Product Liability Litigation*, 506 F.Supp. 750 (E.D.N.Y.1980).

7. GNC is subject to sanctions imposed under the inherent powers of the Court and Rule 37 of the Federal Rules of Civil Procedure, for knowingly and purposefully permitting its employees to destroy key documents and records. This destruction resulted in prejudice to Thompson, since it deprived Thompson of access to the objective evidence needed to build a case against GNC. GNC's conduct creates a presumption that the missing data would have permitted Thompson to prove the bait–and–switch advertising claims that lie at the heart of its complaint.

8. GNC is also subject to sanctions under Rule 37 of the Federal Rules of Civil Procedure, for failure to comply with the Special

Master's orders to produce the supplier documents. GNC failed to comply with four successive orders to produce the documents, issued over a 21–month period between January 1980 and October 1981. GNC's partial last–minute tender of responsive documents does not cure the damage created by this delay, and subsequently does not immunize GNC from the imposition of sanctions. *See Wyle v. R.J. Reynolds Industries, Inc.*, 709 F.2d 585. 591 (9th Cir.1983); *G–K Properties v. Redevelopment Agency*, 577 F.2d 645, 647–48 (9th Cir.1978).

The Choice of Sanctions

9. The "ultimate" sanction of striking GNC's answer and entering default in case no. CV 78–32906 CHH, and dismissing its complaint in case no. CV 78–3891 CHH, is appropriate in this action. GNC's destruction of critical document deprived Thompson of access to the objective evidence it needed to build its case against GNC. Default and dismissal are proper sanctions in view of GNC's willful destruction of documents and records that deprived Thompson of the opportunity to present critical evidence on its key claims to the jury. *See, e.g., National Hockey League v. Metropolitan Hockey Club, Inc.*, 427 U.S. 639 96 S.Ct. 2778, 49 L.Ed.2d 747 (1976); *Professional Seminar Consultants, Inc. v Sino American Technology Exchange Counsel, Inc.*, 727 F.2d 1470 (9th Cir.1984).

10. Default and dismissal are also appropriate sanctions for the repeated violations of the Special Master's orders to produce the supplier documents. *See, e.g., G–K Properties, supra.* This pattern of discovery order violations constitutes an independent basis for imposing the sanctions of default and dismissal.

11. The Court has considered the propriety of the less severe sanction of entering an order precluding GNC from introducing certain matters into evidence; *to wit*, any evidence contesting Thompson's claim that GNC stores stocked only a *de minimus* quantity of Thompson products during the relevant time period. Such a sanction is inappropriate for three reasons. First, entry of an evidence preclusion order would virtu-

ally compel a directed verdict for Thompson on several of its claims, e.g., the business tort claims asserted in Count III of the Lanham Act claim asserted in Count IV. The proposed order would unequivocally establish the truth of Thompson's bait–and–switch advertising claims, which would, as a matter of law, entitle it to relief on several of its claims. Second, the Court may, in its discretion, require proof of additional facts in default judgment hearing that are essential to the proof of Thompson's claims. *See, e.g., Au Bon Pain Corp. v. Artect, Inc.*, 653 F.2d 61, 65 (2d Cir.1981); *McGinty v. Beranger Volkswagen, Inc.*, 633 F.2d 226, 229 (1st Cir.1980). For example, since Thompson's Sherman Act claim asserts that GNC conspired with various unknown co–conspirators, it may be appropriate to require Thompson to produce evidence of the existence and identity of the co–conspirators before treble damages are awarded. Third, the discovery abuses that occurred in this litigation are far more serious in magnitude than in cases such as *G–K Properties, supra*, and *Professional Seminar Consultants, supra.* Imposition of severe sanctions is required in this case by the severity of the abuses that took place. The record shows that GNC deliberately and purposefully undertook a program to impede and obstruct the litigation process, presumably because it believed that the case would be lost if all of the evidence ever came to light. Imposition of a lesser sanction would only reward GNC for its misconduct in this litigation.

12. The Special Master awarded Thompson a total of $453,312.56 in his two reports, reflecting the cost to Thompson of attempting to compel the production of nonexistent documents, attempting to compel the production of the supplier documents in response to the Special Master's orders, engaging in the special discovery ordered to determine the extent of GNC's motions for sanctions that culminated in the Special Master's reports. Imposition of monetary sanctions in addition to default and dismissal are necessary to fully compensate Thompson for the costs entailed by GNC's misconduct. Thompson must, however, provide additional documentation of its attorneys' fees

incurred in these matters. Specifically, Thompson should file a statement showing the number of hours worked by each attorney on these matters and the billing rate for each attorney. Hours may be aggregated on a monthly basis. Thompson should also provide a brief statement specifying the matters worked on by each attorney each month.

13. The Special Master's orders imposing monetary sanctions were issued on April 26, 1982 and July 26, 1982, and GNC sought review by the district court within 10 days as required by the Order of Reference to the Special Master. District court review has, however, taken over two years to accomplish. Thompson is entitled to interest on the monetary sanctions from the date that district court review was sought in order to fully compensate it for the delay occasioned by the review process. Since no specific rate of interest is fixed by either statute or rule under these circumstances, the Court will award interest at the rate specified by 26 U.S.C. § 6621 through the date of entry of the order affirming the Special Master's action.

WOOLNER THEATRES, INC. & Drive–In Movies of Louisiana, Inc. v. PARAMOUNT PICTURES CORPORATION et al.

333 F.Supp. 658

United States District Court, E.D. Louisiana
May 5, 1970

Woolner Theatres, Inc. and Drive–In Movies of Louisiana, Inc., operators of drive–in theatres in the New Orleans area, brought this motion picture anti–trust action against the major motion picture distributors and certain downtown New Orleans exhibitors alleging these defendants conspired to distribute and exhibit better quality first–run motion pictures on an exclusive first–run basis in downtown theatres in violation of 15 U.S.C. § 15. Plaintiffs prayed for injunctive relief and damages.

The plaintiffs urge the admission of Profit and Loss Statements (hereafter P&LS) for their fiscal years which are embraced in the damage period of 1961–1965. They contend that the P&LS should be received under the Federal Business Records Act (28 U.S.C.A. § 1732). They also claim that *McDaniel v. United States* (5th Cir. 1965) 343 F.2d 785, cert. den. 382 U.S. 826, 86 S.Ct. 59, 15 L.Ed.2d 71, holding that summaries of books and records are admissible "provided cross-examination is allowed and the original records are available" (p. 789), requires admission of the exhibits.

The defendants have objected to their receipt in evidence on the grounds that they do not qualify for admission under the Act.

These documents represent critical evidence in the plaintiffs' case to prove injury and damage. In view of the serious charges of fraud on the part of the plaintiffs in the relevant period and in the period 1954–1959, wherein the plaintiffs concede that they defrauded defendants on a film rental of about $78,000.00 of box office admission receipts through a system of underreporting, diversion of box office receipts to another corporation owned, operated and controlled by the individuals who owned, operated and controlled the plaintiffs' corporations in both periods, and fraudulent record keeping, a foundation hearing, out of the presence of the jury, was held.

* * * * *

We believe the authorities support the conclusion that admissibility of records under the Act is to be adjudicated not only as a showing that records were kept in the regular course of business and that it was in the regular course of business to keep the records. *Doss v. United States*, 355 F.2d 663 (8th Cir. 1966), but also on a determination, where the evidence requires, of the character of the records and their earmarks of reliability. *United States v. Grow*, 394 F.2d 182 (4th Cir. 1968). Mechanical compliance with the Act is not always sufficient to qualify business records for admission thereunder. The records or the circumstances under which they are kept should indicate an "inherent probability of trustworthiness for the purpose for which they are offered." *Bowman v.*

Kaufman, 387 F.2d 582, 587 (2d Cir. 1967); *LeRoy v. Sabena Belgian World Airlines*, 344 F.2d 266 (2d Cir. 1965). See also *Palmer v. Hoffman*, 318 U.S. 109, 63 S.Ct. 477, 87 L.Ed 645 (1943); *Hartzog v. United States*, 217 F.2d 706 (4th Cir. 1954); *Mo. Pac. RR Co. v. Austin*, 292 F.2d 415 (5th Cir. 1961); *Sabatino v. Curtiss Nat'l Bank*, 415 F.2d 632 (5th Cir. 1969).

The P&LS were prepared by plaintiffs' Memphis bookkeeper to whom were sent, during a period from early 1960 until about October 1962, re–written copies of the cashier's daily box office reports, and thereafter, a monthly summary of the claimed daily receipts. Additionally, the bookkeeper received duplicate bank deposit slips, check registers and canceled checks. From these records the bookkeeper prepared and maintained a double entry set of formal books. The bookkeeper prepared the P&LS and various tax returns, including income tax returns of the plaintiffs and their sister corporation, Southern Concessions, Inc.

Although the defendants concede that the P&LS reflect accurately the information furnished by the plaintiffs to their bookkeeper, they vigorously challenge the correctness of the gross receipts information furnished by plaintiffs, the reasonableness of certain expenses deducted and the propriety of others.

The evidence shows that the keystone record regularly and usually maintained in a theatre operation is a daily box office report of ticket sales maintained by the box office cashier. Determination of tax liabilities, percentage rentals due film companies and the operator's financial condition, of course, depend, among others, on accurate receipts records. Here, a daily cashier's box office report was made, showing, among other data, gross sales and ticket numbers sold.

The evidence shows that from about April, 1960 to April, 1965 these vital records were destroyed within weeks or months, and perhaps daily on occasions. A partial re–write of those reports was made by Mrs. Betty Woolner, wife of Lawrence Woolner, one of the co–owners of plaintiffs. Until about October, 1962, these re-

writes were sent to the bookkeeper, who was not aware they were not the original box office reports. After October, 1962, the monthly summaries, themselves re–writes scheduled on a single sheet, were submitted to the bookkeeper. This change apparently was designed to eliminate the bulk of the monthly mailing to the bookkeeper (see Deposition of Robert S. Jacobs, p. 48).

The evidence also shows that the plaintiffs fraudulently reported to the film companies lower gross receipts on which they paid percentage film rentals, which they were obligated to pay on true grosses under film license contracts, rather than on the actual receipts. Other records kept by Mrs. Woolner bear out the fraud which, on trial, Mrs. Woolner admitted, but on deposition denied. It is claimed, however, that the fraud was practiced only in about half the 1961–1965 period.

The evidence also shows that similar fraudulent record keeping and other practices which prevailed in the 1960–1965 period also prevailed in the 1954–1959 period. Nevertheless, plaintiffs claim that notwithstanding the fraud practiced on the film companies, their true gross receipts were banked and reported to their bookkeeper. They also maintain that the P&LS are in agreement with their income tax returns.

In this connection it is noted that the income tax returns of the plaintiff, Woolner Theatres, Inc. operator of the Airline Drive–In for the fiscal periods ending January 31, 1961, 1962 and 1963 and of the plaintiff, Drive–In Movies of Louisiana, Inc., operator of the Jeff Drive–In, for the fiscal years ending April 30, 1962, 1963 and 1964, reflect lesser gross profits than the P&LS. Further, the evidence shows that payments made in the period June, 1959 to November, 1962 (see Defendants' Exhibits 32 & 33) to cover film rentals of which plaintiffs defrauded defendants in the period 1954–1959, were included in the film rental figures appearing in the P&LS and the tax returns, the plaintiffs having failed to inform their bookkeepers of the character of such payments. At the same time the amount of receipts to which such payment would be applicable are not included in the gross receipts shown in both.

There is also evidence that even if the cashier's reports were available they themselves, would not guarantee the gross receipts shown in the P&LS because sales of tickets after closing of the box office were not included.

Plaintiffs failed to offer any of the records of their satellite corporation, Southern Concessions, Inc., to which, in the 1954–1959 period, box office receipts were diverted and in whose bank account they were deposited.

Considered along with all other evidence on the issue, the tax returns are themselves suspect and are entitled to no weight in determining whether the gross receipts figures in the P&LS are trustworthy.

Destruction of basic records after lapse of an appropriate time and for legitimate reasons is the regular course of business in some businesses. Tax conscious prudent businessmen may destroy, and their accounting and legal advisors may counsel destruction of, vital records after civil and criminal tax statutes of limitations have run. Destruction in this case occurred, relatively, if not actually, almost simultaneously with the re–write of the primary record. Evidently, some attempt was made to maintain records through re–writes of the originals, which it was hoped would withstand the scrutiny of the Internal Revenue Service, and at the same time thwart discovery by film companies of plaintiffs' fraud as to them. It has not succeeded for the latter purpose and its success for the former is dubious. Re–writes of basic records made for such purposes would not be records kept in the regular course of business. *United States v. Grow*, supra; *United States v. Plisco*, 192 F. Supp. 337, aff'd 113 U.S.App.D.C. 177, 306 F.2d 784, cert. den. 371 U.S. 948, 83 S.Ct. 505, 9 L.Ed.2d 499.

Mrs. Woolner, referring to the change over to keeping the monthly summary, testified the bookkeeper, Jacobs, advised the institution of the system. If she would thus create the impression that Jacobs advised the destruction of the basic records, we are not impressed. Jacobs, testifying on this subject, explained the "only reason" the change from sending the bulk mail (the re–writes of the cashier's reports, which he

did not know were not the original reports) into one sheet (the monthly summary) "was merely for mailing purposes" (Deposition p. 48). He further testified that although he did not specifically recall instructing the plaintiffs how long the basic records should be retained, he would "usually tell a client that they should keep records at least five years (Deposition p. 16, L L 14–18). This suite was filed in April, 1965; no doubt it was contemplated considerably earlier. Had Jacobs' usual advice to clients been observed, or had plaintiffs not had ulterior motives, the basic records, which plaintiff so desperately need now, would have been available back to April, 1960 at least, and would doubtlessly be available today. It is inconceivable that those records would have been destroyed after the suit was filed, or even after the decision was made to file suit, if they would not indict plaintiffs.

We are convinced that the basic records were not destroyed routinely and in the regular course of business. We are convinced that they were systematically destroyed in an effort to conceal fraud.

* * * * *

The perjurious character of some of Mrs. Woolner's testimony, the inconsistencies within other portions and with that of Mr. Talley, Talley's role in the 1954–1959 fraud, the inconsistencies in certain of his testimony with facts otherwise proven, the deceit practice by the plaintiffs on Jacobs and Caldwell, indeed, even on their counsel in the case which, in turn, was calculated to practice fraud even on the jury and Court, the clear proof of fraudulent record keeping in the period involved, the destruction of basic records, other means employed to effect the scheme to defraud the defendants, and the adverse presumption arising from the failure to call witnesses who could be expected to have material information and to produce records of Southern, compelled our conclusions that:

1. The plaintiffs have failed to establish the probable trustworthiness required for admission of the P&LS under the provisions of 28 U.S.C. § 1732.

2. The P&LS are inadmissible under the summaries rule. Cross–examination of some, but not all, persons who would have information concerning the records was available to the defendants. The cross–examination of those available adversely reflect on the trustworthiness of the summaries. The original basic records, the cashier's box office reports, which are the foundation of the summaries, were not, of course, available.

YOFFE et al. v. UNITED STATES

153 F.2d 570

Circuit Court of Appeals, First Circuit
February 14, 1946

Eli Yoffe and William S. Krasnow, in three indictments, were charged with conspiring willfully to attempt and evasion of income and excess profits taxes in connection with Yoffe–Krasnow, Inc., and each with willfully attempting to evade his individual income taxes. Verdicts of guilty were returned, and sentences were pronounced. The two men appealed, claiming error in the trial court's failure to direct a verdict for them in the absence of sufficient evidence to warrant submission of the issues to the jury, in the court's failure to give certain instructions to the jury, and in its failure to submit to the jury for its deliberation the bills of particulars filed by the government.

In 1928 Yoffe, Krasnow, and Lincoln S. Fifield organized "Fifield–Yoffe–Krasnow, Inc.," under the corporate laws of Massachusetts for the purpose of dealing in wool rags. The three incorporators subscribed and paid in cash for all the authorized capital stock of the Company — 50 shares of common stock to each, 300 shares of preferred to Yoffe, and 550 shares of preferred to Krasnow. The shares, preferred and common alike, had a par value of $100 each. All the incorporators had engaged in the wool rag business prior to the formation of the corporation, Yoffe and Krasnow each in partnership with members of his own family and

Fifield as manager of a branch office. At the time the concern was formed the Yoffes and Krasnows had on hand rather large stocks of merchandise, which were not any part of the capital of the new enterprise. Fifield dropped out after two years, selling half his stock to Yoffe and half to Krasnow. The corporate name was then changed to Yoffe–Krasnow, Inc., hereinafter sometimes called the corporation. On January 16, 1936, the corporation voted to dissolve. Krasnow and his family organized a new corporation called Krasnow Wool Stock Company, and Yoffe became interested in another corporation called Glaser–Yoffe, Inc.

Indictment No. 16,101 charged appellants with conspiracy to evade and defeat the income and excess profits taxes of Yoffe–Krasnow, Inc. for the years 1934, 1935, and 1936. According to the allegations of the indictment the conspiracy consisted of filing for those three years tax returns in which the net income of the corporation was grossly understated, of selling goods of the corporation under the name of "YK Associates" and preventing the recordation of such sales on the corporation's books, and of diverting large sums of the corporation's sales receipts into bank and brokerage accounts of appellants.

In 1934 sales of woolen rages were made by YK Associates to B.D. Kaplan and Company of New York. The rags were billed and checks in payment were received in the name of YK Associates. Proceeds from sales of over $100,000 were deposited to personal accounts of Krasnow, Yoffe, and Yoffe's brother–in–law in banks or brokerage firms except for approximately $2000 deposited in Yoffe–Krasnow, Inc., bank account. Appellants claim they were engaged in business as partners under the name of YK Associates and that the goods sold by the partnership belonged to them individually and not to the corporation. Their shares of the total receipts from the sales in 1934 were not reported in the appellants' individual income tax returns for that year.

Similarly, in 1935 sales of merchandise were made by YK Associates to B.D. Kaplan & Company and the proceeds deposited in personal or relatives' bank and brokerage accounts to Yoffe's credit in a finance company, to Yoffe's credit in a finance company, or credited to appellant's accounts on the corporation's books. Also in 1935 the corporation made certain sales for which checks were drawn to the order of the corporation, but, according to the government, the sales were not included in the corporation's books or in its tax return. Instead, they were deposited in or credited to various personal accounts of Yoffe and Krasnow.

In 1936 YK Associates sales and certain sales by the corporation to other firms were not reflected in the corporation's 1936 tax return. Receipts appeared in various accounts of Yoffe and Krasnow. After the corporation voted to dissolve on January 16, 1936, many checks were received in payment for merchandise shipped prior to that date and were deposited by Yoffe and Krasnow in their various accounts. Also, the government accountant determined that the inventory actually distributed at the time of liquidation was considerably larger than the amounts shown on the corporation's books. Therefore, an increased closing inventory which was allegedly not reflected on the corporation's tax returns for 1936 were computed.

Indictment 16,100 and count I of indictment 16,102 charged Yoffe and Krasnow respectively for failing to report the entire amounts of their individual incomes in 1936. The understatements, according to the bills of particulars, involved amounts received in the liquidation of Yoffe–Krasnow, Inc. Those amounts were derived from the same checks discussed in connection with the conspiracy indictment for 1936 and from checks payable to the corporation but credited to personal accounts of Yoffe and Krasnow. Count II of indictment 16,102 charged Krasnow with failing to report his entire income for 1937. The understatement, according to the bill of particulars, involved proceeds from sales of the Krasnow Wool Stock Company diverted to Krasnow's use, amounts recovered from insurance companies on fire losses of the Stock Company, and returned insurance premiums. All the items were credited to Krasnow's account on the Stock Company's

books, or deposited in his personal bank account. Krasnow insists that the Stock Company was a partnership business composed of himself and four others.

* * * * *

There is also substantial evidence consistent with the view that a taxable profit was derived from the YK Associates sales. The books of the corporation were not available to the revenue investigating agent or for evidence in court as appellants explained in the brief that " *** after the liquidation of Yoffe–Krasnow, Inc., on January 16, 1936, the books and records of the business were left in the care of Krasnow in the building at 210 Maple Street, Chelsea, where the Krasnow Wool Stock Company commenced doing business. Yoffe never saw the books or records after that. Krasnow stored the books and records in the basement of the building. In the summer of 1938 during a rainy spell the cellar became flooded. In salvaging the merchandise in the cellar the hopelessly ruined stock was thrown into a dump in back of the plant by the employees. Apparently the old books and records disappeared in that process."

However, Krasnow, in his sworn statement to revenue agents, claimed the books had been destroyed by a storm flood in June or July, 1938, and had been transferred to a dump and destroyed without his knowledge. Appellee in its brief comments, and we think, correctly: "Such seemingly careless concern for records at a time when they were being requested by the revenue agents would clearly support the inference that the information contained therein would be harmful to the defendants. This inference coupled with the other evidence as to the contents of the corporation's sales accounts, is clearly sufficient to justify submission to the jury."

* * * * *

Table of Cases

Page numbers in **bold** indicate the location of the edited text of the case in Appendix C.

Index